UNDERSTANDING
CONTEMPORARY
ASIA PACIFIC

Understanding

Introductions to the States and Regions of the Contemporary World
Donald L. Gordon, series editor

Understanding Contemporary Africa, 4th edition
edited by April A. Gordon and Donald L. Gordon

Understanding Contemporary Asia Pacific
edited by Katherine Palmer Kaup

Understanding the Contemporary Caribbean
edited by Richard S. Hillman and Thomas J. D'Agostino

Understanding Contemporary China, 2nd edition
edited by Robert E. Gamer

Understanding Contemporary India
edited by Sumit Ganguly and Neil DeVotta

Understanding Contemporary Latin America, 3rd edition
edited by Richard S. Hillman

Understanding the Contemporary Middle East, 2nd edition
edited by Deborah J. Gerner and Jillian Schwedler

UNDERSTANDING
CONTEMPORARY
ASIA
PACIFIC

edited by
Katherine Palmer Kaup

LYNNE
RIENNER
PUBLISHERS

BOULDER
LONDON

Published in the United States of America in 2007 by
Lynne Rienner Publishers, Inc.
1800 30th Street, Boulder, Colorado 80301
www.rienner.com

and in the United Kingdom by
Lynne Rienner Publishers, Inc.
3 Henrietta Street, Covent Garden, London WC2E 8LU

Library of Congress Cataloging-in-Publication Data
Understanding contemporary Asia Pacific / Edited by Katherine Palmer Kaup.
      p. cm. — (Understanding)
   ISBN 978-1-58826-061-1 (hardcover : alk. paper) — ISBN 978-1-58826-086-4
(pbk. : alk. paper)
   1. East Asia. 2. Southeast Asia.   I. Kaup, Katherine Palmer, 1968–
DS504.5.U4 2007
   950.4'3—dc22

                                      2006101895

British Cataloguing in Publication Data
A Cataloguing in Publication record for this book
is available from the British Library.

Printed and bound in the United States of America

        The paper used in this publication meets the requirements
  (∞)   of the American National Standard for Permanence of
        Paper for Printed Library Materials Z39.48-1992.

        5   4   3   2

To John—
with love and thanks

Contents

Illustrations

▧ Photographs

Acknowledgments

News of contemporary Asia Pacific fills every major newspaper, and scores of scholarly journals present specialized studies. Yet, few multidisciplinary studies of this diverse and dynamic region exist. Undergraduate students are not alone in their generally cursory understanding of this important area: policymakers in the world's capitals often evidence a poor grasp of the complexity of the region and the interconnectedness of the topics covered in the following pages.

In an effort to compile a single text addressing the most pressing issues facing the region today and providing the background material necessary to appreciate the complexity of Asia Pacific, thirteen leading specialists and dedicated teachers joined to produce this volume. Each of the contributors has spent years, often decades, mastering Asian languages and exploring the area's cultures, histories, international relations, economics, and politics to write original and often highly specialized studies in their respective fields. Over the course of our collaboration, each has shown a commitment and rare ability to condense those years of study into accessible chapters that identify the most important aspects of the region. Each has provided succinct, but by no means superficial, introductions that expose students to key themes in the literature and across Asia Pacific. As editor, I would like to express my thanks and admiration for the contributors' willingness to share their expertise, for their patience, and for their dedication to introducing this so often misunderstood region.

I would like to thank especially Paige Johnson Tan, Brantly Womack, Colin Mackerras, and Richard Palmer for their feedback and encouragement on several chapter drafts. Thanks also go to my family—John, Richard, Rachel, and Rebecca—who endured many evenings, weekends, and holidays on their own over the course of the project.

—*Katherine Palmer Kaup*

1

Introduction

Katherine Palmer Kaup

The countries that stretch from the dry grasslands of northern China to the island tropics of southern Indonesia represent some of the most widely varied in the world: from one of the few remaining monarchies in tiny Brunei, to the world's largest communist regime in the mammoth People's Republic of China (PRC). China's huge and rapidly expanding economy stands in stark contrast to the small and troubled system in neighboring Laos. Dozens upon dozens of ethnic groups live in the area, speaking hundreds of local languages and observing a wide variety of religious and other cultural practices. Why even discuss these countries together? Why write a book that focuses on the People's Republic of China, the Democratic People's Republic of Korea (North Korea), the Republic of Korea (South Korea), Japan, East Timor, and the ten member states of the Association of Southeast Asian Nations (ASEAN: Brunei, Cambodia, Indonesia, Laos, Malaysia, Myanmar, Philippines, Singapore, Thailand, and Vietnam)? Why not divide the region, as so many analysts do, into smaller regions, like Northeast Asia (including the Koreas, Japan, and China) and Southeast Asia (including the ten ASEAN states), or why not focus on the Pacific Rim and include all countries that border both sides of the Pacific, including Russia and the United States, as well as several Latin American states?

Though the ASEAN states, China, Japan, the Koreas, and East Timor constitute one of the most diverse regions of the world, they also represent a group of countries that is increasingly interdependent and aware of common interests. Particularly since the devastating Asian financial crisis in 1997, these countries have been strengthening their regional alliances and interactions and developing a host of "Asia-only" institutions such as ASEAN Plus Three, designed to increase ties among ASEAN states, China, Japan, and South Korea.

1

The United States and others outside the region have had to reformulate plans to retain their presence within, in the face of this rising sense of Asia Pacific community (Revere 2005).

The economic and political rise of Asia Pacific has been characterized by many as threatening. The international community, and perhaps the United States most of all, has been particularly anxious about the rapid rise of China, politically, economically, and increasingly militarily. The US Defense Department's 2006 annual report to Congress on the military power of the People's Republic of China, for example, notes that not only does China have the "greatest potential to compete militarily with the United States . . . and over time offset traditional U.S. military advantages," but China's failure to clarify its reasons for dramatically increasing its military capabilities forces "others to hedge against these unknowns" (Office of the Secretary of Defense 2006:4). One congressman from California was much less diplomatic in his description of China as "an aggressive nuclear-armed bully that now threatens the world with its hostile acts and proliferation" (Rohrabacher 2001). Policymakers, scholars, and casual observers alike have clearly recognized the growing influence of the region, and responded in widely differing ways, from seizing opportunities for greater interactions to the creation of think tanks, associations, and lobbying organizations to counter the region's economic, political, and social rise. The 1997 Asian financial crisis brought into clear relief just how interdependent the world's economies have become, as has the recent popular recognition that China holds $1 trillion in US Treasury bonds. Common interests in thwarting international terrorism and the spread of epidemic diseases have also reinforced the need for greater cooperation.

At what point in time should one begin to explain developments in "contemporary" Asia Pacific? How far back does one need to go to understand contemporary trends, particularly in a region of the world with such a strong sense of pride in its thousands of years of history? Some background of cultural and historical traditions is clearly essential to understanding the key themes and patterns from the past that continue to influence events in Asia Pacific today. Placing our primary focus on events and trends since 1945 seems a clear choice, however, as new regimes emerged in almost all of the region's states from the rubble of World War II and the retreat of the colonial powers in the years that immediately followed.

The historical, political, economic, and cultural dynamics since the end of World War II within Asia Pacific have been so varied and complex that few analysts have dared to examine the region as a whole. Within academia, policymaking circles, and economic organizations, analysts have become increasingly specialized, often focusing their studies on a particular issue within a single country, rather than on broad trends occurring across the region. While it is possible to find experts on individual ethnic groups in China, for example, it is more difficult to find specialists on China's ethnic minorities generally, and extremely rare to find those with expertise on ethnic groups throughout the region. The plethora of languages and diversity of experiences among those living in the region complicate cross-border and transnational studies.

Failure to "connect the dots" among the various disciplines and countries, however, will leave the student at best with a narrow understanding of the region, and at worst with a distorted view of what motivates and influences those within the area. To date, very few attempts have been made to understand the extremely diverse traditions and dynamic changes occurring in Asia Pacific through a multidisciplinary approach. Yet this is exactly what is needed in order to identify common patterns of interaction in the region. We need to understand how each of the topics covered in our volume intersects and informs action within the region, to assist us in navigating relations with those living in the region, and to learn from one another, explore areas of common interest, and avoid conflict bred from miscommunication. In bringing together leading scholars from a variety of disciplines, with decades of fieldwork experience throughout the region, it is our hope to provide a broad, interdisciplinary introduction to the trends occurring across one of the world's most exciting regions. Though each of the chapters in this volume can be studied independently, read as a whole they provide uncommon insights on how culture, economics, politics, and international relations intersect with one another to shape dynamics in Asia Pacific. As the rest of the world charts a course for responding to Asia's rise since World War II, it is crucial to be familiar with each of the issues collected here by leaders in the field.

Asian political and cultural diversity is reflected in the region's varied geographical terrain, which ranges from tropical forests to stark deserts, from imposing mountain ranges to deep gorges, and from vast expanses in the northern grasslands to thousands of islands scattered across the southeast. Historically, the mountains, deserts, and archipelagos have divided communities and left peoples speaking hundreds of local languages, practicing a wide array of religions, and professing loyalty to a variety of ethnic groupings. The impact of Asia's geography can be seen in each of the topics addressed throughout our volume, from its effects on transnational migration patterns across time, to growing economic disparities across the region, to the rise and fall of security alliances.

While the region exudes a sense of forward movement and drive to modernize, it remains heavily influenced by its past. Citizens in the region tend to have a much longer historical worldview than is commonly found in the West. Almost any traveler through China is likely to have heard contemporary issues explained through reference to China's ancient past, for example. After first explaining that "China is a big country, with a long history, and a lot of people," many Chinese are as likely to attribute current weaknesses in rule-of-law development to China's first emperor's brutal use of legalism in the second century B.C.E. as they are to current party controls over the judicial system.

Colin Mackerras's historical overview of migration patterns, agricultural development, traditional ethics, the rise of key states, and the expansion of Western colonialism in the nineteenth and twentieth centuries sets the stage for understanding many facets of contemporary Asia Pacific.

After Ron Hill and Colin Mackerras sketch the geographical and historical setting, our chapters turn to developments since World War II. Asia Pacific lay in utter despair in 1945, after nearly a decade of regional warfare. An estimated 10 million people were killed in China alone during the second Sino-Japanese war (1937–1945), which destroyed infrastructure and economies throughout the region. More than 6 million Japanese soldiers were demobilized after the war, and returned to a shattered economy and a newly restructured political system that seemed incapable of supplying them with jobs. Hundreds of thousands of citizens were left homeless and unemployed throughout the region. Even after more than a decade of recovery efforts, the per capita income of the average Japanese was barely 10 percent of the average American's; South Korea was no better off economically than many of the poorest countries in Africa; and widespread famine was feared across parts of the region. Few analysts predicted the rapid economic and political rise of Asia that would begin to sweep the region by 1960.

The spectacular economic rise of Asia Pacific has led many to describe the phenomenon as "the Asian miracle" (World Bank 1993). Between 1960 and 1985, Japan and the four "little dragons"—Hong Kong, Singapore, Taiwan, and South Korea—doubled their incomes every eight years. By 1990, more than 650 million people in East Asia had been lifted out of abject poverty, leaving less than 10 percent of the population in that category, compared with 25 percent in Latin America, and more than 50 percent in black Africa and on the Indian subcontinent (Rowher 1995). Asia Pacific and South Asia produced only 19 percent of the global gross domestic product (GDP) in 1950, but produced almost a third of total GDP by 1998, and the World Bank predicts that this figure will rise to nearly 60 percent by 2025 (Kristof 2000:12). China's per capita GDP has increased more than tenfold since 1945, and many of the other countries in the region report enviable growth rates.

Each of the regimes that came to power in the years after World War II, many of them governing newly independent states, had to deal with the legacy of the Western powers' involvement in the region. As these new governments tried to build cohesive nations within the often arbitrarily drawn boundaries imposed by the colonial powers, and as they struggled to create effective state institutions to handle the pressing needs of development, they often resorted to coercion and concentrated state control over society. Though heavy state involvement in the economy and tight government control over society may have led to rapid national economic development, they often came at a heavy cost to individuals' liberties. While state economies boomed in many countries across the region, individual living standards remained low. By the 1980s, as their economies improved, as internal challenges to state control gradually became less intense, and as the countries became more involved in the global economy and world order, governments across the region began to loosen their grip over society. Whether the countries chose communism, military rule, or some form of restricted democracy in the first decades after World War II, by the early 1980s the region witnessed a general easing of state repression and a liberalization of political rule, albeit with periodic setbacks.

Despite the generalized trend toward liberalization beginning in the 1980s, the Asia Pacific countries still have extremely diverse forms of government; perhaps in no other region of the world are the differences so pronounced. Brunei is run by an absolute monarch who shows little inclination to reform. Japan's parliamentary democracy continues to serve as a role model for democratizing nations like South Korea, while the military junta in Burma shows little sign of easing its stranglehold on the Burmese population. In Chapter 4, on politics, I note the common challenges of nation building, statebuilding, and economic development in the countries of Asia Pacific; each initially chose some form of communist, military, or restricted democratic rule, yet each has moved away from trying to concentrate power principally in government hands and stepped toward liberalization and granting greater power to citizens. Though students may at times feel overwhelmed as they grapple to understand the radically different forms of governments in the region and the rapidly shifting policies of each, I provide a framework for recognizing general patterns of governance among seemingly disparate systems, and for tracing common trends in shifting power from central governments to the citizens of the region.

How were so many of these countries able to prosper despite their radically different forms of governance? Common patterns arising from diverse experiences also become apparent in Kailash Khandke's analysis of the region's economies in Chapter 5. Focusing on the factors contributing to the rapid economic rise of the high-performing economies and on how these countries' economic choices in many ways paved the way for the Asian financial crisis of 1997, Khandke shows how state policies and unique historical circumstances combined with Asian cultural and political norms to allow these states unprecedented growth from the 1960s through the 1990s. Most of the Asia Pacific states now appear well on their way to economic recovery after the crash of the Thai baht and the "contagious" spread of the economic crisis.

The economic and political development choices made by each of the Asia Pacific states influenced their relations with one another as well as with countries outside the region, as Derek McDougall describes in fascinating detail in Chapter 6. Perhaps the defining choice that most clearly determined patterns of international interaction, particularly in Northeast Asia, was whether states would adopt communism or more market-driven economies. The ideological division between the communist states of China, North Korea, and Indochina and their noncommunist neighbors dramatically affected how the United States and Russia interacted with each state, and thus altered their interstate dynamics. Although the Cold War division was important in both Northeast Asia and in the southeast, the more fragile and newer states in the southeast were more heavily influenced by regional concerns than they were by the great powers. With the collapse of Cold War divisions since 1991, national governments across Asia Pacific have devoted fewer resources to securing domestic control and more to addressing security concerns beyond their respective borders, as Robert Sutter outlines in Chapter 7.

Economic and political choices have also had a dramatic impact on the environment in Asia Pacific, as Peter Hills's sobering account in Chapter 8 reflects. The communist development path imposed a heavy toll on the environment as the communist states raced to industrialize at whatever cost. The failure to tie natural resource use to market prices has led to overutilization of resources and diminished care for sustainable development. Rapid urbanization throughout the region, discussed by Hills as well as Dean Forbes in Chapter 9, has led to startling increases in air and water pollution, and significant global warming. Conversion of land for agricultural use has led to massive deforestation, soil erosion, and water shortages throughout much of the region, particularly in the People's Republic of China. Despite Hills's grim outline of the current state of the Asia Pacific environment, he leaves us with some hope that new awareness of and commitment to sustainable development may be able to ease the region's environmental devastation.

Forbes continues Hills's discussion of rapid urbanization throughout the region, and examines the problems of population controls and managing new demographic challenges. New efforts to control population growth rates, and improvements in health and human services, have contributed to the aging of the Asia Pacific population. While some countries, like the PRC, are banking on economic growth to answer future challenges of caring for the elderly, others, like Japan, where it is predicted that over 40 percent of the population will be age sixty or older by 2050, have begun to experiment with a number of new policies to meet the challenge before it turns to crisis levels. Combating poverty and managing migration into the already overburdened megacities will continue to challenge most of the Asia Pacific countries.

Another challenge governments face in managing their populations is how to handle the diverse ethnic communities living within their borders. As I detail in Chapter 10, Asia Pacific's ethnic mosaic is extraordinarily complex, as ethnic communities have emerged over time in response to intragroup elite efforts to build a sense of common destiny, and in response to changing environments and state policies. Governments have tried a host of approaches to managing ethnic competition, including excluding certain groups, assimilation, integration, preferential treatment for privileged ethnicities, and regional autonomy schemes. As state policies shift over time and in response to new contingencies, they at times are able to control ethnic conflict, while at other times these policies only exacerbate such conflict. More than 10,000 lives have been lost in Indonesia as a result of ethnic strife since the early 1990s, and in China the government's policy in the country's northwest appears to be fomenting interethnic tensions. Only through properly understanding how ethnic groups originate, and properly assessing their needs, can governments hope to formulate proper policies.

Governments have also had to address another important segment of the population: women. While women have traditionally been treated as second-class citizens throughout much of Asia Pacific, improvements have been made, as shown by Yana Rodgers in Chapter 11. While gender inequalities continue and are particularly pronounced in the poorer countries in the region, women have made great strides in health, education, and the labor market. Several legal reforms have been promoted that, while incomplete and not always well enforced, have at least begun to lay the framework for women's rights. Once laws are recorded and a rights regime is developed, women can begin to push for the rights they have been promised theoretically.

Religious influences have affected the position of women throughout Asia Pacific, and have had a major impact on nearly every aspect of life in the region. The richness of diversity in Asia Pacific is perhaps nowhere more apparent than in the religious traditions found throughout the region. All of the world's major religions have played a role in the spiritual life of the region, as Keri Cole describes in Chapter 12, blending with, shaping, and being shaped by one another in the interactions of local and foreign influences. While Buddhism has the largest numerical representation in the region, Islam is not far behind, and the number of Christians, though far below that of Buddhists and Muslims, is on the rise. Though Hinduism is today found primarily only in Bali, it has merged with the other traditions to create a unique blend of faiths in Southeast Asia.

The rich changes occurring in the Asia Pacific societies in terms of cultural, economic, political, ethnic, spiritual, and gender relations are vividly reflected by Fay Beauchamp and Ely Marquez in Chapter 13, on literary traditions found in the region. Ranging from oral storytelling to postmodern theater, the literature of Asia Pacific is as dynamic as the region itself. Beauchamp and Ely trace how the major literary forms reflect themes that preoccupy these diverse cultures.

While few predicted in 1945 that Asia Pacific might one day rival the power of Western Europe and the United States, today it is precisely this concern that keeps attention focused on this vibrant region. In our final chapter, Brantly Womack distinguishes three broad trends in Asia Pacific since World War II that help students both make sense of the complex changes occurring in this dynamic region and inform our understanding of the area's future prospects. He discusses how changes in geography, societal choices, and external interactions have all shaped contemporary developments and future prospects for Asia Pacific.

Casual observers and policymakers alike all seem to have strong opinions about the region, whether they see it as the next frontier for economic development and cooperation or as a dangerous military rival. Yet, quite worryingly, few have the necessary tools for understanding the region. It is our hope that this volume will provide students with a strong foundation for further study. As students explore the interactions among culture, economics, and politics in Asia Pacific, we hope they will begin to appreciate developments in the region and discover common ground for engaging with those living within it. For it is only through increased understanding that we can move toward a future of global cooperation and mutual respect, rather than one of distrust and conflict.

Bibliography

Kristof, Nicholas D., and Sheryl WuDunn. 2000. *Thunder from the East: Portrait of a Rising Asia.* New York: Knopf.

Office of the Secretary of Defense. 2006. *Annual Report to Congress: China's Military Power of the People's Republic of China.* Washington, D.C. http://www.defense link.mil/pubs/pdfs/China%20Report%202006.pdf.

Revere, Evans J. R. 2005. "U.S. Interests and Strategic Goals in East Asia and the Pacific." Acting assistant secretary for East Asian and Pacific affairs, testimony before the Senate Foreign Relations Committee. Washington, D.C., March 2.

Rohrabacher, Dana. 2001. "Rohrabacher Slams U.S. Aid to China." Speech delivered to the House of Representatives. Washington, D.C., April 25. http://www.newsmax .com/archives/articles/2001/4/25/184549.shtml.

Rohwer, Jim. 1995. *Asia Rising: Why America Will Prosper as Asia's Economies Boom.* New York: Simon and Schuster.

World Bank. 1993. *East Asian Model: Economic Growth and Public Policy.* Oxford: Oxford University Press.

2

Asia Pacific:
A Geographic Preface

Ron D. Hill

Nowhere is the theme of diversity and unity better played out than in the Asia Pacific region. The physique of the land ranges from deserts to tropics; from great plains intersected by major rivers, to high plateaus; from mountains to deep gorges that offer major barriers to movement. Asia Pacific constitutes a large section of the Eurasian continent, much of it distant from the sea yet fringed by major archipelagoes easily accessible by water. Its climate includes regions of surpassing dryness and winter cold, such as the Gobi and Takla Makan deserts, as well as some of Earth's wetter places, as along the coast adjoining Myanmar's Arakan ranges or, even wetter, the flanks of some of Java's volcanoes, where an average year may bring more than 26 feet (8 meters) of rain (see Map 2.1). The very land itself is in a semipermanent state of turmoil, as the devastation of the December 2004 tsunami and the smaller Java earthquake of May 2006 so dramatically illustrated. Floods of extraordinary dimensions affect millions at a time in China. Typhoons along China's coast and, more seriously, along the coast of the central and northern Philippines, adjacent to their spawning grounds in the Western Pacific and the South China Sea, may cause serious damage. In the Philippines, Indonesia, and Japan, the risk of serious volcanic eruptions is ever present. Earthquakes offer further threats in such areas, and also in those parts of western and central China that are nearest to the continuing upthrust of the Himalayas.

Historically, the mountains and archipelagic terrains of Asia Pacific have divided communities, leading to a great variety of cultures and peoples, especially in Southeast Asia, essentially a "shatter zone" between the cores of Indic civilization to the west and Sinic to the north. There are several hundred languages in the region. Even in China, where a more or less uniform written language has long existed, the many versions of spoken Chinese are often

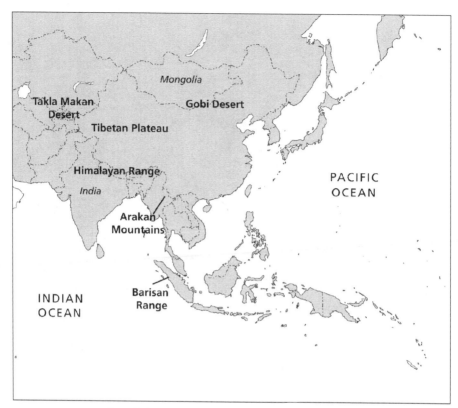

Map 2.1   Mountain Ranges of Asia Pacific

mutually incomprehensible. All the major religious traditions of the world are present in Asia Pacific: Islam in Malaysia, Indonesia, and the southern Philippines; Christianity in the rest of the Philippines and South Korea; Mahayana Buddhism in China, the Koreas, and Japan; and Hinayana Buddhism in Myanmar, Thailand, and Cambodia (see Map 2.2 for the political boundaries of these countries). Ethnically, the region is extremely diverse, as several chapters in this book discuss.

Culturally, there are broad similarities. All parts of the region were externally influenced, notably by Indic and Arabic civilizations, including external religions and languages. Crops include many from outside the region, prehistorically wheat and several other cereals, and more recently a host of "Americans": tobacco, maize, tomatoes, manioc, sweet potato, and many others. Most people now wear much the same kind of clothing and listen to much the same kind of popular Western music. If they know another language, chances are that it will be English.

The terrain ranges widely across Asia Pacific,
shown here *(top)* in the lushness of Java province in Indonesia
and *(bottom)* the stark sands of the Gobi desert in western China.

Map 2.2 Political Map of Asia Pacific

Agriculture is still the prime employer of people in most of the region, though in Japan most of the few remaining farmers now engage in agriculture only part-time. Small, specialist entities such as Singapore, Brunei, and Hong Kong have very limited agricultural sectors. Hunting and gathering as specialist economic activities still survive in the deepest rainforests of Southeast Asia, where region-shifting cultivators continue to fell trees, today almost invariably in already-damaged secondary forest. Manufacturing industry varies greatly from country to country and especially within countries, for little is located in rural areas except that involving the transformation of agricultural produce. The service sectors are developed only to a limited degree in the poorer countries of the region, though dominating in places such as Hong Kong and Singapore.

World Bank photo 00720.

With arable land in short supply, peasants cultivate terraced rice paddies interspersed among mountains in southern China.

Hills and mountains dominate the region, leading to major problems of overland communication. The plains are scattered. Most are densely populated, though this is as much a reflection of their settlement history as of their particular suitability for crops. Most of the long-settled plains see rice as the dominant crop, sometimes almost exclusively. In the north and west of China, where the environment has too short a growing season for rice, wheat replaces it as the major crop, or barley at very high elevations, as in Tibet.

The location of the region in the northwestern quadrant of the Pacific Ocean and its marginal seas has significant consequences for its history, as well as its physical and human geography. Historically, the lands beyond the Ganges, now Southeast Asia, including China, Japan, and the Korean peninsula, were outside the ambit of Europeans until relatively late in human history. Marco Polo in all likelihood visited China when he said he did, though the matter is still debated. But only with the establishment of the Spanish in Manila at the end of the fifteenth century, followed by the Dutch in Java in the early seventeenth century, do we see the beginnings of European territorial control and claims of sovereignty. In northern China, an advanced civilization was established by the Shang dynasty, dating from 1523 B.C.E. This civilization, as it expanded from its core region, centered in the general area of present-day Xi'an, is sometimes claimed to owe little to foreign influences. This is not so. It was generally remarkably open to things foreign. These initially came from southern Asia via what came to be known, by reason of its trade, as the Old Silk Route (there were actually several routes that converged and diverged along its course). The response of the Qing emperor to Britain's Lord Macartney in the nineteenth century, suggesting that China had no need of anything that the West could provide, must be seen as an aberration. This was repeated during the late 1950s in the highly xenophobic era of the Great Leap Forward (today, for many, better called the "Great Leap Backward"). Japan too developed in some degree of isolation. Some suggest that Neolithic Japan was culturally somewhat like Neolithic Southeast Asia, but the modern consensus, noted by Colin Mackerras in Chapter 3, is that both culturally and in terms of ancestral lineage, Japan's cultural origins are to be sought mainly on the Korean peninsula. Xenophobic isolation typified the Tokugawa period, broken forcibly by Commodore Matthew Perry in 1853.

It is perhaps in religious terms that the culturally syncretic nature of the region is best seen. The only two truly indigenous major religions are Shinto in Japan, and "Chinese religion," a variable mix of Taoist, Confucian, and sometimes Buddhist beliefs combined with a healthy measure of ancestor and spirit worship. All the rest were externally introduced. Buddhism and Hinduism were introduced from southern Asia. Islam came from India, partly via missionaries from Aceh, then through the Malay archipelago, and partly across the Silk Routes from what are now the Central Asian republics, to northwestern China. Christianity in its Roman Catholic form came to the Philippines with the Spanish at the very end of the fifteenth century. Elsewhere, in both Roman Catholic and Protestant form, Christianity accompanied Western colonial conquest. Christianity had actually much earlier entered China from the West, though it apparently did not survive into modern times until its reintroduction by Europeans in the sixteenth century. Such examples could be repeated from many other fields, but the basic point is that for much of its history, the Asia Pacific region saw a lively traffic in outside ideas, many of which were incorporated into the cultural fabric. Within the region, too, there was and remains a lively exchange in cultural traits. Consider, for example, the hopefully temporary adulation of the Japanese icon "Hello Kitty."

The location of the region is also fundamental in explaining its climate. Being on the eastern side of the world's largest continent and extending to high latitudes brings winters of extraordinary severity to northern China and the Koreas. In China's Heilongjiang province, for instance, temperatures of –30 degrees Celsius (–22 degrees Fahrenheit) are often accompanied by howling winds. The dryness of western China is to be explained in part by great distance from the sea, exacerbated by the fact that the great mass of the Himalayas and the Tibetan Plateau shields it from the rain-bearing southwest monsoon. By contrast again, the peninsular and archipelagic nature of the band of lands from Japan to Indonesia's Sumatra, to the south and west, leads to climates improved by the influence of the sea, for water both gains and loses heat relatively slowly.

The Asia Pacific region constitutes little more than a tenth of total global land area, though it houses almost a third of the world's people (see Table 2.1).

While distance is a function of technology (and wealth) as much as the size of a country, it nevertheless has a cost, large for transport by airline or human porter, small by water. Thus all large countries have peripheral areas where the hand of government rests lightly. Regional examples include Indonesia's eastern archipelago and the interior of Borneo. Central governments may not know just what is happening in such areas. It is difficult to believe that the recent, staggeringly large smuggling operations in China's Fujian and Hainan provinces could have emerged nearer to the center of power in Beijing. The old saying about the emperor being far away still holds true.

Size has its own advantages. Other things being equal, a large country will have a wider range of climatic zones, allowing the economic production of a broad range of agricultural commodities. It will have a greater chance of possessing a variety of minerals and fuels. Internal production, and with it internal trade, can thus be considerable, along with high levels of self-sufficiency. The China of the 1960s succeeded in being substantially self-supporting, with only about 4 percent of its national income deriving from international trade. Had it been small, China simply could not have done this. Consider the case of Singapore. It has no fuels, no minerals beyond the fabric of the land itself, not even enough water to supply its needs (how far the water shortfall may be is a state secret, but is probably near half; importation from the nearby Malaysian state of Johor supplies the rest). Lest this example be thought extreme, consider also

Table 2.1   Proportion of World Area and Population in Asia Pacific

	Percentage of Area	Percentage of Population
China	7.2	21.1
Japan	0.3	2.1
Korea, North	0.1	0.4
Korea, South	0.1	0.8
Indonesia	1.4	3.5
Malaysia	0.3	0.4
Myanmar	0.5	0.8
Philippines	0.2	1.3
Thailand	0.4	1.0
Vietnam	0.3	0.4
Remainder of Southeast Asia	0.3	0.4
Total	11.1	32.2

Source: Calculated from data in *CIA World Factbook.*

Laos. It has little flat land and no economically developable metallic minerals beyond the scrap left over from war (once the country's first-ranking export). It has no fuels beyond wood and hydroelectricity, the latter of which is today a major export to Thailand.

Size also has strategic implications. In the event of invasion, a small country like Singapore would have little chance of trading space for time, or for developing fallback positions from which to launch counterattacks. The strategic imperative would thus be to launch preemptive strikes in order to forestall invasion. By contrast, a large country like China has great strength in depth, as the second Sino-Japanese war (1937–1945) demonstrated. The subsequent development of heavy industry in the interior was a clear attempt to build an economic and technical base from which counterattacks could be mounted in the event of invasion of its coasts and border areas.

▨ Land and Sea

The Asia Pacific region may be divided into two broad topographical units: a subcontinental-scale section of the Eurasian continent, and a band of peninsulas and islands. The former can be considered to include what is sometimes set off as a separate unit, the Indo-Chinese peninsula. But this is a very broad-based topographical element, substantially joined to China. In part it is linked by drainage basins, notably those of the Irrawaddy, the Salween, and the Mekong (see Map 2.3). In terms of geological structure and composition, the differences between the Indo-Chinese peninsula and the adjoining continent are not major. The ranges of the Indo-Chinese peninsula are no more than a southwestward extension of the great block of terrain that includes the whole of China, though the mountains become lower and the intervening basins broader to the east and south.

The peninsulas and archipelagoes form a distinctly different unit. Though the Korean peninsula is not active volcanically, all the other peninsulas either are or have been within this or the previous geological era. Thus parts of the Malay peninsula still have hot-spring activity and substantial areas of deep, red soils formed on basic volcanic materials of the Tertiary period, poured out just a few million years ago. The areas of current volcanism form arcs (see Map 2.4). One curves south then east from Sumatra's Barisan range, through Java and Bali to Sumbawa. Here, most of the ejected material is chemically basic, on which surpassingly rich soils are formed. Java's relative richness is sometimes unwisely attributed to this geological fact, though the generation of wealth requires much more than just a productive soil. Another arc runs north to south through the central and northern Philippines, where it is partly associated with economically important gold and copper mineralization. A third comprises the Japanese island arc, again an area of nutrient-rich soils.

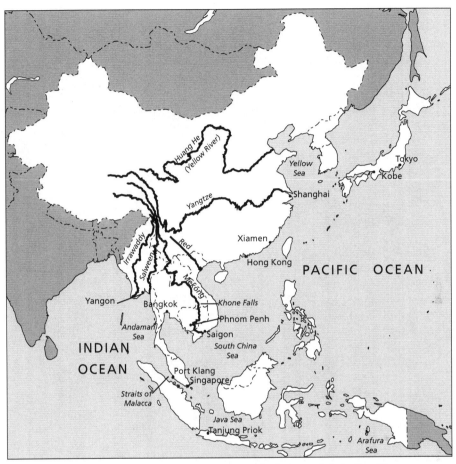

Map 2.3   Major Ports, Seas, and Rivers of Asia Pacific

All such arcs mark the boundaries of great tectonic plates that grind against each other as they slowly move over underlying molten rock. Such regions are notably unstable, experiencing not only the relatively shallow earthquakes associated with eruptions, but also deeper and often more damaging ones resulting from major crustal movements. Along such arcs the possibility of catastrophe is always present. The great Kansai earthquake of 1995 in Japan, which led to several thousand deaths and huge property losses, is only one example of severe environmental and economic damage. Others, involving tens of thousands of deaths, include the Tambora (Sumbawa) eruption of 1815, the Krakatoa eruption of 1883 in Indonesia, and in 1991 the less serious Pinatubo eruption in the Zambales Mountains just north of Manila in the Philippines. All are also thought to have had major effects on global weather,

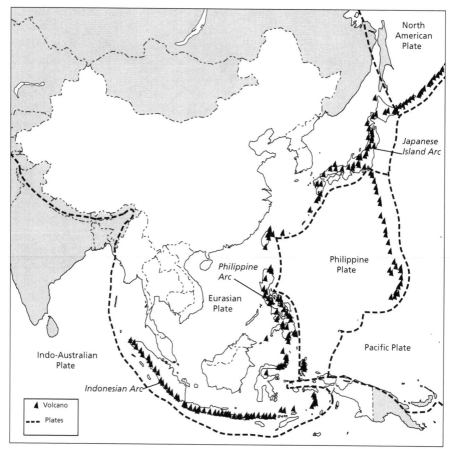

Map 2.4   Tectonic Plates and Major Volcanic Arcs of Asia Pacific

leading to depression of temperatures as a result of their ash and sulfur dioxide emissions.

Two major shared characteristics distinguish the peninsulas and archipelagoes from the continental region: these landmasses are of much lower relief,
and are close to the sea. Permanent snow and ice are thus mostly lacking (only
the tips of New Guinea's highest ranges have them), though the Japanese and
Korean "alps" are snow-clad every winter. Generally, mountains are marked
by temperatures substantially cooler than those of the plains. This leads to the
absence of malarial mosquitoes and to distinctive vegetation types that have
affinities with temperate parts of the globe.

The interlocking of land and sea in the peninsulas and archipelagoes results in relatively mild and stable climatic conditions. It also facilitates trans-

portation, except where coasts are continually exposed to oceanic swells, as along the southern coast of Java and, especially, the eastern coast of the Philippines. A series of seas, from the Andaman in the west to the Timor in the east, assists maritime movement, except at latitudes of about 8 degrees north in the late summer, when warm seas and the effects of the Coriolis force are sufficient to set local air masses spinning in what can be destructive tropical cyclones locally known as typhoons. Like volcanic eruptions and earthquakes, these too can be economically damaging as well as life-threatening, although they also bring substantial rainfall to such areas as the coasts of Vietnam, southern China, much of the Philippines, and Japan. Taken together, the effects of such disasters may be considerable. In the Philippines, for example, it has been estimated that natural disasters cause annual losses equivalent to about 1 percent of national income.

Politically and strategically, the peninsulas and archipelagoes have common interests in the management of fisheries and of seaborne traffic, not least because a major part of the region, the South China Sea, is crucial to the movement of fuels to Japan both from within the region and from the Persian Gulf. Defense needs are also quite different in the archipelagic countries. They need strong navies to keep the sea-lanes open and to control their exclusive economic zones, which may extend to 125 miles (200 kilometers) offshore. Indeed, their island character has required the promulgation of an important principle in international law, the "archipelagic principle." This provides for the drawing of maritime boundaries around outermost islands so that enclaves of "unowned" territory are avoided.

By contrast, the consequences of the continental character of the Chinese massif are rather different. Climate is much more extreme. Natural disasters exclude volcanism and typhoons, though on the western margins especially, except on China's southern and eastern coasts, there are severe earthquakes, for the land is still rising under the effects of the collision of the Indian and Eurasian crustal plates, pushing up the Himalayas and the Tibetan Plateau. In some areas, such as Sichuan, deep earthquakes may trigger massive landslides. Earthquakes may involve massive loss. The Tangshan event of 1976 officially killed about a quarter of a million people, but some estimates double that number of deaths.

Large land areas have large drainage basins, and sustained rain may result in extremely large and persistent floods, in the past sometimes involving major shifts in river channels. China's Huang He (Yellow River), for example, once flowed to the south of the Shandong peninsula, its mouth about 300 miles (500 kilometers) from where it is today. Such shifts are now infrequent because of massive embankments, but the construction of these embankments has had an unintended but serious consequence. The lower courses of many rivers in China, plus some smaller ones in the islands and archipelagoes, are now above the level of the surrounding countryside. The Song Koi (Red River) of northern Vietnam is in some places about 30 feet (10 meters) above the surrounding land, so that a breach in the levees is a matter of utmost seriousness should, for example, a major flood occur. Such levees are strategically vulnerable, as the US bombing during the Vietnam War demonstrated.

Large size also exacts a penalty in the greater cost of overland transportation as compared with movement at sea, except where large navigable rivers reach into the interior, though even these may levy a cost in transshipment. Thus the Chang Jiang (Yangzi River) has been a traditional artery into central China, despite the severe difficulty of navigation through its gorges below Chongqing. By contrast, the Mekong has no arterial function, for its course is severely obstructed at several points, notably at the Khone Falls, though the Chinese authorities are currently removing obstructions to navigation farther north. Distance from the sea also has consequences to human health. Goiter remains a problem in some inland parts of China where people lack access to sea salt and seafoods that contain the trace element of iodine necessary for its prevention.

Accessibility from the sea may thus have important economic consequences. Certainly, the South China Sea, the Yellow Sea, and the series of seas to the south, from the Java Sea in the west to the Arafura Sea in the east, have historically tended to facilitate easy movement at most times of the year. The waters beyond about 8 degrees north latitude are subject to typhoons during the late summer, while those fringing the continental landmass are open to storms during the winter monsoon. Still, navigation is relatively easy for the most part, though as vessels have become larger, water depth has increasingly become a crucial factor. The very largest tankers, for example, can no longer safely navigate the crowded Straits of Malacca. A number of once-important ports have failed to grow because of depth constraints, notably Phnom Penh and Yangon (Rangoon), while others remain limited in the size of vessels they can handle, such as Bangkok and Xiamen (see Map 2.3).

Some coastal regions remain inaccessible from the sea as a result of the nature of the coast itself. For example, the eastern coast of the Malay peninsula lacks any harbor for vessels of more than a few hundred tons, as do the southern coast of Java and the eastern coast of Mindanao, both of which are susceptible to oceanic swells, from the Indian and Pacific oceans respectively. Should hinterlands develop sufficiently to warrant the construction of artificial harbors, these can of course be built, but at a large cost.

The contrast between the region's continental countries, which have a high ratio of land to coastline, and the island and archipelagic nations, which have a low ratio, is very striking (see Table 2.2). The continental countries have relatively long land borders, which has major implications for the conduct of international relations and for military strategy. Thus China shares its land boundary with fourteen other countries, while Japan, the Philippines, and Singapore have no land boundaries at all, unless the causeway from Singapore

Table 2.2   Size, Coastline, and Borders of Asia Pacific Countries

	Area (thousand km²)	Coastline (thousand km)	Border (km)	Ratio of Land Area to Length of Coast	Number of Countries Bordered
China					
Mainland		14,500	22,147	660	14
Taiwan		1,566	—	23	—
Hong Kong		733	30	2	—
Japan	378	29,751	—	13	—
Korea, North	123	2,495	1,673	49	3
Korea, South	99	2,413	231	41	1
ASEAN countries					
Brunei	6	161	381	36	1
Cambodia	181	443	2,572	409	3
Indonesia	1,923	54,716	2,830	35	3
Laos	237	—	5,083	—	5
Malaysia	330	4,676	2,669	71	3
Myanmar	677	1,930	5,876	351	5
Philippines	300	36,289	—	8	—
Singapore	1	193	—	4	—
Thailand	513	3,219	4,863	159	4
Vietnam	331	3,444	4,639	96	3

Source: http://www.odci.gov/cia/publications/factbook/geos (accessed October 30, 2002).

to the neighboring Malaysian state of Johor, about 3,300 feet (1,000 meters) wide, is considered a land boundary (how strategically important even such a tenuous link may be can be illustrated by the relative ease with which Japanese forces crossed the causeway to Singapore in 1943).

Length of coast is also important because each unit of shore length "generates" a corresponding area offshore in each country's exclusive economic zone, except for landlocked Laos. This gives the country a share of fisheries and of such resources as petroleum lying under the sea floor. This in turn generates a number of problems. A major one is China's insistence that the "archipelagic principle" enunciated by the United Nations Conference on the Law of the Sea, a principle designed to ensure that countries like the Philippines and Indonesia do not contain "unowned" sea within their national maritime borders, be applied in the case of the South China Sea. With its large continental landmass, China is manifestly not an archipelago. Moreover, the South China Sea is crisscrossed by a maze of partly overlapping and multiple claims. A few have been resolved, as between Malaysia and Thailand. Most have not, as in the cases of conflicting claims among China, Japan, and Korea farther north.

▨ Climate as Resource

The Asia Pacific region, since it is located on the southeastern side of a continent, has a climate that is markedly more extreme than that of the northwestern sides of continents. This is because the rotation of Earth, coupled with heat
transfer from equatorial to polar regions, pulls cold air in a southeasterly direction at most times of the year. The effect is strongest in winter and weaker
in summer, when heating of the continental interior results in low pressure and
an inflow of warm, moist air from the sea: the monsoon system that affects the
whole region to greater or lesser degree. Its effects are strongest in the north,
where winters are bitterly cold, with temperatures down to −30 degrees Celsius at times, but with hot summers, especially in China's Xinjiang, a desert
interspersed with oases and a few rivers that do not reach the sea. The continental fringes—southern China, the Koreas, Japan, even the northern parts of
Laos, Myanmar, and Vietnam—experience cool winters, with frosts at higher
elevation.

For the equatorial parts of the region, the monsoons mainly affect wind
direction. Thus in most of insular Southeast Asia, winds in the middle of the
year are mainly from southerly directions, bringing much rain where they have
traversed the sea and drought where, as in the eastern archipelago, they blow
across the dry Australian continent. During the northern winter, the predominant wind direction is from the northeast. This brings cool, initially dry air
from the continent, but as it crosses the neighboring seas it rapidly picks up
moisture. For lands around the southern margin of the South China Sea, heavy
rain often results.

This pattern of circulation is paralleled by a broadly similar pattern of
temperatures, but not in the northern summer. July temperatures are quite uniform, ranging from 25 to 35 degrees Celsius (77 to 95 degrees Fahrenheit) in
most places at sea level, with temperatures exceeding 40 degrees Celsius (104
degrees Fahrenheit) in the western deserts of China. By contrast, the winter
temperatures are very low in the north, with −30 degrees Celsius being sustained for weeks on end. At the same time, temperatures are nearly identical in
the equatorial zone in July, around 27–28 degrees Celsius (80–82 degrees
Fahrenheit). There the diurnal temperature range, 8–10 degrees Celsius
(14–18 degrees Fahrenheit), far exceeds the seasonal range. In Singapore the
seasonal range is barely 1 degree Celsius, but father north the range increases.
In Bangkok it is about 4 degrees Celsius, in Hong Kong 13, in Chongqing and
Tokyo 20, and in Beijing 24. Farther west the range is even greater. In Kashi
(Kashgar) the January mean is −6 degrees Celsius (21 degrees Fahrenheit),
with a mean in summer of 26 degrees Celsius (79 degrees Fahrenheit).

This pattern is in turn reflected in the length of the growing season. While
it is true that the length of the growing season depends in part on just which
crops are being grown, freezing weather stops all crop growth. In the low-

lands, such weather never occurs in insular Southeast Asia, and is uncommon in southern Japan and along the coast of southern China, where, however, the growth of some crops, such as rice, may slow or even cease. At higher elevations, the length of the growing season also decreases, so that in parts of Tibet, for example, it may be only a few months.

The region's crop patterns are substantially dependent on temperature and length of the growing season, as well as the availability of water. Thus in northern China, the predominant cereal is wheat, with, farther south, barley and buckwheat at higher elevation. By contrast, throughout Southeast Asia, in southern China, and in Japan, rice is the overwhelmingly common cereal. It was not always thus. For instance, in Japan it was not until the nineteenth century that strains of rice were developed that could tolerate the relatively cool summers of the northern island of Hokkaido. Such areas may be physically suited to particular crops, but to grow them is to defy economic rationality, such that most rice production in northern Japan has ceased. Rationalization in China has also resulted in the disappearance of wheat as a winter crop in the south, and of most rice in Heilongjiang. However, *Hevea* rubber production, though quite marginal, remains in Hainan and other parts of southern China, because it is regarded as a strategic commodity. In principle, China's accession to the World Trade Organization should see rubber production disappear in step with other forms of agricultural rationalization.

Whether the comparative advantage given to most of Southeast Asia in the form of a large range of tropical crops will be fully realized remains to be seen. But this part of the region unquestionably has a major advantage in that temperature is a constraint to cropping only at the highest elevations. In Java, for instance, occasional frosts may occur at elevations above about 5,000 feet (1,500 meters).

Much progress has already been made in taking advantage of the fact that temperature is not a constraint to plant growth in most of the southern half of the Asia Pacific region. In precolonial times, multiple cropping of rice existed only in the densely populated lowlands of southern China, southern Japan, and northern Vietnam. Elsewhere, market demand was such that a single annual crop sufficed. With the growth of export markets and increase of population, multiple cropping spread widely in much of this area, a process greatly aided by the evolution of quick-maturing varieties and stored-water irrigation. In fact, it is water availability, not temperature, that constrains production. In Indonesia, for instance, some 10.3 million acres (4.1 million hectares) of rice is harvested each year, from only 7.5 million acres (3 million hectares) of rice land, a ratio of 1.37. In Sulawesi, the ratio is 1.44, but in the drier lands to the east it falls, to 0.97 in Kalimantan and only 0.42 in eastern Nusa Tenggara, where in any year only about two-fifths of the rice land is actually cultivated.

Tree crops, being deeper-rooted, are less susceptible to dryness than annuals like rice and maize. Coconuts, cacao, *Hevea* rubber, and oil palm need high but equable temperatures and plenty of moisture. These they find in most of Southeast Asia. Their cultivation becomes increasingly uneconomic northward and, except for coconuts, to the east in the archipelago. Rubber and cacao are susceptible to high winds, and their cultivation becomes uneconomic in the typhoon zone. Unfortunately there are no comparably important tree crops that grow farther north, though citrus, lichee, and tea are locally significant. In most of China, Japan, and the Koreas, annual crops are of much greater importance.

Water

Agriculture is the major user of water throughout the region. Very broadly, most of the region has enough to meet the needs of this activity, plus the needs of industry and domestic supply. The major exception to this is the large region north and west of the Yangzi basin. Here, deficits may be very large, but would be even larger except for the fact that rain falling on mountain slopes, little though it is, finds its way into subterranean aquifers, from which it flows or is pumped to supply local needs. Many of the settlement nodes of this region originated as oases. Levels of water use far exceed input in many of these

Water is in scarce supply across much of northwest China. Here, outside Kashgar, China, an adobe home blends into the dusty backdrop.

areas. One indicator of overuse in this large deficit region is the fact that at certain times of the year, the Yellow River, for all its size, fails to reach the sea, so great is the off-take, mainly for agriculture.

Another environment in which water supply can be a problem is that of small islands. Some of these are low and partly coralline in origin, too near sea level to ensure the orographic lifting of water-laden air necessary to rain. Others are too small to develop more than very small rivers and streams, and these may evaporate during dry seasons. Even high islands such as Lombok may suffer from serious shortages during the dry season. Perhaps the most notable island with a water deficit is Singapore. While its deficit is regarded as a state secret, as indicated previously, most observers indicate a shortfall of 40–50 percent of its needs, these almost entirely for industry and domestic uses. Its existing supply from the nearby Malaysian state of Johor has periodically been a political bone of contention, and has led Singapore to improve its water-use efficiency.

For the most part, though, the rest of the region outside of northern China has enough water for all major uses, including hydroelectricity. That happy situation is steadily being eroded by the rapid growth of water demand in cities, as

Though surrounded by water, Singapore does not have enough fresh water to support its citizens.

result of a growth in manufacturing, and especially the adoption of Western-style plumbing and sewage disposal. This in turn has led to the major problems of water pollution analyzed by Peter Hills in Chapter 8. The waste from major cities such as Yangon, Bangkok, Ho Chi Minh City (Saigon), Chongqing, and Shanghai is discharged into waterways with minimal treatment. The coastal waters near major cities are universally suffering from an excess of nutrients, mainly nitrates, contained in waste, while control of the dumping of potentially dangerous heavy metals, mainly from industrial processes, is limited.

Some of the region's rivers are notably large and at first sight would seem to offer great potential for the generation of hydroelectricity. Such include the Yangzi, the Mekong, the Salween, the Irrawaddy, and the Song Koi. All are located in the continental part of the Asia Pacific region where the landmass is large enough to have allowed their development. The catchment of the Yangzi, for example, is about 460,000 square miles (1.2 million square kilometers), with that of the Mekong not much smaller. But even such large rivers suffer from large seasonal variations in their flow. In the wet season, the flow of the Mekong is twenty times greater than that in the dry season. Smaller rivers have even larger disparities. These imply water storage if irrigation and power generation are to operate year-round, which is quite costly. The construction of the necessary dams often results in loss of habitat for large numbers of people and animals. The Three Gorges dam on the Yangzi has required the removal of more than 1 million people. In addition to generating hydroelectricity, the Three Gorges dam is designed to raise the water levels of the Chang Jiang to allow larger shipping vessels access to Chongqing, a central hub of the Chinese government's southwestern development plans. Many observers have questioned the construction of such massive structures, arguing that many small dams on many small rivers would achieve the same results, but would reduce distribution costs and limit environmental damage. But small rivers, especially in the continental part of the region, suffer from much larger seasonal variation in flow, requiring proportionately larger dams to ensure an even supply throughout the year.

Energy and Minerals

Hydroelectricity is a minor contributor to Asia Pacific's energy supply. Only in Laos does it contribute more than half of the total electricity supply. Some countries—Brunei and Singapore—have none at all, depending entirely on fossil fuels. The other renewable source, geothermal power, is only of minor importance, and then only in Indonesia, Japan, and the Philippines, where active volcanism provides the necessary subterranean heat.

Coal and petroleum, as gas or liquid, are the overwhelmingly important sources of energy. Despite being a major producer of petroleum, the region is a net importer of energy, largely as a result of both Japan's and China's large demands. Some of these are met from within the region, with Malaysia, Brunei, Indonesia, and Vietnam being significant exporters, especially of gas. Until the mid-1980s, China was basically self-sufficient in energy resources, relying primarily on coal. Coal mining and use have been fraught with problems in China, as low standards of mining have led to thousands of deaths annually, and coal burning has contributed to massive environmental pollution. The need for petroleum products is growing so rapidly that China will likely soon become the world's largest importer. Vietnam is more than self-sufficient in coal, but finds difficulty in competing with Australian and South African open-cast coal on world markets. Other Southeast Asian countries have some coal, but mostly of poor, sub-bituminous quality, though its use is rising.

The region has adequate supplies of metallic minerals, though only China and Japan have basic heavy industries based on them. Iron ores are widespread, though not always rich enough to be worth working. Much steel manufacture is based on scrap. Bauxite, the ore of aluminum, being a product of rock weathering, is widespread outside the volcanic areas of Southeast Asia. It is smelted mainly in Indonesia. Tin, once widely used in the manufacture of tin plate, is found in local deposits in and around Indonesian islands south of Singapore, in patches on the western side of the Malay peninsula, including southern Thailand, and in parts of Myanmar and China's Yunnan province. But its use is now limited to some electronic goods, and the international market is depressed. Copper, gold, lead, silver, and zinc occur in small quantities in localized patches. Production mostly feeds local or regional markets.

Nonmetallic minerals are available in most of the region. Clay for bricks is found almost universally, as are road and concrete aggregates. Limestone for the manufacture of Portland cement is also widely available, and most countries produce some. Salt is mainly produced by the evaporation of seawater, except in parts of China, where underground deposits are exploited, but nowhere does it form the basis for a significant chemical industry.

Since energy use grows with increasing wealth, the Asia Pacific region, China especially, is likely to see increased demand, especially for petroleum. China is seeking sources to its west in the Central Asian republics and offshore, in the South China Sea, virtually all of which it claims as sovereign territory. China began constructing a US$3 billion gas pipeline from Kazakhstan into the Xinjiang Uighur Autonomous Region in the fall of 2004. In April 2006, China and Turkmenistan signed a framework agreement to begin shipping 1 trillion cubic feet (30 billion cubic meters) of gas from Turkmenistan to China each year beginning in 2009. Various sectors of the South China Sea are also claimed by coastal powers, such as Thailand, Malaysia, Indonesia, the Philippines, and Vietnam. Joint exploitation agreements are already in operation among several of these, and recently China has indicated that it is prepared to set aside thorny issues of ownership and to cooperate in the exploitation of offshore oil and gas.

▧ Natural Vegetation and Its Uses

In step with the north-south temperature gradient lies a vegetation gradient reflecting water supply. Were people, with their long-established penchant for removing trees, not present, this gradient would range from scattered desert vegetation in places like Kashi in western China, where the mean annual rainfall is
only 1/6th of an inch (4 millimeters), to grasslands in Inner Mongolia and
Gansu and Shanxi provinces, to forests in central and eastern China. In the
north, these included coniferous forests, as in the Koreas and adjoining parts of
China; temperate broadleaf forests, which occupied the North China Plain; and
subtropical forests, which covered the rest of the Chinese lowlands, except for
a strip of monsoonal forest along the southern coast of China. Monsoonal forest covered the rest of mainland Southeast Asia as far south as the Isthmus of
Kra. Equatorial forest covered the rest, except at the highest elevations and in
the eastern part of the Indonesian archipelago, where dryness would have led
to a monsoonal forest, in that region one containing a number of species also
found in Australia. At elevations above about 11,500 feet (3,500 meters) along
the Equator, trees give way to grasses and herbs, a fact of little significance
given that such areas occur only in the almost uninhabited mountains of West
Irian. From northern Myanmar and westward rises the great "wall" surmounted
by the Tibetan Plateau, where high elevation, cold, and dryness have led to vast
areas of specialized mountain vegetations.

But this pattern has actually existed for varying periods in the past. In
much of northern China, the human impact has been so long sustained and so
intense that there is real doubt about what the "original" vegetation may have
been. What can be said is that where trees once grew, they can certainly grow
again, but probably not the same kinds of trees that once were there, for local
potential seed sources have mostly long since disappeared. Raising trees and
planting them is the only option.

Most of the grasslands remain, though some have been transformed for
intensive horticulture by irrigation. But most are degraded by the overgrazing
of domestic livestock. In parts of China, it has been policy to encourage the
growth of livestock numbers by providing financial incentives, but there has
been little corresponding expenditure to improve the amount and quality of
fodder needed to support them. Japan has seen an expansion of forest, both by
natural regeneration and by planting, especially since the 1960s, when many
upland agricultural areas began to be abandoned as people moved into industrial cities in the lowlands.

In Southeast Asia, removal of forests began relatively recently. Four hundred years ago, the region was probably more than 90 percent forest-covered,
the only major exceptions being in the Song Koi valley of northern Vietnam
and in parts of Java. The colonial era saw massive deforestation in the course
of converting lowland areas into rice fields, and the hills of the wetter parts of

the equatorial zone into rubber or oil palm "forests." At that time, methods of timber extraction and the proportion of logs extracted, two to five trees per acre, caused relatively little damage to managed forests. By the 1960s, matters had worsened. Changes in the economics of timber extraction led to the use of heavy machines that caused serious damage to that portion of the forest logged over but not actually cut, while the number of trees extracted rose to twenty-five to thirty-eight per hectare. As a result, there have been major decreases in forested areas as well as degradation of what has remained. In Thailand, for instance, in 1953, about two-thirds of the land was still forested. By 1998, only 25 percent remained, and further cutting was prohibited, with the result that Thai loggers shifted their attention to Myanmar and to Cambodia.

The case of Japan suggests that, as in Europe, there may be a cycle of forest exploitation at work that earlier saw massive cutting as international markets for wood products, especially hardwoods, grew. The capital realized by such exploitation aided general economic growth. But as countries become "more wealthy" and come to see that their forests have value other than as timber, so forests increase in area by natural regeneration, where this is possible, and by planting. So far, mostly fast-growing softwoods have been planted in the Asia Pacific region, for these give a quick return and demand is strong. If overlogged land is simply left alone, a forest will recover, but it may never become what once it was in terms of tree variety, largely because selective logging substantially destroys potential sources of seed. However, the Japanese case may be exceptional in that the cost of milling its own forests is so high that many are over-mature. This has occurred because the average timber holding is only about 5 acres (2 hectares), making it cheaper to buy timber abroad. Throughout the region, the current prices of hardwoods are too low to make it worth planting them, for they may take one to three centuries to mature. Softwoods mature in thirty to sixty years, so that planting is feasible.

In the Asia Pacific region generally, several factors will continue to drive the market for wood products. First is the large size of the region's population, together with its continued, though slowing, growth, discussed in detail by Dean Forbes in Chapter 9. Second is the increasing wealth of the region's peoples, though income disparities, both in respect of the areas in which people reside and in terms of the socioeconomic class to which they belong, are clearly becoming greater.

Conclusion

None of the geography of Asia Pacific is immutable, not even the geography of the land itself. China's land area continues to grow as its deltas build seaward, though the completion of the Three Gorges dam will see a substantial reduction in that process. Singapore grows by land reclamation, somewhat to the

chagrin of its neighbors, who thus see the relative size of their territory reduced. Even the climate seems well set to change, in the direction of more heat,
perhaps more rain in the wet parts and less in the dry, probably bringing more
severe and longer-lasting storms. Some kinds of agricultural production, those
based on short-term crops especially, are likely to become more uncertain. The
region's forests seem set to diminish further, especially in Myanmar, Cambodia, and Indonesia, where there is a lack of political will to control deforestation. China has already begun to emerge as a major regional market for timber
while its own supplies are diminishing.

As wealth grows, vulnerability to natural disasters is likely to diminish.
Buildings will be better constructed, though how far even a wealthy country
such as Japan still has to go to mitigate the effects of earthquakes was well illustrated by the Kansai earthquake in 1995. Irrigation will reduce the effects
of drought on agriculture, though ironically, this may come at the price of reduced supplies of water for other purposes. China, with its penchant for
grandiose projects, seems committed to taking water from the wetter south to
the drier north, for lack of water is emerging as a constraint to urban and industrial growth there.

As wealth grows, so too will environmental problems grow. As Peter Hills
shows in Chapter 8, China has major problems, especially with air and water.
Soil erosion is serious. The annual loss of nutrients from soil erosion is equivalent to the whole of the country's annual fertilizer output. In Beijing, spring
dust storms are a regular occurrence, disrupting land and air traffic and causing health problems. There is some evidence that southern China is the epicenter for viral diseases, such as "bird flu" and severe acute respiratory syndrome
(SARS), that may spread in global pandemics. The poorer parts of the region
still lack clean water, while the introduction of waterborne human waste disposal simultaneously deprives agriculture of nutrients for recycling, creates
massive demands for water and huge problems of treating the consequent
waste discharge, while also creating problems of eutrophication (excessive nutrients) in inland and inshore waters. In industry and in the generation of electricity using coal, inferior furnace design leads to excessive fuel consumption
and to massive air pollution problems, aggravated by rapid increases in the
numbers of motor vehicles, especially those with poorly maintained diesel engines. Some of this pollution is exported. For example, about half of Hong
Kong's air pollution comes from elsewhere, while for much of the year most
of China is covered with a dirty brown cloud perhaps over a mile thick.

But with growing wealth comes also the financial means to clean up the
environment, to plant more trees, even in urban areas, and to apply tertiary-
level treatment to water waste to make it drinkable if heavy-metal residues can
be successfully controlled at the source. Throughout the region, government
policy, spoken or unspoken, has been to "grow now, clean up later." Japan has
made good progress with the latter part of this process, in part out of a realiza-

tion that there are very substantial, mainly public, costs of dirtiness. There will always be some risk to living in the Asia Pacific region, but there is real hope that most of its inhabitants will be able to lead lives that are safe, clean, and healthy.

Bibliography

Gupta, Avajit, ed. 2005. *The Physical Geography of Southeast Asia.* Oxford: Oxford University Press.

Hill, R. D. 2002. *Southeast Asia: People, Land, and Economy.* Crow's Nest, NSW: Allen and Unwin.

Leeming, Frank. 1993. *The Changing Geography of China.* Oxford: Blackwell.

Ren Mei-e et al. 1985. *An Outline of China's Physical Geography.* Beijing: Foreign Languages Press.

Smith, Christopher J. 1991. *China: People and Places in the Land of One Billion.* Boulder: Westview.

Spencer, J. E. 1954. *Asia, East by South: A Cultural Geography.* New York: Wiley.

Zhao, Songqiao. 1994. *Geography of China: Environment, Resources, Population, and Development.* New York: Wiley.

3

The Historical Context

Colin Mackerras

There is a good deal in common among the cultures, traditions, and histories of the peoples living within Asia Pacific. Other than in a few areas, like the pastures of Inner Mongolia, the economies throughout most of the region were based originally on agriculture. The staple diet of the great majority of the people was—and still is—rice, a highly productive grain that has dominated the agriculture of most of the region since the early centuries of the common era. Most people lived in villages, and by far the most important calling was farming.

The organization of most Asia Pacific societies was hierarchical, with the welfare of the individual subordinated to that of the group. Almost all these societies were based on the family, with three generations usually living together. In general, young people deferred to old, and females to males. However, the degree of patriarchal dominance varied greatly from society to society. It was generally far stronger in the Confucian and Islamic societies than in the Buddhist, and in China, Japan, and Korea than in Southeast Asia (Murphey 1992:4–6). Anthony Reid argues (1988:146–147) that females had a relatively high degree of autonomy throughout Southeast Asia, except in Confucian Vietnam.

Defined as those territories within the current states that make up China, Japan, and North and South Korea, and within the states of the Association of Southeast Asian Nations (ASEAN), Asia Pacific can be defended as a valid and more or less coherent unit for the purposes of study. Yet there are also great diversities among the peoples of East and Southeast Asia. The traditions of China, Japan, Korea, and Vietnam are strongly dominated by Confucianism, a state-centric ideology covered in more detail later in this chapter. Government in Southeast Asia featured kings and chieftains, but, other than in

Vietnam, was commonly less centralized than in the Confucian states, with no defined, let alone fixed, borders. The political influence of the sovereign diminished the farther away one traveled from the center (Stuart-Fox 2000:84).

It is also worth noting that there are some factors that make the countries of Asia Pacific more diverse than other great civilization centers. If we compare Asia Pacific with Europe, for instance, the differences are quite pronounced. Once Christianity reached its peak, it became a common, if not necessarily unifying, factor throughout almost all Europe until the onset of modern secularism. The most important exceptions were those territories that adopted Islam through belonging to the Turkish Ottoman Empire. In East and Southeast Asia, on the other hand, as Keri Cole details in Chapter 12, we find several major faiths with major influence, and a plethora of folk religions as well. Buddhism, Islam, and Christianity were among the universalist religions competing for influence, with Confucianism, Shinto, and Daoism also enjoying an impact in specific places. There are two broad forms of Buddhism: Mahayana and Theravada. Mahayana Buddhism prevails in Vietnam, Japan, and all of China, except for one portion of Yunnan province. Southeast Asian Buddhists, such as the Thais and Burmese, accept Theravada Buddhism. Theravada is the older form of Buddhism, while the Mahayana tradition claims to represent the Buddha's most complete teachings. Besides religion, a further source of diversity in the region is language and script. In Europe, almost all languages belong to the Indo-European family, the most notable exceptions being Finnish, Hungarian, and Basque. Only three related scripts are in use—Latin, Greek, and Cyrillic—with the Latin alphabet being the overwhelmingly dominant form of writing, except in Greece, Russia, Bulgaria, and Serbia. By contrast, the countries of East and Southeast Asia developed a plethora of languages, belonging to several different language families, including Sino-Tibetan, Tai, Austro-Asiatic, and Austronesian. Traditionally there were many scripts, though several major languages have adopted the Latin alphabet. The most widely used script is Chinese, which differs from most writing systems in being nonalphabetic. Vietnamese is closely related to Chinese linguistically, and used Chinese characters until French Jesuit Alexandre de Rhodes (1591–1660) perfected a script called Quoc-ngu, based closely on the Latin alphabet. Japanese and Korean are unrelated linguistically to Chinese, but have adopted Chinese characters. Japanese still uses Chinese characters and two syllabaries based on Chinese characters. In 1446, King Sejong of Korea ordered the adoption of a specifically Korean syllabary called *hangul*. Aristocratic Korean literature continued to use Chinese, but novels adopted the Korean script.

For the purposes of definition and scholarly classification, it is both appropriate and desirable to define a region according to the political borders of existing nation-states. However, these borders have not necessarily been constant over history. The oldest "state" in the region is probably the one we know today as "China." The Chinese are justly proud of their history of "unity," and there is a long Chinese tradition of a large territory within a state ruled by a single emperor. But it has not always been a Chinese government that has ruled over the territory, much of which has not always been within "China," or whatever name this state was known by at the time. There have been periods when two or several dynasties ruled over the territory.

Even Japan, which has a great advantage in terms of establishing borders and being a set of islands, has seen periods of disunity and civil war. Southeast Asia has been anything but stable politically over its long history. The territories governed by the various Southeast Asian kings, chieftains, and emperors have shifted over time and have often been quite porous. There has been a recognizable Vietnamese kingdom for many centuries, but there have been times when the northern part of what is today called Vietnam was part of China. Kingdoms like Champa (founded 192 C.E.) took up much of the territory of the central and southern coastal areas of Vietnam until the Vietnamese absorbed it in the seventeenth century. The concept of "Indonesia" is mainly a modern one, deriving its legitimacy from the nationalist movement.

▨ The Peopling of Asia Pacific

The earliest finds of the species *Homo erectus* (literally "person standing erect") were made in 1890 by Dutch army surgeon Eugène Dubois. Because he made the discoveries in Java, now in Indonesia, following them up with others on the same island, we usually know this species as "Java man." The 1920s saw the unearthing of *Homo erectus* remains at Zhoukoudian near Beijing, and since the English-language name for the city at the time was Peking, the specimens attracted the name "Peking man." These and other finds in China and Vietnam date from about 500,000 years ago, and there seems little doubt that the species *Homo erectus* had become widespread throughout Asia Pacific by then, and probably quite a bit earlier. These hominids appear to have used chopping tools such as hand axes. At least some of them lived in caves and had mastered fire.

About 200,000 years ago, modern humankind, or *Homo sapiens* (literally "wise person"), superseded *Homo erectus* and became the only human species on the planet. At about the same time, the minor differences in body characteristics that we associate with different peoples began to emerge, including facial features, color of skin, and extent of body hair. This suggests that the *Homo erectus* found in East and Southeast Asia evolved into *Homo sapiens* there, but of course this does not exclude the possibility of migrations from elsewhere or within the region.

However, the earliest evidence of human culture comes not from East and Southeast Asia but from farther west. The earliest known Neolithic cultures in China are based in the Yellow River valley and date from about 6500 to 5000

B.C.E., and thus are considerably more recent than their counterparts in western Asia. These cultures produced unpainted pottery, lived in villages, and practiced agriculture. They domesticated pigs and dogs, and stored grain, mainly millet, underground.

The Yangshao Neolithic culture (about 5000 to 3000 B.C.E.) is well represented in the village of Banpo, which is still preserved as an archaeological site and tourist attraction just outside Xi'an, capital of Shaanxi province, China. The burial places are relatively even in their level of grandeur, suggesting a reasonably equitable society with some measure of gender equality. There is evidence of "a slash-and-burn type of shifting agriculture largely dependent on the cultivation of an indigenous millet" (Fairservis 1997:230). The pottery found here, having colorful painted decorations, is far more elaborate than that created by earlier Neolithic predecessors.

Despite their ethnic similarities with the Chinese, the spoken languages of the Koreans and Japanese are different from any Sino-Tibetan tongue. There are, however, many similarities in the two languages, both with each other and with northern Asian Altaic languages. This suggests that both peoples descended, to a large extent, from migrants from the north. There are signs of cultures in Korea from about the third millennium B.C.E., in Japan probably earlier. Already in those early days, both Koreans and Japanese were able to make pottery, but were not yet able to practice agriculture; they survived through hunting and gathering, with fish a primary part of their diet.

The grains that archaeologists have found signs of in northern China do not include rice, though by late Neolithic times rice may have become a major part of the diet of Chinese in the south, where the climate is milder and wetter than in the north (von Falkenhausen 1991:138–140). However, it is possible that one of the quintessential features of the cultures of East and Southeast Asia, rice cultivation, was found earliest in the region not in China, but in mainland Southeast Asia. Rice and small cattle may have been domesticated in Thailand as early as 6000 B.C.E. (Fairservis 1997:230). Concerning the situation farther east, one Vietnamese author has written: "It is reasonable to assume that at the end of the Neolithic Era, about 5,000–6,000 years ago, most of the primitive human beings living on the territory of present-day Vietnam were entering into the era of rice cultivation. Recent archaeological discoveries have provided evidence of this everywhere, from north to south, from highlands to lowlands, and from littoral areas to islands off the coast" (Nguyen 1993:9).

At a time before written records and from a source that scholars have not determined with certainty, the Malay peoples spread over most of Southeast Asia. A wide range of peoples inhabit island Southeast Asia, in what is today Indonesia and the Philippines, and nonpeninsular Malaysia. However, their languages and ethnicities are broadly similar, pointing to common origins.

Malay peoples also inhabit many parts of mainland Southeast Asia. However, from the third or fourth millennium B.C.E., and extending over many centuries, mainland Southeast Asia sustained a series of migrations from the north and northwest. There was also migration the other way, as shown in the ethnic composition of Yunnan province in China, but the mainstream migration was toward mainland Southeast Asia and from China, including the Tibetan areas.

It is notable that for a long period, southern China and much of mainland Southeast Asia, by today's delineation, formed a single cultural region. Northern Vietnam was similar in language, culture, and ethnicity to southern China, and even today the influence is obvious. The languages of mainland Southeast Asia evince the strong impact of the Sino-Tibetan family, suggesting cultural influence. But there are very important ways in which influence moved in the opposite direction as well. For example, as mentioned, rice cultivation may well have spread from Southeast Asia to China. It was in Southeast Asia that chickens and water buffaloes, and possibly pigs, were first domesticated. And the domestication of these fowl and animals, so crucial to humankind over the ages, spread both north and northwest, to China, India, and Europe (Murphey 1992:12–15).

Cultural diffusion from India greatly impacted all of Southeast Asia, except northern Vietnam, where the Chinese were in control, and the Philippines, which was too distant geographically. Indianization was an extremely gradual process, and probably began in the very early centuries of the common era. It was from India that Buddhism, Hinduism, and writing systems were introduced to Southeast Asia. To this day, Indian influences are obvious in the arts of Indonesia; for instance, Indian themes dominate Javanese shadow plays, and Indian motifs are used in traditional batik designs.

This cultural diffusion did not occur, as one might expect, through mass migration of Indians. On the contrary, it appears that "a relatively limited number of traders and priest-scholars brought Indian culture in its various forms to Southeast Asia where much, but not all, of this culture was absorbed by the local population and joined to their existing cultural patterns" (Osborne 2000:28). And Southeast Asian travelers, traders, and religious specialists may also have taken Indian concepts back to their home countries.

◼ Political Patterns of the Past and "the State"

There is an enormous literature on "the state," and it is beyond the scope of this chapter to contribute to it. For present purposes, I understand "the state" as that complex of institutions and people contributing to governance and holding some degree of sovereignty or control in a territory. In most periods, including the ancient periods under discussion here, a state had access to a writing system and military force, controlled wealth and resources, and to some extent had an ideology or religion. A "kingdom" was territory ruled by a king or monarch, and an "empire" was usually an enormous kingdom ruled by an emperor. A "dynasty" was a territory ruled by a family based on heredity. By definition, most kingdoms and empires are states. However, not all states are kingdoms, with republics being particularly common in modern times.

Among the countries covered in this book, it was in China that we first find politics developed to the stage where we can talk of a recognizable "state." The major states of Korea, Japan, and Southeast Asia belong to a much later period, as is obvious from the brief Asia Pacific timeline presented in Figure 3.1. Also, China exerted considerable influence on the growth of the state in neighboring countries, especially Korea and Vietnam, and also Japan to some extent. The Chinese state has for millennia been the most populous of the world. At the start of the common era, there were some 58 million people living in China (Ebrey 1996:73), somewhat more than in the Roman Empire, while the total world population was about 300 million. For these three reasons—age, influence, and population—any discussion of the growth of the state must devote considerable attention to China.

The Chinese State

Probably the first "state" in Asia Pacific, as defined in this book, was China's Shang dynasty (ca. 1554–1045 B.C.E.). Although skeptics doubted even the existence of the Shang at one time, extensive archaeological finds, especially near its last capital, Anyang in Henan province, have enabled us to piece together some crucial features of this political and cultural entity. The Shang had a capital city and a royal dynasty who exercised power partly through military force, and levied taxes. Many oracle bones have been discovered showing the first cast-iron evidence of writing in the history of Asia Pacific. There was a complex ritual attached to the dynasty, and a religion based in part on ancestor worship. "At the core of the state were groups of ritual specialists, administrators, warriors, artisans and retainers linked to the royal house by blood, belief and self-interest" (Keightley 1991:143).

With the fall of the Shang, another "state" was established, headed by the Zhou dynasty (ca. 1122–221 B.C.E.). In its heyday, the Zhou held control over a fairly extensive territory, certainly far more than had the Shang. In due course, however, the Zhou monarchy declined, its rule relegated to a small area, while more or less independent kingdoms fought for control. This period, called the Warring States, lasted from about the middle of the fifth century B.C.E. to the conquests of the Qin dynasty two centuries later. The constant wars resulted in misery for the people as a whole, but the period was nevertheless a spectacularly great one for the growth of Chinese philosophy and culture.

In 221 B.C.E., one of these warring states, the Qin, achieved power, unity, and dominance over all others. It was Qin Shihuang (literally "the first emperor of Qin"), whose efforts to create a unified country included the imposition of uniform systems of writing and weights and measures. Before his time, there had been significant differences in the writing of characters throughout

Figure 3.1 Brief Asia Pacific Timeline, ca. 9000 B.C.E. to 1950

China/Mongolia	Japan/Korea	Southeast Asia	Other Places
ca. 5000 B.C.E.: Rice and millet crops, fruits, nuts, vegetables, pork, and fish already consumed.	ca. 4000–250 B.C.E.: Jomon and Yayoi Neolithic cultures in Japan.	ca. 9000 B.C.E.: Possible first use of domesticated beans, peas, and water chestnuts in Thailand.	ca. 9000–7000 B.C.E.: Beginnings of agriculture, first in western Asia.
ca. 5000–3000 B.C.E.: Yangshao Neolithic culture in China.		ca. 6000 B.C.E.: Possible first use of rice and of small domesticated cattle.	ca. 3200 B.C.E.: Earliest wheeled transport (Mesopotamia).
ca. 1554–1045 B.C.E.: Shang dynasty, probably Asia Pacific's first "state," includes earliest evidence of Chinese writing.			ca. 2500–1700 B.C.E.: Period of the Indus Civilization, the earliest known urban civilization of the Indian subcontinent.
ca. 1122–221 B.C.E.: Zhou dynasty, including Warring States period (ca. 450–221 B.C.E.).			
551–479 B.C.E.: Life of Confucius.			ca. 563–483 B.C.E.: Life of Gautama, the Buddha, in India.
221 B.C.E.: Qin Shihuang establishes powerful unified state.			334–323 B.C.E.: Alexander the Great's conquests.
206 B.C.E.: Restoration of the Han dynasty (fell 220 C.E.), especially reign of Wudi (141–87 B.C.E.), results in centralized bureaucratic empire based on Confucianism.		111 B.C.E.: China conquers the northern part of Vietnam, which remains part of China for about a millennium.	27 B.C.E.–14 C.E.: Rule of Caesar Augustus, founder of the Roman Empire.
			ca. 6 B.C.E.–30 C.E.: Life of Jesus Christ, founder of Christianity.

continues

Figure 3.1 Brief Asia Pacific Timeline, ca. 9000 B.C.E. to 1950, *continued*

China/Mongolia	Japan/Korea	Southeast Asia	Other Places
589 C.E.: The Sui dynasty reunifies China after period of disunity, followed by the Tang dynasty (618–907), under which Chinese political power, economy, and culture reach an apex.	Second century C.E.: Koguryo, the first native "state," established in Korea.	Early centuries C.E.: Buddhism, Hinduism, and writing systems introduced.	306–337 C.E.: Reign of Constantine I results in the official establishment of Christianity in the Roman Empire.
	372: Koguryo founds a school for Confucian classics.	First–sixth centuries: The first "Hinduized" state: Funan.	Seventh century: Emergence of Islam as major monotheistic religion.
845: Persecution against Buddhism and Manichaeism, ordered by Emperor Wuzong, reaches its climax.	Mid–sixth century: Buddhism begins to spread in Japan.	192: The early Hinduized kingdom Champa is established; absorbed into Vietnam in the seventeenth century.	632: Death of Islam's founder, Muhammad.
960: Foundation of the Song dynasty, which sees urban growth and a cultural flowering, especially in landscape painting.	604: Japanese prince Shotoku adopts ideas of Chinese centralized governance, based on Confucianism, followed by institutionalization of these ideas in the Taika reforms of the mid–seventh century.	939: Vietnam establishes a state independent of China.	800: Charlemagne, who brought about a cultural and political renaissance in western Europe, is crowned Holy Roman Emperor.
			1095–1099: First Crusade against Islam.
1206: In Mongolia, Temüjin is declared Chingghiz Khan, leading over the next decades to Mongol control over most of the Eurasian continent, including the whole of China and Korea, but not Japan.	918–1392: Koryo dynasty in Korea.	1181–ca. 1219: The Hinduized kingdom Khmer reaches its height under Jayavarman VII, builder of one of its greatest monuments, the Bayon.	1198–1216: Papacy of Innocent III exemplifies great age of European medieval Catholicism.
	1192: Minamoto Yoritomo titles himself shogun, founding the 700-year shogunate rule of Japan.		1258–1324: Life of Osman, founder of the Ottoman Turkish state.
		Thirteenth century: Islam spreads to Sumatra.	1347–1351: Black Death (plague pandemic) ravages Europe.

continues

Figure 3.1 Brief Asia Pacific Timeline, ca. 9000 B.C.E. to 1950, continued

China/Mongolia	Japan/Korea	Southeast Asia	Other Places
1368–1644: The Ming dynasty expels the Mongols from China, its economy sparking the "Age of Commerce," lasting to the late seventeenth century.	1338–1573: The Ashikaga shogunate in Japan sees the rise of regional samurai (daimyo), great economic and cultural growth, and urban development.	1350: King Ramadhipati founds the Kingdom of Ayuthia, the first major Thai Buddhist state.	1453: Ottoman Turks seize Constantinople, ending the centuries-old eastern Roman Empire.
		Early fifteenth century: Western Malaya, which rules rising power Melaka, converts to Islam, strengthening Muslim political power.	Fifteenth-sixteenth centuries: Renaissance in Europe.
1405–1433: Chinese Muslim eunuch Zheng He leads seven maritime voyages as far as the Persian Gulf and the east coast of Africa.	1392–1910: Yi dynasty in Korea.		1492: Spaniard Christopher Columbus reaches the Americas.
	1446: Korean king Sejong adopts hangul syllabary.	1511: The Portuguese seize Melaka, beginning major Iberian influence in Southeast Asia.	Sixteenth century: The Reformation in Europe.
1644–1911: Manchus rule China under the Qing dynasty, reaching their height under Kangxi (1662–1722) and Qianlong (1736–1796) emperors.	1603: Tokugawa Ieyasu establishes the Tokugawa shogunate, which leads to a period of high urban culture and prosperity in Japan, but also to isolation from the outside world.	Mid-seventeenth century: Alexandre de Rhodes (1591–1660) perfects romanized Vietnamese writing called Quoc-ngu.	Seventeenth-eighteenth centuries: The Enlightenment leads to a much broader range of ideas in Europe.
		1602: The Dutch East India Company is established, leading to a period of profound Dutch influence over trade and politics in Java, where the company seizes Batavia (Jakarta) in 1619.	Eighteenth-nineteenth centuries: The industrial revolution in Europe expands economy and culture, leading to imperialism.
			1776: United States established.
			1789: French Revolution.

continues

Figure 3.1 Brief Asia Pacific Timeline, ca. 9000 B.C.E. to 1950, *continued*

China/Mongolia	Japan/Korea	Southeast Asia	Other Places
1842: The British impose the Treaty of Nanjing on China, the first of the "unequal treaties."	1867: The Tokugawa shogunate ends.	1802: Nguyen dynasty established in Vietnam, promoting Chinese governance.	1815: Napoleon's defeat at the Battle of Waterloo ends twenty-three years of war between France and other European powers.
1851–1864: Taiping rebellion ravages China.	1868: Japanese emperor Meiji launches the Meiji Restoration; a rapid rise in Japanese power follows.	1819: Stamford Raffles of Britain establishes Singapore as a port.	1857–1858: Rebellion in India against British economic and cultural influence leads to transfer of authority to the British crown; British India becomes the world's largest colony.
1900: The Boxer uprising is suppressed by six European powers, the United States, and Japan.	1895: Japan defeats China in the first Sino-Japanese war.	1824: Anglo-Dutch Treaty returns the Malay archipelago to the Dutch, but the Malay peninsula to the British.	1871: Germany united under Kaiser Wilhelm I.
1901: The European powers impose on China the humiliating Boxer Protocol.	1910: The Yi dynasty falls, and Korea becomes a Japanese colony.	1887: Union of Indochina decreed as a French colony.	
1905: Japan wins the Russo-Japanese War (begun 1904), fought on Chinese soil.		1898: Treaty of Paris ends the Spanish-American War. The Philippines becomes a colony of the United States.	

continues

Figure 3.1 Brief Asia Pacific Timeline, ca. 9000 B.C.E. to 1950, *continued*

China/Mongolia	Japan/Korea	Southeast Asia	Other Places
1912: Nationalist hero Sun Yat-sen (1866–1925) establishes the Republic of China.	1919: Upsurge of anti-Japanese nationalism in Korea following March First Movement.	1912: Protonationalist Sarekat Islam founded.	1914–1918: World War I; Germany defeated.
1919: Anti-Japanese May Fourth Movement takes place in China, associated with the New Culture Movement.	1922: Japan forced to restrict navy by the Washington Conference.	1927: Sukarno establishes the Indonesian National Party.	1917: Bolshevik Revolution in Russia leads to establishment of the Soviet Union.
1921: First congress of the Chinese Communist Party (CCP).	1941: Japan attacks Pearl Harbor in Hawaii, bringing the United States into the war against Japan.	1930: Indochinese Communist Party established under Ho Chi Minh (1890–1969).	1919: Treaty of Versailles sets framework for post–World War I world.
1924: First congress of China's Nationalist Party.	1945: The United States drops nuclear bombs on the Japanese cities of Hiroshima and Nagasaki; Japan surrenders shortly thereafter.	1940: Japanese troops occupy Vietnam.	1922: Washington Conference.
1927: Chiang Kai-shek carries out a coup against the left and seizes power.	1947: A new Japanese constitution, adopted under US occupation, renounces war and upholds democracy.	1942: Japanese troops seize Malaya and Singapore.	1933: Adolf Hitler becomes German chancellor.
1931: Japanese troops seize Manchuria.		1945: Ho Chi Minh declares independence in Vietnam (but France returns in 1946, leading to renewed war); nationalist leaders proclaim independent the Republic of Indonesia.	1939: Britain declares war on Germany, leading to World War II.
1934–1935: CCP forced to undertake the Long March.		1948: Independent Federation of Malaya established.	1941: The Soviet Union and the United States join the war on the Allied side.
1937–1945: Anti-Japanese war.		1949: Dutch concede full sovereignty to Indonesia.	1945: World War II ends.
1949: People's Republic of China established.			

China, but the standard characters his regime enforced remained essentially unchanged until the Chinese Communist Party (CCP) simplified the Chinese script in the 1950s.

Qin Shihuang is famous in Chinese history for his cruelty. Confucian historians have castigated him for his excessive emphasis on punishment as a way of creating social stability. In 213 B.C.E., several scholars recommended the restoration of much of the old system of government, partly because they believed that antiquity should be regarded as a model. Qin Shihuang responded by having many of these scholars buried alive, and ordering the burning of all books except those on farming, medicine, and divination. It was Qin Shihuang's rule that first brought together into a single whole the icon of Chinese civilization, the Great Wall. In the 1970s, archaeologists found thousands of terra-cotta warriors and horses near his grave-mound. This magnificent set of artworks was designed to protect Qin Shihuang in his afterlife.

Qin Shihuang expected that the empire he founded would last ten millennia. However, it lasted only four years after his death in 210 B.C.E. Peasant rebellion had begun to break out against the harsh rule of the Qin, and after a period of civil war a peasant named Liu Bang established the long-lasting Han dynasty (202 B.C.E.–220 C.E.), with himself on the throne as Gaozu (the "High Ancestor" or "Eminent Ancestor"). The initial task of the Han emperors was to establish a state that would be less harsh than under the Qin, but that would nevertheless be stable and strong. It was Wudi (the "Martial Emperor," 141–87 B.C.E.) who succeeded in doing this. His basic formula was a mixture of rigid authoritarianism and "a moral basis of superior-subordinate relations" based

Andrew Reid. Image from BigStockPhoto.com.

Thousands of life-size terra-cotta warriors, each crafted individually, guard the tomb of Qin Shihuang in Xi'an.

The Great Wall was integrated into a single whole
under Qin Shihuang's rule.

on Confucianism (Ebrey 1996:65). He broke and assumed the power of the rival aristocracy by seizing their lands; directed the labor of his subjects into enriching the state and his own court; and established the Grand Academy in 124 B.C.E., with the aim of instructing selected students in the Confucian classics, contributing greatly to implementing the idea of moral bureaucracy in the service of the emperor.

The net effect of the Qin unification and the Han restoration was the creation of what one scholar has called "the bureaucratic empire" (Ebrey 1996:60). This highly developed "state" was centralized and authoritarian, and its emperors, assuming they were competent, were extremely powerful. This notion of a strong central state has survived in China to the present. It had access to immense wealth through taxes and the labor of peasants, and controlled an extremely powerful army. At the same time, the state selected its bureaucracy, in theory, less through hereditary privilege than through learning and morality. Its intent was to value the interests of the people and ensure a good livelihood for them in return for their loyalty.

The basic features of this "bureaucratic empire" remained constant until the twentieth century, and some would argue until the twenty-first. But this is not to imply an absence of change. Chinese history has not been static, and the culture and society of the late imperial age were very different from those of the Han dynasty. Yet in terms of its political nature and culture, China has perhaps been less dynamic than some other great civilizations (see, for instance, Murphey 1999:49–50).

The borders of China waxed and waned throughout the ages, reaching their greatest extent during the Qing dynasty (1644–1911). At times, there were two or more claimants to the throne, or two or more thrones within what we today know as China. But unity remained the ideal: there was never to be more than one emperor at any time, ruling "all under Heaven" *(tianxia),* that is, the empire. Among large continental states, China has a particularly unified history. After the Roman Empire split asunder, it never came together again, and all attempts to reunify Europe have ended in failure. Though China disintegrated in the third century C.E. under the Han dynasty, the state was reunified in 589 C.E. by the Sui dynasty; and though there have been periods of disunity since, they are outweighed greatly in time and importance by periods of unity.

According to the Marxist historiography of China, "feudalism" lasted for 2,000 years or more, essentially from the time the Qin dynasty destroyed the slave-owning system of the preceding period, until the mid–nineteenth century. Western scholars such as Henri Maspero (1883–1945) (1978:34–63), and more recently Rhoads Murphey (1999:34–35), have applied the term "feudalism" to the earlier period of the Shang and Zhou dynasties. The difference is one of definition. Chinese historians understand feudalism as a system dominated by the class who own land as the main means of production. Western historians, on the other hand, tend to see feudalism as a social system in which there is no strong central state, but instead a relationship between the sovereign and a network of "vassals" maintained by loyalties. Both understandings of feudalism are valid, but great confusion can ensue if they are not clearly distinguished. It is ironic that, by defining the whole period from the third century B.C.E. to the nineteenth century C.E. as belonging to the "feudal" era, the Marxist view of China in effect implies no, or very little, basic change in China over those centuries. The implication of change is historical significance, and one might have expected those who were proud of their country and its history to adopt an interpretation that strengthened the case for significance rather than weakening it.

The Non-Chinese State

The earliest "states" in what is now Korea were Koguryo in the north (firmly established in the second century C.E.), Paekche in the southwest (third century), and Silla in the southeast (fourth century). The "three kingdoms," as they are called, were united by Silla, with Chinese help, in the seventh century. The Chinese attempted to conquer Silla, and absorb it into their own empire, during the rule of the Tang dynasty (618–907), but military and political defeat led them to recognize an independent Silla in 735. Since Silla, only two dynasties have ruled over Korea: the Koryo (918–1392), from which derives the English word *Korea,* and the Yi (1392–1910). Korea formally submitted to the Mongols in 1259, but during their century-long rule the Mongols never displaced the Koryo kings, though the latter enjoyed very little power. Koryo survived the collapse of the Mongol Empire in the middle of the fourteenth century.

Other than during the Mongol century, Korea was an independent and united kingdom until 1910. On the other hand, though never a carbon copy, it was heavily influenced by China in political and cultural terms. As early as 372 C.E., the Koguryo king established a school for the specific purpose of teaching Confucian classics and Chinese language in order to train prospective government officials along Chinese lines (Han 1970:63). As a Korean historian noted, Silla also saw "the imposition of Chinese-style bureaucratic government," involving the establishment of numerous educational institutions designed to teach the Confucian classics (Han 1970:102).

At the beginning of the twenty-first century, Japan has the oldest still-surviving ruling dynastic line in the world. Though its legendary origins date back well before the common era, it was not until some centuries afterward that governance developed to the point that we can talk about a "state." The original Japanese community religion, called Shinto (literally, "the way of the gods"), was animistic and naturalistic, and political to the extent that the emperor could be seen as a living spirit *(kami).*

Chinese infusions spread to Japan through Korea, in both political and cultural spheres. By the end of the sixth century C.E., Japan was specifically modeling itself on China. In the mid–seventh century, the Japanese court took several major decisions that firmly implanted the Chinese centralized political

The Shinto Itsukushima Shrine in Hiroshima prefecture, Japan, dates to the sixth century.

system, along with its underlying Confucian ideology. Chinese became the written language of the Japanese elite, and Japan began to produce official histories based on the Chinese Confucian model. The design, structure, and architecture of both the capitals of the period, Nara and Kyoto, were based closely on the Tang Chinese capital Changan.

It was also from China through Korea that Buddhism was introduced into Japan. The religion swept the country, becoming more or less universal, and exerting a stronger influence over Japanese history than over Chinese. Yet Confucianism generally maintained its hold over the educated and official elite. Shinto has retained influence to the present as an emblem of Japanese distinctiveness and, from time to time, of Japanese nationalism.

Despite strong Chinese and Confucian influence, Japan showed quite strong differences from China in its patterns of governance. In the late twelfth century, the shogunate system began, which was to last nearly 700 years, reaching its height in the Tokugawa period (1603–1867), when the shoguns had their capital in Edo (Tokyo), while the emperor stayed in Kyoto. In essence, this system reduced the emperor to a figurehead, even though he held great prestige, while real power was placed into the hands of a military leader called shogun. The highest class were the samurai *(daimyo)*, who were both warriors and administrators.

Himeji Castle was held most famously by a branch of the Ikeda clan, one of the great baronal families *(daimyo)* under Tokugawa shogunal rule.

The other factor that distinguished Japan over these centuries was its feudalism, in the classical non-Marxist sense. The greatest of the *daimyo* were able to exert control over their own domains, but were themselves bound to the shogun through feudal ties of loyalty. However, during the Tokugawa period, the shoguns were able to gain enough control over these *daimyo* that one notable history of East Asia summed up Tokugawa Japan as "a centralized feudal state" (Reischauer and Fairbank 1958:579). They did this through mechanisms like political marriages and forbidding contact between the *daimyo* families without permission from the shogunate. The *daimyo* were forced to spend a good deal of their time in Edo attending to the shogun, and even had to leave their wives and children there as hostages when they returned to their own domains. All this severely restricted their autonomy and gave greater central power to the shoguns.

The northern part of Vietnam was ruled as part of China for about a millennium from the first century B.C.E. There were movements toward independence, but all failed until 938, when China was undergoing one of its periods of disunity called the Five Dynasties (907–960). Ngo Quyen succeeded in defeating an invading Chinese army and the following year established a centralized state. It was, as Vietnamese historians like Nguyen Khac Vien (1993:28) claim, "the first truly independent Vietnamese state." This state lasted less than a decade, but did lead to the establishment of a successful set of dynasties shortly afterward. Apart from a brief interlude in the early fifteenth century, Vietnam has maintained its independence from China. Yet its governance has been based quite closely on the Chinese Confucian model, with emphasis on a strong central monarchical state assisted by a mandarinate.

In the rest of Southeast Asia, states were very different in origin from those of East Asia. With the spread of Indian influences to Southeast Asia through trade and other factors, the impact created, among other entities, what French scholar George Coedès (1948) has called *les états hindouisés* (the Hinduized states). Central to these Southeast Asian states is the notion of the god-king, explained later.

There is some controversy over just how much was Indian in these states and how much was indigenous. The very terms "Indonesia" and "Indochina" imply that much of Southeast Asia is almost like an extension of India, but most scholars are much more inclined to give the peoples of the region credit for a vital role in the creation of their own statecraft. John Legge (1977:38–46) discusses these kingdoms in terms of "borrowed forms and local genius." However, it is highly doubtful that any of the political units antedating the Hinduized states were developed enough to be considered "states" as defined here.

The first of these Hinduized states was Funan, which lasted from the first to the sixth centuries C.E. and covered territories that today belong to southern Vietnam, Cambodia, and Thailand. Its neighbor Champa followed soon after, but lasted much longer. The great maritime and commercial state of Srivijaya,

Built in the twelfth century, Angkor Wat is the best preserved of the many temples in Angkor, capital of the ancient Khmer kingdom.

lasting from the seventh to the thirteenth centuries, dominated most of Java and other parts of the Malay archipelago; and though many of its political formations were similar to those of the Hinduized states, it was ironically Buddhist in its religion, not Hindu. However, a range of Hindu kingdoms were based in Java, the last of them being Majapahit. Arising in the wake of the Mongol invasion of the thirteenth century, Majapahit lasted until the sixteenth century, then succumbed to the spread of Islam and the rise of the Islamic states along the northern coast of Java.

Possibly the greatest of all the Hinduized states was the Khmer kingdom, which had its capital in Angkor from the ninth to the fifteenth centuries. Two kings of particular fame were Suryavarman II (ruled 1113–1150) and Jayavarman VII (ruled 1181–ca. 1219). The former was an ambitious and expansionist warrior whom D. G. E. Hall (1955:103) called "the most powerful king of Khmer history." However, Suryavarman II also exhausted his people to the extent that in 1177, the state of Champa was able to attack and sack Angkor. It was Jayavarman VII who defeated and drove out the Chams, going on to expand the kingdom to its greatest territorial extent, even farther than under Suryavarman II. It dominated most of mainland Southeast Asia, extending into the Malay peninsula into what is now Burma, and even north into what is today Yunnan province in China.

Though Jayavarman VII never abandoned the political forms of the Hinduized state, he is notable among Khmer kings for his conversion to Buddhism, probably at least in part because the sacking of Angkor in 1177 had appeared to throw doubt on the legitimacy of the Hindu cults. Buddhism was not a new religion for the kings of the region. In the Thai Nanzhao kingdom, centered on western Yunnan province, Buddhism had "begun displacing the earlier native religious orientation" in the first half of the ninth century (Backus 1981:129), and the founder of the Burmese Pagan kingdom, Anawrahta (ruled 1044–1077), had already adopted Theravada Buddhism as his official religion. Yet the conversion of Jayavarman VII appears to have strengthened a new notion of kingship in mainland Southeast Asia, one based on Theravada Buddhism.

In the countries of concern to this book, it was in Thailand that Buddhist kingship reached its highest point. Both Nanzhao and Pagan succumbed to the Mongol invasions, in 1253 and 1287 respectively. These events, plus the decline of Khmer power to the east, provided the Thais with a good opportunity to expand their own power. The climax came with the enthronement of King Ramadhipati in 1350, who, according to Hall (1955:151), "is regarded as the first King of Siam," the old name for the country currently called Thailand. His capital was in Ayuthia, which is why the state is often described as the "Kingdom of Ayuthia." The Siamese capital remained there until the Burmese destroyed the city in 1767.

Slightly after the rise of the great Thai Buddhist kingdom, Islam spread into the Malay archipelago and Malay peninsula, mainly in its Sunni form. This was the original, or "orthodox," form of Islam. The other surviving important form is Shi'ite, and derives from a political conflict of the late seventh century; it has been adopted mainly by the Persians (Iranians) and Arabs in Iraq. Both forms accept the main Islamic doctrines, but quite a few differences emerged in the theologies of the sects over the centuries. The "most characteristic" Shi'ite doctrine is its theology of esoteric knowledge, meaning that the Quran, besides having external meanings, has "hidden esoteric meanings that can be known only through spiritual contact" with relevant leaders or imams (Rahman 1987:317).

Through trade and clerical missionaries, Islam had apparently established a foothold in Sumatra by the thirteenth century. From a political point of view, it received a powerful boost through the conversion of the ruler of Melaka on the western coast of the Malay peninsula. The city was the center of a sultanate that had risen as a commercial power early in the fifteenth century. According to Nicholas Tarling, "It became the greatest entrepot of Southeast Asia, and Islam spread to other centres with which Melaka had commercial ties" (2001:315).

Tarling also notes that the existence of strong Hindu-Buddhist kingdoms had at first exercised an inhibiting effect on the political spread of Islam. However, it was "then facilitated by their decline in the fifteenth century" (2001:315). Certainly, Islam spread throughout the Malay peninsula and across most of the islands of Indonesia, though not Bali, and into the southern Philippines.

Though of great significance for the region, the spread of Islam was very uneven politically. In Java, it exerted a far greater impact on the commercial towns of the coast than on the agricultural inland regions. Moreover, the Javanese are known for their syncretism, meaning that they were able to mingle and cross-fertilize different religious traditions with each other, including adapting their local traditions to Islam. As a result, the political impact of Islam on kings and their courts was never total.

Concepts of State Polity and Governance

The most widespread religion in Asia Pacific is Confucianism. Although the doctrine bears his name, Confucius (the accepted romanization of "Kong Fuzi," 551–479 B.C.E.) was actually more of a transmitter than a creator. For example, China was family-centered long before Confucius stressed the importance of loyalty to family; its people had already accepted filial piety *(xiao)* as a major moral virtue. Yet together with his disciples, Confucius did bring together many of the pithy sayings that embody his values and political philosophy.

Confucianism has a strong this-worldly emphasis, meaning that it gives a far higher priority to the present life than to any potential afterlife. So it is often described as a philosophy rather than a religion (see "Confucius and Confucian Thought" on p. 362). However, it has much to say about morality and governance. It also places an enormous weight on rites and the ceremonial, which functioned as an outward manifestation of power and propriety in all traditional Confucian societies. The most basic of Confucian ideas is the virtue of filial piety, as apparent in the family-oriented nature of Chinese and other Confucian societies. Of the "five relationships" *(wulun)* that Confucius emphasized for society to function smoothly, three are associated with family. The five are, in order of importance, ruler-subject, father-son, husband-wife, elder brother–younger brother, and friend-friend. The relationships also suggest a somewhat male-dominated society, as women are explicitly ignored in two of the three family relationships.

The relationships also imply that, historically, Confucianism was generally hierarchical. It was a philosophy that aimed at stable and harmonious governance. Traditional Confucian societies had no time for rebels or anybody who would upset the political applecart. Yet in order to justify loyalty to the ruler and his courtiers and officials, Confucianism imposed on them the duty of granting good government to the people, of caring for their needs and disposing of those forces that would harm their interests.

Confucianism held that it was the virtuous and well educated who should rule. It was study of the Confucian classics that would educate scholars to be good administrators. How should one choose these bureaucrats, or mandarins? From the time of the Han dynasty, the state conducted written examinations to choose recruits into the official bureaucracy. The system waxed and waned over the centuries, but reached its height beginning in the fourteenth century.

It became increasingly rigid and stereotyped, yet bestowed gigantic social prestige and power on those who did well.

Korea and Vietnam both adopted the system of competitive examinations for entry into the bureaucracy. In both cases, the format, style, and content of the examination system were modeled on China's, including the emphasis on Chinese Confucian books and ideology. In both cases, success in the examinations ensured great social prestige and power. There were differences among the systems (on those between Vietnam and China, see Woodside 1988:169–233), but the similarities were more fundamental and numerous.

In theory, education was open to all men, but not necessarily to women. Any man could sit for examinations and enter the bureaucracy, no matter what his social class. So there was something egalitarian about the examination system. Japan experimented with the examination system during the eighth century, but because the hereditary aristocracy guarded their power jealously, the system failed. The Tokugawa government resisted introducing the Chinese way of selecting officials through examinations, again for the same reason: the exams opposed the hereditary system (Dore 1965:194–197).

However, there were major restrictions on the egalitarianism of the system in China. In practice, it was all but impossible for anybody not lucky enough to be born into the educated scholarly elite class to gain the kind of education necessary to have any chance of passing the examinations. Still, the Korean and Vietnamese systems appear to have been less open than was the Chinese. In Korea, the only men eligible to sit for examinations were in effect the members of the *yangban,* the aristocratic, landowning, and official classes. In Vietnam under the Ly and Tran dynasties (eleventh to fourteenth centuries), only the sons of aristocrats or mandarins could present themselves for the examinations.

Another aspect of Confucian governance that states like Korea and Japan repudiated was the ancient doctrine of the "Mandate of Heaven," undoubtedly the most important legacy of the early Zhou period to Chinese political culture (Hsu 1997:280–281). The last king of the Shang had behaved in a tyrannical and wicked way, and it was because of this that Heaven, a vague cosmological force, had withdrawn his right to rule. The same would happen to any other king who failed to carry out his ritual and other duties properly and acted in a tyrannical way toward his subjects. This concept implicitly enforces morality on rulers, but gives the ultimate power to decide on the identity of a ruler to "Heaven." It is the sovereign's duty to look after his people, but they certainly do not have any say in who should rule them. In this sense the notion is at once authoritarian and democratic, but with the emphasis on the former.

Other than in Vietnam, the political patterns of Southeast Asia were very different from those found in Confucian countries. Martin Stuart-Fox sums up the contrasts well, including why Southeast Asian rulers rejected Chinese models in favor of Indian, even though most of them were actually much nearer to China than India:

> Confucian forms of ancestor worship did little to enhance local cults, and Heaven *(Tian)* was too nebulous a concept to serve as a ritual focus for Southeast Asian kings. As for Chinese administration in the form of a centrally recruited and appointed bureaucracy of mandarins educated in the Confucian classics, this was a model inapplicable in kingdoms held together by family ties and tribute which possessed no such tradition of government. The Chinese model was eschewed by Southeast Asian rulers because it could only be adopted *in toto.* The Indian model was acceptable because it could be endlessly modified in relation to local needs. (2000:87)

At the heart of the differences between the Chinese and Indian models was the role of the supernatural, including types of cosmology and ideas of what happened to kings and others after their death. Hinduism, Buddhism, and Islam all rejected Confucianism's lack of concern with such matters, which were extremely important not only for daily life, but for governance as well.

Perhaps the most important of all features of the Hinduized kingdoms was the idea of the god-king, whose powers, wrote John Legge, "underlay the whole system of authority," with the terrestrial order being regarded "as a reflection of the cosmic order," so that "in his splendour and might was expressed the splendour and might of the kingdom" (1977:41). Because of the god-king's quasi-divine power, the state was centralized and the sovereign guarded his authority and legitimacy jealously. There could be no more than one legitimate ruler or one legitimate kingdom at any one time.

In the schema of the god-kings, spirituality was equivalent to power. Society was graded with supernatural sanctions, with people being less virtuous the lower their social rank. Clifford Geertz wrote that "spiritual power flowed outward and downward from its royal fountainhead, attenuating as it sank through each layer in the bureaucracy, draining weakly at last into the peasant masses" (1960:232). One feature that flowed from the notion of the god-king, that supported his authority and gave it symbolic expression, was manifest in the vast buildings designed to resemble enormous pyramids, or mountains, rising up in the capital. As Legge put it, "Just as the kingdom represented a microcosm of the universe, so the royal capital in its turn was also, on a smaller though perhaps more perfect scale, a further microcosmic representation" (1977:43). These buildings were temples or royal sepulchers, or both.

Many of these monuments can still be found scattered throughout Southeast Asia. A particularly large complex of them is located in Angkor, the most famous of which is Angkor Wat, the most important of all Cambodian icons and the largest standing building in the world erected for a religious purpose, though no longer in use as such. The man who ordered this monument built was King Suryavarman II of the Khmer kingdom, who designed this gigantic and magnificent structure as his own mausoleum, placing in its central shrine a golden statue of god Vishnu, a representation of himself deified as the Hindu protector and preserver of the world. The mausoleum of Jayavarman VII also still stands among the Angkor complex. Called the Bayon, it is a pyramidal temple and features the king's sculpted face on each of the four sides of the main tower.

Buddhism was a religion that allowed for personal salvation for all people and had no dependence on the god-king notion. The sovereign was still very powerful, but his rank was far lower than in the Hinduized states. The Siamese kings of Ayuthia, according to Stuart-Fox, sought to emulate the ideal Buddhist king, the "universal monarch, whose rule would be coextensive with the Buddhist Dharma, or truth" (2000:89). It was his duty to accumulate as much merit as he could. This would convince his subjects of his progress toward Buddhahood, reinforcing his status in their eyes. One of the ways he could do this was by building temples, erecting stupas, or molding consecrated Buddha images as gifts to the Buddha. It is not surprising that the religious building programs of the Thai monarchs were grand and magnificent, even if not quite as large in scale as those of rulers like Suryavarman II.

In this profoundly religious and spiritual view of kingship, it is the duty of the king to uphold the Buddhist Dharma as well as the moral order, including in the civil and social spheres. The Theravada Buddhism of the Thais lays far more weight on individual merit and achievement than does Hinduism, far less on divine or cosmic assistance. It follows that the king could take a good deal of the credit for his progress toward Buddhahood. Moreover, his success in preserving the moral order showed his legitimacy to rule. But correspondingly, failure opened him to challenge. There is a parallel here with the "Mandate of Heaven," except that the force bestowing the mandate is very different.

Islam is very different from Buddhism or Hinduism, with its belief in the single god Allah in contrast to the anthropomorphic deities of the religions from India. As pointed out by J. G. de Casparis and I. W. Mabbett, there were stages and degrees of divinity in the notions of Southeast Asian kingship based on Indian thought, and for a king to be "divine" was not even necessarily "an instrument of enhanced power" (1992:322–324). The Melaka rulers could show their adherence to Islamic political philosophy by adopting the title of sultan and claiming to be the deputy of Allah (Tarling 2001:315), but it was hardly appropriate to claim to be the reincarnation of Allah. What Islam shared with Hinduism and Buddhism was the total centrality of religion and the spiritual world in kingship and governance. Obedience to the king was a religious obligation, not merely a this-worldly one.

Yet Islam never actually displaced the old Hindu cults and ideas of kingship in Southeast Asia, but rather mingled and integrated with them. Mataram, in central-southern Java, serves as an example. At the beginning of the eighth century, it had flourished as a major Hinduized kingdom in Java, and again became the center of a Muslim kingdom in the sixteenth century, spreading to take over most of Java in the seventeenth. According to Legge:

Insofar as Islam was able to penetrate below the surface of inland Javanese society, it did so by adapting itself in considerable measure to existing patterns of belief and custom. This was particularly apparent at the Court level, where Mataram was able without difficulty to blend Islam in syncretistic fashion into the existing mixture. In making it the Court religion, Mataram used it to buttress a kingdom which was still essentially Hindu-Javanese in character. Mataram revered the nine walis—supposedly the bringers of Islam to Java . . . ; the ruler adopted the title of Sultan; but the bureaucracy remained, and the sultan, though he could not strictly be held to be a divine figure, was at least seen as the terrestrial representative of God, descended from the god-kings of former dynasties, possessed of mystical power. . . . Islam, in brief, was fitted into the courtly system, was mixed up with Hindu and other symbolism in true Javanese fashion and was made to perform magical functions for the monarchical order in the same way as Hindu concepts had done and continued to do. (1977:57–58)

Commerce, Exploration, and Missionaries

The "age of commerce," which followed a century after the initial spread of Islam to the Malay archipelago, produced extensive economic and social change in the Asia Pacific, especially in Southeast Asia. It was accompanied by the arrival of European powers in the region, bent on trading with the people and converting them to Christianity. The first were the Portuguese, followed by the Spanish, Dutch, French, and British, while the Russians expanded overland to the east.

"Commerce" was by no means new at this period. The overland Silk Routes, which had begun and reached their height under the Han dynasty, linked China with the Roman Empire through Central Asia, allowing for extensive commercial exchange between Europe and Asia; silk sold from China to Rome was only the most important commodity. Also, trade over the Silk Routes was much more important for the Roman Empire economically and culturally than it was for China. Long before the age of commerce, sea routes were also used for trade, although in general they were less important than the overland ones, which the Silk Routes best exemplified.

According to Anthony Reid, the economic boom that led to the "age of commerce" began about the beginning of the fifteenth century, and was sparked by "the explosion of energy from the new Ming dynasty [1368–1644] in China" (1992:460). The increase in trade brought about the rise of cosmopolitan commercial cities in Southeast Asia, and also increased interconnections among them. Reid writes that "states formed and strengthened around the cities, and more secular forms of thought and culture flourished in them" (1988:xv).

The arrival of the Portuguese at the beginning of the sixteenth century contributed to this commerce, but initially they were, in Reid's view, "a consequence, not a cause," of this upsurge in international commerce (1992:460). What is beyond doubt, however, is that the European explorations took place at a time of major economic expansion both in Europe and in Asia. By the end of the age of commerce, which Reid (1993:xiv) dates to 1680, European economic, military, and political power had expanded enormously, preparing the way for further penetration later.

The Portuguese seized Melaka in 1511 and expanded eastward, in effect breaking Javanese dominance of trade on the eastern parts of the archipelago. The Portuguese were aware of the greater wealth and greater variety of products in Asia compared with Europe, and were keen to take advantage of this. In an age when there was no refrigeration and cattle had to be slaughtered because of the lack of winter fodder, fine spices were also of major importance, and the Portuguese wanted to access trade in them.

Spain approached Asia from the opposite direction, through the Americas. It was Asia that the Spaniards had been aiming for when Christopher Columbus discovered the Americas, and after conquering Mexico and Peru they were able to trade across the Pacific, largely in Chinese products for precious metals from Mexico. Economically, this contributed to an early phase of what is today called globalization, because, as Tarling notes, "making the world one by including the Americas created a rudimentary world economy" (2001:171). In the latter part of the sixteenth century, the Spaniards established themselves in the northern and central part of what is now the Philippines, naming it after their king, Philip II (ruled 1556–1598). In these islands, before this time, Chinese traders and tribal communities had made their livelihood through cultivation, hunting, and fishing. The "state," as understood in this chapter, had only emerged in very rudimentary form. The Spaniards established a central government in Manila and made many of the islands into an effective colony.

Following the long economic boom that had characterized the preceding two centuries, the period from about 1620 to 1680 was one of economic recession across Eurasia, especially in China. Prices fell, crops failed, and populations stagnated or fell (Reid 1992:489). Among Europeans, it was the Dutch who were best able to cope with these conditions. They were able to move into Asia, displacing the Portuguese. At the apex of their endeavors was the Vereenigde Oost-Indische Compagnie (VOC; Dutch United East India Company), also known as the Dutch East India Company, which was founded in 1602 and lasted until 1799. Over that period, the VOC exercised an enormous impact on world trade and became perhaps the first global trading company. It was crucial in the process of Dutch domination of Southeast Asian trade and, in the longer term, Dutch colonization of Indonesia. The VOC took Batavia (present-day Jakarta) in 1619, and followed up this victory by conquering other cities of the region. By 1680 the Dutch East India Company had succeeded in forcing most of the trading cities of Indonesia into monopolistic arrangements (Reid 1992:488).

The age of commerce saw what Reid describes as "a religious revolution," with the suggestion that "more than half the population of Southeast Asia adopted Islam or Christianity in some sense during the age of commerce" (1993:132). The period also saw intense competition between the Christians and Muslims. Both Portugal and Spain sent keen missionaries. In addition to gaining profit, they hoped to spread their Catholic religion to Asia. When the Portuguese attacked Melaka, their commander told his soldiers that their primary reason was "the great service which we shall perform to the Lord" in ridding the place of Islam (quoted in Tarling 2000:115). The Spaniards firmly implanted their Catholic faith in the Philippines as early as the sixteenth century, Manila having been a Muslim city when it fell to Spain in 1571.

Saint Francis Xavier (1506–1552) was the first of the great missionaries of the Society of Jesus (Jesuits), a product of the Catholic Reformation of the mid–sixteenth century. Xavier was especially attracted toward Japan, and spent over two years there, helping the Jesuits gain some initial ground. Father Matteo Ricci (1552–1610) lived in Beijing in the last decade of his life, at the time a notable privilege for foreigners and especially Europeans. He and later Jesuits achieved some influence among the Chinese intelligentsia, and established a significant Jesuit presence in China. However, it was in Vietnam in the early seventeenth century that the Jesuits achieved their greatest successes. Most distinguished among them was Alexandre de Rhodes, who converted thousands of Vietnamese to Catholicism in the late 1620s. The Jesuits also devised a Vietnamese writing system based on the Latin alphabet, which Alexandre perfected in the middle of the seventeenth century.

The Dutch, however, took very little part in missionary activity. According to Tarling, "In the two centuries of the VOC's existence, fewer than 1000 predicants left to serve in the East" (2000:115). In some ways this abstention from involvement in missionary work was of great benefit to them. In 1614 the new Japanese Tokugawa regime ordered the expulsion of the missionaries, banned Christianity, and persecuted Christians. By 1639 the Tokugawa regime had imposed a series of measures that amounted to what is called *sakoku* (closed country), a policy that lasted until the middle of the nineteenth century. This meant that Japan was cut off from the rest of the world. However, the Dutch, the only foreigners allowed to stay, were able to retain a colony in Deshima in the harbor of Nagasaki.

In the midst of the seventeenth-century recession, China underwent a major political storm when its corrupt and already tottering Ming dynasty succumbed to a major rebellion. The people who were able to take advantage of the situation were not the rebels themselves, but the Manchus of what is now northeastern China. They established the last of China's dynasties, the Qing.

China was involved in trade, but to a much lesser extent than were the countries of Southeast Asia, since its economy was large enough to be rather self-sufficient. It was not a good market for the expanding European powers. However, an important effect of China's role in the age of commerce was the spread of Chinese people to Southeast Asia. Chinese émigrés found employment as artisans, farmers, and intermediaries in the towns the Europeans had established in Java, the Philippines, and elsewhere. Though of course the Chinese had traded outside their own country before this time, the expansion of the Chinese population in Southeast Asia was significant, and had long-term implications.

The Age of Imperialism and Colonization

The European powers strengthened their trade in Southeast Asia over the succeeding centuries. In the latter half of the eighteenth century, the industrial revolution, which began in Britain and then spread elsewhere in Europe and to the United States, gave Europe added confidence in the superiority of its economic, political, and cultural patterns. Of course, the European powers competed with each other over the spoils of imperialism, especially France and Britain. Britain's victories over Napoleon ensured that it would lead the imperialist push into Asia and elsewhere. However, the nineteenth century saw several of the Western powers increasing their hold on specific parts of Southeast Asia.

Robert Elson distinguishes two phases of what he calls "the creation of a new order" that led to colonialism and the formation of the modern state in Southeast Asia (1992:141–151). The first was the liberal phase, which dominated the second half of the nineteenth century. It can be identified by its laissez-faire character, "a reflection not just of popular ideas about the universal applicability of liberalism but more concretely of the limitations of state power and the lack of private Western investment capital" (1992:142). Beginning about the middle of the century, European economies, led by Britain, moved into a phase of high capitalism, dominated more by industry than by commerce, with the result that influence in Asia merged increasingly into political control. Domination became clear enough that the term "imperialism" is appropriate here, and almost all the countries of Southeast Asia were subjected into colonies.

Elson's second phase began at about the turn of the twentieth century. Characterized by control and management, it saw the creation of bureaucracies larger, wider, and more complex than Southeast Asia had ever seen before. They depended not on personal relationships, as had previous bureaucracies, but on procedures and formal and impersonal institutions. According to Elson, "The result was the creation in Southeast Asia of modern centralized states, with the will and the means to manage, exploit and 'improve' their subjects systematically, rather than simply oversee, motivate or cajole them" (1992:153).

Island Southeast Asia

In the late eighteenth century, the Dutch in Indonesia, or "Netherlands India" as they came to call it, still depended on commercial contracts and treaties they had signed with local rulers. However, European rivalries, in which the British were crucial, changed this pattern. Early in the nineteenth century the British took control of some Dutch possessions in the Malay archipelago, especially Java. But for reasons related more to European politics than to Southeast Asia, it suited the British to allow the Dutch an empire in Southeast Asia, as long as Britain's own commercial interests were protected. In 1824 the British and Dutch signed a treaty by which the islands of the Malay archipelago would be returned to the Dutch, but the peninsula would go to the British, who would be allowed to trade and profit there.

The Dutch soon strengthened economic, political, and social control. A major stage of this process was the introduction of the "cultivation system" in the 1830s by Dutch governor-general Johannes van den Bosch. The aim of the system was to cultivate products that could be exported to Europe for high profit, especially coffee, sugar, and indigo. The method of the system was to compel the peasants to produce not for their own benefit, but for that of the European market, with the local elite taking part in this exploitation. The Dutch soon strengthened their control in Java and elsewhere in the archipelago. The last three decades of the nineteenth century saw an expensive war aimed at subjugating the sultanate of Aceh in northwestern Sumatra, in which many Acehnese and Dutch were killed in battles or through disease and exhaustion. Though the sultan surrendered in 1903, the Dutch never fully pacified the area, which remained reluctant to accept rule from Java to the end of Dutch colonial rule and beyond.

Early in the twentieth century, the Dutch introduced their "ethical policy" to replace the cultivation system. As its name implies, it saw a greater emphasis on the interests of the local people, with attempts to give them a greater share and control in produce, and with more attention given to education and social welfare. Ironically, however, the Dutch extended their control in the early twentieth century both territorially and in terms of management in areas already in their possession.

Britain was also content for Spain to retain control of the Philippines, as long as Britain was allowed a share in the region's trade. In the nineteenth century, Spain extended its control farther over the islands. However, in a war that was in some ways analogous to the one the Dutch fought in Aceh, the Spanish came up against extreme opposition from an Islamic sultanate in the Sulu archipelago to the south.

The Spanish-American War of 1898 began in the Caribbean but spread to the Western Pacific. It marked a very important turning point in East Asia, because the United States, following its victory, was able to enter the region as a colonial power for the first time. Under the Treaty of Paris of December 1898, which ended the war, Spain handed over the Philippines to the United States as its colony. In a series of military campaigns lasting from 1899 to 1913, the United States succeeded in subjugating the Sulu archipelago, but the Muslims there remained uneasy about the prospect of belonging to the Philippines, a sentiment still present today.

In 1819, Stamford Raffles of Britain established a port settlement called Singapore on the island of the same name. Following the Anglo-Dutch Treaty of 1824, Singapore became the main hub of British colonialism in Southeast Asia and the administrative seat of the Straits Settlements, which comprised Singapore, Penang, Melaka, and Labuan, an island just off the coast of northwest Borneo. In 1867, the Straits Settlements became a British crown colony.

Mainland Southeast Asia

The British were able to extend their control over the Malay peninsula, signing agreements with local sultans. For a time, the British asserted power against an expansionary Siamese kingdom and could thus claim to be acting in defense of the sultans. The culmination of the process was the establishment of the Federated Malay States in 1895–1896, with an administrative capital in Kuala Lumpur. The sultanates remained in place, but were under British "protection."

Two commodities promoted British interests on the Malay peninsula. Chronologically, the first was tin. Actually, it was mainly Chinese entrepreneurs who profited from the tin mines, even though it was Malay chiefs who controlled the tin lands. However, the British did not stand aloof, and provided the "political, legal and administrative circumstances for accelerated development" (Elson 1992:147). Certainly, tin production expanded enormously in the second half of the nineteenth century, and by 1895, 55 percent of world tin production came from the western Malay states.

The second commodity that promoted British interests on the Malay peninsula was rubber. Malaya was not the only place in the world that produced the commodity, but the early twentieth century saw an enormous boom in production and required growth of rubber. This was the era when motor vehicles with pneumatic tires made of rubber came to hold an immensely important place in world transportation, especially in the United States.

In Vietnam, the Nguyen dynasty, which began in 1802, reunited the country after a period of division. It established an imperial capital in Hue in central Vietnam, and adopted the Chinese model of governance, making this a period of enormous Chinese influence, despite the fact that the Chinese empire itself was in rapid decline. According to Alexander Woodside, the emperors of the first half of the century "upheld Chinese concepts of empire and of the ways of ruling an empire" (1988:9). However, the Nguyen emperors were themselves subject to pressures they could not manage.

The French had competed with Britain in India in the eighteenth century, but lost. They transferred their attention farther east, especially to Vietnam. In contrast to Netherlands India and other places that had reached agreements protecting British interests, Vietnam made no attempt to play the French against the British. When the French began to attempt colonizing southern Vietnam in the 1850s, Britain took no steps to oppose them. As Tarling notes, "Vietnam had escaped the threat that European rivalry often brought to Asia, but it succumbed to European agreement" (2001:74). The French progressively took over Vietnam, Cambodia, and Laos in the second half of the nineteenth century through a series of conquests and treaties. Decrees issued in October 1887 established the Union Indochinoise (Union of Indochina) as a colony, including Cambodia and the three parts of Vietnam called, from south to north, Cochinchina, Annam, and Tongking. Laos became a French protectorate in 1893, and acquired its present borders in 1907.

After the Burmese ended the Kingdom of Ayuthia with their destruction of the capital in 1767 (see "The Non-Chinese State" on p. 46), a new dynasty arose, the Chakkri, which took Bangkok as its capital. Under Rama III (ruled 1824–1851), Siam itself became an expansionist kingdom, extending its rule in three directions, along the Malay peninsula, into Laos, and into Cambodia. Meanwhile, following three wars with the Burmese kingdom, in 1824–1826, 1852, and 1885, Britain took over the country fully, making it a province of its Indian empire in 1886, and then a separate colony in 1937.

The result was that Siam was squeezed between the two major colonial powers. Fortunately for Siam, neither was prepared to let the other take over the country, and it suited the two to have a buffer state separating their spheres of power. The Siamese kingdom did not stand idly by. Under its king, Rama V, also known as Chulalongkorn (ruled 1873–1910), it undertook a modernization campaign. The kingdom proved quite skillful in diplomatic efforts to adapt to the realities of British and French power in the region, and played each against the other. Though Siam was forced to cede territory won under Rama III to both powers, Laos to France and four Malay states to Britain, it remained the only country in Southeast Asia to maintain its independence and avoid the fate of colonization.

East Asia

Farther north, the great Chinese empire, dominated at the time by a Manchu dynasty that had adopted the Chinese name Qing, reached an apogee of power in the seventeenth and eighteenth centuries, especially under the Kangxi (1662–1722) and Qianlong (1736–1796) emperors. By the late Qianlong, it had begun to decline rapidly. Among other reasons for this decline was a trend toward overpopulation, which began to reach serious proportions by the early years of the nineteenth century. Rebellions erupted throughout the nineteenth century. The largest in scale was the Taiping rebellion, which devastated the country from 1851 to 1864 and was responsible for the deaths of 20–30 million people.

Meanwhile, the foreign powers began encroaching on China, contributing to a period of great humiliation for this once mighty empire. The British were the first. After the Opium War, fought with a small number of troops but with incomparably superior technology, the British were able to impose the first of the "unequal treaties" in 1842: the Treaty of Nanjing. Other Western powers quickly became involved, especially France, imposing their own treaties and taking over slices of Chinese territory or carving out areas where they were able to dominate. Concessions the Chinese were forced to make included:

- the opening of "treaty ports" to foreign trade and influence;
- Christian missionary rights to proselytize;
- extraterritoriality, meaning that foreigners in China were subject not to Chinese law, but to that of their own country;
- the payment of indemnities for wars lost to the powers; and
- the right to control China's tariffs, usually undertaken in a way more to the benefit of foreign than to Chinese interests.

The encroachments of the foreign powers grew worse as the nineteenth century proceeded, and reached a climax in 1900, the year of the famous Boxer uprising. The Boxers, who gained their name from a kind of magic boxing they practiced, attempted to besiege the foreign legations in Beijing. In response, the eight strongest powers of the day—Britain, France, Germany, Italy, Austria-Hungary, Russia, the United States, and Japan—invaded Beijing and lifted the siege, imposing on China the most humiliating treaty it had yet suffered. It was the only time in history these eight had actually fought on the same side against a common enemy. Many at the time thought China would actually succumb to colonization. The foreign powers soon turned to promote their own rather than common interests, while the Qing dynasty undertook an extensive and at least partly successful attempt at reform. The net effect was that China never actually became a colony, but did undergo great humiliation at the hands of the foreign powers.

Chinese influence expanded overseas during this period. Although migration of Chinese to Southeast Asia was by no means new in the imperialist age, it expanded greatly after 1870, because the economic expansion brought by the imperialist age made their skills and labor valuable. The Chinese were already important as entrepreneurs and tin miners, but they could also take on other work. They became of crucial importance in the retail trade in most cities of Southeast Asia. In Siam, they assimilated well into the population, but this was not the case elsewhere; despite their contributions to the economies of Southeast Asia, many felt the Chinese were a bit *too* dominant and successful, and harbored resentment against them.

Moving east from China, we find that Japan presented the most unusual picture of all, since it was by far the most successful in undertaking the reforms that brought it into the modern world and created the modern nation-state. It was the United States that first compelled Japan to abandon its policy of seclusion, through Commodore Matthew Perry's 1853 mission requesting trade and diplomatic relations. In 1867 the last Tokugawa shogun surrendered to the imperial house, with the young Meiji emperor taking over titular control of government in 1868 in a move called the Meiji Restoration. Japan's rise was spectacular. It defeated China in the first Sino-Japanese war, of 1894–1895, thereby increasing its power in Korea and in northeastern China, at China's expense. In 1904–1905, after Russian troops had invaded the northeast in 1900 in the wake of the Boxer debacle, Japan fought against Russia on Chinese soil and without Chinese permission, and became the first Asian country to defeat a European one in the imperialist age. Japan even became a colonial power itself, taking over Korea in 1910 and holding it as a formal colony until its own defeat in World War II in 1945.

■ The Rise and Impact of Nationalism

Imperialism and colonialism gave rise to nationalism, but at different times in each country of Asia Pacific. Nationalism gathered momentum after World War I, at least in part because of the principle of national self-determination as promoted by US president Woodrow Wilson (Fung 2000:140–141). At least in some parts of Asia in the first half of the twentieth century, nationalism was among the most important forces driving history forward, if not the most important.

The Concept of Nationalism

Much has been written about the theory and nature of nationalism. It is based on the concept of the nation, a comparatively modern idea that, in its Asian forms, derives from the era of imperialism. One influential encyclopedia states that "nationalism centers the supreme loyalty of the overwhelming majority of the people upon the nation-state, either existing or desired. The nation-state is regarded . . . as the indispensable framework for all social, cultural, and economic activities" (Kohn 1968:63).

Nationalism is quite different from "culturalism," a term that two well-known specialists have coined and attributed to China before the modern era. This was characterized by "a complete confidence in cultural superiority that is notably lacking in nationalism" (Reischauer and Fairbank 1958:292). A foreign people like the Mongols or the Manchus might conquer China, but they could never overcome Chinese culture. Indeed, they were more likely to succumb to Chinese culture than to conquer it.

Nationalism is also very different from patriotism, which is simply love of the land of birth (Chavan 1973:5) or of country (Amstutz 1999:33). In the stages before the development of nationalism, the focus of loyalty may be a monarch, a cleric, a region, or a village. But if nationalism is to develop, we can expect to find such loyalties changing into a "primitive awareness of shared destiny and of ethnic or cultural distinctiveness" (Duiker 1976:15). Such consciousness might be termed "protonationalist." Only when it develops to the stage where the nation-state becomes the focus of loyalty can we really speak of modern nationalism.

Scholars have categorized nationalism in a range of ways. One way is to distinguish five types: political or civic nationalism, ethnic nationalism, religious nationalism, social revolution, and anticolonialism (Amstutz 1999:33–34). Another way is along a spectrum of reactive to aggressive. Reactive nationalism owes its existence primarily to wrongs done to the nation. Proactive nationalism appeals to pride in the nation as a reason to promote the vigor and prosperity of the nation, but without becoming a threat to other peoples. And then there is aggressive or radical nationalism, or "ultra-nationalism," which promotes the power of the nation to the extent that it wishes to conquer and colonize other peoples. In the first half of the twentieth century, the dominant form of nationalism in the Asia Pacific region was reactive, for the simple reason that it took its origin as a reaction against imperialism and colonialism. However, aggressive nationalism also existed.

Nationalism in Southeast Asia

According to one authoritative study of Southeast Asia, it was in the Philippines that modern nationalism, involving consciousness of a national identity, emerged (Kratoska and Batson 1992:257–258). A period of Spanish repression, following a failed mutiny in 1872, gave rise to an intensely anticlerical movement promoting a form of cultural nationalism, which included such demands as equality for Filipinos, freedom of speech and assembly, and staffing of the clergy with Filipinos rather than Spaniards. US intervention in the Philippines at the end of the nineteenth century was a decisive factor in the expulsion of Spanish colonialism from the country, but the activities of the nationalists certainly contributed greatly.

There were many anticolonial movements in Southeast Asia in the latter part of the nineteenth century and through the first half of the twentieth that were based on traditional religion or ideas. One of particular significance was Sarekat Islam (Islamic League), founded in 1912 and led from the next year by Tjokroaminoto, noted for his splendid oratory. Emerging from an organization of indigenous batik traders in Central Java province in competition with Chinese counterparts, it spread throughout the island. What was extraordinary about this movement was that it gained, and for several years held, a mass appeal and following, reaching over 2 million in 1919 (Steinberg 1985:306). Despite its enormous following, Sarekat Islam was very diverse and regionalized, with associations and sects that varied greatly according to local conditions.

As a result, this movement was more protonationalist than nationalist, especially since its mass following was "secured on a traditional rather than a modern basis" (Tarling 2001:373). Despite its religious coloration, there was a partial merger of Sarekat Islam with the Communists, who in 1924 adopted the formal name Partai Komunis Indonesia (PKI; Indonesian Communist Party). When a PKI-led revolt erupted at the end of 1926, Dutch suppression broke the PKI for many years, and spelled the end of the "great folk movement" that was Sarekat Islam (Steinberg 1985:307).

In most of the countries of Southeast Asia, the factor of "national awareness," so crucial to modern nationalism, developed mainly in the 1920s and 1930s. These two decades also saw "an awakening of interest concerning the nature and purpose of government" throughout Southeast Asia (Osborne 2000: 117), including in Thailand, itself never a colony. Given the importance of the state as a focus of loyalty for nationalists, this concern over government inevitably contributed to nationalist appeal and strength.

Modern nationalism in Southeast Asia took a major step forward in the late 1920s. In July 1927, Sukarno led a small group of like-minded enthusiasts to found the Partai Nasional Indonesia (PNI; Indonesian National Party), its name indicating a national identity that was significant and new. In October 1928, a congress of youth organizations declared the identity of Indonesia in a memorable slogan: "one nation—Indonesia, one people—Indonesian, one language—Indonesian" (see Steinberg 1985:307). The congress also adopted a national flag and national anthem. Educated people in the Dutch East Indies came to identify themselves as Indonesians over those years. According to David Steinberg:

> The idea of Indonesia spread so easily, once launched, that it seemed to later historians as if it had always existed, if not actually explicitly then inchoate in the hearts of the people. But it was, in fact, a new creation, the product of a great and difficult leap of the imagination. The idea of Indonesia required the denial of the political meaning of the societies into which the first Indonesians had been born. It required also the acceptance of the new reality of the Dutch Indies, and then the transmuting of that into "Indonesia." (1985:308)

A Southeast Asian country worth special attention for its Confucian tradition and adoption of Marxism-Leninism is Vietnam. There were protonationalists in the late nineteenth century, most notably the Vietnamese emperor Ham Nghi, who in 1885 led an unsuccessful rebellion against the French, wanting to restore the old traditional system of government. The early twentieth century saw the rise of a group of what one specialist called "scholar-patriots" (Duiker 1976:288), the major representative being Phan Boi Chau (1867–1940). These scholars rejected the traditional model and wanted to modernize the country. Phan Boi Chau visited and was influenced by Japan, which he regarded as a model for Vietnam. These scholars can perhaps claim to have taken "the first step toward modern nationalist movement in Vietnam" (Duiker 1976:287). The representatives of a new stage of urban nationalism grew to maturity just after World War I and were strongly influenced by French culture. Their focus on the cities and their Western orientation cut them off from any traditional roots in the villages, and this could only be a major weakness in their appeal to the Vietnamese masses, since the overwhelming majority of Vietnamese were rural.

The most enduring form of Vietnamese nationalism leading up to 1945 was dominated by socialism, with the most famous representative being Ho Chi Minh (1890–1969), who led a Marxist-Leninist party for almost the entire period from 1925 until his death, though his interest in that doctrine lay not in dialectical materialism but in Lenin's opposition to colonialism and imperialism. Ho admired and loved French culture, but reacted to French colonialism with a deep and abiding hatred. His tract "French Colonization on Trial" is infused with a passion that is rare in the writings of the Marxist-Leninist leaders of Asia. Though Ho's initial revolutionary activities against the French were not particularly successful, they laid the basis for the supremely important postwar struggle against the French and the Americans. Unlike the urban nationalists discussed above, this revolutionary nationalism had deep roots in the countryside and among the peasants. Ho Chi Minh was able to develop a mass following that eluded his nationalist predecessors. His prestige, respect, and affection among the Vietnamese remain very powerful indeed into the twenty-first century, much stronger, for example, than Mao Zedong's in China.

Nationalism in Korea
In East Asia, Korea is the smallest of the region's countries and the only one to become a formal colony. The epochal event in modern Korean nationalism is generally agreed to be the uprising of March 1, 1919. Over thirty prominent people issued a proclamation of independence from Japan in Seoul, and large but peaceful demonstrations flared throughout the country. About 2 million people took part in several thousand demonstrations throughout the rest of 1919.

The Japanese colonial masters reacted by suppressing the demonstrations. During many of the demonstrations they fired at the crowds, killing several thousand over the year. They also changed their policy in Korea, replacing "military" with "cultural" rule. However, historians of both North and South Korea today agree that in fact the change in policy was only superficial and altered nothing essential.

The March First Movement did lead to a rise in the labor and communist movements. It appears to have "greatly developed the spirit of national unity" (Han 1970:477), a matter of some importance given the definition of nationalism presented here. However, in the big picture of Korean history in the first half of the twentieth century, it was probably not as important as it seems. Not only did it fail in its aim of forcing the Japanese to give Korea independence, but "nothing on the same scale was repeated during the colonial period" that might show a gathering of nationalist momentum (Lone and McCormack 1993:58). When Korea did finally win its independence in 1945, it was primarily because of Japan's defeat in World War II, not because of Korean nationalism.

Nationalism in China

In China, Korea's large continental neighbor and a country that had in the past influenced Korea enormously, nationalism developed in several stages over the twentieth century, culminating in a major civil war that resulted in the establishment of the People's Republic of China in 1949. The Boxer uprising (see "East Asia" on p. 62) was an example of a protonationalist religious movement. The Boxers appear to have loved Chinese culture and expressed a deep and even racist hatred for Westerners and Christianity. Yet they can hardly be described as nationalists under the definition offered here, since their allegiance was not to the nation-state. However, their rebellion certainly led to the rise of modern nationalism, and was probably even a cause of it.

According to Mary Wright, a distinguished historian of China, reformers and revolutionaries of the early twentieth century considered the antiforeign uprisings of the nineteenth century, culminating in the Boxers, as examples of "primitive xenophobia." Nationalism was a powerful force emerging from those upheavals, demanding "the organization of a centralized nation-state, capable both of forcing back the imperialists and of forwarding the country's new aspirations in political, social, economic, and cultural life" (1968:3–4). Yet nationalism was initially aimed not only against the imperialists, but also against the Manchus. Many Han Chinese regarded these people as foreigners who had taken over China. This is obvious from the manifesto of the Chinese United League (Tongmeng-hui), established in August 1905 under Sun Yat-sen. There were four main points in the manifesto: expulsion of "the Manchu barbarians," restoration of Chinese rule, establishment of a republic, and equalization of land rights (see translation in Mackerras 1998:97–98).

Sun Yat-sen achieved the first three of these aims through his revolution of 1911, which overthrew not only the Manchu dynasty but also the monarchy as an institution. Admired by Chinese on both sides of the Taiwan Strait, Sun is usually regarded as the father of the republic and sometimes even of the modern Chinese state. Yet in fact his revolution was not particularly successful and China soon fell into disarray, dominated by warlords, most of whom acted more in their own interests than in those of the people, let alone the Chinese nation.

On May 4, 1919, a major movement of political and cultural nationalism erupted first in the capital, Beijing, beginning with a demonstration by students against the Japanese, and then in other parts of China. The impetus of the May Fourth Movement was horror by Chinese intellectuals and students that the Paris Conference, which ended World War I and resulted in the Treaty of Versailles, had handed over formerly German interests in China's Shandong province to Japan. The demonstrators were very concerned about China's national sovereignty, and very nationalist in character. Chow Tse-tsung recorded a "Manifesto of All the Students of Beijing," part of which read: "Japan's . . . diplomacy has secured a great victory; and ours has led to a great failure. The loss of Shandong means the destruction of the integrity of China's territory. Once the integrity of her territory is destroyed, China will soon be annihilated" (1960:106–107). Ironically, the culture the movement's proponents advocated was strongly influenced by Western values and hostile to Confucian ones. It was both modernist and nationalist, and a good example of how the two coexisted and supported each other.

Koreans today point with pride to the fact that their own nationalist movement began over two months before its Chinese counterpart. Yet there is little evidence that the May Fourth Movement derived from the March First Movement. Of course, the nationalists of both countries shared a strong hostility toward Japanese imperialism, but also had their own concerns. One of the contrasts between the two was the successive protest. As noted above, this was sparse for the Korean movement, but in the case of China there were many student nationalist movements in the three decades from 1919 to 1949, and they played a significant role in the history of the period.

Meanwhile in southern China, Sun Yat-sen established another government, based in Guangzhou, and attempted to develop his nationalist and republican ideas. He did reconstitute the Nationalist Party (Guomindang) into a

Library of Congress photo.

Sun Yat-sen is regarded as the founder of the modern Chinese state by Chinese on both sides of the Taiwan Strait.

viable political organization, and presided over its first congress in 1924. His vision was to reunite China, eliminate the warlords and imperialism, and preside over a powerful and prosperous country with a strong, centralized government. He did not succeed. However, from 1926 to 1928, his successor, Chiang Kai-shek, led a military expedition to the north and formally reunited the country with its capital, Nanjing.

Sun Yat-sen and the Chinese Communist Party, which had held its first congress in 1921, established a united front in 1923. As a result, members of the CCP took part in the first two congresses of the Nationalist Party (in 1924 and 1926) and played an important role in the nationalist revolution associated with the reunification of the country. For example, Mao Zedong (1893–1976), later to become the leader of the CCP, was elected an alternate member of the Nationalist Party's central executive committee at its first two congresses. However, in April 1927, Chiang Kai-shek turned against the CCP, ending the united front and carrying out a large-scale purge of the CCP and the labor movement that cost the lives of many thousands of people.

Chiang Kai-shek continued to regard himself as nationalist, and the party he led still called itself "nationalist." However, his was a somewhat right-wing nationalism. The Japanese took over Manchuria in 1931, and persisted in further encroachments on China, yet resistance to Japan was secondary in Chiang's mind to eradicating the CCP. He suppressed the student nationalist movements that demanded resistance to Japan, largely because he thought, rightly, that the Communists had infiltrated them. However, in December 1936, after being kidnapped by one of his own generals, he agreed to resist Japan and played an active leadership role against the country when it launched a full-scale invasion of China in July 1937.

Ironically, Chiang Kai-shek's attempts to eradicate the CCP produced a nationalist backlash that was exceedingly damaging to him in the long term. It was military pressure from Chiang that forced the CCP to undertake the famous Long March of 1934–1935 from Jiangxi in southeastern China to northern Shaanxi. At least one view of history, advanced by Chalmers Johnson, holds that peasant nationalism against the Japanese during the following period was an essential ingredient in the final victory of the CCP. It is for this reason that Johnson considered communism in China to be "a particularly virulent form of nationalism" (1962: xi).

China may have been among the victors in the war against Japan, but the occupation and war devastated the country. By the time Mao and his CCP forced Chiang Kai-shek out of the Chinese mainland in 1949, China was in a state of complete disorder and economic and social disintegration. One scholar even summed up the republican period from 1912 to 1949 under the title "China in Disintegration" (Sheridan 1975).

Johnson's view on the reasons for the CCP's victory is not universally accepted among historians. Yet there is very little doubt that the CCP's ability to appropriate nationalism was at least one of the reasons why it won against Chiang Kai-shek. It is also clear that nationalism was among the major elements in Chinese history in the first half of the twentieth century. The efforts of nationalists at statebuilding were not particularly successful, but they did try to establish strong central governments that would promote China as a nation-state.

Nationalism in Japan

Of all countries in the Asia Pacific, Japan was most successful in responding to the challenges the Western impact imposed. From the time of the Meiji Restoration, Japan showed itself very willing to adopt changes in the direction of Westernization. It adopted policies that led to successful industrialization, such as developing an excellent universal education system and infrastructure, including a central bank and telegraph and railway systems. It also put energy into creating a modern army and navy. In 1889, the Meiji emperor promulgated a constitution in which the "rights of Sovereignty of the State" were paramount (Mason and Caiger 1972:242).

It was not long after the Meiji Restoration of 1868 that Japan began to adopt nationalist policies that were more aggressive than reactive. As discussed previously, Japan began expanding toward other Asian islands and the Asian continent. Its victory against China in 1895 gave it Taiwan as a colony. After several decades of increasing involvement and intervention, it made Korea a formal colony in 1910. The guiding principle of the Meiji government was "a rich country and a strong army" (*fukoku kyohei*) (Morris-Suzuki 2000:152), and in the 1880s it began to develop the nationalist doctrine of *kokutai* (national entity). In 1890, an imperial rescript on education laid down this ideology as a guiding principle for all children. Although mainly a demand for adherence to traditional Confucian virtues, it also included the requirement that "should emergency arise, offer yourselves courageously to the State" (see Mason and Caiger 1972:248).

After Japan defeated Russia in 1905, Japanese nationalism underwent a change that made it "a concomitant of confidence in the future progress of the nation" (Brown 1955:170). Japan remained highly aggressive in its policy toward Korea and China, and keen to expand its modernization program. It joined the Allies in World War I and, though it did not take much part in the fighting, after the war it was able to secure interests in China at Germany's expense. The aftermath of World War I ushered in a comparatively liberal period in Japanese history, with many competing political ideologies, all of them with nationalist or radical nationalist components. At the same time, the military increased in power, even though the government remained in civilian hands. The Nine-Power Treaty, which concluded the Washington Conference of February 1922, forced Japan to restrict the size of its navy, because the major Western powers saw it as a threat, but at the same time provoked great resentment among Japanese nationalists. The fact that a Japanese army was able to move into Manchuria in 1931 against the explicit wishes of the civilian government showed that the power of the military was not only too great for comfort, but also on the rise.

In February 1936, radical nationalists attempted, unsuccessfully, to carry out a coup d'état in Tokyo. Their failure "did nothing to weaken the power of the conservative nationalists in the army's leadership" (Morris-Suzuki 2000:159). No less than four of Japan's ten prime ministers in the 1930s were senior military officers. Although the famous ultranationalist Kita Ikki (1884–1937) was executed for his part in the 1936 coup, the essentials of his ideology triumphed. Japan was well on the path to, and truly confirmed in its pursuit of, aggressive nationalism.

After launching a full-scale war against China in 1937, the Japanese seized the capital, Nanjing, at the end of 1937, and exacted a massacre there famous for the extent and horror of its atrocities. In September 1940 the Japanese occupied Vietnam, but left the French to govern on their behalf until the last months of the war. In December 1941, Japan attacked Pearl Harbor in Hawaii, bringing the United States into the war. The Japanese then went on to occupy almost all of Southeast Asia, including the Philippines, Thailand, Malaya, Singapore, and Indonesia, where the Dutch colonial forces surrendered in March 1942. Despite these successes, the tide soon turned against the Japanese. In June 1942, they were defeated at the Battle of Midway in the Pacific, and later sustained a further succession of reverses, despite increasingly desperate attempts to prevent them. The end came in 1945, hastened by the dropping of nuclear bombs on Hiroshima and Nagasaki, respectively on August 6 and August 9, 1945, by the United States.

▨ Conclusion

Though the above example of radical nationalism ended in total disaster, it certainly did not mean the end of nationalism in Asia Pacific. European colonialists certainly did not simply give up; for example, the French attempted to restore their old control in Vietnam. Yet the postwar period saw a much weaker European colonial power in the region. Indigenous nationalisms became generally more successful and clearer in their ideologies. Both Asian nationalism and the decline of European imperialism were to play a major role in the post-1945 history of Asia Pacific. Indeed, nationalism in the region was just as important in the years immediately after 1945 as it had been before.

▨ Bibliography

Amstutz, Mark R. 1999. *International Conflict and Cooperation: An Introduction to World Politics.* 2nd ed. Boston: McGraw-Hill.

Backus, Charles. 1981. *The Nan-chao Kingdom and T'ang China's Southwestern Frontier.* Cambridge: Cambridge University Press.

Blunden, Caroline, and Mark Elvin. 1990. *The Cultural Atlas of the World: China.* Oxford: Andromeda.

Brown, Delmer M. 1955. *Nationalism in Japan: An Introductory Historical Analysis.* New York: Russell and Russell.

Buss, Claude A. 1964. *Asia in the Modern World: A History of China, Japan, South and Southeast Asia.* London: Collier-Macmillan.

Chavan, R. S. 1973. *Nationalism in Asia.* New Delhi: Sterling.

Chow Tse-tsung. 1960. *The May Fourth Movement: Intellectual Revolution in Modern China.* Cambridge: Harvard University Press.

Coedès, George. 1948. *Les états hindouisés d'Indochine et d'Indonesie.* Paris: Editions de Boccard.

de Casparis, J. G., and I. W. Mabbett. 1992. "Religion and Popular Beliefs of Southeast Asia Before c. 1500." In Nicholas Tarling, ed., *The Cambridge History of Southeast Asia,* vol. 1, *From Early Times to c. 1800,* pp. 276–339. Cambridge: Cambridge University Press.

Dore, R. P. 1965. *Education in Tokugawa Japan.* London: Routledge and Kegan Paul.

Duiker, William J. 1976. *The Rise of Nationalism in Vietnam, 1900–1941.* Ithaca: Cornell University Press.

Ebrey, Patricia Buckley. 1996. *The Cambridge Illustrated History of China.* Cambridge: Cambridge University Press.

Elson, Robert E. 1992. "International Commerce, the State, and Society: Economic and Social Change." In Nicholas Tarling, ed., *The Cambridge History of Southeast Asia,* vol. 2, *The Nineteenth and Twentieth Centuries,* pp. 131–195. Cambridge: Cambridge University Press.

Embree, Ainslie T., and Carol Gluck, eds. 1997. *Asia in Western and World History: A Guide for Teaching.* Armonk, N.Y.: Sharpe.

Fairservis, Walter A. 1997. "The Neolithic Transition: Hunting-Gathering to Sedentary Village Farming and Pastoralism." In Ainslie T. Embree and Carol Gluck, eds., *Asia in Western and World History: A Guide for Teaching,* pp. 217–235. Armonk, N.Y.: Sharpe.

Fung, Edmund. 2000. "Chinese Nationalism in the Twentieth Century." In Colin Mackerras, ed., *Eastern Asia: An Introductory History,* 3rd ed., pp. 139–147. Melbourne: Longman.

Geertz, Clifford. 1960. *The Religion of Java.* Glencoe, Ill.: Free Press.

Gray, Jack. 1990. *Rebellions and Revolutions: China from the 1800s to the 1980s.* Oxford: Oxford University Press.

Hall, D. G. E. 1955. *A History of South-East Asia.* London: Macmillan.

Hall, John W., et al., eds. 1988–1999. *The Cambridge History of Japan.* 6 vols. Cambridge: Cambridge University Press.

Han Woo-keun, trans. 1970. *The History of Korea.* By Grafton K. Mintz. Edited by Lee Kyung-shik. Seoul: Eul-yoo.

Hsu, Cho-yun. 1997. "Empire in East Asia." In Ainslie T. Embree and Carol Gluck, eds., *Asia in Western and World History: A Guide for Teaching,* pp. 280–284. Armonk, N.Y.: Sharpe.

Johnson, Chalmers A. 1962. *Peasant Nationalism and Communist Power: The Emergence of Revolutionary China, 1937–1945.* Stanford: Stanford University Press.

Keightley, David N. 1991. "Shang: The First Historical Dynasty (c. 1554–1045 BC)." In Brian Hook and Denis Twitchett, eds., *The Cambridge Encyclopedia of China,* 2nd ed., pp. 142–145. Cambridge: Cambridge University Press.

Kohn, Hans. 1968. "Nationalism." In David L. Sills, ed., *International Encyclopedia of the Social Sciences,* vol. 11, pp. 63–70. New York: Macmillan and Free Press.

Kratoska, Paul, and Ben Batson. 1992. "Nationalism and Modernist Reform." In Nicholas Tarling, ed., *The Cambridge History of Southeast Asia*, vol. 2, *The Nineteenth and Twentieth Centuries*, pp. 249–324. Cambridge: Cambridge University Press.

Legge, John D. 1977. *Indonesia*. 3rd ed. Sydney: Prentice Hall Australia.

Lone, Stewart, and Gavan McCormack. 1993. *Korea Since 1850*. Melbourne: Longman Cheshire.

Mackerras, Colin. 1998. *China in Transformation, 1900–1949*. London: Longman.

———, ed. 2000. *Eastern Asia: An Introductory History*. 3rd ed. Melbourne: Longman.

Mason, R. H. P., and J. G. Caiger. 1972. *A History of Japan*. Tokyo: Tuttle.

Maspero, Henri. 1978. *China in Antiquity*. Translated by F. A. Kierman. Cambridge: Massachusetts Institute of Technology Press. (Originally published in 1927 in French as *La Chine Antique;* the Kierman translation is from the 1955 edition, published in Paris by Imprimerie Nationale.)

Morris-Suzuki, Tessa. 2000. "Japanese Nationalism from the Meiji to 1937." In Colin Mackerras, ed., *Eastern Asia: An Introductory History,* 3rd ed., pp. 149–162. Melbourne: Longman.

Murphey, Rhoads. 1992. *A History of Asia*. New York: HarperCollins.

———. 1997. *East Asia: A New History*. New York: Addison-Wesley, Longman.

———. 1999. "The Historical Context." In Robert E. Gamer, ed., *Understanding Contemporary China*, pp. 29–62. Boulder: Lynne Rienner.

Nakamura, Hajime. 1987. "Mahâyâna Buddhism." In Mircea Eliade, ed., *The Encyclopedia of Religion*, vol. 2, pp. 457–472. New York: Macmillan.

Nguyen Khac Vien. 1993. *Vietnam: A Long History*. Rev. ed. Hanoi: Gioi.

Osborne, Milton. 2000. *Southeast Asia: An Introductory History*. 8th ed. Sydney: Allen and Unwin.

Rahman, Fazlur. 1987. "Islam: An Overview." In Mircea Eliade, ed., *The Encyclopedia of Religion*, vol. 7, pp. 303–322. New York: Macmillan.

Reid, Anthony. 1988. *Southeast Asia in the Age of Commerce, 1450–1680*. Vol. 1, *The Lands Below the Winds*. New Haven: Yale University Press.

———. 1992. "Economic and Social Change, c. 1400–1800." In Nicholas Tarling, ed., *The Cambridge History of Southeast Asia*, vol. 1, *From Early Times to c. 1800*, pp. 460–507. Cambridge: Cambridge University Press.

———. 1993. *Southeast Asia in the Age of Commerce, 1450–1680*. Vol. 2, *Expansion and Crisis*. New Haven: Yale University Press.

Reischauer, Edwin O., and John K. Fairbank. 1958. *East Asia: The Great Tradition*. London: Allen and Unwin.

Sheridan, James E. 1975. *China in Disintegration: The Republican Era in Chinese History, 1912–1949*. New York: Free Press.

Smith, Anthony D. S. 1979. *Nationalism in the Twentieth Century*. New York: New York University Press.

Steinberg, David Joel, ed. 1985. *In Search of Southeast Asia: A Modern History*. Rev. ed. Honolulu: University of Hawaii Press.

Stuart-Fox, Martin. 2000. "Political Patterns in Southeast Asia." In Colin Mackerras, ed., *Eastern Asia: An Introductory History,* 3rd ed., pp. 83–92. Melbourne: Longman.

Tarling, Nicholas, ed. 1992a. *The Cambridge History of Southeast Asia*. Vol. 1, *From Early Times to c. 1800*. Cambridge: Cambridge University Press.

———. 1992b. *The Cambridge History of Southeast Asia*. Vol. 2, *The Nineteenth and Twentieth Centuries*. Cambridge: Cambridge University Press.

————. 2000. "Mercantilists and Missionaries: Impact and Accommodation." In Colin Mackerras, ed., *Eastern Asia: An Introductory History,* 3rd ed., pp. 113–120. Melbourne: Longman.

————. 2001. *Southeast Asia: A Modern History.* Oxford: Oxford University Press.

Twitchett, Denis, and John King Fairbank. 1978–2003. *The Cambridge History of China.* 15 vols. Cambridge: Cambridge University Press.

van Creveld, Martin. 1999. *The Rise and Decline of the State.* Cambridge: Cambridge University Press.

von Falkenhausen, Lothar. 1991. "Archaeology." In Brian Hook and Denis Twitchett, eds., *The Cambridge Encyclopedia of China,* 2nd ed., pp. 136–142. Cambridge: Cambridge University Press.

Wilbur, C. Martin. 1983. *The Nationalist Revolution in China, 1923–1928.* Cambridge: Cambridge University Press.

Woodside, Alexander Barton. 1988. *Vietnam and the Chinese Model: A Comparative Study of Vietnamese and Chinese Government in the First Half of the Nineteenth Century.* Boston: Harvard University Press.

Wright, Mary C., ed. 1968. *China in Revolution: The First Phase, 1900–1913.* New Haven: Yale University Press.

4

Asia Pacific Politics

Katherine Palmer Kaup

Politics within Asia Pacific has changed with lightning speed since the end of World War II, which left the region shattered and impoverished. Hundreds of thousands were homeless across the region, economic infrastructure lay in tatters, and millions of demobilized soldiers returned to their homes with no prospects of civilian employment. A decade after the war ended, Japan's per capita income was still less than one-eighth that of the United States, even though it was the wealthiest country in the region. Today, Japan boasts one of the largest economies in the world. China, home to 650 million citizens living below the poverty line in the early 1980s, has now lowered the number of people living in abject poverty by more than 90 percent and today confronts the challenge of an overheated economy with soaring growth rates rather than the declining rates of productivity it faced in the late 1950s and 1960s. Politically, the region is in the midst of one of the largest transformations in state-society relations the world has ever seen. Since the 1980s, citizens in Asia Pacific have begun demanding new rights and involvement in politics, transforming some of the most repressive military and authoritarian regimes into fledgling, though fragile, democracies.

At the end of the Pacific War, across the region newly emerging nationalist forces sought to wrestle control from the colonial powers in the vacuum left by the Japanese withdrawal in 1945. Even China, Japan, and Thailand had to respond to the imperial challenge, though they managed to avoid formal colonization. The nationalist response to colonialism varied greatly, both as a result of the traditional patterns of governance in the colonized areas and as a result of the differing policies pursued by the colonizers. Each of the new regimes that arose after 1945 faced similar challenges, however, though their approaches to handling them varied drastically. Even in countries that had long histories of relatively unified state rule, as in China and Japan, all of the new governments faced the challenge of building a strong sense of national community in regions with strong centripetal challenges to central rule. In many countries, ethnic, regional, or religious minorities challenged the state's right to rule. Before the Asia Pacific states could hope to build state capacity and develop effective governmental structures, they had to focus on nation building to convince the local populations to commit their loyalty to the new states.

Nation-building challenges were particularly vexing in China and throughout Southeast Asia in places like Indonesia and Malaysia. In China, large segments of the country's landmass were controlled by ethnic minorities with different cultural and historical backgrounds than the majority Han population. In Tibet, Xinjiang, and Inner Mongolia, large segments of the local population argue that they belong to separate countries that were illegally occupied by communist forces after 1949. The Chinese Communist Party (CCP) has developed an elaborate system of regional autonomy for these areas and for the fifty-five minority groups recognized by the party, in hopes of integrating them into a unified multinational state. What emerged from Dutch rule as Indonesia comprises more than 17,000 islands, a multitude of local languages, diverse religious and ethnic traditions, and areas with separate histories of independent rule. Crafting a nation from such diverse traditions has proved an intractable challenge to the Indonesian government through to the present. Malaysian political institutions are designed specifically to distribute political power among the main ethnic groups, while ensuring the dominance of the Malay population.

In addition to the challenges of nation building and statebuilding, the Asia Pacific governments were forced to focus much of their energies on economic development. How each regime handled these three main challenges—nation building, statebuilding, and economic development—radically affected the dynamics of state-society relations and the consequent degree of individual liberty throughout the region. Three primary competing forms of rule emerged in Asia and were pursued to varying degrees by different countries and at different times. States chose among communist rule, military rule, or some form of restricted democratic rule. The implementation of these different forms of government differed over time and differed markedly from their counterparts outside of Asia. Asian communism took on unique characteristics that distinguish it quite clearly from that found in the West, though there are important variations within the Asian form itself. Likewise, the military regimes in Asia Pacific shared certain characteristics, while differing quite markedly by country and across time. Perhaps the widest variation of rule can be found in those nations that pursued some form of restricted democratic rule. The term "restricted democracy" usefully highlights the fact that even in nations modeled directly after Western liberal democracies, as in Japan and the Philippines, what emerged from those democratic structures looked quite different from the Western models largely due to the historical and cultural traditions found in the Asian states. Historical contingencies and practical developmental requirements in the post–World War II order also influenced how these democracies operated.

All of the countries in Asia Pacific (with the sole exception of Brunei, which has tenaciously clung to monarchical rule) have experimented with at least one form of the above patterns of governance to address the challenges of nation building, statebuilding, and economic development. Throughout the region, regardless of the form of governance chosen, the countries' political development reflects two important, similar trends. First, in addressing their common challenges, each state initially tended toward strong state control over society, what many analysts refer to as authoritarian rule. Even Japan, the most liberal democratic government in the region, though careful to hold regular and free elections, continues to be ruled largely by a cooperative arrangement among the Liberal Democratic Party, big business, and the bureaucracy, what many analysts call "Japan, Inc." or "the Japanese developmental state." Only recently, since the mid-1980s, has the Japanese citizenry begun to demand, and receive, greater real participation in the governing process. The communist regimes perhaps most vividly demonstrated the dominance of the state over society as they often sought to control not only individual actions, but even individual thoughts, as seen most clearly in North Korea since the end of World War II and in China during the Cultural Revolution, from 1966 to 1976. The communist regimes sought (though not always successfully) to either co-opt or crush the private realm throughout the first decades of their rule. The military regimes differed in the degree of individual liberty they were willing to tolerate if it did not challenge their rule, but the private sphere was carefully monitored for signs of dissent. Ironically, this trend toward concentrating power in the state arose in part because of the initially low levels of state capacity and poorly developed state institutions. Many of the states faced serious challenges to their rule, including from ethnic, regional, or religious minority groupings, military forces, contending political groupings with opposing ideologies, and outside international threats.

The second, more recent trend, however, has been toward liberalization and a greater opening for societal influence in the governing process. This trend began quite dramatically in the early 1980s in China, Japan, South Korea, and Taiwan, and spread throughout the region. With the sole exceptions of Brunei, Burma, and North Korea (Democratic People's Republic of Korea), which continue resolutely to reject calls for greater opening, all of the regimes, regardless of their form of governance, have loosened the authoritarian controls of the central state organizations. This reform process has come in fits and starts, and many of the most promising openings have often proved ineffective or compromised, as in Indonesia's efforts to move toward greater civilian control of politics since 1998 and in China's frequent large-scale crackdowns on dissent.

Even within China, however, which remains communist in name and governing structure, the capitalist economic reforms and limited state-sanctioned political reforms have given the Chinese citizenry the greatest degree of individual liberty it has known in nearly a century. In countries such as South Korea and areas such as Taiwan, the change has been at least as dramatic, as the entire rules of governance and political ideology supporting them have changed since the late 1980s.

By examining the three main forms of governance utilized in Asia Pacific by various countries at different times—communist, military, and restricted democratic—this chapter will trace the initial challenges that led each state to adopt governments with strong state control over society and the process of liberalization since the late 1970s. Ironically, the governments' successes in meeting early challenges were often the cause of their weakening position vis-à-vis society. As nationalism took root throughout most of the Asia Pacific states and the sense of urgent national and economic crisis faded, new social groups emerged that demanded greater attention to individual needs over state interests. Economic globalization and the resultant international exchange of ideas and normative international expectations have also influenced the authoritarian regimes to loosen their strangleholds on society. Regimes hoping to engage in the global economy have difficulty overtly rejecting international norms regarding human rights, labor conditions, minority rights, and other areas of concern to the international community. As the central state has loosened its control over society, many of the groups previously tightly controlled or suppressed by the national government have begun to reemerge. The rise of politicized Islamic groups throughout Indonesia, the Philippines, and other parts of Southeast Asia is but one example, as is the increase in subnational demands for independence in Indonesia and in the southern Philippines. The Asia Pacific governments are struggling to find a balance that will allow greater societal freedom while maintaining order.

An introductory chapter cannot hope to delve into the complexities of each and every one of the region's countries. Instead, several countries have been selected that best illustrate the mode of governance discussed. China is the most important and dynamic example of Asian communism, and will be addressed in most detail here, though the chapter will also briefly discuss some features of the North Korean and Vietnamese strands of communism. The forms of military rule differ dramatically in Asia Pacific, as will be demonstrated by examining Indonesia, Thailand, and South Korea. Likewise, Asia Pacific countries have experimented with a variety of restricted democratic forms of governance. Japan will be examined in some detail, as it is often hailed as the first (some would say, along with Taiwan, the only) successful Asian democracy, and several other Asian governments adopted its model of the developmental state, hoping to reap the economic benefits of Japan's "economic miracle." The Philippines will be discussed briefly, as it offers a solid example of how patron-client, personalistic patterns of association often influence politics in Asia Pacific. Malaysia follows a similar pattern of patron-client relations, though state rewards were parceled out to communal (ethnic) groups rather than to individuals.

■ The Communist Regimes

Asian communism emerged in large part as a reaction to imperialism. Although China was never formally colonized by European powers, its ancient pride had been bruised by the territorial concessions established throughout several of China's coastal cities beginning in the mid–nineteenth century. The Japanese attempt to colonize China in the 1930s significantly contributed to the decline of the ruling Nationalist Party (Guomindang) and to the soaring popularity of Mao Zedong and the Chinese Communist Party. Indeed, some scholars (Johnson 1962) argue had it not been for the Japanese invasion, the Nationalist Party might well have been able to combat the fledgling Communist Party. Others warn against overemphasizing the influence of outside powers. In Vietnam, Ho Chi Minh emerged as a nationalist figure in the north in the early 1940s. As the French and Americans struggled to keep his regime at bay, his appeal only increased domestically, as he appeared to be a Vietnamese loyalist fending off foreign invaders. Although the Soviet Union was instrumental in bringing Kim Il Sung to power in North Korea, he also emerged as a nationalist hero as he struggled to expel the occupying powers in South Korea.

The Asian communists' careful manipulation of their rhetoric to blend communism and nationalism greatly strengthened their ability to seize power. Mao Zedong adopted Marxist-Leninist theory, for example, to include the concept of the "national bourgeoisie." According to this principle, even if a Chinese factory-owner would typically be considered a member of the bourgeoisie, as long as that factory-owner was himself being exploited by foreign imperialists, he would then be considered a *national* bourgeoisie and would be welcomed into the revolution as long as he was willing to struggle against the foreign imperialists. This policy allowed the Chinese Communist Party to include many entrepreneurs in the cities in the revolutionary struggle and wait to overturn them once the party had consolidated more power in the mid-1950s.

Nationalism was certainly not the only key to the Asian Communist parties' successes in the late 1940s and early 1950s. The appeal of the egalitarian communist ideology and promises to fulfill basic subsistence needs equitably resonated well in societies that were wracked with poverty and huge gaps in wealth and landholdings. The parties' skillful use of guerrilla warfare also worked to their advantage, as did their ability to mobilize the masses through land reform.

Having seized power in the nationalist struggle against invading forces, the Communist parties faced three primary challenges. First, they had to establish effective governing institutions to implement the promises they had made during the revolutions. Second, they had to build on and strengthen national unity. The protracted nature of the revolutions themselves, both in China and Vietnam, strengthened the nation-building process greatly, but challenges still remained. Third, the parties had to develop an economic plan to achieve the goals of the revolution that had put them into power.

Statebuilding

The communist leaders increasingly centralized their rule through a union of the party and their newly established governing institutions. The governing systems they established tended to be wracked with inefficiencies and uncertainties caused by overlapping chains of command within the party and state structure and the multiple administrative levels in which they operated. Each of the Asian communist regimes rose to power through armed struggle led by a Communist party and its military arm: the Chinese Communist Party and its People's Liberation Army, the Communist Party of Vietnam and its People's Army of Vietnam, and the Korean Workers' Party and the Korean People's Army. Once the previous ruling regime had been defeated, these parties found it necessary to build a complex set of state institutions that were carefully monitored and controlled by the Communist parties, in part to repress remaining resistance to the armed takeover. For each state institution, then, there was a parallel party institution. The National People's Congress in China, for example, is the highest-ranking legislative organ in the state structure. There is a parallel National Party Congress that actually sets the agenda for the National People's Congress, however. A new people's congress is selected every five years and plenary sessions are held annually. Though the National People's Congress has begun to gain some independence since the late 1980s, its agenda continues to be set by the National Party Congress, which meets several months before the People's Congress. Each of the many state commissions, ministries, and agencies has a corresponding parallel party organization that oversees its work.

The party-state system is also hierarchical: directives are given from the center and disbursed down a chain of administrative levels. Each of the communist states is unitary, and the power granted by the center to the lower levels can therefore be withdrawn at any point and the leadership of the lower levels can be recalled by the center. Nonetheless, a careful line of command has been established, with directives being passed from the center down to the grassroots level. In China, for example, directives are passed down from the center to the province or municipality, then to the city or county, then to the township or district, and then finally to the village. While local governments have been granted a number of responsibilities and privileges, important national decisions are made through "democratic centralism" at the highest levels of the administrative hierarchy and then passed down. According to the Leninist principle of democratic centralism, decisions are reached through democratic consensus within the party at the highest levels. Once decisions are reached, however, they are not to be questioned by lower levels of the party or government, nor are they to be challenged by the decisionmakers themselves. As decisions are passed down through the state administrative hierarchy, each level of the hierarchy is supervised by a parallel party organization.

The Chinese system is also pyramidal in that directives within both the party and the state organizations flow from an apex of power down through a more disbursed body. Although in theory and according to the Chinese Communist Party's constitution, power is vested in the lowest rungs of the pyramid, in fact real power rests at the highest levels of the pyramid. At the central level, the National Party Congress is the lowest rung of the pyramid and, according to Chapter II, Article 3, of the CCP constitution, is the "highest leading body of the party." In actuality, its more than 3,000 members have very limited power and the congress typically does little more than rubber-stamp directives issued from higher up the organizational pyramid. The Central Committee, composed of about 300 members, is next up the chain of command, followed by the Politburo, composed of 15–30 members, then the Standing Committee, composed of 5–10 members, with the general secretary perched on top. Though the current general secretary, Hu Jintao, has less power than his predecessors Mao Zedong or Deng Xiaoping possessed by virtue of their revolutionary credentials and immense personal networks, he is the highest-ranking party official. With former leader Jiang Zemin's resignation from his last official post as the State Central Military Commission chairman in March 2005, and Hu Jintao's acceptance of the post, Hu has made great strides in consolidating his power. Hu now concurrently holds the top posts in the party, state, and military as the general secretary of the CCP, president of the People's Republic of China, and chair of the Central Military Commission. Along with the state premier, Wen Jiabao, and the chair of the National People's Congress, Wu Bangguo, Hu Jintao wields a great deal of power. The transfer of power from Jiang to Hu represents an institutionalization of the succession process and reflects party efforts since 1978 to remove a degree of personalized rule and power concentration in a single leader. The degree of liberalization that these measures provide, however, must be questioned in light of the government's increased crackdowns on political dissent since late fall of 2004, when Hu's leadership became more secure.

The parallel party-state organization and the hierarchical chain of command from the central government down to the grassroots organizations lend themselves to what Kenneth Lieberthal terms "fragmented authoritarianism" (2004:187). Each body within the system must seek permission to act from both the state or party organization above it and the party organization that resides

US president George W.
Bush and Chinese president
Hu Jintao at the arrival
ceremony for the Chinese
delegation in April 2006.

Eric Draper, White House photo.

at its same administrative level. For a county ethnic affairs commission in Tibet to grant a foreign scholar access to certain materials, for example, as a state organization it must be sure not to contradict the policies and wishes of the county party organization in charge of ethnic affairs or the provincial ethnic affairs commission. The provincial commission must be careful not to go against the provincial party organs involved with ethnic affairs, which in essence means the county commission must consult the county-level party department that is in charge of minority relations, the provincial commission, *and* the provincial-level party organizations that are monitoring nationality affairs. For very controversial decisions, this process may proceed all the way up to the central level, involving numerous decisionmakers and convoluting the policymaking process to such a degree that decisions are often slow or simply shelved. Since Deng Xiaoping's launch of economic and political reforms in 1978, the party has claimed its intention to separate itself from micromanaging state affairs. The party has reduced the number of party organizations with direct counterparts in the state, and has allowed the state a gradual increase in legislative powers and management of the economy.

Party-state relations appear differently in North Korea, though it is exceedingly difficult to obtain solid details on governance within this reclusive regime, which is hidden from the world in a self-imposed policy of *juche* (self-reliance). According to a high-ranking defector from the North Korean government, Kim Jong Il has been strengthening the position of the military toward the People's Workers' Party since as early as 1974. In September of 1998, a year after becoming head of the Korean Workers' Party, Kim Jong Il revised the state constitution to abolish the state presidency and instead named the chairman of the National Defense Committee (a post he himself had held since 1993) as head of state. This in effect elevated the role of the military. In addition, state media began to mention the military and its officials more regularly than the party and its top leadership, indicating a tilt toward greater military control in North Korea at the cost of party dominance (*Far Eastern Economic Review* 1998:30–31).

Nation Building

Nation-building challenges have been more pronounced in China and Vietnam than in North Korea. This is true largely because North Korea's population is ethnically more homogeneous, and because the country has not yet had to confront the challenge of building a common sense of purpose after the reunification of two deeply divided political and economic systems in the north and south, as in the case of Vietnam after 1976. China and Vietnam both contain what they call minority nationalities, which are minority ethnic groups with territorial homelands. Some of these groups, such as the Uighurs and Tibetans in China, lay claims to histories of independent statehood. In China, in fact, by official accounts ethnic groups now occupy 64 percent of the country's entire landmass. Although the minorities constitute only 8 percent of the total population, in absolute terms this equals more than 104 million people, or a population larger than all but a few of the world's largest countries. More than 90 percent of China's international border rests in minority territory, and more than thirty of the fifty-five officially designated minority nationalities in China have counterparts across international borders; as a result, securing their loyalties is of particular concern to the Communist Party. In addition to the minority nationalities, the Chinese government has had to struggle against historical tendencies toward regional fragmentation. Since the country was nominally unified in the second century B.C.E., China's central leaders have struggled to keep the county from dividing into smaller kingdoms or, more recently, into separate states.

Both China and Vietnam sought to appeal to their minority nationalities by promising them regional autonomy. Because the communists in China and Vietnam believed, in accordance with Marxist-Leninist views of nationality, that nationality consciousness was a reflection of class consciousness and would fade with the development of communism, they felt little concern promising the nationalities the right to govern themselves in the early years of the communist takeover. The party assumed that the nationalities would see the benefits of communism and of remaining within the increasingly powerful communist states, and would gradually become more and more integrated into the unified nation-state. The minorities were thus guaranteed the right to become the "masters of their own homes" and were awarded regional governments in areas with a heavy concentration of minorities. Within these regional autonomous areas, the head of the state government was required to be drawn from the titular minority, and minorities were guaranteed the right to develop their own languages, religions, and cultures, allowed to adapt and reject central directives that ran counter to minority cultures, and given "appropriate" control over their natural resources. That the minority territories are actually more tightly controlled than their nonautonomous counterparts has been well documented (Kaup 2000; Bovingdon 2004; Bulag 2002; Congressional-Executive Commission on China 2005), and can be clearly seen in China's numerous political campaigns against "splittism" and "ethnic chauvinism," like the ongoing "strike hard" campaign launched against Uighur separatism in 1997. Vietnam abolished its regional autonomy system in the late 1970s after the Vietnamese Communist Party successfully unified the northern and southern parts of the country.

Nation-building efforts have continued unabated since 1949 and have largely been tackled through careful party censorship of the press, control over the media, and educational campaigns. The CCP tightly controls the content of books, popular songs, television shows, museums, and other means of transmitting views of history that might conflict with the official representation of minorities' historical relationship with the majority Han population and with a central Chinese state. The government strictly forbids any discussion that might show, for example, that Uighurs or Tibetans or Mongols were resistant to their incorporation into China in the early 1940s, or that they historically had strained relations with the Han. Tohti Tunyaz, a Uighur student studying for his doctorate in Japan, was arrested in 2000 after collecting materials on Uighur history from Xinjiang University's archives that the government feared might be used to present a view of history different from the official interpretation of the Uighurs' past. Tunyaz was sentenced to ten years' imprisonment for "advocating splittism" in his writings (Congressional-Executive Commission on China 2005).

The Chinese government's nation-building efforts have been more successful in the southwestern areas of the country, while the government believes its repressive stranglehold on expression remains the only means of ensuring minority compliance in the northwest.

Economic Development

In addition to legitimizing their seizure of power on nationalist grounds, the Asian Communist parties also based their legitimacy on their ability to improve the national economy and individuals' economic well-being. Communism promised "from each according to his ability, to each according to his needs." Though the communist regimes experimented with a variety of economic plans, until 1978 in China and 1986 in Vietnam, the regimes were built on and relied on command economies. It will be necessary to examine the key features of a command economy below in order to grasp fully the degree of state control over individuals such systems provide. The reforms launched after 1978 have had a major impact not only on the citizens within China and Vietnam, but also on the global economy as a whole. The economic reforms have also radically altered state-society relations within the communist countries. Though North Korea implemented several market reforms in the summer of 2002, it has proved unwilling to carry out the type of reforms launched by Deng Xiaoping in his "new era of socialism" or by Vietnam's "restructuring" *(doi moi)*.

Early communist economic policies in China concentrated on heavy industrialization in the cities, largely financed by extracting limited surpluses from collectivized rural farms. In 1950, the CCP began a staged collectivization of the countryside, with farmers eventually forced onto communes, where they were all compensated equally regardless of the amount of work they did. Farmers were compensated well below what they could have received were market forces allowed to prevail rather than the state setting all of the prices. In the cities, workers were organized into units affiliated with large state-owned enterprises (SOEs). Within these SOEs, which employed more than 80 percent of the urban workers, the central government set the prices for goods, production and purchasing quotas, and workers' wages. Productivity was low, goods were shoddy, and bottlenecks or surpluses were quite common. The government subsidized the price of foodstuffs so that farmers were supporting the urban work force. The peasants were forced to stay in the countryside through the *hukou* (household registration) system, in which each citizen had to register his or her residence with the state and could not move without prior approval. This system ensured that peasants would not flock to the urban areas and overburden the infrastructure, as occurred in many Latin American developing countries. By 1978, the SOEs actually *cost* the government more than 90 billion yuan (nearly US$11 billion) to remain operating. According to official Chinese government sources, in 1985 more than 5 percent of gross domestic product went to prop up inefficient state-owned enterprises, and these figures are extremely low estimates of real costs (China Internet Information Center 2003).

In December 1978, the new paramount leader, Deng Xiaoping, announced "a new era of socialism" and launched a series of market reforms. Over the next two decades, China gradually moved toward a full-blown capitalist economy with a small state-owned sector, and continued intermittent heavy governmental interference. Detailed analysis of the economic reforms can be found elsewhere quite readily (Lardy 1998, 2002; Wu 2004). A brief sketch here of the key features of the economic reforms is enough to show the central government's deliberate reduction of state control over the economy and the gradual, albeit highly controlled, reduction of state controls over society.

China's economic reforms, as one can easily imagine, have been extremely complex. Rather than leaping forward with a shock-therapy approach as tried in European transitional economies such as Russia and Poland, however, the Chinese pursued a gradualist approach. The architect of the reforms, Deng Xiaoping, described the Chinese experimental approach as "crossing the stream by groping for each stone." The Chinese Communist Party would experiment with an economic reform in a particular province; if the experiment proved successful, the government would expound upon it and promote it nationwide. This approach can be easily seen in the development of the one child policy (promoted as necessary for economic development), for example, which was first tried in Sichuan province, and in the agricultural responsibility system, which was also allowed to unfold there in the early 1980s.

Among the extremely complicated and intricate reforms, three of the most important, both for the economy and for the development of an increasingly independent civil society, were the agricultural responsibility system, price and wage reforms, and changes in the SOE system. After years of forced communalization and a decade of economically destructive political campaigns during the nationwide chaos of the Cultural Revolution, from 1966 to 1976, productivity in the countryside was extremely low. Morale of peasants was low, as they were not compensated for the quality of their work. One of the first reforms pushed through after Deng Xiaoping took power in December 1978 was the agricultural responsibility system, which divided the communes into individual household units. Each household entered into a contract with the state. The state continued to own the land, which was leased to peasant households in exchange for the household's agreement to sell a quota of its production at a low, state-mandated price. Anything beyond the quota could be sold by the household at whatever price the market would bear. Several other major economic reforms followed as the agricultural responsibility system created new economic conditions and needs. As households strived to become economically efficient and the communes no longer supported the surplus rural labor force, for example, nonagricultural jobs needed to be found for more than 100 million surplus laborers. This led to a series of new policies and reforms, including, for example, the allowance of township and village enterprises, which in essence brought industries to the agricultural work force to prevent large numbers of agricultural workers from flooding the cities, as occurred in developing economies elsewhere. Over 125 million surplus laborers were absorbed by the township and village enterprises.

Price and wage reforms were another crucial area of change. The government gradually stopped setting prices for goods and allowed many products to be sold on the burgeoning open market. By the mid-1980s, the government had also loosened wage controls, which in effect allowed the cost of labor to be determined by the market as well. The rampant inflation that ensued throughout the 1980s, as food prices in particular soared, was one of the main factors that drove students and workers to take to the streets in protest against government policies in 1989.

A third major area of economic reform that affected not only economics but state-society relations was reform of state-owned enterprises. Simply stated, through a series of increasingly daring maneuvers, the state gradually withdrew its control over the urban industries and allowed the nonperforming SOEs to downsize, privatize, or eventually even declare bankruptcy. More than 80 percent of the urban work force in 1978 was employed by state-owned enterprises, and the reform of these enterprises has thus been extremely problematic and sensitive for the CCP, which came to power as a party of the proletariat and was now overseeing one of the world's largest downsizing campaigns. Millions of workers have lost their jobs, and more, under the reforms. When the reforms were begun, state-owned enterprises supplied workers not only with their cradle-to-grave jobs, but also their housing, healthcare, retirement, and children's education. Losing a job in an SOE meant losing social welfare privileges as well as one's housing. By 2001, the state announced that more than 80 percent of previously state-owned enterprises had been privatized (China Internet Information Center 2005). No longer dependent on the state for their livelihoods, workers and peasants have proven more willing to challenge the state in at least limited areas (see Congressional-Executive Commission on China 2005).

Changing State-Society Relations

It is a common misperception that the Asian communist countries have carried out their economic reforms without corresponding political reforms. The political reforms have in fact been quite profound. Whereas in the mid-1970s peasants in China lived on collective farms and could be arrested simply for having a relative living abroad or for "Western imperialist" practices like listening to classical European music, today hundreds of thousands of Chinese have studied in the West, own their own private businesses, and listen to Western rock music while driving in privately owned cars. I provide here a brief sketch of a few representative reforms in China since 1978 that have increased individual liberties and societal influence in politics.

Prior to 1979, China functioned with no written laws. The government closed the nation's law offices and arrested most of the country's lawyers during the anti-rightist political campaign in the late 1950s. The Chinese Communist Party's policies became the law of the land. The party adjusted its policies rapidly to fit its changing needs, leaving the population guessing on just what would and would not be tolerated. What might be allowed, and indeed *encouraged,* by the party one month might be attacked as a "counterrevolutionary crime" the next. The rapid shift from the Hundred Flowers campaign to the anti-rightist campaign in late 1957 and early 1958 provides an excellent example. Mao Zedong, assuming that the masses would support him against his opponents in the CCP, called for the people to offer their criticisms of corrupt party members and of the progress of communism in the spring of 1957. "Let a hundred schools of thought contend, let a hundred flowers bloom," the party propaganda sounded as it urged, and then demanded, citizens to voice their opinions. As the initial tepid response became gradually more heated, and as citizens began to show true discontent with the course of the revolution, Mao demanded an end to the campaign. Within just months after the start of the Hundred Flowers campaign, Mao claimed that the entire exercise had been nothing more than a way for him to "shake the grass to get the snakes out," and he declared most of those who had criticized the party as "rightists" or "counter-revolutionaries." Thousands were rounded up, struggled against in mass campaigns, or imprisoned with no legal recourse. Lawyers were arrested, and political dissent in any form definitively was no longer tolerated. The party's ever-changing policies were the law of the land.

With the introduction of economic reforms in 1978, however, and after decades of political turmoil, Deng Xiaoping began to promote legal development. In 1979 the State Council passed laws on civil and criminal procedures, and since then China has developed hundreds of national and thousands of local laws and written regulations. Family planning is even defined by law now. Equitable enforcement of laws remains a real problem, and laws remain subject to the party's ultimate interpretation, but citizens' gradual understanding of laws and rights may enable them to demand fair implementation in the years ahead.

In addition to legal reforms, the CCP has promoted a host of other political reforms. The party has set new term limits for government officials, and an open civil service examination is in place for government positions that previously were appointed by the CCP as rewards for ideological loyalty. Popular local elections are now used to select delegates to local people's congresses as well as village administrators. Importantly, the party has declared that the state should be given more control over daily affairs without being micromanaged by party officials, and that both the party and the state should let the market play a stronger role in the economy.

While the communist regimes of Asia Pacific remain flagrant violators of human rights, seeking to stamp out any direct challenge to their rule or policies, the private realm of citizens has expanded and civil society has begun to take root, particularly since the early 1980s. No single factor or set of factors can explain these profound changes that have occurred in state-society relations in the communist bloc. Several factors deserve brief mention, however. First, the decades of instability, particularly during the chaotic years of the Cultural Revolution in China and during Vietnam's succession of wars with France, the United States, and eventually China and Cambodia, led to a general consensus that change was necessary. Economic and political reforms were pushed through with less traumatic results than they were in the Soviet Union, in large part because the Chinese leadership in 1978 and the Vietnamese party members in the mid-1980s generally were in agreement that both economic and political change was necessary to prevent the terrible destruction of Cultural Revolution–type movements from occurring again. Whereas Mikhail Gorbachev felt compelled to carry out democratic reforms in order to pressure the hard-liners within the Communist Party of the Soviet Union, Deng Xiaoping did not face the same hard-line resistance within the party.

Second, the economic reforms required certain institutional reforms to be successful. As China sought to attract international investors, for example, it was necessary to develop previously nonexistent contract law and to develop a legal system to enforce these laws, otherwise foreign investors would stand clear of the unstable investment environment. Increased globalization brought with it demands not just for greater economic convergence, but also for the sharing of international norms such as human rights.

Finally, the economic reforms created several practical openings for society's separation from state control. Under the commune system, for example, China was not a highly monetized society. Workers depended on the communes and on the state-run work units for their housing, healthcare, and food ration coupons. As citizens gained a degree of economic independence, they could retract from their everyday forced interaction with the state. Bruce Dickson (2003) convincingly argues that the new middle class in China will not necessarily play the democratizing role scholars have noted of the middle class in Latin America, Eastern Europe, and other parts of Asia such as South Korea and Taiwan. The middle class and entrepreneurs have actually been some of the greatest beneficiaries of the recent CCP reforms, and may prove unlikely to push for the removal of party control. Nonetheless, the party now has less daily contact with individuals and appears willing to allow greater freedom for a private realm of activity as long as it does not challenge ultimate party power.

Military Rule

While Asia Pacific military regimes have maintained tight control over their citizens, military rule has functioned quite differently from communist rule. During Suharto's New Order regime, from 1966 until his ouster in 1998, the military played both a defense and a sociopolitical function in a system known as *dwi fungsi* (dual function). Though a military-state structure was established with the military supervising government structures at each administrative level much like the party-state structures established in communist countries, the intentions of the New Order military and its economic development strategies were radically different from those of the communist states. Militaries have played a varied role throughout Asia Pacific, with their influence gaining and waning across different countries and over time. Militaries have played an important role in nearly all of the Asia Pacific countries, though less so in post–World War II Japan, where the military is officially banned from playing any role in politics or foreign policy. Militaries have also played a minimal role in Malaysia and Singapore. In the communist regimes, militaries have played a particularly crucial role in aiding the parties in their initial seizure of power. In China and Vietnam, the parties have managed to maintain their dominance of the military. Kim Jong Il seems to have resuscitated the primacy of the military in North Korean politics since at least 1993. Indeed, the military consumes nearly 23 percent of North Korea's national budget (Central Intelligence Agency 2005), despite the fact that more than 13 million North Koreans suffer from malnutrition, including 60 percent of all its children (*Frontline World* 2005).

Militaries have played the most overt, direct role in governance, however, in Thailand, South Korea, Indonesia, and Burma. Civilian regimes were dominant throughout the region at the moment each state declared its independence, with the sole exception of Thailand. Militaries, or regimes backed by them, gained control throughout most of the region beginning in 1958, and held on to power until the early 1980s, when the civilian governments began to reassert their influence. Militaries stayed in power in Thailand and Indonesia until 1992 and 1998 respectively. The military once again stepped into control in Thailand in September 2006, though it argued it was only interested in ousting the corrupt civilian prime minister and pledged to reestablish democratic rule within the year. The rise of the militaries followed a pattern somewhat different from that found in Latin America or Africa, as has been eloquently argued by Muthiah Alagappa. A favored explanation as to why military coups overthrew civilian regimes in Latin America and Africa is that the military was often the only institution committed to national development that was organized enough to step in when weak civilian regimes failed to meet high popular demands in the years surrounding independence, what scholars label "the institutional imbalance argument" (Alagappa 2001:452). This argument does not work well in Asia Pacific, Alagappa contends, because it fails to take into account the degree of cooperation and common interests between players in the civilian government and the military. Most of the militaries in Asia Pacific were initially weak, faction-ridden, nonprofessional, and lacking in domestic and international standing. In the years immediately surrounding independence, however, in each of the states that eventually utilized military rule, civilian rulers opted to use a heavy dose of coercion to control the numerous threats to their rule. In the process, these rulers built up their militaries in ways that increased the militaries' unity, strength, administrative capabilities, and prestige. The civilian governments then paved the way for the militaries to step in during the 1960s and 1970s. As they faced the challenges of nation building and statebuilding, these young regimes turned to coercion to such an extent that they eventually lost power to their militaries. Not all scholars agree with Alagappa's theory, asserting instead that the Asia Pacific militaries, though at times quite fragmented, nonetheless were a force to be reckoned with from the time of independence, and that many of the region's militaries never accepted the legitimacy of civilian rule.

As export-led growth in these countries (with the exception of Burma, which remains relatively isolated) integrated them into the global economy by the 1980s, international political and social norms accompanied economic convergence. The increasingly complex economies could no longer be competently managed by militaries, which contributed to their willingness to step aside gradually and concentrate instead on developing professional and technically advanced military corps. The end of the Cold War, and the global media focus on the military capabilities of the United States demonstrated in the Gulf War in 1991, led many governments in Asia Pacific to work closely with their militaries to improve their technical and professional training and to acknowledge that the militaries would have to focus their attention on nonpolitical matters if they hoped to become competitive.

Liberalizing reforms that have attempted to decrease the role of the military in politics since the late 1970s have met with mixed results, with Thailand fluctuating between civilian and military rule, Indonesia steadily curbing the military's power, and South Korea successfully moving to fully civilian political systems.

Thailand

Thai politics has been marked by instability, with a series of military coups replacing the few civilian governments that have managed to rise to power. Although Thailand, like Indonesia and South Korea, moved toward reducing the military's role in politics in the 1990s, after fifteen years of civilian rule the military again staged a coup, on September 19, 2006. Civilians held the position of prime minister for less than one-quarter of the time over the period 1932–1992, after which the military gradually began to give up some of its control. Many of those civilian prime ministers ruled on behalf of the military. There were two periods of civilian rule between 1932 and 1992, each lasting only three years, from 1944 to 1947 and from 1973 to 1976. Ten governments were formed and fell under five prime ministers during the first period of civilian rule, seriously undermining societal confidence in nonmilitary rule. The current Thai constitution is the sixteenth since 1932, and the new prime minister, former general Surayud Chulanont, will oversee the drafting of a new constitution due to be put to a popular referendum in 2008.

The term "bureaucratic politics" was coined by Fred Riggs in 1966 to explain patterns of governance in Thailand. Although the Thai revolution of 1932 established constitutional controls over the monarch, the masses remained largely disenfranchised, while the real power-holders, the bureaucrats, ran the country for their own benefit. In this framework, the military was the most important bureaucracy. Civil society remained quite weak during military rule, though not always because of overt crackdowns by the military. The military was extremely factionalized, and each faction created its own political party to promote its agenda. Parties thus were created and disbanded as rapidly as political tides changed, and there was no unified party representing the military itself. The country's few nongovernmental organizations had largely been co-opted by the military's civilian affairs branch.

Pressures to reduce the role of the military began in 1973 with a student movement demanding a series of political reforms. Students clashed with police and the military, but the military was divided over how best to handle the uprising, with several factions refusing to crack down on the unarmed students. A civilian government was initiated, and people believed that democracy was on its way. This civilian government managed to maintain power for only three years, though, before another military coup, Thailand's bloodiest, occurred. Perhaps the most dramatic and, to date, longest-lasting move toward democratization began in 1992. This time, a student-led movement resulted in the military firing on the students and a series of mass arrests, in what came to be known as "Black May." Peace was restored only after the king stepped in, criticized both the military and the protest leaders for setting their followers on a course of conflict, and called for new democratic elections.

The 1997 constitution pushed through a series of reforms to reduce the influence of the military. While several previous constitutions had allowed the appointment of top-ranking government officials, the 1997 constitution provided for direct elections. Though by the end of 2000 no active servicemen were serving in parliament, the military reasserted its control in late September 2006 by ousting Prime Minister Thaksin Shinawatra while he was in New York preparing to address the United Nations. Though the military's explanation of the coup as a "pro-democracy military coup" may seem a contradiction to outside analysts, many urban citizens in Thailand may appear to have welcomed the coup, which removed the increasingly corrupt Prime Minister Thaksin Shinawatra from power. Nonetheless, many worried that Thailand would never escape from what one Thai analyst described as a "vicious cycle of constitution, election, corruption and coup" (Mydans 2006).

Indonesia

Indonesia did not immediately adopt a political system dominated by the military; in fact, the nation's first president, Sukarno, worked diligently to balance the influence of the military against various Islamic forces and the Partai Komunis Indonesia (PKI; Indonesian Communist Party). Sukarno struggled to unite a country spread across 3,000 miles and 17,000 separate islands, torn apart by competing ethnic and regional loyalties, and fractured by linguistic and religious divides. His failure to successfully forge a unified nation led to assumption of power by his successor, General Suharto, who imposed military rule over the country. Suharto's military only gradually co-opted other forces, such as the bureaucrats and later Islamic forces, under the *dwi fungsi* system. Under this system, the military supervised the bureaucrats at each level of the government hierarchy, much as the Communist parties paralleled their governments in other parts of Asia. To understand the rise and rule of the military in Indonesia and the movement under way since 1998 to keep the military out of power, we must first briefly examine the societal makeup of the country and early efforts to forge a sense of national unity.

Indonesia has more than 200 ethnic groups scattered across the country's more than 6,000 inhabited islands. The Javanese are the largest group, making up 45 percent of the total population, with the Sundanese (14 percent), Madurese (7.5 percent), Malays (7.5 percent), and Chinese (5 percent) falling far behind numerically and in terms of the political power they have been able to obtain. Muslims make up close to 90 percent of the population, though they are split into a number of smaller divisions. In an effort to bring these diverse groups together, Sukarno promoted a national ideology known as *pancasila* (the five pillars): nationalism, humanism, representative government, social justice, and monotheism.

The peoples of Indonesia were initially brought together in their efforts to expel the colonial Dutch, and the fledgling sense of nation was reinforced with the adoption of Bahasa Indonesia (rather than Javanese) as the national language and the use of a series of state symbols and nationalist rhetoric. The rebel calls of nationalism in opposition to Dutch rule helped unify much of the country, though the Dutch policy of favoring certain ethnic groups over others, and of utilizing local ethnic bureaucrats in a system of indirect rule, led to lasting divisions within the Indonesian population and lasting resentments toward those who "colluded" with the Dutch, like the Dayaks, who are still discriminated against (Bertrand 2004).

Indonesia initially experimented with a parliamentary democracy from 1950 to 1957, but a series of uprisings by communist, Islamic, and regional military leaders led Sukarno to suspend elections in 1957 and establish a system of "guided democracy," or "democracy with leadership," based on what he called traditional Indonesian values, including consultation, consensus, and mutual assistance. Guided democracy limited the number of political parties and concentrated power in the hands of the president. Sukarno was not all-powerful, though, as he worked to balance the rising strengths of both the military and the PKI.

In September 1965, a murky coup was launched that resulted in the deaths of six top military generals. To this day, the exact happenings surrounding this coup are unknown. The results are known, however. General Suharto, commander of military forces in Jakarta, took control and blamed the coup on the Indonesian Communist Party. With the suggestion that Sukarno himself was involved, Suharto pushed him aside and began to consolidate his regime, the New Order. In contrast to the chaos and poverty of the "Old Order" under

Sukarno, the New Order was to be peaceful and development-oriented. Accompanying the changeover in power, perhaps 500,000 people were killed, among them communists, communist sympathizers, and simply the unlucky (including many ethnic Chinese who were "assumed" to be communists, like the Chinese of the People's Republic). Tens of thousands of others were imprisoned, internally exiled, or deprived of their political rights.

Suharto used Golkar, a military-linked coalition of "functional groups" (groups of veterans, youth, women, farmers, etc.), as the military's electoral vehicle during the New Order, linking these social groups with the military and the bureaucrats. Parties and partisanship became anathema. Controlled elections were held in 1971, and in 1973 the remnants of opposition political parties were forced to merge into two toothless parties: the United Development Party, to represent Islamic forces, and the Indonesian Democracy Party, to serve as an umbrella for nationalist forces. These parties were not permitted to organize at the grassroots level, and were not even allowed to oppose the government's programs.

Under the New Order regime, the military established a parallel administration to the civilian government throughout Indonesia. Close to one-third of the military was involved primarily in nonmilitary functions such as occupying positions of state power, including ministerships at the national level and governorships of provinces. The military also engaged in development efforts, the regime's primary claim to legitimacy.

The economic crash in 1997 was the immediate cause of Suharto's fall, though popular resistance movements against him had been gaining ground in the years immediately preceding the crash, particularly since the government's thinly veiled efforts to rig the 1996 overthrow of Megawati Sukarnoputri, Sukarno's daughter, as head of the Indonesian Democracy Party. Megawati's ouster was followed by violent protests that left perhaps scores dead.

The post-Suharto governments have pushed through a series of reforms to reduce the role of the military in politics. The police force was separated from the military in 1999, though the two still retain close links. President Abdurrahman Wahid tried to assert civilian dominance over the military by dismissing several top-ranking generals, and appointed a civilian as defense minister. The post had been held by a military official throughout Suharto's reign.

Even the current civilian minister of defense, Juwono Sudarsono, however, acknowledges that despite the democratic presidential election in 2004, the military "retains the real levers of power" (Perlez 2005). The civilian government has been unable to bring to justice the military officers responsible for the widespread slaughter of East Timorese in 1999, when the citizens of that area declared their independence. The military has seized upon the devastation of the December 26, 2005, tsunami to reassert its control over the rebellious Aceh region. Whether or not newly elected president Susilo Bambang Yudhoyono (the first directly elected president, though a retired general) will be able to rein in the country's generals remains to be seen, though efforts to do so, in and of themselves, are significant. While the military still maintains influence in Indonesia, the reforms since 1998 have significantly curbed its power and paved the way for further reductions in its sway over politicians.

South Korea

The Korean military largely dominated politics until the first president elected in over thirty years with no military background, Kim Young-sam, pushed through a series of forceful reforms between 1993 and 1998. Although the military only actually replaced the civilian government twice, through a military coup on May 16, 1961, that placed General Park Chung Hee in charge of the country, and through another coup immediately following his assassination in December 1979, its influence limited the civilian leaders' ability to act independently. The leaders of the second military coup orchestrated nominally democratic elections just over a year after taking power. Korean politics, society, and the economy were largely dominated by the military until the end of the 1990s.

Just as the governments in our other case studies were radically affected by the colonial powers, so South Korea's politics and the rise of the military have been influenced by outside powers. South Korean politics has been dramatically influenced not so much by outside colonialism per se, but by the Allies' decision following World War II to divide the Korean peninsula. This decision, along with the impact of the North Korean invasion of the south in 1950, contributed to the consolidation of central executive power in the south and the justification for an increasingly militarized society throughout the 1960s, 1970s, and 1980s. The South Korean government justified the concentration of power in the executive branch and the restrictions on social liberties because of the urgent need to stop the expansion of communism from the north, and to fend off communist sympathizers even within the south. It was not until 1987 that South Korea began to reverse the trends of authoritarian rule and move toward more open politics.

The South Korean political system was born out of popular opposition. Numerous Koreans in the south protested against the division of the Korean peninsula and the creation of separate governing structures for the south. Nonetheless, the Allies' occupation forces created a new political system and placed Syngman Rhee at its head in 1946. The popular response was immediate, as people took to the streets to protest the new administration. President Rhee's response was to enact a national security law that gave the state sweeping powers to crush any opposition forces. With the onset of the Korean War in 1950, the Rhee regime found justification for increasing the military's role in the need to squelch global communism. The increasingly repressive police state imposed by the Rhee regime, despite the facade of an ineffective democratic institutional structure, led to an ongoing struggle between the authoritarian state and irrepressible groups within civil society. Even this facade was dismantled in 1972 with the passing of the Yushun constitution, which further restricted what few civil liberties remained for the population. In 1980, General Chun Doo Hwan led a ruthless and bloody crackdown against the citizens of Kwangju, who took to the streets demanding greater democratic maneuvering room. Though protesters for the most part went underground for several years following the Kwangju massacre of 1987, General Chun's officer corps refused to participate in another Kwangju-type crackdown. Under massive popular pressure as well as pressure from within his own military's ranks, General Chun finally agreed to allow democratic elections, which were held in December 1987. The opposition forces were so divided, however, that they failed to place a civilian president in office, and retired general Roh Tae Woo assumed the post with only 36 percent of the popular vote.

The shift toward democratic elections and increasing civilian control was partly facilitated because the military viewed the new president as friendly toward its cause. The new civilian leadership tacitly accepted an amnesty for military leaders, and civil-military relations continued on much as they had until the 1987 civil protests. The military did not have to retain the formal reins of power to assert great influence over the political system. Korean society and economics were highly militarized. A universal mandatory term of service for all young men heightened the citizenry's awareness of the military. A home-defense corps system provided military training to all high school and university students, making the military a key actor in the socialization of Korean youth and a force not to be ignored by the civilian leadership. In addition, after finishing their military commitments, retired military personnel were placed in solid positions within the bureaucracy and business community. Scholar Auriel Croissant describes the military at this time as "the single most important channel for upward mobility in Korean society." More than 27 percent of cabinet officers and nearly 12 percent of National Assembly representatives were retired military, for example, during the period 1963–1979. These figures declined only slightly during the 1980–1988 period, to 21.5 percent and 10.5 percent respectively. The fact that these numbers dropped to 4.5 percent and 2.7 percent during the last half of the 1990s is significant, though the government continues to struggle to keep the military out of the civilian governing organizations (Croissant 2004). This important role began to diminish slightly as the private sector began to provide alternate sources of upward mobility, and the role was further redefined beginning in 1993, when Kim Young Sam took office as president.

Kim was the first civilian to hold the nation's top political position. He placed reform of civil-military relations at the top of his agenda from the beginning. Among the most important moves he launched was a campaign to "rectify the authoritarian past." Widely supported by the general public, the campaign led to the arrest of former presidents Chun Doo Hwan and Roh Tae

Woo, along with several of their leading generals, and a guilty verdict on charges of rebellion, conspiracy, and corruption in office. Kim portrayed the arrests as an attack on military corruption and the ascendance of civilian checks on such practices.

In 1997, Kim Dae Jung, the first opposition candidate ever to overthrow the incumbent party's candidate, became president. Many analysts point to this transfer of power as the definitive end of military domination. Kim was able to further reduce the military's influence by pushing through his famous "Sunshine" policy, which held that North Korea could be encouraged into good behavior given proper engagement. This controversial policy (one largely opposed by the Bill Clinton and George W. Bush administrations) stripped the South Korean government of its argument that democratic opening would lead to chaos in a system under constant threat of military attack from the north.

▧ Restricted Democracies

A number of Asia Pacific states avidly rejected communism, and established civilian political institutions designed to provide a degree of democracy to their populaces. But even within Japan, probably the most democratic of the Asian states, individuals' ability to influence politics in order to promote their desires or to improve their standards of living were largely restricted until the early 1990s. Scholars debate the root cause of the limited success of Western-style liberal democracies in Asia Pacific, though many cite Confucianism and other Asian cultural patterns (Pye 1985; Bell 1995). According to these culturalist arguments, at least two features of Asian culture limit the growth of democracy. First, Asians tend to place a higher priority on the group rather than on the individual, and are thus reluctant to push for a liberal democracy that stems from the Hobbesian and Lockean premise that government's legitimacy is based on its ability to protect the individual and his or her interests. Second, Asian culture emphasizes proper observance of hierarchical relationships and the duties and obligations derived from one's position within clearly defined hierarchical relationships. Democracy must be based on a system in which the views of all individuals have equal importance. The individual and egalitarian base of democracies (at least in theory) thus does not mesh well with traditional Asian values. Others, such as Amartya Sen (1997), argue that there is little more in Asian culture than in Western that would limit democracy's growth. Sen, in fact, questions using the term "Asian values" at all to refer to the plethora of diverse and competing values held by those in the region.

Confucian thought outlines five hierarchical relationships: ruler-led, father-son, husband-wife, older brother–younger brother, and friend-friend. In each of these relationships, duties and obligations are clearly spelled out for each partner. Even in the seemingly equal friend-to-friend relationship, there are responsibilities for respect and paternalistic care due to age differences, just as in the other relationships. Although Confucian teachings dictate that superiors in hierarchical relationships are not to violate certain norms, and that they have certain obligations to their lower partner in the relationship, nonetheless a great deal of power is vested in the higher role in the relationship. Barring mass starvation, famine, or war (in China, what is known as loss of the "Mandate of Heaven"), subjects have no right to control or influence their rulers. Rulers gain their authority based not on general consent, but on their divine mandate to promote the good of the whole land, rather than to protect individual rights.

Confucian values have contributed to the prevalence and importance of patron-client relationships throughout much of Asia Pacific. Ties of mutual obligation, known by various terms such as *utang na loob* in the Philippines and *guanxi* in China, bind clients to patrons who hold important positions, with the patrons helping to support the clients financially, socially, or politically. These personalistic hierarchical ties have limited the growth of political parties and other civil interest groups and nongovernmental organizations that require horizontal linkages to flourish. A series of reforms pushed through beginning in the 1980s throughout many Asia Pacific countries have begun to weaken the near-monopolistic importance of patron-client relationships, paving the way for growth of the more independent civil societies so crucial for democratic transitions.

Japan

Although Japan was never formally colonized, its present political and economic system evolved in part as a response to Western pressures. Feudal Japan had tried to hide from Western influence by barring all contact with outsiders in 1639. With the arrival of US commodore Matthew Perry's fleet in 1853, however, Japan was forced to open its borders to trade. Aware of the powerful capabilities of the West, Japan realized that it would have to adopt radical reforms to resist being fully colonized by the West. After witnessing China's humiliating defeat to the British in the Opium War in 1842, a group of Japanese ousted the ruling shogunate and placed the young Meiji emperor on the throne. The emperor launched a series of reforms that radically transformed traditional Japanese society and the system of government that managed it, contributing to the rise of Japanese economic might and a military machine that would seek to conquer the world just a few decades later.

The Meiji Restoration had an important influence on what has come to be called "the Japanese developmental state," the Japanese political and economic system that emerged after World War II. First, while many of the other Asia Pacific countries confronted the simultaneous challenges of nation building and statebuilding at independence, when Japan was given a new set of political institutions after World War II, it already had a firmly established sense of nationalism that developed rapidly under the Meiji reforms. While the myth of common origin in the Sun Goddess had a long history in Japan, modern nationalism was given a boost by the leaders of the Meiji Restoration. Compared with all of the other Asia Pacific countries with the exception of Korea, Japan is relatively homogeneous ethnically. The lack of major ethnic divides simplified nation-building challenges, which largely required only the weakening of regional loyalties to specific local military leaders. Determined to unify the numerous feudal domains in order to strengthen the country and resist foreign occupation, the samurai leaders of the Meiji Restoration actively promoted a number of nation-building policies. The government created a universal system of education to teach a unified history of the proud Japanese nation. The government also used the Shinto religion to promote nationalism. The state withdrew its support for Buddhism in 1868 and launched a campaign to promote "an official creed, teaching respect for the gods, reverence for the emperor, love of country, and obedience to the government" (Simone 1999:105). The Meiji reformers moved to centralize the government and strip the traditional warrior class of its monopoly on bearing arms. By centralizing the military and making it a conscription force, the Meiji reformers created an army that became a nationalizing force. By the turn of the nineteenth century, in fact, the army had become so nationalistic that it began to expand Japan's influence beyond its borders. Ironically, it was the immense strength of the Japanese military that led to its dismantlement under the terms of Japan's surrender in 1945. Though Japan now has one of the most advanced fighting forces in the world, the Self-Defense Force, the country is barred from using force as a component of its foreign policy by Article 9 of its constitution, the peace clause.

Another important feature of the Meiji reforms that continues to play an important role in Japanese politics is the close relationship that was forged between government and big business. The comprehensive Meiji reforms radically transformed traditional society and were purchased at an immense financial cost. Determined to transform Japan into a modernized state, the new government invested heavily in such industries as mining, shipbuilding, textiles, transportation, and other industries it felt crucial for Japan's national security. Private sources for these investments were minimal at the time, forcing the government to take on this leading role. This top-down pattern of industrialization was quite different from the path pursued in the most advanced nations of Western Europe, where the merchant and middle classes gradually accumulated enough capital to invest in private industries. Industry was not the only arena for government investment. The government created a new centralized system of universal education, along with a new postal and banking system and other social services.

Within less than a decade after launching the reforms, the new Meiji administration had overextended itself to the brink of bankruptcy. It began to auction off its new industries to private businesspeople, usually to those who had close personal ties to government officials. Most of these industries were sold at well below the government's initial investment costs. Through this process, a few key households were able to garner control of several industries by working closely with the government. It was through this means that the *zaibatsu* (conglomerates) emerged.

The *zaibatsu* were large holding companies that owned a group of industries. The various industries were like spokes on a wheel, with the center being the main holding company. One *zaibatsu* might own a shipbuilding industry as well as the steel factory and the various companies supplying parts to the shipyard. These *zaibatsu* did not have to pay dividends to private shareholders and could thus base their policies on long-term planning rather than the need to raise short-term profits. The industries within a given *zaibatsu* also had a strong incentive to buy from one another, even if there were lower-priced alternatives outside of the *zaibatsu,* as all of the revenue rolled back into the central hub of the wheel. The government worked closely with these *zaibatsu,* which were seen as the engine of Japan's industrial growth. The *zaibatsu* were dismantled briefly after World War II, only to reemerge as the slightly transformed *keiretsu.*

The preparations for World War II also greatly influenced postwar politics. As the Japanese military propelled the country into war, the bureaucrats were responsible for developing a system to maintain the war machine. As Bai Gao explains, the national mobilization law, enacted by the government in 1938, "gave the state bureaucracy unprecedented power to shape the managed economy by using administrative decrees. From then on, the state bureaucracy could issue orders directly to the private sector without consulting with the Diet. This has had a long-lasting impact on the post-war Japanese economy" (Bai 1997:62).

The current state institutions were developed at the end of World War II in conjunction with the US occupation forces. All of the features of a democratic system were clearly articulated in the 1947 constitution, though many scholars question the degree of democracy actually practiced in the informal political system. The sense of national crisis after World War II led the majority of Japanese to allow individual interests to take a backseat to national growth. Throughout the first four decades after the war, the average Japanese citizen's standard of living was far below what would be suggested by the national per capita gross domestic product and income levels. A number of governmental policies promoted national growth at the expense of the individual consumer. It was not until the economic bubble burst in 1990 that the average Japanese citizen began to assert demands for greater representation and reform of the existing balance of powers. A unique set of circumstances existed at the end of World War II that allowed the Liberal Democratic Party (LDP) to rise to power in 1955 and retain its hold on power through to the present, with only a brief interlude of opposition rule in 1993.

The constitution created a parliamentary system with regular elections. A system of checks and balances was established, with the Supreme Court granted the power of judicial review, and the elected legislature in charge of selecting the prime minister. Despite the holding of free and fair elections, the LDP managed to hold power effectively unchallenged until after the economic bubble burst in 1990. A unique set of circumstances contributed to the LDP's long-lasting rule. The unusual multimember district election system resulted in disproportionately high representation for the LDP-supporting rural districts, and the LDP worked extremely closely with the bureaucracy and with big business to propel the country's economy into the top global ranks. Although scholars disagree on exactly which component of this "iron triangle" holds the most power, the success of the Japanese developmental state model led most Japanese citizens to feel disinclined to challenge the arrangement.

The relationships among the LDP, the bureaucracy, and big business are quite complex, and have been the focus of many volumes on Japanese politics; because of their unique patterns of interaction, many scholars use terms such as "Japan, Inc." or "the Japanese developmental state." The power of elected officials is more limited in Japan's democracy than in the US system. The LDP, riddled with factions, tends to rotate the assignment of ministry heads in order to satisfy the demands of the numerous competing factions for cabinet representation. Ministers are often in office less than a year, while the bureaucrats working below the minister tend to serve their entire careers within a single ministry, and thus have extensive expertise. Most of the ministry work, then, is carried out by career bureaucrats rather than elected office holders. In effect, this means that Japanese citizens have little control over who is running their country, since the bureaucrats are not popularly elected. Laws are typically written quite broadly within the Diet, leaving a great deal of interpretation to the ministries responsible for implementing them. Bureaucrats are vetted through a rigorous civil service exam that only a small percentage of the top graduates from Japan's premier universities pass. The power of the bureaucracy transcends the work done within the various ministries, in a system known as *amakudari,* best translated as "descent from heaven." Under this system, retired bureaucrats are snatched up by big businesses to serve on their boards or as key executives. The bureaucratic background creates a bond between the business community and the bureaucracy, which many see as strengthening their position in relation to the more isolated and less powerful elected officialdom.

The ties between the LDP and big business have come with the state's commitment to develop Japan's economy. After the devastation of World War II and the national humiliation of the surrender, the Japanese population was generally willing to sacrifice individual improvements in standard of living for the good of the nation. Several factors in the international environment came together in just the right way at just the right time to contribute to Japan's miraculous economic success in the 1960s through the collapse of the bubble in 1990. Because several changes in these conditions led to mass questioning of the entire political base of the development model, they must be examined at least briefly here.

Gary Allinson (1997) outlines several important features of the Japanese political economy that contributed to Japan's phenomenal rise in the 1950s through the 1970s, but that began to change by the mid-1970s, contributing to the creation of the bubble economy from 1985 to 1990. First, international factors favored Japan's export-oriented growth strategy. Raw materials for Japan's industrial machine were relatively low-cost, and the stable currency system of Bretton Woods from 1944 to 1971 allowed Japan to set its currency artificially low in order to encourage exports. High global demand, particularly after the Korean War began in 1950, and an international tolerance for Japan's policies allowed exports to soar. Big business, Allinson argues, was able to exert a great deal of influence over Japan's elected officials, in part because management and labor were much more closely united than in most Western counterparts. The amount of time lost in 1987 due to strikes, measured in thousands of workdays, for example, was 256 in Japan, compared with 4,469 in the United States.

Changes in this international environment in the 1970s included the heavy costs to Japan from the oil embargo imposed by the Organization of Petroleum-Exporting Countries in 1973, the collapse of the Bretton Woods system, growing international concerns over Japan's "unfair trade policies," and increased competition from within the region. When Japan finally agreed to revalue its currency at urging by the United States in the mid-1980s, it tried to temper the impact on its exporting sector by dropping interest rates, setting off a bubble boom from 1985 until its burst in 1990.

The push to increase popular participation in the political process came after the shock of the bubble bursting in the 1990s. The stock market began to plummet on the first trading day of 1990, and by August 1992 the Nikkei stock market index had dropped from 38,915 to 14,309. The market value of stocks and land plunged at a rate of 10 trillion yen (approximately US$100 billion) per month; over a thirty-month time period, owners of stocks and land lost over US$2.5 trillion. The horrified and nearly numb Japanese citizenry no longer accepted the notion that the LDP-bureaucrat-business alliance knew the correct path to national growth, nor were they willing to continue sacrificing their own standard of living for this now elusive national growth. A series of government scandals and government mishandlings of national crises (the Kobe earthquake of 1995, for example) further shook popular confidence in the leadership, and citizens began to demand reform.

Though Japan's democracy clearly functioned quite differently from its US counterpart and many counterparts in Western Europe, it was by no means simply a facade for authoritarian rule. Of all the cases examined in this chapter, Japan has consistently been the most democratic, even during the periods of tight elite consensus and popular acquiescence. Nonetheless, the common pattern of increasing space for society in relation to the state can be seen in Japan after 1990, just as it can in most of the rest of Asia Pacific. Popular pressure led to the LDP's first electoral loss in 1989 and to a revision in the odd multimember-district electoral system that had helped ensure LDP dominance at the polls since 1955. While scholars debate why Japan has not been able to push through greater reforms since 1990, despite governmental and popular assertions of the necessity of doing so, it seems clear that average Japanese voters have more influence and are more willing to make their voices heard than before 1990.

Philippines

As in Japan, the political institutions in the Philippines were largely influenced by the United States, which ruled the Philippines as one of its few colonies from 1898 to 1946, when it regained control after the Japanese occupation during the Pacific War. Modeled after the US system, the Philippine government was divided into executive, legislative, and judicial branches, each with supervisory powers over the others. The nation-building challenges of bringing together more than 100 linguistic, cultural, and racial groupings spread across many of the country's 7,000 islands and the dire economic conditions within the Philippines contributed to Ferdinand Marcos's manipulation of these institutions and of the traditional Filipino culture. He imposed martial law and ruled as a dictator beginning in 1972. As in the other countries examined here, this concentration of state power, particularly in the executive branch, reached its peak in the 1970s and led to the reassertion of citizen demands for greater involvement in the 1980s.

Using some of the same anticommunist rhetoric used by Suharto in Indonesia and Syngman Rhee in South Korea, Marcos used the military to clamp down on regional challenges and Muslim discontents in the south. Seizing on fear of disorder felt by the military and some segments of the population, Marcos declared martial law in 1972. He suspended the constitution to avoid being subject to the two-term limit it imposed on the president, and then suspended parliament itself. The military increased from 60,000 to 200,000 under his rule, and human rights abuses during this time were flagrant.

The Philippine economy plummeted under Marcos's watch. Second only to Japan in the 1960s, by the end of Marcos's rule the Philippine economy was near the bottom of the Asia Pacific countries in all socioeconomic indicators. Marcos nationalized industries and handed over their management to his loyal clients and relatives, dubbed "cronies." Corruption soared under Marcos, as vividly reflected in the discovery of opulent spending by his immediate family members despite appalling levels of widespread poverty throughout the country. His wife owned more than a thousand pairs of expensive shoes, for example, while citizens watched their children die from malnutrition and waterborne diseases carried through the open sewers running throughout many of the country's cities.

Following the pattern seen throughout much of the region, the Philippines experienced dramatic reforms in the mid-1980s. Economic crisis and soaring international debt, together with newly created fissures in Filipino society (such as among the established oligarchs and the newly rich created by Marcos's crony capitalism, or among the factions within the military, and between it and civilians), led to growing support for change. Citizens took to the street in the bloodless "People Power Revolution" after the opposition candidate, Corazon Aquino, was denied the electoral victory that most citizens felt she had earned in the February 1986 election. When the military, with the backing of Marcos's own defense minister, came to the aid of the people rather than the government, Marcos fled with his family into exile in Hawaii.

The transition toward a more democratic system has not been easy in the Philippines, but the changes have certainly been dramatic. Aquino managed to resist six military coup attempts against her leadership during the six years she was in office. A year after coming to office, Aquino pushed through a pro-people constitution and mandated popular elections, along with a devolution of power to local governments. She stripped the bureaucracy of Marcos loyalists and weakened the power of the military by dividing it from the police force and making the police subject to local civilian governmental control. Although Aquino's successor, Fidel Ramos, won the presidency with less than 24 percent of the popular vote in a crowded field, the peaceful transfer of power confirmed that the era of dictatorial rule had been successfully eliminated by the Aquino reforms, though Joseph Estrada's presidency, from 1998 until his ouster in 2001, saw the return of much corruption and crony capitalism, as well as a resurgence in regional conflicts. The new administration continues to try to consolidate the reforms.

Malaysia

Also heavily influenced by patron-client relationships, the Malaysian political system is nonetheless different from that of the Philippines, and from other patron-client systems in Asia Pacific, in that preferential treatment and benefits have been distributed on the basis of communal ties in addition to purely personal ones. The Malaysian political system in place today has evolved out of a unique combination of traditional practices, altered yet reinforced by British colonial policies, and shaped through the ongoing struggle to achieve universal citizen commitment to the Malaysian state while maintaining preferential standing for the Malay majority.

Malaysia's population of 21 million comprises 51 percent Malay, 27 percent Chinese, 8 percent Indians, and 12 percent from a wide assortment of groups indigenous to the area. The Malays traditionally controlled the territory of the Malay peninsula (which together with parts of the island of Borneo forms today's Malaysia), with the Chinese and Indians arriving in large numbers only after British recruitment in the nineteenth and early twentieth centuries. Before the Portuguese arrival in 1511, the Malay peninsula was dominated by the sultanate of Malacca (today, Melaka). Several sultanates accepted Malaccan rule and the empire wielded great influence through the entire Southeast Asian region. Over the next three centuries, regional sultans reasserted a degree of independence from Malacca as European powers jockeyed for colonial control of the region. The British began to gain greater influence in the region in the late eighteenth century, and tried to use these sultans to implement colonial policy, allowing a high degree of autonomy to those who cooperated in Britain's indirect rule.

British rule from the late nineteenth to the mid–twentieth century altered the dynamics of Malaysian demographics and corresponding policies, in ways that have continued to influence Malaysian politics through to the present. By the 1930s, Malays had learned through a British-run census that they had become a minority in "their" own country. Colonial policies altered ethnic demographics while reinforcing the political dominance of the Malays, laying the institutional foundations for a unique political system that disperses privileges on the basis of communal divisions rather than individual patron-client relationships. As in the other countries discussed here, in Malaysia the nationalist forces that were jockeying for independence from the colonial powers were forced to forge some type of national identity out of the fragmented and loosely associated regions, ethnic groups, and religious organizations that had been manipulated and played against one another under the colonial administration. In the Malaysian case, the effort to forge a national identity directly impacted the unusual set of state institutions selected to manage the new country. These institutions, in turn, greatly affected the economic development model selected by Malaysia and the economic distribution system used to propel Malaysia into a successful and flourishing export economy by the 1990s. To understand this complex process, we must first turn to Malaysia under British rule.

British rule had a major impact on ethnic demographics within Malaysia. The British needed additional laborers for their tin and rubber plantations, and brought in numerous Indians from their nearby colony as well as a large number of Chinese. The colonial administrators granted the Malays special privileges, including preferential access to education, greater landownership rights, and a near-total domination of the bureaucracy. The British ruled the region indirectly by granting powers to the traditional Malay sultans and training an extensive Malay bureaucracy to support them in their implementation of colonial policies. Colonial policies created a system that privileged the Malay, yet significantly increased the number of non-Malays living within the territory.

The country's ethnic makeup has had a dramatic impact on politics from before the current nation's inception, through the present efforts at reform, and from the most local level to the country's international dealings. Ironically, but perhaps not surprisingly, the beginning of a strong Malaysian nationalism arose from Malay resistance against British efforts to unify the country and to award citizenship rights to all those living within the territory, regardless of ethnicity. In 1946, Britain tried to create a "Malayan union" by abolishing the power of the sultans. To block the British, Malays from across the numerous sultanates joined to create the United Malays Nationalist Organization (UMNO). The British failure to impose a Malayan union highlighted that the British could in fact be successfully challenged by a popular movement, and in 1952 the Malayan Chinese Association joined with UMNO to create an alliance. They were joined two years later by the Malayan Indian Congress. The alliance successfully negotiated the withdrawal of the British, and the Malayan Federation gained its formal independence on August 31, 1959. The alliance, which adopted the name Barisan Nasional (BN; National Front) in 1974, has dominated Malaysian politics since its inception.

Malaysia's ethnic makeup also weakened the communist challenge to Malay rule, as the Communist Party was associated with the Chinese and comprised primarily ethnic Chinese. While the Communist Party therefore had much less power and impact than it did in Indonesia, for example, political events surrounding the early years of the nation's independence were nonetheless turbulent and explosive. Popular expectations for the new leadership were unrealistically high, and governmental shortfalls were met with protests and eventually mass rioting. The postindependence political system was built on a premise of elite interethnic cooperation supported by ethnic-based political parties. From 1957 to 1969, "the bargain" among the ethnic groups was that Malays would dominate political power while other groups, primarily the Chinese and foreign investors, would be allowed to dominate the economy. After intercommunal rioting in 1969, however, the bargain was drastically revised, as Malay leaders perceived that Malay economic backwardness had contributed to severe nation-building challenges. A new pro-Malay economic affirmative action policy, begun in 1971, was initiated to help to "eliminate the identification of race with economic function." This led the government to grant greater favoritism to Malays in university enrollment, overseas scholarships, business development, and shareholding/capital accumulation.

The fall of seven parliamentary governments within the first decade after independence, and the ethnic rioting in 1969, led the king to disband parliament and declare emergency rule. The system after 1969 concentrated power in the executive branch, and several new policies were launched to further strengthen Malay economic and political dominance.

The Malaysian political order, which evolved out of the legacy of colonial rule, preserved elements of the traditional governing system and crafted a system that propelled the nation forward economically. Malaysia is a constitutional monarchy. The federal parliamentary system vests most of the governing power in the central government, with states given limited control over only land, water, and Islam (Sabah and Sarawak have a few additional powers, including control over educational policy). Local government officials are appointed by state governments, rather than popularly elected. The unique role of ethnicity in politics can clearly be seen in the election process of the king, who is the "apex of Malaysia's political structure . . . the Supreme Head of the Federation, the repository of executive, legislative, and judicial authority, the Supreme Commander of the Armed Forces, and the Head of Islam in the Federal Territories" (Funston 2001:172). The king is elected every five years on a rotational basis from among the nine traditional state sultans. The nine sultans, together with the appointed governors of the other four states, make up the Conference of Rulers, which must be consulted before any constitutional changes can be made that would affect ethnic harmony. Most of the king's powers are in name only, with real rule left to the head of the executive, the prime minister, along with the prime minister's cabinet. The trend to diminish the powers of the king and state sultans became especially pronounced under Malaysia's long-serving prime minister, Mahathir Mohamad, who ruled from 1981 to 2003.

Governing powers have been concentrated in the executive, particularly since the prime minister imposed a number of power-aggrandizing policies in the months following the declaration of emergency rule in 1969. As an act of parliament is required to annul a state of emergency, and none has been issued to revoke the four states of emergency, declared in 1964, 1966, 1969, and 1977, the prime minister can technically rule by decree without being checked by either the legislature or the judiciary. The ruling coalition's strong dominance of parliament (it usually controls more than two-thirds of the seats and can thus change the constitution at will) has reinforced the power of the executive.

The Malaysian political system was created to ensure continued Malay dominance of the policymaking process. Malays were also assured preferential treatment in economic affairs, particularly after the race riots of 1969 and as the state played an ever-increasing role in the economy in the 1980s. The Malaysian economic system has led many observers to label it "Malaysia, Inc.," as UMNO joined the bureaucracy and big business in ways similar to those found in Japan. Executive control over the privatization process, however, was largely influenced by ethnic concerns in ways not found in Japan. When Malaysia began a push to privatize in the early 1980s, UMNO retained control over establishing state institutions to invest in private companies as trustees for Malays. UMNO thus increased its patronage capabilities, and the favors that it dispensed were largely based on ethnicity or communal ties rather than purely on personal ties (though these have also been quite important).

Despite the communal nature of politics in Malaysia and the direct subsidies to promote Malay education and affirmative action economic programs, communal politics has remarkably not led to huge divisions in standard of living. Non-Malays, in fact, often vote for the governing Malay coalition. In 1995, for the first time in history, the majority of non-Malays endorsed the governing National Front coalition, affirming their view of its legitimacy. In 1999, when the Malay vote was divided over a variety of issues, non-Malays saved the ruling government.

Conclusion

Dynamic political changes in Asia Pacific are ongoing. The transition away from centralized authoritarian rule that began in the early 1980s has been anything but smooth. The financial crisis in 1997 simultaneously pushed reform forward in some areas, Indonesia for example, while challenging the fragile progress in others, as in Malaysia. As authoritarian rule has receded, social divisions that were repressed by these regimes have begun to reemerge in some areas, as the violence in Mindanao in the southern Philippines, and in Aceh province in Indonesia, vividly demonstrates. Personalistic politics continues to undermine institutional reforms, as seen perhaps most vividly in China, South Korea, and Vietnam, but the gradual expansion of legal reform and institutional development has led citizens throughout Asia Pacific to believe in their right to political, social, and economic liberties. All three types of political systems in Asia Pacific—communist, military, and restricted democratic—have shifted away from centralized rule, granting more liberties to their citizens. Human rights abuses continue throughout much of Asia Pacific, but have diminished since the early 1980s. As ties with the global community continue to expand with global trade and cultural exchanges, it seems likely that the private sphere will continue to expand, and that civil society will continue to grow, within this dynamic and exciting region.

Note

I would like to thank Paige Johnson Tan, of the University of North Carolina at Wilmington, for her expertise on Indonesia and suggested revisions on an earlier draft of this chapter.

Bibliography

Alagappa, Muthiah. 2001. *Coercion and Governance: The Declining Political Role of the Military in Asia.* Stanford: Stanford University Press.
Allinson, Gary. 1997. *Japan's Postwar History.* Ithaca: Cornell University Press.
Bai Gao. 1997. *Economic Ideology and Japanese Industrial Policy.* Cambridge: Cambridge University Press.

Bell, Daniel. 1995. *Towards Illiberal Democracy in Pacific Asia.* New York: St. Martin's.

Bertrand, Jacques. 2004. *Nationalism and Ethnic Conflict in Indonesia.* Cambridge: Cambridge University Press.

Bianco, Lucien. 1971. *Origins of the Chinese Communist Revolution, 1911–1949.* Stanford: Stanford University Press.

Bovingdon, Gardner. 2004. *Autonomy in Xinjiang: Han Nationalist Imperatives and Uyghur Discontent.* Policy Study no. 11. Washington, D.C.: East-West Center.

Brill, Jennifer. 1998. "North Korean Famine Claims Two Million Lives." http://www.disasterrelief.org/disasters/980824northkorea.

Bulag, Uradyn Erden. 2002. *Mongols at China's Edge: History and the Politics of National Identity.* Lanham: Rowman and Littlefield.

Central Intelligence Agency. 2005. *World Factbook: Democratic People's Republic of Korea.* February. http://www.cia.gov/cia/publications/factbook/geos/kn.html#military.

China Internet Information Center. 2003. "Marketization of State Owned Enterprises." http://www.china.org.cn/english/2003chinamarket/79517.htm.

Congressional-Executive Commission on China. 2005. *Annual Report.* Washington, D.C.: Government Printing Office.

Croissant, Auriel. 2004. "Riding the Tiger: Civilian Control and the Military in Democratizing Korea." *Armed Forces and Society* 30, no. 3 (Spring): 357–381.

Dickson, Bruce. 2003. *Red Capitalists in China: The Party, Private Entrepreneurs, and Prospects for Political Change.* Cambridge: Cambridge University Press.

Eberstadt, Nicholas. 2000. "Disparities in Socioeconomic Development in Divided Korea: Indications and Implications." *Asian Survey* (November–December): 867–893.

Far Eastern Economic Review. 1998. "North Korea: Running Against History— Hwang Jang Yop Interview with Olaf Jahn." October 15: 30–31.

Frontline World. 2005. "North Korea." http://www.pbs.org/frontlineworld/stories/northkorea/facts.html#04.

Funston, John. 2001. *Government and Politics in Southeast Asia.* London: Zed.

Hernandez, Carlina. 1985. "The Philippines." In Z. H. Ahmad and H. Crouch, eds., *Military-Civilian Relations in South-East Asia,* pp. 157–158. New York: Oxford University Press.

Johnson, Chalmers. 1962. *Peasant Nationalism and Communist Power: The Emergence of Revolutionary China, 1937–1945.* Stanford: Stanford University Press.

———. 1995. *Japan: Who Governs? The Rise of the Developmental State.* New York: Norton.

Kaup, Katherine Palmer. 2000. *Creating the Zhuang: Ethnic Politics in China.* Boulder: Lynne Rienner.

Kristof, Nicholas D., and Sheryl WuDunn. 2000. *Thunder from the East: Portrait of a Rising Asia.* New York: Knopf.

Lardy, Nicholas. 1998. *China's Unfinished Economic Revolution.* Washington, D.C.: Brookings Institution.

———. 2002. *Integrating China into the Global Economy.* Washington, D.C.: Brookings Institution.

Lieberthal, Kenneth. 2004. *Governing China: From Revolution Through Reform.* 2nd rev. ed. New York: Norton.

Maidment, Richard, et al., eds. 1998. *Governance in the Asia-Pacific.* London: Routledge.

Marx, Karl. 1970. "Critique of the Gotha Programme." In *Selected Works of Karl Marx and Frederick Engels,* pp. 13–30. Moscow: Progress Publishers.

Mydans, Seth. 2006. "Thailand Reinterprets the Rules of Democracy, Again." *New York Times,* September 20.

Perlez, Jane. 2005. "U.S. Takes Steps to Mend Ties with Indonesian Military." *New York Times,* February 7.

Pye, Lucien. 1985. *Asian Power and Politics: The Cultural Dimensions of Authority.* Cambridge: Belknap.

Riggs, Fred W. 1966. *Thailand: The Modernization of a Bureaucratic Polity.* Honolulu: East-West Center.

Rohwer, Jim. 1995. *Asia Rising: Why America Will Prosper as Asia's Economies Boom.* New York: Simon and Schuster.

Sen, Amartya. 1997. "Human Rights and Asian Values: What Lee Kuan Yew and Li Peng Don't Understand About Asia." *New Republic* 217, nos. 2–3 (July).

Simone, Vera. 1995. *The Asian Pacific: Political and Economic Development in a Global Context.* White Plains, N.Y.: Longman.

Wu, Yanrui. 2004. *China's Economic Growth: A Miracle with Chinese Characteristics.* New York: Routledge.

5

The Economies of Asia Pacific

Kailash Khandke

It is difficult to provide an in-depth economic survey of all the Asian economies, or even the entire group of Asia Pacific economies, in a concise and succinct manner. Conventional definitions of the region make the task more difficult still. For example, the United Nations Economic and Social Commission for Asia and the Pacific (UNESCAP) lists fifty-one nations as member states and nine associate members.[1] The list includes nations as diverse as Afghanistan and the Maldives, on one end of the development spectrum, to the newly industrialized economies of Thailand and Malaysia. Similarly, the Asia-Pacific Economic Cooperation (APEC) forum lists twenty-one member states, not all of which are in Asia; the list nevertheless includes Vietnam and the Philippines, which have had a slightly less conventional development path compared with the economies of, say, Japan, Singapore, South Korea, and Taiwan.[2] The primary purpose of this chapter is to provide a core understanding of the economic and political factors that have made the economies of Asia Pacific some of the fastest growing in the world. The chapter primarily focuses on the development records of nine of the Asian economies: Japan, the "four dragons" or "four tigers" (South Korea, Taiwan, Hong Kong, and Singapore), three newly emerging industrialized economies (Malaysia, Thailand, and Indonesia), and the newly emerging liberalized economy of China. A broad economic perspective is used to examine institutional changes, policies, and the roles of the government and the private sector in these economies.

Concentrating on these nine countries allows us to recognize some commonalities in policy choices pursued by the economies in this region. I will proceed for the most part by identifying these commonalities, rather than presenting a case-by-case country approach. This focus, combined with a brief

examination of four less-developed economies in the region, will help us identify the development strategies that can lead to sustained and rapid economic
development.

The World Bank (1993:1) labels the economies of Japan, South Korea,
Taiwan, Hong Kong, Singapore, Malaysia, Thailand, and Indonesia as "high-
performing Asian economies" (HPAEs). They are among the few economies
since the end of World War II that have overcome the label of "underdevelop-
ment." As such, they provide a real test case for the story of economic development, the role of policy choices, and the factors that can lead to rapid economic growth, such as trade, investment, and industrialization. Unfortunately,
these economies are also a reminder that bad things can happen to good
economies, and the Asian crisis of 1997 provides a classic real-world labora-
tory lesson on the importance and the role of institutions in the incorporation
of economic development strategies.

The chapter begins with an analysis of the factors and policy choices that
sustained economic growth and development between 1960 and 1995, highlighting the traditional focus on policies and institutions. Next it examines the
East Asian financial crisis. The crisis hit the region with the dramatic devaluation of the Thai baht in the summer of 1997, and rapidly spread to the entire
East Asian region by 1998. A brief digression follows, in which I explore some
of the countries that were not part of the Asian success story. Here the economic
development in the Indo-Chinese region—in Vietnam, Laos, and Cambodia, as
well as in the Philippines—is briefly outlined, and the role of the Association
of Southeast Asian Nations (ASEAN) in promoting that development is explored. The chapter next provides a brief overview of the sudden rise of the
Chinese economy, especially in light of the fact that a cautionary tale may be in
place given the East Asian crisis in the region in 1997. In conclusion, I offer
some remarks on the track records of the Asia Pacific economies, as well as lessons and remedies that will be necessary to avoid future crises in the region. Of
importance are whether the region as a whole can sustain economic growth
well into the twenty-first century, and the set of factors that will be necessary
to integrate these economies into the world economy.

◾ The East Asian Miracle

At the end of World War II, most of the East Asian and Asia Pacific economies
were underdeveloped. These economies were still largely dependent on agriculture. The manufacturing base was weak, and investment in capital in Korea
and Singapore, for example, was quite low. Levels of literacy across the region
were fairly low, and consequently there was widespread inequality in income.
In addition, all of the leaders in the HPAEs (except Japan) faced questions
about their political legitimacy and either external or internal threat in one

form or another. South Korea, for example, was threatened from the north by communist Korea; Taiwan was threatened from mainland China; and Thailand, Malaysia, Indonesia, and Singapore faced internal political strife from formidable Communist parties (Campos and Root 1996:28).

The political leaders in each of these economies were prompted to address the needs of the poorer sectors of the population. These leaders determined that political legitimacy would follow economic growth, and they sought to achieve this through a policy of shared economic growth, which necessitated two straightforward principles. First, given existing low levels of investment, it was necessary to encourage businesses to invest in industry and management. Second, it was important to persuade the low-income sectors of the economy to think long-term. This would necessitate short-term sacrifices, for example by increasing current savings and postponing consumption of goods and services (Campos and Root 1996:29).

For more than a quarter of a century, between 1965 and 1995, the countries of East Asia experienced rapid economic change. The spectacular economic performance of these countries was nothing short of a miracle, according to many analysts (Woronoff 1986:6; Nelsen and Pack 1999:416; Stiglitz 1996:151). Average life expectancy at birth rose from fifty-seven years in 1970 to sixty-eight years in 1995. The adult literacy rate jumped from 73 to 91 percent over this period, and per capita income more than quadrupled in each of the countries. In fact, the World Bank (1993:8) dubbed a set of eight economies—Japan, Korea, Taiwan, Hong Kong, Singapore, Thailand, Malaysia, and Indonesia—as the "East Asian miracle." From the mid-1960s to the mid-1990s, these eight HPAEs underwent rapid and sustained economic development. With an annual income per capita growth rate of 5.5 percent, they outperformed all other low- and middle-income countries in the world. Moreover, the average Gini coefficient, the most widely recognized measure of income distribution, was 0.38 between 1965 and 1990, while the average for all other low- and middle-income economies in the rest of the world was 0.49 (Campos and Root 1996:9).[3]

The importance of economic growth is difficult to overstate. All countries in the world desire rapid economic growth and a better standard of living. Yet understanding economic growth and, more importantly, attributing economic growth to a particular set of factors, prove to be quite difficult in practice (Easterly 2002:23, 145). The conceptual framework that is employed here to analyze the Asia Pacific economies follows the standard neoclassical model of economic growth.

Coupled with the basic precepts of the neoclassical model of economic growth, the eight HPAEs all exhibited prudent macroeconomic management. Budget deficits were maintained within limits that the economy could absorb, inflation was kept under control, and internal and external debt was managed extremely well. Macroeconomic stability proved to be significant, since it created a favorable environment from which other policy initiatives could be launched, such as the policies that emphasized physical and human capital investment, and the role of international trade in the growth process. With the interaction of these different policy prescriptions, the East Asian economies experienced three decades of sustained and rapid economic growth and development.

High Levels of Savings and Physical Capital Investment

High and growing savings rates constituted one of the principal engines for growth in the HPAEs. High savings, both public and private, fostered high levels of public and private investment in these economies. The public sector mostly invested in construction and improvement of new and existing infrastructure, while private investment took the form of accumulation of capital goods and renovating or adding to existing infrastructure (World Bank 1993:40; Stiglitz 1996:151). High and growing savings rates in the HPAEs were facilitated by the low to moderate inflation and stable interest rates that existed in the 1960s and 1970s. This spurred greater public confidence and increased savings rates. The East Asian governments used a wide array of policies to develop savings. Singapore, Taiwan, Japan, and Malaysia encouraged high private savings through mandatory pension and provident funds. The accumulation of the pension and provident funds filled the void for consumer credit, which was then rationed toward the purchase of durable goods such as housing in Singapore. In Japan, household savings were channeled into financial assets that contributed to strengthening financial markets. Japan and Korea also resorted to fiscal policy to encourage private savings, including such measures as high rates of interest on loans for consumer items, and taxes on luxury consumption.

On the other hand, to ensure that banks did not undertake risky loans, HPAE governments facilitated close contact between supervisors and banks. Regular meetings allowed both parties to assess the risk level of the bank portfolios. Government regulation was aimed at reducing the risk of loan default. Moreover, all the HPAEs adopted the capital adequacy requirements outlined by the Bank for International Settlements to make certain that banks did not take inappropriate risks (World Bank 1993:277; Leipziger 1997:555).

The HPAEs regulated or intervened in the banking sector by limiting competition in the early 1980s. Traditionally, all governments regulate the creation of new financial institutions. In the economies in East Asia, it was believed that restriction of entry into the financial sector would give the government more control over bank behavior and would increase the profitability of the banking sector. Joseph Stiglitz (Stiglitz and Shahid 2001:514) points out that some of the benefits of this limiting competition strategy were passed on to borrowers in the form of lower lending rates, which facilitated increased growth in the mid-1980s. High and growing savings rates proved important, as they led to increasing levels of public and private investment. Private investment was most impressive, with the HPAEs averaging nearly 7 percent higher growth in gross domestic product (GDP) compared with some of the other low- and middle-income economies of Latin American and sub-Saharan African nations. Public investment was mostly used to either create or provide the conditions necessary for infrastructure, such as electrification and telephone service, but was particularly significant for export-oriented manufacturing activities.

To combat the problems of missing capital markets that are prevalent in developing economies, the HPAEs predominantly used three techniques—bond and equity markets, development banks, and low relative prices for capital goods (World Bank 1993:224–228). The creation of bond and equity markets, while important for the overall financial development of the HPAEs, did not play a role in the rapid economic takeoff of the HPAEs, because of their late development. Development banks were one of the measures used to fill the gaps from the missing capital markets, and provided long-term credit to industries that the other existing credit entities could not. Since the relative prices for capital goods were on average lower during the growth period, 1960–1990, compared with the period immediately following World War II, the East Asian economies were able to invest the same nominal amount as before but reap greater returns on their investments, and this led to higher growth rates.

Human Capital Investment

One of the most significant accomplishments of the East Asian economies was the creation of a skilled and educated work force. The region's transformation from an agrarian society to an industrial one necessitated investment in education and resulted in an increase in human capital.

"Every government spends on education, but the HPAE's spent their money more wisely, emphasizing universal primary, and later, secondary education. . . . The allocation of public expenditure between basic and higher education is the major public policy factor that accounts for East Asia's extraordinary performance with regard to the quantity of basic education provided" (World Bank 1993:191–192). The East Asia economies did not begin their rapid economic expansion with a better human capital base compared with other developing countries. In fact, schooling averaged 2.3 years in East Asia in 1960, compared with 3 years in Latin America and the Caribbean. By 1985, however, East Asia had climbed to an impressive average of 5.2 years of schooling, while the averages for Latin America and the Caribbean, and the rest of the developing world, were 4.5 and 3.6 years respectively (Barro and Lee 1993:384).

In addition to accomplishing universal primary education, the HPAEs focused on improving vocational training. Vocational training is known to have high spillover effects, with training for one worker having the potential to increase the productivity of coworkers. The issue here is whether investment in human capital through vocational training can create growth in other sectors of the economy, for example exports. The effects of this training were particularly prominent in the export sector in Taiwan, and were dependent on the level of technology present within the individual firms (San 1990:416). Whereas the government financed primary education, firms financed vocational training, because it was firm-specific and aimed at developing new products based on market trends and innovations. High firm-specific skills led to greater success in management, information technology, finance, marketing, accounting, law, and adaptive innovations on the shop floor, which in turn led to productivity gains in the HPAEs. Thus, human capital development in East Asia created a better-trained and better-skilled labor force who were able to fill high-technology positions in both the public and the private sector (Galenson 1992:41).

The government was also actively involved in vocational training. In Japan, for example, policymakers recognized the need for government-supported vocational programs. In 1996, the Council of Science and Technology, headed by the Japanese prime minister, proposed a five-year plan of US$37 billion in expenditure on science and technology aimed at basic research and training. The Chinese education system is modeled along the lines of the Japanese system, with the main emphasis on the quality of primary and secondary education. The Chinese government, which has begun to invest heavily in vocational training, is recognizing the spillover effects of basic skill developments and enhanced productivity. Not just schools and vocational training but also colleges were expanded in China to graduate more than 2 million students in 2003 (Prestowitz 2005:27)

Interaction Between Human and Physical Capital

Although the East Asian economies succeeded in acquiring human and physical capital, growth resulted largely from the interaction of these two factors. Robin Grier (2002:891–892) contends that human and physical capital are more successful at increasing output when policies are designed to effectively match them together. William Easterly (2001:48, 67) points out that, while many developing countries acquired human capital and invested enormous amounts of money in physical capital, most of them failed to achieve notable economic growth. The East Asian economies differed from the rest of these developing nations, because they actively created policies to match human capital with technologically advanced physical capital. For example, governments lowered barriers to trade, which allowed firms to import technologically advanced physical capital, while seeking policies to educate and mobilize labor (Stiglitz 1996:153). These policies were effective at matching human and physical capital together. By having a smarter, more efficient work force, equipped with sophisticated and technologically superior physical capital, workers in the HPAEs were able to produce more goods. Not only did production increase, but production processes also improved, and the final products were vastly superior. In fact, the quality of the products improved enough to make them competitive in the global market, resulting in increased export activity and growth.

The emphasis on human capital and savings and investment in the Asian context allows us to return to the conceptual framework postulated in Figure 5.1. All growth models start by postulating that there is a certain amount of labor *(L)*, which when combined with physical capital *(K)* and human capital *(H)*, yields output (income) *(Y)*. From this income, some proportion needs to be saved. Choosing the right savings rate *(s)* in the economy is important. Too high a rate implies that the economy is not currently consuming enough. If consumption *(C)* is low, this implies that there is low demand for goods and services and hence too little production. On the other hand, too low a savings rate implies that the absolute level of savings *(S)* available for investing in infrastructure, and in the financial, manufacturing, and service sectors of the economy, is low. If investment *(I)* is low, the subsequent buildup of capital stock will be low, and consequently output, or GDP, and ultimately economic growth will be low. This analysis seems to indicate that by combining high-quality physical capital with a well-educated labor force and choosing an appropriate savings rate in the economy that maximized consumption yet maintained high levels of investment, the East Asian economies were able to optimize production and achieve sustained rates of high economic growth between 1960 and 1995.

International Trade

As with human and physical capital investment, macroeconomic prudence created a favorable climate for international trade between the Asia Pacific economies and the rest of the world. For example, because the HPAEs never had

Figure 5.1 Conceptual Framework for Analyzing Economic Growth

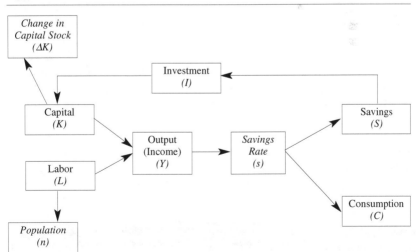

large trade deficits, they did not have to resort to measures such as import restrictions as did the other developing countries in the 1950s and 1960s. Barriers to trade such as tariffs and quotas deprive businesses of beneficial imported inputs and are especially harmful to exporters. However, trade liberalization in the absence of macroeconomic stability or appropriate exchange-rate policy is a recipe for disaster. Most developing countries have to resort to devaluation of their currencies to encourage exports. The HPAE governments were no exception. Government assistance to exporters varied across these economies and over time. Preferential financing, promotion subsidies, tax incentives, subsidized infrastructure, and foreign investment incentives were all part of the trade equation (Bhagwati 1996:18). Most of the HPAEs allowed exporters access to imports at world prices. Usually, when imported inputs are taxed, they become relatively more expensive to the exporting firm of the tax-levying country. Even though the HPAEs did maintain some types of import tax, the creation of free trade zones, export-processing zones, bonded warehouses, duty drawbacks, and tariff exemptions allowed exporting firms to purchase imports at world prices.

HPAE governments also provided export financing and assistance in market penetration to the export firms. The governments offered both long- and short-term financing, usually in the form of some type of credit program. To overcome challenges in export markets, governments directly subsidized export activity or market penetration, or pushed for the creation of international trading companies. Over time, as the HPAEs became more involved and adept in the export sector, the composition of exports changed from primary food products and textiles to manufactured goods. By 1991, machinery exports comprised a greater share of total exports in the HPAEs, averaging some 40 percent of manufactured exports (Chow and Kellman 1993:165).

The export industry contributed to growth by serving as a catalyst to industrialization, and by facilitating the exchange of technological know-how. The HPAEs increased their share in world exports from 7.9 percent in 1965 to 18.2 percent in 1990. Similarly, their share of the developing-economy exports over this same time period increased from 12.2 percent to 56.3 percent (World Bank 1993:38). As the HPAEs increased their exports, they were able to build up foreign exchange reserves. With these increased reserves, they were able to forge new investments in other countries, pay off existing foreign debt, and, perhaps more important, import technologically superior capital goods. By incorporating these capital good imports with high levels of human capital, the HPAEs were better able to diffuse the learning spillovers compared with other developing economies. Thus trade served as an engine of growth in East Asia and facilitated rapid industrialization and the push to developed-nation status.

Growth Incentives

Sustained growth in developing countries has failed to materialize either because of a failure to implement policy or due to misplaced incentive structures.

William Easterly states that "neither aid nor investment nor education nor population control nor adjustment lending nor debt forgiveness proved to be the panacea for growth. Growth failed to respond to any of these formulas because the formulas did not take heed of the basic principles of economics: people respond to incentives" (2001:143). Poor people often do not have the incentive to grow out of poverty, because they become trapped in it and often require direct, government-created incentives to break the cycle. On the other hand, government mismanagement often kills growth. In developing countries that have high levels of income inequality, government officials often have an incentive to act in the interest of a particular class and not in the interest of the nation as a whole. Thus, incentives to ensure growth require fundamental social and institutional reforms. The East Asian economies thrived for more than three decades due to government policies that succeeded in placing incentives in the proper areas. Most of these policies were aimed at improving income inequality, increasing education, and insulating economic technocrats to minimize their susceptibility to interest-group or class pressure.

Income Inequality

Many of the East Asian economies were able to achieve a more equitable income distribution by creating policies that benefited the elites as well as the nonelites. To garner the support of the nonelites, the leaders of these countries introduced mechanisms that drastically increased opportunities to share and participate in the benefits of growth. "These mechanisms varied from economy to economy but included land reform (in Japan, Korea, and Taiwan), support for small and medium-size industries (Hong Kong, Japan, Korea, and Taiwan), and government provision of such basic amenities as housing and public health services (Hong Kong and Singapore)" (World Bank 1993:159). The income redistribution procedures differed from the typical wealth-sharing approach of most developing economies. Instead of granting direct income transfers (such as welfare checks) or subsidizing specific commodities (for example, food or fuel), the East Asian governments favored techniques that increased opportunities for upward mobility. By focusing attention on landownership, for example, the governments in East Asia cultivated a climate of reasonable faith in the agricultural sector. They established an environment in which wealth would accumulate in the traditional agricultural sector as returns to land and returns to cultivated crops increased. As the benefits of higher education became clearer, the segments of the population in the lower income groups maintained the hope that their children would be able to take advantage of high-paying jobs in a rapidly industrializing nation.

Housing and homeownership remain a significant constraint for low-income individuals in the developing world. The governments of Hong Kong, Singapore, and Malaysia recognized this and developed relevant intervention programs in their housing markets. In Singapore, for example, an ambitious project was undertaken to develop public housing for low-income families. With attractive low-interest loans and the ability to borrow against their mandatory pension plans, today nearly 90 percent of the population in Singapore own their homes (Campos and Root 1996:74–75). The wide availability of low-cost housing for workers in these economies helped to hold down wage demands, thus subsidizing labor-intensive manufacturing (World Bank 1993:163; Campos and Root 1996:56). Low-cost housing for the majority of residents also helped to decrease inequality and minimize social unrest, thus providing the long-term stability attractive to investors.

Table 5.1, which shows the Gini coefficient for the HPAEs and other developing countries in Asia and Africa, reflects the relatively low levels of income disparity in Asia. It demonstrates that policies aimed at achieving a more egalitarian distribution of income were quite successful in the HPAEs. The average Gini coefficient fell from 0.41 between 1965 and 1970 to 0.36 between 1981 and 1990. In comparison, for the other group of selected developing countries, the Gini coefficient fell from a high of 0.50 to 0.48 across the same two time periods.

Budget constraints in developing countries prevent poor households from investing in education, even when it is patently obvious that the returns to education are high. By reducing income inequality, the governments in the HPAEs provided the incentive for more families to send their children to school. As East Asian governments simultaneously implemented other policies, such as physical capital accumulation, export promotion, and rapid industrialization, people were able to see firsthand the high potential returns to education and the potential for upward mobility.

Greater equity was also fostered through governmental land redistribution policies. In China, the government seized land from landlords and as compensation issued shares in state-owned enterprises (SOEs). Beginning in the 1950s, Korea took over landed properties, made nominal compensations, and redistributed this land to nearly 90,000 tenants, in the process effectively eliminating tenancy (World Bank 1993:160–161). To understand how these countries achieved a more egalitarian landholding and gave all parties the incentive to foster growth, consider the case of Taiwan, in which the government took land from the landlords in the 1950s and compensated them with shares in state enterprises. It then sold the seized land to the farmers at favorable credit terms and prices. The government then helped the farmers improve production methods for domestic and export markets. The program worked both economically and politically, as land reform allowed Taiwan to achieve one of the world's most equitable income distributions. "Political stability benefited in two ways. Newly landed farmers, focused on boosting production, had little interest in radical activities. Former landlords, as new shareholders in state enterprises, had a vested interest in the success of the Taiwanese authorities' eco-

Table 5.1   Gini Index, Period Averages, 1965–1990[a]

Region	1965–1970	1971–1980	1981–1990
High-performing Asian economies (HPAEs)			
Korea	0.34	0.38	0.33
Taiwan	0.32	0.36	0.30
Singapore	0.50	0.45	0.41
Indonesia	0.40	0.41	0.30
Thailand[b]	0.44	0.38	0.46
Malaysia	0.50	0.48	0.42
Hong Kong	0.49	0.42	0.39
Japan	0.31 (1965)	0.28 (1979)	—
Average	0.41	0.39	0.36
Others			
India	0.40	0.41	—
Pakistan	0.37	—	—
Nepal	—	0.53	—
Bangladesh	—	0.37	—
Sri Lanka	0.41	0.35	—
Philippines	0.48	0.45	0.39
Argentina	0.43	0.41	0.43
Brazil	0.57	0.60	0.60
Colombia	0.56	0.58	0.51
Chile	0.50	0.53	0.53
Mexico	0.58	0.52	0.53
Peru	0.59	0.57	0.40
Venezuela	0.52	0.53	0.44
Gabon	0.65	—	—
Sudan	0.44	—	—
Zambia	0.49	0.53	—
Kenya	—	0.59	—
Average	0.50	0.50	0.48

Sources: World Bank, Economic and Social Database, Washington; for Latin America, Psacharopoulos and others (1992). Reprinted with permission from Jose Edgardo Campos and Hilton L. Rout, *The Key to the Asian Miracle* (Washington, D.C.: Brookings Institution, 1996), tab. 1-1, p. 9.

Notes: a. Average across all available index values for the period.

b. Oshima's (1993) estimates indicate that the average for 1981–1990 may be around 0.43, and the average for 1965–1970, 0.43.

nomic program" (World Bank 1993:160). Thus, both the farmers and the elite had an incentive to support the government's policies.

Just as multitudes of small landholdings improved equity and efficiency, the East Asian governments benefited from an abundance of small and medium-size enterprises (SMEs). For example, in Korea, rapid growth of labor-intensive manufacturing in these firms absorbed large numbers of workers, reducing

World Bank Photo: CN 10/S17.

State-owned enterprises, such as the one pictured here,
continue to operate at a great cost to China's central government,
and at great risk to the banks that subsidize them.

unemployment and attracting rural labor (Galenson 1992:49). As early as the
1980s, the SME sector began to grow. The SME share in total manufacturing
employment rose from 37.6 percent in 1976 to 51.2 percent in 1988. At the same
time, the SME share in manufacturing value-added rose from 23.7 percent to
34.9 percent (World Bank 1993:163). Consequently, unemployment dropped
and real wages rose in Korea.

As firms shifted to improved production methods, efficiency increased and
workers' incomes rose. For example, Korea's economic development resulted
largely from the expansion of conglomerates, or *chaebols,* which are diversified groups of businesses with concentrated ownership structures. A similar
system exists in the Japanese economy, known as *keiretsu* (linked group), under
which a group of large corporate houses are all connected to one large commercial bank. Korea's *chaebols* consist mostly of horizontally diversified corporations rather than vertically diversified corporations (Huh and Kim 1993). Horizontal diversification in this instance implies that Korean firms developed
products that appealed to their current customer base. Vertical diversification is
said to occur when the firm tries to move into the manufacturing lines of its
suppliers. This horizontally diversified firm structure with a concentrated ownership pattern allowed the Korean government to control and monitor the flow
of credit to corporate borrowers more effectively. The emergence of *chaebols*

is thus closely linked to government intervention, and is yet another mechanism of industrial policy that facilitated an equitable distribution of income.

Isolation of Policymakers from Social Pressures

Historically, corruption in developing economies tends to favor certain areas of the economy, which leads to inequality in opportunities for the middle- and lower-income sectors of the population. For example, vested interests doomed land reform in the Philippines. Mo Pak-hung (Mo 2001:67) argues that the more isolated policymakers are from outside pressure such as lobbying and special-interest groups, the more effective their policies are likely to be at stimulating economic growth. Many of the successful Asian governments dealt with this problem by insulating their technocrats from such outside pressure. Economic technocrats were able to formulate and implement policies that were in line with politically formulated national goals, with little pressure from lobbyists, politicians, and interest groups. Without this, technocrats in these economies would have been unable to introduce and sustain rational economic policies.

The clearest case of technocratic insulation has occurred in Japan, where insulation is prevalent not only for the economic technocracy, but also for nearly the entire bureaucracy. "Japanese bureaucrats draft laws in consultation with the policy committees of the ruling Liberal Democratic Party and private sector representatives. Since the bureaucracy has independent power, it can often ignore pressure from individual actors in the private sector" (World Bank 1993:168). Further, the Japanese bureaucracy can accomplish policy objectives through nonbinding recommendations. That is, objectives can be imposed with generous incentives, such as licenses and foreign exchange allocations, and the implicit threat to withhold them from companies that refuse to cooperate. Thus, by separating the technocrats from the rest of the governmental structure, Japan and the rest of the Asian economies were able to maximize efficiency and effectiveness in policymaking, and this had far-reaching effects in the economy.

From about 1960 to 1990, the East Asian economies experienced tremendous economic growth through creating policies that encouraged the accumulation of human and physical capital, emphasizing the interaction among various resources and adopting incentives in the proper areas, together with effective governance that minimized corruption. Even though these economies would suffer a crisis in 1997, the policies they have implemented have more than likely paved the way for sustained economic growth in the twenty-first century.

Miracle or Myth?

Since 1950 we have seen a remarkable transformation in the economies of Hong Kong, Singapore, Taiwan, Korea, Malaysia, Thailand, and China. These economies have transformed themselves from "less-developed countries"

(LDCs) to developed status, with significant increases in per capita income. The question that the "East Asian miracle" inevitably raises in policy circles is, if investment in human and physical capital, coupled with sound outward-oriented trade policies and high savings rates, constitutes a recipe for growth, why can this not be duplicated in other parts of the developing world?

Growth theory suggests that simply increasing labor (more workers entering the work force) and capital (machines) is not a recipe for economic growth. Robert Solow (1956:85) argued that in addition to human and physical capital, efficiency of inputs, or technology, is the driving force behind economic growth. The World Bank's report on the matter (1993:4) is quite emphatic that the "miracle"-like economic performance in East Asia was indeed a result of increased productivity or increased efficiency. Thus efficiency of inputs, or total factor productivity, is a large component of the story in East Asia.

The World Bank's report (1993) created a healthy debate in the economics profession. On the one side, economists such as Paul Krugman (1994), Jong-il Kim and Lawrence Lau (1994), and Alwyn Young (1994) questioned the very notion of a miracle. On the other side, Jagdish Bhagwati (1996), Joseph Stiglitz (1996), and Richard Nelsen and Howard Pack (1999), among others, furthered the notion that growth in Asia was unprecedented, the likes of which had never before been seen in the growth records of modern economies.

Krugman seems to suggest that East Asia's growth is a myth more than a miracle: "It is only when one actually does the quantitative accounting that the astonishing result emerges: all of Singapore's growth can be explained by increases in measured inputs" (1994:71). Using the estimates of Kim and Lau (1994) and Young (1994), Krugman believes that the rest of East Asia, except Japan, exhibited startlingly little evidence of improvements in efficiency. He suggests that Japan had both high rates of input growth and high rates of efficiency growth. The latter was undoubtedly a factor in the post–World War II convergence of the Japanese economy and technological catch-up with the US economy. Further, Krugman suggests that Japan's miracle growth is "well in the past" (1994:73), a fact borne out by Japan's recent economic woes in the banking and financial sectors. On the surface, this alternative model of East Asian growth is useful, because it suggests that growth in inputs without increases in technical know-how and efficiency is doomed to failure, or in economic terms, will inevitably face diminishing returns. The former command-style economy of the Soviet Union is a good example of sheer increases in physical capital and labor with no attention to the mix or efficiency of the two.

Krugman's thesis of the lack of a miracle and the implication that East Asia's growth was "hollow" is also important in light of the Asian crisis that followed in 1997. Bhagwati (1996:5) suggests that Krugman is wrong in arguing that there was no miracle in East Asia. The HPAEs did not in fact experience diminishing returns to capital as predicted by Krugman. The crisis that followed in 1997 had its roots instead in panic-driven capital flight, facilitated in large measure by crony capitalism and overvalued currencies in the newly industrialized economies of Thailand, Malaysia, and Indonesia.

Bhagwati (1998:5) thus counters that the miracle consisted of the large increase in the rates of private investment in the HPAEs, the likes of which have not been seen historically. He thus favors the "exceptional private investment" explanation for the miracle, coupled with export-promotion policies followed by East Asia, as opposed to import-substitution policies followed by the Soviet Union and the economies of South Asia, notably India. The inducement to invest provided in turn the surplus that created the basis for the import of new capital and technology. The effective return to this capital was provided by a literate and technologically advanced labor force.

Nelsen and Pack (1999:418) make a theoretical argument in favor of the miracle explanation. In essence they ask whether the Asian miracle can be explained merely in terms of capital investment. They divide the Asian miracle into two groups or theories—accumulation versus assimilation. Accumulation theory stresses the role of capital investment. In this theory, rapid economic development is predicated on very high levels of savings and investment. Assimilation theory stresses some intangibles in the development process, including entrepreneurship, innovation, and learning. Marshaling of inputs is a necessary but not sufficient condition for economic growth. Assimilationists thus see the increasing returns to a sharply rising and educated work force. A well-educated work force of managers and engineers has the advantage of seeing new opportunities and effectively learning new things. The firm has an explicit role to play, since it must quickly learn to innovate, as was the case with the Hyundai corporation in Korea. Nelsen and Pack (1999:420) point out that Taiwan had virtually no production in electronic goods in 1960, but that by 1990 this sector accounted for 21 percent of manufactured exports. The export promotion strategy encouraged by the governments in these economies meant that a significant proportion of a firm's trade was with the established world traders, including the United States, and later Japan as well, both of which demanded high performance standards. Thus the accumulation versus assimilation hypothesis is important, because it enables us to better understand why the East Asian miracle occurred. Moreover, if growth has a recipe, it enables us to better understand the development policy involved.

Nelsen and Pack's thesis (1999) may in fact enable us to sort through the myth-versus-miracle debate. It appears that both sides in the debate are evaluating whether or not a miracle occurred in terms of sustained economic growth in East Asia. Those opposed to the miracle explanation "see investment in human and physical capital as necessary but far from sufficient in the production process" (Nelsen and Pack 1999:418). For them, clearly, economic growth is "the steady process by which the productive capacity of the economy is increased over time to bring about rising levels of national output and income."

The pro-miracle group, on the other hand, seems to have a broader definition of economic growth and development in East Asia, "one that was accompanied by a major change in structure of their economies including shifts in the size of firms and the sections of specialization" (1999:416).

The debate between myth and miracle in East Asia may simply come down to economic semantics between growth and development. This is not to say that growth and development are distinct. In fact, sustained economic growth contributes to economic development. Stiglitz (1996:174) suggests that no single policy was responsible for economic success in East Asia. The miracle was achieved in large measure due to a combination of factors: high savings rates interacting with high levels of human capital accumulation, promotion of the export sector by the government, and the nexus between technology and education, all in a market-oriented environment that was conducive to the transfer of technology.

The East Asian Crisis

Following nearly three decades of phenomenal and sustained economic growth and development, the East Asian economies were becoming a model for developing nations. Budget deficits and inflation were low, the leading economic indicators predicted more growth, and investors were optimistic about the future. However, in late 1996 and early 1997, the East Asian economies were hit with a crisis much deeper than anyone first imagined. With phenomenal growth came a change in production methods. As East Asia became more integrated into the global economy, production methods became more complex and heavily integrated into the global economy. As a result, a more sophisticated financial sector was needed to support domestic firms. Steven Radelet and Jeffrey Sachs (1998:22–23) point out that the rapid economic growth led to weaknesses in both the microeconomic and the macroeconomic sectors of the East Asian economies.

First, the East Asian economies looked toward financial market liberalization and opened up channels for foreign capital to enter the economy. Indonesia instituted a series of deregulation packages, expanding the banking sector. Thailand created the Bangkok International Banking Facility, which fueled an increase in the number of financial institutions with the ability to lend and borrow in foreign-denominated currencies. Korea underwent several financial market reforms by increasing the access of domestic banks to short-term international loans. The consequence was that foreign liabilities in South Korea more than doubled, from 4.5 percent of GDP in 1993 to 9.5 percent of GDP in 1997 (Radelet and Sachs 1998:25).

Before the Asian crisis of 1997, the East Asian economies had highly regulated financial markets. Caps on interest rates, limits on asset holdings by financial institutions, monitoring and limitations on foreign entry into the banking system, and restrictions on foreign direct investment were the norm rather than the exception. The rapid nature of the financial market liberalization and reforms in the banking sector without adequate regulation or supervision led to an increasingly fragile financial system. In both Korea and Thailand, for example, deregulation of the banking sector took the form of loosened regulations on bank lending and the removal of restrictions for many types of consumer and capital investment lending. Liberalization of the financial sector often necessitates adequate training of managers in the areas of credit assessment and monitoring of risky loans. In arguing that financial liberalization increases the probability of a country's exposure to a financial crisis, Jason Furman and Joseph Stiglitz point out that "the prevalence of complex financial instruments further taxed the often limited expertise of bankers and supervisors" (1998:17).

For the most part, therefore, the strategy of prudent regulation of the banking and financial sectors prior to the 1990s seemed to have worked in these economies. But a push for more liberalization in the 1990s necessitated that this intervention and gradualist approach to banking be replaced with reduced government involvement. This should have strengthened the banking sector, but perhaps increased the scope for risk-taking. For example, the restrictions on speculative risk-taking, a hallmark from the miracle period, were eliminated and replaced by risk-taking in certain sectors of the economy, notably the real estate industry in Thailand.

As a result, the economies of Thailand, Malaysia, Indonesia, and South Korea suffered from financial services that were not carefully regulated or supervised, and "crony capitalism" became the norm in many of these economies. Under this type of capitalism, investment funds are directed to favored businesses or industries, such as in Indonesia, where Suharto engaged in a pattern of clear and blatant nepotism. Regulatory reforms were almost never completely instituted, and the rapid expansion and growth of the economy made management difficult. Government-owned banks in Korea and Indonesia regularly broke rules and regulations without penalty

Rapid financial market liberalization and inadequately regulated markets in capital goods can result in an influx of short-term capital. Capital predominantly took the form of short-term foreign currency–denominated debt (short-term borrowing from foreign creditors) and foreign direct investment. Moreover, foreign investors were already attracted to East Asia due to its successful track record. The annual capital inflow of funds for investment for the five crisis economies averaged over 6 percent of GDP between 1990 and 1996. In dollar terms for the same period, these economies received almost US$300 billion in foreign investment (Radelet and Sachs 1998:23). In Thailand, inflows consisted primarily of short-term foreign debt accumulated by domestic banks and were the most vulnerable to quick reversal. That is, investors were more readily able to withdraw their investments. Foreign short-term capital in Malaysia predominantly took the form of foreign direct investment, which was less susceptible to quick reversals. In Indonesia, short-term inflows mostly consisted of private borrowing from offshore lenders.

Second, export growth, which had fueled much of the economic development during the previous three decades, began to slow in the mid-1990s, and declined significantly in each country. It should be noted that the exchange-rate regimes varied across East Asia in 1997. Hong Kong maintained a unilateral peg to the US dollar, while Indonesia, Singapore, Malaysia, and Thailand all maintained fixed or adjustable pegs to a basket of world currencies. Korea, on the other hand, had a managed float, while Japan was on a floating exchange-rate regime. The countries that pegged their currencies to a currency basket all tended to "overvalue" them. For example, at the beginning of 1997, the Thai baht was valued at about twenty-five to the dollar, whereas most experts believed that the true rate should have been at least thirty to the dollar (Moreno 1995, 1996). In other words, the Thai baht was overvalued by nearly 20 percent. The reason an economy may choose to overvalue its currency under a pegged exchange-rate regime is to create a cheaper import bill (prices of imports for inputs in the production process are cheaper with an overvalued currency). On the other hand, the overvalued exchange rates made the exports of these countries relatively more expensive to the rest of the world. In addition, the overvaluation of exchange rates, caused mainly by the large capital inflows, worsened the terms of trade for East Asia. The competitive effects of Mexico's participation in the North American Free Trade Agreement, and the global slump in semiconductor production, also contributed to the slowdown in export growth.

Third, an increasing portion of foreign borrowing was in the form of short-term debt. Short-term debt to overseas banks in Korea, Thailand, and Indonesia had reached US$68 billion, US$46 billion, and US$34 billion respectively (Radelet and Sachs 1998:25). Moreover, the ratio of short-term debt to foreign exchange reserves in Korea, Thailand, and Indonesia was greater than 1.0 after 1994 (Furman and Stiglitz 1998:14). The latter is not unhealthy for an economy as long as creditors are willing to roll over their loans. However, a high ratio of debt to exchange is an indicator of vulnerability. Once creditors sense vulnerability, they have an incentive to withdraw their capital as soon as possible, since they are aware that there are not enough foreign reserves to repay all the lenders.

On the eve of the Asian financial crisis, the majority of the economic imbalances lay in the private sector. The public sector had continued to maintain low inflation, fiscal surpluses, and declining government foreign debt. The private sector, on the other hand, had built up tremendous debt, and many companies, large and small, were beginning to file for bankruptcy (Wade 1998:365). In early 1997, the financial problems of Thailand became apparent to the rest of the world. Property prices had been falling since late 1996, and Somprasong Lang, a major property developer, was unable to meet foreign debt payments.

In late 1996 and mid-1997, the baht came under speculation. By this time, it had become clear that the property markets and financial institutions in Thailand were in trouble. In an effort to save troubled businesses and ward off speculative attacks against the baht, the Thai government mistakenly tried to bail out businesses instead of trying to close them down or rehabilitate them. It also tried to maintain its pegged exchange rate, instead of allowing the baht to float immediately. As a result, foreign reserves in Thailand were severely depleted. Finally, on July 2, 1997, the Thai government was forced to float the baht.

With the devaluation of the baht, foreign creditors began to withdraw massive quantities of capital not only from Thailand, but also from the rest of the region. Investors feared that Thailand's neighbors suffered from the same set of problems, and started removing capital on the expectation that others would do so soon. What started in Thailand in July 1997 shifted to Malaysia and Indonesia in August, and to South Korea in November. This spread of the crisis, referred to as the "Asian contagion," first affected the currencies of each country and consequently led to the outpouring of capital that each of these economies had sought to carefully build through responsible macroeconomic policies. The contagion was now afoot, and expectations and speculation on currencies in the region were a prime source of the instability that followed. By the end of 1997, Indonesia, Malaysia, and Thailand were experiencing a rapid decline in the external value of their currencies, and a sudden reversal of private capital followed. Foreign creditors were unwilling to give new loans or allow existing loans to roll over (Pesenti and Tille 2000:3). The net capital outflow, nearly US$100 billion, constituted a staggering 10 percent of the combined GDPs of five economies hit by the crisis.

In response to the impending crisis, international financial institutions, notably the International Monetary Fund (IMF), tried to restore confidence in the region. The urgent task at hand was to stop the drain on foreign reserves caused by the currency crisis, and stem the outflow of capital. As investors rushed to convert local currencies back into stable currencies like the dollar, the countries faced a dilemma: should interest rates be raised to persuade investors to keep funds in local currencies, or should the value of the currency be allowed to drop to its true value? The IMF recommended a temporary tightening of monetary policy that would raise interest rates. The IMF's objective here was twofold: first, a rise in interest rates would control the capital outflow and prompt foreign investors not to pull their assets out of the Asian markets; second, an increase in the interest rates would stabilize exchange rates and prevent further depreciation in the value of the Asian currencies. In addition, the IMF approved about US$35 billion in loans for the financial reform and stabilization of reserves in the three countries that were mainly affected—Korea, Thailand, and Indonesia.

The IMF proffered three recommendations: raise interest rates in the banking sector, close down the weak banks in Thailand, and maintain the pegged currency as an anchor against domestic inflation. A number of prominent policy scholars, including Jeffrey Sachs (1997) and Barry Eichengreen (2002), were critical of these recommendations. Both advocated the opposite: lowering interest rates rather than raising them, to encourage domestic lending and ward off a slowdown in production in the economy. Sachs (1997:3) argued that the IMF policy of shutting down weak banks would not strengthen foreign investors' confidence, but rather would signal to them that the banking sector was in more trouble than previously imagined, and would thus lead to more investor flight. Recapitalization of the banking system and reform of its regulatory structure were therefore urgently needed.

Recapitalization and reform of the banking sector in the five economies hit by the crisis did not happen fast enough, and indeed more investor flight followed in countries less affected by the crisis, such as Singapore and Japan. A more judicious policy would have been to try to merge the weak banks with some of the healthier banks. Indonesia was at first reluctant to raise its interest rates, but Thailand, Korea, and Indonesia eventually acceded to the IMF recommendation. Despite the criticism that is levied against the IMF, it is important to note that countries usually approach international financial institutions only during a crisis, not necessarily during a period of sustained economic growth. The East Asian economies did not consult or approach the IMF during their miracle period. One should also note that it is difficult to devise a short-term rescue operation in the midst of a monetary or financial panic, as was the case here.

The IMF policies did stem the outflow of investors from Asian markets to some extent. On the other hand, the policy for a high interest rate impacted local companies, driving many into bankruptcy and depressing consumer spending. As the economies of East and Southeast Asia let their exchange rates fall and float against the dollar, the export sector began to pick up, and by late 1998 the trade deficits of the impacted countries began to decline significantly. In summary, the proximate causes of the Asian crisis were:

- An Asian development model with an emphasis on growth through overvalued currencies.
- Structural imbalances that resulted due to an overemphasis on export promotion and export-led growth. East Asia's folly may have been the emphasis on the link between exports and growth, rather than trade and growth. There is growing evidence, for example from the United States, that productivity and efficiency drive exports, not the other way around. Focusing on imports forces the import-competing sector to either compete or get out of the way (see Stiglitz and Yusuf 2001:9, 34). By favoring the export sector relative to the import sector, the Asia Pacific economies may well have bred inefficiency in the trade sector, which only surfaced as Asia began to face challenges from other

emerging economies like China and India and a globally integrated world economy intent on competitive price industries. Domestic markets and consumption may well have suffered in an aggressive pursuit of export markets.

- A buildup of excess productive capacity in large measure due to crony capitalism. For example, favoritism and nepotism toward family members of politicians in Indonesia and the cozy relationship between the corporate and banking sectors in Thailand.

- Moral hazard and overinvestment in the banking and financial sectors. A number of East Asian governments played a large role in the establishment of the financial institutions in the economy. In turn, they acted as regulators and guaranteed the funds of the banking institutions. Financial institutions, whose liabilities are guaranteed against bank failure by the government, expose the economy to the moral hazard problem. Knowing that their deposits are guaranteed by the government, financial intermediaries often engage in risky behavior, as was the case in Thailand, where there was a rush of loans to the real estate market. The government thus implicitly underwrote the risky loans. Both creditors and debtors misallocated resources because there was no regulation in place. This led to a buildup of short-term credit, which was unhedged and ultimately left the Asian economies vulnerable to speculative attacks on their currencies and asset bases. A sudden panic-driven collapse of domestic and international confidence followed.

The economies of Thailand, Malaysia, Indonesia, and South Korea in particular suffered devastating financial and economic woes from 1997 to 1998, ranked among the worst since the Great Depression (Stiglitz 1999:2). The severe economic downturn ultimately affected the lives of millions of people. Although the magnitude of the impact on income, output, and poverty differed across countries, all were hit hard.

Output in industrial production in 1998 was approximately 25 percent below its 1997 level. Further, unemployment in Korea increased from 2.0 percent in 1996 to 6.8 percent in 1998, while in Thailand it increased from 2.0 percent to 6.5 percent, and in Indonesia it increased from 2.3 percent to 7.1 percent. In many cases, those who retained their jobs suffered from declines in real wages of about 25 percent to 35 percent in Indonesia and 10 percent in Korea (Stiglitz 1999:5). Real per capita GDP fell by 16 percent in Indonesia, 12 percent in Thailand, 10 percent in Malaysia, and 8 percent in South Korea (Barro 2001:4).

While there is anecdotal evidence that poverty, education, and healthcare were significantly impacted during the crisis, quantifying these measures has been a more difficult task. Poverty levels, especially among the urban working class, increased significantly. Education, which prior to the crisis was a free, government-provided service, became a private service during and after the crisis in almost all the HPAEs. As a result, the rising unemployment levels and falling real per capita GDP levels made privately funded education almost impossible to obtain for many people (Stiglitz 1999:5). The crisis thus undermined the effort made by these economies between 1960 and 1996.

The crisis took a severe toll on the economies of the region, and points to the need to prevent future accumulations of large foreign currency denominated assets. Paolo Pesenti and Cedric Tille (2000:12) suggest that there is an urgent need for regional cooperation over debt expansion. Regional cooperation among the economies of the Asia Pacific region could well be underscored by a more effective role by institutions like APEC and ASEAN. These institutions need to step in and establish supervisory and regulatory mechanisms to prevent future such crises.

▩ The Economies of Southeast Asia and the Role of ASEAN

The rapid growth and miracle status that East Asia achieved from 1960 to 1990 have inevitably generated discussion as to whether the policies and strategies may be generalized to other parts of the world, particularly some of the poorer regions of Southeast Asia, including Vietnam, Laos, and Cambodia. The question is often raised as to why a country like the Philippines, which experienced steady economic growth in the 1950s and 1960s, remained an outlier in the robust growth performance of the East Asian economies. This section provides a brief review of some of the economies that remained outside the realm of rapid growth and development in Asia. It also looks at the institutional development of the Association of Southeast Asian Nations and the role that it has played in the economic and political development of some of these Southeast Asian economies.

Vietnam
Vietnam continues to be an extremely poor country, with a per capita income of only about US$650 in 2006. Decades of isolation from most of the world, and a communist regime that in essence forbade contact with its neighbors, left the country dependent on the Soviet economy for economic aid and staple goods such as fuel, fertilizers, and cotton. Throughout the post-1975 period, after North Vietnam unified the country, the Marxist, centrally planned economy curtailed economic growth through collectivism in agriculture and state-owned bureaucratic enterprises. Vietnam had virtually no prospects for take-off economic growth, let alone a miracle like some of its East Asian neighbors experienced. Possibly as a reaction to economic growth in the region, the Vietnamese government began moving from a centrally planned economy to a

market-based economy. The collapse of the Soviet Union in 1991 precipitated economic reforms that prompted the IMF and the World Bank to proclaim that Vietnam was among the most successful countries to have moved from socialism to market capitalism (Kim 1995:86–87).

The reforms included a decentralization of the price system in most commodity markets, the adoption of property rights, and a revival of the banking sector through the introduction of bond and other capital instruments. The result was high, real economic growth in the mid-1990s of about 8 percent, reminiscent of the East Asian miracle at its height. Growth slowed in the middle to late 1990s, in part due to tension between the reformists and the conservatives in the government on the pace and path of economic reform. The East Asian crisis and the contagion that followed did not spare Vietnam, whose growth fell to about 2 percent in the late 1990s. Vietnam's economy has grown steadily since, and averaged nearly 7 percent in the period 2000–2003. In 2005, economic growth reached its highest rate, 8.4 percent, largely due to growth in construction, telecommunications, and tourism. The government is in the process of reducing the number of state-owned enterprises, revising its investment laws to foster a climate of higher investment, and committing itself more fully to regional institutions like ASEAN (see the World Bank's country briefs, at http://www.worldbank.org/eapupdate). Vietnam is also committed to joining the World Trade Organization (WTO). As a precondition for accession to the WTO, the government of Vietnam will be required to accelerate domestic economic reforms (Luong 2005:152; see *Asian Survey* 46, no. 1, for other Asia Pacific economy surveys).

Laos

Like Vietnam, Laos is still classified as a less-developed economy, and had a per capita income of just US$490 in 2006, making it one of the poorest countries in the world (Forbes and Cutler 2005:176). The country's geographic location, landlocked dependence on Thailand, and relationships with the socialist governments of China, Vietnam, and the Soviet Union plagued the economy and resulted in subsistence agriculture. Unlike its neighbor Vietnam, which initiated reforms in 1986, Laos did not begin the process toward a working market economy until the complete collapse of the Soviet Union in 1991 (Kim 1995:94). The IMF has guided economic reforms since 1989. Although modest in scope compared with its neighbors, the decision to free up interest rates, for example, reduced inflation from 85 percent in 1989 to only 6 percent in 1993. Laos was hit particularly hard by the Asian crisis. Inflation returned with a vengeance in the late 1990s. Government reforms initiated in 2000 and 2001 reduced the triple-digit inflation, and economic growth approached 5.5 percent. Real economic growth was 6.4 percent in 2004, and 7.2 percent in 2006. The pace of reforms remains relatively slow, however, and the small size of the economy makes it particularly vulnerable to external global shocks. Recently,

Francis Dobbs, World Bank photo KH002S02.

Though the high-performing Asian economies have experienced
rapid economic growth, many parts of Asia Pacific remain impoverished,
as illustrated in this view of a Cambodian shanty home.

the government of Laos has begun to exploit the country's export capacity in mining and energy (see the World Bank's country briefs, at http://www .worldbank.org/eapupdate).

Cambodia

Of the three countries in Indochina, Cambodia is perhaps the poorest and least developed, with a per capita income of roughly US$450 in 2006. The economic, political, and cultural upheaval that followed with the Khmer Rouge regime in the mid-1970s, coupled with the invasion and occupation of the country by Vietnam in 1978, left Cambodia with few institutions on which to build sustainable economic growth. So drastic was the destruction of the economy and the political order that, in 1991 under a UN Security Council initiative, a peacekeeping force was assigned to reconstruct the society. In October 1991, under an agreement on a comprehensive political settlement in Cambodia, signed by nineteen nations of the UN Security Council and the warring Khmer parties, the United Nations Transitional Authority in Cambodia (UNTAC) was permitted to temporarily take over the responsibility for governing and for the future of the economy. Reform was of little initial importance, as the country had been decimated by years of aggression and conflict. Instead, the urgent task in the early 1990s was to build basic infrastructure, water and irrigation supplies, and the school system. Elections were held in 1993 (Kim 1995:96).

The Asian crisis affected Cambodia less than it did Vietnam and Laos. Instead, civil violence and political infighting slowed the economic progress that the country made in the first term of elected leader Norodom Sihanouk. The IMF and the World Bank suspended their aid and development program to Cambodia from 1997 to 1999. Since 1999, the IMF has resumed its structural adjustment program for Cambodia, with nearly US$100 million in loans. In response, Cambodia has begun to reduce tariffs and is participating more fully in the trade arena as part of its obligations to ASEAN. In September 2003, Cambodia was granted entry into the World Trade Organization. Financial and banking reforms were initiated in 2000–2001. Cambodia's economic growth in the early part of the twenty-first century has been below expectations. The economy grew at about 6 percent in 2005, and about 8 percent in 2006. The country will have to undertake a comprehensive reform strategy, including provisions to induce investment, diversify exports, and reduce income inequality as a means to alleviate the extreme poverty in the nation (see the World Bank's country briefs, at http://www.worldbank.org/eapupdate). Cambodia's national strategic development plan for 2006–2010 calls for speeding up economic growth to 6–7 percent, eradicating corruption, and reforming education and healthcare. Focusing on growth in human capital will likely be Cambodia's biggest challenge in the twenty-first century (Weggel 2005:158).

Philippines

While the miracle economies of East Asia grew on average by 8.2 percent between 1966 and 1980, and by 6.9 percent in the 1980s, the Philippine economy grew on average by 5.7 percent and 0.9 percent respectively (Leipziger 1997:444). The economy of the Philippines is largely agricultural, with most of the country's export revenue coming from agricultural products as well. Even as late as the 1970s, export-led agricultural economic growth, coupled with a literate population, seemed to bode well for the country's economic future. But as in Indochina, some of the blame for the anemic economic growth in the Philippines from 1965 to 1980 can be placed on the martial law regime of Ferdinand Marcos. This mostly took the form of excessive foreign borrowing and unproductive investments in industrial capital. Rather than the export promotion strategy employed by all of the miracle economies, the Philippines relied on an import substitution strategy, based on protection and increased production in consumer goods behind a veil of high tariff barriers (Hughes 1988:307). Despite this, growth averaged 5–6 percent through the 1970s, and the Philippines did possess some of the prerequisites for the miracle growth that occurred in some of its Asian neighbors. In 1970, 83 percent of the population was literate, and the country's domestic savings rate, at 20 percent, was comparable to Taiwan's and Korea's.

The economic record of the Philippines thus suggests that despite favorable economic prerequisites, its poor development can be attributed to policy mistakes. Outside agriculture, industrialization of public infrastructure was accomplished through external debt. In 1984, the country had difficulty servicing its debt obligations. The overvalued peso was devalued repeatedly, and capital flight followed the political upheaval of the 1980s. In addition, internal public debt grew, from 28 percent of GDP in 1976 to 112 percent in 1986 (Leipziger 1997:448). "The poor economic performance of the Philippines since 1946 is due to the shortcomings of the elite, which has little incentive to want to change the basic socio-economic structure. This stands in stark contrast to the miracle economies that instead concentrated on laying out incentives and policies for the non-elites—increased education, reducing income inequality and shared growth through high rates of savings" (Hughes 1988:309). Beginning in the mid-1990s, however, the presidencies of Fidel Ramos, Joseph Estrada, and Gloria Macapagal Arroyo introduced a range of policy-based economic reforms, including liberalization of the banking, trade, and commerce sectors. The country continues to be plagued with poverty, social inequality, and rising budget deficits (Hedman 2005:192). The economy grew on average by just 4 percent from 1999 to 2003, and 5 percent in 2006.[4] This should improve some of the social outcomes of poverty reduction and primary education, albeit a decade or two too late compared with the HPAEs.

Institution Building in Asia: The Role of ASEAN

The Association of Southeast Asian Nations was formed on August 8, 1967, in Bangkok, Thailand. The original five members were Indonesia, Malaysia, Thailand, the Philippines, and Singapore. The declaration signed by the founding countries sets out the twofold purpose of the association: (1) to accelerate economic growth, social progress, and cultural development in the region through joint endeavors in the spirit of equality and partnership, in order to strengthen the foundation for a prosperous and peaceful community of Southeast Asian nations; and (2) to promote regional peace and stability through abiding respect for justice and the rule of law in the relationship among countries in the region, and adherence to the principles of the UN Charter (see the ASEAN website, at http://www.apec.org). When the foreign ministers of the founding countries first conferred in 1967, they realized that cooperation in the economic, social, cultural, technical, and educational arenas was greatly needed. In part, they realized that their economies were economically fragmented and had experienced colonization (by the Americans in the Philippines, the Dutch in Indonesia, and the British in Singapore and Malaysia). Further, in their postindependence periods, all faced some form of ethnic conflict as well as communist insurgencies. It was proposed that ASEAN, as an institution, represented the potential to enhance economic growth and development through cooperation and even integration.

ASEAN has contributed to the economic development of the region in a number of significant ways. First, before ASEAN was established, trade among the member countries was insignificant. In the spirit of economic co-operation, preferential trading arrangements were established in 1977, which accorded tariff preferences for trade among ASEAN economies. In 1992, the ASEAN Free Trade Area (AFTA) was established, whose strategic objective, economic regionalism, was already well under way in the global economy. Paul Bowles (1997:221) argues that ASEAN's main objectives in forming AFTA were to address the changing international political economy in the 1980s, which was rapidly moving toward regionalism in trade, and the rise in business influence in the ASEAN region and the general predisposition toward regional trade liberalization.

Second, ASEAN facilitated substantial economic development in the region through its stability as an institution and the commitment of its member nations to foster a climate of economic growth. ASEAN's share in global flows of foreign direct investment (FDI) increased from less than 1 percent in 1980 to 9 percent in 1993 (Tongzon 1998:145). Jose Tongzon states, "During their initial stages of economic development, the ASEAN countries were constrained by the shortage of capital. . . . The inflow of foreign direct investment has provided not only more employment opportunities, much required capital and technology to boost its productivity and output, but also has reinforced its export competitiveness through outward-oriented foreign investments and the foreign firms' international networks and management know how" (1998:204). Thus ASEAN as an institution filled the savings gap between foreign and domestic savings in the region, and arguably played an important catalyst role in the miracle growth of at least four of its member countries—Singapore, Thailand, Indonesia, and Malaysia.

The third and perhaps most important role of ASEAN, which it continues to play today, is the absorption of the smaller Southeast Asian nations of Indochina that are outside the high-growth countries. Brunei Darussalam joined ASEAN in 1984. Vietnam became the seventh member on July 28, 1995. Vietnam had demonstrated its intent by this time to participate in trade by declaring that it was ready to join AFTA as well. Laos had been granted observer status earlier, in 1992, and both Laos and Myanmar were granted member status on July 23, 1997. Cambodia's admission was delayed until the political and domestic crisis in the late 1990s improved. With resumption of structural aid from the IMF in 1999 and an improvement in civil unrest, Cambodia was granted ASEAN member status on April 30, 1999. Cambodia's inclusion fulfilled the vision of ASEAN to have as members all of the Southeast Asian nations (see Table 5.2).

Given the weak economic records of Vietnam, Laos, Cambodia, and the Philippines, the question arises as to the potential benefits to these countries and the region at large of membership in ASEAN. From ASEAN's standpoint, the inclusion of these smaller Southeast Asian nations is an expression of their willingness to abide by the two pillars of ASEAN: to liberalize trade and to increase

Table 5.2   ASEAN Member Countries

	Date of ASEAN Membership
Indonesia	August 8, 1967
Malaysia	August 8, 1967
Philippines	August 8, 1967
Singapore	August 8, 1967
Thailand	August 8, 1967
Brunei Darussalam	January 8, 1984
Vietnam	July 28, 1995
Laos	July 23, 1997
Myanmar	July 23, 1997
Cambodia	April 30, 1999

Source: http://www.aseansec.org.

investment in the region. Tongzon suggests that "any potential conflicts can be resolved diplomatically and peacefully using the institutional machinery of ASEAN, and thus reduce the possibility of violent confrontation" (1998:173). From the vantage point of the smaller Southeast Asian economies, membership signals their willingness to free themselves from the vestiges of state-owned capital and move toward a market-oriented economy. For example, Vietnam has begun an ambitious program of privatization with the help of the IMF and the World Bank. Membership in ASEAN provides credibility to these smaller nations, indicating that their quest to introduce competition and private ownership is sincere. In turn, ASEAN will be able to provide a credible voice in international negotiations for its smaller member nations.

Finally, trade creation implied in AFTA will bring about new markets for goods and services for the ten members of ASEAN. For example, Vietnam and Myanmar are a valuable source of cheap labor and natural resources that can complement the functioning of capital-intensive Singapore and Malaysia. The "common effective preferential tariff" scheme for AFTA, signed in Singapore on January 28, 1992, and the decision of the thirteenth AFTA council meeting in Singapore on September 29, 1999, call for the elimination of import duties on all products to achieve the eventual objective of a true ASEAN-wide free trade area by 2015 for the five original ASEAN member countries, and by 2018 for the remaining members. However, trade creation and the implied reduction in tariffs agreed on by member nations drive a wedge into labor markets. Tongzon (1998:182) suggests that some of the costs to Vietnam, Laos, Myanmar, Cambodia, and the Philippines will surface in the form of unemployment in some sectors, particularly the historically state-owned industries. As part of its economic development strategy, ASEAN will need to provide leadership along these avenues in directing and establishing adequate safety nets and training programs for displaced workers. This may prove to be a crucial challenge if the full impact of economic benefits is to be experienced across the region.

■ The Emergence of China in the Asia Pacific Region

China's post-Mao economic reforms have resulted in the country becoming one of the world's fastest-growing economies. Rapid and sustained growth, and unprecedented rises in income and living standards, have transformed what was one of the most insular economies into the world's third largest trading nation (after the United States and Germany). Since the reforms in 1978, China's real GDP has grown at an annual average rate of 9.6 percent. Average incomes have quadrupled, and 300 million people have been lifted out of poverty. In 2005, China's trade continued to grow at astounding rates. Exports grew by 28.4 percent, to US$762 billion, while imports grew by 17.6 percent, to US$660 billion, creating a trade surplus of over US$100 billion (Morrison 2006:1).

China's rise as a global trading power stands in contrast to the economic growth of HPAEs and other economies of the Asia Pacific region. First, while high domestic savings, both public and private, were largely responsible for propelling the HPAEs, China's impressive trade volume is largely the result of heavy inflows of foreign savings or FDI. The total amount of FDI into China was $58 billion in 2005 (Fung 2005:11). This has allowed foreign firms, including a large number from the United States, to have immediate access to China's industrial exports. Second, while the HPAEs, particularly Japan and Korea, encouraged entrepreneurship and technical innovation within private firms, China's transition has been gradual, with public industry protected rather than subjected to competition and privatization. The government has deliberately forestalled independent private firms, focusing instead on economic reforms in state-owned enterprises. George Gilboy (2004:34) points out that these SOEs have been granted preferential access to technology, capital, and markets.

The "gradualist" view described above is disputed by some economists, notably Wing Thye Woo (1999:116), who attributes China's rapid economic growth since 1978 to the same factors that promoted economic growth in East and Southeast Asia—increased liberalization, internationalization of the economy, privatization of economic activities, and export-led growth. This observation is important because it suggests that China's economic success is the product of allowing its institutions to harmonize more easily with the nonsocialist sectors of the economy. In this sense, Woo (1999:118, 136) is of the opinion that China is more like its East Asian neighbors, and is likely to adopt large-scale market reforms more quickly than previously imagined. The debate is likely to continue, and the ultimate proof may lie in China's ability to easily absorb workers from the agricultural sector into the technologically advanced industrial sector of the economy.

Economic Reform in China

Before the reforms in 1978, China maintained a command and control–type economy. A large percentage of China's economy was controlled by the state, which set production goals, controlled prices, and directed resources to various industries, resulting in widespread distortion in the economy. Various government policies that provided few incentives for farmers and firms kept the Chinese economy slow and inefficient. Further, competition was nearly non-existent. In the 1950s, China's individual household farms were consolidated. To further support rapid industrialization, the government invested heavily in physical and human capital in the decades that followed. By 1978, nearly three-fourths of industrial production came from centrally controlled, state-owned enterprises, according to centrally planned output targets (Morrison 2006:2).

In 1978, China introduced a number of reforms. Initially, the government initiated price and ownership incentives for farmers that allowed them to start working in the free market. The government further established five specific economic zones, in Shenzen, Zhuhai, Shantou, Xiamen, and Hainan, directed toward improving exports, improving imports, and increasing FDI. To accomplish this, certain regions and cities were allowed to experiment with tax and trade incentives. Additional reforms were implemented in stages. The primary goal was to decentralize economic decisions in a number of different areas, particularly trade. The control of a number of sectors and enterprises was handed over to local and provincial governments, which had the choice to operate on free market principles. Gradually, state price controls on a wide range of products were eliminated.

Foreign Direct Investment and Trade in China

Prior to the reforms, the goal of the Chinese government was to make China's economy self-sufficient, and foreign trade was limited to those goods that were not produced or available locally. However, with the introduction of reforms, FDI and trade have become important components of the country's GDP. Today, China is the largest recipient of worldwide FDI. Further, China's trade constitutes as much as 50 percent of the country's GDP (Fung 2005:3–4).

In 1978, at the beginning of the reform period, China's exports to the world were valued at US$9.8 billion. In 2005, exports stood at US$762 billion. In the same time frame, China's imports to the world increased from US$11 billion to US$660 billion. China's trade continues to grow at unprecedented rates. From 2002 to 2005, China's foreign sector more than doubled, and in 2005 alone, China's trade surplus tripled, from a US$32 billion surplus to a US$102 billion surplus (Morrison 2006:7).

At the end of 2004, China's five biggest trading partners were the European Union, the United States, Japan, Hong Kong, and the ASEAN group of countries. With its abundance of cheap labor, China has an advantage in low-cost, labor-intensive manufacturing. As a result, manufactured products form a large part of China's trade. In 2004, China's main imports were electrical machinery; boiler machinery, mechanical appliances, crude oil, and plastics; and organic chemicals. China's main exports in 2004 were apparel, furniture, bedding, lamps, photo equipment, and medical equipment (Morrison 2006:10).

China is not just an exporter of goods. Its growing economy and large population make it one of the largest importers in Asia. While it has a trade surplus with the United States, a little-known fact is that it runs trade deficits with Japan and Korea and a US$16 billion trade deficit with members of ASEAN (Gilboy 2004:36). In comparing and contrasting the other Asia Pacific economies with China, Gilboy (2004:36) points out that while Japan and Korea rejected imports and investment from the United States and Western Europe, in its early stages of development China became a large import and investment market for the United States. Over 50 percent of China's trade comes from foreign-funded enterprises. Since 1984, the amount of FDI flowing into mainland China has increased by a factor of over forty, from US$1.4 billion to US$58 billion. FDI in China results in over 10 percent of gross fixed capital formation, 29 percent of industrial output, and half of exports (Fung 2005:11).

The dramatic increase in FDI has resulted in large-scale capital investment, and has improved total factor productivity by bringing to China new technology and processes that improve efficiency. Nevertheless, as Gilboy (2004:34) notes, China's dependence on foreign technology and investment has restricted its ability to be a world leader in industrial and technological production.

Twenty-three years after China first initiated economic reform, and fifteen years after China began lobbying for access to the World Trade Organization, China was finally granted WTO membership in 2001, at the Doha ministerial round. China's entry into the WTO has been viewed for some years with mixed emotion. On the one hand was elation that China would initiate its own domestic pace of economic reforms in the trade arena much more quickly than previously expected. On the other hand was fear that China would use its power and establish a hegemony in global trade relations and quite possibly even reshape the WTO to serve its own self-interest. Nicholas Lardy (2002:157, 164) suggests instead that China's integration into the global trading economy will likely make it a more constructive participant in new global trading negotiations.

Challenges to Economic Growth in China

China has made great strides in the past quarter century, ever since the reforms of 1978. The Asian financial crisis presents a cautionary tale for China. Several issues need to be addressed if China plans to sustain its exemplary growth record. State-owned enterprises have been putting a heavy strain on the Chinese economy and consequently on the banking sector. Over half of SOEs are believed to be losing money, and must be supported by subsidies and loans from state banks. One of the preconditions for liberalizing the flow of capital is reform of the financial and banking sector. This point was reflected all too well during the Asian crisis. The central government often forces the banks to issue low-interest, nonperforming loans, estimated at US$480 billion, or 43 percent of China's GDP, in 2004 (Morrison 2006:12). With continued support of these SOEs, there is the urgent sense that valuable resources are being misdirected and wasted. Janet Yellen (2004) points out that China has recently separated the supervisory and regulatory role of the banking sector from its central bank. Yellen believes that the recently created China Banking Regulatory Commission faces a real challenge, since curtailing credit to SOEs will impact employment for thousands of workers.

The key issue in China will be how to manage an explosive growth of nearly 10 percent without triggering inflation. Rising investment of nearly 50 percent of GDP, together with a rapidly growing export sector, is likely to cause an excess demand in sectors like real estate, cement, and steel (Yellen 2004). The fear that China may fail to control the overheating in the economy is exacerbated, since the conduct of monetary policy is not full proof of the contrary. Raising interest rates to ward off inflation is difficult, since the People's Bank of China (PBOC) has until recently pegged its currency, the reminbi, to the dollar. Continued altercations with its trading partners, notably the United States, prompted the PBOC to rethink this fixed exchange-rate policy. On July 21, 2005, after more than a decade of enforcing this peg, the PBOC announced that the reminbi exchange rate would be allowed to float against the dollar, but only within a band of plus or minus 0.3 percent (Spiegel 2005). This quasi-floating exchange-rate mechanism was an attempt to bring the Chinese currency more in line with domestic and international markets for goods and services. Constant pressure from the United States for China to revalue its currency as a way to improve the trade imbalance between the two countries has resulted in a steady upward revaluation of the reminbi, from approximately 8.3 to the dollar in July 2005 to about 7.8 in February 2007.

The East Asian economies were able to achieve a more equitable income distribution by catering to the elites as well as the nonelites, thus fostering a climate where the benefits of growth were shared by a majority of the population in these economies. The HPAEs were able to reduce their Gini coefficients from about 0.45 in the 1960s to 0.36 in the 1990s. In 2006, China's Gini coefficient was still high by comparison, at 0.48. The gaps between various regions in the country have also enlarged since the reforms. In 1980, the share of the eastern region's GDP in the whole country was 50 percent. By 2003, that share had risen to 59 percent. In terms of per capita GDP, the eastern region was 34 percent higher than the average level in 1980. By 2002, that share had risen to 53 percent. Wayne Morrison (2006:10) points out that this unequal distribution of development has already led to social unrest and rising levels of corruption in the SOEs.

The short-term and long-term future for China is bright, however. China's real GDP has been growing at an average of 8–10 percent, and this is likely to continue until 2010. If it does, China will become the world's largest exporter by 2010, will double the size of its economy by 2015, and will become the world's largest economy by 2020 (Morrison 2006:13). However, to achieve these goals, China needs to continue its reforms of inefficient SOEs and its reforms of the financial and banking sectors.

China is an industrial nation striving to grow and provide a better livelihood for its teeming billion people. Behind the allure of 10 percent economic growth remain a backward agricultural sector, mismanaged SOEs, and limited political participation. China's trading partners, and institutions like ASEAN, should continue to encourage the country to develop its economy and liberalize its political institutions. It is likely that, with economic reform, political reform will follow, and political reform in China is in the interests of the world at large.

The Future of Asia Pacific Economies

The East Asian miracle was characterized by sound public policies. The public and private sectors worked together in these economies and thus promoted prudent macroeconomic management, high levels of savings, high levels of investment, efficient allocation of investment, investment in human capital, competition, and export-oriented policies. In essence, these were the policies that led to thirty years of rapid and sustained growth. The urgent task ahead for the Asia Pacific economies is to build on these fundamentals and restore growth in the region once again.

The macroeconomic situation of the Asia Pacific economies has improved since the 1997 crisis. Most of these economies performed very well in the latter half of 1999, particularly in 2000, before a global slowdown set in and once again lowered growth expectations in the region. Annual GDP growth rates for the region increased from –1.4 percent in 1998, to 6.9 percent in 1999, to 7.6 percent in 2000, before slowing down to 4.3 percent in 2001. Since the slowdown of 2001, annual growth rates have increased once again. The region performed strongly in 2005, as it firmly established itself as the most open regional bloc in world trade, surpassing even the European Union. Trade within the region was about 6.5 percent of total global trade in 2006, and can largely be attributed to the dynamism of the export sector and initiatives taken toward regional integration in the trade arena by institutions such as ASEAN and APEC. The World Bank estimates that growth in East Asia and the Pacific region will average about 6.5 percent from 2006 to 2009, which will be a difficult time in the global economy given rising oil prices as well as rising interest rates (see "East Asia and Pacific Overview" at the World Bank's website, at http:// www.worldbank.org/eap). Still, some countries in the region, including China, Vietnam, Laos, and Cambodia, face challenges to sustaining income growth, reducing poverty, and decreasing income inequality. In terms of other general economic indicators in the region, inflation and interest rates are low, savings rates are high, public and private investment is increasing, and investment in human capital, which declined sharply during the crisis of 1997, is now approaching precrisis levels. Most of the short-term foreign debt that contributed to the crisis has been repaid or rescheduled. Currencies, except for those of Hong Kong and Malaysia, are no longer pegged to the dollar, and central banks have increased foreign currency reserves.

The crisis has shown the urgent need for the region to strengthen financial institutions as well as regulatory systems. The countries of Asia Pacific also recognize that maintaining strong fundamentals such as price stability, low unemployment, and low budget deficits, which proved so crucial during the miracle years, is equally important in order to return to precrisis growth levels. Weak financial institutions were a major source of instability, and contributed directly to the deepening of the crisis of 1997. The countries of Asia Pacific mistakenly pursued financial market liberalization instead of developing appropriate regulatory structures to strengthen their financial systems. Presently, commercial banks need to create more comprehensive regulatory measures and approaches, such as implementing exposure limits on foreign-denominated liabilities (that is, regulatory measures on short-term capital inflows) and assessing borrowers. Restrictions on risky lending and the speed at which bank portfolios can increase should also be considered.

South Korea has been the leader in many of these financial reforms. As the crisis began to consume East Asia in late 1997, Korea recapitalized its banks and established a system to buy up bad loans, freeing banks to conduct business. Korean banks have made two major changes. First, financial regulators have laid down guidelines for managing credit, including independent credit committees insulated from internal as well as external pressures. Second, banks are more responsive to competitive pressures. Since the initial financial liberalization packages, banks have now had adequate time to adjust their systems to be more competitive with newer, more innovative banks. The rest of the region has been slow to follow Korea's example.

In addition to weak financial institutions, short-term capital inflows were a major source of instability and a primary factor in spurring the crisis. Essentially, investors engaging in transactions involving short-term capital rarely take into account or bear the social risks, which they impose on others. This warrants urgent government intervention. Governments should work to stabilize these short-term capital flows and discourage those capital flows that are unrelated to trade. Malaysia has used intervention to curtail the outflow of capital and, to the surprise of many critics, has experienced an increase in foreign direct investment (Stiglitz 1999:10).

Since 2005, recovery in the East Asian and Pacific economies is being fueled by some of the same factors that established the platform for miracle growth in the 1965–1995 period—growing exports, low interest rates, and high investment in the region, particularly in China, Vietnam, and Thailand. A cautionary tale is in order. There will always be spurts of growth and slowdowns in any economy. Diminishing returns, not just to labor and capital but also to the stock of technical know-how and entrepreneurship, are an inevitable consequence of the development process. Joseph Stiglitz (2001:521) suggests that the countries of East and Southeast Asia not sit on their laurels from the precrisis era. This seems all the more important given that sleeping giants India and China have emerged as a force to reckon with. The traditional comparative advantage that East Asia had in the precrisis era, particularly in manufacturing, is being imitated in China and India today. This necessitates the active pursuit of new sources of "dynamic comparative advantage." One possible new source of investment to consider for the economies of Singapore, Malaysia, Thailand, and Indonesia is research and development, an area largely ignored outside Japan and Korea.

The fundamentals of economic policy are strong in the entire Asia Pacific region. The challenge of maintaining traditional policies of growth, while determining how best to take advantage of global liberalization and integration, remains. This may well require the cultivation of ideas and institutions, not just investment in capital and labor. To the extent that the region is able to do so, the economies involved will once again be easily integrated into the global economy. The lesson from the Asia Pacific region is clear: economic policy is important, and the role of institutions and governance is the key to sustained growth for those regions of the world that find themselves in the midst of development.

◼ Notes

1. For a complete listing, see the UNESCAP website, http://www.unescap.org.
2. For a complete listing, see the APEC website, http://www.apec.org.
3. The lower the coefficient, the lower the income inequality. A value of 0 denotes perfect equality, while a value of 1 implies perfect inequality. Gini coefficients for countries with highly unequal income distributions typically lie between 0.50 and 0.75.
4. See the World Bank's country briefs, at http://www.worldbank.org/eap.

◼ Bibliography

Asian Development Bank. 2003. *Asian Development Outlook Update, 2003.* New York: Oxford University Press.

Barro, Robert J. 2001. "Economic Growth in East Asia Before and After the Financial Crisis." NBER Working Paper no. 8330. http://www.nber.org/papers/w8330.

Barro, Robert, and Jong-wha Lee. 1993. "International Comparisons of Educational Attainment." *Journal of Monetary Economics* no. 32: 383–384.

Bhagwati, Jagdish. 1996. "The Miracle That Did Happen: Understanding East Asia in Comparative Perspective." Ithaca: Cornell University Press, May 3. http://www.columbia.edu/~jb38.

Bowles, Paul. 1997. "ASEAN, AFTA, and the New Regionalism." *Pacific Affairs* 70, no. 2: 219–233.

Campos, Jose Edgardo, and Hilton L. Root. 1996. "The Key to the Asian Miracle." Washington, D.C.: Brookings Institution.

Chow, Peter C. Y., and Mitchell H. Kellman. 1993. *Trade: The Engine of Growth in East Asia.* New York: Oxford University Press.

Cooper, Richard N., and Barry P. Bosworth. 1998. "The East Asian Financial Crisis: Diagnosis, Remedies, Prospects, Comments, and Discussion." *Brookings Papers on Economic Activity* no. 1: 75–90.

Easterly, William. 2001. *The Elusive Quest for Growth: Economists' Adventures and Misadventures in the Tropics.* Cambridge: Massachusetts Institute of Technology Press.

Eichengreen, Barry. 2002. "Globalization Wars: An Economist Reports from the Front Lines." *Foreign Affairs* (July–August): 157–164.

Forbes, Dean, and Cecile Cutler. 2005. "Laos in 2005." *Asian Survey* 56, no. 1: 175–179.

Fung Hung-gay. 2005. "China's Foreign Trade and Investment: An Overview and Analysis." *China & World Economy* 13, no. 3: 13–16.

Furman, Jason, and Joseph Stiglitz. 1998. "Economic Crises: Evidence and Insights from East Asia." *Brookings Papers on Economic Activity* no. 2: 1–114.

Galenson, Walter. 1992. *Labor and Economic Growth in Five Asian Countries.* New York: Praeger.

Gilboy, George. 2004. "The Myth Behind China's Miracle." *Foreign Affairs* (July–August): 33–48.

Grier, Robin, 2002. "On the Interaction of Human and Physical Capital in Latin America." *Economic Development and Cultural Change* 50, no. 4: 891–913.

Hedman, Eva-Lotta. 2005. "Philippines in 2005." *Asian Survey* 56, no. 1: 187–193.

Hughes, Helen, ed. 1998. *Achieving Industrialization in East Asia.* Cambridge: Cambridge University Press.

Huh, Chan, and Sun Kim. 1993. "Japan's Keiretsu and Korea's Chaebol." *Federal Reserve Bank of San Francisco Weekly Letter* no. 25 (July 16).

Kim Jong Il and Lawrence J. Lau. 1994. "The Sources of Economic Growth of the East Asian Newly Industrialized Countries." *Journal of the Japanese and International Economies* no. 8: 235–271.

Kim, Young, C. 1995. *The South East Asian Economic Miracle.* New Brunswick, N.J.: Transaction.

Krugman, Paul. 1994. "The Myth of Asia's Miracle." *Foreign Affairs* (November–December): 62–78.

Lardy, Nicholas. 2002. *Integrating China into the Global Economy.* Washington, D.C.: Brookings Institution.

Leipziger, Danny M. 1997. *Lessons from East Asia.* Ann Arbor: University of Michigan Press.

Luong Hy. 2005. "Vietnam in 2005." *Asian Survey* 56, no. 1: 148–154.

Mo Pak-hung. 2001. "Corruption and Economic Growth." *Journal of Comparative Economics* 29, no. 1: 66–79.

Moreno, Ramon. 1995. "Is Pegging the Exchange Rate a Cure for Inflation? East Asian Experiences." *Federal Reserve Board of San Francisco Weekly Letter* no. 37 (November 3).

———. 1996. "Models of Currency Speculation: Implications and East Asian Evidence." *Federal Reserve Board of San Francisco Weekly Letter* no. 13 (April 19).

Morrison, Wayne M. 2006. "CRS Issue Brief for Congress: China's Economic Conditions." July. http://www.fas.org/sgp/crs/row/ib98014.pdf.

Nelsen, Richard R., and Howard Pack. 1999. "The Asian Growth Miracle and Modern Growth Theory." *Economic Journal* no. 109: 1–21.

Oshima, Harry. 1993. *Strategic Processes in Monsoon Asia's Economic Development.* Baltimore: Johns Hopkins University Press.

Pesenti, Paolo, and Cedric Tille. 2000. "The Economics of Currency Crises and Contagion: An Introduction." *Federal Reserve Bank of New York Economic Policy Review* 6, no. 3: 3–16.

Prestowitz, Clyde. 2005. *Three Billion New Capitalists: The Great Shift of Wealth and Power to the East.* New York: Basic.

Psacharopoulos, George, et al. 1992. *Poverty and Income Distribution in Latin America: The Story of the 1980's.* Washington, D.C.: World Bank.

Radelet, Steven, and Jeffrey D. Sachs. 1998. "The East Asian Financial Crisis: Diagnosis, Remedies, Prospects." *Brookings Papers on Economic Activity* no. 1: 1–90.

Rowen, Henry. 1998. *Behind East Asian Growth.* London: Routledge.

Sachs, Jeffrey D. 1997. "IMF Is a Power unto Itself." *Financial Times,* December 11.

San, G. "Training in Taiwan: Results from the Vocational Training Needs Survey." *Economics of Education Review* 9, no. 4: 411–418.

Solow, Robert. 1956. "A Contribution to the Theory of Economic Growth." *Quarterly Journal of Economics* 70, no. 1: 65–94.

Spiegel, Mark. 2005. "A Look at China's New Exchange Rate Regime." *Federal Reserve Board of San Francisco Weekly Letter* no. 23 (September 9).

Stiglitz, Joseph. 1996. "Some Lessons from the East Asian Miracle." *World Bank Observer* 11, no. 2: 151–177.

———. 1999. "Back to Basics: Policies and Strategies for Enhanced Growth and Equity in Post-Crisis East Asia." Bangkok: World Bank, July 29. http://www.worldbank.org/knowledge/chiefecon/articles/bangkok.htm.

Stiglitz, Joseph, and Yusuf Shahid. 2001. *Rethinking the East Asia Miracle.* Oxford: Oxford University Press.

Todaro, Michael. 1997. *Economic Development.* 6th ed. Reading, Mass.: Addison Wesley.

Tongzon, Jose. 1998. *The Economies of Southeast Asia: The Growth and Development of ASEAN Economies.* Cheltenham, UK: Elgar.

Wade, Robert. 1998. "The Asian Crisis and the Global Economy: Causes, Consequences, and Cure." *Current History* 97, no. 2 (November): 361–373.

Weggel, Oskar. 2005. "Cambodia in 2005." *Asian Survey* 56, no. 1: 155–161.

Woo, Wing Thye. 1999. "The Real Reasons for China's Growth." *China Journal* 41 (January 1999): 115–137.

World Bank. 1993. *The East Asian Miracle: Economic Growth and Public Policy.* New York: Oxford University Press.

Woronoff, Jon. 1986. *Asia's "Miracle" Economies.* New York: Sharpe.

Yellen, Janet. 2004. "Reflections on China's Economy." *Federal Reserve Board of San Francisco Weekly Letter* no. 31 (November 5).

Young, Alwyn. 1994. "Lessons from the East Asian NICS: A Contrarian View." *European Economic Review* no. 38: 964–973.

———. 1995. "The Tyranny of Numbers: Confronting the Statistical Realities of the East Asian Growth Experience." *Quarterly Journal of Economics* 110, no. 3: 641–680.

6

International Relations

Derek McDougall

An understanding of international relations in Asia Pacific can best be obtained by dividing the region into two parts: Northeast Asia, consisting of China, Japan, and the Koreas; and Southeast Asia, comprising all ten members of the Association of Southeast Asian Nations (ASEAN) and East Timor. In examining international relations within Asia Pacific it is not sufficient to consider only the states within these two subregions, however, as these nations are often dramatically affected by their relations with the broader Asia Pacific, including Russia, Australia and New Zealand, the Pacific Island region, Canada and the United States in their Pacific aspects, and the countries of Latin America with Pacific coastlines. It is important also to examine the role of states and other actors that have their centers elsewhere. Most important in this respect is the United States, which plays a very important role in Northeast Asia and (to a lesser extent) in Southeast Asia. China and Japan, although centered in Northeast Asia, also play an important role in Southeast Asia.

In examining international relations in Asia Pacific, we need to keep in mind a working definition of "international relations." In the "realist" framework developed from the 1940s on, international relations has focused on the relationships among states. States pursue their "national interests" using various instruments such as diplomacy and, in extreme circumstances, military force. They align with or oppose other states depending on judgments about what best advances national interests. More recently, new approaches have developed to take account of the way in which the position of states has been weakened in various respects. International relations now encompasses a broader range of issues, with more emphasis on economic and social developments. Issues such as refugees, drug trafficking, international crime, and the environment are part of the "new international agenda." More emphasis is placed on domestic politics as an influence on international behavior. Globalization as a phenomenon suggests both a broadening of the international agenda and the way in which states have become relatively weaker than was previously the case. Within international relations as a discipline, "liberal institutionalists" make a similar argument, pointing out also the way in which international organizations (both regional and global) have assumed a greater importance. There is also the argument that most general approaches to international relations have been developed by Western scholars and relate primarily to Western experience and perceptions. In the East Asian context an alternative view is that approaches to international relations need to put more emphasis on the features of international relations that are distinctive to the region. Particularly important is the historical experience of the region, covering such issues as the role of traditional civilizations (preeminently China) and the impact of Western imperialism. In many cases, particularly in Southeast Asia, states as entities have faced significant opposition and have been weaker than their Western counterparts.

This chapter takes into account a number of these different approaches. The discussion of the historical context indicates the way in which past experience is relevant to understanding more recent international relations. It also highlights some of the more distinctive features of Asia Pacific international relations. The examination of international relations in Northeast Asia is primarily state-centered. However, many of the issues have an important domestic dimension. In the case of Southeast Asia the state system is frequently more fragile. Therefore, a broader conception of international relations will underlie the discussion, taking account of the role of both states and nonstate actors. The final section, dealing with the Asia Pacific concept more broadly, draws attention to regionalism as one of the newer forces in the international relations of the region.

◼ The Historical Context

Any understanding of international relations in Asia Pacific today must be grounded in how the situation has evolved historically, in three phases: the era of traditional civilizations, the era of imperialism, and the 1945–1989 period. These will provide the foundation for our subsequent focus on the post–Cold War period.

Traditional Civilizations

Contemporary Asia Pacific is organized as a system of states based on the Westphalian model, developed in Europe. The shift to this model, which only became the norm in Europe after 1648, as discussed in Chapter 3 by Colin Mackerras, was the outcome of the impact of Europeans in the region. The Westphalian system historically was not the dominant model in East Asia. China, the dominant force in the region, functioned as a "civilization" rather than as a "state" or "sovereign power" in the modern Western sense. Viewing itself as the "Middle Kingdom," China developed as a distinctive civilization over a period of thousands of years. While the writ of the emperors ran wide, China saw itself primarily as a model for others within its "civilization area" to follow. Chinese influence was particularly strong in Korea and Vietnam. This influence was not just cultural, as the leaders of these entities were also required to pay tribute to the Chinese emperor. China also contributed to Japanese cultural development, though Japanese rulers were never forced to pay tribute to China. In the Chinese view of the world, people living beyond its civilizational influence were characterized as "barbarians." There was minimal interaction.

In Southeast Asia the situation was more complex again. While China was an important influence in the northern part of Southeast Asia, particularly in Vietnam, Indian civilization also had a major impact. No single empire dominated Southeast Asia. Significant political entities included Angkor, Champa (central and southern Vietnam), Srivijaya and Majapahit (successive states covering an extensive region of modern Indonesia), Pagan (Burma), and Sukhothai and Ayutthya (successive states in the area of modern Thailand). Rather than being based on Western principles of sovereignty, these entities were based on a *mandala* (circle) system. Power was concentrated at the center of the entity, but was more diffuse the further one moved from the center. This meant that between adjoining centers of power, there would be "gray" areas where local leaders might hold sway, or where there might be overlapping layers of authority (see Acharya 2000:18–29).

The Era of Imperialism

The advent of extensive European involvement in the region from the fifteenth century did not mean the immediate replacement of the existing international system by a Western-oriented one. The Chinese tributary system, for example, lasted in a formal sense until the late nineteenth century. Europeans were particularly interested in trade, and missionaries also became involved in some areas. Trade did not necessarily require the establishment of political control, however, and many colonial powers opted to rule indirectly or through cooperative relationships with local rulers. From the sixteenth through the eighteenth centuries, European powers, including the Portuguese, Dutch, British, and French, expanded their influence over the region. One vehicle for European penetration was through mercantile companies such as the Dutch United East India Company. Trading centers and forts were established in some regions, and these often came under the political control of European powers.

The greatest external pressure on the existing international system in East Asia occurred during the course of the nineteenth century, with coercion being used in a number of situations. The form this pressure took differed between Northeast Asia and Southeast Asia. In Northeast Asia the imperialist powers generally sought domination but, with some exceptions, did not emphasize the acquisition of territory. There were means other than annexation to ensure the achievement of strategic and economic objectives. The changing situation was most obvious in relation to China. Particularly from the time of the Opium War in 1842 between Britain and China, China was forced to make a number of concessions to Western powers through a series of "unequal treaties." Some of these concessions involved the cession or lease of territory, Hong Kong being a notable example. Another sign of China's weakness was the imposition of a system of extraterritoriality, whereby Westerners were generally subject to the laws of their own countries rather than to Chinese law. Western powers established spheres of influence in different parts of China: Britain in the Yangzi valley and adjoining Hong Kong, France in Yunnan next to Indochina, Germany in the Shandong peninsula, and so on. The United States pursued an "open door" policy with the aim of giving all external powers equal access to China. Russia was the Western power that put the most emphasis on territorial expansion at China's expense. This reflected Russia's economic weakness: annexation would allow Russians to be given preferential treatment in a way that was not possible when open competition prevailed. Its expansion into Siberia dated from the seventeenth century. During the nineteenth century it acquired parts of Central Asia from China, as well as the area adjacent to Vladivostok. Northern Manchuria became a Russian sphere of influence.

In Northeast Asia, Japan was also subjected to strong Western pressures, but the outcome there was very different from what occurred in China. In 1853, Commodore Matthew Perry of the US Navy was instrumental in bringing Japan's self-imposed isolation to an end. Japan too faced "unequal treaties" and the imposition of a system designed to bring commercial advantages to Westerners. However, with the Meiji Restoration of 1868, Japan took steps to strengthen its political and economic system from within. The aim was to resist Western encroachments and to compete with the Western powers on their own terms. Japan achieved remarkable success in this respect. By the end of the nineteenth century, Japan had joined the Western powers in making gains at China's expense, and was also competing strongly with Russia in Northeast Asia. Following its success in the first Sino-Japanese war (1894–1895), Japan acquired Taiwan from China. Competition with Russia was most marked in Manchuria and Korea. Japan won a stunning victory in the Russo-Japanese War (1904–1905). Manchuria came predominantly under Japanese influence. Following a short period of Japanese "protection," by 1910 Korea was a Japanese colony.

During the 1930s and early 1940s, the main territorial threat to China came from Japan. The inability of the Qing dynasty to resist imperialist encroachments had led to its downfall in the 1911 revolution. However, China remained weak. Warlords controlled important regions of the country. From 1927, conflict between the Communists (led by Mao Zedong) and the ruling Nationalists under Chiang Kai-shek contributed to China's weakness. In 1931,

Japanese forces seized Manchuria and established the puppet state of Manchukuo. In 1937, war broke out between Japan and China, first in the north, but extending subsequently to large parts of eastern China. In 1941, this conflict became the China theater of the Pacific War.

As compared with Northeast Asia, in Southeast Asia there was a stronger emphasis on territorial expansion by the Western powers. Japan became involved in this territorial expansion during the Pacific War. As previously indicated, up until the early nineteenth century the Western powers in Southeast Asia had established some centers and limited areas where they had political control. During the course of the nineteenth century there was greater competition among those powers, which encouraged the acquisition of colonies. The form colonial control took could vary depending on the particular situation; local political factors were often important. The main changes in Southeast Asia involved Britain, France, and the Netherlands. Britain became the colonial power in Burma, the Malayan peninsula, Singapore, and northern Borneo. France acquired Indochina: Vietnam (administered as Tongking, Annam, and Cochinchina, running from north to south), Cambodia, and Laos. The Netherlands extended its control throughout the entire Indonesian archipelago to constitute the Netherlands East Indies. In addition to the three European powers, the United States became a colonial power when it acquired the Philippines from Spain following the latter's defeat in the Spanish-American War (1898–1899). Within Southeast Asia, only Thailand, then known as Siam, escaped colonial rule. This was largely due to the country's location as a buffer zone between the British and French spheres in mainland Southeast Asia.

During the early decades of the twentieth century, nationalist movements developed as a challenge to Western rule in a number of Southeast Asian countries. The most significant movements were in Vietnam and Indonesia. However, the greatest challenge to the existing colonial system came with Japanese expansion into the region during the Pacific War (1941–1945). Japan wished to incorporate Southeast Asia into its "Greater East Asia Co-Prosperity Sphere." In this scheme, Southeast Asia would be an important source of raw materials for Japanese industry. Japan occupied all the British, Dutch, and US possessions in Southeast Asia. In Indochina, Japan had the cooperation of the Vichy French government in Indochina for much of the war, but took more direct control in the closing phases. Thailand (Siam) also cooperated with Japan. Nationalist movements in Indonesia and Burma worked with Japan as a means of advancing their own goals. With Japan's defeat in 1945, clearly the reimposition of the previous colonial system would be no easy task.

The 1945–1989 Period

The main dimensions of international relations in Asia Pacific in the post–Cold War era emerged during the 1945–1989 period. This is sometimes referred to as the era of the Cold War, but to say that the Cold War was the

dominant theme in the region's international relations would be an oversimplification. Important themes in the history of international relations in Asia Pacific during this period included the new international roles of China and
Japan, the position adopted by the United States, the Cold War conflicts in the
1950s and 1960s, the decolonization in Southeast Asia, the Sino-Soviet conflict, the Sino-American rapprochement of the 1970s, the emergence of Southeast Asian regionalism, and postcolonial conflicts in Southeast Asia. To appreciate the significance of these various themes and their interrelationships, it
will be helpful to focus on key phases: the late 1940s, the 1950s and 1960s,
and the 1970s and 1980s.

The late 1940s laid the foundations for international relations in the Asia
Pacific for the entire postwar period. Defeated Japan came under the occupation of the United States from 1945 to 1951. At first the United States was intent on democratizing and demilitarizing Japan. The aim was to ensure that
Japan would never again become a threat. By 1947, however, the United States
had shifted tack due to changes occurring at a global level. The onset of the
Cold War meant that the "containment" of communism, specifically of the Soviet Union, became the first priority for the United States, which wished to ensure that Japan would be an ally in that struggle. Hence the more radical objectives of the early occupation were superseded in favor of a more
conservative policy. The United States concluded a lenient peace treaty with
Japan in 1951; at the same time, a mutual security treaty linked Japan to the
emerging alliance system of the United States.

While developments in Japan were consistent with the objectives of the
United States in the Cold War, developments in China were more of a setback.
At the time of World War II the United States had looked to China to play a
major role as a replacement for Japan in East Asia. On that basis, China became
one of the permanent members of the United Nations Security Council. However, with Japan's defeat, full-scale civil war resumed between the Communists
and Nationalists in China. Although the United States initially had hopes of effecting compromise, for the most part it leaned toward the Nationalists. However, the position of the Nationalists had been weakened by the war with Japan,
and the Communists extended their political support in many areas. Over the
period 1945–1949 the Communists advanced from their bases in northern
China and by late 1949 controlled the whole of the mainland. Mao Zedong proclaimed the establishment of the People's Republic of China (PRC) on October
1, 1949. Clearly, this development had major implications for the international
situation in Asia Pacific. The United States interpreted the emergence of the
PRC as beneficial for the Soviet Union, which seemed to be confirmed by a
Sino-Soviet alliance concluded in 1950. The Chinese revolution had received
little support from Joseph Stalin, however, who maintained diplomatic relations
with the Nationalist government until well into 1949. Sino-Soviet tensions
would remain largely hidden, but by the 1960s there was open conflict.

Although Cold War issues had some impact in Southeast Asia in the late 1940s, the major changes occurring there related to the issue of decolonization. With the defeat of Japan, the two colonial powers most intent on restoring their prewar positions were France and the Netherlands. In both cases, conflict ensued with the relevant nationalist movements. In Vietnam, war between France and the communist-led Viet Minh lasted from 1946 to 1954. The Viet Minh's communist orientation made it suspect in the eyes of the United States. From the US perspective, the success of the Viet Minh would bolster the position of China and the Soviet Union in the region. In Indonesia the conflict was a more straightforward contest between colonialism and nationalism, and by 1949 the Netherlands had conceded independence. The United States granted independence to the Philippines in 1946, as did Britain to Burma in 1948.

In the 1950s and 1960s the confrontation between China and the United States dominated international relations in Asia Pacific. Direct conflict between the two powers occurred in the context of the Korean War (1950–1953). This war had commenced with (communist) North Korea's attack on (anticommunist) South Korea on June 25, 1950. With UN authorization, US forces (supported by forces from a number of other countries) had come to the assistance of South Korea. However, instead of stopping at the dividing line between the two Koreas (the Thirty-eighth Parallel), the United States decided to take the conflict into the north. China felt threatened, and Chinese "volunteers" entered the war from late 1950. China had also been affected at the very start of the war when the deployment of the US Seventh Fleet to the Taiwan Strait meant that Chinese communist forces could not liberate Taiwan from the Nationalists. The Nationalist government was able to consolidate its position as the Republic of China. The United States continued diplomatic relations with the Nationalists, and a mutual defense treaty was concluded in 1954. The PRC became the main object for the US containment in Asia Pacific. The PRC saw US protection of Taiwan as unwarranted interference in the Chinese civil war. From the Chinese perspective, the United States was attempting "encirclement" of China.

In the 1960s the emergence of the Vietnam War also highlighted the Sino-American confrontation. The United States interpreted the conflict between Vietnamese communist forces and the anticommunist Saigon government from the perspective of its global strategy of containment. Both the Soviet Union and China were seen as supporting the Vietnamese communists. It was believed that the defeat of South Vietnam would mean an extension of Chinese power.

The United States slowly came to realize the significance of the emerging Sino-Soviet conflict. Rather than being allies, China and the Soviet Union saw each other as rivals. There was an important element of "power politics" in this conflict. China and the Soviet Union competed for influence in various regions of the world. In Vietnam, for example, China and the Soviet Union were each vying for influence rather than engaging in a cooperative endeavor. There were territorial differences, with their origins in earlier expansion by Tsarist Russia at China's expense. Racial tensions recalled the earlier imperialist era. The fact that both powers espoused communism added an important ideological dimension to the conflict. Each side accused the other of "revisionism" as their development strategies took different paths, particularly after China's launch of the Great Leap Forward in 1958. Irrespective of whether ideology was a fundamental cause of the rivalry, it certainly added to the bitterness of the exchanges.

During the 1950s and 1960s, Japan gradually emerged once again as an important economic power in Asia Pacific, though there was a mismatch between Japan's growing economic strength and its very limited international political role. Under Article 9 of the 1947 "peace constitution," Japan had foresworn the use of force in its international relations, and it relied on the United States for defense after 1945. There were significant US forces in Japan, and Okinawa remained under US control until 1972. Japan acted as a rear base for the United States during the Korean War, and Japan also gave low-level support to the United States during the Vietnam War. Under the Yoshida Doctrine, dating from the early 1950s, Japan concentrated on its own economic development and spent no more than about 1 percent of gross domestic product (GDP) on defense. Although Article 9 barred Japan from acquiring military forces, it developed a technologically advanced "self-defense force."

In Southeast Asia, issues of decolonization continued to have an impact in the 1950s and 1960s. From the Vietnamese communist perspective, the Vietnam War was simply a continuation of the earlier struggle against the French for independence. Malaya became independent from Britain in 1957, and was joined in 1963 by Singapore and the northern Borneo territories in the new Federation of Malaysia. This development provoked a conflict with Indonesia. Sukarno saw the new federation as a neocolonial scheme to perpetuate British influence, and mounted an anti-Malaysia campaign known as Konfrontasi (Confrontation). Under Sukarno's leadership, Indonesia had espoused an increasingly radical direction, but Sukarno himself fell following an attempted leftist coup in September 1965. The military regime, or New Order, that emerged under President Suharto was strongly anticommunist, and in fact hundreds of thousands of alleged Communists and their sympathizers were massacred (see Chapter 4 for further details). The changes in Indonesia brought an end to Confrontation. They also prepared the way for a new regionalism when the Association of Southeast Asian Nations was founded in 1967. This was a way of strengthening the relations among the noncommunist countries in Southeast Asia and of integrating Indonesia into regional affairs. Apart from Indonesia, the founding members were Malaysia, the Philippines, Singapore, and Thailand.

During the 1970s and 1980s, the most significant development in international relations at the broadest regional level was the emergence and development of the Sino-American rapprochement. The Richard Nixon administration, which took office in the United States at the beginning of 1969, sought to achieve improved relations with both China and the Soviet Union. Such a situation would improve US leverage with both communist powers. China regarded its conflict with the Soviet Union as more threatening than its conflict with the United States. Improved relations with the United States would enable China to focus its efforts on the conflict with the Soviet Union. This convergence in perspectives paved the way for a visit to China by President Nixon in February 1972. In the "Shanghai Communiqué," signed by the two sides, the United States recognized the "one China" principle,[1] while also maintaining its interest in a peaceful resolution of the Taiwan issue. The United States and the PRC did not establish formal diplomatic relations until 1979, at which point US recognition of Taiwan (as the "Republic of China") ceased and the mutual security treaty also ended. Taiwan became more isolated, although the United States provided for "unofficial" relations with Taiwan and continuing arms sales through the Taiwan Relations Act (1979). Apart from the changes in the relationships among the United States, China, and Taiwan, the effect of the Sino-American rapprochement was to end polarization in the region and to allow for more fluidity in international relationships. There was more scope for regional countries to develop relations with both China and the United States, and to pursue more independent policies.

From the US perspective, the Sino-American rapprochement made withdrawal from the Vietnam conflict easier. Such withdrawal would have been much more difficult for the United States had it been presented as a boost for the major communist powers, China in particular. Such an argument was difficult to sustain in the light of the accommodation between China and the United States. US withdrawal was provided for in the Paris Accords of 1973; by April 1975 the Saigon government had fallen. While Vietnam as a whole now came under communist rule, and communist governments also emerged in Cambodia and Laos, this did not bring peace to Indochina. The Khmer Rouge government in Cambodia pursued radical communist policies, resulting in extensive loss of life. It was also strongly anti-Vietnamese. Vietnam intervened in Cambodia in late 1978 and deposed the Khmer Rouge government. The resulting conflict, lasting until 1991, was known as the Third Indochina War. Vietnam installed a pro-Vietnamese government in Phnom Penh. Arrayed against Vietnam and its Cambodian supporters was the anti-Vietnamese resistance. While the Khmer Rouge was the strongest element in the resistance, rightist and royalist (Sihanoukist) groups were also involved. At the international level the strongest dimension of the conflict related to the Sino-Soviet conflict. The Soviet Union backed Vietnam, while China supported the anti-Vietnamese resistance. The ASEAN countries and the United States also supported the opposition to Vietnam. In fact, China invaded northern Vietnam in 1979 in reaction to Vietnam's invasion of Cambodia, but withdrew upon encountering stiff resistance from the Vietnamese.

A major development affecting the Third Indochina War was the Sino-Soviet rapprochement of 1989. While this had implications for international politics more broadly, in relation to Indochina it meant that the main external parties had agreed on a framework for resolving the conflict. Securing agreement among the Cambodian parties required a further two years, after which the UN became involved in a process of transition, culminating in elections in 1993.

The greater fluidity in international relations in Asia Pacific following the Sino-American rapprochement had implications for Japan. There was more scope for Japan to expand its international role. Okinawa reverted to Japanese rule in 1972, but it remained the major US base in the region. The United States encouraged Japan to expand its international role, but Japan remained cautious. The "peace constitution" was a limitation, but it also reflected widely held sentiment in Japan. Neighboring countries, particularly China and South Korea, were suspicious of any moves by Japan to expand its security role. There was more scope for Japan in terms of economic diplomacy and arenas such as aid. Japan was active in the Group of Seven and expanded its links with Southeast Asia. However, Japanese strength also led to resentment in many countries.

Japanese economic development provided a model for certain other East Asian countries to follow. The emergence of the Asian "tigers," who followed Japan's model of export-led industrialization and heavy state involvement in the economy, was an important development in the 1970s and 1980s. South Korea, Taiwan, Hong Kong, and Singapore were the main examples. In the case of South Korea, its economic development contributed to tensions with North Korea. Whereas in the 1950s and 1960s the two countries were comparable in their economic situations, in terms of measures such as per capita GDP, by the 1970s and 1980s South Korea had become much more economically successful. This possibly contributed to various acts of terror undertaken by North Korea during these decades, including the assassination of members of the South Korean cabinet in Yangon in 1983 and the destruction of a South Korean airliner in 1987.

Apart from the Third Indochina War, an important development in the international politics of Southeast Asia during the 1970s and 1980s was the strengthening of regionalism. While ASEAN had been founded in 1967, it assumed a new importance after the Bali summit of 1976. ASEAN became the major regional focus for the noncommunist countries in a much more significant way than had been the case previously, in part as a result of the end of the Vietnam War. With the reduction of the US presence in the region, the strategic landscape in Southeast Asia required reassessment. The noncommunist Southeast Asian countries saw themselves assuming a more significant role in the region, and a reduced involvement by external powers. Ironically, ASEAN's enhanced role came about through another conflict centered on Indochina (the Third Indochina War), involving not just ASEAN but also external powers, particularly China and the Sovet Union, as well as the United States.

In the 1970s and 1980s the major unresolved issue of decolonization in Southeast Asia was East Timor. The Portuguese presence in this territory was a vestige of the colonial era dating back to the sixteenth century. Political changes in Portugal in 1974 raised the question of Portuguese Timor's future. Indonesia preferred to see East Timor become part of Indonesian territory, but was frustrated by the strong popular support for the Frente Revolucionária do Timor-Leste Independente (FRETILIN; Revolutionary Front of Independent East Timor), a radical nationalist movement. Indonesia invaded the territory in late 1975 and later incorporated it as the twenty-seventh Indonesian province. Resistance to Indonesian rule continued for some decades.

While East Timor was an issue relating to Western colonialism, the subsequent development of the conflict there highlighted the way in which the postcolonial state system in Southeast Asia was often imposed against the will of significant groups. Many groups within Southeast Asian states saw themselves as "nations" in their own right and wished to establish their own states. In Indonesia, for example, there were significant separatist movements in Aceh and West Papua, at the western and eastern ends of the archipelago respectively. In the southern Philippines, Muslims resisted rule from Manila. In Burma, the various hill peoples (Karen, Kachin, Wa, Mon, and so on) had opposed the Rangoon government from the time of independence. These conflicts weakened the states in Southeast Asia. Separatist movements sought international support for their cause.

These various developments in Asia Pacific in the 1970s and 1980s indicate some of the main features of the regional context at the time of the end of the Cold War. There is no precise date for this event, although the fall of the Berlin Wall in late 1989 is often given major symbolic importance. The impact of the end of the Cold War was greater in Europe than in Asia Pacific. Europe was more polarized between East and West. The Sino-Soviet conflict had been a complicating factor in Asia Pacific in terms of any simple polarization. As far as the United States was concerned, the main contest in Asia Pacific had been with China, and that relationship had been transformed with the achievement of rapprochement in 1972. In Asia Pacific, the major developments relating to the end of the Cold War involved relationships concerning the Soviet Union. The achievement of Sino-Soviet rapprochement has already been noted. Soviet-Japanese relations did not change significantly. Soviet-American relations clearly changed at the global level, particularly in Europe, but there were also implications in the North Pacific. Tensions relating to the opposing military deployments of the United States and the Soviet Union in this region did ease at this time.

▪ Northeast Asia in the Post–Cold War Era

Any overview of the roles played by the United States, China, and Japan in Northeast Asia during the post–Cold War era must consider how these states define and pursue their national interests, as well as the relationships these powers have with each other. Russia's influence in the region is also important to consider, as are the roles of Taiwan and Korea, the two major "hot spots" of Northeast Asia.

Roles of the United States, China, and Japan

There are certain key questions to keep in mind when examining the roles played by the United States, China, and Japan in post–Cold War Northeast Asia. What objectives have been important to each state? How have they pursued those objectives? What factors have influenced the Northeast Asian policies of the three states?

It is useful to compare the United States, China, and Japan in terms of power. Clearly, the United States is the strongest power in terms of quantitative indices. Japan comes second to the United States as an economic power and, despite its claim to have a limited security role, still has significant military power. China is widely regarded as the rising power of the region, but is still well behind the other two powers in economic strength. It has considerable military strength (including nuclear weapons) and is undergoing significant military modernization. However, China is technologically behind the United States and Japan, and its ability to project its military power is limited. Of course, specific figures, as indicated in Table 6.1, provide just one insight into comparative power. Subjective dimensions, such as quality of leadership, political support, various aspects of a population's well-being, and the ability to use military force, also need to be considered. An assessment of a state's power also needs to take into account what that state aims to do with its power. The importance of the subjective dimension becomes clearer when we examine each power in terms of the objectives, strategies, and relevant influences affecting its behavior.

Table 6.1   Measures of Power, United States Compared with China and Japan

	United States	China	Japan
GDP (US$, 2005)	12.5 trillion	1.89 trillion	4.7 trillion
Per capita GDP (US$, 2005)	42,207	1,450	36,850
Population (2006)	295.7 million	1,306.3 million	127.4 million
Defense spending (US$, 2004)	455.9 billion	84.3 billion	45.2 billion
Defense spending as percentage of GDP (2004)	3.9	1.5	1.0

Source: International Institute for Strategic Studies 2006.

In the case of the United States, its objectives encompass political-strategic, economic, and liberal democratic dimensions. Strategically, the United States has aimed to prevent any one power from becoming dominant in Northeast Asia. During the post–Cold War era, this objective has been directed particularly at China. The US role is stronger than that of "balancer," and in some respects the United States can be seen as the dominant power of the region. The United States also has major economic interests in the region. Japan, China, Taiwan, and South Korea are important trading partners. The United States is also a major investor in the region. The relationship between Japan and the United States is important for global as well as regional economic stability. The liberal democratic objective relates to the US emphasis on human rights and support for democracy. Sometimes this objective clashes with one or another of the other two, but it is nevertheless an important element of US policy. It derives from the development of the United States as a liberal democratic society and the belief that the United States can provide a model for other societies to follow.

To some extent, the strategies employed by the United States vary with the particular objective, but there is also overlap. Military, political-diplomatic, and economic strategies are all used. The emphasis on bilateralism or multilateralism can vary depending on the context. At the military level, the United States has deployed a forward defense presence in Asia Pacific, with a focus on Northeast Asia. This presence generally involves over 100,000 US military personnel, with command centered on the Commander-in-Chief Pacific (CINCPAC), based in Hawaii. The most important countries for the forward military presence are Japan and South Korea, with US military personnel in 2006 numbered at 38,660 in the former and 30,983 in the latter (International Institute for Strategic Studies [IISS] 2006:42). The United States has bilateral security treaties with both Japan and South Korea. A considerable emphasis in US strategy in the region is placed on political-diplomatic means—that is, attempting to persuade other countries to support US objectives. However, the US military presence is often seen as providing "ballast" for these diplomatic efforts. In the economic context, the significance of the United States for the various economies of the region strengthens it in the pursuit of its goals. The US military alliances with Japan and South Korea are on a bilateral basis. Diplomacy might be conducted bilaterally or multilaterally, depending on the context. The Asia-Pacific Economic Cooperation (APEC) has provided one multilateral context for dealing with economic issues, although more broadly political issues can be considered. Generally, the United States has focused on bilateral approaches, but without excluding multilateralism in some situations.

In determining how it approaches Northeast Asia, the United States is influenced by the other powers in the region and by relevant international developments. However, it is not simply reactive. US policies in the region are influenced by domestic politics. On many issues the US executive branch has considerable scope for formulating policies toward the region. The Department of State and the Department of Defense are particularly relevant in formulating security policies. The Treasury and Department of Commerce are involved in formulating economic policies. The president and the relevant secretaries become involved when major policies are under consideration or when a crisis develops. Congress can use its power over legislation and financial measures to influence US policy in Northeast Asia. Congressional hearings are also relevant in this context. While Congress plays a role in relation to the whole range of US policies, it is often the forum where issues of human rights and democracy are given a particular emphasis. This situation reflects the general sentiments of the American people. On specific issues, particular interest groups (whether economic or more generally political in nature) can attempt to lobby Congress and also the executive branch.

Turning next to China, we find that its objectives in Northeast Asia are broadly political-strategic and economic in nature. China puts a lot of emphasis on maintaining its territorial integrity and has a more traditional view of sovereignty. It resists outside interference. Maintaining territorial integrity means that China is sensitive to any claims for "self-determination" in outlying regions such as Tibet or Xinjiang (northwest China). It also puts much emphasis on recovering Taiwan, as we shall see below. China attempts to influence developments in neighboring areas that are relevant to its own security. The Korean peninsula is a good example. Extending beyond Northeast Asia, China sees mainland Southeast Asia (Indochina, Thailand, Burma) in a similar light. Developments in South Asia, Central Asia, and Russia also have a bearing on China's security, as do the positions adopted by the United States and Japan.

In the economic sphere China emphasizes its goal of modernization. This in turn provides a means of achieving economic development and enhancing the welfare of its large population. Simply ensuring that the basic needs of such a large population are met is a daunting task. Failure to achieve these goals could bring suffering to untold millions and also lead to political instability. China justifies its authoritarian political system on the grounds that this is the best means of ensuring stability and meeting the needs of the population. The development of international trade and the encouragement of foreign investment are seen as facilitating economic modernization. Access to Western technology is also important.

In relation to its political-strategic objectives, China employs both military and more broadly political strategies. It has a large defense force, of about 2,255,000 in 2006 (IISS 2006:264). It has some capacity to intervene in neighboring areas. The technological modernization of the defense force will increase China's capacity for regional influence. China is also a nuclear power, with a small force of intercontinental and intermediate-range ballistic missiles and one nuclear-armed submarine (IISS 2006:264). Alliances in a formal sense do not feature in Chinese strategy. China attempts to exert influence through political means in the areas that are of particular concern for its security. Military forces play some role in enhancing the use of diplomatic means, but the strategy is more broadly based. An expanding economy also adds to China's weight in this respect. In the pursuit of economic modernization, China has followed a liberalizing strategy in its external relations. Barriers to foreign involvement in the Chinese economy have been reduced, and this process was taken further with Chinese entry into the World Trade Organization in 2001.

While China is clearly influenced by the positions adopted by the United States and Japan as the two other major powers in the region, and by developments in the areas adjoining its own territory, there are also important domestic influences. As indicated, the international objectives adopted by China are partly a means of dealing with important domestic issues. More broadly, one can see tensions between important elements in Chinese politics in relation to China's international role. On the one hand, a more conservative element tends to be more "nationalistic" and inward-looking. It is more likely to espouse the traditional symbols of communism in Chinese foreign policy. The other and dominant group is more "moderate" and emphasizes the ways in which the external world can assist China's modernization. There is always scope for the balance between these two tendencies to shift depending on both external and domestic circumstances.

Japan's situation is different again as compared with the other two major powers. Its objectives cover political-strategic and economic aspects. Influenced by the "peace constitution" of 1947, Japan emphasizes "self-defense" rather than national security as more traditionally conceived. It gives particular attention to its relationship with the United States and to the situation in neighboring parts of Northeast Asia: China, Taiwan, Korea, and Pacific Russia. Recent debate in Japan has focused on issues concerning its broader international role. Should the United States relationship remain central, or should there be a move toward a more clear-cut independence? Should the peace constitution be modified as a factor in Japan's international orientation? Should there be a stronger regional role? What role should Japan play in the United Nations? Economically, Japan seeks to maintain its position as an economic superpower, second only to the United States. In more recent years, however, Japan's situation has been complicated by a slowdown in its economy. Dealing with this situation and its international ramifications has been an important objective.

In terms of strategy, Japan's approach to political-security issues has emphasized the importance of the US relationship while also gradually expanding its own security role. Japan has taken a cautious approach to cultivating relations with neighboring countries such as China, South Korea, and Russia. This is partly because those countries in turn are cautious about Japan as a result of their wartime and other historical experiences. Japan has sought to "multilateralize" its regional involvement to some extent through groupings such as APEC and the ASEAN Regional Forum (ARF). However, the multilateral context has provided another dimension to that involvement rather than substituting for bilateral relationships, particularly the US relationship. In terms of economic strategy, Japan has operated at a number of levels. At the global level, it has sought to pursue its goals through the Group of Seven (Group of Eight if Russia is included). Given the significance of the United States to the Japanese economy, the bilateral relationship is also very important. Bilateral relations with China, South Korea, and Taiwan (at an "unofficial" level for the latter) also play a role in Japanese economic strategy. A multilateral forum such as APEC is of some significance, but generally less so than the bilateral relationships.

Factors influencing Japan's role in Northeast Asia are both external and domestic. In the former category, the relationship with the United States is of particular importance, but developments affecting other regional countries also have an impact. Economic changes within the broader Asia Pacific (such as the Asian economic crisis of 1997) are directly relevant to Japan's economic situation. In 2005, 22.6 percent of Japan's exports went to the United States, and 46.7 percent went to East Asia; 12.4 percent of Japan's imports were from the United States, and 42.3 percent from East Asia.[2] In the same year, 26.7 percent of Japan's foreign investment went to the United States; 35.0 percent went to East Asia, with China, Thailand, Hong Kong, and South Korea as the leading recipients (in order).[3] In terms of the debate about Japan's future direction, the different options are not well reflected in the system of political parties. The Liberal Democratic Party has traditionally been dominant, but in the post–Cold War era this party has mostly governed as part of coalitions. The bureaucracy and interest groups have a strong influence in the political process. Going beyond these political structures, the clearest choice has been between a nationalist right (favoring an assertive independence) and a pacifist left (favoring the values underlying the peace constitution). The middle and generally dominant position, as articulated by various governments, has supported an expanded international role for Japan, but in the context of continued close ties with the United States. Dealing with Japan's economic problems has been difficult because of the lack of clear policy choices in the system and the way in which vested interests are able to exercise influence. This is sometimes referred to as "immobilism."

Relationships Among the United States, China, and Japan

It is clear from the above discussion of objectives and strategies that each major power in Northeast Asia gives particular attention to its relationship with the other two powers. The relationships between the United States and China, the United States and Japan, and China and Japan provide an important structural element in the international politics of the region. However, the situation should not be seen simply in terms of three bilateral relationships. There is a triangular dimension as well. The relationship between the United

States and China is important also to Japan. The relationship between the United States and Japan affects China. Likewise, the relationship between China and Japan is relevant to the United States.

The relationship between the United States and China might be seen as the most difficult of the major power relationships in the region. From the US perspective, China is important for political-strategic, economic, and human rights reasons. In political-strategic terms, China is important as the "rising power" of the region. For the United States, as for other powers, there is the issue of how to respond to China's growing strength. In general, the US debate about China has been framed in terms of "containment versus engagement." Should China be treated as an adversary or as a partner with which the United States has many interests in common? China has important influence in a number of situations in adjoining areas: Korea, mainland Southeast Asia, Central Asia. It is a factor related to developments in South Asia. There is also the issue of Taiwan; the United States, although having diplomatic relations with the People's Republic, also has strong "unofficial relations" with Taiwan and is committed to a peaceful solution (see "The Taiwan Issue" on p. 172 for more details). In economic terms, China is important to the United States as a trading partner and as a destination for investment. From 2000 to 2005, exports to China grew from 2.1 to 4.6 percent of the US total; more strikingly, imports from China over the same period increased from 8.2 to 14.6 percent of the US total.[4] Between 1995 and 2004, US-contracted direct investment in China rose from US\$7.47 billion to US\$12.17 billion; in percentage terms over the same period, there was a slight decline in the US share of contracted investment in China, from 8.2 to 7.93 percent.[5] From the perspective of its liberal democratic ideology, the United States also seeks to influence the human rights situation in China, particularly political freedoms (treatment of dissidents, freedom of religious expression, and so on).

In practice, all US administrations in the post–Cold War era have maintained a certain level of engagement with China. Nevertheless, there can be differences of emphasis between administrations, and also within the course of an administration. An early shock for the United States was the massacre of prodemocracy supporters in Tiananmen Square in Beijing in June 1989. Despite official condemnation of this event by the United States, the relationship with China soon resumed, due to strong pragmatic interests. Similarly, though the George W. Bush administration indicated in early 2001 that the United States would treat China as at least a potential adversary, in practice there has been significant cooperation between the two countries, such as China's espoused support for the US-led "war on terrorism" following the events of September 11, 2001. Nevertheless the more assertive US posture that has resulted from the US campaign against terrorism could also lead to tensions with China.

From China's perspective, there are important political-strategic and economic interests involved in its relationship with the United States. The United

States plays a key role in Northeast Asia, and China wants to ensure that US policies are not detrimental to Chinese interests. In terms of China's modernization, the United States plays a crucial role in trade, investment, and access to technology. In 2005 the United States took 21.4 percent of China's exports and provided 7.4 percent of China's imports; the United States was the most important destination for Chinese exports and held fourth place for imports.[6] Figures for US investment in China have already been given, with the United States accounting most recently for about 8 percent of foreign investment in that country. The United States is the most important destination for Chinese exports, and was a key player in China's admission to the World Trade Organization in 2001. More conservative elements in China tend to be hostile to the United States, but in practice the views of moderates, with an emphasis on the benefits of cooperation, have prevailed. Setbacks, such as the accidental US bombing of the Chinese embassy in Belgrade during the Kosovo war in 1999, have not been sufficient to derail the relationship.

While Sino-American relations have been central to international politics in Northeast Asia in the post–Cold War era, important developments have also occurred in the relationship between the United States and Japan. These developments have been affected by the debates about Japan's international role and by reconsiderations of the future international role of the United States. The US-Japanese alliance has remained a central feature of the international politics of the region, but the substance of the relationship has changed in some respects. It is useful to focus on the political-strategic aspects of the relationship in the first instance, and then move to the economic aspects.

At the political-strategic level, there has been strong pressure from the United States for Japan to assume a more prominent security role. This pressure has been fueled by US resentment that Japan has been too much of a "free rider" on the United States for defense. At the same time, in terms of the domestic debate in Japan, one cannot assume that an enhanced Japanese security role would simply mean the continuation of the relationship as before, but with Japan assuming a greater share of the burden of defense. A more prominent Japanese security role could also encourage greater independence of Japan from the United States. A major development was the signing of a joint security declaration by President Bill Clinton and Prime Minister Ryutaro Hashimoto in April 1996. This led in 1997 to revised US-Japanese defense guidelines and the passage of implementing legislation by Japan in 1999. While Japan's defense role had previously focused on the defense of Japan itself, the declaration indicated that this role would expand to include "situations in areas surrounding Japan." This move was viewed with both suspicion and resentment by the Chinese government, which questioned whether Japan was thus committing itself to the defense of Taiwan from a PRC takeover. During the post–Cold War era, Japan's peacekeeping role has gradually expanded, with involvement in situations such as Cambodia, Mozambique, East Timor, and Iraq. Generally, Japanese peacekeeping forces have been confined to noncombat roles. In the US-led war in Afghanistan from late 2001, Japan sent naval vessels to the Indian Ocean to play a support role. After the Iraq War of 2003, Japan agreed to send some of its Self-Defense Force personnel to assist in Iraqi reconstruction, even though there was some risk of hostile activity (*The Economist* 2003).

The role of US bases in Japan has occasioned some controversy. Japan plays host to about 38,000 US military personnel, and is thus crucial to the forward US deployment in Asia Pacific. At the same time, when there are domestic pressures for Japan to assume a more independent role, the presence of US forces suggests that Japan is subordinate to the United States. The US presence is most controversial in Okinawa, where about 60 percent of US forces are stationed. With Okinawa having only a small land area, the US bases are very intrusive. In addition, there is local resentment because of the behavior of some US personnel. There have been a number of rape cases involving US servicemen. Japanese governments have opposed moving the bases to the Japanese home islands, largely because this would make the US presence there (and the US relationship more generally) more controversial.

Economic issues have also been significant in the relationship between the United States and Japan. Given that the balance of trade invariably favors Japan, this has sometimes caused resentment in the United States, where it has been argued that many aspects of the Japanese market are unnecessarily restrictive. The role of the United States as the world's leading debtor, and the role of Japan as the leading lender, can also cause resentment. In the late 1990s, Japan's economic malaise became a major concern, signaled by static or negative growth and an inability to achieve effective reform. The United States has pressured Japan to deal with several of these issues, favoring such goals as greater market access and neoliberal reform. The Japanese government has resisted specific targets for market access. The problem with achieving economic reforms lies in the many domestic groups who have vested interests in the existing system. The opposition of these groups means that reforms are often blocked or are only minor in scope. At a more general level, there is also resistance to change imposed from outside Japan. Since the United States and Japan are both economic superpowers (the European Union being the third), any difficulties in their economic relationship have an adverse effect not just regionally but also globally. With Japan returning to moderate rates of economic growth in recent years, US pressure for greater liberalization in the Japanese economy has eased to some extent.

The third major bilateral relationship in Northeast Asia is that between China and Japan, a relationship that has a strong historical and cultural dimension. Essentially, China sees itself as the superior civilization from which Japan was the offshoot; China resents Japan's imperialist depredations from the late nineteenth century through to the Pacific War. Japan sees China as a less successful society that has been much more economically backward during the modern era. China wants to gain from economic ties with Japan, while also ensuring that Japan will not challenge China's own rise to power within the region. Japan, too, sees benefits deriving from trade and investment with China. At the same time, there is concern that some Chinese imports might threaten certain sectors of the Japanese economy (agriculture, for example). In terms of the political-strategic relationship, the issue for Japan is whether it should accommodate China's rise and therefore focus on cooperation, or whether it should attempt to contain China. The latter course would involve developing at least a tacit alignment with other powers in the region that might also have an interest in restraining China, including Taiwan. This course would also normally include strengthening the relationship with the United States. However, the nationalist right in Japan also tends to be critical of China, while at the same time asserting independence from the United States.

In each of these three major bilateral relationships in Northeast Asia, it is important to consider the way in which the third power is relevant. Japan is relevant to Sino-American relations in a number of ways. The United States looks to Japan to support US strategy in relation to China. The United States needs to ensure that its China policy is not perceived as giving China a higher priority than Japan. George W. Bush claimed that this is what occurred under the Clinton administration. In Bush's view, Japan, as a US ally, should be assigned a higher priority. From China's perspective, it might be assumed that there is an interest in detaching Japan from the United States. It could be argued that this would weaken US engagement in the region. However, a more assertive Japanese posture is associated with the nationalist right in Japan, and such a development could thus be contrary to Chinese interests. In practice, therefore, China could have an interest in a continuation of the US-Japanese alliance as a means of restraining Japan.

This last point makes clear the way in which the relationship between the United States and Japan is relevant to China. Clearly there is scope for considerable ambiguity in China's attitude. The remaining point about the "triangle" is the way in which the United States is affected by the relationship between China and Japan. Various possibilities suggest themselves. One would be an "Asia for the Asians" approach based on close Sino-Japanese cooperation. In general, this is unlikely to occur, although there may be specific issues (in relation to Korea, for example) on which China and Japan might favor a similar approach in opposition to the course being advocated by the United States. In the case of intense Sino-Japanese hostility, the United States is more likely to align with Japan as an ally rather than with China. There is also the possibility that the United States could act as a "peacemaker" in such a situation. The most likely situation is that there will be continuing multipolarity and a certain fluidity in major power relationships in Northeast Asia. The US alignment with Japan will continue, but with Japan becoming increasingly more independent. The relationships of both powers with China will be problematic, but with elements of both cooperation and tension.

Russia and Its Relationships

Russia's role in Northeast Asia during the post–Cold War era has been less significant than that of the Soviet Union during the Cold War. Nevertheless, Russia is a factor in the international politics of this region, and the key dimensions of its role, and its relationships with China, Japan, and the United States, should be considered.

Russia has both geopolitical and economic interests in Northeast Asia. These interests manifest themselves both at a general level and in terms of protecting the position of the Russian Far East (also known as Pacific Russia). At a geopolitical level, Russia wishes to maintain its status as one of the major powers of Northeast Asia. It opposes domination of the region by any one power, and prefers multipolarity. Economically, Russia sees advantages for itself in developing further its ties with China, Japan, and South Korea.

Unlike the United States, Russia has a territorial presence in Northeast Asia, focusing on the Russian Far East. The Russian Far East is sparsely inhabited (about 7 million people in 2002), large in area (2.4 million square miles, or 6.2 million square kilometers), and inhospitable. Khabarovsk is the major city, with Vladivostok the main port. The region is resource-rich, but underdeveloped. Russia would like to see further economic development take place in the region. At the same time, there are concerns about vulnerability, given the location of the Russian Far East in such a strategically sensitive area. Despite these concerns, there has been a decline in Russia's military presence in the region. There have been reductions in ground forces in the Far Eastern Military District and, even more so, in the naval forces making up the Pacific Fleet; Vladivostok has become well known for its rotting ships. This decline means that Russia is not only less able to protect the Russian Far East, but also less influential in the affairs of Northeast Asia more generally.

Russia has significant relationships with all three of the major powers in Northeast Asia. In the case of China, there has been speculation from time to time about the development of a "strategic partnership" between the two countries. However, such a development assumes that Russia and China have a common interest in aligning against Western countries, and the United States in particular. While there have been difficult periods for both Russia and China in their relations with the United States since the 1990s, the situation has never reached the point where Russia and China have sought to establish an anti-Western alignment. There is scope for both conflict and cooperation in some of the areas where Russia and China are both involved. The border issue has been largely quiescent, with a demilitarization agreement in 1996 and some agreements on delimitation during the 1990s. Russian and Chinese interests in

Central Asia have been largely complementary, with both powers opposed to radical Islamic movements. China is Russia's most important trading partner in Asia Pacific, and a major customer for Russian weapons sales.

Russia's relationship with Japan has been traditionally antagonistic, and this situation has changed only gradually during the post–Cold War era. Russia would like to develop its trading relationship with Japan and to attract Japanese investment. Such investment would be particularly helpful for the economic development of the Russian Far East. A particular obstacle in the way of improving Russo-Japanese relations is the Japanese insistence that the four southernmost islands of the Kuril chain be returned to Japan. Japan refers to these four islands as the Northern Territories (the Soviet Union occupied the whole of the Kurils in 1945). For nationalist reasons, including political pressures from the Russian Far East, Russia is reluctant to concede on this issue. However, Japan is unlikely to respond warmly to Russian overtures for improving the general relationship until the specific issue of the Northern Territories is dealt with to its satisfaction.

Russia's relationship with the United States in Northeast Asia is only a minor aspect of the overall Russo-American relationship. However, Russia does have some influence in Northeast Asia, and this can have a bearing on the way in which the United States pursues its objectives. Similarly, Russia wishes to ensure that the United States does not behave in a way contrary to Russian interests. Russia opposes US domination of Northeast Asia. It does not wish to see the US-Japanese or US-Chinese relationships directed against Russia's position. It wishes to have an influence in Korea, where the United States is a major factor. Russia is opposed to US plans for developing missile defense. The Russian argument is that such a development, even though not ostensibly directed against Russia itself, would undermine the ability of its existing military forces to maintain a deterrent.

The Taiwan Issue

Taiwan is one of the major points of tension in the contemporary international politics of Northeast Asia. While the Sino-American rapprochement of 1972 had led subsequently to the formalizing of relations between the People's Republic of China and the United States, the Taiwan issue itself was not resolved. The United States maintained "unofficial" relations with Taiwan, including continued arms sales. The PRC remained committed to reunifying Taiwan with the mainland. China's rhetoric shifted from "liberation" to "peaceful reunification," but the goal remained the same. In 1984, China declared that the "one country, two systems" model proposed for Hong Kong could also apply to Taiwan. Fearing a trap, Taiwan sought to minimize contact with the mainland. The communist authorities were generally castigated as "bandits."

During the post–Cold War era, there have been significant changes relating to the Taiwan issue. China has maintained its "peaceful reunification" approach. At the same time, it has indicated its unwillingness to renounce the use of force. From China's perspective, force would be an option if Taiwan were to declare independence or be seen as dealing with the reunification issue too slowly. The Chinese codified this position in an antisecession law of March 2005 that specifically declares that China will attack Taiwan militarily if needed to prevent Taiwan's secession. The "one country, two systems" model remains the preferred solution for the PRC. This could include Taiwan retaining its own military forces. Because China does not recognize the government of Taiwan in any sense (even as a provincial government), its preference for dealing with the issue has been on the basis of party-to-party talks—between the Chinese Communists and Chinese Nationalists (Kuomintang), or between a combination of Taiwanese parties—rather than through bilateral talks between governments.

Taiwan's own position has also changed quite significantly during the post–Cold War period. While continuing to describe itself as the "Republic of China" and asserting its sovereignty as a state, Taiwan abandoned any claim to govern the mainland. Its guidelines for national unification, in March 1991, foresaw a number of phases in dealing with the reunification issue. These would begin with people-to-people contacts, the renunciation of the use of force by the PRC, and the ending of the PRC's restrictions on Taiwan's international role. Later there would be economic reforms and democratization in the PRC. Government-to-government contacts and talks would not occur until the final phase. In 1999, President Lee Teng-hui spoke of the PRC-Taiwan relationship as a "special state-to-state relationship." This underlined Taiwan's position that the relationship was between independent governments. In March 2000, Chen Shui-bian, from the pro-independence Democratic Progressive Party, was elected as president. This raised fears that there would be an overt push toward independence. However, in his inauguration speech of May 2000, Chen said his policy would be based on "five nos": no declaration of independence, no referendum on independence, no change in Taiwan's title, no reference to the "state-to-state" formula in the constitution, and no change in the guidelines for national unification.

The process of democratization in Taiwan has had an important impact on the reunification issue. Up to the late 1980s, Taiwan had been under the authoritarian rule of the Kuomintang, first under Chiang Kai-shek, who died in 1975, and then under his son Chiang Ching-kuo, who ruled from 1975 to 1988. In Taiwan there was tension between the mainlanders, who came to the island in the late 1940s, and the Taiwanese. While the authoritarian system prevailed, these tensions were suppressed. In 1988, Lee Teng-hui became president; in 1996 he was confirmed in office in the first fully democratic presidential election. Lee was from the Kuomintang, but was also a native-born Taiwanese. Chen Shui-bian's election in 2000 not only confirmed democratization, but also indicated the strength of Taiwanese sentiment in favor of at least de facto independence. As a democratic political system, Taiwan also had greater international legitimacy.

After Chen's narrow win in the presidential elections of March 2004, he continued to push for measures that would give a stronger legal basis to Taiwan's de facto independence. In January 2006, he announced a plan for a referendum on a new constitution in 2007 with this aim in mind. A strong measure of consensus would be necessary to proceed in this direction. Opinion in Taiwan is largely divided between those supporting Chen's stance and those preferring the stability of the status quo.

While these political changes were occurring in Taiwan, there were also increasing nonofficial links between China and Taiwan. Until the late 1980s, Taiwan had barred visits to the mainland, and economic contacts were also forbidden. After this time, the situation changed dramatically. In terms of people-to-people links, there were 16 million visits from Taiwan to the mainland in the period 1987–1999.[7] As there were no direct travel links between China and the mainland, visitors traveled through third ports, most commonly Hong Kong. The development of economic links was such that by the end of the 1990s, China (including Hong Kong) had become Taiwan's third most important trading partner after the United States and Japan, and its second most important destination for exports after the United States. In 2004, China (including Hong Kong) took 31.6 percent of Taiwan's exports, and was Taiwan's leading export destination. From China's perspective, Taiwan in 2005 was its third most important source of imports (11.3 percent); in 2004, Taiwan was the sixth most important source of foreign investment in China.[8] Overall, this situation means that both Taiwan and China have a very strong interest in maintaining a stable relationship. Though China's bargaining power may be stronger than Taiwan's, China would also be adversely affected (although on a smaller scale than would Taiwan) if the economic relationship with Taiwan were damaged.

In light of these recent developments relating to the Taiwan issue, what strategies are available to the two sides to advance their respective positions? The difficulties for the PRC in using economic pressures against Taiwan have been indicated. There is more reliance on political pressures of various kinds. These include direct political pressures on Taiwan to indicate the costs of any moves toward overt independence. The antisecession law of March 2005 states that China will use military force in certain circumstances. At an international level, the PRC acts to isolate Taiwan. China refuses to have diplomatic relations with any country that recognizes Taiwan as a state. Since China is of much greater significance than Taiwan, most countries do not have official diplomatic relations with Taiwan. China is similarly insistent on excluding Taiwan from the United Nations. Direct military action against Taiwan would be difficult, and not only because the United States would be likely to come to Taiwan's assistance in such circumstances. Taiwan's mountainous terrain and extensive mud flats on the west coast would make invasion difficult, quite apart from the

Home-ported in Japan, the US Navy's only permanently forward-deployed aircraft carrier was moved into the Taiwan Strait following China's decision to conduct live-fire war games off the coast of Taiwan following Taiwan's first direct presidential elections in March 1996.

deterrent capacity of Taiwan's armed forces. Military pressure, such as the missile tests and exercises carried out in 1996, would be more likely. A blockade of Taiwan's ports would be another possibility, although again China would have to contend with countermeasures from Taiwan and possibly the United States. A combination of political and military pressures on Taiwan could have damaging psychological and economic effects.

Taiwan's strategy for protecting its position has various dimensions. Having a strong economy is one way of bolstering international support. As noted previously, democratization has also strengthened Taiwan's international legitimacy. Taiwan's military forces assist its defensive strategy. However, unlike China, Taiwan does not have nuclear weapons. China's military modernization is also leading to a bigger gap between its armed forces and Taiwan's. This increases Taiwan's dependence on the United States for the supply of more advanced equipment and for actual assistance in the event of certain scenarios.

The US position toward Taiwan has generally been characterized as one of "strategic ambiguity." The aim has been to maintain relations with the PRC while at the same time signaling the dire consequences if military action were taken against Taiwan. The US interest is to deal with the issue peacefully. While the United States thus gives tacit support to Taiwan, it does not wish to do this in such a way that Taiwan will move to declare independence openly. Such a move by Taiwan would clearly lead to a major crisis, with consequences for the United States as well as for China and Taiwan. There have been developments during the George W. Bush administration indicating that the United States will give stronger support to Taiwan than was previously the case. In April 2001, Bush said that the United States would do "whatever it took" to defend Taiwan. US defense links with Taiwan have also become stronger.

In the near future, the most likely course for the Taiwan issue is a continuation of the status quo. The key parties have too much to lose if major conflict develops. Nevertheless, one can expect China to resist strongly any moves by Taiwan toward a more overt independence. Nationalist sentiment in China in relation to this issue is very strong. At the same time, the people of Taiwan clearly do not wish to unify with China; they prefer at least the continuation of the status quo and many support open independence. The US interest lies essentially in a continuation of the status quo, but its involvement is only one factor influencing the situation. One problem in dealing with the situation is that Taiwan and China have different understandings of "one China." For China, the concept means the PRC as a legal entity. Reunification would mean Taiwan accepting its position as a province of the PRC. Taiwan might be able to accept "one China" in the sense of "one Chinese nation." However, short of major political change in China, Taiwan's preference is to recognize the PRC and Taiwan as two separate states.

Conflict on the Korean Peninsula

Another major point of conflict in Northeast Asia is the Korean peninsula. In the period since the Korean War, the two Korean states have developed in completely different directions (for further details, see Chapter 4). By the end of the 1980s, South Korea (Republic of Korea) had emerged from its earlier authoritarianism and was undergoing democratization. This was signaled most directly in the election of Roh Tae Woo as president in 1987, and again by the election in 1997 of Kim Dae Jung, who had been an opposition leader in the 1970s and 1980s and had survived several attempts made on his life. Roh Tae Woo embarked on a policy of Nordpolitik (Northern policy), designed to broaden South Korea's international links and to isolate North Korea. The most notable feature of the policy was the establishment of diplomatic links with communist countries, beginning with Eastern Europe in the late 1980s and then extending to the Soviet Union in 1990 and China in 1992.

Whereas South Korea was known as one of the "tigers" of economic development in East Asia, North Korea (Democratic People's Republic of Korea) remained very much a third world country under authoritarian communist, and indeed Stalinist, rule. The North Korean political system featured a cult of personality centered on its leader, Kim Il Sung, until his death in 1994, and then on his son, Kim Jong Il. Another characteristic was the emphasis on "self-reliance" as embodied in the term *juche*. However, this approach did not facilitate economic development in North Korea. Its weakness in relation to South Korea made North Korea more vulnerable. Self-reliance did not mean isolationism as such. North Korea's major international links were with the Soviet Union and China as the two major communist powers. The Sino-Soviet conflict had meant that there was some competition between the two powers for influence in North Korea. However, that conflict had come to an end, in 1989, at the very time that communism was collapsing in Eastern Europe; by 1991 the Soviet Union itself had disintegrated. While China remained a communist power, the direction of its development was very different from that of North Korea. North Korea has become increasingly isolated since 1991. Table 6.2 presents the underlying disparities between North and South Korea.

Although North Korea has more military personnel than South Korea, the latter's forces are more technologically advanced. South Korea also receives support from 30,983 US military personnel (2006), with a reduction of several thousands having occurred during the course of the George W. Bush administration. Nevertheless, North Korea's forces are structured in such a way as to inflict maximum damage on South Korea in the event of conflict.

It is misleading to refer to "the Korean issue," as some do, as if it consisted of just one issue. Since the 1990s there have been at least three crucial issues facing the Korean peninsula. One of these issues is reunification. Another is North Korea's role as a "problem state." A third issue concerns North Korea's position in relation to weapons of mass destruction. On the first issue, both Korean states are committed to reunification in principle. This is understandable given Korea's long tradition as a unified political entity. However, they differ on what reunification should entail and how it should be achieved. North Korea wishes to see reunification take the form of a confederation to be known as the

Table 6.2 North and South Korea Compared

	South Korea	North Korea
Population (2006)	48.6 million	22.9 million
GDP	817.0 billion (2005)	22.0 billion (2004 estimate)
Per capita GDP (US$)	16,791 (2005)	969 (2004)
Defense spending (US$, 2004)	16.4 billion	1.8 billion (defense budget, estimate)
Defense spending as percentage of GDP (2004)	2.4	12.3
Armed forces personnel (2006)	687,700	1.1 million

Source: International Institute for Strategic Studies 2006.
Note: Figures for defense spending as a percentage of GDP for North Korea calculated by the author.

"Democratic Confederal Republic of Koryo." The two existing political systems would be preserved and unity would be minimal and largely symbolic. Confederation would enable most of the existing features of the North Korean system to be preserved. The South Korean approach favors a more complete integration. Although a number of phases would be involved, the ultimate goal is to have an all-Korean government chosen by democratic elections. A deterrent for South Korea in moving too quickly on reunification (quite apart from the problem of securing agreement) is North Korea's economic backwardness and its very different political system. Korean unification would be a much more difficult task than was German unification, as the disparities between the Koreas dwarf those that existed between the two German states, and because North Korea is far more isolated than East Germany ever was.

This situation highlights the way in which North Korea is generally a "problem state" in ways that challenge reunification, but that are in many ways more pressing. North Korea's parlous economic situation has deleterious consequences for its own population, as well as implications for South Korea and the region. North Korea is in economic decline, with its gross national product at the turn of the twenty-first century estimated at one-half to two-thirds its 1990 level. Estimates for the number of people killed due to famine vary, from a cautious 600,000 to 1 million (1995–2000) (Goodkind and West 2001:220), to as high as 3.5 million (cited in Noland, Robinson, and Tao 2001:741). North Korea has failed its people economically, and the elite emphasize preserving their own position. This involves not just political repression, but provocative behavior designed to win concessions (both political and economic) from states that are concerned about the implications of a North Korean collapse. While North Korea appears to have moved on from the terrorist actions of the 1970s and 1980s, there have been various incidents since, involving infiltration into South Korea from North Korean submarines and fishing boats.[9]

Part of North Korea's provocative behavior concerns its policy toward weapons of mass destruction. Although North Korea had become a signatory to the Nuclear Nonproliferation Treaty in 1985, by the early 1990s the issue of inspections of its nuclear facilities by the International Atomic Energy Agency (IAEA) had still not been resolved. In 1994 a crisis arose when it became clear that plutonium being reprocessed from an existing North Korean reactor could be used for nuclear weapons. In October 1994 a framework agreement was concluded between North Korea and the United States whereby the former would forego development of its own nuclear plants in return for assistance to meet its energy requirements. The Korean Peninsula Energy Development Organization was established, with the task of building two light water reactors for North Korea by 2003. Most of the finance came from South Korea (70 percent), with Japan also assisting (20 percent). The United States would supply crude oil on an interim basis until the new reactors were completed. Completion of the new energy infrastructure would be accompanied by ongoing IAEA inspections.

During this period, the North Korean leadership also acted provocatively in developing missiles. From North Korea's perspective, missile development enhanced its bargaining power. Though the missiles would not necessarily carry nuclear weapons, they could do so in the event of North Korea acquiring such weapons. During the 1980s, North Korea developed a medium-range ballistic missile, known as the No Dong, and in 1998 test-fired the Taepo Dong 1 over Japan. The Taepo Dong 1 is capable of reaching Hawaii and Alaska, and research continues on the Taepo Dong 2, which could reach the western coast of the United States.

The election of Kim Dae Jung as South Korean president in 1997 had a major impact on the situation on the Korean peninsula. Kim was more committed to reconciliation with North Korea than any previous South Korean leader had been, and hoped that his "Sunshine" policy would induce North Korea to behave less aggressively and pave the way for a smoother reunification process. Kim's policy was designed to build bridges with North Korea as a means of improving the economic situation there, and to promote people-to-people links. Kim Dae Jung's visit to Pyongyang in June 2000 symbolized the new policy. The United States was supportive, through the Clinton administration, as were the neighboring powers of China, Japan, and Russia.

When George W. Bush took office, his administration rejected the assumptions behind the "Sunshine" policy and instead advocated a more confrontational approach with North Korea. As indicated in his "axis of evil" speech of February 2002, Bush was particularly concerned about North Korea's position in relation to weapons of mass destruction. Engagement with North Korea would continue, but any assistance would be based on North Korea's "good behavior." Provocative behavior could lead to penalties, including the use of military options.

The situation concerning North Korea became more complex in late 2002, when it became clear that Pyongyang was developing nuclear weapons. This might have been in response to its being included among the "rogue states" listed in Bush's "axis of evil" speech. An additional factor was that North Korea believed that the United States had not lived up to its commitments under the framework agreement. James Kelly, US assistant secretary of state for East Asian and Pacific affairs, highlighted the situation, in his statement in early October 2002, that the United States had evidence of a North Korean uranium enrichment program. In January 2003, North Korea announced its withdrawal from the Nuclear Nonproliferation Treaty. The United States wanted to deal with this situation through multilateral negotiations involving the other Northeast Asian states; North Korea wanted direct negotiations with the United States alone. South Korea, Japan, and China, while being concerned about the acquisition of nuclear weapons by North Korea, generally favored a conciliatory approach. Following presidential elections in December 2002, Roh Moo Hyun emerged as the new leader of South Korea, with an even stronger commitment to engagement with the north than had been the case under Kim Dae Jung.

With China taking the lead, six-party talks on the North Korean nuclear issue commenced in August 2003, involving the two Koreas, the United States, China, Japan, and Russia. The talks met the US requirement for a multilateral format, although it was also possible for the United States and North Korea to meet directly within this context. Some progress was apparent by September 2005, with the announcement that North Korea would abandon existing nuclear weapons and nuclear weapons facilities, while the United States would declare it had no nuclear weapons in South Korea and no intention to attack North Korea. Both North Korea and the United States would work toward a normalization of relations. The issue of a light water reactor for North Korea was left unresolved. The agreement provided a framework for proceeding, but issues of implementation still had to be dealt with. North Korea did not say when its declaration would take effect, whereas the United States would want complete verification of nuclear disarmament before implementing its side of the bargain. This stalemated situation was a factor in North Korea's test launching of Taepo Dong 2 missiles in the Sea of Japan in July 2006, and its nuclear test in October 2006. In February 2007 the United States agreed to provide emergency energy assistance to North Korea in return for the latter's freezing of plutonium production at its Yongbyon nuclear plant and allowing international inspectors to verify this. These steps were essentially "initial actions" to enable negotiations toward a comprehensive agreement to continue.

Southeast Asia

While Northeast Asia is the subregion of Asia Pacific that receives the most attention in global terms, Southeast Asia also warrants consideration. The major powers, which relate to each other directly in Northeast Asia, are also involved in Southeast Asia. Indonesia has global significance as having the highest Muslim population of any country in the world.

Major Features

While the major powers are involved in Southeast Asia, their role is less central than in Northeast Asia. Although it would be an oversimplification to explain the dynamics of international politics in Northeast Asia in terms of the US-Chinese-Japanese triangle, the relationships of the three powers are more important than any other single feature. In Southeast Asia the three powers have a strong influence without necessarily being dominant. They are one influence among several. Another difference between the two subregions is that the state system is more fragile in Southeast Asia than in Northeast Asia. In Northeast Asia, China, Japan, and Korea are based on civilizations that count their history in terms of millennia. Despite the China-Taiwan and Korean conflicts, Chinese and Koreans, irrespective of their political allegiances, generally relate to the long history of their civilizations. In Southeast Asia, while there are some states that are based on prior entities with long histories, generally the impact of the colonial era on current ways of organizing the region has been greater. Significant elements in Southeast Asia do not identify with the existing states and indeed might be in opposition to them. A third difference is that regionalism is far stronger in Southeast Asia than in Northeast Asia. While there is some low-level regionalism in Northeast Asia, and there is participation in groupings extending beyond the subregion (at both an Asia Pacific and an East Asian level), there is nothing to rival the Association of Southeast Asian Nations. This is because the major powers in Northeast Asia relate directly to each other and prefer to avoid the constraints of an organization simply for that region. The small number of states in Northeast Asia also means there is less need for a regional organization there. China would not agree to Taiwan's membership in such an organization. The larger number of states in Southeast Asia is a fourth area of difference between the two subregions. With East Timor's accession to independence in May 2002, the total number of states in Southeast Asia is eleven. The sheer number of states provides a layer of complexity in the international politics of the subregion. Even if we include the United States, Russia, and Taiwan, the number of states in Northeast Asia is only seven. The more states there are in a subregion, the more possibilities there are for interrelationships. There are also more possibilities for more localized patterns to emerge within the wider subregion.

State boundaries in Southeast Asia are largely a colonial legacy. With the exception of Thailand, which survived as an independent kingdom (known as Siam) during the colonial era, all the states of Southeast Asia are successor entities to the previous colonial territories, as discussed in Chapter 3. Within these early empires, the mandala system meant that power was concentrated at the administrative center. "Gray" zones existed in the areas between these centers of power. This helps to explain why the authority of Southeast Asian states, even though based on Western notions of sovereignty, might be weaker in outlying areas.

Given that the modern states of Southeast Asia are the successors to the colonial entities, their acceptance within their particular boundaries is not necessarily universal. Just as some groups regarded colonial rule as an imposition, so they view the postcolonial state as lacking in authority. This is particularly the case given the assumption underlying the modern state system that states derive their legitimacy from being "nation-states." That is, a legitimate state derives its authority from being based on a group having a shared culture and known as a "nation." Many groups within the existing Southeast Asian states claim to be separate nations and wish to form their own nation-states. This attitude has been encouraged in some cases by democratization. As long as authoritarian rule prevails, it is easier to repress groups who reject the legitimacy of a particular government. Groups who wish to secede and form their own states are more likely to come to the fore in a democratic environment. Post-1998 Indonesia is a good example, as will be discussed below. The southern Philippines is another situation where a particular group, in this case Muslims, has wished to constitute its own state. In Burma, where military rule has prevailed for much of the time since independence in 1948, the minority peoples have also fought for separate status. The legitimacy of a state can also be challenged by groups who want the state to be run along different lines. The aim might be a democratic system, as with the National League for Democracy in Burma, led by Aung San Suu Kyi. In Malaysia, some groups (notably Parti Islam Se-Malaysia) aim for an Islamic state; other groups (for example, the Democratic Action Party) aim for a system in which Malays would not have political dominance. Sometimes there can be conflicts in particular regions within a state, without secessionism being an aim. The conflicts might involve attempts to change the balance of power between the center and the region, or within the region. Many of the regional conflicts within Indonesia fall into this category.

There are numerous international consequences arising from the tensions between state and society in Southeast Asia. States are often preoccupied with conflicts within their own borders. Their writ does not necessarily run large. If the legitimacy of states is widely contested, then this will mean significant internal division and often result in weak government. In this situation governments find it more difficult to deal with international developments that affect their state. Weak governments will not be very effective in dealing with internal issues that can be internationally destabilizing or harmful, for example controlling drug trafficking or people smuggling. Where there are major conflicts within a state, neighboring countries can easily be affected. Refugees might move from one country to another. Groups in conflict with a government might try to win support from their neighbors. In fact, such groups often mount broadly based international campaigns to assist their cause. Secessionist groups will justify their struggles in the name of self-determination. Groups struggling for democracy, as in Burma, will claim the support of all people who support democratic values. Such campaigns can easily extend beyond a region and become global in scope.

A second major feature of international relations in Southeast Asia concerns the relationships to be found among the states of the subregion. No single power is clearly dominant in Southeast Asia, leading to complex, subregional power relations. With over 240 million people, Indonesia has the highest population, but there are four states in the 45–90 million range: Burma, the Philippines, Thailand, and Vietnam (see Table 6.3). Although smaller in population, both Malaysia and Singapore are economically significant. It is possible to discern subregional patterns within Southeast Asia. In maritime Southeast Asia, there is

Table 6.3 GDP and Population, Southeast Asian States

	GDP (US$, 2005)	Per Capita GDP (US$, 2005)	Population (2006)
Brunei	5.2 billion (2004)	14,250 (2004)	372,361
Burma (Myanmar)	69.0 billion (2004)	1,483 (2004)	46.9 million
Cambodia	5.4 billion	399	13.6 million
East Timor	355.0 million	378	1.0 million
Indonesia	277.0 billion	1,145	241.9 million
Laos	2.8 billion (2004)	455 (2004)	6.2 million
Malaysia	128.0 billion	5,339	23.9 million
Philippines	96.2 billion	1,095	87.8 million
Singapore	114.0 billion	25,862	4.4 million
Thailand	178.0 billion	2,279	64.1 million
Vietnam	52.2 billion	625	83.5 million

Sources: International Institute for Strategic Studies 2006. Data for GDP and for East Timor's per capita GDP from Australian Department of Foreign Affairs and Trade, "East Timor Fact Sheet," http://www.dfat.gov.au/geo/fs/timo.pdf (accessed August 1, 2006).

US secretary of state Condoleezza Rice at a meeting with the foreign ministers of ASEAN states at the thirty-ninth ASEAN ministerial meeting in Kuala Lumpur, July 2006.

a triangle consisting of Indonesia, Malaysia, and the Philippines. There are generally close relationships within this triangle, with Indonesia as the leading but not dominating state. Singapore, as a small but economically significant city-state, has important relationships with both Malaysia and Indonesia. These relationships are also shaped by Singapore's character as a predominantly Chinese society. Brunei, too, as a small but wealthy sultanate, puts a strong emphasis on its relationships with Malaysia and Indonesia. Both Singapore and Brunei feel some sense of threat from Malaysia in particular. There is a pattern of relationships involving Malaysia, Singapore, and Brunei, whereby the latter two look to each other for mutual support. Malaysia is not viewed as the "enemy," but there is a strong rivalry between Malaysia and Singapore, as well as a perception that Malaysia would prefer Brunei to be within its own federation.

In mainland Southeast Asia one can also see important patterns among the various states located there. Thailand has a pivotal role. In relation to the Thailand-Indochina complex, there has been a historical rivalry between Thailand and Vietnam. This rivalry can still exert an influence, as when the two states compete for influence in relation to Cambodia and Laos. In terms of the western part of mainland Southeast Asia, the relationship between Thailand and Burma is important. Again there is a historical rivalry at play here, although more recently Thailand has been more concerned about the spillover of internal conflicts in Burma into Thailand, and the resulting refugee flows into the latter. There are also concerns about drug trafficking from Burma. If Indochina itself were regarded as a distinct subsystem, Vietnam might be seen as the dominant power. However, as indicated, Thailand has a role in balancing Vietnam. China, with influence in both Cambodia and Laos, also fulfills that role.

Despite the various subregional patterns in Southeast Asia, there is no "balance of power" as such. There is some fluidity in interstate relations, and the prevailing patterns can change depending on the particular issue. These patterns manifest themselves at one level in the context of regionalism, through the Association of Southeast Asian Nations in particular. Regionalism is much more significant in Southeast Asia than in Northeast Asia, but how significant? During the Third Indochina War, there had been a balance of power in Southeast Asia centering on the relationship between ASEAN and Vietnam. Clearly this involved other elements, particularly the Sino-Soviet dimension and the role of the United States, but there was nonetheless a Southeast Asian dimension. Since the end of that conflict in 1991, there have been important issues about ASEAN's future direction to consider. One emphasis has involved strengthening ASEAN's economic role. Although economic cooperation had been part of ASEAN's original rationale, the fact that the ASEAN economies largely compete with each other has proven an impediment. There has been more success when the ASEAN countries combine to pursue common interests they have in relation to external powers, for example, in gaining greater market access. In January 1992 an agreement was concluded to establish the ASEAN Free Trade

Area (AFTA), effective from the beginning of 1993. AFTA applied only to manufactured goods, with agreement to reduce tariffs gradually over a period of years. ASEAN also became involved in negotiations to establish free trade agreements with other countries. Most notable in this respect was the framework agreement on comprehensive economic cooperation between China and the ASEAN states, concluded in November 2002; an agreement was concluded with South Korea in May 2006 (excluding Thailand), and discussions have also been taking place with Japan, the European Union, Australia, and New Zealand.

A more significant development for ASEAN was the decision to make it a comprehensive Southeast Asian organization. The countries of Indochina and Burma were admitted over a period of years. Vietnam was first, in 1995, followed by Burma and Laos in 1997, and then Cambodia in 1999. Although there were big differences between the new and the old ASEAN members in terms of economic development and political systems, the rationale for the expansion was that ASEAN would provide a forum where regional differences could be dealt with regionally. ASEAN could also foster the economic development of the new members and assist in engaging those countries with the outside world in cases where there were significant conflicts. Particularly important in this respect was the situation in Burma, with ASEAN arguing that Burma's membership would facilitate gradual change in that country as opposed to the imposition of sanctions favored by Western countries such as the United States and the European Union. The difficulty for ASEAN was that the new members had very traditional views of sovereignty and therefore resisted too much engagement if that was seen as threatening. The new ASEAN members were strongly opposed to attempts by Thailand and the Philippines in the late 1990s to promote "flexible engagement," a formula to allow greater ASEAN involvement in "domestic" issues having international implications.

On the issue of assessing ASEAN's significance in the post–Cold War era, one might note the argument of Amitav Acharya (2001) that the organization has contributed to a sense of regional identity. Keeping in mind the various patterns of interstate relationships in Southeast Asia, ASEAN has contributed to the reduction of interstate tensions. Conflicts between states within Southeast Asia have generally been managed within the ASEAN framework. On the other hand, one could argue that major issues have arisen in Southeast Asia to which ASEAN has not made a major contribution. An example would be the East Timor crisis of 1999. Though ASEAN members did play a role in responding to the crisis, they did not lead on the issue. ASEAN countries were cautious about damaging their relations with Indonesia, but were prepared to contribute once a direction for dealing with the crisis had been established, largely by Australia and the United States. Nor did ASEAN play a leading role in responding to the Asian economic crisis of 1997. Again, that was left largely to external bodies, most notably the International Monetary Fund. While ASEAN did reject "flexible engagement" as an approach in the late 1990s, the compromise

formula of "enhanced interaction" (allowing more limited ASEAN involvement) was accepted. There is a need for Southeast Asian states to work together
in dealing with "domestic" issues that transcend national boundaries. In some
cases, a bilateral approach is appropriate, but ASEAN does have a role in facilitating multilateral arrangements.

One reason that ASEAN does not deal with issues on its own results from
the significant external involvement in Southeast Asian affairs. Most significant
in this respect is the role of the major powers. The interests of the United States
in Southeast Asia embrace political-strategic, economic, and human rights concerns. In maritime Southeast Asia, the United States has a strategic interest in developments in Indonesia, given both the geographic extent of that country and
its significance as the world's largest Muslim state. This interest has strengthened in the context of the "war on terrorism." The United States has historical
links with the neighboring Philippines, having provided assistance to combat the
Abu Sayyaf group since late 2001. There is close defense cooperation between
the United States and Singapore. In mainland Southeast Asia, US involvement
provides some balance to the strong Chinese presence. Historically, the closest
US links in Southeast Asia have been with Thailand. Diplomatic ties with Vietnam (established in 1995) are also relevant to US relations with China.

Economic ties with Southeast Asia are important to the United States, without being crucial. They are far more important to the Southeast Asian countries.
In 2004 the United States was the principal export destination for Cambodia, as
it was in 2005 for Malaysia, the Philippines, Thailand, and Vietnam; in 2005 it
was the second most important export destination for Indonesia and Singapore.
For imports in 2005, the United States ranked first for the Philippines, second
for Malaysia and Singapore, and third for Thailand.[10] In contrast, for the United
States in 2001 the ASEAN countries accounted for 5.5 percent of exports and
5.9 percent of imports.[11]

Human rights issues have been important to the United States in relation
to a number of Southeast Asian countries, including Indonesia, Burma, Vietnam, and Malaysia. US military ties with Indonesia have been sharply cur-
tailed in response to human rights abuses, particularly in East Timor. There has
been some pressure to modify this policy in light of the "war on terrorism,"
but change has been limited. A small opening emerged after the tsunami devastation in December 2004. The United States reinstated stalled training programs with the Indonesian military in the spring of 2005. In the case of Burma,
the United States has given support to the prodemocracy movement, led by
Aung San Suu Kyi, through a policy of limited sanctions. The authoritarian
policies pursued in Vietnam have also colored US relations with that country.
With Malaysia, the treatment of Anwar Ibrahim, the former deputy prime minister, was an important issue for the United States.

China's interests in mainland Southeast Asia have primarily revolved
around political-strategic concerns. China wishes to ensure that the states on

its southern flank do not pursue anti-China policies. It has developed close relations with Burma and Thailand. In Indochina, its closest relationship is with Cambodia, but it also seeks to influence and restrain Vietnam. China is in dispute with several Southeast Asian countries over the South China Sea. China claims this area as its own "historical waters," but Vietnam, the Philippines, Malaysia, Brunei, and Indonesia contest this. China has an interest in protecting the position of the ethnic Chinese in the various countries of Southeast Asia. It also seeks to restrict Taiwan's influence in the region. In maritime Southeast Asia, there have been tensions from time to time in China's relations with Indonesia and Malaysia. The position of ethnic Chinese in those countries has affected their relationships with China. China has a strategic interest in developments in Indonesia, but without exerting a strong influence.

As with the United States, China is more important to the Southeast Asian countries as a trading partner than vice versa. As an export destination, China ranked third for Burma in 2004, and for the Philippines, Thailand, and Vietnam in 2005. As a source of imports, China ranked first for Burma in 2004, and for Vietnam in 2005; second for Laos in 2004, and for Thailand in 2005; and third for Cambodia in 2004, and for Indonesia and Singapore in 2005.[12] For China, the ASEAN countries took 7.2 percent of exports and provided 11.4 percent of imports in 2005.[13]

Japan clearly has important economic interests in Southeast Asia. Indonesia is Japan's fifth most important source of imports (mainly oil). Otherwise, the general pattern of economic relations is similar to that of the other two major powers, with Japan being more important to the Southeast Asian countries than vice versa. Japan was the most important export destination for Indonesia in 2005, and for Brunei in 2004; second for Vietnam in 2005, and for East Timor in 2004; and third for Malaysia in 2005. For imports, Japan ranked first in 2005 for Malaysia and Thailand, second in 2005 for Indonesia and the Philippines, and third in 2004 for Brunei. Overall, Japan is the single most important source of imports for the Southeast Asian countries as a whole, and second only to the United States as a destination for exports. From Japan's perspective, the ASEAN countries took 12.7 percent of exports and provided 14.4 percent of imports in 2005.[14]

Japan plays a low-key political role in Southeast Asia. This is partly to ensure that its high economic profile does not lead to political resentment. Lingering resentments from World War II are also a restraining influence. Japan is an important aid donor in the region. In 2003–2004, nearly half of Japan's foreign aid went to "other Asia and Oceania" (including China, but excluding South and Central Asia). Among the top ten recipients of Japan's bilateral aid in the same year were Indonesia (second), the Philippines (third), Thailand (fourth), Vietnam (sixth), and Malaysia (ninth).[15] Japan's aid is based on the assumption that economic development can facilitate political stability and the development of civil society. For this reason, Japan has been prepared to develop aid relationships with authoritarian regimes such as the military government in Burma. More broadly, Japan has an interest in ensuring the protection of the sea-lanes through Southeast Asia. It is concerned about piracy in Indonesia. Japan's oil imports from the Persian Gulf pass through the Straits of Malacca.

The involvement of the major powers is clearly a complicating factor in the international politics of Southeast Asia. While there might be problems for ASEAN as a regional organization because of the current situation of its members, the role of the major powers in Southeast Asia does make it more difficult to proceed on the basis of "regional solutions to regional problems." Similarly, in terms of any local situation in Southeast Asia, one cannot assume that such a situation will develop simply on the basis of the local factors involved. The major powers will frequently be a significant influence.

Indonesia

Indonesia is the largest of Southeast Asia's eleven states and has played a leading role in the region. For that reason, it merits special attention. Before 1998, Indonesia's international involvement had gone through a number of phases. The radical orientation of Sukarno in the late 1950s and early 1960s had been succeeded by the more cautious and pro-Western policies of Suharto. In both cases, domestic influences had been an important influence on Indonesia's international orientation. Sukarno saw his radical orientation as a means of uniting a divided population behind his leadership. Under Suharto, the government's domestic anticommunism encouraged a similar orientation in its foreign policy. The emphasis of Indonesia's New Order on economic development led it to strengthen links with countries, such as Japan and the United States, that could assist that development. At the same time, Indonesia sought to play a leading role in Southeast Asia and in wider contexts such as the nonaligned movement and the Islamic world. The authoritarian political system meant the suppression of domestic political differences. While Indonesia's occupation of East Timor since 1975 attracted foreign criticism, internal divisions did not greatly impede the country's international role.

Since Suharto's downfall in May 1998, Indonesia's domestic problems have greatly affected its international situation. The collapse of the New Order has been followed by a period of democratization in Indonesia, as discussed in Chapter 4. Democratization has encouraged the various regional, ethnic, and religious groups in Indonesia to express themselves politically. At the same time, the government has not been in as strong a position to act as under the New Order. A higher level of consensus has to be achieved. The contending groups and the need for consensus have undermined the authority of the central government. This situation extends to the regions, which are now in a stronger position to bargain with Jakarta. The role of the military has become less formal under democratization. However, the military retains great influence as the major institution holding Indonesia together.

Democratization has had an impact not simply at the national level, but also in terms of regional politics in Indonesia. Various regional groups have been able to assert themselves more forcefully. The most dramatic development was in relation to East Timor. B. J. Habibie, who assumed the role of president when Suharto stepped down in May 1998, agreed that the people of East Timor should have the opportunity for self-determination. While Indonesia had effectively occupied the territory since 1975, most countries still recognized Portugal as the sovereign power. In May 1999, Portugal and Indonesia agreed that there would be a popular vote on the territory's future, with the United Nations responsible for electoral arrangements. When this occurred, on August 30, 1999, 78.5 percent of those voting supported independence. The Indonesian military had worked with local militias to try to effect a pro-Indonesian outcome. These groups responded to the vote by unleashing a campaign of destruction. Only the intervention of a UN-authorized military force, led by Australia, put an end to this situation. Subsequently, the United Nations Transitional Administration for East Timor (UNTAET) took responsibility for effecting the decision of the East Timorese, with independence being achieved in May 2002.

East Timor's situation in relation to Indonesia was unique, in the sense that its international status had not been resolved. In Aceh and West Papua, there was also strong support for independence, but these territories were internationally recognized as part of Indonesia. In Aceh, the memory of the province's independent political status before 1873 and the long struggle with the Dutch nurtured separatism. The Acehnese regarded Indonesian rule as an unwanted imposition. The Gerakan Aceh Merdeka (GAM; Free Aceh Movement) led the struggle for independence. The aim was to establish an Islamic state. The conflict was highly militarized, with GAM guerrillas arrayed against the Indonesian armed forces. While Acehnese independence was unacceptable to Indonesia, moves to give the province "special autonomy" did proceed. Under a law passed in July 2001, Aceh was to receive 70 percent of government revenue from natural gas in the province, and would also have more self-government than other provinces. Islamic law would receive special recognition. In early 2002 an agreement was concluded in Geneva to provide a basis for ending the conflict, but this agreement collapsed when President Megawati Sukarnoputri declared a military emergency in Aceh in May 2003.[16] There was renewed international attention on Aceh following the tsunami that struck on Boxing Day 2004; 130,000 were killed in the province as a result of this natural disaster. In August 2005 there was another agreement to end the conflict. GAM agreed to accept "special autonomy," and the Indonesian government undertook to end its military campaign; both the European Union and ASEAN would play a monitoring role.[17]

The conflict in West Papua was less militarized. Papuan nationalists resented the way in which the territory had been transferred from the Netherlands to Indonesia in 1962–1963. The "act of free choice," conducted by Indonesia in

1969, involved consultation with carefully selected local leaders so that a pro-Indonesian outcome was predetermined. The main organization campaigning for independence since the 1960s had been the Organisasi Papua Merdeka (OPM; Free Papua Movement). However, the ability of the OPM to mount an armed struggle had been limited. In the context of the post-1998 democratization, a more broadly based political movement emerged, with the Papuan Presidium Council as its focus. The OPM was linked to this body, but did not dominate it. One of the hopes of the independence movement was that the West Papuan issue could be internationalized. The basis of such a strategy involved questioning whether the 1969 "act of free choice" was legitimate. While Indonesia opposed independence for the province, "special autonomy" was an option. Like Aceh, West Papua was rich in resources. The renaming of the province as "Papua" (previously Irian Jaya) was a concession to West Papuan sentiment by President Abdurrahman Wahid, but Megawati Sukarnoputri subsequently reversed direction on this matter.

Other regional conflicts within Indonesia often derived from tensions between indigenous peoples and immigrants (particularly from Java and more crowded parts of the archipelago). The most serious of these conflicts was between Christians and Muslims in Maluku. Although the situation varied throughout Maluku, in Ambon the Christians were the indigenous group and the Muslims were predominantly immigrants. The intervention of Laskar Jihad, an Islamic extremist group from Java, swung the situation in favor of the Muslims. In central and western Kalimantan and in central Sulawesi, there were also conflicts between indigenous and immigrant groups (although not necessarily along Christian-Muslim lines). In other regional situations there was less tension, excepting demands for greater autonomy in relation to Jakarta. Resource-rich regions, such as Riau, came to the fore with such demands.

In assessing the international impact of Indonesia's domestic situation, one needs to be aware of developments both at the national level and at the regional level. The major international consequence of weak government at the national level is an inability to control many situations that adversely affect other countries. There are numerous examples. Unregulated population movements, involving illegal immigrants and refugees, are facilitated by weak states such as Indonesia. People-smuggling by criminal groups highlights this problem. Criminal groups can also take advantage of a weak state for such purposes as drug trafficking and money laundering. Piracy is also a big issue in Indonesian waters; in 1999, 25 percent of all such attacks worldwide occurred in Indonesia (IISS 2001:xxii). The inability of the central authorities to control unauthorized forest fires in Kalimantan and Sumatra has caused significant problems with smoke haze in Singapore and Malaysia. Islamic extremism, although attracting small numbers in Indonesia, can exacerbate regional conflicts within the country, and add to the general picture of weakness and instability. Islamic extremism, insofar as it nurtures terrorism, can have consequences for many other countries.

The regional conflicts within Indonesia also have international implications. At a general level, there are often human rights issues involved, with savage killings undertaken simply on the basis of the group to which people belong. Widespread suffering attracts international attention. International agencies can become involved in dealing with refugees and internally displaced people. Neighboring countries can be affected by specific conflicts. In the case of Aceh, the relevant countries are Malaysia and Singapore. Refugees could become an issue, and there are some Acehnese exiles based in Malaysia. With West Papua, there is a shared border with Papua New Guinea. Governments in Papua New Guinea have been careful not to become involved in the issue, but Papua New Guineans generally sympathize with the West Papuans as fellow Melanesians. In the Pacific Island Forum, Nauru and Vanuatu have unsuccessfully urged support for West Papuan independence. Australia (also a member of the forum) has played a role in moderating such views. Australia wants to maintain its relationship with Indonesia, and is concerned about any conflict developing between Papua New Guinea and Indonesia over the West Papua issue.

The domestic situation in Indonesia has an impact on regional dynamics in Southeast Asia. While ASEAN's problems have many sources, one issue is Indonesia's weakness. A strong and stable Indonesia would be able to give more attention to ways of strengthening ASEAN. Indonesia's neighbors are affected in various ways in addition to the regional conflicts already discussed. Malaysia and Singapore have concerns that Indonesia's problems might spill over and affect their own situations. Singapore is particularly concerned in this respect, being a predominantly Chinese city-state in a Malay world. The Philippines has its own problems in dealing with Muslim separatism in the south; in current circumstances, it is more difficult to expect assistance from Indonesia in dealing with that situation. Papua New Guinea and Australia are affected not just by the West Papua situation, but also by the general instability in Indonesia. Issues such as people-smuggling have been a particular concern for Australia. Given the circumstances of East Timor's accession to independence, relations with Indonesia relate directly to the new state's viability. Indonesia's ability to assist East Timor is adversely affected by lingering resentment among some elements within Indonesia, including among the military. An overtly hostile stance would be very destabilizing for East Timor.

Among the major powers, the United States has taken a renewed interest in Indonesia in the context of its "war on terrorism." As previously mentioned, congressional bans on US cooperation with the Indonesian military were largely lifted in 2005. These bans had related to previous Indonesian policy toward East Timor and to dissatisfaction with the Indonesian response to the murder of two Americans near the Freeport mine in West Papua in August 2002. The United States is very conscious of the strategic importance of Indonesia, not just in relation to Southeast Asia, but also within the Islamic world. Japan has important economic interests in Indonesia, including the import of oil from the latter. The sea-lanes through and adjoining Indonesia are important for Japanese trade, including the supply of oil from the Persian Gulf. Japan has proposed action to deal with piracy in Indonesian waters. China's interests in Indonesia concern not just strategic issues, but also more specifically the position of the ethnic Chinese.

In discussing the international impact of Indonesia's domestic situation, an important issue concerns the implications of possible balkanization. At one level, there is an argument as to whether or not fragmentation is likely. The most sustained campaigns for separation relate to Aceh and West Papua. However, greater autonomy appears a far more likely outcome than independence. Even if independence were achieved, this would not necessarily mean that other regions would break away. Such a development depends on the situation in the relevant areas and also on the policies of the Jakarta government. A more likely outcome would be the continuation of weak government, with various regions having greater autonomy in practice (and sometimes legally too). Balkanization, or even increasing de facto fragmentation, would complicate the way in which outside countries involve themselves with the region. The situations in relation to the former Yugoslavia and the former Soviet Union provide a precedent. A bigger concern is that the process whereby separate states might emerge would probably be accompanied by great conflict. While Indonesia's legitimacy would be strengthened if all its constituent peoples freely gave their consent to the existing state, the ideal of self-determination sometimes has to be balanced against the costs involved in attaining such a goal.

An Asia Pacific Dimension?

This chapter has focused on Northeast Asia and Southeast Asia in discussing the substance of international relations in Asia Pacific. But how much substance is there in Asia Pacific more broadly as a region? Many writers define Asia Pacific to include not just Northeast Asia and Southeast Asia, but also Australasia, the Pacific Islands, and the Eastern Pacific (the Pacific seaboard of the Americas). While international relations occur within each of these subregions, there is also some focus on Asia Pacific as a whole. This is evident from at least two perspectives: the development of regionalism, and the approach adopted by the United States and other Western powers.

At the Asia Pacific level there are two main instances of regionalism. One is the Asia-Pacific Economic Cooperation, established in 1989 as a forum focusing on economic issues. The other is the ASEAN Regional Forum (ARF), which commenced in 1994 with a focus on security issues. Since 1993, APEC has held annual leaders' meetings. It is the only such forum where the leaders of Asia Pacific gather for discussion and consultation. Although the emphasis is ostensibly on economic issues, there is scope for consultation on broader political and security issues. This was important, for example, in the formulation of a response to the East Timor crisis in 1999, and in coordinating the campaign against terrorism in late 2001. In terms of economic issues, APEC has had two main functions. In the context of the Uruguay round of global trade negotiations (completed in 1994), APEC supported greater liberalization, against the more protectionist approach favored by the European Union in particular. In facilitating economic cooperation among members, the emphasis has been on "open regionalism." This involves reducing barriers among members, but in such a way that nonmembers are not discriminated against. At the Bogor meeting in 1994, APEC set itself the goal of achieving free trade among its industrialized economies by 2010, and by 2020 for its developing economies. While APEC is certainly a feature of international relations in Asia Pacific, one should not exaggerate its overall importance. Its role in responding to the Asian economic crisis in 1997 was limited, as was ASEAN's, and APEC is not a prominent factor in the major bilateral economic relationships in the region.

A similar point could be made about the ASEAN Regional Forum. Despite the use of the term "ASEAN" in the title, ARF is Asia Pacific in scope and, in addition to the ASEAN members, includes the European Union, Australia, Canada, China, India, Japan, South Korea, Mongolia, New Zealand, North Korea, Papua New Guinea, Russia, and the United States. Meetings are held annually, with foreign ministers of member countries normally attending. The emphasis is on exchanging views about important security issues in the region. Conflict resolution negotiations do not take place under the auspices of ARF. Because of China's opposition, Taiwan is not a member of the forum, and so ARF is prevented from becoming involved in the Taiwan issue. North Korea became a member in 2000. While ARF does engage in some intersessional activities, these focus on practical matters and do not relate to broader strategic issues. ARF fulfills a role as a security forum, but is not a significant factor in the overall dynamics of international politics in Asia Pacific.

An important factor in explaining the relevance of the Asia Pacific concept is the fact that it suits the interests of the United States and other Western powers (Canada, Australia, New Zealand). The term "Asia Pacific" legitimizes the involvement of these powers in the affairs of East Asia (i.e., Northeast and Southeast Asia). All of these powers have important economic and strategic interests in East Asia. "Asia Pacific" makes these powers local actors in the region, whereas "East Asia" would make them external. Having the status of local actors gives the Western powers (particularly the United States) greater influence than would otherwise be the case. Hence all of these powers have a strong interest in promoting the use of the Asia Pacific concept. The involvement of Latin

American countries (Mexico, Peru, and Chile are members of APEC) weakens any suggestion that the Asia Pacific concept is simply a vehicle for promoting the interests of developed Western states.

The major alternative to the Asia Pacific concept is a focus on East Asia. Soon after the establishment of APEC, Mahathir Mohamad, then–prime minister of Malaysia, promoted an East Asian economic grouping or caucus as a means of excluding or minimizing Western influence. His proposal was not realized, although Southeast Asian and East Asian countries might caucus in some international contexts. Most of these countries did have an interest in promoting their relationship with the United States, not to mention the other Western powers. Japan in particular feared that an East Asian focus would give too much power to China. In the context of the 1997 East Asian economic crisis, a stronger East Asian orientation did emerge. The "ASEAN Plus Three" group brought together the ASEAN countries with China, Japan, and South Korea. This group complemented rather than superseded the Asia Pacific groupings, with Japan acting as an important bridge. In December 2005, Malaysia played host to an East Asian summit involving not just ASEAN Plus Three but also India, Australia, and New Zealand. With annual meetings planned, this grouping will also strengthen the East Asian focus.

Overall, it appears that the Asia Pacific concept is a weak one. To understand the substance of international politics in the region, much can be gained by focusing on the subregions, the most important of which are Northeast Asia and Southeast Asia. There is a broader Asia Pacific dimension, involving APEC and the ASEAN Regional Forum as regional groupings, but particularly the United States. Although the major interests of the United States are in Northeast Asia, it is involved in all of the subregions. The "Asia Pacific" approach enables the United States to portray itself as a regional actor rather than as simply a global power pursuing interests in a number of regions throughout the world.

▨ **Notes**

1. In 1972 the "one China" principle was the view that there should be one government for the whole of China, including Taiwan, irrespective of whether this government was the People's Republic of China (Communist) or the Republic of China (Nationalist).

2. Japan External Trade Organization (JETRO), *Japanese Trade in 2005,* app. 1, "Foreign Trade by Country and Region," p. 134, http://www.jetro.go.jp/jpn/stats/data/pdf/trade2005.pdf.

3. Calculated from figures in JETRO, "Japanese Trade and Investment Statistics: Japan's Outward and Inward Foreign Direct Investment, FDI Flow (Based on Balance of Payments, Net), by Country and Region, Historical Data, Outward," http://www.jetro.go.jp/en/stats/statistics.

4. Calculated from US Department of Commerce, International Trade Administration, TradeStats Express, http://tse.export.gov/ntdmap.aspx?uniqueurl=efzn5f45pgw0 esvhtakfci55-2006-8-4-1-27-4.

5. United States–China Business Council, "FDI in China (Total and US) 1995–2005," http://www.uschina.org/statistics/fdi_cumulative.html.

6. "China: Economy," in Central Intelligence Agency, *The World Factbook,* http://www.cia.gov/cia/publications/factbook/geos/ch.html#econ.

7. "China White Paper," February 2000, http://www.china.daily.com.cn/highlights/chinainbrief/taiwan/principle.html.

8. Trade figures are from Australian Department of Foreign Affairs and Trade, "Taiwan Country Information and China Fact Sheet," http://www.dfat.gov.au. Investment information is from United States–China Business, "Foreign Investment in China," http://www.uschina.org/statistics/2005foreigninvestment.html.

9. In late June 2002 a small-scale naval incident involving North Korea and South Korea led to deaths on both sides.

10. Country information provided by Australian Department of Foreign Affairs and Trade, http://www.dfat.gov.au.

11. Based on information from US Department of Commerce, International Trade Administration, TradeStats Express, http://tse.export.gov/itahome.aspx?uniqueurl= 4qqb0k55rhxxsuqn5ggo3l45-2006-8-1-1-3-37.

12. See http://www.dfat.gov.au.

13. Calculated from figures in International Monetary Fund, *Direction of Trade Statistics Quarterly* (June 2006): 96–97.

14. JETRO, *Japanese Trade in 2005,* app. 1, "Foreign Trade by Country and Region," p. 134, http://www.jetro.go.jp/jpn/stats/data/pdf/trade2005.pdf.

15. See http://www.oecd.org/dataoecd/42/5/1860382.gif.

16. International Crisis Group, "Aceh: How Not to Win Hearts and Minds," *Indonesia Briefing,* July 23, 2003, http://www.crisisweb.org/projects/asia/indonesia/reports/a401059_23072003.pdf.

17. See "Memorandum of Understanding Between the Government of the Republic of Indonesia and the Free Aceh Movement," August 15, 2005, http://www.thejakartapost.com/ri_gam_mou.pdf. There is a comprehensive analysis in International Crisis Group, "Aceh: A New Chance for Peace," *Asia Briefing,* August 15, 2005, http://www.crisisgroup.org/library/documents/asia/indonesia/b040_aceh_a_new_chance_for_peace.pdf.

Bibliography

Acharya, Amitav. 2000. *The Quest for Identity: International Relations of Southeast Asia.* Singapore: Oxford University Press.
———. 2001. *Constructing a Security Community in Southeast Asia: ASEAN and the Problem of Regional Order.* London: Routledge.
Aspinall, Edward, and Mark T. 2001. "The Breakup of Indonesia? Nationalisms After Decolonisation and the Limits of the Nation-State in Post–Cold War Southeast Asia." *Third World Quarterly* 22, no. 6: 1003–1024.
Australian Department of Foreign Affairs and Trade. East Asia Analytical Unit. 1996a. *Asia's Global Powers: China-Japan Relations in the 21st Century.* Canberra.
———. 1996b. *Pacific Russia: Risks and Rewards.* Canberra.

Beeson, Mark, ed. 2004. *Contemporary Southeast Asia: Regional Dynamics, National Differences.* New York: Palgrave Macmillan.

Bernstein, Richard, and Ross H. Munro. 1997. *The Coming Conflict with China.* New York: Knopf.

Bertrand, Jacques. 2004. *Nationalism and Ethnic Conflict in Indonesia.* Cambridge: Cambridge University Press.

Buckley, Roger. 2002. *The United States in the Asia-Pacific Since 1945.* Cambridge: Cambridge University Press.

Buzo, Adrian. 2002. *The Making of Modern Korea.* London: Routledge.

Caballero-Anthony, Mely. 2005. *Regional Security in Southeast Asia: Beyond the ASEAN Way.* Singapore: Institute of Southeast Asian Studies.

Cha, Victor D., and David C. Kang. 2003. *Nuclear North Korea: A Debate on Engagement Strategies.* New York: Columbia University Press.

Connors, Michael K., Rémy Davison, and Jörn Dosch. 2004. *The New Global Politics of the Asia-Pacific.* London: RoutledgeCurzon.

Cumings, Bruce. 1981. *The Origins of the Korean War.* Vol. 1. Princeton: Princeton University Press.

———. 1990. *The Origins of the Korean War.* Vol. 2. Princeton: Princeton University Press.

———. 1997. *Korea's Place in the Sun: A Modern History.* New York: Norton.

Davis, Sue. 2003. *The Russian Far East: The Last Frontier?* London: Routledge.

Deng Yong and Wang Fei-ling, eds. 2005. *China Rising: Power and Motivation in Chinese Foreign Policy.* Lanham: Rowman and Littlefield.

Dirlik, Arif, ed. 1998. *What Is in a Rim? Critical Perspectives on the Pacific Region Idea.* 2nd ed. Lanham: Rowman and Littlefield.

Drifte, Reinhard. 2003. *Japan's Security Relations with China Since 1989: From Balancing to Bandwagoning?* London: RoutledgeCurzon.

Drysdale, Peter, and Zhang Dong Dong, eds. 2000. *Japan and China: Rivalry or Cooperation in East Asia?* Canberra: Asia Pacific Press.

Dupont, Alan. 2001. *East Asia Imperilled: Transnational Challenges to Security.* Cambridge: Cambridge University Press.

The Economist. 2003. "Into Harm's Way." July 26–August 1.

Foot, Rosemary. 1995. *The Practice of Power: US Relations with China Since 1949.* New York: Oxford University Press.

———. 2000. *Rights Beyond Borders: The Global Community and the Struggle over Human Rights in China.* Oxford: Oxford University Press.

Funston, John, ed. 2001. *Government and Politics in Southeast Asia.* London: Zed.

Garrison, Jean A. 2005. *Making China Policy: From Nixon to G. W. Bush.* Boulder: Lynne Rienner.

Gertz, Bill. 2000. *The China Threat: How the People's Republic Targets America.* Washington, D.C.: Regnery.

Goldstein, Avery. 2005. *Rising to the Challenge: China's Grand Strategy and International Security.* Stanford: Stanford University Press.

Goodkind, Daniel, and Loraine West. 2001. "The North Korean Famine and Its Demographic Impact." *Population and Development Review* no. 27: 219–238.

Green, Michael Jonathan. 2001. *Japan's Reluctant Realism: Foreign Policy Challenges in an Era of Uncertain Power.* New York: Palgrave.

Gurtov, Mel. 2002. *Pacific Asia? Prospects for Security and Cooperation in East Asia.* Lanham: Rowman and Littlefield.

Harrison, Selig. 2002. *Korean Endgame: A Strategy for Reunification and U.S. Disengagement.* Princeton: Princeton University Press.

Hatch, Walter, and Kozo Yamamura. 1996. *Asia in Japan's Embrace: Building a Regional Production Alliance.* Cambridge: Cambridge University Press.

Henderson, Jeannie. 1999. *Reassessing ASEAN.* Adelphi Paper no. 328. London: International Institute for Strategic Studies.

Hill, Hal. 1999. *The Indonesian Economy in Crisis: Causes, Consequences, and Lessons.* Singapore: Institute of Southeast Asian Studies.

————. 2000. *The Indonesian Economy.* 2nd ed. Cambridge: Cambridge University Press.

Hoare, James, and Susan Pares. 1999. *Conflict in Korea: An Encyclopedia.* Santa Barbara, Calif.: ABC-CLIO.

Hook, Glenn D., Julie Gilson, Christopher W. Hughes, and Hugo Dobson. 2005. *Japan's International Relations: Politics, Economics, and Security.* 2nd ed. London: Routledge.

Hughes, Christopher W. 2004. *Japan's Security Agenda: Military, Economic, and Environmental Dimensions.* Boulder: Lynne Rienner.

Huxley, Tim. 2002. *Disintegrating Indonesia? Implications for Regional Security.* Adelphi Paper no. 349. London: International Institute for Strategic Studies.

International Institute for Strategic Studies (IISS). 2001. "Global Trends: Piracy Hot-Spots." In *Strategic Survey 2000–2001.* London: Oxford University Press.

————. 2006. *The Military Balance 2006.* London: Routledge.

Johnson, Chalmers. 2002. *Blowback: The Costs and Consequences of American Empire.* London: Time Warner.

Kingsbury, Damien. 2001. *South-East Asia: A Political Profile.* South Melbourne: Oxford University Press.

————. 2005. *The Politics of Indonesia.* 3rd ed. South Melbourne: Oxford University Press.

Klien, Susanne. 2002. *Rethinking Japan's Identity and International Role: An Intercultural Perspective.* New York: Routledge.

Kornberg, Judith F., and John R. Faust. 2004. *China in World Politics: Policies, Processes, Prospects.* Boulder: Lynne Rienner.

Lampton, David M. 2001. *Same Bed, Different Dreams: Managing U.S.-China Relations, 1989–2000.* Berkeley: University of California Press.

Lardy, Nicholas R. 2002. *Integrating China into the Global Economy.* Washington, D.C.: Brookings Institution.

Leifer, Michael. 2000. *Singapore's Foreign Policy: Coping with Vulnerability.* London: Routledge.

————. 2001. *Dictionary of the Modern Politics of South-East Asia.* 3rd ed. London: Routledge.

Lincoln, Edward J. 2004. *East Asian Economic Regionalism.* Washington, D.C.: Brookings Institution.

Mackerras, Colin, ed. 2000. *Eastern Asia: An Introductory History.* 3rd ed. Sydney: Longman.

Mann, Jim. 1999. *About Face: A History of America's Curious Relationship with China, from Nixon to Clinton.* New York: Knopf.

McCormack, Gavan. 2004. *Target North Korea: Pushing North Korea to the Brink of Nuclear Catastrophe.* New York: Thunder's Mouth/Nation Books.

McDougall, Derek. 1997. *Studies in International Relations: The Asia-Pacific, the Nuclear Age, Australia.* 2nd ed. Rydalmere, NSW: Hodder Headline.

————. 2002. *Historical Dictionary of International Organizations in Asia and the Pacific.* Lanham: Scarecrow.

————. 2007. *Asia Pacific in World Politics.* Boulder: Lynne Rienner.

Murphey, Rhoads. 2005. *A History of Asia*. 5th ed. New York: Longman.

Nathan, Andrew J., and Robert S. Ross. 1997. *The Great Wall and the Empty Fortress: China's Search for Security*. New York: Norton.

Neher, Clark D. 2002. *Southeast Asia in the New International Era*. 4th ed. Boulder: Westview.

Noland, Marcus. 2004. *Korea After Kim Jong-il*. Washington, D.C.: Institute for International Economics.

Noland, Marcus, Sherman Robinson, and Tao Wang. 2001. "Famine in North Korea: Causes and Cures." *Economic Development and Cultural Change* 49: 741–767.

Oberdorfer, Don. 1999. *The Two Koreas: A Contemporary History*. London: Warner.

O'Hanlon, Michael, and Mike Mochizuki. 2003. *Crisis on the Korean Peninsula: How to Deal with a Nuclear North Korea*. New York: McGraw-Hill.

Pempel, T. J., ed. 2005. *Remapping East Asia: The Construction of a Region*. Ithaca: Cornell University Press.

Ricklefs, M. C. 2001. *A History of Modern Indonesia Since c. 1200*. 3rd ed. Stanford: Stanford University Press.

Roy, Denny. 1998. *China's Foreign Relations*. Houndmills, Basingstoke: Macmillan.

———. 2003. *Taiwan: A Political History*. Ithaca: Cornell University Press.

Saich, Tony. 2001. *Governance and Politics of China*. Houndmills, Basingstoke: Palgrave.

Shambaugh, David, ed. 2000. *Is China Unstable? Assessing the Factors*. Armonk, N.Y.: Sharpe.

———. 2002. *Modernizing China's Military: Progress, Problems, and Prospects*. Berkeley: University of California Press.

Siddique, Sharon, and Sree Kumar, comps. 2003. *The 2nd ASEAN Reader*. Singapore: Institute of Southeast Asian Studies.

Sigal, Leon V. 1998. *Disarming Strangers: Nuclear Diplomacy with North Korea*. Princeton: Princeton University Press.

Söderberg, Marie, ed. 2002. *Chinese-Japanese Relations in the Twenty-First Century: Complementarity and Conflict*. London: Routledge.

Stephan, John J. 1994. *The Russian Far East: A History*. Stanford: Stanford University Press.

Stockwin, J. A. A. 1999. *Governing Japan: Divided Politics in a Major Economy*. 3rd ed. Oxford: Blackwell.

———. 2003. *Dictionary of the Modern Politics of Japan*. London: RoutledgeCurzon.

Suettinger, Robert L. 2003. *Beyond Tiananmen: The Politics of U.S.-China Relations, 1989–2000*. Washington, D.C.: Brookings Institution.

Sutter, Robert G. 2005. *China's Rise in Asia: Promises and Perils*. Lanham: Rowman and Littlefield.

Terrill, Ross. 2003. *The New Chinese Empire: And What It Means for the United States*. New York: Basic.

Tow, William T. 2001. *Asia-Pacific Strategic Relations: Seeking Convergent Security*. Cambridge: Cambridge University Press.

Tucker, Nancy Bernkopf, ed. 2005. *Dangerous Strait: The U.S.-Taiwan-China Crisis*. New York: Columbia University Press.

Vogel, Steven K., ed. 2002. *U.S.-Japan Relations in a Changing World*. Washington, D.C.: Brookings Institution.

Weatherbee, Donald E., with Ralf Emmers, Mari Pengestu, and Leonard C. Sebastian. 2005. *International Relations in Southeast Asia: The Struggle for Autonomy*. Lanham: Rowman and Littlefield.

Weeks, Stanley B., and Charles A. Meconis. 1999. *The Armed Forces of the USA in the Asia-Pacific Region.* St. Leonards, NSW: Allen and Unwin.

Wesley, Michael, ed. 2003. *The Regional Organizations of the Asia-Pacific: Exploring Institutional Change.* Basingstoke: Palgrave Macmillan.

Wit, Joel S., Daniel B. Poneman, and Robert L. Gallucci. 2004. *Going Critical: The First North Korean Nuclear Crisis.* Washington, D.C.: Brookings Institution.

Yahuda, Michael. 2004. *The International Politics of the Asia-Pacific.* 2nd rev. ed. London: RoutledgeCurzon.

Zagoria, Donald S., ed. 2003. *Breaking the China-Taiwan Impasse.* Westport: Praeger.

Zhao, Suisheng, ed. 2004. *Chinese Foreign Policy: Pragmatism and Strategic Behavior.* Armonk, N.Y.: Sharpe.

Zheng, Yongnian. 1999. *Discovering Chinese Nationalism in China: Modernization, Identity, and International Relations.* Cambridge: Cambridge University Press.

7

Military and Security Issues

Robert Sutter

The collapse of the Soviet Union and the end of the Cold War coincided with a marked upswing in East Asian economic power and political assertiveness. Though dampened by setbacks during the Asian economic crisis later in the 1990s, regional initiatives and leadership continued, mainly by way of national governments. Government leaders generally endeavored to meet growing popular demands for greater economic development and nationalistic respect through balanced nation-building strategies that placed a premium on encouraging economic growth beneficial to broad segments of their societies. Most tended to eschew radical ideologies and to emphasize conventional nationalism.

With the weakening of armed insurgencies and interstate conflict driven by Cold War rivalries, Asia Pacific states reoriented military priorities. Protecting the states' environs and trading routes, and projecting power, became more important. Navies and air forces received more resources than in the past, when counterinsurgency and homeland defense had given top priority to armies. Military power developed in tandem with economic power, but few regimes (North Korea and Burma were exceptions) emphasized the former at the expense of the latter when faced with international opposition and domestic pressures for more effective development of overall national power.

Most Asian militaries followed the direction of their civilian government leaders and focused greater attention on professional development of their armed forces to deal with external threats and the requirements of modern warfare. In a few authoritarian Asian countries (e.g., North Korea, Burma) and states transitioning to democracy (e.g., Indonesia), militaries continued to exert important influence in political, economic, and social development, and to stand against efforts by civilian leaders or others to reduce their power and influence (discussed in Chapter 4). Regardless of the role militaries played, the region's nations shared two basic characteristics:

- Regional government leaders remained well aware that failure to meet domestic expectations could result in being voted out of office in democratic states, or in widespread demonstrations and violence in authoritarian states, leading to regime collapse.
- People of the region generally recognized that national governments were important in advancing and protecting their interests, and that national governments needed to be accountable and effective in pursuing goals beneficial to citizens of the state.

Despite these commonalities, Asia Pacific remained the world's most diverse region, with a wide variety of cultural, historical, and other differences; unlike Europe, Latin America, and even Africa, there were few established mechanisms for substantial intraregional security cooperation. The region had only recently begun to experiment with such cooperative mechanisms, and would continue to do so.

■ The Importance of Global Trends

Specialists have identified a series of salient global trends that have affected and will continue to affect security issues in Asia Pacific. In general, though there were exceptions, Asian governments dealt with these trends pragmatically and effectively.

Population
The countries of Asia Pacific generally demonstrated good control regarding population growth, though growth remained a serious problem in Vietnam and the Philippines. East Asia was not facing serious problems posed by an aging population, except for Japan, and only recently China. There was some labor migration among states; communal tension and minority issues were serious problems affecting countries like Indonesia, the Philippines, China, Malaysia, and Thailand; and infectious diseases, notably AIDS and severe acute respiratory syndrome (SARS), were also of concern.

Food, Water, and Energy
Food security was generally adequate in the region, though there were major difficulties in some places (e.g., North Korea). China could meet most of its needs by increasing its importation of products that were not likely to cause major upset in world markets. The same was basically true with energy, although the search for offshore energy sources exacerbated maritime territorial

disputes in the region. The water problem in northern China was serious, but the People's Republic was taking remedial steps, including plans to divert water to northern China from better-watered territory in its southern provinces.

Economic Growth
Asia Pacific would follow the path of other regions toward greater economic integration and growth. The splits between haves and have-nots in some countries, notably China, would be a serious problem. Given its overall assets, Asia Pacific was likely to grow in importance in the overall world economy.

Permeation of Science and Technology
Information empowers greater civil society and enables economic growth. Because of the latter, even authoritarian Asian governments were likely to promote technological development, though North Korea, Vietnam, Burma, and perhaps some others might lag behind.

Erosion of Nation-State Power?
The ability of Asian states to promote authoritarianism, especially corporate control of social, economic, and political life, was in decline. But nationalism was not declining, and the nation-state would remain an essential vehicle for bringing nationalism to fulfillment.

Some authoritarian states like North Korea and Burma continued to use military power to sustain the regime and exert strong control over social, economic, and political life. States in transition from authoritarian rule—notably Indonesia—also allowed continued strong military control over social, political, and economic realms. Chinese leaders sustained authoritarian political control while largely freeing social and economic life. They used police and internal security forces to sustain domestic stability, and encouraged the military to hone professional skills to secure Chinese regional and international interests.

■ Key Determinants of Recent Regional Security Dynamics

Five main factors affected the post–Cold War policy environment in determining the security issues and trends in Asia Pacific:

- Reactions to changes in major regional power relationships. These changes included China's rising power, Japan's prolonged economic slowdown, and Indonesia's weakness and leadership drift.
- Changed relations in Korea.
- Regional effort to sustain economic growth amid increasing challenges of economic globalization.

- Challenges posed by the freer flow of information.
- Regional concern over US security, economic, and political policies and objectives, including perceived US unilateralism and pressures, and US intentions to stay involved in the region.

With the exception of the Korean factor, these determinants were not new, though all have become stronger in recent years. They have led to Asian security and power relationships becoming more fluid than at any time since the Cold War. Their relative importance depends on circumstances and the priorities of regional leaders. For example, security determinants were of particular importance on those occasions when regional leaders focused on the evolving balance of power in Asia Pacific and its implication for their interests in the particular crisis or situation, such as the repeated crises over North Korea's nuclear weapons program from 2002 to 2006, the thaw in North Korean–South Korean relations during 2000, and the 1996 US-Chinese military face-off over Taiwan. Globalization and the information revolution were of key importance when regional leaders faced economic crises or instability brought on by these forces. Taken together, the determinants provided impetus for Asian governments to become more active in promoting their own interests in an increasingly challenging and fluid environment.

The US-led "war on terrorism" after the attacks of September 2001 also affected the region. However, the US antiterrorism effort in Asia Pacific focused on Southeast Asia and was a secondary front; primary attention was devoted to Central and Southwest Asia. Asia Pacific governments and their military forces cooperated in sharing intelligence, coordinating investigations, and endeavoring to root out terrorist groups active in the region. US-led efforts to capture and destroy terrorists received mixed responses in Southeast Asia. The US-led Iraq War was especially unpopular, notably among Muslim populations in Indonesia, Malaysia, and elsewhere in Southeast Asia. This reduced the willingness of those governments to cooperate closely with US antiterrorism efforts in Southeast Asia.

Regional Power Relationships

Governments in Asia Pacific watched carefully and took measures to deal with several major changes in regional power relationships:

- The rise of China as an economic and increasingly capable military power. Freed from the Soviet threat and buttressed by layers of internal security forces, Chinese leaders focused more military resources on power projection—notably air, sea, and missile forces. Backed by rapid economic growth and burgeoning foreign trade, China's rise was likely to remain among the most important regional changes for years to come. It raised angst particularly in Taiwan, Japan, and some Southeast Asian nations. The implications of Beijing's political power and influence, developing in tandem with its economic and military power, coincided with some concerns over Chinese internal stability. The authoritarian regime faced numerous internal problems associated with accession to the World Trade Organization (WTO), as well as economic reforms and political and ethnic dissidence.

- The implications of Japan's poor economic growth and seeming political weakness for its regional leadership aspirations and capabilities, especially in comparison with China. The combination of China's rise and Japan's stagnation led to competition between the two for influence in the region, among other things. This rivalry was evident in the increased Japanese military engagement abroad, notably in support of US-led operations in South and Southwest Asia, which developed despite controversy in Japan and among some neighboring states, including South Korea and China.

- Heightened tensions over Taiwan, which posed the risk of a conflict or confrontation between China and the United States, and possibly involving Japan.

- Indonesia's leadership decline, which contributed to the weakening of the Association of Southeast Asian Nations (ASEAN) and to uncertainty in Southeast Asia (as discussed in Chapter 6). China and Japan were stepping up competition for influence in Indonesia. Despite ongoing reform efforts, the Indonesian military remained deeply involved in the country's politics, economic development, and social life, and seemed likely to remain deeply involved in these areas given its standing as the single most powerful and influential element of Indonesian society.

Other developments, though less central, also affected regional power relationships: Russia's efforts, especially under President Vladimir Putin, to work with China; the efforts of North Korea and others to gain more influence in regional politics; the more active role of India in security dialogues, exchanges, and other interactions, especially with Japan and Southeast Asian countries; the enhanced efforts of the European Community after the Cold War to develop greater regional influence, largely to foster advantageous economic interchange; and the growing prominence of Middle Eastern and Central Asian countries in long-term Asia Pacific economic and security calculations (particularly energy security).

Korean Relations

Most government leaders were surprised by North Korean leader Kim Jong Il's positive response in 2000 to South Korean president Kim Dae Jung's policy of accommodation with the north. The success of the North Korean–South Korean summit of June 2000, and the related flurry of positive North Korean international activity—notably high-level negotiations with the United States under the Bill Clinton administration—prompted widespread reevaluation of what had heretofore been viewed mainly as a dangerous military standoff on the Korean peninsula. The thaw proved to be short-lived. Changes in US and North Korean policy led to a major and prolonged crisis, from 2002 to 2007, over North Korea's resumption of nuclear weapon building and its assertions that it possessed functioning nuclear weapons beginning in the fall of 2004.

The brief thaw in North Korean–South Korean relations in 2000 led to diplomatic initiatives by Russia, China, ASEAN, and others to influence Korean affairs. High-level contacts between the Clinton administration and North Korean officials invigorated bilateral relations, but were suspended by the George W. Bush administration during a protracted policy review in 2001. Anxious not to be left out of decisions affecting Korea that had broad implications for regional stability and security, Japan tried to manage public bilateral differences with North Korea and to renew engagement with Pyongyang. The thaw in North-South relations also led to some decline in South Korean popular support for the large US troop presence there, and prompted diverse reactions in Japan about the size, scope, and mission of US forces based in Japan. The diplomatic thaw of 2000 continued toward South Korea, even while tensions resumed on the Korean peninsula in 2002, when North Korea broke away from international restrictions and openly sought to develop nuclear weapons. The six-party talks established in 2003 to deal with the nuclear crisis saw South Korea, China, and Russia maintain generally conciliatory positions toward North Korea, while the United States and Japan took a harder-line stance.

Economic Concerns

The improved performance of most Asia Pacific regional economies following the 1997–1998 Asian economic crisis was a source of some optimism to government leaders, but it failed to mask continuing anxiety about future performance. The previous model of government-directed, export-oriented growth faced increasing challenges from economic globalization. Japanese officials were particularly concerned about how to reform in order to generate growth after a decade of stagnation. China's growth figures were impressive, but were seen by Beijing as the minimum required to sustain social stability; a heavy imperative was placed on continued growth. Recent growth in South Korea and other economies often came without significant structural reform, potentially setting the stage for another downturn like the one in 1997–1998.

The Asian economic crisis not only hit regional economies hard, but also sidetracked military modernization programs, seriously undermined social stability, challenged the standing of political regimes whose legitimacy rested heavily on providing economic growth, and weakened national security. It was a leading factor in the collapse of the Suharto government in Indonesia. It also prompted widespread popular and elite resentment over economic globalization and International Monetary Fund (IMF) rescue efforts. Most governments nonetheless continued to accept the need to accommodate norms on ownership, markets, trade, and investment. To seriously resist those norms could jeopardize economic development, and thereby undermine domestic political support for Asia Pacific leaders, whose political legitimacy was based heavily on their effectiveness in promoting economic growth and overall national power.

Information vs. Control
Regional states generally continued to accommodate the freer flow of information needed to modernize their economies, open markets, and promote common efforts to improve the environment and fight terrorism, international crime, and disease. To do otherwise risked economic downturn and stagnant development; these in turn could undermine national security and the legitimacy and popular support of Asia Pacific governments, which depended on improving economic conditions and living standards to support their continuation in power.

The freer flow of information stemming from the global communications revolution promoted greater political pluralism, democracy, and respect for human rights, all of which challenged Asian authoritarian regimes. Several of these governments sought to control the Internet and other forms of information exchange, in order to secure their political control. Most governments remained concerned that the Internet and other means of communication could be used by ethnic, regional, religious, terrorist, or other groups to challenge national identity and control and weaken the ability of the state to establish cohesive policies and programs.

US Policy
After the Cold War, many countries in the region feared a US withdrawal (Van Ness and Gurtov 2005). Although still present in some quarters, this concern has been superseded by regional uncertainty over US regional objectives and angst over US unilateralism. For instance, at the start of the Kosovo crisis in 1999, Asian observers did not expect the United States to use political, economic, and especially military power and influence to achieve its goals, which they did not see as warranting such a strong US effort. US decisions to move ahead with national and regional missile defense programs were seen as a serious disruption to Asian security, and notably as a challenge to China's security interests. The US-led war against the Taliban regime in Afghanistan and against Saddam Hussein in Iraq, combined with the broader antiterrorism efforts taking aim at Iran in the Persian Gulf and North Korea in East Asia, prompted mixed regional reactions, with some governments concerned that the rapid rise of the US military presence and influence in Asia could negatively affect regional security and their national interests.

Perceived US unilateralism and unpredictability led to widespread criticism of the United States and added to the difficulties of Japan and South Korea in balancing US basing requirements with domestic pressures to reduce or adjust the US military presence. Among other considerations, this unreliability of the United States prompted the Asian powers to seek ways to work out important international security problems on their own, or in conjunction with other regional or non-US outside powers. In addition to South Korea's opening to North Korea, South Korea and Japan at times tried to improve security relations; the increase in these countries' respective security dialogues with China, Russia, and India, as well as Japan's efforts to engage more closely with Southeast Asian countries on some regional security issues, was part of this broad trend.

Governments of Asia Pacific, including US allies in Japan, South Korea, and Thailand, resented what they perceived as heavy-handed or unhelpful US demands for reform and other measures during the Asian economic crisis. The governments of Asia Pacific also tended to view US efforts as fostering political issues and values, such as human rights and democracy, and as driving often unpredictable US domestic interests that came at the expense of the regional states' national sovereignty and security.

Regional Dynamics and Trends

In general terms, the determinants noted above resulted in regional security and other trends that diffused leadership and power, adding to the unpredictability of the types of tactical alliances or ad hoc blocs that might emerge on specific issues (similar patterns of fluid alliances and shifting government priorities are discussed in Chapter 6). The increase in policy initiatives coming from Asia Pacific governments was based more on insecurity and uncertainty over growing challenges and changing regional trends than on careful, long-term strategic plans.

Regional security and economic trends pushed power relations in Asia Pacific in various and often complicated or seemingly contradictory directions, so that a static bloc of countries dominating Asian affairs did not emerge, though an increase in Asia-only forums as an outgrowth of intraregional interaction was evident:

- While staying engaged with the United States for economic and other benefits, China sought to diminish US influence in order to enhance its own power and prominence. China endorsed Japan-led regional economic measures that ignored or were at odds with US policy, but it also continued to guard against rising Japanese influence as a result of those measures.

- Japan sought to strengthen its regional influence by solidifying the US alliance while simultaneously promoting initiatives that were often at odds with or in disregard of US policy.
- Thailand, the Philippines, and Singapore sought stronger demonstrations of US support, but they also continued at times to join with China in criticizing US policy, and with Japan, South Korea, China, and the EU in pursuing economic initiatives that ignored or opposed US interests. For example, all the Asian governments endorsed the economic and other initiatives considered at the December 2005 summit of Asian leaders, which excluded the United States.

Sometimes, significant developments caused reactions and initiatives by individual countries to converge, leading to a broader pattern of cooperation. Regional cooperation to deal with terrorism grew markedly with the encouragement of the United States after September 11, 2001. The regional powers also continued reaching out beyond their immediate neighbors in seeking leverage from expanded exchanges with Russia, India, and powers in Europe, the Middle East, and Central Asia.

Security Initiatives and "Hedging"

All regional powers continued "hedging"—using more diversified diplomacy, military preparations, and other means to ensure that their particular security interests would be safeguarded, especially in case the regional situation should change for the worse. All powers wanted generally positive relations with the United States, but sought diversified ties to enhance their security options. They differed on a strong US regional security presence, with China notably encouraging a gradual weakening of the US position as it sought expanded regional influence, while most others backed a strong US presence. Regional governments were divided over US missile defense plans, and offered mixed support to the US antiterrorism campaign (Green and Dalton 2000).

Chinese civil and military leaders appeared to agree that Chinese military forces should focus both on building power-projection capabilities and on coping with technical advances in modern warfare. In this effort, China relied on Russian arms and technical support to modernize its military in preparation for possible contingencies involving the United States in the Taiwan area. Chinese and Japanese leaders remained deeply suspicious of the other side's intentions. China opposed the strengthening of the US-Japanese alliance and US-Japanese efforts to develop theater missile defenses. Additionally, China wished to join with Russia, India, and some ASEAN states to use the ASEAN Regional Forum (ARF) and other forums to oppose US-backed security policies that would intrude on Chinese interests. Chinese collaboration with India remained limited by deeply rooted territorial and security differences, however. China worked with the six-member Shanghai Cooperation Organization

(SCO) to restrict US influence in Central Asia. Though it was forced by the imperative of the US-led antiterrorism campaign to support US military actions there, the SCO in 2005 said the United States should declare a timetable for withdrawing troops from the area.

Economic and other ties bound Japan and China, but historical, territorial, and strategic differences lingered. Japanese leaders at times showed diminished certainty that they could rely on the alliance with the United States to deal with security contingencies, notably China's rise. Rather, Japanese leaders were more determined to try to solidify the US alliance while also handling security issues more independently.

The Japanese government welcomed the George W. Bush administration's priority treatment of Japan. Japanese leaders overcame significant domestic political opposition and complaints from neighboring governments to deploy Japanese military forces abroad in support of US-led missions related to the wars against Afghanistan and Iraq. Though strongly supporting the US alliance, Japan also prepared for possible serious difficulty in the US security relationship as a result of a major incident involving US bases or a military crisis in East Asia (e.g., the Taiwan Strait) involving US forces in Japan. It pursued some initiatives internally and overseas that were designed to ensure Japanese interests without direct reference to the US alliance. For example, the Japanese government developed reconnaissance satellites independent of the United States. It maintained political and other relations with Iran and Burma, despite strong US opposition to those governments. Japan also worked to improve security and other ties with India, South Korea, Southeast Asia, and Russia, partly as a hedge against a possible crisis in its ambivalent relationship with China.

South Korea strove to diversify contacts to protect its interests in dealing with North Korea and other powers concerned with the peninsula. While maintaining its US alliance, it increasingly moved on its own to improve relations with North Korea, China, Japan, and Russia to safeguard its interests on the Korean peninsula. South Korean military leaders appeared to support a strong, close alliance with the United States, while government political leaders reflected the greater ambivalence regarding the US connection prevalent in South Korean society.

North Korea focused on ties with the United States in the 1990s but sought improved relations with a variety of powers and gave new priority to North Korean–South Korean dialogue at the time of the Pyongyang summit in June 2000. It returned to a strong, albeit negative, focus on relations with the United States in 2001–2002, foreshadowing a major crisis over North Korea's nuclear weapons program beginning in 2002. Meanwhile, Kim Jong Il's "military first" policies underscored the regime's close identity with the North Korean armed forces (see Chapter 4 for further details).

Less preoccupied with internal threats, Southeast Asian military leaders followed their governments in seeking improved security relations with Japan,

India, and others as they endeavored to deal constructively with China's growing power and influence in the area. Typical of the balanced approach followed by many in Southeast Asia, Thailand carefully weighed relations with the United States, Japan, and China, striving to remain on good terms with the three powers. It backed the US-Japanese alliance, constructive US-Chinese ties, and also greater involvement of the European Union (EU) in Asia.

The major flanking powers—Russia and India—used diplomacy, military exchanges and sales, and other interactions to heighten their respective influence in regional security affairs. They remained open to Asia Pacific powers interested in using contacts with Moscow and New Delhi to hedge against negative contingencies. Their influence remained constrained by geography, economic limitations, and more pressing policy priorities, and their policies often contradicted each other. For example, closer security contacts between Japan and India probably were motivated, in part, by their respective concerns over China's rising military capabilities, as a result of transfers of advanced Russian weapons and military technology to China.

Economic and Political Trends
Meanwhile, economic and political trends affected broader regional dynamics and thereby had a general impact on security trends in the region. While generally recognizing the need to conform to international economic norms, Asia Pacific governments sought to block or slow perceived adverse consequences of economic globalization by greater cooperation with similarly affected governments within and outside the region in existing organizations like ASEAN, the Asia-Pacific Economic Cooperation (APEC), and the WTO, and in emerging regional and broader groupings, notably ASEAN Plus Three. Annual ASEAN Plus Three summits began in 1997, and ministers met on a regular basis. Regional officials welcomed proposals for a China-ASEAN free trade agreement, and for a possible free trade agreement that would also include South Korea and Japan. National rivalries and other regional differences were less of an obstacle than in the past to Asia Pacific multilateral economic cooperation. These rivalries and differences remained more of an obstacle to multilateral cooperation over more sensitive security issues, though nascent multilateral security dialogues and interchange became more common in ASEAN and ASEAN Plus Three forums.

Regional governments strongly opposed outside pressure for political rights and democracy that came at the expense of national sovereignty and stability. Firm in their own convictions, regional powers—including US allies—consulted with one another at the UN General Assembly, the annual UN Human Rights Commission meetings in Geneva, and other forums in finding independent paths for dealing with regional human rights and other political issues. Some appealed to nationalism—a powerful force in many of the newly emerged regional states—in efforts to mobilize their populations against the perceived outside pressure and domination.

▨ Key Security Issues

Korea

The situation on the Korean peninsula posed major security issues. On the one hand, the United States worked with allies and other interested powers to deter a North Korean attack on South Korea and to curb North Korea's development and proliferation of weapons of mass destruction (WMD). The main concerned powers—the United States, South Korea, Japan, China, and Russia—sought to avoid conflict or increased military tensions on the peninsula. The United States worked closely with its allies, South Korea and Japan, in formal consultative mechanisms to arrive at broadly compatible policies on Korean security questions. US officials consulted closely with China on such questions, and also discussed Korean issues with the Russian administration of President Putin, which showed a much more active interest than had its predecessor regarding Korean and other East Asian affairs. The main arena of such consultation was the six-party talks that began in 2003, involving the five concerned powers and North Korea. The talks made little progress until February 2007.

Though all five concerned powers agreed that the Korean peninsula should be nuclear-free, they disagreed on the best approach for achieving this common goal. The Japanese government appeared to support the George W. Bush administration's reserved and firm posture toward North Korea. South Korea's president Kim Dae Jung and his successor, Roh Moo Hyun, seemed to chafe under restrictive US policies toward North Korea, while China and Russia advised against the rise of tension on the peninsula as a result of US–North Korean differences. South Korea sought to ease tensions with North Korea through a policy of engagement, beginning in the late 1990s, known as the "Sunshine" policy. The north-south political détente arguably brought greater stability to the peninsula, but clearly reduced the US leadership role in Korean security issues. This changed dynamic raised the possibility of greater independent action by South Korea, North Korea, and other concerned powers, as each sought specific interests and greater influence in the increasingly fluid situation governing Korean affairs. In this context, the upsurge in military tensions beginning in 2002–2003 caused some South Korean, Chinese, and Russian officials to lay blame on the United States. Some accused the United States of keeping tensions high on the peninsula for self-serving reasons—such as to support the continued US military presence in Korea and Japan and to justify US missile defense programs targeted against the North Korean threat.

The upsurge in tension on the peninsula also increased already active debate within the United States over the appropriate US posture toward North Korea. US congressional members and media commentators were critical of the Bush administration's posture toward North Korea, with some urging more US–North Korean engagement. In 2001, some of these critics echoed the accusations made by South Korean, Chinese, and Russian officials that the administration was pursuing a firm stance toward North Korea in order to sustain an image of a North Korean WMD threat that helped to justify the Bush administration's strong push for an expensive and controversial missile defense program designed to protect the United States from missile attack from North Korea and other hostile states. The contrast between the Bush administration's diplomatic approach to the North Korean nuclear weapons development and the harsher US approach to Saddam Hussein over Iraq's WMD programs has been a salient issue in congressional and media commentary since 2002.

Through 2006, little progress had been made in resolving the North Korean crisis, and it appeared likely that it would take a protracted process involving diplomacy, negotiations, and possible sanctions and military moves to seek safeguards regarding North Korea's nuclear program. North Korea's testing of a nuclear weapon in October 2006 further heightened tensions. After months of no progress, North Korea finally returned to the negotiating table and on February 13, 2007, agreed to halt its nuclear weapons program in exchange for approximately US$300 million in aid and steps toward renormalization of relations with the United States and Japan.

As of March 2007, it remained too early to tell if North Korea would abide by its agreements or how the arrangement might impact relations among the six parties to the talks. It is possible that this forward movement in curbing North Korea's nuclear missile threat might challenge some of the arguments in favor of US missile defense programs. Any rapid reconciliation between North and South Korea could greatly heighten regional uncertainty over the long-term security framework in Northeast Asia, could make more difficult US alliance management efforts with both South Korea and Japan, and could add to questions about the overall US force structure in East Asia. South Korean anger and frustrations over a perceived decline in the rationale for a US military presence, when linked to better ties with the north, could prompt Seoul to speed the downsizing of the US military presence or to give less attention to US interests.

Friction Between China and the United States

China's differences with the United States over security issues in Northeast Asia, especially Taiwan, complicated security and US relations in the region. In addition to opposing US support for Taiwan, China worked against US efforts to strengthen the alliance with Japan, and probably would oppose a US military presence in Korea in the event of reunification. Beijing also tried to move discussion and decisions in regional bodies like ASEAN Plus Three, the SCO (Russia, China, Kazakhstan, Kyrgyzstan, Uzbekistan, and Tajikistan), and ARF in directions that impeded US strategic leadership in the region. China supported the US-led antiterrorism campaign, but worked against a long-term US military presence along China's western flank. Among the world powers (e.g., Russia, Europe, Japan, India), China was one of the most reserved in its support for the US-led war against the Taliban, and maintained substantive differences with the United States on Taiwan, Tibet, Xinjiang, human rights, WMD proliferation, and other issues.

Even close US allies were reluctant to take sides in US-Chinese disputes over regional security issues, and they were particularly worried about Taiwan. The Chen Shui-bian administration in Taiwan, and China's reaction to it, underlined trends toward greater separatism on the island and Beijing's determination to rely on military power to press Taiwan to return to "one China" talks. Although a large attack by the People's Liberation Army (PLA) was unlikely (barring major provocation by Taiwan or the United States), some military conflict or large-scale show-of-force exercises in the next few years would add substantially to regional tensions. Under such circumstances, Japan, South Korea, and Australia probably would urge restraint on all sides.

US ability to manage the volatile tensions in the Taiwan Strait was questionable. Many analysts judged that cross-strait relations would remain a dangerous hot spot in the region for the foreseeable future. The prospects for a repetition of the large-scale PLA exercises like those in 1995–1996, or of small military incidents between PLA and Taiwan forces, were significant, even though China probably would not be in a position to militarily coerce or defeat Taiwan for several more years, if then. Such demonstrations or incidents could escalate into broader military confrontation and combat, despite the intent of concerned leaders to avoid such an outcome.

The determinants of continued tensions in cross-strait relations were strong. In recent years, Beijing viewed Taiwan's movement toward greater political separatism as antithetical to China's core concern with national sovereignty and reunification. Chinese officials remained deeply distrustful of President Chen Shui-bian. They tended to view him and his party as endeavoring to appear moderate on cross-strait issues in order to assuage US and world opinion and to win favor in Taiwan, preparing to move toward greater independence when the time becomes ripe.

Beijing officials showed some satisfaction that China's recent tactics weakened the Chen Shui-bian administration and helped to slow the movement toward political separatism on Taiwan. These tactics saw Beijing shun Chen and his party while warmly interacting with opposition-party leaders who were willing to voice positions on cross-strait issues somewhat compatible with Beijing's "one China" stance. The booming cross-strait economic relations also braked independence sentiment on Taiwan, as Taiwan's economy increasingly relied on trade and investment with the Chinese mainland.

Nevertheless, the pattern of China's military modernization and buildup in the Taiwan area continued and intensified. This expensive, multifaceted effort involved some extraordinary measures, notably the wide-ranging purchases of advanced Russian military equipment targeted to assist the PLA in dealing with military contingencies focused on Taiwan, including the possible intervention of US forces to protect Taiwan. This effort demonstrated that senior Chinese leaders relied on military means both to halt Taiwan's move toward separatism and to press Taiwan to seek talks with China leading to eventual reunification. China's 2005 antisecession law definitively articulated Beijing's obligation to use force should political means fail to reunify the country.

The military buildup probably did not mean that China was prepared to attack Taiwan—analysts pointed to continuing weaknesses and the dire consequences for Beijing leaders if they failed to win victory in the face of Taiwanese and possible US resistance. The military buildup nonetheless significantly added to regional tension and increased the danger of massive negative consequences for regional peace and stability if conflict were to break out due to either an unexpected escalation of cross-strait skirmishing or actions by Taiwan (e.g., declaration of independence) seen to fundamentally challenge China's vital interests.

Taiwan, meanwhile, seemed unready to give ground to Beijing on significant cross-strait political issues. The Chen Shui-bian administration's limited flexibility was due in part to its political base in the Democratic Progressive Party, which had long championed Taiwan's status independent of mainland control. The previous ruling party, the Nationalist Party, and the People's First Party, of breakaway Nationalist Party leader James Soong, were more flexible in comments on cross-strait issues, discussing possible eventual reunification and appealing to Beijing's "one China" sensitivities. Popular sentiment on the island remained cautious, however. Opinion polls showed little support for pursuit of greater Taiwan independence in ways that would antagonize Beijing, and strong support for the status quo in cross-strait relations.

ASEAN Weakness

ASEAN's problems, notably the drift in Indonesia, added to internal weaknesses, complicating security and stability in Southeast Asia. Under pressure from domestic forces, several Southeast Asian governments provided only mixed support for the US antiterrorism campaign after 2001:

- A rift persisted between, on the one hand, some ASEAN states (like Thailand and the Philippines), which exerted pressure, individually as well as through multinational organizations, to intervene to address internal strife in neighboring countries and, on the other hand, ASEAN states like Vietnam, Burma, and Cambodia, which strongly resisted any outside interference in domestic affairs. These conflicts weakened ASEAN and added to instability in Southeast Asia.
- ASEAN weakness and divisions, notably on issues dealing with the authoritarian regimes in Burma and Cambodia, undermined the ability of Southeast Asia to balance or impede China's expanding influence in those two countries. The fractures also made it more difficult for ASEAN members to deal with South China Sea territorial disputes, terrorism in Southeast Asia, piracy, and crime.

Regime Decay

The example of Indonesia's instability after Suharto underlined a set of major security issues—how to deal with significant decay or possible collapse of important Asian states. Indonesia's political decay was arrested by the coming to power of a more effective administration under President Megawati in 2001, but the underlying political, economic, and social issues facing the country portended continued instability and challenged governance.

The Indonesian military remained a big part of this problem. Its continued prominence assured it a strong role in Indonesia's political, economic, and social affairs. Military leaders' views generally differed with those of ardent reformers in Indonesia and abroad. Opinion among military leaders tended to range from those who supported democratization, but stressed that steady implementation of reforms was needed to ensure the continued high stature of the military, to those who sought a return to the autocratic system of the past, but under a new leader who more fully appreciated the power and support of the armed forces.

Meanwhile, declining economic conditions elsewhere in Southeast Asia added to the fragility of other governments, notably the Philippines. Unlike many of its neighbors, the Philippines remained preoccupied with domestic instability and was unable to modernize its armed forces in order to protect its offshore territorial claims and monitor its lengthy coastline.

The United States, Japan, China, and other concerned powers proved to be relatively ineffective in dealing with trends in post-Suharto Indonesia. Continued decay there, combined with political decline in other Southeast Asian countries, seriously challenged US and other foreign policymakers, who had few levers at their disposal to influence such circumstances. Increased US government attention to fighting terrorism in Southeast Asia after September 11, 2001, unfortunately did not reverse these important negative political and economic trends.

Regime decay in Northeast Asia would have more serious security implications. The most immediate concern focused on North Korea. Though Kim Jong Il consolidated his power following the death of his father, the economy remained in a collapsed state, starvation continued, and regime survival depended heavily on coercive means. The United States, South Korea, and other concerned powers appeared in general accord that gradual change and not rapid collapse in North Korea was in their collective interests, and each was pursuing policies toward this end, despite significant differences on tactics.

A less likely but much more serious set of problems for regional security would come in the event of significant regime decay or collapse in China. The United States and other powers were poorly prepared to deal with this possibility. US policy attention focused on China as a possible danger or threat to US interests in the context of Taiwan, WMD proliferation, and competition for influence in Asian and world affairs. Yet the danger of potentially serious regime decay or even collapse was significant. Chinese leaders faced a wide range of challenges to their authority and legitimacy as they endeavored to manage economic and social order. The demands of WTO accession, broader economic globalization, and the information revolution compounded existing problems. The regime strove to preserve unity as it proceeded through a sensitive leadership transition from Jiang Zemin to Hu Jintao.

Management of US Alliances

Japan and South Korea supported their respective alliances with the United States, yet both Tokyo and Seoul, like many US allies in Europe and elsewhere, continued to chafe over the asymmetry of their alliance relationship with the US superpower. Each sought adjustments in the US military presence to accommodate their own nationalistic or local concerns. Further reduction of military tensions between North and South Korea would appear to reinforce this tendency. In particular, Japanese and South Korean authorities could seek modifications in US military bases, pursue status-of-forces agreements, and host nation support arrangements. Both governments remained sensitive to accidents or crimes by US military personnel that could give rise to strong popular pressure against US bases.

John A. Lee. US Defense Department photo.

A South Korean soldier in the demilitarized zone between North and South Korea. In 2003 the United States and South Korea announced that 12,500 of the 37,000 US troops based in the zone would be redeployed elsewhere.

Southeast Asian allies and friends, notably Thailand, the Philippines, and Singapore, saw US interests much less involved in, and the United States much less committed to, Southeast Asia in comparison with Northeast Asia. This pattern continued despite the uptick in US antiterrorism cooperation with many Southeast Asian governments after September 11, 2001. They continued to be concerned that the United States might pull back militarily from the region. Southeast Asian allies and friends of the United States viewed ASEAN and related security dialogues in ARF and other bodies as no substitute for a continued strong US regional presence. The nations sought reassurances of US commitment and participated in some US military activities, notably multifaceted military exercises and exchanges. The Philippines welcomed the US antiterrorism campaign beginning in 2001, in part to build closer military ties with the United States. However, others in Southeast Asia—pressed by domestic groups critical of the US war effort—were more wary of close US ties.

The Southeast Asian countries eschewed strong public signs of support for the US military presence, particularly to avoid antagonizing China; they sometimes even joined with China and others in criticizing US security policies in the region or globally. They were well aware that China, a growing power and one permanently involved in the region by virtue of geography, opposed a strong US military presence in the area. Meanwhile, they worked pragmatically with Russia, India, Japan, and other countries to deal with security issues, such as piracy and smuggling.

US Missile Defense

Russia's grudging acquiescence in late 2001 to the George W. Bush administration's missile defense programs somewhat reduced the salience of missile defense as a divisive issue in Asian security. China still strongly opposed the US programs, however. Much of the rest of the region disapproved of a strong US push to develop and deploy national and theater missile defenses that disregarded Chinese concerns. If the United States were to move forward with a national missile defense program in conjunction with stepped-up theater missile defense programs in East Asia, this would divide the region. Japan most likely would support the United States and continue collaboration on theater missile defense, but few other regional governments (South Korea included) would support such a US stance. Regional complications would be heightened if the United States were to provide missile defenses for Taiwan.

▓ Japan

Japan's armed forces have long had minimal domestic responsibilities and have been concerned almost entirely with external defense. They have focused on professional development under the control of civilian leaders since the end of World War II, and have avoided interference in Japanese politics or other domestic affairs.

Continuing serious economic difficulties, security issues, and other recent challenges raise serious questions in Japan about the viability of its long-standing post–World War II national strategy for development and security. The goal of Japan's postwar national strategy, as laid out by Prime Minister Shigeru Yoshida just after the war, was to gradually reestablish Japan's national power and preeminence. The strategy emphasized economic recovery and expansion to rebuild Japanese national wealth, and with that wealth, power and influence. The primacy of economics fit well with widespread Japanese postwar aversion to militarism and the use of force. But with the bipolar Cold War heating up, Japan could pursue economic growth only if its security were guaranteed. It thus relied on the United States for external security in exchange for hosting a large, permanent US military presence.

Japan's strategy was successful. Legally, politically, and socially constrained from rebuilding a credible military capability, Japan grew and became an economic superpower and leader by the 1980s. Not only did this strategy benefit Japan, but the bilateral security arrangement supported the US Cold War security strategy in the Pacific, and was quietly endorsed by the rest of Asia as a check against future Japanese militarism.

Forces for Change
In the 1990s, Japan's national strategy for development and security came under challenge and changed because of several key factors.

Post–Cold War threats and uncertainties. The end of the Cold War and collapse of the Soviet Union altered Japan's threat environment. It dismantled the Cold War strategic framework for the East Asian security equation; it removed Japan's foremost security threat, against which Japan's force structure was configured; and it took away the initial rationale for Japan's post–World War II geostrategic bargain with the United States. Japanese leaders viewed the strategic situation in East Asia as more unsettled than during the Cold War, with a number of near-term flashpoints and longer-term uncertainties shaping Japan's security calculus.

North Korea was the most pressing security issue. Pyongyang's Taepo Dong missile flight over Japan in August 1998 galvanized a national sense of vulnerability. Japan previously had viewed North Korea as posing an indirect threat in terms of regional instability and refugee flows, as well as a potential problem for the alliance should rifts emerge with the United States over expected Japanese involvement in a Korean contingency. The missile launch, combined with North Korea's active nuclear program evident after 2002, elevated North Korea to a direct military threat to Japan.

The prospect of a unified Korea added to future uncertainty. History and geography make Korea an important security concern for Japan. Despite efforts to improve bilateral ties with South Korea, Japan continued to be suspicious of Korea. The external orientation of a future unified Korea—how it would relate to Beijing, the type of military capability it would possess, and the posture it would assume toward Japan—was seen in Japan as a major factor in the future security equation in Northeast Asia.

Taiwan was a near-term concern. Japanese leaders feared that an outbreak of hostilities in the Taiwan Strait, involving US forces, would draw in Japan under the US-Japanese Defense Guidelines. The extent and role of Japanese involvement in a military conflict among China, Taiwan, and the United States would have required difficult decisions of Japan, which would have been forced to weigh the need to support its ally against the costs such actions would entail for its future relationship with China.

China was a growing factor in Japan's security calculations. Neither Japan's policymakers nor its public defined China as an inevitable threat, however. China was seen more as an uncertainty that Japan must actively position itself to deal with on many fronts, rather than as a threat to be actively countered. Some in Japan expressed fears that China might become more aggressive and coercive—for example, in the disputed Senkaku/Diaoyu Islands—as it sought regional preeminence. Others, however, were more concerned by the perceived economic threat China posed to Japan, and still others saw the potential for instability in China and worried about the physical and economic implications for Japan's security of a weak, fragmented, and unpredictable China.

Instability in Southeast Asia posed a threat to Japanese political, economic, and security interests. Disruption could jeopardize lines of communication at sea, threaten Japanese nationals, and complicate regional security dynamics. Japan's security interests were largely compatible with those of Southeast Asia—preventing regional hegemony, maintaining a regional US presence as a stabilizing force, carefully managing China's regional role as it grows in power, and coping with terrorism, piracy, and crime.

Russia was low on the list of Japan's security worries, but this view could change if Russian nationalism were to grow and to look eastward. One Japanese concern was Russian weapons proliferation and the problems this posed in Asia, particularly Russian-Chinese arms deals. Although the Northern Territories dispute remained a traditional security issue, Japan continued to deal with the problem in the diplomatic arena, subordinating it to the broader goal of good relations with Russia.

Long-term energy and economic concerns drove much of Japan's diplomatic and economic activity in the Middle East. Japan saw its interests well served by strong support for the US-led antiterrorism operations in Central and Southwest Asia beginning in 2001.

Perceptions of US security policy. Until the 1990s, Japanese policymakers were confident that the United States needed Japan, and that the alliance was just as critical for Washington's security strategy as it was for Tokyo's. In the post–Cold War period, this confidence was questioned for several reasons.

Japan was unsure how Washington defined its strategic role in the post–Cold War era. The updated US-Japanese Defense Guidelines notwithstanding, Japanese observers envisioned a crisis in the alliance, provoked either by Japan's failure to provide expected assistance to the United States in a contingency or by the US decision not to engage on a security issue important to Japan. Prime Minister Junichiro Koizumi endeavored to avoid an image of Japan failing to provide expected assistance by adopting a high profile in support of the US antiterrorism campaign after 2001.

Japanese leaders assessed that Japan's economic stagnation made the country less important to the United States. Japan also was uncertain of US policy on China. It feared a zero-sum dynamic in which the United States would conclude that its long-term national interest depended most importantly on a strategic understanding with China, and would therefore pull back from Japan if it became an obstacle to this agenda. At the same time, however, Japan feared that poor US management of its China relationship could lead Washington to use Japan explicitly to counter growing Chinese power, a role Japan did not want and presumably would actively resist.

Other factors also came into play. Japan's economic stagnation in the 1990s severely shook the long-standing Japanese belief in economic power as its key lever of international importance and influence. The post–World War II Japanese political system was undergoing major changes, weakening the political leadership. Generational change produced greater pride and assertiveness: growing nationalism in Japan highlighted the country's postwar accomplishments and its desire to be viewed as a modern, responsible state.

Constraints and Continuities

The forces for change in Japanese security policy ran up against strong constraints and continuities that curbed Japanese tendencies toward increasing assertiveness in security affairs:

- Support for the US alliance remained high. Any deliberate actions that would directly undermine the alliance would have been hugely controversial and unlikely to succeed.
- Consensus building in a democracy in which power was increasingly diffuse made change in sensitive security areas difficult.
- Japanese leaders remained cautious and oriented toward the status quo.
- Low economic growth reinforced a status quo security orientation and limited the resources available to substantially increase Japan's current plans for force modernization.

- Antimilitarism and pacifist sentiment remained strong, especially among the elderly. This sentiment dictated a cautious, incremental approach to any changes in how Japan used its military, as demonstrated by the difficulties of achieving even modest changes in Japan's peace-keeping legislation.
- Japanese leaders also were wary of drawing a negative reaction from Asian neighbors, either by strengthening defense capabilities or by taking steps that appeared to pull away from the US alliance.

Defense spending in Japan increased slowly or stayed constant in the early 2000s. It continued to amount to just under 1 percent of Japan's gross domestic product (GDP)—valued at around US$40–50 billion. Japan proved to be an active ally in the US war against terrorism, passing legislation allowing Japanese forces to support US military operations in Afghanistan and Iraq, and committing resources to reconstruction efforts in both countries. The Japanese government also worked closely with the US government in seeking to resolve issues over the extensive US bases in Okinawa, burden-sharing questions, and coordinating policy toward the volatile situation in Korea. Signs of change in Japanese security posture tended to be subtle.

Anxiety about the US alliance. Japanese observers continued to raise serious questions over the nature, relevance, and flexibility of the alliance. The alliance remained central to Japan's security—Japan needed and wanted the alliance to continue, and deeply feared the consequences if it did not. Nonetheless, Japanese leaders had major concerns about asymmetry and sought a more reciprocal arrangement in which the United States would engage in prior consultations on security matters of importance, and would not seek to dictate Japanese government policies or actions related to the alliance, resulting in greater autonomy for Japan. It was uncertain how far the George W. Bush administration's efforts to bolster Japanese autonomy allayed this concern.

Greater assertiveness/activism. Japanese government leaders, backed by military leaders, demonstrated increased initiative in security matters. The decision in 1999 to build indigenous reconnaissance satellites, unusually aggressive responses to the North Korean spy-ship encroachments, and the stepped-up pursuit of foreign military contacts and regional diplomacy all exemplified this more forward-leaning posture. Tokyo expended considerable effort to pass legislation on US-Japanese Defense Guidelines, and sought new ways to cooperate with the United States in the antiterrorism campaign, but it was slow to engage in bilateral planning under the defense guidelines or to tackle a variety of other long-standing base-related issues.

Wider, more active security debate. The notion that Japan would seriously consider constitutional change to ease strictures against military activity had long seemed implausible. However, discussion on that issue has now become acceptable. The constitutional debate, along with moves to pass antiterrorism legislation and to modify peacekeeping legislation, demonstrated a growing maturity and normalcy in thinking about the purpose of the military. Humanitarian interventions and peacekeeping operations increasingly were viewed within Japan as valid roles for the country's Self-Defense Force. Moreover, firing at North Korean spy vessels moved in the direction of using military force as a deterrent, while sending naval destroyers to South Asia during the antiterrorism campaign reflected a more assertive approach. Some Japanese commentators even discussed the possibility of Japan developing nuclear weapons in response to North Korea's nuclear weapons program (Barnabie and Burnie 2005).

China

Chinese Communist Party leaders relied on the military to put down popular insurrection associated with the Tiananmen demonstrations of 1989, but they afterward reached a consensus with military leaders that strengthened internal police and public security forces and allowed the Chinese armed forces to focus on professional development in order to better secure Chinese interests in the international post–Cold War environment. China remained dependent on its economic connections with the developed countries of the West and with Japan. Nonetheless, Chinese nationalism exerted pressure to push policy in directions that resisted US "hegemony" and the power of the United States and its allies in East Asia, notably Japan. Beijing resolved these contrasting pressures by attempting to stay on good terms with its neighbors and by keeping economic and other channels with the United States open, while simultaneously attempting to create a more "multipolar" world through endeavors to weaken overall US power and influence in East Asia and elsewhere. The pace of Chinese military modernization increased in the 1990s and posed some challenge to the already modern and advancing militaries of the United States and its allies and associates in Asia, especially in such nearby areas as Taiwan, where the Chinese development of ballistic and cruise missiles and acquisition of advanced Russian weaponry presented notable dangers.

China also faced a challenging international security environment and was apprehensive about several international security trends. It was concerned about the perceived US "containment" and military "encirclement" of China, US national and theater missile defense programs, and the potential for Japan to improve its regional force-projection capabilities. One concern for China regarding the US-led antiterrorism campaign was that it sharply increased US influence and presence along China's western and southern periphery—adding to Beijing's overall sense of being surrounded by US power and influence. Despite some successes in military modernization, the PLA remained limited in its ability to quickly absorb sophisticated weapon systems and to develop the joint-operations doctrine necessary to use these weapons effectively.

Taiwan, however, was China's main security focus and the biggest problem in US-Chinese relations, both politically and militarily. The issues of continuing US arms sales and missile defense deployments in the region were persistent threats. China and the United States attempted to find common ground in rebuilding relations in the wake of the 1999 US bombing of the Chinese embassy in Belgrade, and they did so again following the downturn in relations resulting from the crash of a US reconnaissance plane and a Chinese jet fighter in 2001. After the September 11, 2001, terrorist attacks against the United States, however, the United States and China resumed cooperation in a number of areas.

Strategic Objectives and Perception
of Chinese Power and Influence

Debate among specialists over the security goals of Chinese leaders is wide-ranging and often intense. In the middle view, Chinese security priorities and practices support and are consistent with several broad regime objectives that enjoy the support of both civilian and military leaders in the country:

- Perpetuation of power, to avoid the fate of the Soviet Union and other East European communist regimes.
- Pursuit of territorial unification and integrity, especially through the reintegration of Taiwan into the People's Republic and, to a lesser degree, through regaining territories in the East and South China seas.
- Modernization of China's economy, technology, and military capabilities and improvement of social conditions, while maintaining stability.

In addition, China has strategic objectives that reflect its status as a rising power.

Regional preeminence. China wants to be in a position of sufficient strength (with both positive and negative incentives) such that other countries in the region will routinely take China's interests and equities into account in determining their own policies. Beijing wishes to be seen as the leading power in Asia, and not as lower in prestige or regional influence than its neighbors. It also wishes to project sufficient power to counter hostile naval and air power.

Global influence. As a permanent member of the UN Security Council, China desires status and prestige among the community of nations. It intends to be a major player in the IMF, the World Bank, the WTO, and other key international institutions. It seeks to assert its influence on all issues that it deems important, not only to protect and defend its interests, but also to bolster its standing as a major power. Chinese leaders believe that international power and prestige are an extension of national economic and technological prowess, which they intend to develop.

In seeking these objectives, Chinese leaders were influenced by their perceptions of power relations in the post–Cold War world. Chinese perceptions of global trends appeared to be in flux, and were a matter of considerable internal debate. Chinese leaders had believed the world was becoming multipolar, with the United States as the single superpower but decreasingly able to exert its will as other countries and regions opposed US initiatives. This view was sharply rebutted beginning in the late 1990s, owing to the striking disparities between economic performance of the United States and those of other major powers, and also to US leadership in the Balkans crisis, US policy on missile defense, the US war on terrorism, and other issues.

The Chinese apparently concluded that the world would be unipolar in the near term, with the United States exerting greater influence than Beijing had originally calculated. Chinese leaders often perceived that this influence might not be benign in relation to China's core interests. They were ambivalent about the spread of US influence along China's flank in Central Asia as a result of the US-led antiterrorism campaign of 2001–2002. Chinese commentary expressed concern about the expansion and strengthening of the US alliance structure and the ability of US-led alliances to intervene globally.

Preoccupied as it was with domestic issues of modernization and stability, Beijing tended to react to international developments. Deng Xiaoping stated that China should not take the lead on key issues, but should take advantage of opportunities, and his successors held to this view. In international forums (the United Nations, the WTO, arms control forums, and other arenas) and in multilateral regional organizations like ASEAN Plus Three, however, China increasingly tried to ensure its place among the rule-makers in the global and regional environment of the twenty-first century. Beijing also perceived that it must continue to build its military capabilities to be able eventually to back up its diplomacy with the threat of force, especially over the status of Taiwan. There appeared to be no notable difference between civilian and military leaders over this and other policy priorities.

Chinese leaders averred that the overall external threat to China was significantly lower than it had been during the Cold War. China nevertheless perceived that internal threats to its stability were often encouraged from the outside. China was convinced that the United States, directly or indirectly, was interfering with Beijing's ability to recover Taiwan and maintain control in Tibet and even Xinjiang.

China saw the United States as colleague in that the two sides spoke of building a "strategic partnership" after 1997, but this ended with the start of the George W. Bush administration. At the same time, China saw the United

States as a competitor and adversary, partly in reaction to perceived anti-China rhetoric and action by the United States. State-fostered nationalism bolstered the common perception among Chinese that the United States was behind many of China's problems:

- Chinese leaders saw the need to construct a US policy that protected China's economic interests while resisting what they saw as the domination of US security arrangements.
- Nevertheless, the prevailing view of China's leaders was that China should not risk opposing the United States directly.
- China also saw many areas of common policy ground between itself and the United States, notably regarding the broad-gauge objectives of both countries to promote regional and world stability, to encourage economic development, and to combat common threats such as terrorism and narcotics trafficking.

Effects of China's Behavior on Asia Pacific Security

Though focused on regime survival and domestic modernization and stability, China's behavior affected security in Asia Pacific in several ways.

Preventing Taiwan's independence. The long-term objective of the People's Republic of China is reunification with Taiwan, but for the foreseeable future, Beijing's focus will be on preventing further steps by Taiwan toward permanent separation. If necessary, China seems prepared to conduct a major military exercise near Taiwan, as it did in March 1996. Also, small-scale incidents between the military forces of the two sides are possible, ranging from an accidental air incident to the seizure by Beijing of a lightly manned offshore island. It remains unlikely, however, that Beijing—unless provoked by extreme actions of Taiwan or the United States—would actually follow through with such large-scale combat operations as invading Taiwan or any of its heavily defended offshore islands, conducting missile attacks against targets on Taiwan, or blockading Taiwan with air or naval forces. Notably, Beijing does not have the military ability to carry out these operations successfully. The international community nonetheless reacted with concern when Beijing announced its antisecession law in March 2005, which pledged a Chinese military response should Taiwan declare independence.

Enhancing military capabilities. China perceived that it needed a long period of peace and stability to improve the economic foundation of its national power. China continued to view economic growth as the basis of military power, but in the 1990s it accorded the improvement of military capabilities a higher priority than previously. This resulted in annual double-digit increases in China's defense budget. The US Defense Department estimated China's overall defense spending in 2002 to be US$65 billion, and in 2006 the estimate was US$65–95 billion.

China's increase in military spending stemmed from its evaluation of the results of US and Western advances (seen notably in the Kosovo intervention and the wars in Afghanistan and Iraq), and from the perceived implications of Taiwan's formulation of "state-to-state" relations and other moves toward greater separatism. A key component of the military priority was to sustain the credibility of China's strategic nuclear and missile capabilities in the face of advancing US technology.

Although competing priorities arose from economic and social objectives, the government nevertheless was able to devote additional resources to military modernization. China, long disappointed by its defense industries, continued to rely heavily on Russia and Israel for advanced weapons and production technologies. China also tried to obtain military technology from the United States, Europe, Japan, and elsewhere via purchase, joint ventures, or espionage.

Emphasizing quality over quantity, China's conventional military acquisitions were designed to counter US and Taiwanese military capabilities that could be brought to bear in a Taiwan Strait crisis, to advance China's claims in the East and South China seas, to secure sea-lanes for Chinese trade, and generally to project Chinese regional power. China emphasized missile, naval, and air modernization, because its military specialists identified these as its most immediate needs. By 2006, purchases of over US$1 billion a year for several years had seen the delivery of advanced Russian destroyers and submarines, a wide array of air defense, air-to-air, and surface-to-surface missiles, and over 200 advanced fighter aircraft.

China also developed its strategic programs, information warfare, and electronic countermeasures. It will soon have operational road-mobile, solid-fueled intercontinental ballistic missiles capable of striking Washington, D.C. (US-China Economic and Security Review Commission 2005). Regarding WMD proliferation, China continued to engage in some sales of military equipment and technology, an activity strongly opposed by the United States. At times, Beijing used proliferation behavior in part as a lever to influence US decisions on weapons sales to Taiwan.

Rising regional influence. China promoted regional stability—that is, stability according to Beijing's definition. Besides preventing Taiwan's steps to independence, China had several priorities in Asia Pacific:

- Counter Japan's growing military cooperation with the United States and prevent a rebirth of Japanese "militarism," but at the same time engage Japan to obtain economic benefit.
- Maintain stability on the Korean peninsula by engaging South Korea without further straining ties to North Korea, and curb North Korea's

nuclear weapons program while avoiding military confrontation and conflict.
- Prevent the development and implementation of theater missile defense in the region.
- Cope with challenges to its claims in the East and South China seas.
- Support its economic interests via bilateral and multilateral mechanisms, while building its political influence in and avoiding challenges from a coalition of states via ASEAN, APEC, or ARF.

The United States remained central to these regional priorities. Consequently, Beijing's actions in the region reflected its assessment of US policies, particularly with respect to US alliance relations, including those with South Korea and Japan. While recognizing the centrality of the United States, China tried to marginalize Washington when opportunities to do so arose. It had tried to keep US influence out of Central Asia and away from China's western flank, felt compelled to reverse course and endorse the upswing in US influence there as part of the antiterrorist campaign launched in 2001, and moved again in 2005 to positions once again directly challenging US military presence in Central Asia.

Meanwhile, Taiwan's defense modernization program, unveiled in 2000, called for three main operational requirements:

- Maintaining air superiority over the strait and contiguous waters.
- Conducting effective counterblockade operations.
- Preparing to defeat an amphibious or aerial assault on Taiwan.

The strong statements of support and large arms packages offered by the George W. Bush administration heartened Taipei. Economic decline and partisan politics resulted in a decline in Taiwan's defense spending, though military reforms under the Chen Shui-bian administration began to make the military more responsive to the central administration's direction. Closer interaction with US defense officials after a long period of relative isolation also foreshadowed improvements in Taiwan's military capabilities.

Korea

Change in North Korean and US policy, along with uncertainty over North Korea's priorities, has made the Korean peninsula the most dynamic area of regional interaction since 2000, and one with direct and important implications for security in Asia Pacific. North Korea's shift in 2000 from confrontational policies to a more moderate, cooperative approach toward South Korea complemented South Korea's efforts to engage the north, resulting in the most significant thaw in north-south relations since the Korean War. Both sides espoused complementary views on the future of the Korean peninsula—at least outwardly envisioning a prolonged coexistence of two distinct governments, though their long-term goals on Korean unification probably remained at odds. Relations cooled in 2001 as North Korea halted progress with South Korea as a means to pressure the George W. Bush administration to be more forthcoming and flexible in policy toward North Korea. Relations between North Korea and the United States reached a major impasse in late 2002, as North Korea admitted to a clandestine nuclear enrichment program and broke international safeguards on its nuclear production sites. South Korea publicly disagreed with US tactics favoring international censure and sanction, and endeavored to pursue an engagement policy toward the north.

Key Determinants of North Korea's Shifting Approach

Kim Jong Il's consolidation of control. The North Korean leader used purges and other means to solidify his personal rule following the death of Kim II Song in 1994. With support from foreign food aid, his regime endured the multiyear famine that began in earnest that same year. Summits with Chinese, South Korean, and Russian leaders, and high-level meetings with the Bill Clinton administration, all reflected Kim's personal diplomacy. He was able to secure important benefits for North Korea while preserving key interests involving internal regime control, military preparedness, WMD capabilities, and long-term goals regarding Korean unification.

Regime needs. North Korean leaders appeared anxious to revitalize the moribund North Korean economy, both to ensure political stability and to achieve the avowed goal of building a strong and prosperous nation. They were stymied by serious obstacles: decrepit power generation and distribution systems; the resulting lack of electric power for industry, agriculture, and transportation; a continuing commitment to collective ownership and a command economy; and lack of international creditworthiness.

US relations and new international priorities. During the 1990s and especially after the 1994 framework agreement, North Korea focused heavily on relations with the United States as its top foreign policy priority; until 2000 it generally endeavored to isolate and marginalize South Korea in discussions concerning peninsula-wide issues. The new millennium saw a change in the north-south relationship, however. While trying to sustain various negotiations with the United States, North Korea decided to work directly with South Korea in pursuing developments on the peninsula and in seeking additional assistance, probably calculating that Kim Dae Jung's engagement efforts were genuine, that the south could offer the largest, most rapid deliverables, and that improved north-south relations would spur the United States and other countries to engage more actively with Pyongyang. The George W. Bush administration, however, curbed contacts with the north, which prompted strong North Korean complaints, slowed North Korean contacts with South Korea, and set the stage for a US–North Korean impasse by late 2002.

*   *   *

North Korea's new openness to South Korea was welcomed in the south, where Kim Dae Jung's engagement policy persisted with the clear objective of seeking a breakthrough in North-South Korean relations. Kim's "Sunshine" policy evolved from an approach that sought to erode public support for Kim Jong Il to one that sought to work with the North Korean leader. As elite and popular opinion became more familiar with costs associated with rapid reunification, South Koreans became more supportive of a prolonged engagement with North Korea that assumed the coexistence of separate governments in the north and south for the foreseeable future. Kim also had his own domestic motivations for promoting the Sunshine policy (for more details, see Chapter 4).

As time passed, the factors that drove the breakthrough in North Korean–South Korean relations in 2000 remained operative, but many positive factors were conditional, and subsequent events revealed that they could turn negative with changes in the pace of north-south progress, the role of the United States and other powers, and the extent of achievements. Both North Korea and South Korea appeared in 2000 to desire incremental, controlled improvements in ties that afforded each progress on their key interests—money and other economic inputs for the north, tension reduction and person-to-person openings for the south. Tension arose out of Pyongyang's fear that it would lose control and out of Seoul's impatience to achieve meaningful results. The shift in US policy from the forward-leaning Clinton stance to the critical and reserved Bush stance also clearly affected North Korea's calculus.

Possible Alternative Outcomes

The zigs and zags in North Korean policy since 2000 underlined the difficulty of predicting trends on the peninsula. Possible alternative outcomes for the security situation in the Korean peninsula varied widely. Analysts were uncertain if recent trends would persist or be overturned by countervailing factors.

Reversion to Cold War tensions. The situation on the peninsula might revert to the tensions and Cold War atmosphere that prevailed prior to the June 2000 summit if prompted by one or more conditions:

- If Kim Jong Il were to determine that the price of continuing along a path of reconciliation with South Korea and others would be too high in terms of social, political, and economic control. His fear of a Romanian scenario could lead him to reverse direction.

- If collective pressure from the United States, South Korea, and other donors were to result in restricted aid to North Korea until Pyongyang met specific demands on sensitive issues like reducing the military threat and curbing WMD, and widely opening and reforming North Korea's economy. The restrictions would prompt a negative North Korean response.
- If Kim Jong Il were to take rapid initial moves toward South Korea but ultimately wane in pursuing them. He would then repeat the pattern successively with the other powers, offering concessions on their respective priorities to obtain needed aid, but then back off and use the gains to shore up his regime and the North Korean system.
- If a major dispute among foreign powers in the region (e.g., China and the United States over Taiwan) were to increase great-power tension on the peninsula and subsequently reduce the likelihood for positive maneuver by North and South Korea.

Continued moderation and some forward movement. North Korean–South Korean relations could continue to develop in important symbolic and substantive ways:

- Continued government-to-government dialogue at expanded levels.
- Growing, but still limited and controlled, economic and commercial interactions and people-to-people exchanges.
- Limited, largely symbolic military gestures in confidence building and tension reduction on the peninsula.
- Shared political will to avoid military, political, or other incidents, and in the event that such incidents continue to occur, to endeavor to neutralize their negative consequences.
- Improving North Korean relations with the United States and other interested foreign powers; continued high priority given to improving North-South relations.

Strategic shift. South Korean and international support could move Kim Jong Il to become increasingly flexible should he decide to allow the momentum of improved relations to broaden and deepen. In this scenario, prospects for much-expanded external assistance and investment would lead Kim to accelerate north-south improvement by making major concessions, including on the military front, and to undertake changes previously considered unlikely—such as economic restructuring and adherence to standards and conditions of international financial institutions.

North Korean collapse. The lessons of the transitions in Eastern Europe after the Cold War, in South Africa, and in other formerly authoritarian regimes underscore the potential for regime collapse in North Korea. How this could come about given Kim Jong Il's multiple layers of security controls in North Korea remains unclear, but the impact of more extensive and hard-to-control foreign contacts, continued dire domestic material needs, and ideological weakness and political corruption would challenge regime stability.

▓ Southeast Asia

The Asian economic crisis had its most serious impact in Indonesia, bringing down the authoritarian Suharto government, but it also provided a central challenge to other leading states of ASEAN. Overall, the crisis weakened Southeast Asian ability to handle security issues. Defense spending declined markedly in several states. Piracy rose along the critical Southeast Asian waterways, prompting Japan, India, and other affected powers to lend a hand to ensure safe communications. The Southeast Asian governments were slow to respond to regional crises such as the fallout from Indonesia's bloody withdrawal from East Timor. They were fortunate that China adopted a more moderate stance toward the region, seeking to build influence through conventional economic, military, and political interchange and through cooperation with the protracted procedures of the various ASEAN-supported dialogues and discussion groups. Disputes among the ASEAN members and China over the Spratly Islands and the South China Sea were relatively dormant, though these could escalate in the future.

US-backed efforts to curb terrorism saw several pacts among regional powers for greater intelligence sharing, joint police operations, and other measures. Nevertheless, there remained a strong reluctance by Indonesian officials and others to take a hard line against Muslim extremists in their countries, despite assertions by the United States and others that the extremists were linked to international terrorist organizations targeted at them.

The founding members of ASEAN in 1967 were Indonesia, the Philippines, Thailand, Malaysia, and Singapore. Five notably weaker Southeast Asian states—Brunei, Burma, Cambodia, Laos, and Vietnam—joined later (for details, see "Southeast Asia" on p. 180). The latter ASEAN members tended to be preoccupied with difficult internal problems and international pressures. Burma's military-dominated regime continued to walk a fine line between seeking greater international legitimacy and maintaining tight controls on domestic political opponents. Vietnam, Cambodia, and Laos to varying degrees faced the problems of authoritarian leaders trying to maintain their monopoly of political power in the face of the pressures of globalization and the information revolution. In general, the militaries in these countries remained subordinate to the ruling civilian authorities.

Singapore

Only Singapore, with its modern and globally integrated economy and efficient civil service, was relatively well positioned to weather the economic crisis and pursue its security and other interests forthrightly in regional and world affairs. However, even this technically successful city-state, with a modern, disciplined, and professional military force, was increasingly unsettled by the massive difficulties in neighboring Indonesia, and by a broader cycle of economic and political weakness throughout ASEAN. It sought assurance through closer security and other ties with the United States, Australia, the EU, Japan, and China. Giving a lower priority to fostering ASEAN unity, Singapore sought a diversified range of security and other contacts and guarantees that would help to sustain and preserve its interests in the prevailing atmosphere of economic and political uncertainty.

Indonesia

Indonesia's instability stemmed from several important contradictions and conflicts that were far from resolved in 2007. The Indonesian military remained a main contributor to ongoing problems. Military leaders ensured that the reforms that took place under the auspices of more democratic civilian leaders did not undermine the stature of the armed forces. Many military officers worked with considerable success against reforms that would cut back the military's extensive power in Indonesian political, economic, and social development. The thinking among the military ranged from those who favored steady implementation of reforms that would preserve the military's high standing to those who yearned for a return to the military-dominated system that prevailed under President Suharto. An analysis of Indonesia's security situation must recognize several key points:

- The desire for an open political system clashed with the practical need for strong central power to force difficult changes. The inefficiencies of an open political system worked against consensus on national priorities and policies. Democratic processes were tested by the complexity of economic and social problems. Failure of the fragile democracy either to prevent conditions from deteriorating or to enact positive change produced pressure to revert to a more authoritarian system. Indonesia's outer islands had long chafed under Jakarta's control, and wanted a more equitable balance of authority and resources. It became evident that the centralization of the Suharto years was no longer tenable, but managing the devolution process, with its inequities and corruption, was difficult.
- Subnational ethnic and religious identification surfaced strongly following the collapse of Suharto's regime. Management of the long-

suppressed ethnic and religious allegiances and tensions was critical to maintaining stability, political credibility, and possibly even national unity.

- With authoritarian restraints now weakened, Muslim groups were testing the limits of a greater role for Islam.
- Economic trends and military developments, among other variables, threatened overall stability. External influence on domestic stability was relatively small.

Philippines

The Philippines followed Indonesia as the most seriously challenged government among the founding members of ASEAN. President Joseph Estrada's mismanagement and corruption after his election in 1998 were met by increasingly strong, military-backed opposition from a range of elite constituencies. Led by Vice President Gloria Macapagal Arroyo, the anti-Estrada movement was an unlikely alliance of elites, moderate labor groups, rival left-wing labor elements, and leftist radicals. It was united by the goal of removing Estrada from power, but had little else in common. Factional and personal rivalries periodically surfaced, demonstrating the alliance's fragility. Though Philippine military leaders remained far from united on controversial issues like intervention in national politics, Estrada's ouster in January 2001 came in part after active duty and retired military officers shifted their support to Vice President Arroyo.

Succeeding Estrada, Arroyo brought strong economic, technocratic, and managerial talent to the presidency. Based on her past behavior, she maintained close and cooperative relations with the United States. While serving in the Philippine Senate from 1992 to 1998, she championed Manila's defense relationship with the United States and supported ratification of the Visiting Forces Agreement. She strongly supported the US-led antiterrorism campaign beginning in 2001, providing US forces with access to Philippine bases and welcoming US military support against terrorist groups in the country.

Nevertheless, overall conditions in the Philippines remained poor, and the security situation began to worsen significantly, especially in the southern Philippines. Both the Philippine armed forces and the insurgents remained at a stalemate; communist and Muslim groups had not ruled out escalating violent action. Lacking resources for the acquisitions that it would need to increase its capabilities, the military welcomed the strong US interest in cooperating with the Philippines on antiterrorism campaigns, in part to gain needed equipment and training. Modernization and professional development of Philippine armed forces were lagging to the point that the Manila government was basically unable to protect its territorial claims in the South China Sea or effectively monitor its coastline.

Thailand

Military leaders in Thailand appeared no longer interested in direct involvement in politics. Their concerns were no longer related to the internal turmoil prevalent during the Cold War, but focused on border conflicts with Burma and to some degree Cambodia. The resistance of Muslim people in southern Thailand posed a continuing internal security concern, however. Although they were constrained by limited resources because of the aftermath of the economic crisis, Thai government authorities, with the support of the armed forces, pursued foreign and security policy interests with increasing assertiveness and independence. Thailand continued to back the US-Japanese alliance, constructive US-Chinese ties, and also greater EU involvement in Asia. Bangkok was cordial to Beijing, improving relations and engaging in summits. Thai assertiveness in ASEAN over engaging Burma, calming Cambodia, and pacifying East Timor helped to fill a gap posed by Indonesia's decline and ASEAN's growing weakness and disunity.

Unlike in the past, Thailand faced no major security threats. Thus, Bangkok's perception of its need for close US security cooperation changed. US noncontribution to the IMF's Thai rescue, a reduced US diplomatic and military presence, and perceived US unilateralism, notably over ASEAN engaging on Burma, also prompted Thai officials to affirm their interests by seeking a more equal and less subservient relationship with the United States. As a result, irritants over arms sales, WTO leadership, and other issues were harder to solve. The George W. Bush administration took some steps to improve military ties, but Thai support for US policies in UN and US regional military initiatives seemed less reliable.

Thailand's foreign policy activism developed in tandem with the government's gradual institutionalization of democratic politics and its experience in coping with the economic crisis. Building on many years of civilian democratic rule, government politics were more regularized under terms of the 1997 reform constitution. The military, recalling its negative ruling experience in 1991–1992, and having few answers to Thailand's economic and social problems, avoided direct intervention in politics and sought resources through normal government channels until the September 2006 coup.

Malaysia

Malaysia's armed forces remained focused on professional development and modernization under the command of civilian authorities. An important change in foreign and security policy was Kuala Lumpur's signaling in early 2001 that it wanted to improve relations with the George W. Bush administration. US-Malaysian relations had soured in 1998 when Prime Minister Mahathir Mohamad was angered by a speech Vice President Al Gore gave in Kuala Lumpur lauding Malaysia's opposition movement. Admiral Dennis

Blair, commander in chief of the US Pacific Command, in January 2001 received an unusually warm welcome from Mahathir. Cultivating better economic and security ties with the United States—Malaysia's top trade and investment partner—was consistent with Kuala Lumpur's efforts to increase direct investment to ease the impact of an anticipated economic slowdown. This pro-US trend was offset by serious Malaysian reservations over the US antiterrorist war against Afghanistan and Iraq, though US officials were pleased with Mahathir's tough stance against domestic extremists and terrorist suspects.

▨ Conclusion

Military and security issues in Asia Pacific in the post–Cold War period have reflected the dynamics and relations between and among Asian Pacific states. Though using military force to safeguard internal security against domestic insurgents and dissidents had been the top priority of many regional armed services since the end of World War II, post–Cold War conditions saw national governments become more confident of internal control and devote more attention and resources to deal with national security issues beyond their respective borders.

The security situation in post–Cold War Asia Pacific sometimes was tense and appeared to be subject to change; the actual degree of tension and change was held in check by several stabilizing factors—notably the US alliance system and the forward-deployed US military presence, which enjoyed generally strong support on both sides of the Pacific. The United States remained by far the region's most capable military power. In the wake of the September 11, 2001, terrorist attacks, US power and influence in Asia expanded markedly, especially in South and Central Asia, adding to reasons why most East Asian powers sought to stay on good terms with the United States, at least for the time being. Nonetheless, salient issues posed serious challenges to US leadership and interests, and to overall regional stability. They included regional "hot spots" in Korea and Taiwan, and weaknesses in Southeast Asia stemming from the 1997–1998 Asian economic crisis and regime decay in several key states. The US war in Iraq was very unpopular in the region, leading to a decline in the US image in Asia at a time of the rising prominence of China as a leader in Asian affairs.

Despite a certain comfort level provided by US involvement, Asia Pacific governments nonetheless reflected considerable anxiety that their security concerns could be negatively affected by changes after the Cold War. They were not so worried that they saw a need to align closely with one power or group of powers. More common was a tendency to "hedge"—using more diversified military preparations and other means to ensure that their particular security interests would be safeguarded, especially in case the regional security situation should change for the worse. The result was regional security trends that tended to diffuse regional leadership and power, adding to the unpredictability of the types of tactical alliances or ad hoc blocs that might emerge on specific issues. The increase in policy initiatives coming from Asian governments, pervasive hedging, and other regional security trends pushed power relations in Asia Pacific in various and often complicated or seemingly contradictory directions.

▩ Bibliography

Abramowitz, Morton, and Stephen Bosworth. 2006. *Chasing the Sun: Rethinking East Asian Policy.* New York: Century.

Abuza, Zachary. 2003. *Militant Islam in Southeast Asia: Crucible of Terror.* Boulder: Lynne Rienner.

Alagappa, Muthiah, ed. 1998. *Asian Security Practice: Material and Ideational Influences.* Stanford: Stanford University Press.

———. 2001. *Coercion and Governance: The Declining Political Role of the Military in Asia.* Stanford: Stanford University Press.

———. 2003. *Asian Security Order.* Stanford: Stanford University Press.

Baker, Richard, and Charles A. Morrison. 2005. *Asia Pacific Security Outlook 2005.* Tokyo: Japan Center for International Exchange.

Barnabie, Frank, and Shaun Burnie. 2005. "Thinking the Unthinkable: Japanese Power and Proliferation in East Asia." *Japan Focus,* September 8.

Blackwill, Robert D., and Paul Dibb, eds. 2000. *America's Asian Alliances.* Cambridge: Massachusetts Institute of Technology Press.

Blair, Dennis C., and John T. Hanley Jr. 2001. "From Wheels to Webs: Reconstructing Asia-Pacific Security Arrangements." *Washington Quarterly* 24, no. 1: 7–17.

Blasko, Dennis. 2006. *The Chinese Army Today.* London: Routledge.

Buckley, Roger. 2002. *The United States in the Asia Pacific Since 1945.* Cambridge: Cambridge University Press.

Bush, Richard. 2005. *Untying the Knot: Making Peace in the Taiwan Strait.* Washington, D.C.: Brookings Institution.

Calder, Kent E. 2001. "The New Face of Northeast Asia." *Foreign Affairs* (January–February): 106–122.

Carpenter, William, and David Wiencek. 2005. *Asian Security Handbook.* Armonk, N.Y.: Sharpe.

Central Intelligence Agency. 2002. *Unclassified Report to Congress on the Acquisition of Technology Relating to Weapons of Mass Destruction and Advanced Conventional Munitions 2002.* Washington, D.C.

Cha, Victor D. 1999. "Engaging China: Seoul-Beijing Détente and Korean Security." *Survival* 41, no. 1: 73–98.

Cha, Victor, and David Kang. 2003. *Nuclear North Korea: A Debate on Engagement Strategies.* New York: Columbia University Press.

Christensen, Thomas J. 1999. "China, the US-Japan Alliance, and the Security Dilemma in East Asia." *International Security* 23, no. 4: 49–80.

———. 2001. "Posing Problems Without Catching Up: China's Rise and Challenges for US Security Policy." *International Security* 23, no. 4: 5–40.

Cohen, Warren I., ed. 1996. *Pacific Passage: The Study of American–East Asian Relations on the Eve of the Twenty-First Century.* New York: Columbia University Press.

Collins, Alan. 2003. *Security and Southeast Asia.* Boulder: Lynne Rienner.

Council on Foreign Relations. 2001. *The United States and Southeast Asia: A Policy Agenda for the New Administration. Report of an Independent Task Force.* New York.

———. 2003. *Task Force on Chinese Military Power.* New York.

Dibb, Paul, David D. Hale, and Peter Prince. 1998. "The Strategic Implications of Asia's Economic Crisis." *Survival* 40, no. 2: 5–26.

———. 1999. "Asia's Insecurity." *Survival* 41, no. 3: 5–20.

Dupont, Alan. 1998. *The Environment and Security in Pacific Asia.* Adelphi Paper no. 319. London: International Institute for Strategic Studies.

———. 2001. *East Asia Imperiled.* Cambridge: Cambridge University Press.

Eberstadt, Nicholas, and Richard Ellings, eds. 2001. *Korea's Future and the Great Powers.* Seattle: National Bureau of Asian Research and University of Washington Press.

Ellings, Richard, and Aaron Friedberg, eds. 2001. *Strategic Asia 2001–2002.* Seattle: National Bureau of Asian Research.

———. 2002. *Strategic Asia, 2002–2003.* Seattle: National Bureau of Asian Research.

———. 2003. *Strategic Asia, 2003–2004.* Seattle: National Bureau of Asian Research.

Feigenbaum, Evan A. 1999. "China's Military Posture and the New Economic Geopolitics." *Survival* 41, no. 2: 71–88.

Freeman, Charles. 1998. "Preventing War in the Taiwan Strait." *Foreign Affairs* (July–August): 6–11.

Friedberg, Aaron. 2005. "The Future of US-China Relations: Is Conflict Inevitable?" *International Security* 30, no. 2 (Fall): 7–45.

Funabashi, Yoichi. 2001. "Japan's Moment of Truth." *Survival* 42, no. 4: 73–84.

Gallucci, Robert, and Joel Wit. 2004. *Going Critical: The First North Korean Crisis.* Washington, D.C.: Brookings Institution.

Green, Michael J. 2001. *Japan's Reluctant Realism.* New York: Palgrave.

Green, Michael, and Toby Dalton. 2000. "Asian Reactions to US Missile Defense." *NBR* [National Bureau of Asian Research] *Analysis* 11, no. 3. http://www.nbr.org.

Gurtov, Mel. 2002. *Pacific Asia? Prospects for Security and Cooperation in East Asia.* Lanham: Rowman and Littlefield.

Han Sung-joo. 2001. "The Koreas' New Century." *Survival* 42, no. 4: 85–95.

Henderson, Jeannie. 1999. *Reassessing ASEAN.* Adelphi Paper no. 328. London: International Institute for Strategic Studies.

Hughes, Christopher. 2004. *Japan's Security Agenda: Military, Economic, and Environmental Dimensions.* Boulder: Lynne Rienner.

Huntington, Samuel. 1999. "The Lonely Superpower." *Foreign Affairs* (March–April): 35–49.

International Institute for Strategic Studies. 2006. *The Military Balance, 2006–2007.* London.

Johnson, Chalmers. 2000. *Blowback: The Costs and Consequences of American Empire.* New York: Holt.

Kang, David. 2003. "Getting Asia Wrong: The Need for New Analytical Frameworks." *International Security* 27, no. 4 (Spring): 57–85.

Kim, Samuel S., ed. 2000. *East Asia and Globalization.* Lanham: Rowman and Littlefield.

———. 2004. *The International Relations of Northeast Asia.* Lanham: Rowman and Littlefield.

Lincoln, Edward. 2004. *East Asian Economic Regionalism.* Washington, D.C.: Brookings Institution.

Manning, Robert A., and James J. Przystup. 1999. "Asia's Transition Diplomacy: Hedging Against Futureshock." *Survival* 41, no. 3: 43–67.

Medeiros, Evan. 2005–2006. "Strategic Hedging and the Future of Asia-Pacific Stability." *Washington Quarterly* 29, no. 1 (Winter): 145–167.

Morley, James, ed. 1999. *Driven by Growth: Political Change in the Asia-Pacific.* Armonk, N.Y.: Sharpe.

National Intelligence Council. 2000a. *East Asia and the United States: Current Status and Five-Year Outlook.* Conference Report no. 2000-02. Washington, D.C.

———. 2000b. *Global Trends 2015: A Dialogue with Non-Government Specialists.* Washington, D.C.

———. 2001a. *Foreign Missile Developments and the Ballistic Missile Threat Through 2015.* Washington, D.C.

———. 2001b. *North Korea's Engagement.* Conference Report no. 2001-01. Washington, D.C.

Neher, Clark D. 1994. *Southeast Asia in the New International Era.* Boulder: Westview.

O'Hanlon, Michael. 2000. "Why China Cannot Conquer Taiwan." *International Security* 25, no. 2: 51–86.

O'Hanlon, Michael, and Mike Mochizuki. 2003. *Crisis on the Korean Peninsula: How to Deal with a Nuclear North Korea.* New York: McGraw-Hill.

Pape, Wolfgang, ed. 1998. *East Asia by the Year 2000 and Beyond: Shaping Factors.* New York: St. Martin's.

Pierre, Andrew J. 2000. "Vietnam's Contradictions." *Foreign Affairs* (November–December): 69–86.

Ross, Robert S., ed. 1995. *East Asia in Transition: Toward a New Regional Order.* Armonk, N.Y.: Sharpe.

———. 1999. "The Geography of Peace: East Asia in the Twenty-First Century." *International Security* 23, no. 4: 81–118.

Roy, Denny. 2000. "Tensions in the Taiwan Strait." *Survival* 42, no. 1: 76–96.

Rozman, Gilbert. 2004. *Northeast Asia's Stunted Regionalism: Bilateral Distrust in the Shadow of Globalization.* Cambridge: Cambridge University Press.

SarDesai, D. R. 1997. *Southeast Asia: Past and Present.* Boulder: Westview.

Scobell, Andrew. 2001. *The US Army and the Asia-Pacific.* Carlisle, Pa.: US Army War College, Strategic Studies Institute.

Shambaugh, David. 2002. *Modernizing China's Military.* Berkeley: University of California Press.

———. 2004–2005. "China Engages Asia: Reshaping the Regional Order." *International Security* 29, no. 3 (Winter): 64–99.

Simon, Sheldon. 2000. "Asian Armed Forces." *NBR* [National Bureau of Asian Research] *Analysis* 11, no. 2. http://www.nbr.org.

———, ed. 2001. *The Many Faces of Asian Security.* Lanham: Rowman and Littlefield.

———. 2002. "Managing Security Challenges in Southeast Asia." *NBR* [National Bureau of Asian Research] *Analysis* 13, no. 4. http://www.nbr.org.

Suh, J. J., Peter Katzenstein, and Allan Carlson, eds. 2004. *Rethinking Security in East Asia: Identity, Power, and Efficiency.* Stanford: Stanford University Press.

Sutter, Robert G. 2003. *The United States and East Asia.* Lanham: Rowman and Littlefield.

———. 2005. *China's Rise in Asia: Promises and Perils.* Lanham: Rowman and Littlefield.

Swaine, Michael, with Loren Runyon. 2002. "Ballistic Missiles and Missile Defense in Asia." *NBR* [National Bureau of Asian Research] *Analysis* 13, no. 3. http://www.nbr.org.

Tellis, Ashley, and Michael Wills, eds. 2004. *Strategic Asia, 2004–2005*. Seattle: National Bureau of Asian Research.

———. 2005. *Strategic Asia, 2005–2006*. Seattle: National Bureau of Asian Research.

Tien Hung-mao and Cheng Tun-jen, eds. 2000. *The Security Environment in the Asia-Pacific*. Armonk, N.Y.: Sharpe.

Tow, William T. 2001. *Asia-Pacific Strategic Relations*. Cambridge: Cambridge University Press.

Tucker, Nancy B. 1998. "China-Taiwan: U.S. Debates and Policy Choices." *Survival* 40, no. 4: 150–167.

———. 2002. "If Taiwan Chooses Unification, Should the US Care?" *Washington Quarterly* 25, no. 3: 15–28.

———, ed. 2005. *Dangerous Strait: The US-Taiwan-China Crisis*. New York: Columbia University Press.

US-China Economic and Security Review Commission. 2002. *Report to Congress*. http://www.uscc.gov.

———. 2005. *Report to Congress*. http://www.uscc.gov.

US Department of Defense. 1998. *The United States Security Strategy for the East Asian–Pacific Region*. Washington, D.C.

———. 2001a. *Proliferation: Threat and Response, January 10, 2001*. Washington, D.C.

———. 2001b. *Report on Theater Missile Defense Architecture Options for the Asia-Pacific Region*. Washington, D.C.

———. 2005a. *Annual Report on the Military Power of the People's Republic of China, 2005*. Washington, D.C.

———. 2005b. *Quadrennial Defense Review 2005*. Washington, D.C.

———. 2006. *Annual Report on the Military Power of the People's Republic of China, 2006*. Washington, D.C.

Valencia, M. J. 1997. *China and the South China Sea Disputes*. Adelphi Paper no. 298. London: International Institute for Strategic Studies.

Van Ness, Peter, and Melvin Gurtov. 2005. *Confronting the Bush Doctrine: Critical Views from the Asia-Pacific*. London: Routledge.

Weeks, Stanley B., and Charles E. Meconis. 1999. *The Armed Forces of the USA in the Asia-Pacific Region*. New York: St. Martin's.

Woo, Wing Thye, Jeffrey D. Sachs, and Klaus Schwab. 2000. *The Asian Financial Crisis: Lessons for a Resilient Asia*. Cambridge: Massachusetts Institute of Technology Press.

World Bank. 1993. *The East Asian Miracle: Economic Growth and Public Policy*. Cambridge: Oxford University Press.

Yahuda, Michael. 1996. *The International Politics of the Asia-Pacific, 1945–1995*. London: Routledge.

———. 2004. *The International Politics of the Asia-Pacific*. London: RoutledgeCurzon.

Zheng Bijian. 2005. "China's 'Peaceful Rise' to Great Power Status." *Foreign Affairs* (September–October): 18–24.

Zweig, David, and Bi Jianhai. 2005. "China's Global Hunt for Energy." *Foreign Affairs* (September–October): 25–38.

8

The Environment

Peter Hills

The Asian environment is extremely diverse and complex. It contains an enormous variety of terrestrial and marine habitats and ecosystems, extending across a number of distinct climatic zones. It is also an environment under great pressure, and one that is experiencing many threats to its longer-term viability and sustainability. These threats arise from a variety of sources, including population growth, continuing rapid urbanization and industrialization, widespread poverty, mismanagement and abuse of natural resources, and inadequate and often ineffective institutions and laws for environmental protection and resource management. It is also a region of great contrasts. It contains some of the least densely populated regions in the world, but many of the world's largest cities. Amid the poverty of much of Asia are pockets of great affluence with patterns of consumption matching and sometimes exceeding those found in much of the United States and Europe. Although much of the natural environment of Asia is under threat, there remain large tracts of tropical rainforest and numerous rich and diverse coral reef ecosystems, as well as an amazingly diverse flora and fauna.

Within this region, environmental issues have attracted increasing attention since the early 1980s. The state of the regional environment has been extensively documented in recent years in numerous reports, books, and journals. Two of the most comprehensive reviews are provided by the United Nations Environment Programme (UNEP) in *GEO-2000: Global Environmental Outlook* (UNEP 1999) and, more recently, *Global Environment Outlook 3* (UNEP 2002). These UNEP reports present some startling and deeply troubling statistics.

It is estimated, for example, that approximately 20 percent of Asia's vegetated land is affected by soil degradation (UNEP 1999). From 1990 to 1995,

241

43 million acres (17 million hectares) of forest were lost in the Mekong basin. Between 1961 and 1993, it is estimated that more than half of Thailand's mangrove forests were lost. Some 70 percent of major vegetation types in the Indo-Malayan realm and possibly 15 percent of associated terrestrial species have been lost. Annual per capita availability of freshwater in developing countries of the Asia Pacific region declined from 357,000 cubic feet (10,000 cubic meters) in 1950 to 150,000 cubic feet (4,200 cubic meters) in the early 1990s. In Asia's rivers, biological oxygen demand—a key indicator of pollution—is 1.4 times the world average.

Although levels of urbanization in the region are relatively low (about 35 percent in the late 1990s) in comparison with the developed economies of Europe, Japan, and North America, urban population growth in Asia has been very rapid in many countries, has typically been concentrated in major cities, and has had pronounced impacts on surrounding agricultural and forest areas, on air, water, and noise pollution, and on the generation of solid municipal and industrial wastes. Slum areas have expanded, growing populations have often outpaced the development of urban infrastructure, and many cities throughout the region face growing problems associated with traffic congestion (e.g., air pollution, extended travel times), as discussed in greater detail in Chapter 9. East Asia generated 46 percent (327 million tons) of Asia Pacific's total municipal solid waste in 1992. By 2010, this figure is projected to increase to 60 percent (UNEP 1999). In South Korea, for example, the amount of industrial waste grew by 50 percent from 1991 to 1995. Although figures are not available, it is quite likely that much of the industrial waste produced across the region—including potentially hazardous chemicals—is discharged and released into the environment without any form of treatment. These discharges represent both an immediate and a long-term threat to the region's environment, and to the health of its people.

The Asia Pacific region is therefore under threat from a wide variety of environmental hazards. The future welfare of its population will be strongly influenced by the ability of policymakers to control and manage these numerous environmental risks in the decades ahead. The concept of sustainable development offers one framework or model within which to address such concerns; later in the chapter we shall briefly examine the progress that has been made in the region's implementation of policies for environmental sustainability since the 1992 United Nations Conference on Environment and Development (the "Earth Summit," held in Rio de Janeiro, Brazil).

This chapter explores the nature of the threats to this rich and complex environment, and some of the manifestations of Asia's environmental crisis. It also discusses some of the policies that are being implemented to tackle these problems, and looks toward the future by offering an assessment of the prospects for achieving greater environmental sustainability in Asia in the decades ahead. Clearly, given the geographical scale of Asia and the potential vastness of the topic, only selected issues and policy responses can be examined here. Nonetheless, this chapter should provide a useful snapshot of overall environmental conditions at the beginning of the new millennium and trajectories for change.

■ The State of the Environment in Asia Pacific

Although environmental problems are widespread throughout Asia, it is difficult to generalize about the extent and severity of particular problems, because these can vary across subregions and among the countries of the region. A detailed review of the situation in each country falls outside the scope of this chapter, but it is informative to examine some of the information that has already been compiled for recent regional analyses such as the *State of the Environment in Asia and the Pacific* report (United Nations 2000), prepared by the United Nations Economic and Social Commission for Asia and the Pacific (UNESCAP) and the Asian Development Bank (ADB). Like UNEP's *GEO* reports, the *State of the Environment* report presents a bleak picture of environmental conditions across much of the region. The report notes, for example, that China's overreliance on low-grade coal, inadequate infrastructure for management of urban effluent, deforestation and soil erosion, and poverty in general all contribute to a host of environmental problems, including acidification of inland waterways, loss of agricultural land and biodiversity, and vulnerability to natural disasters such as drought and flooding. Japan suffers from excess volumes of industrial waste, increasing greenhouse gas emissions, and loss of biological diversity, which are all exacerbated by unsustainable consumption patterns, lack of emissions controls, increasing vehicle ownership, and rapid development.

Before considering in greater detail some of the specific environmental problems confronting countries in the region, it is important to consider the population dimension, because this is the factor responsible for creating most of the pressures on the regional environment. The rate of population growth in the Asia Pacific region is expected to slacken over the next two decades. The annual growth rate in East Asia, for example, is expected to decline from 1.3 percent to 0.7 percent by 2020. However, even with a reduction in the rate of population growth, rising income levels and patterns of increased consumption will continue to drive a growth in demand for energy and other important resources. Furthermore, even as the annual rate of population growth declines, we must keep in mind that the base population itself is very large and consequently the population of the region will increase substantially over the next twenty years. The resource demands of this population growth will remain one of the most significant drivers of environmental degradation in the region (ADB 2001).

Since the 1970s, the region has also experienced rapid urbanization, as Dean Forbes explains in Chapter 9. Rapid economic growth—particularly until 1997—and structural economic change associated with industrialization and the growth of the service sector have been powerful factors driving this urbanization process. Urbanization has been underpinned by the continuing movement of people from rural to urban areas in search of better economic opportunities. Urbanization is proceeding at a rapid rate across all subregions of Asia Pacific (UNEP 1999). The annual rate of growth in the urban population is expected to average more than 2 percent between 2001 and 2015. Japan and South Korea already have urbanization rates in excess of 75 percent, while in the city-state of Singapore the figure is 100 percent. The urban population in Southeast Asia tends to be concentrated in a limited number of major industrialized centers, a number of which are also national capitals. Jakarta, for example, has grown to a population of 8 million in one-tenth of the time that it took New York City and its environs to reach the same population (UNEP 1999). In East Asia, China's urban population increased from 192 million to 377 million between 1980 and 1996. The country now boasts the largest urban population in the world. In Japan, 50.3 percent of the total population lived in urban areas in 1950. By 1996, this figure had increased to 78 percent. In South Korea, Seoul's population increased tenfold between 1950 and 1990, and now represents more than 25 percent of the country's total population (UNEP 1999). Asia Pacific already contains a number of the world's megacities with populations exceeding 10 million people, including Beijing, Jakarta, Metro Manila, Seoul, Shanghai, and Tokyo (UNEP 2002).

Although there is still significant growth in the urban population, the majority of people in Asia Pacific still live in rural areas. Indeed, across much of the region the rural population continues to grow, and large numbers of people remain dependent on agriculture, forestry, and fishing. However, the rate of growth of the rural population is lower than that of the urban population. While many millions of Asians will continue to be rural dwellers for decades to come, Asia will nonetheless become increasingly urbanized in the future (United Nations Population Division [UNPD] 2001).

Population growth in Asia will create unprecedented challenges to environmental sustainability. It will contribute to increased consumption of energy, raw materials, food, and a host of other natural resources, and will produce ever-increasing amounts of waste products and pollutants, which the environment will have to absorb. Unless effectively managed through appropriate policies, population growth will result in even more pronounced resource depletion and will impose even greater stresses on the environment. Income growth, grander expectations, and the consumerist sentiment that already characterizes many Asian societies will intensify demand from this growing population (ADB 2001).

Asia's contemporary environmental crisis manifests itself in several key issues: air quality; waste generation, disposal, and management; water pollution and water use; deforestation; desertification; and climate change and its

A woman in China covers her face to
protect against heavy air pollution.

implications. To help combat these various types of environmental problems,
clean technologies and production techniques are being promoted in Asia, as
is sustainable development.

Air Quality Problems

Degradation of air quality is a serious environmental issue throughout much
of the region. Air pollution levels in some of the largest cities are among the
highest in the world, producing serious health problems and affecting local
ecosystems. Levels of air pollution substantially exceed the international
guidelines for air quality recommended by the World Health Organization
(WHO), and the levels of ambient particulates, smoke particles, and dust are
generally twice the world average (ADB 2001). Of the fifteen cities in the
world with the highest levels of particulate matter in the air, several are located
in the Asia Pacific region. Cities such as Beijing, Jakarta, and Shanghai are
well known for high levels of suspended particulates.

Air pollution is exacerbated by the growth of road traffic and of industrial
activities. Transport is a significant, often major, source of urban air pollution,
as the motorized fleet has been growing rapidly in Asia. In China, more than 11
million motorcycles were produced in 1999—some 50 percent of the world's
total and reflecting a 28 percent increase over the 1996 figure. The Chinese
motor vehicle industry is growing rapidly; with rising personal incomes, car

Some of the worst traffic congestion can be found in
Asia Pacific, as pictured here in Bangkok.

ownership is now a reality for an increasing number of people in China, especially in the major cities. In countries such as Indonesia, Malaysia, and Thailand, vehicles with two-stroke engines, such as motorcycles and three-wheel taxis, constitute more than half of all motor traffic and are major polluters (UNEP 2002).

Other sources of air pollution include industrial emissions, burning of solid and liquid fuels for power generation, and burning of biomass and other fuels such as charcoal for household use. The burning of fossil fuels and biomass is the most significant source of the air pollutants sulfur dioxide, carbon monoxide, nitrogen oxide and nitrogen dioxide, suspended particulate matter, volatile organic compounds, and some heavy metals. It is also the major anthropogenic source of carbon dioxide. In Asia, coal accounts for the highest proportion of fuel consumption, and the level of use is far higher than in other regions of the world. Air pollution is particularly serious in rapidly industrializing countries such as China, which is a major coal producer (BP Amoco 1999). Here, coal constitutes 73 percent of the country's overall energy consumption, and is responsible for the country's major contribution in greenhouse gas emissions (UNEP 2002).

Indoor air pollution is also a serious problem encountered in the Asia Pacific region. In rural areas, many families rely heavily on biomass (e.g., wood and charcoal) or kerosene as household fuels. This fuel consumption pattern, coupled with inadequate ventilation, gives rise to highly contaminated indoor air. Given the concentrations of harmful emissions and the number of people using traditional cooking fuels, the scale of exposure to unacceptable and unhealthy levels of indoor air pollution is high (UNEP 2002). In areas where high levels of indoor air pollution are prevalent, such as the rural and hilly areas of China and Vietnam, acute respiratory diseases are common. The cost of indoor air pollution is enormous. It is not just traditional fuels such as wood that can give rise to health problems. Recent studies have shown that coal burning can also lead to health problems. It is thought that one reason why China has one of the highest rates of lung cancer in the world among nonsmoking women is the widespread use of coal for cooking and heating within homes (Mishra, Retherford, and Smith 2002)

Air pollution in Asia has resulted in declining air quality, reduced sustainability of ecosystems, and serious health problems. Haze and acid rain have become major regional issues as a result of the heavy reliance on coal by countries like China. In the spring of 1999, a dense, brownish pollution haze layer covered most of South and Southeast Asia and the tropical region of the Indian Ocean, resulting in reduced levels of sunlight reaching the surface of the Indian Ocean. Acid rain is reported in many parts of China, particularly in the Sichuan basin, resulting in massive destruction of forests.

High levels of urban outdoor air pollution are a further major threat to human health. In Japan, sulfur dioxide and particulate emissions have been significantly reduced since the country introduced stricter emission standards and other energy-related policies on vehicles. However, emission levels have still not declined sufficiently, because the effects of improved standards and technical developments have been offset by dramatic increases in the number of road vehicles. This pattern is common throughout Asia Pacific in cities with growing levels of private transport (UNEP 2002).

To combat increasingly high levels of air pollution, many countries have introduced a combination of economic measures and regulatory policies, as well as other preventative mechanisms. These include the introduction of cleaner fuels and technologies targeting key emission sources such as power plants, industries, and vehicles. For instance, Hong Kong and many countries have introduced unleaded petrol and mandatory catalytic converters for new cars. The use of liquefied petroleum gas and low-sulfur diesel fuel has also been encouraged. Alternative technologies such as electric vehicles are being explored.

In Singapore, an integrated, sustainable commuting system has been progressively introduced to combat air pollution and to reduce losses due to traffic congestion. Vehicle numbers are strictly controlled, drivers must pay additional charges to use roads in the central business district, and the tax system is designed to encourage residents to use public transport rather than own and use cars. Vehicle inspection centers carry out mandatory testing of cars more than three years old, and exhaust emissions are rigorously tested to ensure that they do not exceed levels set by the Ministry of Environment. The government has also introduced tax incentives to encourage the use of electric and hybrid vehicles (UNEP 2002). With regard to indoor air pollution, similar measures have been introduced, including the use of cleaner fuels to substitute for low-grade highly polluting biomass fuels, the introduction of clean technologies, and improvements in environmental awareness and education. In China, technological developments have resulted in the introduction of 200 million improved cooking stoves (Mishra, Retherford, and Smith 2002).

Waste Generation, Disposal, and Management

The waste disposal problem has grown tremendously since the 1970s as a result of population increases, rapid urbanization and industrialization, and rising living standards, particularly in the cities of the region. Much of the solid waste generated in cities remains uncollected and is either disposed of in surface waters and empty lots or burned in the streets. Collected waste is mainly disposed of in open dumps, many of which are not properly operated or maintained. In East Asia alone, over 320 million tons of industrial and solid waste were being generated annually in the early 1990s, and this figure is expected to grow significantly through 2010 (UNEP 1999, 2002). Countries in the region are also having to adjust to new kinds of waste problems as their economies develop and change. For example, a growing problem throughout the region concerns the disposal of obsolete computer equipment. To answer this concern, small towns in southern China actually specialize in waste recovery and recycling of discarded computer equipment.

Throughout the region, especially in the poorer countries, there remains concern about the international trade in hazardous waste, which despite greater international control is still a significant problem. Dumping of hazardous waste is widespread throughout the region, and hazardous chemicals are often discharged without being adequately treated. These materials not only affect the health of workers who come into contact with them, but can also harm residents living nearby.

Though some of the more developed and prosperous Asian cities have installed progressive solid-waste disposal programs, such measures may be insufficient. Hong Kong is a case in point. Here, large sums of money have been invested in state-of-the-art landfills, but these are filling up much more rapidly than expected. The Hong Kong government has therefore turned its attention to alternative methods to encourage waste reduction, reuse, and recycling. However, it has been unable to introduce a scheme for charging for waste disposal at local landfills, due to intense opposition from various interest groups.

In Metro Manila in the Philippines, the rate of solid-waste generation has also outpaced landfill carrying capacity. An average of 6,300 tons of solid waste is being generated daily, but the landfill carrying capacity is only about half that amount. Similar problems also exist in Indonesia, especially in the major cities such as Jakarta (UNEP 2002).

Serious public health and environmental problems can result from improper and inadequate waste disposal methods and facilities. Improper waste disposal can lead to water contamination, resulting in the spread of intestinal diseases, eye infections, and even large-scale epidemics. Despite these problems, some improvements in waste management services have occurred after concerted stakeholder efforts to formulate national waste management policies and strategies. In countries such as Japan, South Korea, Malaysia, and Thailand, waste management services have been privatized (UNEP 2002). This appears to be an effective way of improving services and can generate additional local employment opportunities. There is also a clear trend toward liberalization in the international trade in environmental service, promoted through the General Agreement on Trade in Services (GATS), which is being negotiated among members of the World Trade Organization (WTO). This will almost certainly result in a growing number of large international companies becoming directly involved in the waste disposal and other "environmental" businesses (e.g., water supply, sewage treatment) in various countries in the Asia Pacific region in the years ahead.

Water Pollution and Use

The Asia Pacific region accounts for about 36 percent of global water runoff. In absolute terms, China and Indonesia have the largest water resources: more than half of the region's total. However, as the region has the lowest per capita availability of freshwater, water scarcity and water pollution remain the key issues. Renewable water resources amounted to about 132,000 cubic feet (3,690 cubic meters) per capita in mid-1999. Some countries, such as South Korea, suffer from water scarcity or water depletion, while in other countries, such as China, there are major regional imbalances in supply. In China, agriculture is the largest consumer of water (i.e., for irrigation), accounting for 86 percent of freshwater demand, with the domestic and industrial sectors accounting for the remaining 14 percent. The availability situation is expected to worsen with increasing population and consumption (UNEP 2002).

Water scarcity is common in many countries due to overextraction of water resources. Reduced stream levels, lowered water tables, degraded wetlands, and diminished freshwater aquatic diversity are often associated with deforestation. In coastal cities such as Bangkok and Manila, excessive demand for groundwater has led to salinization and ground subsistence (UNEP 2002).

Water pollution has emerged as an increasingly serious problem since the 1980s, especially in Southeast Asia. China's Yellow River is among the world's most polluted. This river, which runs through one of China's most important agricultural regions, is heavily polluted and ran dry due to overextraction of water and low rainfall on 226 days in 1997 (ADB 2001). The Three Gorges dam project on the Yangzi River, which is one of the largest civil engineering projects ever undertaken anywhere in the world, has highlighted the problems of pollution in one of China's other great rivers. The lake behind the dam wall will be seriously polluted unless strict control of pollution sources can be maintained in upstream areas. In cities of the developing countries, most water bodies are heavily polluted with domestic sewage, industrial waste, chemicals, and solid wastes. In Southeast Asia, almost 50 percent of the population lacks access to safe drinking water as a result of contamination by untreated sewage. Only 10 percent of sewage is treated even at the most basic level (ADB 2001).

Water pollution also gives rise to serious public health concerns and problems. In Asia Pacific, more than 500,000 infant deaths per year and many illnesses and disabilities are attributed to water shortages and poor sanitation. About 8–9 percent of total disability adjusted life years (DALYs) are caused by diseases relating to these factors (UNEP 2002). The DALY is the only available quantitative indicator of the burden of disease, and indicates the total time of healthy life lost from either premature death or some period of disability.

To address the problem of water shortages, government policies and strategies in a growing number of countries have increasingly relied on an integrated approach to water resource management by emphasizing demand management measures, such as efficient water use, conservation and protection, institutional arrangements, regulatory and economic instruments, public information, and interagency cooperation. For example, North-South cooperation between organizations in Indonesia and the United States has contributed to enhanced water catchment management in the Lake Toba watershed, covering about 1,500 square miles (4,000 square kilometers). Lake Toba, the world's largest volcanic crater lake, suffers from degraded water quality, loss of biological diversity, and invasion from nonnative plants and animals, though it has benefited from institutional cooperation between the Lake Toba Heritage Foundation and the Lake Champlain Basin Program, in Vermont in the United States. An exchange program has helped address freshwater management issues in the catchment area. The success of the program reflects the benefits of sharing experience, undertaking partnerships between jurisdictions, and engaging citizen and stakeholder participation (UNEP 2002). To address water pollution issues, various countries have implemented plans for water improvement since the 1980s, including China, Thailand, the Philippines, and South Korea. In addition, cleanup campaigns for different types of water bodies have been undertaken, and many of these activities have been successful in improving water quality as well as increasing awareness of both voluntary and mandatory measures for water and wastewater control. Successful water pollution management initiatives are usually those that adopt a multisectoral and multidisciplinary approach (UNEP 2002).

Deforestation

Deforestation threatens biodiversity, ecosystem stability, and the long-term availability of forest products, and also depletes the natural resource base underpinning many national economies. Asia Pacific still accounts for a substantial proportion of global forests, about 14–16 percent. Within the region, the

Northwest Pacific and East Asia have the largest forest area (29.3 percent of the regional total), with Southeast Asia (29.1 percent) close behind (UNEP 2002).

The latest Global Forest Resources Assessment shows that within the region, annual deforestation rates were highest in Southeast Asia, at 5.8 million acres (2.3 million hectares) per year (equivalent to 1 percent), whereas the Northwest Pacific and East Asia had an increase of 4.6 million acres (1.85 million hectares) annually due mainly to afforestation efforts in China (Food and Agriculture Organization 2005: chap. 2). However, doubts remain concerning the effectiveness of afforestation programs in China, and many newly planted trees may not survive to maturity. More than half of the world's mangroves are found in Asia Pacific. However, these mangrove forests are disappearing at an alarming rate. More than 60 percent (some 28 million acres [11 million hectares]) of Asia's mangroves have already been converted for aquacultural or urban and industrial land use. Those that remain are exploited for timber, fuel wood, tannin, and food items.

The dependence on natural forests for fuel wood contributes significantly to deforestation. Many Asian countries rely on fuel wood for a significant component of national energy needs. Much of the forest degradation in the Pacific Island countries results from large-scale logging induced by the high commercial value of the timber available. Other factors, such as overgrazing, construction of reservoirs, and mining and land clearances, also put pressure on the forests in the region. The underlying causes of these problems include poverty, population growth, markets and trade in forest products, and macroeconomic policies (UNEP 2002).

Fire is a significant and recurring influence on the region's forests. Serious forest fires have occurred in China and Indonesia in recent years. The severity of forest fires has been exacerbated by droughts and by land clearance.

Many governments have implemented forestry legislation and programs aimed at conservation and afforestation. While plantation forests are usually a poor substitute for natural forests in terms of maintaining biodiversity, they can be a supplement and reduce pressure on and disruption of natural resources. Plantation forests also perform many of the environmental services of natural forests, including carbon sequestration, watershed protection, and land rehabilitation. Some countries are also opting to control the clearance of land outside conservation and protection areas. Logging bans exist in Cambodia, Indonesia, and Thailand, but have met with mixed success. Zero-burning policies have been adopted by Thailand and Malaysia. Some countries have introduced economic instruments for the conservation of forest resources. For example, afforestation fees and licenses are used in China to encourage the cultivation and strengthen the protection and management of forests. In Laos, logging quotas are issued and distributed to the individual provinces of the country (UNEP 2002).

Local community participation in the management of forests has been gathering momentum since the late 1970s. It is often referred to as "community forestry." In the Philippines, community-based forest management has been adopted as the national strategy for the management and sustainable development of forest resources. By 2001, more than 1.25 million acres (500,000 hectares) of national forest had been turned over to communities for management purposes. This has proved to be a successful strategy against illegal logging in the country (ADB 2001).

Desertification

Desertification takes many forms across Asia and is a critical issue in some parts of the region. Degraded areas include the deforested and overgrazed highlands of Laos and large parts of northern, central, and western China (UNEP 2002). A recent assessment of soil degradation in Southeast Asia found that agricultural production has been substantially reduced by degradation in dryer areas. In China, nearly 180 million hectares of land, including 90 percent of its grasslands, are regarded as degraded drylands.

Desertification is defined by the Intergovernmental Panel on Climate Change (IPCC) as land degradation in arid, semiarid, and dry subhumid areas brought about by factors such as climatic variations and human activities. Desertification occurs because dryland ecosystems, which cover over one-third of the world's land area, are extremely vulnerable to overexploitation and inappropriate land uses. Poverty, political instability, deforestation, overgrazing, and inappropriate irrigation practices can all undermine the land's productivity (United Nations Convention to Combat Desertification [UNCCD] 2002b).

Desertification reduces the land's resilience to natural climate variability, which has both physical and socioeconomic consequences. Physically, as a result of land degradation, the soil becomes less productive. Vegetation becomes damaged. Degraded land may cause downstream flooding, reduced water quality, sedimentation in lakes, and siltation of reservoirs and navigation channels. Dust storms and air pollution are also documented effects. The physical consequences of desertification subsequently contribute to health problems, including eye infections, respiratory illnesses, and allergies. In addition, desertification usually contributes to a series of social problems, including reduced food production, famine, and social instability. Economically, desertification is a huge drain on resources. The annual income foregone in the areas immediately affected by desertification is enormous, and may extend to tens of billions of dollars each year (UNCCD 2002a, 2002b). Losses in China have been estimated at 15 billion yuan—nearly US$2 billion per year.

As the causes of desertification are many and complex, ranging from international trade patterns to unsustainable land management, the problem continues to worsen. Combating desertification is essential to ensuring the long-term productivity of inhabited drylands. In Asia, activities to combat desertification include watershed management, soil and water conservation, sand-dune stabilization, reforestation, reclamation of waterlogged and saline lands, forest and rangeland management, and soil fertility restoration.

Climate Change and Its Implications

Climate change is an extremely complex and politically sensitive topic. Despite the different positions adopted by national governments toward the issue, the scientific community has moved progressively toward a consensus that the world's climate is indeed undergoing change; the precise nature and extent of these changes, and their implications, remain matters for debate.

Continuing emissions of greenhouse gases from human activities are likely to result in significant changes in mean climate and its intraseasonal and interannual variability in the Asian region. Currently available general circulation models suggest that the area-averaged annual mean warming would be about 5.5 degrees Fahrenheit (3 degrees Celsius) in the 2050s and about 9 degrees Fahrenheit (5 degrees Celsius) in the 2080s over the land regions of Asia, as a result of future increases in the atmospheric concentration of greenhouse gases. General circulation models indicate an enhanced hydrological cycle and an increase in area-averaged annual mean rainfall over Asia. An annual mean increase in precipitation of approximately 7 percent in the 2050s and approximately 11 percent in the 2080s over the land regions of Asia is projected (IPCC 2001).

Climate change is likely to induce various vulnerabilities in Asia, including physical, ecological, and associated economic consequences. Physically, climate change is likely to induce dangerous processes of permafrost degradation in some countries, and drought in others. Melting of permafrost regions would result in floods and increased volume of runoff. Sea-level rise would cause large-scale inundation along the Asian coastline and recession of flat, sandy beaches. Many of Asia's major cities are located in coastal areas and could be seriously threatened by a significant rise in mean sea levels.

Arid and semiarid regions of Asia could experience severe water stress if affected by global warming. Countries in temperate and tropical Asia are likely to experience increased exposure to extreme events, including forest die-back and increased fire risk, typhoons and tropical storms, floods and landslides, and vector-borne diseases. The monsoons in tropical Asia could become more variable if El Niño–Southern Oscillation events become stronger and more frequent in a warmer atmosphere. Ecologically, the dangerous processes of permafrost degradation would threaten the forest systems in boreal Asia. In addition, the stresses of climate change are likely to disrupt the ecology of mountain and highland systems. High-elevation ecosystems of Asia can expect major changes as a consequence of the impacts of climate change.

Many species of mammals, birds, and plants could be exterminated as a result of the synergistic effects of climate change and habitat fragmentation. Glacial melt is also expected to increase under changed climate conditions, which would result in reduction in flow of the river systems as the glaciers disappear. On the other hand, disruption of coastal zones caused by sea-level rise would place the ecological security of mangroves and coral reefs at risk. Economically, climate change is likely to have its most profound impact on the socioeconomic environment of the water and agricultural sectors in Asia. Agricultural productivity is likely to suffer because of higher temperatures, severe drought, flood conditions, and soil degradation, putting at risk the food security of many developing countries in the region. There are also likely to be large-scale changes in the productivity of warm-water and cool-water fish populations in many countries in Asia (IPCC 2001), with major implications for the availability of protein in the food supply.

The impacts of climate change are likely to be felt most severely in the developing countries of Asia, because of those countries' resource and infrastructure constraints. Climate change and its associated impacts therefore have important implications for the future planning, design, and implementation of development activities. The IPCC (2001) suggests that incremental adaptation strategies and policies must be developed and implemented by countries to exploit "no regret" measures and "win-win" options. Detailed and reliable regional scenarios of climate change must be developed and used in rigorous vulnerability analyses. Emphasis must be given to characteristics of system vulnerability such as ecosystem resilience, critical thresholds, and coping ranges, which are highly dependent on local conditions. In addition, such plans and activities are particularly important to areas of Asia where climate change may have irreversible or catastrophic effects.

Adaptation strategies for subregions in Asia have been identified by the IPCC (2001). A mixture of micro- and macro-level strategies has been proposed for various sectors that are particularly vulnerable to climate change, including water resources, agriculture and food security, coastal resources, human health, ecosystems, and biodiversity. Each subregion suits its adaptation strategy to its own situation. Food security, disaster preparedness and management, soil conservation, and human health sectors appear to be crucial for countries with large populations, such as China. Adaptations for sea-level rise, potentially more intense cyclones, and threats to ecosystems and biodiversity should be considered a high priority in temperate and tropical Asian countries.

▨ Industry, Technology, and the Environment

Despite the rather bleak state of the environment in Asia Pacific and the many environmental pressures the region faces, there are encouraging signs that at least some of these pressures are recognized and that changing business attitudes and practices will assist in the promotion of efforts to improve environmental quality, particularly in the manufacturing industry, whose rapid expansion has been a key factor in the region's economic growth.

Throughout Asia Pacific, industry is becoming increasingly sensitive to environmental concerns. Waste minimization, energy efficiency, waste recycling, and substitute chlorofluorocarbon programs are among the initiatives being undertaken. Some countries, such as Japan, are pioneers in environmental auditing. In addition, there is growing recognition of the importance of clean technology, as reflected in growing interest in International Standardization Organization (ISO) 14000 certification in the manufacturing sector in countries such as Malaysia, Singapore, and Thailand. Companies meeting these standards for environmental management set by the ISO are eligible for the certification. Ecolabeling is also being promoted in a number of countries, including Indonesia and Singapore, to encourage cleaner production and to raise awareness among consumers of the environmental implications of consumption patterns.

In Indonesia and Thailand, partnerships are emerging between governments and the private sector to provide environmental services and infrastructure, including the development of technologies for environmental management. Some countries are leading the way in pursuing policies to encourage cleaner production and to develop the required technologies. For instance, Japan provides financial incentives for research developments in cleaner technologies. In South Korea, legislation on "green" production systems and factories was passed in 1994.

Since the early 1990s, corporate environmental excellence has been seen as an increasingly important issue. At the first Global 500 Forum international conference, titled "Towards Corporate Environmental Excellence: Challenges and Opportunities in Asia-Pacific" and conducted from October 17 to October 20, 1995, general guiding principles on corporate environmental management were established (United Nations Economic and Social Council [UNESC] 1996). These included a statement on the responsibility of government for business and industry set out by the United Nations (1993) in *Agenda 21* (the blueprint for sustainable development endorsed at the 1992 Earth Summit); the sixteen principles for environmental management as set out by the International Chamber of Commerce in its "business charter for sustainable development"; and the nine approaches to ecoefficiency advocated by the World Business Council for Sustainable Development (WBCSD). The advocacy of ecoefficiency by the WBCSD emphasizes that companies that are environmentally efficient are also likely to be economically efficient.

There exist many incentives for, and benefits of, both pursuing the concept of ecoefficiency and introducing relevant policy mechanisms for the promotion and implementation of ecoefficiency programs. However, there are fundamental barriers facing nonmarket or mixed-market economies (e.g., China) that impede the progress and effectiveness of such initiatives. In China, market failures have impeded the development, transfer, and diffusion of renewable energy and energy-efficiency technologies. From a macro perspective, these market failures include a lack of capital and flexible financing mechanisms, lack of information about potential markets and partners, lack of technical and market-oriented managerial expertise, and inappropriate incentives to promote ecoefficiency initiatives. Institutional barriers that prevent the energy market from functioning effectively compound this. While energy prices are increasingly set by the market, subsidies still remain in some important sectors, particularly for state-owned enterprises. Industries that are able to purchase factor inputs, such as electricity, water, timber, coal, and the like, at subsidized prices have no incentive to conserve these resources. As the Chinese government progressively divests itself of these enterprises through privatization or closure, these problems will diminish.

From a micro perspective there are also problems. For example, many enterprises are not well placed to receive substantial technical assistance in the field of energy efficiency. Both the pattern of joint ventures and the potential for technology transfer in China differ among the various forms of enterprises: state-owned, rural township and village enterprises, and private sector firms. Township and village enterprises, which account for over one-third of total industrial production, and which are therefore major energy consumers, often lack human and capital resources to improve the efficiency of both their production processes and their products. They could benefit greatly from ecoefficiency programs involving technology transfer and joint-venture partnerships with foreign firms (Martinot, Sinton, and Haddad 1997).

D. Angel and M. Rock suggest that environmental problems in East Asia reflect rapid urban and industrial growth. Until recently, "the core focus of environmental policy for industry continue[d] to be that of reducing negative environmental 'outputs' and on improving local environmental 'outcomes'" (2000:12). Predictably, the trends of industrialization and urbanization will escalate in East Asia in the next few decades, resulting in further declines in environmental quality. To remedy the worsening trend, a new policy response is needed. Governments and companies must recognize that "sustainable development, industrial transformation, a cleaner environment, increased corporate responsibility, greater citizen participation and concern for those left out of the growth phenomenon must move from a *choice* to an *imperative*" (2000:10). The real challenge, as Angel and Rock observe, lies in "shifting to patterns of economic development that are less intensive in use of energy and materials and in production of pollution and waste" (2000:12).

Since 2000, greater resources have been committed to pollution control and to the remediation of existing pollution. Investments have also been made in urban infrastructure, particularly in water supply and sanitation systems, and, to a lesser extent, in mass transit systems. Environmental regulatory systems are being strengthened in most countries in the region using market-based instruments, information disclosure, public participation, clean-technology diffusion, and other innovative policy approaches. However, simply modifying the regulatory system does not guarantee positive improvements: the benefits of incremental improvement are often "overridden by the scale effects of energy- and materials-intensive economic development" (Angel and Rock 2000:10).

Existing patterns of economic growth in the Asia Pacific region have created or exacerbated a wide range of local and national environmental problems. For example, transboundary environmental problems are becoming increasingly significant in Asia (Hills and Roberts 2001). Transboundary air pollution can be traced to economic changes across the region, including both a scaling-up of industry and an increase in consumption of polluting products and services. The increased regional and global integration of Asia Pacific economies has also led to increased pressure from the major importing markets to conform to trade-related and investment-related environmental standards, and as Angel and Rock (2000) argue, increasing globalization and integration of economies lead to some loss of autonomy over domestic environmental policy.

In terms of the evolution of environmental policy responses within the region, it is possible to identify three groups of countries, based on the extent, strength, and effectiveness of their regulatory systems. M. Rock, O. Ling, and V. Kimm suggest:

> One group of economies (Korea, Taiwan, Hong Kong and Singapore) has relatively strong command-and-control environmental agencies, economies that are nearing the end of their industrial revolutions and firms with strong technical capabilities. A second group of economies (China, Indonesia, Thailand, Malaysia and the Philippines) has much weaker environmental protection agencies, economies that are in the midst of their industrial revolutions and firms with weaker technical capabilities. A third group of economies (Cambodia, Laos People's Democratic Republic and Vietnam) has extremely weak environmental protection agencies, economies that are at the start of their industrial revolutions and firms with extremely limited technical capabilities. (2000:100)

The authors also point out that, since the first group of countries are already engaged in rapid technological adoption and learning processes, it should be relatively easy for them to engage in a similarly high-speed adoption of advanced environmental management practices and extend learning at the firm level to achieve cleaner production and performance solutions to pollution. The second group of countries lack strong environmental regulatory agencies and landmark environmental legislation for setting standards for emissions and the like. Performance monitoring and enforcement of compliance are widely lacking. Economies in this group are still engaged in their own industrial revolutions, and will probably experience substantial increases in industrial output in the next twenty years. It might be best for the regulatory agencies to develop the capacity to manage command-and-control programs through an opportunistic and strategic approach. A problem-specific approach to capacity building has been conducted in several countries in East Asia. For instance, the Department of Environment in Malaysia took advantage of growing community and public dissatisfaction over pollution from crude palm oil mills to fashion a highly effective intervention strategy that successfully delinked palm oil production and exports from water pollution.

The countries in the third cohort have largely agrarian economies, relatively small industrial bases, and even smaller export-oriented industrial bases. Countries in this group might benefit from a regional investment code of environmental conduct that binds foreign investors to a commonly agreed set of environmental practices. Export-oriented industrial plants might also gain from greening the supply chains and other external environmental market measures (Rock, Ling, and Kimm 2000).

Clearly, technology is widely seen as one of the most important drivers for the kinds of changes that can help to combat environmental pollution in the region. Three broad categories of technological applications exist (Angel, Rock, and Feridhanusetyawan 2000):

- Increased use of end-of-pipe pollution control equipment by industry, ranging from air filters on smokestacks to catalytic converters on cars.
- Development and use of "environmental technologies" such as renewable energy systems and electric cars, which can reduce energy use and greenhouse gas emissions.
- Improvements in existing products and processes to generate environmental benefits from increased operational efficiency.

The second and third options embody the concept of clean production. Cleaner production adopts a more wide-ranging and sustainable approach to environmental performance, by taking into account the total impacts of producing and using a product or service, thereby minimizing aggregate environmental costs. A key notion of cleaner production is the concept of natural capitalism, which promotes energy and resource efficiency per unit of output produced (Angel, Rock, and Feridhanusetyawan 2000).

Cleaner production is a more effective approach to achieving environmental improvements, and is more cost-effective than end-of-pipe solutions because it seeks to minimizing aggregate environmental costs and improves energy and resource efficiency. As D. Angel, M. Rock, and T. Feridhanusetyawan (2000) suggest, from the perspective of businesses, the benefits of cleaner production include reduced operating costs and improved profitability through greater production efficiency, improved corporate image, better access to certain types of financing, reduced business risk arising from regulatory enforcement, and a stronger competitive position, especially in international trade.

The promotion of cleaner production in Asia requires the development of new policy instruments that will encourage companies to move beyond mere compliance to achieve higher levels of environmental performance. Angel, Rock, and Feridhanusetyawan (2000) recommended four broad policy initiatives that are appropriate to all the newly industrialized Asian countries:

- Strengthening nonregulatory drivers of environmental performance, such as cost reduction and community pressure (supported by the adoption of effective systems of environmental performance measurement and disclosure).
- Identification and implementation of development goals for cleaner production.
- Enhancing the capability of firms and industries in Asia to develop, adopt, and improve product and process technologies and associated manufacturing practices.
- Enhancing institutional capabilities for cleaner production both locally and nationally, and encouraging participation in regional and international agreements.

The promotion of cleaner production (CP) is not without its problems, however. There are major barriers that countries, especially developing countries, need to overcome. In China, these barriers include a variety of conceptual, organizational, economic, technological, and informational concerns (Zhang 2001), such as:

- Lack of pollution prevention and environmental awareness.
- Lack of effective management systems fit with CP in enterprises.
- Lack of specific objectives and implementation planning for CP, due to the national environmental management focus on end-of-pipe solutions and lack of cooperation between government departments.
- Lack of financial support for CP from both banks and enterprises, and lack of supporting economic policies (taxes, appropriate pollution discharge fees) for promoting CP and an inadequately developed pricing system.
- Backward production processes and equipment, lack of research and development and transfer mechanisms for CP technology, limited access to CP information, and lack of skilled professionals with expertise in CP.

■ The Challenge of Sustainable Development

The entire development debate has been profoundly influenced by the emergence of the sustainable development model. Discourses on sustainable development dominate contemporary perspectives on the environment (Torgerson

1995) in Asia as elsewhere in the world (see, for example, Itoga 1998; Smith and Jalal 2000). Nonetheless, despite the dominant position achieved by the sustainable development model, it is far from problematic, both as a model for and of development and as a framework for informing and guiding policy formulation. The essence of the problem is neatly expressed by J. Dryzek, who argues: "It is at the discursive level that dilemmas are dissolved by sustainable development, not at the level of policies and accomplishments. That is, sustainable development is not proven or demonstrated but rather asserted" (1997:123).

Sustainable development is certainly a difficult concept to define—though many have attempted to. The concept has a relatively long history, certainly extending back before the 1980 World Conservation Strategy, which is generally regarded as marking the model's emergence as a central construct of contemporary environmentalism. This strategy also marked a turning point in the evolution of sustainable development. Its meaning started to change as the linkages between development and the environment became increasingly explicit, culminating in the famous 1987 Brundtland Report (World Commission on Environment and Development [WCED] 1987). This report, according to Dryzek, "developed a vision of the simultaneous and mutually reinforcing pursuit of economic growth, environmental improvement, population stabilization, peace and global equity, all of which could be maintained in the long term. Such a vision was seductive [though] Brundtland did not go so far as to demonstrate the feasibility of the vision, or indicate the practical steps that would be required to bring it about" (1997:126).

The subsequent history of the concept—as reflected, for example, in the 1991 sustainable development strategy devised by the International Union for the Conservation of Nature and Natural Resources (now known as the Conservation Union), the United Nations Environment Programme, and the World Wildlife Fund; the outcomes of the 1992 Earth Summit; the UN's *Agenda 21;* the World Bank's 1992 world report on the environment; and the formation of the World Business Council on Sustainable Development—has served to further reinforce the dominance of this development model.

The critical objectives (or strategic imperatives) for environment and development, which, as argued in the Brundtland Report (WCED 1987:49), followed from the concept of sustainable development, included:

- Reviving growth.
- Changing the quality of growth.
- Meeting essential needs for jobs, food, energy, water, and sanitation.
- Ensuring a sustainable level of population.
- Conserving and enhancing resources.
- Reorienting technology and managing risk.
- Merging environment and economics in decisionmaking.

These objectives can then be restated as a set of requirements that must be met to pursue sustainable development (WCED 1987:65):

- *Political system:* must secure effective citizen participation in decisionmaking.
- *Economic system:* must be able to generate surpluses and technical knowledge on a self-reliant and sustained basis.
- *Social system:* must provide for solutions to the tensions that arise from disharmonious development.
- *Production system:* must respect the obligation to preserve the ecological base for development.
- *Technological system:* must search continuously for new solutions.
- *International system:* must foster sustainable patterns of trade and finance.
- *Administrative system:* must be flexible and have the capacity for self-correction.

Thus sustainable development is a concept that extends well beyond simply reducing pollution and conserving natural resources. It is potentially a radical political agenda for change, something that becomes much clearer in *Agenda 21* itself (United Nations 1993).

Scholars have been exploring and evaluating the concept of sustainable development since the early 1990s, and the concept continues to command considerable attention. Its application has been vigorously promoted through the widespread adoption of *Agenda 21* initiatives through bodies such as the UN's Commission on Sustainable Development (established after the 1992 Earth Summit). Many countries have made progress toward the formulation of national sustainable development strategies for submission to the commission. But many of the proposed policies appear to represent little more than a continuation or an intensification of existing environmental management and pollution control measures, and many are weak in the area of specifying appropriate measures of sustainability.

The concept of sustainable development has attracted considerable attention in Asia (Hills and Ng 2000); many countries throughout the region have adopted various aspects of *Agenda 21;* and some, like China, have formulated more elaborate national sustainable development strategies. Nevertheless, only limited progress has been made in framing comprehensive policies that promote sustainable development in a multisectoral way. And it is unlikely that there have been significant improvements in the overall environmental sustainability of countries in the region; rather the opposite has occurred, as the discussion in this chapter suggests.

Many of the issues surrounding sustainable development issues in the region were reviewed in Phnom Penh in late 2001 at a meeting of government

ministers from countries of the region. This meeting produced a regional platform on sustainable development for Asia Pacific, which reviewed progress in
the implementation of *Agenda 21* objectives in the region and identified policy issues, priorities, goals, and actions in preparation for the Johannesburg
World Summit on Sustainable Development of September 2002 (United Nations 2002).

The regional platform acknowledges that, while significant gains have
been made in various economic, social, and environmental aspects of sustainable development (e.g., infrastructure provision, poverty alleviation, the development of environmental policies, institutions, and legislation), environmental degradation has continued and the number of poor has continued to
increase. Lack of progress is attributed to a number of factors:

- continuing widespread poverty and lack of financial resources;
- the regional financial crisis of 1997;
- recurrent natural disasters;
- inadequate institutional and technical capacity;
- nonavailability of environmentally sound technologies; and
- problems arising from the lack of peace, stability, and security in some
  parts of the region.

In response, the regional platform identifies seven priority areas for follow-up
action:

- capacity building for sustainable development;
- poverty reduction;
- cleaner production and sustainable energy;
- land management and biodiversity conservation;
- protection and management of freshwater resources;
- improved management of ocean, coastal, and marine resources, and
  sustainable development of small island states; and
- action on atmosphere and climate change.

Mobilizing resources to fund sustainable development is a matter of crucial concern to developing countries in the region. The regional platform urges
developed countries to attain the UN's overseas development assistance target
of 0.7 percent of gross national product, and to facilitate the transfer of environmentally sound technologies on favorable terms to developing countries in
accordance with the guiding principles embodied in *Agenda 21*.

In many ways, the regional platform provides a sobering assessment of
the progress of Asia Pacific in moving toward sustainable development. It also
demonstrates the challenges that lie ahead and the numerous constraints that
will have to be overcome. Though by no means ensured, the achievement of

sustainable development in the region is in the interests of not only the Asian community, but also the global community.

Conclusion

The quality and sustainability of the environment in Asia Pacific, the world's most populous region, should be of concern to the entire world. Any further serious deterioration in the Asia Pacific environment over the coming decades could give rise to a variety of economic, social, and political problems that may have global ramifications. For example, the prospect of large numbers of "environmental refugees" displaced by collapsing food production systems, drought, or desertification is a growing source of concern to politicians and the public in various parts of the world. Furthermore, the ability of the global community to tackle problems such as climate change will depend to a considerable degree on cooperation from countries like China. Although China currently produces far less carbon dioxide per capita than the United States or European Union countries, it nonetheless accounts for an increasing proportion of the global total by virtue of its much larger and still-growing population.

Economic progress and social and political stability in Asia will be facilitated in the longer term by development strategies that are guided by the principles of sustainable development. The formulation and implementation of such strategies, however, are no easy task; making the transition from rhetoric to concrete programs for managing change will pose enormous challenges for the countries of the region. The economic growth imperatives that have driven development throughout Asia Pacific since 1950, but especially since the early 1980s, must be tempered by one realization: while economic advancement is essential to address issues of poverty and social injustice, economic development will serve little purpose if the natural systems upon which it depends are mismanaged and overexploited to the extent that their long-term sustainability is seriously compromised. Addressing the environmental imperatives that confront Asia Pacific is just as important as promoting economic growth; indeed, effective management of environmental resources can itself significantly contribute to this growth.

Bibliography

Angel, D., and M. Rock, eds. 2000. *Asia's Clean Revolution: Industry, Growth, and the Environment.* Sheffield: Greenleaf.
Angel, D., M. Rock, and T. Feridhanusetyawan. 2000. "Toward Clean Shared Growth in Asia." In D. Angel and M. Rock, eds., *Asia's Clean Revolution: Industry, Growth, and the Environment,* pp. 11–37. Sheffield: Greenleaf.
Asian Development Bank (ADB). 2001 *Asian Environment Outlook, 2001.* Manila.

BP Amoco. 1999. *BP Amoco Statistical Review of World Energy.* United Kingdom: Group Media and Publications.

Dryzek, J. S. 1997. *The Politics of the Earth: Environmental Discourses.* Oxford: Oxford University Press.

Food and Agriculture Organization. *Global Forest Resources Assessment 2005: Progress Towards Sustainable Forest Management.* Rome: United Nations.

Hills, P., and M. K. Ng. 2000. "Pathways to Sustainability: A Critical Review of the Sustainable Development Paradigm." *Asia Development Monitor* 2, no. 1: 1–31.

Hills, P., and P. Roberts. 2001. "Political Integration, Transboundary Pollution, and Sustainability: Challenges for Environmental Policy in the Pearl River Delta Region." *Journal of Environmental Planning and Management* 44, no. 4: 455–473.

Intergovernmental Panel on Climate Change (IPCC). 2001. "Impacts, Adaptation, and Vulnerability." Executive summary. http://www.grida.no/climate/ipcc_tar/wg2/021.htm.

Itoga, S., ed. 1998. *APEC: Cooperation for Sustainable Development.* Tokyo: Institute of Developing Economies.

Martinot, E., J. E. Sinton, and B. M. Haddad. 1997. "International Technology Transfer for Climate Change Mitigation and the Cases of Russia and China." *Annual Review of Energy and Environment* 22: 357–401.

Mishra, V., R. D. Retherford, and K. R. Smith. 2002. "Indoor Air Pollution: The Silent Killer." *Asia Pacific* 62: 1–8.

Rock, M., O. G. Ling, and V. Kimm. 2000. "Public Policies to Promote Cleaner Shared Industrial Growth in East Asia." In D. Angel and M. Rock, eds., *Asia's Clean Revolution: Industry, Growth, and the Environment,* pp. 88–103. Sheffield: Greenleaf.

Smith, D., and K. Jalal. 2000. *Sustainable Development in Asia.* Manila: Asian Development Bank.

Torgerson, D. 1995. "The Uncertain Quest for Sustainability: Public Discourse and the Politics of Environmentalism." In F. Fischer and M. Black, eds., *Greening Environmental Policy: The Politics of a Sustainable Future,* pp. 3–20. Liverpool: Chapman.

United Nations. 1993. *Agenda 21.* New York.

———. 2000. *State of the Environment in Asia and the Pacific 2000.* Report of the Economic and Social Commission for Asia and the Pacific, and the Asian Development Bank. New York.

———. 2002. *Phnom Penh Regional Platform on Sustainable Development for Asia and the Pacific.* New York.

United Nations Convention to Combat Desertification (UNCCD). 2002a. "Fact Sheet 12: Combating Desertification in Asia." http://www.unccd.int/publicinfo/factsheets/showfs.php?number=12.

———. 2002b. "United Nations Convention to Combat Desertification: An Explanatory Leaflet." http://www.unccd.int/convention/text/leaflet.php.

United Nations Economic and Social Council (UNESC). 1996. "Cross-Sectoral Issues with Particular Reference to the Critical Elements of Sustainability." Commission on Sustainable Development, 4th sess., April 18–May 3. http://www.un.org/documents/ecosoc/cn17/1997/ecn171997-5.htm.

United Nations Environment Programme (UNEP). 1999. *GEO-2000: Global Environmental Outlook.* Nairobi. http://www.grida.no/geo2000/index.htm.

———. 2002. *Global Environment Outlook 3.* United Kingdom: Earth Scan.

United Nations Population Division (UNPD). 2002. *World Urbanization Prospects: The 2001 Revision—Data Tables and Highlights.* http://www.un.org/esa/population/publications/wup2001/wup2001dh.pdf.

World Commission on Environment and Development (WCED). 1987. *The Report of the Brundtland Commission: Our Common Future.* Oxford: Oxford University Press.

Zhang, T. Z. 2001. "Design of Policy Mechanism to Promote Cleaner Production in China." *Journal of Environmental Sciences* 13, no. 3: 346–350.

9

Population and Urbanization

Dean Forbes

P opulation matters. The large number of people, the rate at which the population is growing, and the distribution and settlement patterns are all vital characteristics of the Asia Pacific region. The nations of Asia Pacific range in size from newly independent microstates such as East Timor to global giant China. The nations strung along the Pacific coast of the Asian continent are very populous. Collectively the population of the sixteen major Asia Pacific countries (Taiwan and East Timor, along with Japan, China, the Koreas, and the ASEAN states) totaled over 2 billion in 2000, one-third of the world's population of about 6 billion. But size alone is just one characteristic of the population. Asia Pacific populations are far from static, and understanding the nature of population dynamics is critical to understanding the region.

Several critical aspects of population will be examined in this chapter. First the size, structure, and dynamics of population growth will be considered, followed by a review of attempts to manage population increases. Second, the chapter will explore the process of urbanization as Asia Pacific nations' underlying economic structures evolve, resulting in substantial numbers of people shifting from rural to urban areas. Third, the growth of cities will be discussed, with an emphasis on the growth of megacities and the key issues raised by this new form of concentrated population settlement.

▨ Population Growth

In population terms, Asia Pacific is heterogeneous, with a wide distribution of population sizes and growth rates. China is at the upper end of the spectrum, with a population of 1.3 billion in 2005 (see Table 9.1). Indonesia is the next

Table 9.1   Population Growth in Asia Pacific Nations

	Population in 1950 (millions)	Population in 2005 (millions)	Projected Population in 2015 (millions)	Population Growth Rates, 1995–2000 (% per annum)
Northeast Asia				
China	555.8	1,315.8	1,410.2	0.90
Japan	83.6	127.8	127.5	0.26
Korea, North	10.8	22.5	24.4	0.82
Korea, South	20.4	48.5	50.6	0.78
Taiwan	9.4	22.3	n/a	0.9
Southeast Asia				
Brunei	0.1	0.4	0.4	2.18
Cambodia	4.3	13.8	18.6	2.80
Timor Leste	n/a	0.9	n/a	−2.60
Indonesia	79.5	222.8	250.0	1.41
Laos	1.8	5.9	7.3	2.38
Malaysia	6.1	26.0	27.9	2.09
Myanmar	17.8	50.5	55.3	1.48
Philippines	20.0	85.2	95.9	2.03
Singapore	1.0	4.3	4.8	2.90
Thailand	19.6	64.3	72.5	1.34
Vietnam	27.4	84.2	94.4	1.40

Sources: United Nations 2001: tabs. 2, 6; Asian Development Bank 2002; Directorate-General of Budget, Accounting, and Statistics 2002; United Nations Economic and Social Commission for Asia and the Pacific 2005: tab. 1.

Note: n/a = data not available.

largest country, with a population of 222.8 million, followed by Japan with 127.8 million. Next are Vietnam (84.2 million people), the Philippines (85.2 million), Thailand (64.3 million), Burma (50.5 million), South Korea (48.5 million), Taiwan (22.3 million), North Korea (22.5 million), Malaysia (26.0 million), and Cambodia (13.8 million). A cluster of smaller countries gather at the opposite end of the population spectrum: Laos (5.9 million), Singapore (4.3 million), Brunei Darussalam (374,000), and East Timor (947,000), the latter of which achieved independence from Indonesia in 2002 after years of struggle.

Global population growth from 1950 to 2000 averaged 1.8 percent per year (United Nations 2000:2). In general, population growth rates are slower in richer countries, and faster in poorer countries. In the more developed regions of the world, the population growth from 1950 to 2000 was 0.8 percent per year, but in the less developed regions, which encompass most Asia Pacific nations, growth rates averaged 2.1 percent per year. On a continental basis, population growth rates were fastest in Africa (2.5 percent per year) and Latin America (2.3 percent), followed by Asia (1.9 percent). In contrast, populations grew at just 1.2 percent per year in North America and 0.6 percent in Europe.

Demographic transition theory proposes that countries pass through a series of four demographic stages, each marked by different patterns of population growth. In the first stage, high, albeit fluctuating, birthrates intersect with high death rates, resulting in low population growth. All Asia Pacific nations have moved beyond this stage, which was a common experience in the nineteenth century and earlier.

In the second stage of the demographic transition, economic development brings improvements in health, and this results in a decline in mortality and illness, though birthrates remain at a higher level. Cambodia, Laos, and the Philippines are in the latter phases of this stage, with relatively high growth rates: 2.8 percent, 2.4 percent, and 2.0 percent per year respectively. Other countries maintain high population growth rates for specific reasons. As East Timor recovers from years of disruption, and as independence encourages a sense of political stability, it too is likely to experience a surge in population growth. Cambodia has stabilized in recent years. After suffering a troubled recent history that included mass killings experienced under the Khmer Rouge, the country is rebuilding its population. Malaysia's fast growth rate, 2.1 percent per year, reflects government strategies to bolster the place of the Malay population, while Brunei is a small, wealthy enclave where government services support larger family size.

In the third stage, birthrates begin to decline. There are two chief causes: the impact of accelerating economic development, which creates a middle class and changes the status of women; and government attention to family planning programs. A number of Asia Pacific countries, all in Southeast Asia, have experienced slowdowns in population growth and hence are situated in this stage of the demographic transition. These include Indonesia (1.4 percent population growth per year), Malaysia (2.1 percent), Thailand (1.3 percent), and Vietnam (1.4 percent).

In the fourth stage of the demographic transition, both birth and death rates stabilize at low levels, resulting in slow rates of population growth, and sometimes net population declines. All the Northeast Asia nations—Japan, China, the two Koreas, and Taiwan—have experienced population growth rates below 1.0 percent per year. China's growth rate has been kept low by government policy; as that policy is slowly relaxed, birthrates may increase, but this will likely be countered by the increasing affluence of the Chinese population. Singapore's growth rate, 2.1 percent per year, is an exception, as the government is trying to encourage population growth after concerns about low growth in the preceding decades.

Through 2015, population growth rates for China, Japan, North Korea, South Korea, Brunei, Cambodia, Indonesia, Laos, Malaysia, Myanmar, the Philippines, Singapore, Thailand, and Vietnam are projected to fall below the late-twentieth-century levels (see Table 9.1). However, the impact on total population numbers will vary. As the twenty-first century progresses, Japan's population is expected to decline after 2010. China, South Korea, and Singapore, based on current projections, will also begin to experience declines in population. In contrast to its Asia Pacific neighbors, East Timor increased its population by 5.4 percent per year from 2000 to 2005; the boost was a result of citizens returning from surrounding countries, especially Indonesia, but is expected to drop to 1.5 percent growth per year from 2005 until 2010.

Several key processes affect population dynamics and underpin the broad demographic patterns discussed above: fertility, morbidity and mortality, the aging of the population, poverty and inequality, and migration.

Fertility and Family Planning

Total fertility rate (TFR) is a calculation of the number of children a woman would have in a lifetime if she had children at the standard rate for each age band. In other words, it is a composite picture of births per women at a given point in time. A TFR of 2.1 represents replacement-level fertility. The TFR is 2.1, not 2.0, to compensate for mortality among children and among women before they complete their reproductive years. The more economically developed countries, especially in Northeast Asia—Japan, South Korea, Singapore, China, and North Korea—have TFRs below replacement level. Thailand, Vietnam, Indonesia, and Brunei have TFRs from 2.1 to 2.8, reflecting the impact of economic development and family planning programs. Malaysia, Myanmar, and the Philippines have TFRs from 3.2 to 3.6. East Timor, Cambodia, and Laos have TFRs in excess of 4.3.

Although many countries have already achieved replacement levels of fertility, and might be expected to sustain TFRs around the 2.1 mark, their populations will continue to grow for decades. As an illustration, China's population is projected to grow from 1.3 billion in 2000 to 1.4 billion in 2015, despite the country's achievement of replacement-level fertility in the early 1990s. The continued increase will result from the age structure of the population and from population momentum. China's population has a bulge in the reproductive age range, due to large numbers of men and women born prior to the drop in fertility levels. This additional population will continue to fuel increases in China's overall population until well into the twenty-first century.

Family planning programs, combined with overall economic development, have played key roles in slowing population growth. Contraceptive use is reasonably high throughout the Asia Pacific region. In China, about 84 percent of married women aged fifteen to forty-nine use contraceptives, about half through sterilization and half through a range of modern methods. In Thailand, about 74 percent of married women in the reproductive age range use contraceptives, compared with 65 percent in Vietnam, 57 percent in Indonesia, and 47 percent in the Philippines (Retherford and Westley 2002:18).

Concerns that China's large and growing population would be a barrier to economic development surfaced in the 1970s, leading to a policy emphasizing the importance of later marriage, longer intervals between births, and fewer children. Then, in 1979, the Chinese government promulgated its "one child" policy. The policy set in place a series of incentives for couples to restrict themselves to a single child, and backed this up with extremely harsh penalties for those who defied the policy, including mandatory abortions in many areas. Minority groups were exempted from the one-child requirement, and the policy was uneven in its impact, being more effectively implemented and policed in urban areas than in rural areas. The use of coercive practices to achieve reproductive policy goals attracted much criticism from the international community.

China's management of fertility successfully reduced the country's TFR from 6.1 in 1965–1969 to 1.8 in 1995–2000, and hence slowed population growth. In recent years, enforcement of the one-child policy has slackened. The government intended to pursue this policy for about thirty years, from 1979 to around 2009. A growing middle class in China is bound to increase pressure on the government to dilute the policy, if not abandon it altogether. Chinese policymakers are no doubt mindful of the problems the policy will create as China's population ages, and are aware that rapid economic growth will help to contain large family size. Projections suggest that China's TFR will remain at 1.8 until 2010, and then shift slightly upward to 1.9 until the middle of the twenty-first century (United Nations 2001: tab. 3).

Japan's reduction in TFR has been the product of a different set of circumstances compared with China, as Japan has not adopted a national family planning program. The TFR began to decline in Japan in the 1950s, halving to 2.1, but then stabilized over the next fifteen years. The fertility rate then dropped further, to 1.3 in 2005, but is expected to steadily climb to 1.8 in 2045–2050. Economic and social circumstances, and their impact on the status of women, have been decisive in explaining the Japanese experience. Whereas in 1955 just 5 percent of Japanese women completed secondary school and progressed to college or university, by 2000 this had increased to 49 percent. As a consequence, 99 percent of Japanese women take on paid work before they get married. About half of married Japanese women in the reproductive age group now have either full-time or part-time work. Thus, average age at marriage in Japan has increased to twenty-eight for women, and this, combined with the difficulties of juggling work and childbearing, has depressed fertility levels (Retherford and Westley 2002:19).

In addition to China, a number of Asia Pacific countries have embarked on successful family planning programs designed to reduce fertility levels, including South Korea, Taiwan, Thailand, Indonesia, and Singapore. During the 1960s and 1970s, governments were able to develop national programs and specific fertility reduction targets. Family planning clinics, where advice on contraception could be obtained, were an important part of the mix. Public campaigns were initiated, and popular slogans were developed, such as *dua anak cukup* (two is enough) in Indonesia (see Adioetomo 1997). And various other economic incentives and policies were introduced to support the main thrust. For example, in Korea, legislation was introduced to reduce gender bias, so that couples would have less of a preference for sons. This, it was hoped, would reduce fertility levels by lessening couples' desire to have extra children in the hope of bearing a son (Retherford and Westley 2002:19). Singapore introduced a strategy to reduce population growth in the 1960s, but later reversed it when the government realized that fertility levels were dropping to dangerous levels.

Population Morbidity and Mortality

Life expectancy at birth (see Table 9.2) provides an indication of the health prospects of the newborn. East Timor is the worst positioned, with a life expectancy for infants at birth of just 47.5 years for those born in the period 1995–2000. Lao residents are not much better off, with a figure of 52.5 years, followed by Myanmar at 55.8 years, and Cambodia at 56.5 years. North Korea, Indonesia, Vietnam, the Philippines, Thailand, and China had life expectancies in the 60s. The most economically developed countries within the Asia Pacific region had life expectancies in the 70–79 range, including Malaysia at 71.9, South Korea at 74.3, Brunei at 75.5, and Singapore at 77.1. Japan topped the Asia Pacific list with a life expectancy of 80.5 years, also the highest life expectancy of all nations in the world. The comparable figure for the United States was 76.5.

Infant mortality, defined as the number of infant deaths for every 1,000 live births, is closely connected to life expectancy at birth. High levels of infant mortality decrease overall life expectancy. Not surprisingly, therefore, infant mortality patterns reflect a similar trend as revealed by life expectancy. East Timor, which had an infant mortality of 135 for those born in the period 1995–2000, is by far the worst-positioned country in Asia Pacific. Next, with infant mortality levels in the 70–100 range, are Laos, Cambodia, and Myanmar. Indonesia, North Korea, China, Vietnam, the Philippines, and Thailand follow, with infant mortality levels in the 25–50 range. Finally, the more economically developed countries (Malaysia, Brunei, South Korea) have infant mortality levels below 12, with Singapore (4.9) and Japan (3.5) having the lowest.

Morbidity patterns reflect many aspects of a population: economic development, culture, lifestyle, and so on. HIV/AIDS is a relatively recent illness that has a devastating impact on human populations. HIV is estimated to have infected 33 million people (as of 1999) throughout the world. Though the HIV/AIDS epidemic most seriously impacted Africa, three Asia Pacific countries—Cambodia, Myanmar, and Thailand—are on the UN's list of forty-five highly affected countries. About 2.2 million Asians were expected to die of AIDS in the period 2000–2005 (United Nations 2001:9–13). In addition to human suffering and economic costs, AIDS will impact population dynamics. The United Nations has estimated that in 2000, there were about

Table 9.2 Population Characteristics of Asia Pacific Nations

	Total Fertility Rate, 1995–2000	Life Expectancy at Birth, 1995–2000 (years)	Infant Mortality Rate, 1995–2000 (infant deaths per 1,000 live births)	Proportion Aged 60+ in 2000	Projected Proportion Aged 60+ in 2050
Northeast Asia					
China	1.80	69.8	41.4	10.1	29.9
Japan	1.41	80.5	3.5	23.2	42.3
Korea, North	2.05	63.1	45.1	10.0	22.4
Korea, South	1.51	74.3	7.9	11.0	33.2
Taiwan	n/a	75.5	6.0	8.6	n/a
Southeast Asia					
Brunei	2.80	75.5	9.6	5.1	23.8
Cambodia	5.25	56.5	83.4	4.4	11.7
Timor Leste	4.35	47.5	135.0	4.7	18.0
Indonesia	2.60	65.1	48.4	7.6	22.3
Laos	5.30	52.5	96.6	5.6	13.3
Malaysia	3.26	71.9	11.6	6.6	20.8
Myanmar	3.30	55.8	78.5	6.8	21.6
Philippines	3.64	68.6	34.4	5.5	19.5
Singapore	1.60	77.1	4.9	10.6	35.0
Thailand	2.10	69.6	25.4	8.1	27.1
Vietnam	2.50	67.2	40.1	7.5	23.5

Source: United Nations 2001: tabs. 4, 7.
Note: n/a = data not available.

560,000 fewer people living in Cambodia, Myanmar, and Thailand as a result of AIDS (see Table 9.3). The United Nations projects that by 2015, these Southeast Asian countries will have about 2.8 million fewer people than if there had been no AIDS epidemic, and the impact will increase to about 6 million in 2050.

The HIV/AIDS problems of Africa are of far greater concern than those of the Asia Pacific countries. Nevertheless, the problems confronting a country such as Thailand are severe. The epidemic first became apparent in 1985, and by the mid-1990s there were more than 600,000 HIV/AIDS cases, about 1 percent of the population. About 90 percent of those who contract AIDS in Thailand are aged twenty to forty-nine, and the peak age range is twenty-five to thirty-four. About 80 percent have acquired the disease through heterosexual transmission. Deaths due to AIDS reached their peak in 2002, about 60,000 per year, and are expected to drop to 40,000–50,000 each year by 2010 (Rhucharoenpornpanich and Chamratrithirong 2001:71–79).

The social and economic impact of HIV/AIDS in Thailand is significant, and the impact on children is particularly severe. It is estimated that 25–33 percent of children whose mothers are HIV-positive will also contract the disease. The inevitable outcome, unless new treatments are discovered, is that mortality rates of children aged one to five in Thailand will be 30 percent higher in 2010 than they would have been without AIDS in the community. Another concern is further increases due to AIDS in the already large number of orphans in Thailand. AIDS orphans were expected to increase from 60,000 in 2000 to 120,000 by 2005 (Rhucharoenpornpanich and Chamratrithirong 2001:83–87). More generally, HIV/AIDS is most prevalent in those aged twenty to forty-nine, the core of the labor force. Thus the disease reduces the productivity of the most economically active, and increased mortality levels deprive the country of significant parts of its work force. But the economic impact at the household level is even more serious, particularly among poor households. The loss of key income earners, and the burden of looking after the ill and dying, impose an unbearable human cost on families.

Table 9.3   Projected Population Differences in Southeast Asia Due to AIDS

	Population Difference, 2000	Projected Population Difference, 2015	Projected Population Difference, 2050
Cambodia	46,000	621,000	1,986,000
Myanmar	192,000	1,166,000	2,870,000
Thailand	322,000	1,025,000	1,175,000

Source: United Nations 2001: tab. 18.

Aging of the Population

Another significant product of declining fertility and increased life expectancy is the aging of the population. The median age of the world population in 1950 was 23.6 years; in 2000 it had increased to 26.5, and by 2050 it is projected to be 36.2 (United Nations 2001: tab. 7). Continentally, Africa will have the lowest median age in 2050, 27.4 years, and Europe will have the highest median age, 49.5. The median age of Asia's population increased from 22.0 in 1950 to 26.2 in 2000, and is projected to reach 38.3 in 2050. Japan has the oldest population in the world, with a median age in 2000 of 41.2 years. No other Asia Pacific country is in the top ten, which is dominated by European countries.

A corollary of increasing median ages is the increasing proportion of the population over sixty years of age (see Table 9.2). In 2000 the majority of Asia Pacific nations had populations in which less than 10 percent were over sixty. The exceptions were South Korea (11 percent), North Korea (10 percent), China (10.1 percent), and of course Japan, where 23.2 percent of the population was over sixty. However, by 2050 the situation is projected to change significantly. Most Asia Pacific countries will have populations in which 10–25 percent are over sixty. Furthermore, more than a quarter of the population in Thailand (27.1 percent), China (29.9 percent), South Korea (33.2 percent), and Singapore (35.0 percent) will be over sixty, and in Japan this group will account for 42.3 percent of the population.

Concerns about managing aging populations of Asia Pacific countries, and the impact of this on national economies and societies, are receiving growing attention. The mandatory retirement age for men and women is fifty-five in Singapore and Indonesia, sixty in the Philippines and South Korea, and sixty-five in Japan. It is sixty for men and fifty-five for women in China and Vietnam (Westley and Mason 2002:89). Aging populations will force mandatory retirement ages to be increased or discarded altogether. Sustaining levels of economic development will require the work force not to retire early, but to stay employed longer. In addition, increased demands on healthcare programs and public pensions will stress the taxation base in many nations, forcing governments to encourage workers to remain employed.

Population aging is also putting increased stress on Asia Pacific family structures. During the 1980s, about three-quarters of the elderly lived in multigenerational households in which they were cared for by spouses, children, and other family members. By the 1990s, the proportion had dropped to about two-thirds. It is likely to drop further. In Japan, 80 percent of the elderly lived with their children in 1950, but this decreased to 50 percent in 1990. Some 82 percent of elderly Taiwanese parents lived with a married son in 1973, whereas by 1986 this decreased 70 percent (Westley and Mason 2002:86). Declining fertility has resulted in fewer children, thus increasing the burden of caring for aged parents. As well, increasing numbers of women are entering the work force, thus reducing the time available for providing care, and changing attitudes are placing a greater premium on personal growth and career development.

Dramatic drops in fertility levels, combined with a consistently fast pace of economic growth, have propelled care of the elderly to prominence in China. A 1992 national survey on the old-age support system found that 12.2 percent of the elderly (aged sixty and over) lived alone in households, and another 29.6 percent as couples. Some 51.1 percent lived in two-generation or three-generation households. The overall pattern was similar for both urban and rural residents. However, urban elderly residents were better off, as government-sponsored pension schemes largely benefited city residents, especially males. Whereas 92.6 percent of men and 54.5 percent of women in cities received retirement pensions, in rural areas 11.3 percent of men and just 0.7 percent of women received them. Inevitably, rural elderly women depend heavily on financial assistance from their children, but many need to keep working in order to survive (Hao 1997:201–217).

Poverty and Inequality

Despite significant improvements in economic conditions in the Asia Pacific region, poverty remains an important concern in most countries. There is considerable variation in overall income levels across countries within the region. Gross national income (GNI) per capita in Cambodia was just US$350 in 2004, almost the lowest in the whole Asia Pacific region. It was only slightly higher in Laos (at 111 percent of the Cambodia figure), Vietnam (154 percent), and East Timor (157 percent). GNI was much higher, relative to Cambodia, in Indonesia (326 percent), China (429 percent), and the Philippines (334 percent). Middle-income nations Thailand (711 percent of the Cambodia figure) and Malaysia (1,291 percent) had much higher per capita incomes. However, there has been a gigantic gap, in terms of per capita incomes, between Cambodia and the richest Asia Pacific nations, including South Korea (4,400 percent) and Singapore (7,074 percent) (derived from data in Asian Development Bank 2006: tab. 11).

Governments and international agencies are able to define poverty differences within nations in a variety of ways. Despite the difficulties of obtaining good poverty indicators to compare countries, there was evidence of significant levels of poverty in the 1990s, the highest of which occurred in East Timor (41.0 percent of the population below the poverty line), Cambodia (34.7 percent), Laos (33.5 percent), the Philippines (30.0 percent), and Vietnam (19.5 percent) (Asian Development Bank 2006: tab. 1). Comparable data are harder to obtain for North Korea, though its poverty level is probably higher than Vietnam's.

People living in poverty suffer from low incomes and a shortage of adequate food. In Laos, for example, 26.3 percent of the population lived on less than US$1 per day in 2000 (in terms of purchasing power parity). In Cambodia that same year, 46 percent of children under the age of five years were seriously underweight, and 36 percent of the population survived on dietary energy consumption below the minimum levels needed for human survival (Asian Development Bank 2003). There is consistent evidence in the Asia Pacific region that a greater proportion of the rural than urban population exist at incomes below the poverty line (see Table 9.4).

Nevertheless, urban poverty remains an important issue in many Asia Pacific countries. The economic crisis that swept through the Asia Pacific region during 1997 (discussed in detail in Chapter 5) had a significant impact on poverty in the countries worst affected, such as Thailand and Indonesia (United Nations Population Fund 1998:16–17). Whereas in 1997 about 11 percent of the Indonesian population was in poverty, the figure in 1998 had increased to 18 percent. The urban population, particularly of the largest Indonesian cities, such as Jakarta, contributed disproportionately to the increased poor, as the economic crisis had a more significant negative impact in the cities, where many construction projects came to a halt and industries shed staff as they struggled with the higher costs of imported inputs and as lines of credit disappeared. In contrast, many subsistence farmers and informal sector workers were less affected than wage employees, while rural exporters benefited from the lower value of the rupiah, as it reduced the price of their export commodities, for which international demand increased.

Migration

Asia Pacific populations are far from static. Migration into and out of the region, and travel around the region, stretch far back into history. Indians and Arabs have been settling in small trading communities for centuries. The spread of religions such as Hinduism and Islam brought with it religious practitioners.

Table 9.4   Asia Pacific Urban and Rural Populations Below Poverty Line

	Urban Population Below Poverty Line (%)	Rural Population Below Poverty Line (%)	Total Population Below Poverty Line (%)
Northeast Asia			
China (1998)	< 2.0	4.6	4.6
Southeast Asia			
Cambodia (1999)	13.9	40.1	35.9
Indonesia (1999)			27.1
Laos (1998)	26.9	41.0	38.6
Malaysia (1989)			15.5
Philippines (1997)	21.5	50.7	36.8
Thailand (1992)	10.2	15.5	13.1
Vietnam (2002)	6.6	35.6	28.9

Source: World Bank, various years.

Japanese communities were established at strategic locations to support trade, such as at Hoi An on the coast of Vietnam. The Chinese diaspora spread in several directions, but significantly to the south, creating ethnic Chinese communities in all the Asia Pacific countries, and having a profound impact on places such as Singapore and Malaysia. During the 1940s and 1950s, the emergence of new nation-states resulted in the repatriation of colonial populations.

Refugee movements have been a significant feature of recent decades. In 1989, it was estimated that over 7 million refugees were living in Asia, but this figure dropped to 5.1 million in 1995 and 4.5 million in 1996, though still representing about one-third of official refugees worldwide. The most significant refugee movements affecting the Asia Pacific region were the flights of residents from Vietnam, Laos, and Cambodia in the 1970s and 1980s. Smaller but still significant flows have included the departure in the 1990s of Muslims from Myanmar into Bangladesh, and of students and intellectuals from Myanmar to Thailand. It is estimated that there are about 300,000 Burmese in Bangladesh and an equivalent number in Thailand. Up to 90,000 Muslims have shifted from the Philippines to Malaysia, and about 10,000 residents of the eastern Indonesian province of Papua (formerly Irian Jaya) have fled to neighboring Papua New Guinea (Hugo 1997:268–270). Estimates of the number of North Korean refugees hiding in China range from 30,000 to over 300,000 (Congressional-Executive Commission on China 2005:114).

A socialist regime acquired power in northern Vietnam in 1954, and in a reunified Vietnam in 1975. The socialist Khmer Rouge took control of Cambodia, which they renamed Kampuchea, also in 1975. The socialist Pathet Lao entered into a power-sharing arrangement in Laos in the early 1970s, and came into power in their own right in December 1975. Soon thereafter commenced an exodus of people from all three countries. Ethnic Chinese started to leave Vietnam in the late 1970s, often in small boats, and hence became known as "boat people." Those who survived the dangerous journey ended up in refugee camps in Hong Kong, Thailand, Malaysia, Indonesia, and the Philippines. Many more Vietnamese crossed the border into China, settling in the southern parts of the country. A major exodus occurred from Laos, dominated by the Hmong and significant numbers of lowland Lao people. In Cambodia, the Khmer Rouge forced the residents of the capital city, Phnom Penh, to evacuate and move to the countryside. The action wreaked havoc on the population, and those who could escape fled to Thailand. Ethnic Vietnamese, persecuted by the Khmer, fled back to Vietnam. Between 1975 and 1994, over 900,000 Indo-Chinese refugees ended up settling in the United States, 200,000 in Europe (especially France), and about 150,000 in Australia and in Canada (Forbes and Cutler 2000:523–524).

International labor migration has been another important aspect of population mobility. Rises in oil prices in 1973, due to the embargo imposed by the Organization of Petroleum-Exporting Countries, saw Middle Eastern countries expand infrastructure, requiring them to recruit workers to take up jobs in construction. This created a significant demand in Asia. It is estimated that there were about 500,000 Filipinos, 200,000 Indonesians, 97,000 South Koreans, and 81,000 Thais working in the Middle East in 1992 (Hugo 1997:273). The Philippines has been the most significant Asia Pacific exporter of workers, with over 7 million going abroad between 1976 and 1995 (see Table 9.5). Key destinations have been Japan, the Middle East (especially Saudi Arabia, the United Arab Emirates, and Qatar), Hong Kong, Taiwan, Malaysia, and Singapore (Tyner and Donaldson 1999). South Korea, Thailand, Indonesia, and China have also sent significant numbers of contract workers abroad.

Indonesia has been a significant source of laborers, who have traveled to Malaysia (see Mantra 1999), Hong Kong, Singapore, Taiwan, and Saudi Arabia. About 4 million Indonesians are emigrant workers, and about 70 percent of these are women. Growing concerns about the torture and abuse of Indonesian female domestic workers in Saudi Arabia have made more local destinations increasingly attractive, with the result that over half of the 150,000 foreign domestic workers in Singapore are from Indonesia (Rahman 2002:14). Recruitment of domestic workers occurs through specialized agents and recruiters who operate throughout the island of Java, from where most workers originate. In Singapore, domestic work is not legally recognized as formal employment, thus reducing the protection afforded to foreign domestic workers. However, this is partially offset by the rigor of Singapore's control of work permits and its 1998 amendment of the penal code to inflict heavy penalties on those who physically harm foreign domestic workers. Singapore's Ministry of Manpower assists in the resolution of contractual disputes and operates a telephone help line.

Although the conditions under which foreign domestics operate in Singapore are better than in most of the alternative destinations, working and living conditions can be very demanding. Housing in Singapore is usually small in terms of living space, which means that conditions for domestic workers can be extremely cramped. Moreover, social attitudes toward foreign domestic workers are negative; many workers claim they are scorned in Singapore, and

**Table 9.5   Asia Pacific Official Overseas Contract Workers from
            Sending Countries**

	Period	Total Workers Deployed
China	1982–1994	1,163,496
Indonesia	1969–1995	1,312,263
Korea, South	1963–1992	1,884,606
Myanmar	1989–1992	35,248
Philippines	1976–1995	7,275,011
Thailand	1973–1995	1,529,644

Source: Hugo 1997: tab. 1.

treated without respect. Domestic workers are also a very vulnerable group, and are often ruthlessly exploited, especially during their recruitment and travel from Indonesia to Singapore and upon their return to Indonesia (Rahman 2002:14–15).

Urbanization and Urban Growth

Cities have existed for centuries in the Asia Pacific region, and reflect a long historical tradition of urban growth. Beijing has been a site of settlement for more than 2,000 years. Tianjin and Osaka can be traced back to the sixth century. Shanghai dates its origins to the tenth century, Hanoi the eleventh, and Seoul the late fourteenth. Tokyo, or Edo, had a population of 1 million in the eighteenth century and was perhaps the world's largest city.

Urbanization, however, whereby towns and cities have grown more quickly, resulting in the balance of the population shifting from rural to urban, is a more recent process. Beginning in Europe at the time of the industrial revolution, the urbanization process in Europe accelerated through the nineteenth century, quickly spreading to North America and other settler regions such as Australia and New Zealand. By the middle of the twentieth century, significant proportions of the populations of North America (64 percent), Oceania (62 percent), Europe (52 percent), and Latin America and the Caribbean (75 percent) were urban. By contrast, just 17 percent of Asia's population lived in towns and cities, a proportion similar to Africa's (15 percent).

The middle of the twentieth century was a watershed. With the emergence of many newly independent regimes in Asia Pacific and an emphasis on postwar economic reconstruction and the development of poor countries, the process of urbanization escalated across the whole region. Between 1950 and 2000, Asia's urban population (that of Asia Pacific, plus South Asia) increased at an average of 3.4 percent per year, growing to 594 million by 1975 and to 1.4 billion by 2000. Also by 2000, 48 percent of the world's urban population lived in Asia. The proportion of the population living in urban areas more than doubled between 1950 and 2000, rising from 17 percent to 37 percent (see Table 9.6). Nevertheless, Asia remained, along with Africa, the least urbanized of the world's major regions. Whereas just over one in three Asians lived in

Table 9.6   Asia Pacific Urban Population, 1950–2030

	1950	1975	2000	2030
Urban population (millions)	244	594	1,352	2,605
Urban population (%)	17	25	37	53

Source: United Nations 2000: tab. 2.

cities, more than three-quarters of the populations of North and Latin America, Europe, and Oceania were urban residents.

Because of the relatively low proportion of Asia's population living in urban areas, the urbanization process is expected to continue over the coming decades. The United Nations anticipates that Asia's cities will grow at about 2.2 percent per year between 2000 and 2030. If this is achieved, Asia's urban population may increase to an estimated 2.6 billion by 2030, or 53 percent of the world's total urban residents. About 53 percent of Asia's population will reside in towns and cities by 2030.

Levels of urbanization, measured by the proportion of people living in urban areas, vary significantly throughout the Asia Pacific region, reflecting the history and economic development of each country. Asia Pacific countries can be grouped into three categories according to level of urbanization. The first group is headed by Singapore, a city-state that is wholly urbanized. South Korea is the next most urbanized nation, with 84 percent of its population living in towns and cities in 1998 (see Table 9.7). It is followed by Japan, which is 79 percent urban. Japan, Singapore, Taiwan, and Korea have the highest per capita gross national products (GNPs) in the region, and all have a history of

Table 9.7 Asia Pacific Urban Population as a Proportion of Total Population, 1980 and 2005

	Urban Population, 1980 (%)	Urban Population, 2005 (%)
Northeast Asia		
China	20	41
Japan	76	79
Korea, North	57	62
Korea, South	57	81
Taiwan	n/a	60
Southeast Asia		
Brunei	n/a	78
Cambodia	12	20
Timor Leste	n/a	8
Indonesia	22	48
Laos	13	22
Malaysia	42	65
Myanmar	24	31
Philippines	37	63
Singapore	100	100
Thailand	17	31
Vietnam	19	27

Sources: World Bank 2000: tab. 2; Asian Development Bank 2003: tab. 6; United Nations Economic and Social Commission for Asia and the Pacific 2005: tab. 1.

Note: n/a = data not available.

market economies in which populations have been reasonably free to move from rural to urban areas in response to economic pressures and opportunities.

The second group of countries also have market economies, but with lower levels of economic development. As a result, fewer people live in urban areas. Levels of urbanization range from 57 percent in the Philippines and 56 percent in Malaysia to 38 percent in Indonesia and 21 percent in Thailand.

The third group of countries includes China (33 percent urban), Myanmar (27 percent), Cambodia (22 percent), Laos (22 percent), Vietnam (20 percent), and East Timor (8 percent). In the case of four of these countries—China, Cambodia, Lao, and Vietnam—a commitment to a socialist strategy of development for periods up to the late 1980s placed serious barriers on migration to the cities, resulting in lower overall levels of urbanization (see Table 9.6). Cambodia (or Kampuchea, as it was known at the time) took an anti-urban strategy to the extreme, essentially forcing the population out of Phnom Penh, the main city, in April 1975 (Forbes 2000:518–523).

There are three main processes that lead to the growth of city populations. The first is natural population growth (births minus deaths), the second is migration, and the third is changes in how city boundaries are defined. All three processes can have a significant impact on city growth. Jakarta, Indonesia's capital and largest city, is a good illustration. Though Jakarta has the status of a province, and reports directly to the national government, its population spills beyond the formal boundaries into surrounding parts of the province of West Java. Planning for the population overflow, in the mid-1970s the Indonesian government established the region known as Jabotabek, which consists of Jakarta plus the surrounding areas of Bekasi, Bogor, and Tangerang. Whereas in 1990 Jakarta had a population of 9.1 million, Jabotabek's population was 20.1 million (Firman 2001:45).

The population of the Jabotabek region grew at a fast pace during the 1980s, averaging 3.5 percent per year between 1980 and 1990. Net migration, or the excess of in-migrants over out-migrants, accounted for the largest component—35.3 percent—of the overall growth of Jabotabek. Natural increases, or the excess of births over deaths, accounted for 34.5 percent of the growth, and the reclassification of areas and boundaries accounted for 30.3 percent (Gardiner 1997:125). In other words, the population growth of Jabotabek was a product of migration, natural growth, and boundary changes, in approximately equivalent proportions. A similar pattern occurred in the Indonesian metropolitan areas of Surabaya, Medan, and Bandung, though the impact of net migration was considerably lower than in the Jabotabek case.

Examining the pattern of population movement into and out of Jakarta in the period 1990–1995 reveals some interesting trends. The largest numbers of migrants to Jakarta were from the provinces of Central Java and West Java, with fewer numbers from East Java, North Sumatra, and West Sumatra (Firman 2001:49). As has been clear for many years, the bulk of migrants to Jakarta are from the island of Java, although there is at least a trickle from every province of Indonesia. Overall, from 1990 to 1995, some 57 percent of these migrants were female (female migrants from several provinces, such as Central Java, exceeded 60 percent). This reflected a shift from the migration pattern during the 1960s and 1970s, which favored males (Hugo 1996:167). The increases in female migration to Jakarta stem from higher levels of female education and the growing number of jobs for women in export-oriented industries in Jakarta.

Migration patterns are more complex than simply a shift from one place to another. During the period 1990–1995, as Tommy Firman (2001) has shown, there was significant out-migration from Jakarta; over 823,000 people left the city, resulting in a net loss of about 220,000. Some 356,000 of those out-migrants simply crossed the border from Jakarta into the West Java sections of the Jabotabek area. In addition, many migrants to Jakarta are "circular" migrants, or commuters. They have homes in the villages surrounding Jakarta, and travel to the city to engage in cash-earning opportunities on a weekly, monthly, or seasonal basis. Yoshifumi Azuma's study (2001) of trishaw riders from the Indramayu region of West Java described this pattern and examined how the riders integrated their urban and rural lifestyles and income-earning activities (a trishaw is a three-wheeled bicycle used for transporting passengers). As the Jakarta government squeezed out trishaw riders from most parts of the city in the 1990s, the riders were forced to curtail their visits to the city, resulting in increased poverty in the villages as their income-earning activities dried up.

▪ Megacities and Extended Metropolitan Regions

Growing urban populations are distributed among a wide range of towns and cities of different sizes. Across the globe in 1995, small and medium-sized cities with under 1 million people accounted for 63.5 percent of the worldwide urban population. Cities of 1 million or more accounted for just 36.5 percent of the global urban population (World Bank 2000:128). Looking ahead to the period 2000–2015, the United Nations (2000: tab. 4) anticipates that while smaller cities will continue to be significant, about 52 percent of the growth of the world's urban population will occur in cities of more than 1 million. Thus it is expected that the larger cities will grow more rapidly than smaller cities. Moreover, 93.3 percent of the growth in global urban populations will occur in the less-developed regions, and just 6.7 percent in cities in more-developed regions. The conclusion to be drawn from these projections is that the most rapid growth in urban populations, which will inevitably result in greater tensions due to growing populations of largely poor people, will be in larger cities in poorer countries.

Some Asia Pacific countries have what is known as a "primate city." Primate cities are cities that dominate, in population or other terms, the smaller cities within the country. Thailand has a primate city structure. Bangkok in 1990 accounted for 69 percent of the total urban population of Thailand. It was thirty-four times the size of the second largest city, Nonthaburi, and fifty-one times larger than Chiang Mai (Goss 2000:113). Manila, Phnom Penh, and Yangon also dominate their respective national urban systems, though not to the same extent as Bangkok does in Thailand.

Seoul's population in 1990 represented 33 percent of South Korea's urban population, and 25 percent of the total population of the nation. However, its share of the urban population had dropped from a high of 41 percent in 1970. The small decline in its primate status was due to a shift of industry and population out of Seoul and into smaller cities, as a result of reduced government incentives to stay in Seoul, increased autonomy for local authorities, and improved regional infrastructure (World Bank 2000:129).

Megacities are defined as cities with a population of 10 million or more. There were just two—Tokyo and Shanghai—in Asia Pacific in 1975, but in 2000, with the addition of Jakarta, Osaka, Manila, and Beijing, the number had grown to six, and is projected to increase to eight by 2015 (see Table 9.8). Tokyo in 2000 was considered the largest megacity in the world, and is expected to retain that rank well into the twenty-first century. Six of the world's nineteen megacities in 2000 were in Asia Pacific, and another four were in

Tokyo is the largest megacity in the world.

Table 9.8   Asia Pacific Megacities, 1975, 2000, 2015

	Population, 1975 (millions)	Population, 2000 (millions)	Projected Population, 2015 (millions)	Projected Global Ranking, 2015
Tokyo	19.8	26.4	26.4	1
Shanghai	11.4	12.9	14.6	13
Jakarta	—	11.0	17.3	9
Osaka	—	11.0	11.0	20
Metro Manila	—	10.9	14.8	12
Beijing	—	10.8	12.3	18
Tianjin	—	—	10.7	21
Bangkok	—	—	10.1	23

Source: United Nations 2000.

South Asia. By contrast, there were four in Latin America, three in Africa, and two in North America.

As large cities have spread outward from their historical centers, they have leapfrogged administrative boundaries and drawn surrounding rural populations into their orbits. Sometimes these regions extend up to sixty miles from the urban core. These are referred to as extended metropolitan regions

Image from morguefile.com.

The eighty-eight-story Petronas Twin Towers were built in 1998 as an integral component of Kuala Lumpur's new business center.

(EMRs) (McGee 1997:35–37). EMRs are characterized by suburban residential expansion, industrial development, and the proliferation of transportation networks. Functionally, the populations of the EMRs, whether traditional villagers or new residents, are almost totally dependent on the urban economy. There are many examples of EMRs in the Asia Pacific region. Singapore is one, as its influence has spread into neighboring Malaysia (Johor) and Indonesia (e.g., Batam Island), both regions having been incorporated into the expanding Singaporean economy. The EMR has a formal title: the SIJORI (Singapore-Johor-Riau) Growth Triangle.

As the balance of the population shifts to the cities of the Asia Pacific region, new patterns of urbanization will emerge along with new city structures and processes. The megacities are, of course, of unprecedented size. Many expect them to continue to grow, but how large? For decades, scholars have expected the process of counterurbanization to accelerate—that is, for out-migration to exceed in-migration, and hence for net population to flow out of cities and not into them. However, there is no convincing evidence that this is occurring in the Asia Pacific region. Thus the challenge for cities is to deal with the major problems they confront, not to expect these problems to disappear.

The Urban Environment: Tianjin

Countless environmental challenges confront Asia Pacific cities. An example is Tianjin, a large Chinese industrial city located southeast of the capital, Beijing. Along with Shanghai, it is one of four municipalities directly under the central government. Tianjin municipality extends over an area of 4,300 square miles (11,300 square kilometers). In 1995 the municipality had a population of 10.7 million, which has been growing slowly, achieving levels of 1.4 percent per year in the 1970s, 1.5 percent in the 1980s, and 0.6 percent from 1990 to 1995. The city of Tianjin, which is located in the center of the municipality, has a population of about 3.7 million. Tianjin city is connected to a series of satellite cities that together constitute Tianjin municipality.

Gross domestic product (GDP) per capita in Tianjin is US$1,242, which is high by Chinese standards. Tianjin is a major industrial city in which industry accounts for 56 percent of GDP. Specialties include machinery, metallurgy, automobile production, electronics, textiles, chemicals, sea salt, and petroleum as well as plastics, pharmaceuticals, packaging, and processed food. The Dagang and Bohai oil fields have important reserves that are under the control of the municipality. Tianjin has been actively expanding its services industries to help diversify its economy, with a particular emphasis on its education facilities. Tertiary activities increased from 19 percent of GDP in 1984 to 38 percent in 1995.

The environmental problems confronting Tianjin illustrate a major challenge confronting urban managers in the Asia Pacific region. The air in Tianjin, because of the city's industrial economy, can be gritty, with plumes of colored smoke known as "yellow dragon," "black dragon," and "white dragon." Thus much effort has gone into reducing industrial emissions of airborne pollutants in recent years. Another major source of air pollution is coal, which residents burn for heating and cooking, though since 1987 the supply of natural gas has reduced dependence on coal.

Because of the harsh environment of the Tianjin region, much effort has gone into "greening" the city. Urban parks expanded from 125 acres (50 hectares) in 1949 to 1,563 hectares in 1988, including extensive landscaping along the banks of the Hai River and the expansion of Bei Ning Park. Green areas now amount to 13 percent of the six districts of Tianjin city. Northern China suffers from water shortages, and Tianjin has been attempting to supplement its surface and underground water. For example, in 1983, it completed diversion of the Luan River into the Jin River, and completed construction of Panjia dam, which supplies 35 billion cubic feet (1 billion cubic meters) of water to Tianjin.

In 1976 a major earthquake, with its epicenter in the nearby industrial city of Tangshan, caused considerable damage in the Bohai Rim. It is estimated that 30,000 people died in Tianjin, and much of the city's housing and infrastructure was damaged or destroyed. In the aftermath of the earthquake, some 800,000 rooms in residences were repaired and reinforced, and the construction of new housing became a priority, with 14 new residential areas constructed in the early 1980s.

Although local pollution of the atmosphere has been reduced, dust storms often sweep over Tianjin, bringing fine-grained sand particles from China's northwestern regions. Visibility can be reduced to several feet, causing many activities to close. While working or riding bicycles, women cover their faces with scarves to reduce the impact of the grit. While the Chinese government is actively promoting tree-planting in the northern regions to reduce the impact, it remains a major problem for cities such as Beijing and Tianjin, as Peter Hills notes in Chapter 8.

World Cities and Megaurban Regions

Increased levels of urbanization and the growing size of cities have been closely connected to the economic growth that has characterized large parts of the Asia Pacific region. Some 55 percent of Asia Pacific GNP in 1987 was generated by urban areas in low-income countries, 73 percent in middle-income countries, and 85 percent in high-income countries (World Bank 2000:126). Cities are engines of growth due to the agglomeration economies they generate. As the influence of globalization on economies has increased, cities have been forced to become more competitive in order to secure their niches in the global economy. This has meant greater attention to physical and human infrastructure, the development of symbols and cultural capital, and the global branding and marketing of city assets.

The term "world cities" refers to the extent to which a city is able to compete for and host the services by which the global economy is managed. Global cities are therefore the control centers of the global economy. New York and London are on all contemporary lists of world cities, and Tokyo is on many. Although there is no entirely satisfactory way of measuring the degree to which cities direct the world economy, a useful approach is to determine the location of the key global firms that provide accounting, advertising, banking, and legal services. By scoring 122 individual cities according to the level of representation, Jonathan Beaverstock, Richard Smith, and Peter Taylor (1999) have developed a composite measure of the strength of these firms in particular cities, and categorized the cities into four tiers (see Table 9.9). Tokyo, Hong Kong, and Singapore are all categorized as "alpha" world cities, because they have global-service corporations across all four sectors. Seoul is the only Asia Pacific representative of the "beta" world cities. A significant number of Asia Pacific cities are "gamma" world cities: Jakarta, Osaka, Taipei, Bangkok, Beijing, Kuala Lumpur, Manila, and Shanghai. Ho Chi Minh City and Hanoi have a very small number of world city characteristics.

Clearly, Tokyo is the major urban economic powerhouse of the Asia Pacific region, although the poor performance of the Japanese economy since 1990 has inevitably narrowed the gap between Japan and its fast-growing neighbors, such as China. Hong Kong and Singapore have shored their positions as the gateways into China and Southeast Asia respectively. The remaining beta and gamma world cities are strong centers for their regional economies, with some broader world city influence. The only Asia Pacific megacity not represented in the world city list is Tianjin, which reflects the dominance of Hong Kong, Beijing, and Shanghai in connecting the Chinese economy to the global economy.

Table 9.9   Asia Pacific World Cities by Category and Corporate Services Score

Alpha World Cities	Beta World Cities	Gamma World Cities	Some Evidence of World City Formation
Tokyo (12)	Seoul (7)	Jakarta (6)	Ho Chi Minh City (2)
Hong Kong (10)		Osaka (6)	Hanoi (1)
Singapore (10)		Taipei (6)	
		Bangkok (5)	
		Beijing (5)	
		Kuala Lumpur (4)	
		Manila (4)	
		Shanghai (4)	

Source: Beaverstock, Smith, and Taylor 1999: tab. 7.
Note: Categories of world cities are based on scores of their advanced services in accountancy, advertising, banking, and legal services. Alpha world cities score from 10 to 12, beta world cities from 7 to 9, and gamma world cities from 4 to 6.

World cities talk to one another through a network of companies, governments, professional associations, and personal business networks. Infrastructure, in the form of airline networks, telephone and facsimile systems, Internet linkages, video connections, and road, rail, port, and shipping, facilitates the interaction. Some argue that these corridors are creating megaurban regions that draw people and activities to the corridors between the cities. Within the Asia Pacific region, there are arguably three emerging megaurban corridors: northeastern Asia, the Yangzi River region, and southern China and Southeast Asia (see Table 9.10).

Urban Mega-Projects: Shanghai

Urban megaprojects (UMPs) are giant infrastructure development projects in large cities. They are a product of the intersection of globalization and the growth of significant urban economies that, according to Kris Olds (2001), are centered on a "space of flows." In Asia Pacific, money and ideas are channeled by financiers through the Chinese diaspora and synthesized with the creative inputs of the "global intelligence corps"—architects, designers, and engineers—to create massive, often iconic, urban redevelopment schemes. Olds has identified several Asia Pacific UMPs, including the Tokyo Bay Waterfront project, which was completed in 2004 at an approximate cost of US$64 billion, and the Suntec City development project in Singapore, which cost US$1.5 billion and was completed in 1998.

Another is the Lujiazui Central Finance District project in Pudong, the region on the eastern bank of the Huangpu River, opposite from the historical core of Shanghai. Shanghai originated as a tenth-century fishing village, but rose to prominence in the second half of the nineteenth century, when it emerged as China's main trading city. During its heyday in the 1920s and 1930s, Shanghai was the seventh largest city in the world. With independence in 1949, Mao Zedong shifted China's focus away from the decadent Shanghai, and the city was neglected for several decades, until the opening of the Chinese economy beginning in the late 1970s. In recent years, Shanghai has experienced rapid economic growth, facilitated by the industrial boom in the Yangzi River valley, and the city is once again emerging as the major economic center of China. The

Table 9.10   Emerging Asia Pacific Megaurban Regions

Megaurban Region	Key Cities	Core City
Northeast Asian	Tianjin, Beijing, Seoul, Osaka, Tokyo	Tokyo
Yangzi River	Shanghai, Nanjing, Wuxi	Shanghai
Southern China	Guangzhou, Hong Kong, Taipei	Hong Kong
Southeast Asia	Bangkok, Kuala Lumpur, Singapore, Jakarta	Singapore

growth of service industries is beginning to make Shanghai a serious competitor for Hong Kong.

Lujiazui was an initiative of the Shanghai municipal government, with the support of French interests. Shanghai's showpiece waterfront, which was historically focused on the Bund, has been significantly enhanced by the Lujiazui development. Shanghai experienced an overheated land and property market from 1991 until 1994, forcing the municipality to revise its initial plan for the Lujiazui Central Finance District. Shanghai and French authorities responded by devising an international consultation process to provide foreign input into revising the plan for this high-profile development.

Olds (2001) argues that the Shanghai municipal government was attracted to the symbolism of modernist high-rise developments, and to the social order associated with urban planning in strong states such as France. The consultation process thus was a key symbolic move that aligned Shanghai's new financial center with the strong brand names of major international architectural firms. Four prominent international architectural firms and a local group submitted plans for Lujiazui; the Shanghai authorities modified earlier plans and incorporated a few ideas from the submissions. Although the architectural firms won no direct follow-up work in Shanghai, participating in the consultation added a new layer of luster to their own brands.

There are many other examples of UMPs throughout the Asia Pacific region. Competition among cities to attract UMPs is intense. Work commenced in 1999 on the building of a major Disney theme park in Hong Kong. Costing about US$1.35 billion, this joint project, between the Disney Corporation and the Hong Kong government, involved major reclamation work and was completed in 2005. Critical to the success of the project is the theme park's ability to attract Chinese tourists from the rest of China to the Hong Kong Special Administrative Region, into which Chinese visitors need special passes to enter, and where costs of hotels are much higher than in other parts of China. While China represents the largest internal tourist market in Asia Pacific, there is intense competition among cities to secure major UMPs to help underpin future economic growth. For example, an agreement has been struck to build a Disney theme park in Shanghai, which is scheduled to open in 2008, coinciding with the Beijing Olympics.

Kuala Lumpur and the Multimedia Supercorridor

Changes occurring in Kuala Lumpur and adjacent regions also illustrate how Asia Pacific cities are seeking to compete more effectively in the global economy. Tying Kuala Lumpur's development projects together is the city's "multimedia supercorridor."

Kuala Lumpur originated as a mining settlement in Malaysia, but began to grow in the mid–nineteenth century due to rising tin prices, the development of a road and rail network, and flourishing trading enterprises. It was proclaimed the capital of Malaysia when the country achieved independence in 1957. Population growth accelerated, and the city had 1.4 million residents by 1998. However, much of the recent population growth in this part of Malaysia has occurred in the fringe areas outside the boundaries of Kuala Lumpur, and in towns in the Klang River valley. In the late 1990s, Kuala Lumpur embarked on a strategy to make itself a "world-class city" and open itself to greater integration with the global economy (Morshidi 2001:101). A review was commenced of the city's 1984 plan, but with few conclusive outcomes so far.

Coinciding with Kuala Lumpur's intention to become internationally competitive has been the establishment of the city's multimedia supercorridor, which is about 10 miles wide and 30 miles long, stretching south from the city. Integral features of the supercorridor include a new business center (located a couple of miles to the east of the old center) and an international airport (located at Serpang, to the south of Kuala Lumpur), which was opened in 1998. Malaysia's new capital, Putrajaya, is also located inside the supercorridor. In addition, the supercorridor features designated cybercities (see Table 9.11), including Petronas Towers in the city center, Menara KL (a telecommunications tower), Technology Park Malaysia, Universiti Putra Malaysia–Malaysia Technology Development Corporation, and Cyberjaya, an "intelligent city."

The supercorridor project is a comprehensive plan to propel Malaysia into the information age. It is strongly supported by the Malaysian prime minister and his government. However, critics point to the limited progress made with new developments, such as Putrajaya. The new capital is located on the eastern

Table 9.11   Multimedia Supercorridor–Designated Cybercities of Asia Pacific

Cybercity	Year in Operation	Area	Theme
Technology Park Malaysia	1996	92.7 hectares	Symbiosis between nature and the built environment.
Menara KL (KL Tower)	1996	11,174 square meters	Telecommunications and broadcasting tower that reflects Malaysia's Islamic culture.
Universiti Putra Malaysia–Malaysia Technology Development Corporation	1997	15.7 hectares	Incubator to enhance technology development activities.
Kuala Lumpur City Center	1997	381,450 square meters	Petronas Towers' city within a city.
Cyberjaya	1998	2,890 hectares	Intelligent city in harmony with nature and having an ecofriendly environment.

Source: Adapted from MSC.comm 2001, pp. 19–21.

side of the supercorridor, about midway between Kuala Lumpur and the international airport. The Office of the Prime Minister and the Ministry of Home Affairs were among the first government entities to move into the city. Remaining government departments are not expected to make the move until 2012, when Putrajaya will have a projected population of 330,000. While an expressway provides a good vehicular connection to Kuala Lumpur and the international airport, the rail link has not yet been constructed, and Putrajaya often seems deserted (Holland 2001:61–62).

Conclusion

While population growth was the main preoccupation of Asia Pacific countries in the twentieth century, a slowdown in population growth rates is beginning to shift attention to new issues. Concerns about population aging and management, and changing patterns of population morbidity, are becoming increasingly prevalent. In some countries, the implications of pandemics, such as that caused by the AIDS virus, will remain a high priority. Increasing international population mobility, precipitated by either labor force migration or the needs of refugees and asylum-seekers, will continue to complicate the situation.

The escalation of urbanization that began in the second half of the twentieth century will continue, but at marginally slower rates. Nevertheless, as the proportion of Asia Pacific's population in urban areas starts to exceed, and then dwarf, the population in rural areas, new challenges will emerge. The swelling of smaller cities, the growth of the megacities, the emergence of megaurban regions, and the trend toward massive urban megaprojects will create new population growth and distribution problems. These new patterns of urbanization will intensify interest in sustaining and improving Asia Pacific cities.

Bibliography

Adioetomo, S. M. 1997. "Fertility and Family Planning: Prospects and Challenges for Sustainable Fertility Decline." In G. W. Jones and T. H. Hull, eds., *Indonesia Assessment: Population and Human Resources,* pp. 232–245. Canberra: Australian National University Press.

Asian Development Bank. 2002. *Basic Statistics Developing Member Countries Including Millennium Development Goals.* Manila: Development Indicators and Policy Research Division, Economics and Research Department.

———. 2003. *Key Indicators, 2003: Education for Global Participation.* Manila.

———. 2006. *Key Indicators, 2006.* http://www.adb.org/documents/books/key_ indicators/2006.

Azuma, Y. 2001. *Abang Beca: Sekejam-Kejamnya Ibu Tiri Masih Lebih Kejam Ibukota.* Jakarta: Trans Wardah Hafids, Pustaka Sinar Harapan.

Beaverstock, J. V., R. G. Smith, and P. J. Taylor. 1999. "A Roster of World Cities." *Cities* 16, no. 6: 445–458.

Brown, T. 2002. "HIV/AIDS in Asia." In *The Future of Population in Asia,* pp. 69–82. Honolulu: East-West Center.

Congressional-Executive Commission on China. 2005. *Annual Report, 2005.* Washington, D.C.: US Government Printing Office.

East-West Center. 2002. *The Future of Population in Asia.* Honolulu.

Economic and Social Commission for Asia and the Pacific. 1993. *State of Urbanization in Asia and the Pacific, 1993.* New York: United Nations.

Firman, T. 2001. "Metropolitan Expansion and the Growth of Female Migration to Jakarta." *Asia Pacific Viewpoint* 40, no. 1: 45–58.

Forbes, D. K. 1996. *Asian Metropolis.* Melbourne: Oxford University Press.

———. 1997. "Regional Integration, Internationalisation, and the New Geographies of the Pacific Rim." In R. F. Watters and T. G. McGee, eds., *Asia-Pacific: New Geographies of the Pacific Rim,* pp. 13–28. London: Hurst.

———. 1999. "Imaginative Geography and the Postcolonial Spaces of Pacific Asia." In T. C. Wong and M. Singh, eds., *Development and Challenge: Southeast Asia in the New Millennium,* pp. 1–22. Singapore: Times Academic.

———. 2001a. "Socio-Economic Change and the Planning of Hanoi." *Built Environment* 27, no. 2: 68–84.

———. 2001b. "Tianjin." In L. Beckel, ed., *Megacities: The European Space Agency's Contribution to a Better Understanding of a Global Challenge,* pp. 184–187. Salzburg: Geospace Verlag.

Forbes, D. K., and C. Cutler. 2000. "Vietnam, Laos and Cambodia." In T. R. Leinbach and R. Ulack, eds., *Southeast Asia: Diversity and Development,* pp. 508–548. Englewood Cliffs, N.J.: Prentice Hall.

Gardiner, P. 1997. "Migration and Urbanisation: A Discussion." In G. W. Jones and T. H. Hull, eds., *Indonesia Assessment: Population and Human Resources,* pp. 118–134. Canberra: Australian National University.

Goss, J. 2000. "Urbanization." In T. R. Leinbach and R. Ulack, eds., *Southeast Asia: Diversity and Development,* pp. 110–132. Englewood Cliffs, N.J.: Prentice Hall.

Hamnett, S., and D. K. Forbes, eds. 2001. "Pacific-Asian Cities: Challenges and Prospects." *Built Environment* 27, no. 2: 64–155.

Hao, Y. 1997. "Old-Age Support and Care in China in the Early 1990s." *Asia Pacific Viewpoint* 38, no. 3: 201–218.

Holland, L. 2001. "Birth of a City." *Far Eastern Economic Review* 164, no. 18: 61–62.

Hugo, G. 1996. "Urbanization in Indonesia: City and Country Linked." In J. Gugler, ed., *The Urban Transformation of Developing Worlds,* pp. 132–183. New York: Oxford University Press.

———. 1997. "Asia and the Pacific on the Move: Workers and Refugees—A Challenge to Nation-States." *Asia Pacific Viewpoint* 38, no. 3: 267–286.

———. 2000. "Demographic and Social Patterns." In T. R. Leinbach and R. Ulack, eds., *Southeast Asia: Diversity and Development,* pp. 74–109. Englewood Cliffs, N.J.: Prentice Hall.

Hull, T. 1997. "The Setting: Demographic Mosaic of the Asia Pacific Region—Issues Defining the Future." *Asia Pacific Viewpoint* 38, no. 3: 193–200.

Jones, G. W. 1997. "The Thoroughgoing Urbanization of East and South-East Asia." *Asia Pacific Viewpoint* 38, no. 3: 237–250.

Jones, G. W., C. L. Tsay, and B. Bajracharya. 2000. "Demographic and Employment Change in the Mega-Cities of South-East and East Asia." *Third World Planning Review* 22, no. 1: 1–28.

Lever-Tracy, C., D. Ip, and N. Tracy. 1996. *The Chinese Diaspora and Mainland China: An Emerging Economic Survey.* New York: St. Martin's.

Mamas, S. G. M., G. W. Jones, and T. Sastrasuanda. 2001. "Demographic Change in Indonesia's Megacities." *Third World Planning Review* 23, no. 2: 155–174.

Mantra, I. B. 1999. "Illegal Indonesian Labour Movement from Lombok to Malaysia." *Asia Pacific Viewpoint* 40, no. 1: 59–68.

McGee, T. G. 1997. "Globalisation, Urbanisation, and the Emergence of Sub-Global Regions: A Case Study of the Asia-Pacific Region." In T. R. Leinbach and R. Ulack, eds., *Southeast Asia: Diversity and Development,* pp. 29–45. Englewood Cliffs, N.J.: Prentice Hall.

Morshidi, S. 1998. "Producer Services and Growth Management of a Metropolitan Region: The Case of Kuala Lumpur, Malaysia." *Asia Pacific Viewpoint* 39, no. 2: 221–236.

———. 2001. "Kuala Lumpur, Globalization, and Urban Competitiveness: An Unfinished Agenda?" *Built Environment* 27, no. 2: 96–111.

MSC.comm. 2001. "Cybernews: MSC Designated Cybercities." December.

Olds, K. 2001. *Globalization and Urban Change: Capital, Culture, and Pacific Rim Mega-Projects.* Oxford: Oxford University Press.

Rahman, N. A. 2002. "Singapore Girl?" *Inside Indonesia* no. 69: 14–15.

Retherford, R. D., and S. B. Westley. 2002. "Fertility and Family Planning." In *The Future of Population in Asia,* pp. 15–28. Honolulu: East-West Center.

Rhucharoenpornpanich, O., and A. Chamratrithirong. 2001. "Demographic Impact of AIDS on the Thai Population." *Asia-Pacific Population Journal* 16, no. 3: 71–88.

Taiwan Directorate-General of Budget, Accounting, and Statistics. 2002. *General Report of 2000 Population and Housing Census in Taiwan-Fukien Area.* Taipei.

Tyner, J. A., and D. Donaldson. 1999. "The Geography of Philippine International Labour Migration Fields." *Asia Pacific Viewpoint* 40, no. 3: 217–234.

United Nations. 2000. *World Urbanization Prospects: The 1999 Revision.* New York: Population Division, Department of Economic and Social Affairs.

———. 2001. *World Population Prospects: The 2000 Revision.* New York: Population Division, Department of Economic and Social Affairs.

United Nations Economic and Social Commission for Asia and the Pacific. 2005. *ESCAP Population Data Sheet 2005.* Bangkok.

United Nations Population Fund. 1998. *Southeast Asian Populations in Crisis: Challenges to the Implementation of the ICPD Programme of Action.* New York.

Westley, S. B., and A. Mason. 2002. "Asia's Aging Population." In *The Future of Population in Asia,* pp. 83–95. Honolulu: East-West Center.

Wong, T. C. 1999. "Urbanisation and Sustainability of Southeast Asian Cities." In T. C. Wong and M. Singh, eds., *Development and Challenge: Southeast Asia in the New Millennium,* pp. 143–170. Singapore: Times Academic.

World Bank. 2000. *Entering the 21st Century: World Development Report, 1999/2000.* New York: Oxford University Press.

World Bank Group. 2006. "World Development Indicators, April 2006." http://web.world bank.org/wbsite/external/datastatistics/0,,contentmdk:20535285~menupk:1192694 ~pagepk:64133150~pipk:64133175~thesitepk:239419,00.html.

10

Ethnicity

Katherine Palmer Kaup

With the end of the ideological conflict that marked the Cold War, many hoped that peace and stability would characterize the post-1991 world order. Even before the formal collapse of the Soviet Union, however, it became clear that new fissure points were emerging, this time along ethnic lines. Though ethnic conflict is certainly not new in Asia Pacific, it erupted with new strength in the 1990s, particularly in the years immediately surrounding the 1997 Asian financial crisis and following the terrorist attacks on the World Trade Center in the United States in September 2001. More than 10,000 people died, and hundreds of thousands lost their homes, as a result of ethnic violence in Indonesia alone in the first five years following the Asian financial crisis (Bertrand 2004:1). The global effort to rout out terrorism has encouraged the Chinese government to conflate expressions of ethnic identity with international terrorism in western China. The government has stripped ethnic groups of many of their constitutionally provided rights, further straining ethnic relations in those parts of the country (Congressional-Executive Commission on China [CECC] 2005:13–23). The Chinese government views with suspicion members of predominately Muslim ethnic groups living in Xinjiang province, particularly the Uighurs, and assumes that their practice of Islam and interest in preserving their culture indicate a desire for independence from the Chinese state, one that they might even pursue through violent means in conjunction with international terrorist groups.

Asia Pacific is home to one-third of the world's population. Over several thousand years, an extraordinarily complex ethnic mosaic has emerged from the movement of peoples across the expansive and varied terrain, from their interactions with one another and outsiders, and from efforts by the ruling elite and by the state to manage the disparate groups within their territories. There are hundreds of different groups living in the region, speaking a wide variety of languages, adhering to diverse religions, practicing different forms of social organization, and interpreting their communal interests and loyalties quite differently. Given the complexity of ethnicity in the region, it is not surprising that ethnic concerns have impacted states and regions quite differently. Without doubt, however, ethnicity has been an important factor in shaping both state policy and self-identity for the majority of those living in Asia Pacific. An understanding of ethnicity in Asia is necessary to explain key developments throughout the region. Much of the pioneering anthropological and political science fieldwork on ethnicity has been conducted in Asia, and these theoretical findings have then been applied elsewhere. Benedict Anderson's seminal work *Imagined Communities,* for example, which has been important in reshaping how scholars understand ethnic identity and formation, grew out of his study of Indonesia.

Though developing a suitable definition of the term *ethnicity* is fraught with numerous challenges, the term has generally been used to refer to any group of people with either real or purported common origins, who share historical traditions, agree on some common symbols that mark their shared culture, and are conscious of their collective membership in the group. Many people in the region claim lineage from inhabitants who preceded them by thousands of years. Asia Pacific's geographical position as a cultural and trade hub, with constant movements of peoples in and out of the region, complicates understandings of which groups are the "rightful heirs" to these ever-evolving categories. The often harsh geographical terrain that divided human settlements among thousands of islands, in valley pockets amid rugged mountains, or in scattered oasis settlements in inhospitable desert stretches, contributed to the growth of hundreds of mutually unintelligible dialects and languages and a host of localized religious and cultural practices. Many of these regional differences have been seized upon by local communities, by ethnographers from outside the region, or by ethnic and state elites as markers of separate ethnic groups.

Given the complexity of the subject, it is clearly impossible to describe each ethnic group in the region, or even ethnic relations within each of the states in the region. The vast majority of scholarly works on ethnicity in Asia either examine a single ethnic group or examine ethnic relations within individual states, rather than attempting to introduce ethnic dynamics across the region as a whole. Even the excellent volume *Ethnicity in Asia,* edited by Colin Mackerras (2003), which is one of the best studies of ethnicity throughout Asia and provides a solid introduction to many of the issues in the region, examines ethnicity only within individual countries rather than across the region broadly. Which approach is most useful: focusing on ethnic groups themselves, or on nation-states, as the unit of analysis? Is it most helpful, for example, to introduce the Tai ethnic group (which spans several countries) as a whole, or to examine which ethnic groups reside in Thailand and how they have interacted with and been influenced by others within boundaries of the territorial state? Either approach is limited: those identifying themselves as members of the Tai ethnic group, or identified as such by state actors, are not confined neatly within state boundaries, but rather flow across several state borders. Furthermore, government policies in these different states and the different social environments in each have led some members of the Tai ethnic group to identify more closely with smaller ethnic subgroupings or categories, which, depending on the understandings of ethnicity one brings to the analysis, could be considered separate ethnic categories in their own right. For example, there is an ongoing scholarly debate among scholars, analysts, and members of ethnic communities in China, Vietnam, Burma, Thailand, and Laos over which ethnic groups in these areas share common origins and traits and should be considered part of the broader Tai nation, and which are rather separate ethnic groups who may have at one time shared common ancestry but who no longer are part of a single unit. Many members of the Zhuang ethnic group in China, for example, in the early 1990s began exploring common ties with the Dai, Shui, Dong, Buyi, and Li groups in China, the Thai of Thailand, the Lao of Laos, the Nong of Vietnam, and the Shan of Burma. Several influential members of the Zhuang Studies Association assert that all of these groups are part of a greater Tai nation with many millions of members, and that they therefore warrant greater scholarly and governmental attention.[1] The Tai cannot be understood by limiting the study to those living within Thailand, nor can the boundaries of Tai ethnicity itself be understood if divorced from the specific context of state policies and the social environment of the territory within which they live. The existing literature on ethnicity gives students some understanding of how different states have managed and manipulated ethnic groups, but an unclear sense of what are the main groups in the region as a whole, and how they interact with one another. This chapter attempts to offer both by first sketching, in broad strokes, a picture of the ethnic mosaic stretching across the region and examining a few of the largest ethnic categories in Asia Pacific. The chapter then turns to three case studies to examine in more detail how these ethnic categories have evolved and how they in turn influence both broad state ethnic policy and the lives of ethnic minorities.

Scholars continue to debate how to define ethnicity, the origins of ethnic loyalties, and the impact of interethnic relations on ethnic identities, state policies, and the distribution of resources. Most modern scholars, however, now recognize that ethnicity is largely "constructed" rather than "primordial"; that is, ethnicity is often crafted by elites or members of a particular community rather than objectively defined by some clear set of immutable, inherited traits. Assessing this construction process, then, should be a key focus of this chapter. To recreate the process by which the peoples of Asia Pacific perceive themselves as belonging to a given ethnic group, and how they understand the ethnic categories assigned to others in the region, this chapter offers a brief sketch of the main groupings in the region, as generally acknowledged by contemporary scholars and by members of these groups through their own self-identification, and briefly examines how several of these ethnic categorizations arose and were strengthened in response to colonial policies and the subsequent policies of the regimes that emerged after World War II.

In examining the interplay between local communities and state players that has contributed to the drawing of contemporary ethnic boundaries, the chapter will address five methods that have been variously used throughout Asia Pacific to respond to power imbalances between minority and majority ethnic populations: policies of exclusion, assimilation, integration, preferential support for favored groups, and regional autonomy. Exclusionary policies bar certain minorities from claiming to be part of the national culture. The Dayaks in Indonesia, for example, have been excluded from mainstream Indonesian culture by nationalist images of a modernizing and predominately Muslim nation. Assimilationist policies attempt to subsume ethnic minorities into the majority population by having them adopt the majority practices. A policy of integration allows the maintenance of ethnic differences, but seeks to increase ties of mutual interdependence among groups within a single, unified state. Affirmative action policies in some countries favor particular ethnic groups, while in other regions ethnic groups share power through arrangements granting them control over their ethnic homelands. Several states have pursued more than one of these policies simultaneously, or have fluctuated among the different approaches over time and in direct response to changing ethnic frameworks and challenges. Each approach has dramatically impacted how ethnic groups within the given territories conceive of themselves and of their relationship with other ethnicities and the state. The policies have also affected how resources are distributed among ethnic groups, and have directly impacted the standard of living for many of these peoples. These issues are not merely of intellectual interest, as securing stable interactions among the ethnicities is crucial to limiting the types of hostilities that have marked the post–Cold War era.

Definitions and Terms

What exactly do we mean by the terms *ethnicity, nation,* and *ethnonationalism*? When and why does ethnicity become an important concern for individuals, at times so important, in fact, that they may be willing to die fighting for rights of their ethnic group? What defines an ethnic group and what are the criteria for membership? Scholars and analysts have been debating these questions for decades, and seem incapable of even agreeing on common usage of their terminology, much less of reaching consensus on how best to manage these ethnic relations. Read any text on Asian ethnicity and you will discover that authors do not agree on key concepts and often interchangeably use the terms *tribal, ethnic, community, nationality, nation,* and *state,* even in the process of highlighting the importance of clarifying usage of these terms (Connor 1978).

Despite the confusion, several main schools of thought and main points of contention can be extracted from the voluminous writings on ethnicity and nationalism that have emerged since the 1940s. How one defines ethnicity and explains its origins radically impacts policy prescriptions, and is thus not merely of scholarly interest but also decisive in reaching some plan for limiting ethnic strife and promoting ethnic equality.

First, there is a debate regarding the relationship between "ethnic groups" and "nations." Most prominent writers on ethnicity and nationalism place them somewhere along a spectrum of growing self-awareness, though each views the importance of ethnic consciousness slightly differently. Almost all theorists agree that ethnic groups are unique from other social groupings, in that membership is based on real or imagined common descent. One of the preeminent scholars in the field, Walker Connor, defines a nation as a self-conscious or self-aware ethnic group. Others, such as Paul Brass and Karl Deutsch, contend that an ethnic group must be politicized, with recognized group rights in the broader political system (Brass 1991:20), or share a common desire to avoid external influence on its membership (Deutsch 1966), before it can be considered a nation. Many political leaders in Asia Pacific have tried to merge ethnicity and nationalism in their nation-building efforts. In Thailand, for example, King Vajiravudh, who ruled from 1910 to 1924, sought to unify his citizens by creating a sense of Tai-ness to counter the influence of both European colonialists and ethnic Chinese living within state boundaries. The king promoted a notion that "the Tai" comprised all those who spoke the Thai language, practiced Buddhism, and professed loyalty to the ruling Chakkri monarchy (Wyatt 1984:229).

Next, there is a divide among scholars on whether ethnicity and nations should be defined purely subjectively (that is, based purely on members' belief that they constitute a unique group), or whether certain objective criteria distinguish one group from another (in other words, only those who speak a given language, share certain physical characteristics, practice common religious customs, or wear particular clothing, for example, might be considered members of the same ethnic group or nation). Ernest Renan, a founder of the subjectivist school, contended that nations cease to exist the moment people stop perceiving of themselves as a nation: in his words, a nation is "an everyday plebiscite" (1882:26). Others, like former Soviet Union leader Joseph Stalin, rejected this subjectivist definition, contending that nations can exist even if members are not aware of their membership. Nations, according to this school, are defined by specific, objective criteria. Each writer in this school offers different means of determining what these objective markers might be. Stalin, whose definition was particularly influential in Asia Pacific, as it was formally adopted by the Chinese Communist Party (CCP) to classify the now more than 100 million people officially designated as "ethnic minorities" in China, asserted that four "objective" criteria must be present for a nation or ethnic group to exist: "a common language, territory, economic life, and psychological make-up manifested in a common culture. . . . It is only when all these characteristics are present together that we have a nation" (Stalin 1953:307). However, states that adopted Stalin's "objective" criteria soon discovered the impossibility of objectively and definitively distinguishing between one group and another. Even if one accepts Stalin's objective criteria, at exactly what point are certain objective markers similar enough to mark the boundaries of a unique ethnic group, and at which point are they different enough to indicate separate ethnic groups? It is true, for example, that many of the people who today are considered Thai speak languages belonging to the Tai language family. Many of these people, however, are not able to understand one another, given the prominent regional differences in language—whether one calls them accents, dialects, or separate languages. Should only those who can understand 90 percent or more of each other's language be considered speakers of the same language, and therefore of the same ethnic group? Is a 75 percent understanding enough? Should even groups who no longer understand each other nonetheless still be considered members of the same ethnic group if they share common linguistic roots? Even within China, where the government, using Stalin's criteria, recognizes only fifty-six separate ethnicities, there are groups who do not understand each other's languages and practice different local customs, yet are nonetheless officially labeled as members of a single ethnic group; there are groups who arguably should be recognized as ethnic groups (such as the Hakka) who are not; and there is one officially recognized ethnic group (the Hui) who do not have their own language at all.

The debate that evolved from this conflict over subjective versus objective definitions of ethnicity has led scholars to recognize that even if objective criteria could be used to draw distinct boundaries between ethnic groups, human agency becomes crucial in determining the selection of these cultural markers, and in determining which of these myriad symbolic markers might incite individuals to feel subjective identity with a particular group. From this realization emerged new lines of debate, each of the literally hundreds of theories generally falling into one of four main approaches: primordial, instrumental, structural, or hegemonic (Kaup 2000:16).

Primordialists contend that individuals *inherit* their ethnicity; that is, people are born into cultures that share certain "givens" or commonalities such as language or religion. Ethnicity does not become important to people simply because they think they will be able to improve their political or economic position by appealing to ethnic rights or by rallying fellow members of their ethnic group in opposition to other groups, but simply because of some innate, unaccountable loyalty and primordial attachment to the group into which they are born. Instrumentalists, on the other hand, contend that these "givens" only become important when they are highlighted or manipulated by elites in order to encourage mass allegiance to a particular group in order to gain something in relation to others outside of the group. Structuralists, like the instrumentalists, agree that ethnic markers are fluid and can be manipulated, but rather than focusing on how individuals and elites influence ethnic identity formation, they examine how the broader environment influences the development of ethnic groups and ethnic loyalties. For example, Michael Hechter asserts that the uneven distribution of economic resources logically leads to the formation of ethnic groups as a means of strengthening individuals' bargaining positions within society (Hechter and Levi 1979:263). The communist regimes in Asia Pacific closely adhere to this view of ethnic formation, and contend that greater economic development and opportunities will lead to the weakening of ethnic sentiments. The Chinese Communist Party's reliance on this view has led to policies that exacerbate ethnic conflict in western China, particularly in Xinjiang and Tibet. Finally, many scholars believe that ethnic loyalties and divisions are largely a result of hegemonic state policies, particularly evident in Asia Pacific in the colonial powers' strategy of rewarding certain groups at the expense of others, precisely to keep the population divided and weakened under their colonial administrators. Several governments in Asia Pacific have also pursued hegemonic policies since the colonial powers were expelled, including all those that have tried to force their citizens into objective ethnic categories, such as the Chinese, Thai, and Malaysian governments.

Different states have been influenced by these competing approaches to understanding ethnicity, and have responded with radically different means of addressing ethnic cleavages and challenges. States have attempted at various times over the past five decades to assimilate, integrate, or favor one ethnic group over another. In some countries, governments have tried to grant ethnic groups cultural and political control over their own autonomous territories, in the hope of keeping them satisfied within a larger, multiethnic state.

■ A Brief Sketch of the Contemporary Ethnic Mosaic

Though the boundaries of ethnicity are mutable for many of the peoples in Asia Pacific, protecting and developing their ethnic traditions and their rights as members of an ethnic community can become matters worth sacrificing bloodshed and lives over. While Asia Pacific comprises thousands of islands, dozens of religious traditions, and hundreds of local languages and ethnic groups, there are a handful of ethnic groups who account numerically for a large proportion of the population in the region, and who have held a great deal of cultural and political influence historically and into the contemporary, post–World War II period. Primary among them are the Han, Japanese, Koreans, Malay, Kinh, and Tai. Even a cursory look at how they explain their own ethnic categories reveals that there are numerous subdivisions even within these fairly accepted categories, distinguished by their languages, regional origins, religious traditions, or other characteristics.

The vast majority of peoples (92 percent) living in China belong to an ethnic group the Chinese government refers to as Han. Though the term *Han ren,* meaning "Han people," has existed for many centuries and refers to the descendants of the Han dynasty (206 B.C.E.–220 C.E.), the modern use of the term as an ethnic category appeared much more recently. The term seems to have originated during the Qing dynasty (1644–1911) in an effort to unify opposition against Manchu rule (Mackerras 2003:15), and was further refined and promoted as a tool to unite disparate regional groupings by Sun Yat-sen at the turn of the twentieth century. Sun claimed that all Han Chinese were part of the same "race." There are great differences among Han members, however, who speak a number of mutually unintelligible languages and hold strong regional loyalties. Speakers of Cantonese, though the language is entirely incomprehensible to speakers of Shanghaiese, Mandarin, or Minnan, are all considered Han, both by the Chinese government and by themselves.

Han Chinese are found across the globe, having begun their migration originally from the Yellow River region over 3,000 years ago. Chinese migrated to areas throughout Southeast Asia, Europe, and North America in search of new opportunities and employment. Han Chinese today comprise nearly a quarter of Malaysia's population, and over three-quarters of Singapore's. Fourteen percent of Thailand's 64.6 million citizens are ethnically Han Chinese. In many of these countries, the Chinese populations maintain close affiliation with members of their own ethnic group, many continuing to remit funds to relatives remaining in China, or reinvesting their earnings in Chinese enterprises. In some countries, Indonesia and Vietnam, for example, tensions between the Chinese and other ethnic communities have turned quite violent. Several hundred thousand ethnic Chinese fled or were expelled from Vietnam in 1978, for example, contributing in part to the Chinese military's invasion of Vietnam in 1979 (it is interesting to note that over 150,000 ethnic Vietnamese were expelled from Cambodia during this same period, and as many as 10,000 were killed by the Pol Pot regime [Ovesen and Trankell 2003:195]). Anti-Chinese riots in Indonesia in May 1998 left hundreds dead. Dozens of Chinese women were raped during the riots, and Chinese businesses were destroyed. There is evidence to suggest that the Indonesian military seized upon anti-Chinese sentiment to incite the violence and to blame ethnic Chinese for triggering the Asian financial crisis, which heavily impacted Indonesia in the years surrounding 1997.

Those who consider themselves Japanese, though less dispersed throughout the region, are also numerically strong. As scholar Kosaku Yoshino notes, the Japanese historically formed an image of themselves as racially and culturally distinct and as an ethnically homogeneous people (1998:19). Modern Japanese ethnic identity stems from the Meiji era (1868–1912), when cultural and political elites promoted the notion of Japan as a nation of people related by common ancestry and common race. Scholarship since the 1970s has pointed out that race, just like ethnicity, is a socially constructed category, and that "in historical times, Japan has never been a homogenous country" (Refsing 2003:50). Despite a host of scholarly works debunking the notion of a racially homogeneous Japan, such as *Japan's Minorities: The Illusion of Homogeneity* (Weiner 1997), *Multiethnic Japan* (Lie 2001), and *Multicultural Japan* (Denoon 1996), the notion of "Japanese" as a distinct and homogeneous category remains strong in Japanese popular culture.

The overwhelming majority of the 72 million citizens who call the Korean peninsula their home consider themselves ethnically Korean. The Korean Overseas Information Service (of the South Korean government) emphasizes that Koreans have maintained a separate sense of ethnic cohesion for well over a thousand years. The Koreans trace their ethnic origins from those who lived in or near the Altaic mountains in Central Asia. These believed ancestors of the Korean people began migrating to the Korean peninsula and northern China in the third millennium B.C.E. According to official Korean government renditions, numerous Altaic-speaking peoples were unified into a single kingdom, the Shilla, in the seventh century, which crystallized their sense of ethnic solidarity as they began to use a common language and build a common culture. Over 500,000 Koreans live in Central Asia, at least 600,000 in Japan, and 2 million in China. The Korean government notes with pride that members of the Korean diaspora often retain strong cultural ties with other Koreans, maintaining the Korean language, worshipping with other Koreans, and remaining conscious of their ethnic affiliations (Korean Overseas Information Service 1993:48). Within China, Koreans and Tibetans are the only ethnic groups who currently have schools through the postsecondary level that use their native language as the medium of instruction (the same was true of the Uighurs in northwestern China until a government policy in 2002 banned use of the Uighur language at Xinjiang University).

The term "Malay" is variously used, often subsuming several smaller ethnic groups inhabiting the Malay archipelago, including the Aceh, Bataks, and Javanese of Indonesia, and the Tagalogs of the Philippines. Within the Federation of Malaysia, where the government lists 60 percent of the 21 million population as being ethnically Malay, the constitution (Article 160, Clause 2) specifies that one must practice Islam and Malay culture, habitually speak the Malay language, and claim Malay heritage to be considered ethnically Malay. The Malay language belongs to the Austronesian language family. Bahasa Indonesia, adopted as Indonesia's national language in 1945, is considered a standard dialect of Malay. The Malay are spread across Southeast Asia, with large populations in Indonesia, Singapore, the Philippines, and Brunei.

Vietnam's dominant ethnic group is the Kinh, who comprise over 86 percent of the country's total population according to official Vietnamese government census data (General Statistics Office 2001:21). There are large

Vietnamese communities scattered across Southeast Asia, and many have fled to Europe and North America since the 1950s to escape the ravages of war and poverty. The Vietnamese have historically clashed with the Khmer peoples, who are based now in Cambodia. Animosities toward the Vietnamese population in Cambodia led Lon Nol, the general who seized power in 1970 and declared the Khmer Republic, to demand that all ethnic Vietnamese leave the country within forty-eight hours (Ovesen and Trankell 2003:197). Thousands who were not able to meet the demand were slaughtered, and eventually over 200,000 were forcibly repatriated to Vietnam. Pol Pot expelled another 130,000 Vietnamese, and killed most of the few thousand who remained.

Exactly which peoples should be considered Tai is still very much contested, as mentioned above. A host of different groups, typically considered to have originated in southern China and to have migrated south starting in the fifth century, are typically described by scholars and by government officials as ethnically Tai or loosely falling within the category of "Tai peoples," though these analysts and policymakers, as well as members of these ethnic groups themselves, differ as to which groups they assert as belonging to the broader Tai category and which should be considered separate ethnic groups or members of other, larger groupings. Many anthropologists use language as the key marker to identify those who belong to Tai ethnic groups. Yet even determining which local languages fall within the larger Tai family is greatly debated. To get a feel for the complexity of the debate, one need only peruse the *Sino-Tibetan Etymological Dictionary and Thesaurus* (see http://stedt.berkeley.edu/index.html), the publication of a linguistics research project at the University of California at Berkeley that has received funding from the National Science Foundation and the National Endowment for the Humanities over the course of its more than two-decade-long effort to classify and trace the etymology of the Sino-Tibetan language family and place the more than 200 languages, including Thai, that some (though not all) linguists assert fall within it. The publication notes that more than 45 million people speak Thai, while linguists J. Edmondson and D. Solnit (1997) place the number higher, at 80 million. As such scholars, as well as researchers like those at China's Central Nationalities University, continue to refine how various languages should be classified, elites from those language groups may begin to see commonalities among different groups that could create new ethnic boundaries. Some members of the 16 million–strong Zhuang ethnic group in China, for example, have begun to increase ties with other groups they consider to share common ancestry with them, including the Thai in Thailand and the Lao in Laos. While the government of Thailand has promoted a notion of Tai-ness based on Buddhism, loyalty to the king, and the ability to speak Thai, other groups currently considered within the Tai ethnic family practice animism or shamanism, and speak languages incomprehensible to those living in Bangkok.

▪ The Crafting of Ethnic Categories and State Policies

It is impossible to divorce the crafting of ethnic categories from both state policies and efforts by ethnic groups to gain power within the state, whether it be simply the power to define and articulate the boundaries of their ethnicities, or benefits that are more material, such as the right to certain territories, political positions, or natural resources. By examining three case studies drawn from states with widely divergent ethnic compositions and state policies, we can track several patterns in the evolution of ethnic groups and the interplay among ethnic identity, group mobilization, and state policies. While it is beyond the scope of this chapter to introduce all of the various theories of ethnonationalism in Asia Pacific, a brief sketch of ethnic relations in three countries of the region will provide a valuable foundation for further research.

China, Indonesia, and Malaysia prove useful cases due to both the vastly different ethnic compositions of their populations and their different approaches for dealing with them. Though all ethnic categories have been constructed over time and are mutable, it is important to note that China purports to have a large ethnic majority, while the Malaysian population is divided among three relatively large ethnic categories, and Indonesia comprises a plethora of ethnic groups, the largest of whom account for less than half the total population. These demographics have influenced the evolution of ethnic policy and ethnic relations within each of these states in important ways, and have greatly influenced the status of the various ethnic groups living there.

China
Numerous works have been published since the early 1980s on China's ethnic minorities. In addition to ethnologies based on anthropological fieldwork, several works have assessed state policies toward the more than 100 million people whom the Chinese government classifies as members of an ethnic minority. Though fewer in number, several important works have also examined how the notion of a majority "Han" population has been crafted. Examining the Chinese government's contemporary ethnic policy allows us to observe in clear relief how ethnic groups influence, and are in turn influenced by, state policy. Ethnic groups and ethnic boundaries are not static concepts, but are invented and negotiated by peoples in their interactions with those around them, and by concerted government efforts to shape ethnic identity.

China's territory has been inhabited for thousands of years. As populations moved across the plains, mountains, and deserts, settlements of various size emerged that were often segregated from one another by harsh geography and poor infrastructure. Peoples speaking different languages and observing different cultural practices interacted to varying degrees over time, often intermarrying or merging or, conversely, coming into conflict with one another and reinforcing their awareness of group differences. A host of factors influenced their self-identities and group loyalties; some groups focused on regional or clan alliances, while others were more conscious of their linguistic similarities or religious communities. Even the Chinese government's basic introductory texts on each of the ethnic groups are extremely complex, attempting to trace the origin of each as the names of purported ancestral groups change and merge throughout time.

In an effort to build national cohesion, Sun Yat-sen, the ideological leader of the nationalist revolution that overthrew the imperial order in 1911, promoted the notion that all Chinese citizens were related by blood. Though he recognized five separate nationalities in China, the new republic pursued an openly assimilationist strategy that was designed, as Sun articulated in 1921, to "facilitate the dying out of all names of individual peoples inhabiting China, i.e. Manchus, Tibetans, etc." (Sun 1970:229). "Strict implementation of racial assimiliation" was listed as one of five points in the Nationalist Party's first manifesto (Mackerras 1994:55). Chiang Kai-shek, who assumed power from Sun Yat-sen in 1924, further promoted a notion of common ancestry shared by Chinese citizens, and argued that "the differentiation among China's five peoples is due to regional and religious factors, and not to race or blood" (Chiang 1947:40).

The Chinese Communist Party has pursued a markedly different policy than the Nationalists since coming to power in 1949, one that has radically impacted ethnic relations and ethnic identities throughout the country. The CCP and the Chinese government, like many other parties and governments in the region, have employed a policy that combines assimilation, integration, preferential support for certain groups, and regional autonomy. The state has shifted among these various policy options across time and regions, at times applying stronger-armed assimiliationist approaches to the groups most resistant to central control, while at other times attempting to woo them with promises of regional autonomy.

The Chinese government, like the communist government in Vietnam, bases its minority policy on the Marxist-Leninist notion that "nationality" (the term used by many Marxist states to refer to ethnic groups) is a reflection of class divisions. The CCP has contended, since before it took power in 1949, that as exploitation of minorities ceases with the end of class conflict, and as minorities' economic circumstances improve, ethnic loyalties and divisions will fade and a more unified national consciousness will emerge. Though the notion of class conflict has been downplayed in CCP ideology in recent years, the party continues to be highly influenced by the Marxist assertion that inequalities exacerbate ethnic divides. Reflecting its ideological foundations, and in an effort to differentiate its policies from those of the Nationalist Party, in the early 1920s the CCP promised minorities the right to regional autonomy, even before formally seizing control of the country, firmly believing that as the minorities' economic conditions improved under communism, they would be less inclined to seek independence from the state. Under this policy, each ethnic group, living in a concentrated community within a specific territory, would have the right to self-government within the larger, multinational state. Though local policy within these regional autonomous areas was not allowed to conflict with the spirit of the central laws and policies, ethnic communities could alter central policy to make it fit local circumstances, and could thus more effectively implement central directives. Under the regional autonomy plan, the CCP also promised minorities the right to preserve and develop their own cultures, languages, and religions, the right to proportional or "appropriate" representation at all levels of government, and greater control over, and central assistance with, their economies, as compared with nonautonomous areas. Closer examination of how the CCP has implemented this regional autonomy policy reveals how ethnic identities have been influenced by state policy and the variable success of that policy in alleviating ethnic conflict within the country and protecting the rights of ethnic groups.

The CCP developed its regional autonomy policy without a thorough understanding of the ethnic context throughout the country. The party clearly did not anticipate that over 400 groups would seek official recognition when the first census was taken shortly after the CCP took control. Recognizing that it would be infeasible to grant 400 separate groups true autonomy, the government dispatched teams throughout the country to clarify which groups should receive recognition, that is, to define the boundaries of "authentic" ethnic groups. After more than four years of data collection and discussion by more than a thousand anthropologists, linguists, historians, political scientists, and officials, the government recognized fifty-six separate "nationalities" or ethnic groups, including the majority Han, whom the government explained accounted for over 92 percent of the country's population. The classification teams used Stalin's definition of "nationality," and sought to clarify which groups truly had unique languages, territories, economies, and common cultures, and which were simply members of larger ethnic categories that had been divided for political purposes by the "feudalist" or "imperialist" leaders of the past. Confronted with the numerous and disparate communities in the border regions, however, the government realized how difficult, if not impossible, it would be to delineate definitively these ethnic groups.

During the classification process, numerous ethnic categories were merged or divided to fit them relatively neatly into Stalin's compartmental schema. Families living on opposite sides of provincial boundaries, for example, often found themselves labeled as members of different nationalities because different classification teams were operating on either side of the border (Kaup 2002). The classification teams also merged many linguistic, religious, and regional divisions that had marked dynamics in different areas for centuries. In Guangxi and Yunnan provinces, for example, several groups of people who referred to

In Guangxi and Yunnan provinces, the government labeled as "Zhuang" several groups who referred to themselves by a variety of separate names. Representatives from the Nong, Sha, and Tu groups based in Yunnan are pictured here (clockwise from right).

themselves by a host of separate ethnonyms spoke mutually unintelligible languages, wore distinctly different ethnic dress, worshipped a variety of different local gods and spirits in distinct rituals, and rarely had any sense of belonging to a larger ethnic category were grouped together under the label "Zhuang." Disparate groups with varying levels of observable similarities or collective identities were also merged to form the Yao, Miao, Yi, Uighur, and other ethnic categories. Likewise, the government at times divided ethnic groups into categories that seemed arbitrary to many participants in the process.

Once having determined which groups should receive formal recognition and thus the benefits of regional autonomy, the government went about establishing autonomous areas. That political calculations were involved seems clear, as even high-ranking officials involved with the classification teams acknowledged to me in private interviews. In northwestern China, for example, Xinjiang province was divided into several autonomous administrative areas for different ethnic groups, much to the dismay of the ethnic Uighur, who viewed the land as their own homeland. Though over 75 percent of the population in Xinjiang were classified as ethnically Uighur in the 1953 census, more than half of the provincial landmass was set aside as autonomous territory for other minorities. More than a quarter of Xinjiang territory was designated the "Bayingolin Mongol Autonomous Prefecture," where Mongols make up just over 4 percent of the population and Uighurs nearly 33 percent, according to 2000 census data.

Ironically, the CCP's early minority policy was designed to facilitate the erosion of ethnic differences, yet at times required the CCP to highlight and promote ethnic awareness. As I have argued in greater detail in *Creating the Zhuang: Ethnic Politics in China* (Kaup 2000), after forcing disparate groups together under the single rubric of the Zhuang nationality, the party set about creating a sense of community and unified ethnic pride for these groups. It felt compelled to do so in order to convince people who historically felt little sense of community that if someone from this larger group were elevated to a position of power, then "their" autonomy was being preserved, and that the preservation of the larger cultural markers was synonymous with the preservation of their unique cultures. Whereas some groups in northwestern China have been barred from emphasizing their unique ethnic heritages and many people have suffered long prison terms for writing unofficial histories of their ethnic groups (CECC 2005), in Zhuang areas the government has banned writings suggesting that the Zhuang have anything less than a glorious past. One regional magazine was temporarily closed, for example, after publishing an article that asked why Zhuang ethnic consciousness was so weak (Lan 1988).

Although the government has never completely abandoned its regional autonomy policy, it has at different times and in different regions emphasized politics of assimilation or integration. There has been a particularly large emphasis on economic integration since 1978, and this emphasis has reached new crescendos since the government launched its "Open the West" campaign in

2000. Government rhetoric clearly emphasizes that economic integration and development are the key to handling successfully the "ethnic question." Based on this assumption, the government is pursuing rapid economic development in both Xinjiang and Tibet. Rapid industrialization and construction of infrastructure require trained personnel, however, and in its efforts to rush the pace of development, the government has encouraged a mass movement of educated Han Chinese into the area (CECC 2005:13–23). By state mandate, government workers who move to western border areas from coastal regions (the coast is overwhelmingly populated by Han Chinese) are better paid than locals. The thousands of new workers arriving in Xinjiang each year often take the most highly skilled, and thus most highly paid, jobs. In its rush to develop, the government is also offering scholarships for minorities to study in Han areas, where the educational opportunities are better. There are clearly political motivations for sending the minorities into Han areas to be integrated or assimilated, however, rather than investing the funds required to bring the quality of education in minority areas up to national standards. By promoting rapid industrial growth before enough local ethnic minorities have been trained to participate in the modernizing process, the government has exacer-

Of Turkic descent, members of the Uighur ethnic group are overwhelmingly Muslim and speak a language entirely different from that of the majority Han population.

bated ethnic tensions. Uighurs resent seeing the best jobs taken by outside Han, so much so, in fact, that some refer to it as "internal colonialism" (private communications). In areas where the government questions the loyalties of ethnic minorities to the state, however, it has pursued assimilationist policies with new emphasis since 2001. In Xinjiang, for example, where the Uighurs in the past established the independent (though short-lived) East Turkestan Republic, and where many Uighurs still would prefer their own state, the government has tightened controls over expressions of ethnic identity. Of particular concern to many who have accepted their destinies as citizens of the People's Republic of China are the government's efforts since 2002 to reduce use of the Uighur language in schools (Dwyer 2004).

Indonesia

Indonesia is extremely diverse. A number of societal divisions have influenced ethnic relations, with groups utilizing them differently to define their ethnicity. It is unclear exactly how many ethnic groups reside in Indonesia, particularly since the methods for attempting to classify them have changed so rapidly over the past century. A 1930 census conducted by the Dutch, for example, identified 137 ethnic groups, while census-takers in 2000 identified 1,072 different ethnic categories. The Dutch census-takers grouped several self-identified groups into larger categories (Klinken 2003:68). They simultaneously lumped many of the small ethnolinguistic groups in Borneo, such as the Kenyah, Iban, Lawangun, and Ot Danum, into a single category they called "Dayaks," a pejorative term borrowed from coastal Muslims in the area to refer to "pagans from the interior" (King and Wilder 2003:215).

A warrior from one of the many indigenous ethnic groups living in Indonesia.

Though there are a host of divisions throughout the more than 17,000 islands in Indonesia, three main divisions have been particularly important in
shaping ethnic identities: religious, linguistic, and regional. Rarely does a group
base its identity solely on one of these markers, though one may be dominant in
defining the often fluid boundaries of ethnicity. Place of origin is clearly important to the Javanese, for example, though they are not the only group living in
Java, and have had to reconstruct a common heritage for themselves in part centered on court rituals practiced in central Java (King and Wilder 2003:215). The
importance of different ethnic markers also changes over time and in response
to changing circumstances. As conflict erupted in January 1999 among local
Ambonese on Moluccas Island, for example, its nature shifted from a conflict
based largely on place of origin to a conflict among religious groups.

Religion is a key marker of ethnic identity for many living within Indonesia, and has been a flashpoint for ethnic conflict in recent years. Though approximately 90 percent of the population considers itself Muslim, there are important
divides among Muslims, and at times these differences have crystallized and
been utilized by elites as tools for building a sense of ethnic cohesion and solidarity (Brown 1994:118). Some groups also define their ethnic affiliation by
what language they speak. Scholars typically describe Indonesia as having about
25 different language groups and over 250 different dialects (Brown 1994:118).
Regionalism also shapes the ethnic layout of Indonesia, and is often the form of
ethnic competition between those claiming to be indigenous inhabitants of a region and those migrating to the region from outside. In Aceh, for example,
where a strong secessionist movement has troubled the central government for
years, the largest ethnic group, the Acehnese, claim the land as their own. Place-
of-origin ethnic groups usually distinguish themselves from other groups by
using a host of other ethnic markers. The Acehnese sense of identity has been influenced by many of the ethnic markers discussed above, as their devotion to
Shi'a Islam and use of their own language inform their sense of community and
distinctiveness from Sunni neighbors.

There are clear divisions in the way that Javanese, who comprise 45 percent of the country's population; the Sundanese of western Java, who comprise
15 percent; the Malays along the coast, who comprise about 7 percent; the
Achenese; the immigrant Chinese; and the numerous other smaller groups
such as the Dayaks, Madurese, Minangkabau, Bataks, and Bugis perceive of
themselves and their ethnic identities. These groups use a mixture of regional,
religious, linguistic, and other cultural markers to give themselves ethnic co-
herence. Their historical encounters with the colonial administration, and afterward with the Indonesian government, have further greatly influenced their
ethnic identities and mobilizations. None of these groups has emerged in isolation from the others or from the state.

The Dayaks, who are largely concentrated in Kalimantan in northern-
central Indonesia, have developed their ethnic identity largely in reaction to

outsiders (Klinken 2003:72). The category carried little salience until late in colonial rule, as the Dutch began penetrating into the interior hills where the Dayak peoples lived. The colonial administrators lumped several smaller hill tribes into the single category of Dayak. As we observed in the Chinese case, once the state created ethnic categories and required citizens to be identified as belonging to one of them, these newly created categories often took on importance and influenced affiliations among members in ways unseen before the classification process. Those labeled "Dayaks" spoke a variety of languages and observed a plethora of distinct animist religious practices. As they came into contact with the Muslim coastal Malay, they also became more conscious of their commonalities as non-Muslim hill peoples, particularly as they began competing with the Muslim Banjarese for scarce resources and jobs in the 1920s. As Jaques Bertrand (2004) describes in great detail, as the Dayaks jockeyed for greater political and economic autonomy and resisted the Muslim nationalist movement to replace the Dutch with an Islamic Indonesia, the Dayaks lent their support to the Dutch during the independence movement in the 1930s and 1940s. Though they were initially rewarded by the Dutch with their own "Great Dayak" state, they were stripped of autonomy in 1950 with the establishment of a unitary state. The Dayak were thereafter viewed with suspicion by the New Order Indonesian government and marginalized both politically and economically. Bertrand views the eruption of ethnic violence in Kalimantan, which left hundreds dead, as evidence of the Dayaks lashing out against the Madurese in an expression of frustration with their marginalized position.

As in China and other states in the region, in Indonesia the government has utilized a variety of tools to manage ethnic divisions and build a cohesive nation-state. When Indonesia gained its independence in 1945, it was confronted with the challenge of building a unified state amid a fragmented social setting. The New Order government responded first by banning any political discussion of ethnicity (Klinken 2003:71), banning ethnically based political parties, and promoting nationalism based on "unity in diversity." The Sukarno and then Suharto regimes kept tight controls over ethnic groups, and centralized power in Jakarta. It was hoped that modernization and economic integration would help assimilate the disparate groups into a new common nation of "Indonesians." The new nation-building propaganda promoted the notion of Indonesia as a "modern" nation, thereby marginalizing many of the less modern tribes and peoples in the periphery. All Indonesians were expected to pledge loyalty to one country, one nation, and one language. In its nation-building campaign, the central government appealed to "Indonesian" traditions focused on a newly invented Javanese cultural history. Though the national motto was "unity in diversity," at times the government pursued openly assimilationist policies, particularly in its policies toward ethnic Chinese. Government suspicions of Chinese exceptionalism were particularly pronounced throughout the 1950s and 1960s, as the Indonesian government battled to control the Partai Komunis Indonesia (PKI; Indonesian Communist Party). The government attempted to force Indonesian Chinese into casting aside their ethnic loyalties, banned use of the Chinese language in schools, and banned observance of Chinese festivals.

Only recently has the government experimented with offering any of the regions true autonomy. Though Aceh was designated a "special territory" in 1959, Acehnese were never satisfied with the arrangement, and a guerrilla se-cessionist movement, Gerakan Aceh Merdeka (GAM; Free Aceh Movement), began an armed conflict against the central government, in 1976. Only in the summer of 2006 did the Indonesian legislature pass a regional autonomy law according Aceh the right to self-rule in all arenas save foreign policy, and the right to retain 70 percent of the revenue from its rich natural resources. Ana-lysts disagree whether regional autonomy schemes will ultimately create con-crete boundaries that will strengthen ethnic divisions, or whether they will ease ethnic dissatisfaction to the extent that these groups will be willing to par-ticipate fully and meaningfully in a unified state.

Though many analysts still puzzle over how Indonesia has been able to maintain its territorial integrity in the face of vast ethnic disparities and the ab-sence of a history of unified centralized rule before independence, others sug-gest that the extent of ethnic differences may actually contribute to Jakarta's ability to keep the country intact. Gerry Klinken, for example, argues that the only ethnic group large enough to exert a significant impact on the central gov-ernment is the Javanese, and they have no need to do so, since they have been privileged in the administrative system. He argues that because ethnic diver-sity is more pronounced in the outlying areas away from the capital, and be-cause rarely is there a dominant ethnic group capable of imposing its will on the other groups living in these regions, local ethnic elites typically look to Jakarta to help them resolve their local disputes. These place-of-origin ethnic disputes, according to Klinken, may actually lend credence to Jakarta's asser-tion that only a strong central government can manage and alleviate ethnic conflicts in the outlying regions (2003:79).

Markedly different from the Chinese case, in which the Han Chinese as a whole are economically, socially, and culturally dominant throughout the coun-try, ethnic groups in Indonesia can be seen as operating in what Donald Horo-witz calls an "unranked" system (2000:21–36). In an unranked system, though there are certainly groups who are more powerful than others and those who have been significantly marginalized, the ethnic groups are relatively equal in wealth and influence. Ethnic conflicts, therefore, are often not about poor groups as a whole seeking greater wealth from privileged groups, but rather take the shape of conflicts that ultimately end up aiding the ethnic elite rather than the common members of the group. Elites within the central government are also influenced by ethnic concerns, and many factions within the central government take shape around religious or place-of-origin lines rather on the basis of political ideologies or policy platforms.

Malaysia

Any attempt to understand Malaysian politics or society must consider how ethnicity, class, status, and power interact (King and Wilder 2003:208). As Colin Mackerras describes in detail in Chapter 3, the Malaysian government that took power from the British in 1957 had to find some means of managing and controlling the ethnic groups who had been rigidly divided and manipulated by colonial policies. Just as in China and Indonesia, the ethnic makeup of the Malay peninsula until the nineteenth century was extraordinarily complex, and there were few large ethnic groupings. The British encouraged immigration from China and India into Malaysia, to fill certain crucial jobs. Through their system of indirect rule, the British appointed Malays to fill administrative positions and to head the police force and army. Chinese immigrants largely filled urban and commercial positions, while the Indian immigrants brought in by the British from their other colonies took on a host of different jobs, ranging from police work to manual labor on rubber plantations. Once the British had introduced these groups into the territory, they contributed to the crafting of ethnic divisions by asserting that each group was particularly suited to its chosen profession because of innate racial characteristics (King and Wilder 2003:204; Nagata 1979:81–82). Over time, the Chinese and Indian immigrant populations came to fare better economically than the Malays under the British.

The origin of current ethnic boundaries can be traced to decennial censuses taken by the colonial government beginning in 1871 (Shamsul 1998:136), which, like those of the Dutch in Indonesia or the CCP in China, merged several disparate cultural communities into more inclusive categories. The three main ethnic categories that emerged from the census and continue to shape policy today, the Malay (51 percent), Chinese (24 percent), and Indian (7 percent), were each divided by a host of intraethnic schisms that the colonial administrators did not consider important enough to warrant listing as separate ethnic categories. These included, for example, divisions among the Indian immigrant community centered on varied religions, castes, places of origin, occupations, languages, and other societal divisions. The Malay comprised a host of subregional groupings who had markedly different religious practices, languages, and local cultural practices. Even the Chinese, who were perceived by many Malays as a unified group, were divided by linguistic and regional differences.

Though these intraethnic divisions can still be seen in Malaysian society today, anthropological studies have shown that the broader ethnic categories overlay citizens' understanding of their place in society, even when objective analyses would suggest otherwise. Judith Nagata discovered, for example, that by the 1970s there were clear class divisions in Malaysian society that cut across ethnic lines. Her interviews revealed, however, that the vast majority of Malaysians did not perceive of their place in society along class lines, but rather primarily in ethnic terms. Class consciousness was subsumed by ethnic identities, barring the weakening of ethnic divisions in favor of class cooperation (Nagata 1975:130–133, 1979:164–172, referenced in King and Wilder 2003: 205–206). The centrality of ethnicity as an identifying force in society, with state policies since 1971 reinforcing ethnic divisions, should come as no surprise. Ethnicity is also central in social and political alliances, as can be seen in the dominance of ethnic political parties. Though the United Malays Nationalist Organization (UMNO), the Malayan Chinese Association (MCA), and the Malayan Indian Congress (MIC) formed an alliance (now known as the Barisan Nasional [BN; National Front]), the importance of ethnicity in politics is clearly demonstrated in the parties' ethnic composition and activities.

Like those seeking independence from their colonial occupiers in Indonesia, Malaysian nationalists had to build a sense of common identity for the peoples of Malaysia to enable them to function as a nation-state. There were several approaches that the new leaders could have used to meet this goal, including forced assimilation of all the groups into Malay culture, the creation of a new definition of "Malayness" through merging different ethnic categories, or allowing the existing ethnic framework to continue and crafting a pluralist political system to incorporate these communal interests. The leaders arguably attempted all three. There was a great debate among the nationalists over exactly who should be considered Malay. Though there emerged consensus that Malays should be given political and economic privileges as the "original rulers of the land," exactly who could be considered Malay was hotly debated. Three main strands, or *aliran,* competed to define who should be considered Malay. According to one strand, anyone adopting Malay customs could be considered Malay, irrespective of where he or she was born, while according to another strand, only those residing within Malay territory could be considered Malay. Ultimately it was agreed, and incorporated into Article 160 of the constitution, that a "Malay" would be defined as one born within the territory or to parents born within the territory and who "professes the religion of Islam, habitually speaks the Malay language, [and] conforms to Malay custom." Furthermore, Malay cultural markers were emphasized in the crafting of a generalized Malaysian identity, such as using the Malay kite as the emblem of the national airline, listing Islam as the national religion, and establishing a sultan as head of state (King and Wilder 2003:207).

Though there was an initial bargain among the ethnic groups that Malays would be allowed greater influence in the political arena while other groups, particularly the Chinese, would be allowed to dominate the economy, in 1971 the government changed course and launched a new pro-Malay affirmative action economic policy, set to last from 1971 to 1990. The shift to this policy, and to a second policy in 1971 that emphasized the forging of national culture from indigenous Malay culture, came as a result of ethnic riots in 1969, as Malays' resentment against economic marginalization erupted. The new economic policy sought to eradicate the identification of certain economic positions with specific ethnic groups and to elevate the economic position of the Malays. The policy pledged to raise the Malay share of corporate capital from less than 2 percent in 1970 to 30 percent by 1990 (Jesudason 1989:114–115). To reach this goal, the government established a number of specific policies favoring Malays over other ethnic groups. The central bank set targets for lending to Malays, many of whom were offered loans at below-market interest rates. The Malay community's share of bank loans rose from a low of 4 percent in 1968 to 28 percent by 1985 (Jesudason, in Liew 2003:94). Nearly a third of all new public construction projects were reserved for Malay companies, and entry into several low-tech industries was limited exclusively to Malays. Affirmative action policies in education required lower test scores for Malays to enter university, and established a number of special Malay scholarships.

Though many non-Malays still managed to flourish economically, the government's policies were viewed by many as openly discriminatory. Ethnic tensions increased and ethnic divisions were reinforced. Though Prime Minister Mahathir Mohamad pushed for policies to improve ethnic relations after the 1971 economic policy ended in 1990, tensions remained. Tensions between Muslim Malays and non-Muslims have also been strained in a climate of distrust since the terrorist attacks against the United States in 2001 highlighted the activities of radical elements within the Islamic faith.

Conclusion

Though ethnicity is a fluid category and ethnic loyalties can be shaped and manipulated by group interactions, elites, state policies, and changing structural environments, its influence remains strong in shaping communal identities and activities. This brief sketch of the ethnic mosaic in Asia Pacific depicts a complex network of groups and individuals encountering one another in a variety of settings and over time, all in a near-constant process of reaffirmation or reconstruction of what defines their place in society. State policies have at times reinforced or exacerbated ethnic tensions in the very process of trying to alleviate them. How political and cultural elites understand the process of ethnic formation and the importance of various processes of identity formation directly impacts what type of policies they will employ. Many important questions surrounding the nature, process, and consequences of ethnic identity formation remain to be answered. Through more detailed study of both the successes and the failures of ethnic conflict management, and the historical evolution of ethnic categories, formulas need to be developed that will enable differences and similarities among peoples to be respected and protected across the globe.

■ Note

1. David Wyatt (1984) wrote that there were 70 million Tai in Southeast Asia.

■ Bibliography

Anderson, Benedict. 1983. *Imagined Communities: Reflections on the Origins and Spread of Nationalism.* London: Verso.

Bertrand, Jacques. 2004. *Nationalism and Ethnic Conflict in Indonesia.* Cambridge: Cambridge University Press.

Brass, Paul, ed. 1991. *Ethnicity and Nationalism: Theory and Comparison.* Newbury Park, Calif.: Sage.

Brown, David. 1994. *The State and Ethnic Politics in Southeast Asia.* London: Routledge.

Chiang Kaishek. 1947. *China's Destiny and Chinese Economic Theory.* Notes and commentary by Philip Jaffe. New York: Roy.

Congressional-Executive Commission on China (CECC). 2005. *Annual Report, 2005.* Washington, D.C.

Connor, Walker. 1978. "A Nation Is a Nation, Is a State, Is an Ethnic Groups, Is a . . ." *Ethnic and Racial Studies* 1, no. 4: 379–388.

Denoon, Donald, et al., eds. 1996. *Multicultural Japan: Paleolithic to Postmodern.* Cambridge: Cambridge University Press.

Deutsch, Karl W. 1966. *Nationalism and Social Communication.* Cambridge: Massachusetts Institute of Technology Press.

Dwyer, Arienne. 2004. *The Xinjiang Conflict: Uyghur Identity, Language Policy, and Political Discourse.* Washington, D.C.: East-West Center.

Edmondson, J. A., and D. B. Solnit, eds. 1997. *Comparative Kadai: The Tai Branch.* Dallas: Summer Institute of Linguistics and University of Texas at Arlington.

Evans, Grant, ed. 1993. *Asia's Cultural Mosaic: An Anthropological Introduction.* Singapore: Prentice Hall.

General Statistics Office (Vietnam). 2001. *1999 Population and Housing Census Completed Census Results.* Hanoi: Nha Xuat Ban Thong Ke.

Gladney, Dru, ed. 1998. *Making Majorities: Constructing the Nation in Japan, Korea, China, Malaysia, Fiji, Turkey, and the United States.* Stanford: Stanford University Press.

———. 2007. "Internal Colonialism and the Uyghur Nationality: Chinese Nationalism and Its Subaltern Subjects." *Cemoti* 25. http://cemoti.revues.org/document48.html.

Hechter, Michael, and Margaret Levi. 1979. "Ethno-Regional Movements in the West." *Ethnic and Racial Studies* 2, no. 3: 262–274.

Horowitz, Donald. 2000. *Ethnic Groups in Conflict.* 2nd ed. Berkeley: University of California Press.

Hutchinson, John, and Anthony Smith. 1994. *Nationalism: A Reader.* Oxford: Oxford University Press.

Jesudason, James V. 1989. *Ethnicity and the Economy: The State, Chinese Business, and Multinationals in Malaysia.* Singapore: Oxford University Press.

Kaup, Katherine. 2000. *Creating the Zhuang: Ethnic Politics in China.* Boulder: Lynne Rienner.

———. 2002. "Ethnicnationalism Versus Regionalism in the People's Republic of China." *China Quarterly* 172 (December): 863–884.

King, Victor. 1993. *The Peoples of Borneo*. Cambridge: Blackwell.

King, Victor T., and William D. Wilder. 2003. *The Modern Anthropology of South-East Asia: An Introduction*. London: Routledge.

Korean Overseas Information Service. 1993. *A Handbook of Korea*. Seoul.

Lan Jianning. 1988. "Lun zhuangzu sixiang yishi, xinli jiegou ji qizhong de beiruo chengfen" [On the Weakness of Zhuang Ideology and Psychological Structure]. *Guangxi Minzu Yanjiu* [Guangxi Nationalities Research] 4: 7–16.

Lian, Kwen Fee, and Ananda Rajah. 1993. "The Ethnic Mosaic." In Grant Evans, ed., *Asia's Cultural Mosaic: An Anthropological Introduction*, pp. 234–259. Singapore: Prentice Hall.

Lie, John. 2001. *Multiethnic Japan*. Cambridge: Harvard University Press.

Liew, Leong H. 2003. "Ethnicity and Class in Malaysia." In Colin Mackerras, ed., *Ethnicity in Asia*, pp. 88–100. London: Routledge.

Mackerras, Colin. 1994. *China's Minorities: Integration and Modernization in the Twentieth Century*. Hong Kong: Oxford University Press.

———, ed. 2003. *Ethnicity in Asia*. London: Routledge.

Nagata, Judith, ed. 1975. *Pluralism in Malaysia: Myth and Reality*. Leiden: Brill.

———. 1979. *Malaysian Mosaic: Perspectives from a Polyethnic Society*. Vancouver: University of British Columbia Press.

Ovesen, Jan, and Ing-Britt Trankell. 2003. "Cambodia." In Colin Mackerras, ed., *Ethnicity in Asia*, pp. 194–209. London: Routledge,

Refsing, Kirsten. 2003. "*In* Japan, but Not *of* Japan." In Colin Mackerras, ed., *Ethnicity in Asia*, pp. 48–63. London: Routledge.

Renan, Ernest. 1882. *Qu'est-ce qu'une nation*. Translated by Ida Mao Snyder. Paris: Calmann-Levy.

Shamsul, A. B. 1998. "Bureaucratic Management of Identity in a Modern State: 'Malayness' in Postwar Malaysia." In Dru Gladney, ed., *Making Majorities: Constructing the Nation in Japan, Korea, China, Malaysia, Fiji, Turkey, and the United States*, pp. 133–150. Stanford: Stanford University Press.

Stalin, Joseph V. 1953. "Marxism and the National Question." In *Works*, vol. 2. Moscow: Foreign Languages Publishing House.

Sun Yat-sen. 1970. *Memoirs of a Chinese Revolutionary: A Programme of National Reconstruction for China*. New York: AMS.

Van Klinken, Gerry. 2003. "Ethnicity in Indonesia." In Colin Mackerras, ed., *Ethnicity in Asia*, pp. 64–87. London: Routledge.

Weiner, Michael. 1997. *Japan's Minorities: The Illusion of Homogeneity*. London: Routledge.

Wyatt, David. 1984. *Thailand: A Short History*. New Haven: Yale University Press.

Yoshino, Kosaku. 1998. "Culturalism, Racialism, and Internationalism in the Discourse on Japanese Identity." In Dru Gladney, ed., *Making Majorities: Constructing the Nation in Japan, Korea, China, Malaysia, Fiji, Turkey, and the United States*, pp. 13–30. Stanford: Stanford University Press.

11

Women and Development

Yana Rodgers

Women and men in Asia Pacific have experienced sweeping economic and political changes in recent decades. Economic growth paths are often based on international trade and foreign direct investment (FDI), meaning that individuals are participating directly in economies that are becoming increasingly integrated in world markets. This growing integration in the world's goods markets has progressed concurrently with increased integration in the world's financial markets, and these forces have contributed to the adoption of market-oriented economic reforms across many of the Asia Pacific economies as well as to growing pressures to privatize state-owned enterprises. Rapid financial sector liberalization, particularly during the 1990s, had a major impact, as did the 1997–1998 East Asian financial crisis (discussed in Chapter 5). Throughout, women and men have often experienced differential effects from these forces.

As incomes in the Asia Pacific economies have risen in recent decades, so has the region's social well-being, reflecting a well-documented two-way relationship between income on the one hand and health and education on the other. As countries grow richer, households, enterprises, and governments have more resources available for improving health and education outcomes. More abundant and better equipped facilities can be built, and access to those facilities can be improved. At the same time, individuals who are healthier, better skilled, and more educated are more productive, thus contributing directly to a country's potential to grow richer. Just as countries within Asia Pacific have recorded widely disparate outcomes in terms of overall economic performance, women and men have also recorded varying improvements in health status, educational attainment, and labor market performance. Comprehensive and readily available information on social indicators for women and men can provide a more tangible measure of how women's well-being has changed relative to that of men in recent decades of economic growth and structural change. After providing an overall context for understanding the broad economic changes that have affected gender equity, this chapter presents some revealing indicators on gender differences in health, education, labor market, and social outcomes across Asia Pacific. Consistent with the findings of the World Bank (2001) for the world's other regions, gender disparities tend to be largest in Asia Pacific's poorer countries. The chapter closes with a discussion of more detailed legal reforms that have affected women's rights and well-being.

The Impact of Globalization

With rapid economic growth for most of the Asia Pacific economies since the 1960s have come equally rapid changes in the economic environment that women face in their daily lives. In Asia Pacific's higher-income economies, early manufacturing production was concentrated in lower-skill, labor-intensive products—such as textiles, garments, and shoes—and in more recent decades has shifted toward higher-skill, technology-intensive products. These structural shifts in economies, such as in Singapore, Taiwan, and South Korea, have led to substantial challenges for female workers. In these economies, women tend to be clustered in industries that have started to shed their work force, upgrade, and even move abroad to lower-wage countries such as China and Indonesia. Women in these lower-wage countries, in turn, have felt the impact of globalization as their employers face severe pressures on international markets to keep costs low.

Two schools of thought are emerging to explain why increased integration in the world economy may have differential effects for women and men, particularly in the labor market. The forces of globalization are expected to create increasing pressures on employers to undergo cost-cutting practices, particularly if sex discrimination plays a role in employers' hiring and wage decisions. According to the dynamic implications of Gary Becker's neoclassical theory of discrimination (1959), if discrimination is costly, then increased competition from foreign investors and international trade will reduce the ability of employers to discriminate against women. Hence, according to the neoclassical school of thought, over time, competition from international forces is not compatible with persistent discrimination against women, and any gender wage gap due to discrimination should shrink. In contrast, non-neoclassical approaches to discrimination maintain that, rather than being an abnormality that occurs when market conditions are imperfectly competitive, discrimination is entirely consistent with the labor market outcomes of competitive firms and groups of workers acting in economically rational ways. In other words, wage discrimination can persist in the face of growing competition from abroad if women work in an environment of employment segregation and if they have little ability to negotiate for wage gains in bargaining situations.

The jury is still out on which school of thought is better supported by the empirical record for Asia Pacific. Several studies that include East Asian economies among a larger group of industrialized and developing countries have found some evidence supporting the neoclassical theory. That is, increased competitive pressure due to openness to international trade is associated with higher relative wages for female workers (Behrman and King 2002; Oostendorp 2004). In contrast, several case studies focusing on individual East Asian economies have found that greater integration in the world economy has proven less beneficial for women. For example, in Taiwan, the male-female wage gap, even after controlling for gender differences in worker skills and for domestic market structures, appears to have actually grown in industries that became relatively more open to international trade (Berik, Rodgers, and Zveglich 2004). In addition, South Korean *chaebols* (conglomerates), which own firms in a range of industries, may have paid female workers in export industries lower wages in order to support continued export competitiveness and also to maintain profitable operations in the more capital-intensive firms. In an effort to support competitiveness in export industries based on low-cost labor, some Asia Pacific governments have suppressed collective bargaining in export industries such as textiles, garments, and footwear. Because women workers are concentrated in

Women working in export industries, such as these textile workers in China, may face discrimination despite the forces of globalization.

these industries, these controls on worker organization have disproportionately affected women's bargaining efforts. Hence, gender discrimination in East Asian economies may have persisted in the face of, or even due to, international competition (Seguino 1997; Cheng and Hsiung 1994; Nam 1994).

Not only have global changes in recent decades involved dramatic growth in the international trade of goods and services, but physical capital has also increasingly flowed across borders in the form of foreign direct investment. FDI flows into Asia accelerated after the mid-1980s, with a jump from US$5 billion to US$148 billion in FDI to all Asian countries between 1985 and 2004 (United Nations Conference on Trade and Development [UNCTAD] 2005:51). The bulk of this investment has been fairly concentrated. By 2004, China alone was receiving over 40 percent of all FDI flows into Asia, with Hong Kong, Singapore, South Korea, and Malaysia also ranking among the top ten recipient destinations in Asia (UNCTAD 2005:52). These international capital flows have involved consequences for workers in both the sending and the receiving economies, the extent to which is still disputed in the literature. One such consequence that appears to have had particularly large effects on female workers in Asia Pacific is the subcontracting by final-goods producers—both foreign and domestically owned—toward smaller-scale, sometimes home-based operations. These smaller-scale operations are appealing to larger firms for their low labor costs: workers, predominantly female, are paid lower wages and typically remain uncovered by costly labor regulations that stipulate certain benefits and the right to organize. In addition to low pay, which is often piece-rate, and no benefits, working hours are long and shop conditions, such as lighting and ventilation, are often poor. These jobs tend to be filled by women who are displaced from the formal sector, or by new labor market entrants who need to work while caring for their children at the same time (Balakrishnan 2002).

Hand in hand with greater integration in global markets have come broad economic reform strategies in a number of Asia Pacific economies. The privatization of public services and public enterprises, widespread since the 1980s, constitutes an integral part of these broad strategies. Privatization is motivated by the need to trim government budget deficits, correct staffing and skill imbalances in public enterprises, improve efficiency of public sector operations, and refocus the priorities of national governments. Privatization will hurt workers in the short term as they experience layoffs and earnings losses, particularly when governments are unable to support displaced workers with adequate compensation packages, and public sector downsizing is likely to affect women differently from men. Downsizing often involves layoffs for those workers with lower levels of tenure, education, and other qualifications. Hence women are disproportionately affected by downsizing if, on average, they are less qualified than men.

Once they have lost their public sector jobs, women may face relatively larger obstacles in finding comparable formal sector jobs, forcing them to turn to low-paying and informal sector work, or to detach from the labor market altogether. Such obstacles include employer preferences to hire temporary and part-time workers in order to avoid labor market regulations that raise the cost of hiring female workers (such as maternity leave policies), as well as outright sex-based discrimination in employment. Although some female employment in the informal sector is temporary as countries undergo adjustment, women with low levels of education and skills may be displaced to the informal sector for a longer period of time. Among workers who lose their jobs due to privatization of public enterprises, women are more likely than men to exit the labor force or obtain jobs in the informal sector after displacement (Aslanbeigui, Pressman, and Summerfield 1994). Hence privatization has become an important force behind the persistently large informal sectors in many Asia Pacific economies.

Since the 1980s, two Asian countries have experienced particularly large economic and political transitions away from state control and toward greater market orientation: Vietnam and China. Vietnam's massive transition from a centrally planned economy to a more market-based economy involved the shift of about one-third of its public-enterprise work force (over 2.4 million workers) into the private sector, mostly into agricultural and urban informal jobs. A closer look at Vietnam's labor force data suggests that public sector job displacement has been relatively more tumultuous for female workers. Employment statistics indicate that a disproportionate share of women shifted from public sector work into unpaid work, or they left the labor market altogether. For example, among individuals surveyed who had experienced a job change out of public sector employment in 1991, 77 percent of men reported to have entered into unpaid work or were currently out of the labor force, but for women this share stood at 84 percent (Rama 2002:175). Women experienced an additional setback when cooperative-provided childcare services ended with the economic reforms, thus making their attempts to find and hold paid jobs more difficult. Overall, though, Vietnam's structural reforms contributed to rapid and sustained economic growth, which in turn contributed to improved living standards for households across most of the country (Dollar, Glewwe, and Litvack 1998).

In China, the movement away from a centrally planned economy toward greater emphasis on market forces included substantial labor market reforms in which wage determination shifted from a centralized administrative process to a more decentralized market-oriented system, and wages were linked more closely to worker productivity. In addition, employers were given more flexibility and authority in their own hiring and firing decisions (Kidd and Meng 2001). Increased labor-market flexibility, combined with sustained economic growth of 8–9 percent per year well into the 2000s, has contributed to a surge in new nonagricultural job opportunities, especially in labor-intensive industries such as clothing and textiles. The evidence on whether these labor market reforms affected women and men differently is mixed (World Bank 2001; Meng 1996). One set of studies has found that women living in urban areas experienced disproportionate job losses from the public sector; men were more likely in the early years to gain access to new nonfarm jobs, while women stayed behind on the farm; and less government involvement in the private sector translated into the weakening of antidiscrimination laws and a resurgence of traditional attitudes toward the unequal roles of female and male workers. In contrast, another group of studies has found that women have made more recent gains in access to new nonfarm employment opportunities in rural areas; in absolute terms, women's private sector wages are higher than women's state-enterprise wages; and the overall gender wage gap has not changed much. Conclusions on changes in the wage gap can differ depending on the years and the sector of economic activity. For example, in the early years of reform (1981–1987), the overall gender wage gap in the state-enterprise sector did not change much (Kidd and Meng 2001), while during the late 1980s to mid-1990s the gender wage gap in the rural sector grew (Rozelle et al. 2002).

Strong economic growth records, increased participation in international goods markets, and market-oriented reforms were accompanied by rapid and widespread financial sector liberalization during most of the 1990s. The 1997–1998 financial crisis put a quick halt to Asia Pacific's strong economic progress, with particularly large economic and social costs in Thailand, Indonesia, and South Korea (see Chapter 5 for further details). Although careful studies on the full social impact of the financial crisis are still limited, it is clear that effects did differ across gender, but not always to the disadvantage of women (Lim 2000; Aslanbeigui and Summerfield 2000; Manning and van Dierman 2000). The largest effects in the short term occurred in the region's labor markets. For example, men's employment losses in Thailand were generally larger than those of women, while wage cuts for women and men were comparable. In Indonesia and the Philippines, more women were entering into paid work and a higher proportion of women were working long weeks to help households cope financially during the crisis. In Korea, both women and men experienced large declines in regular jobs, but women saw a sizable increase in job openings for less secure positions as daily workers.

The lower-income economies also saw short-term withdrawals from school and reductions in nutrition. These short-term school interruptions and nutrient deprivation can potentially have more significant, longer-term repercussions in terms of gender equality in health status, school performance, and labor market outcomes. In particular, some families pulled their children out of primary school so they could contribute to household income, thus maintaining a sustainable level of household consumption. These school withdrawals were more severe in Indonesia, particularly for girls aged seven to twelve. A similar pattern, albeit less pronounced, seems to have emerged in Thailand, with younger girls of primary school age being disproportionately affected. Although older teenaged boys also experienced disproportionate withdrawals, the withdrawals for girls in the primary school years are more disturbing because of the negative impacts on basic literacy and future economic and social status. The poorer economies also showed some tendency to redistribute nutrient and caloric inputs away from women in poor households, and to forego higher-quality healthcare for pregnant women.

Economic development and increasing integration in world markets are not the only broad forces to have affected women's lives in Asia Pacific. Social norms, customs, and religious views of women form an ever-present backdrop to the way women engage their daily lives. Gender-related customs and beliefs often prescribe the types of work and activities that are considered appropriate for men and women, and they create strong incentives for people to behave in accepted ways as members of the family, community, and work force. Not surprising given its vast geographical size, gender customs vary considerably across the Asia Pacific region. This variation comes with differences across and within countries in social classes, ethnic groups, and religions. For example, Muslim women in Indonesia and Malaysia generally experience less freedom of movement than non-Muslim women, yet religion does not appear to impede women's power in making family-related decisions (World Bank 2001). Although Muslims in Southeast Asia are generally less conservative in their attitudes toward female roles compared with Muslims in the Middle East, there is still considerable agreement among both men and women that men are better political leaders and men have more right to a job than women. In Confucian-based societies such as China, Japan, and Vietnam, women face similar obstacles, with traditional patriarchal attitudes toward women's standing in the family and in the labor market. More generally, Ronald Inglehart and Pippa Norris (2003) argue that the strength by which a society supports principles of gender equity depends critically on that society's attitudes and commitment toward the proper role of women. Such attitudes slowly become less conservative as countries progress along the development ladder.

Asia Pacific stands out among developing regions for its sustained economic growth in recent decades. As most economies in the region have prospered, they have become increasingly integrated into the world's goods and financial markets, have undergone major structural reforms, and have made varying steps toward greater market orientation. These shifts in the macroeconomic environment are associated with considerable health, education, labor market, and social changes in the lives of women and men.

Health

Health status is one of the most important determinants of how people feel, care for their children, engage in their community, and achieve economic satisfaction. For example, poor health can reduce an individual's productive capacity and wage returns in the labor market, which could then have economic repercussions for the entire family in terms of poverty and debt. Numerous indicators are appropriate for measuring the health status of individuals, ranging from more subjective self-reports of well-being to more objective measures such as life expectancy, mortality (deaths), and morbidity (sickness). Access to healthcare facilities and fiscal expenditures on healthcare are also considered in discussions of health status. Across developing countries, data on mortality tend to be much more reliable and accessible as a source of health status information compared with data on morbidity. Most deaths are formally registered, and the information is compiled and disseminated by national ministries of health. Because the mortality data usually include information on age and sex, indicators related to life expectancy and mortality are useful for assessing gender differences in health status.

As shown in Table 11.1—which reports life expectancies at birth by sex in 1980 and 2004—life expectancy has risen for women and men in all the Asia Pacific economies except North Korea. This gain in life expectancies is consistent with gains seen in the world's other developing regions. Trends in the one exception case, North Korea, reflect the growing incidence in recent years of severe poverty, malnutrition, and hardship for most people as macroeconomic and political conditions have worsened. In all countries in both years, women had an advantage in life expectancy over men, reflecting evidence that females have a biological advantage in survival over males. However, the female advantage was not uniform across countries. In 2004, women's advantage in life expectancy in

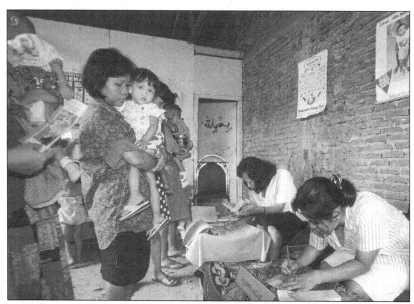

Women register at a rural health clinic in Indonesia.

Table 11.1 Comparative Statistics on Life Expectancy and Child Mortality in Asia Pacific, by Gender, 1980 and 2004

| | Life Expectancy at Birth (years) | | | | Life Expectancy at Birth (Ratio F/M) | Under-5 Mortality Rate, Female[a] | Under-5 Mortality Rate, Male[a] |
| | Female (F) | | Male (M) | | | | |
	1980	2004	1980	2004	2004	2004	2004
ASEAN							
Brunei	73	79	69	75	1.05	8	10
Cambodia	41	60	38	53	1.13	127	154
Indonesia	56	69	53	66	1.05	36	41
Laos	46	57	44	54	1.06	78	88
Malaysia	69	76	65	71	1.07	11	14
Myanmar	54	64	51	58	1.10	93	116
Philippines	63	73	59	69	1.06	28	40
Singapore	74	81	69	77	1.05	3	4
Thailand	66	74	61	67	1.10	20	23
Vietnam	65	73	61	68	1.07	22	24
East Asia							
China	68	73	66	70	1.04	36	27
Hong Kong	77	85	71	79	1.08	n/a	n/a
Japan	79	85	73	78	1.09	3	4
Korea, North	70	67	64	61	1.10	54	56
Korea, South	70	81	64	74	1.09	7	5
Taiwan	75	80	70	73	1.10	n/a	n/a

Sources: World Bank various years; WHO 2005; Taiwan Department of Health various years.
Notes: n/a = data not available.
a. Per 1,000 live births.

the higher-income economies, such as Japan, Hong Kong, and South Korea, averaged about six to seven years. In contrast, the female advantage stood at about three years in lower-income economies such as China, Indonesia, and Laos.

The smaller female advantage is driven by a combination of cultural and economic conditions that favor males and create discriminatory treatment toward young girls and women in access to healthcare and nutrition. These conditions cause women to experience lower longevity than would be expected in the absence of the discriminatory treatment (Coale 1991:519; Sen 1989:14). Just as women's life expectancy relative to men's varies across countries, changes over time in the female advantage also differ across countries. In many countries, including China, the female advantage has grown over time. Possible explanations for this increase are improvements in women's diets and medical care relative to those of men, better medical treatment for infectious diseases that had a relatively larger impact on women, changes in occupational roles that have actually increased occupational health risks for men, and shifts away from agricultural sector work (Schultz 1993; Mellor and Rodgers 2001). The relative importance of these alternative explanations is not known, and they do not explain the stagnation or even the slight decline in the female advantage over time for several economies, including Cambodia, the Philippines, and Thailand.

Infant and child mortality rates are still severe in the poorest Asia Pacific economies. As shown in Table 11.1, in Cambodia, Laos, and Myanmar, more than 75 young children out of every 1,000 live births will not reach the age of five. Infant and child mortality rates fall sharply as income rises, with under-five mortality rates as low as 3 or 4 per 1,000 live births in rich economies such as Japan and Singapore. China stands out for having a considerably higher under-five mortality rate for females than for males. Globally, during infancy, female mortality rates are lower than those of males, mostly due to genetic differences in health at the time of birth. However, in some poor countries, including China, female mortality exceeds that of males for children aged one to four (Waldron 1987:194; Hill and Upchurch 1995:128). This excess female mortality is associated with a relative lack of caloric intake, nutritional content, immunization, and medical treatment that adversely affects young girls, as well as patterns of son preference by parents.

Advances in the reproductive health of women in recent decades have made significant contributions to the improvement in women's overall well-being across Asia Pacific. Several indicators depict these changes in reproductive health, including a substantial reduction in fertility rates across countries, declines in maternal mortality, increased availability of family planning programs and contraceptive devices, and greater access to skilled health staff during childbirth. Consistent with a well-documented relationship across developing regions and over time between total fertility rates and per capita income, fertility rates are highest in Asia Pacific's poorer countries and lowest in its richest economies (see Table 11.2). Dean Forbes traces this relationship between development lev-

Table 11.2 Indicators of Women's Reproductive Health in Asia Pacific, Various Years

	Total Fertility Rate (births per woman)		Maternal Mortality Rate (per 100,000 live births) 2000	Contraceptive Prevalence (%) 2004[a]	Prevalence of Anemia Among Pregnant Women (%) 1999[a]	Births Attended by Trained Health Personnel (%) 2004[a]
	1980	2004				
ASEAN						
Brunei	4.0	2.4	37	n/a	n/a	99
Cambodia	4.7	4.0	450	24	n/a	32
Indonesia	4.3	2.3	230	57	64	72
Laos	6.7	4.6	650	32	62	19
Malaysia	4.2	2.8	41	n/a	56	97
Myanmar	4.9	2.3	360	34	58	57
Philippines	4.8	3.1	200	49	48	60
Singapore	1.7	1.2	30	n/a	n/a	100
Thailand	3.5	1.9	44	72	57	99
Vietnam	5.0	1.8	130	79	n/a	90
East Asia						
China	2.5	1.8	56	87	52	96
Hong Kong	2.0	0.9	n/a	n/a	n/a	100
Japan	1.8	1.3	10	n/a	n/a	100
Korea, North	2.8	2.0	67	n/a	71	97
Korea, South	2.6	1.2	20	81	n/a	95
Taiwan	2.5	1.3	6	n/a	n/a	n/a

Sources: World Bank various years; UNDP 2001; Taiwan Department of Health various years; Directorate-General of Budget, Accounting, and Statistics various years.

Notes: n/a = data not available.

a. For given year or closest year available.

els and population growth rates through the lens of demographic transition theory in Chapter 9. In 2004, women in Laos had 4.6 children on average, and women in Cambodia had 4.0 children on average. In contrast, numerous higher-income countries recorded fertility rates below 2.0, too low for the population to replace itself (given infant and child mortality, a fertility rate of about 2.1 is required). For these economies, any future population growth will come from immigration rather than from natural increase.

In addition, fertility rates fell in all Asia Pacific countries between 1980 and 2004. Fertility declines were particularly large in Vietnam, Myanmar, and Indonesia, due in large part to rising incomes, greater female educational attainment, and also strong commitments by these governments to provide family planning services and make contraception options more easily available. In China, because the country's fertility rate was already fairly low in 1980, the decline in fertility rate has been less pronounced, but in terms of sheer magnitude of the number of people affected, China's family planning program is one of the most effective and large-scale efforts by any government to control a country's population. At its inception in 1971, the government's "planned births" campaign emphasized marriage delay, more time between births, and fewer children, with voluntary participation but extensive pressure from local administrators. Concerns over continued population pressures in the late 1970s led to the current "one child" campaign. Although this campaign has succeeded in lowering the fertility rate, when coupled with traditional preferences for sons, it has also contributed to an increase in abortions of female fetuses, female infanticide, and neglect of female babies (Johnson 1996:80–82; Klasen and Wink 2003:282).

While most of the Asia Pacific economies have recorded considerable declines in fertility rate, maternal mortality remains disturbingly high in a number of countries, particularly those with lower per capita incomes. In fact, three countries (Cambodia, Laos, and Myanmar) still experience female deaths from pregnancy-related causes in excess of 300 women per 100,000 live births. High by any standard, these rates are associated with low rates of contraceptive usage, which raises the number of pregnancies, as well as shorter time durations between births. Gestational anemia can also be quite severe in the poorer economies, with the prevalence of anemia among pregnant women as high as 71 percent in North Korea and 64 percent in Indonesia. Complications during pregnancy and childbirth, such as hemorrhage, high blood pressure, labor obstructions, and infection, increase the risk of maternal mortality (Mellor and Rodgers 2001). By comparison, maternal mortality rates in South Korea, Taiwan, and Japan are among the lowest in the world. One explanation for why East Asia's higher-income economies have been able to successfully prevent or treat childbirth complications is that virtually all births are attended by skilled health staff. In contrast, less than 35 percent of births in Cambodia and Laos are attended by trained health personnel. In general, contraceptive prevalence and births attended by skilled health staff have risen over time alongside rising per capita incomes.

▨ Education

Just as healthy workers benefit from and contribute to the process of economic development, so do better-educated workers, as Kailash Khandke highlights in Chapter 5. Education builds workers' cognitive and analytical skills, thus making them more productive to society. Economic studies also show that countries with high levels of educational attainment for their workers can adopt a wider range of existing technologies and contribute to the development of new technological advances. Not only does education have a strong impact on entire economies, but individuals, families, and communities also benefit profoundly from the opportunities presented by literacy gains, higher educational attainment, and increased resources devoted to quantity and quality of schooling. Educating girls yields particular benefits over and above the schooling effects on boys. In particular, educated women have lower fertility rates, use public health facilities more efficiently, and have healthier and more highly educated children. Although the benefits of educating girls and women are well documented, and despite efforts by most Asia Pacific governments to promote education across the population, many countries in the region still have some gender inequity in educational participation and achievement.

One of the most basic indicators of educational achievement is the adult illiteracy rate. Consistent with other developing regions, women in Asia Pacific experience higher illiteracy rates than men. However, the severity of the gender discrepancy has fallen over time, and is not as high as that found in South Asia, the Middle East, and Africa, where some religions and social norms actually discourage the education of girls. As seen in Table 11.3, both women and men across Asia Pacific have experienced sizable declines in illiteracy since 1980. For example, the illiteracy rate in Indonesia dropped from 41 percent in 1980 to 13 percent in 2004 for women, and from 21 percent to 6 percent for men. Just as illiteracy rates are higher in the lower-income economies, the gender discrepancy was and continues to be higher in lower-income economies such as Cambodia, Laos, and China. Relatively small gender discrepancies by 2004 in the Philippines and Thailand reflect the aggressive use of education policies to achieve universal, full enrollment rates at the primary school level.

Most Asia Pacific economies have closed the gender gap in primary school enrollment rates. As demonstrated in Table 11.4—which reports gross enrollment rates in primary school in 1980 and 2004—by the latter year enrollment rates either exceeded 100 percent or stood close to 100 percent for both females and males. Note that because some students who are enrolled in primary school

Table 11.3   Comparative Statistics on Adult Illiteracy in Asia Pacific, by Gender, 1980 and 2004 (percentages)

	Female Adult Illiteracy Rate[a]		Male Adult Illiteracy Rate[a]	
	1980	2004	1980	2004
ASEAN				
Brunei	33	10	15	5
Cambodia	62	36	25	15
Indonesia	41	13	21	6
Laos	90	39	59	23
Malaysia	38	15	20	8
Myanmar	34	14	15	6
Philippines	12	7	10	7
Singapore	26	11	9	3
Thailand	17	9	8	5
Vietnam	19	13	7	6
East Asia				
China	48	13	22	5
Hong Kong	24	n/a	6	n/a
Japan	n/a	n/a	n/a	n/a
Korea, North	n/a	n/a	n/a	n/a
Korea, South	11	n/a	3	n/a
Taiwan	23	n/a	9	n/a

Sources: World Bank various years; Directorate-General of Budget, Accounting, and Statistics 2000.

Notes: n/a = data not available.

a. Proportion of people aged 15 and older who cannot read and cannot write a short statement on everyday life.

are outside of the age range for the population of primary school–aged children, the reported rates can exceed 100 percent. Net enrollment rates, which exclude enrolled students who are outside the age range from those enrolled in primary school, are considerably lower for some of the poorer economies. Gross enrollment rates at the secondary school level (not reported) are also lower for the poorer countries, and the male advantage is more pronounced. In contrast, the richer economies of South Korea, Japan, and Taiwan each have full enrollment at the secondary school level for both females and males, mostly reflecting legislation that mandates school enrollment through the secondary level for all children. This pattern for Asia Pacific is consistent with other developing regions: income growth typically translates into improved gender equality in education, particularly at the secondary school level (World Bank 2001:19). The rightmost two columns in Table 11.4 show that in most Asia Pacific economies, females have a small disadvantage in their representation among primary school and secondary school students. This disadvantage is considerably greater in the lower-income economies at the secondary school level.

Table 11.4 Comparative Statistics on School Enrollment in Asia Pacific, by Gender, 1980 and 2004 (percentages)

| | Primary School Gross Enrollment Rate[a] | | | | Female Primary School Pupils 2004[b] | Female Secondary School Pupils 2004[b] |
| | Female | | Male | | | |
	1980	2004[b]	1980	2004[b]		
ASEAN						
Brunei	106	109	111	109	48	49
Cambodia	n/a	131	n/a	142	47	38
Indonesia	100	115	115	117	49	49
Laos	104	109	123	124	46	42
Malaysia	92	93	93	93	49	51
Myanmar	89	93	93	92	50	48
Philippines	110	112	114	113	49	51
Singapore	106	n/a	109	n/a	48	47
Thailand	97	96	100	101	48	50
Vietnam	106	94	111	101	47	48
East Asia						
China	104	115	121	115	47	47
Hong Kong	106	105	107	111	48	49
Japan	101	101	101	100	49	49
Korea, North	n/a	n/a	n/a	n/a	n/a	n/a
Korea, South	111	105	109	105	47	47
Taiwan	102	102	101	100	48	49

Sources: World Bank various years; UNESCO various years; Taiwan Ministry of Education various years.

Notes: n/a = data not available.

a. Ratio of children of all ages who are enrolled in primary school to the country's population of primary school–aged children.

b. For 2004 or closest year available.

A woman walking with her ox in southern China.

World Bank photo.

◾ The Labor Market

As countries in Asia Pacific have developed, women's participation in the labor market has changed, following a pattern that closely matches trends observed around the world. In particular, in countries with sizable agricultural sectors and household-based farm production, women's participation in the labor market is usually high. In such economies, women are active in paid work, home production, and farm maintenance. As countries embark on the industrialization process, women's labor force participation begins to decline as they devote less time to household farm production and more time to nonmarket activities such as childcare and household chores. In highly industrialized economies, women's participation in the labor market begins to rise again as women combine paid work with raising children. This U-shaped function, which has been observed for numerous countries around the world, is supported by data for countries at different stages of development in Asia Pacific (Cagatay and Ozler 1995; Goldin 1995).

The first two columns of Table 11.5 report the proportions of the adult female and male populations who participated in the labor market in 2004. Some of the highest labor force activity rates for women are found in the relatively poorer economies of China, Cambodia, and Vietnam. In contrast, some of the lowest female labor force activity rates are found in the middle-income economies of Malaysia and Brunei. Female activity rates appear to move up-

Table 11.5 Indicators of Women's Labor Market Status in Asia Pacific, 1980, 1990, and 2004 (percentages)

	Labor Force Activity Rate[a]		Female Share of Labor Force		Female-to-Male Wage Ratio in Manufacturing	
	Female 2004[b]	Male 2004[b]	1980	2004[b]	1990	2004[b]
ASEAN						
Brunei	46	82	23	34	n/a	n/a
Cambodia	78	81	55	51	n/a	n/a
Indonesia	53	87	35	38	n/a	n/a
Laos	56	82	39	41	n/a	n/a
Malaysia	48	84	34	36	50	63
Myanmar	70	88	44	45	97	91
Philippines	56	85	35	39	76	76
Singapore	57	83	35	40	55	61
Thailand	71	85	47	46	64	75
Vietnam	78	83	48	49	n/a	n/a
East Asia						
China	76	88	43	45	n/a	n/a
Hong Kong	61	81	34	46	69	74
Japan	60	85	38	41	55	60
Korea, North	50	81	45	39	n/a	n/a
Korea, South	54	77	39	41	50	56
Taiwan	48	68	33	42	64	74

Sources: World Bank various years; ILO various years; Directorate-General of Budget, Accounting, and Statistics various years.

Notes: n/a = data not available.

a. Percentage of population aged 15–64 who participate in the labor force.

b. For 2004 or closest year available.

ward again for the higher-income economies of Hong Kong and Japan. In all the economies, men have higher labor force activity rates than women. In addition to women's choices about entering the labor market, religion and social attitudes toward women's presence in the work force contribute to the gender differences in labor force activity rates.

Also supporting the U-shaped function are data for Asia Pacific on the female share of the labor force. As indicated in the third and fourth columns of Table 11.5, women in the poorer economies of Cambodia and Vietnam tended to comprise the highest share of the labor force in both 1980 and 2004. In fact, women's share of Cambodia's labor force actually exceeded that of men, a characteristic that is unusual by most standards, and most likely reflects atrocities during the genocidal Pol Pot regime from 1975 to 1979. Consistent with this high female representation in the labor force, Cambodia also has one of the highest female shares in the overall population among developing countries, also reflecting the years of political turmoil, war, and enforced hardship that appear to have had a relatively greater impact on male mortality. The female share of the labor force fell for the middle-income economies and began to rise again for high-income economies such as Taiwan and Hong Kong. For the majority of countries, women's labor force share rose slightly between 1980 and 2004. The jump was particularly large for Brunei, perhaps reflecting attempts by the country's public and private sectors to strengthen the labor force as the country diversified its economic base away from oil and gas.

Because international standards do not include unpaid work within the home as a labor force activity, and because women perform the bulk of unpaid household work, these official statistics present a misleading account of the time that women allocate to work activities. Detailed studies of how individuals use all their time in all paid and unpaid activities have found that in almost all regions around the world, women work more hours and have less leisure time than men (Ilahi 2000). Differences between women and men in time-use records are greatest when the household includes young children. Gender disparities in time-use also tend to be larger among poor households than richer households, particularly if richer households have access to hired help. For example, in the Philippines, women and men in richer agricultural households have more similar time-use profiles partly because these households can hire workers to perform household work on the family farm that women would otherwise be performing (Brown and Haddad 1995).

In formal labor markets, gender differences in wages occur around the world, and Asia Pacific is no exception. In recent years, female-male wage ratios in the manufacturing sector have ranged from 56 percent in South Korea to 91 percent in Myanmar (see Table 11.5). Japan and South Korea are notorious for having among the lowest manufacturing sector wage ratios in the world, and wage ratios in most East Asian economies are generally lower than those found in Western Europe, the United States, Australia, and New Zealand.

Although the male wage premium has persisted over time across the region, most countries for which comparable data are available show some improvement in women's relative wages since 1990. For example, in Singapore, the female-to-male wage ratio rose from 55 percent in 1990 to 61 percent in 2004. This increase in relative wages for women in Asia Pacific is consistent with a trend in numerous countries in other regions: women's wages have been rising relative to those of men in recent decades (World Bank 2001).

These gender discrepancies in wages, as indicated by the unadjusted ratio of female-to-male wages in Table 11.5, may be capturing gender differences in worker productivity characteristics such as education and skill. In particular, some of the gender gap in wages may be explained by lower educational attainment or experience on the job for women compared with men. In addition, the wage discrepancies may be capturing gender differences in occupations. For instance, the relative concentration of women in lower-paying occupations will contribute to an overall gender wage gap. Finally, because most of the wage ratios are based on daily, weekly, or monthly earnings, the reported wage discrepancies may also be capturing gender differences in the number of hours worked per day, week, or month. Numerous studies have attempted to explain the extent to which these gender differences in productivity characteristics, occupations, and hours worked help to explain the overall gender wage gap in countries around the world. The portion of the gender wage gap that cannot be explained by these factors is commonly attributed to wage discrimination against women. This unexplained portion is surprisingly large across industrialized and developing countries. For example, the percentage of the overall gender wage gap that remains unexplained by gender differences in productivity characteristics, occupational attainment, and hours worked was about 60 percent for Taiwan and Indonesia and 33 percent for Korea in the 1990s (Zveglich, Rodgers, and Rodgers 1997; Rodgers 1998; Horton 1996). Although gender differences in skills not captured in the data could be responsible for some of this unexplained gap, wage discrimination by gender must also be considered as a source of the disparity in wages between women and men.

In addition to the pay they receive on the job, women may be facing discrimination in hiring, training, and promotion decisions. This source of discrimination contributes to the clustering of women in certain lower-paying occupations and industries. Across Asia Pacific, women are clustered in clerical jobs, service and sales work, and elementary occupations. Men, on the other hand, dominate production work in crafts and trades, as well as factory and machinery operations. More significantly, men dominate the high-paying legislative and supervisory positions across countries. Some of this employment segregation by gender in Asia Pacific can be explained by employment decisions and labor control policies in a context of patriarchal gender norms (Seguino 1997; Cheng and Hsiung 1994; Nam 1994). Inequitable access to training, gender-specific advertisements for jobs, employer practices of the "marriage bar," and state promotion of home-based work have all contributed to the exclusion of women from higher-paying occupations and industries. Marriage bars are explicit employer policies that allow employers to avoid hiring married women and to fire single women if they become married. Some employers favor such policies, because they want to avoid investing in the training of women who may later quit their jobs for family reasons, or they want to avoid paying maternity-leave benefits for women who choose to combine work and family. Not only have these policies restricted women's employment opportunities, they have also reduced women's bargaining power with employers in wage negotiations. With economic development, the employment distribution across occupations and industries has become more similar for women and men in a number of Asia Pacific economies. For example, both female and male employees in Taiwan and Korea have recorded dramatic shifts out of low-skilled jobs—especially textiles and garments—into higher-skilled jobs—especially electrical and electronic equipment. This decline in job segregation may be partly responsible for the small improvement in women's relative wages in much of the region.

Political and Social Status

Economic development and increasing integration have also brought substantial changes to women's position in society more broadly. Women have achieved improvements in their political representation and autonomy, they have benefited from the political advocacy of a growing number of women's organizations, and their positions in local communities and even within the family have slowly strengthened. The progression toward women's more visible role in politics, and in society at large, began well over a century ago. Before the 1900s, under patriarchal-feudal or colonial systems of government, women generally did not hold political office or even formal jobs; most of their activity was constrained to farmwork and housework. Growth and political change brought new employment opportunities, including positions in political parties and formal office. Two brief examples illustrate the gains women experienced toward increasing their political power.

After the founding of the People's Republic of China in 1949, new opportunities became available for women as government administrators, Communist Party members, and leaders of social organizations (Xiaojiang and Jun 1998). The new communist government made it a top priority to establish women as valued members of families and also as valued citizens of the country. Policy reforms actively supported women's participation in politics, and also helped to create new women's organizations. In particular, the electoral law of 1953 first allowed women to run for public office, and a series of Communist Party mandates set quotas for the proportion of men and women in the top positions. In practice, gender gaps in party membership and in the holdings of formal office have narrowed across the rural and urban sectors, although inequities have not disappeared.

In another illuminating example, women in South Korea have also experienced slow but steady changes in their participation in the political arena. The end of the Korean War in 1953 and the onset of rapid industrialization brought an infusion of women's groups who pushed for a greater presence for women in political positions. These groups worked to mobilize women at the grassroots level, educate female voters, recruit and support female candidates for office, and stipulate numerical quotas by gender for party positions (Kim et al. 1998). By the beginning of the twenty-first century, South Korea was home to well over 4,000 women's organizations, including two powerful umbrella organizations (the Korean National Council of Women and the Korean Women's Associations United) that have continued to press for women's improved social status.

China and South Korea do not stand alone in Asia Pacific in terms of the important role played by governments and women's organizations in promoting improved political, social, and economic opportunities for women. At all levels—including grassroots movements, nongovernmental organizations, national women's rights groups, and research institutions—women-centered groups have been pushing for changes in laws, institutions, and attitudes toward women's roles for well over a century. Women's movements in individual countries also gained strength from newly liberalized labor unions and the lifting of government restrictions on the rights of workers to organize and to strike. For example, Taiwan's government lifted martial law in 1987 and legalized strikes in 1988, resulting in increased bargaining power for all workers, male and female. Further adding support to causes pushed by women's movements, in recent decades industrialized countries have placed increasing pressure on Asia Pacific economies to adopt core labor standards, which include the elimination of discrimination. Bilateral and multilateral aid agencies have added further pressure for governments in Asia Pacific to improve gender equality in basic legal and social rights, to prevent discrimination by sex, and to improve the provision of public services. These changes have slowly translated into gains for women in their access to schooling, healthcare, new job opportunities, bank credit, and political positions.

Asia Pacific now stands out among all regions for having a high female representation in parliament. On average from 1985 to 1995, women in Asia Pacific economies held 20 percent of parliamentary seats, compared with less than 10 percent for the world's other regions (World Bank 2001). The relative advantage for Asia Pacific in women's political representation and autonomy reflects the slow but steady erosion in recent decades of social norms and traditions favoring men. This erosion has occurred largely in response to pressures from extremely rapid economic growth in recent decades, and also in response to many governments' ideological commitment to gender equity (Chou, Clark, and Clark 1990; Das Gupta et al. 2000). Yet even with 20 percent of parliamentary seats, women are still very much underrepresented in political office. Within the region, some of the highest female representation rates are found in the socialist economies of China (20 percent), Laos (23 percent), and Vietnam (27 percent), and lower shares are found in Malaysia (9 percent) and Thailand (11 percent) (United Nations Development Programme [UNDP] 2005). Women's representation among executive offices is considerably lower: in 2004, women made up less than 10 percent of cabinet ministers in most Asia Pacific countries (UNDP 2005). As in South Asia, female presidents—often the widow or orphaned daughter of a former male president—are not unusual in Asia Pacific. For example, at least two female presidents have ruled in Southeast Asia since 2001, including Megawati Sukarnoputri of Indonesia and Gloria Macapagal-Arroyo of the Philippines. In Myanmar, a Nobel Prize–winning female activist and politician—Aung San Suu Kyi—has been leading the main opposition party that won the 1990 multiparty elections, but was not yielded power by the military junta.

Rapid industrialization, changing labor market structures, and legal reforms since the 1960s have brought changes not only to women's economic and political status, but also to their status within the household. With the strong increase in labor force participation rates since the 1970s, women are waiting longer to become married and have children, are having fewer children, and are relying more on alternative childcare arrangements such as childcare centers. For example, in South Korea between 1970 and 1990, the aver-

Aung San Suu Kyi, leader of the National League for Democracy Party in Myanmar, has spent more than a decade under house arrest. Her party won the general elections in 1990, but the military junta refused to recognize the results.

Image from usinfo.state.gov.

age age at marriage for women rose from twenty-three to twenty-six years, the share of young women (aged twenty to twenty-four) who were never married rose from 57 percent to 81 percent, and the fertility rate fell from 4.3 births to 1.8 births per woman. Revisions in family law and property law have also made divorce a more feasible option for women. The traditional view of the family—in which husbands are the primary breadwinners and wives are the primary caregivers—has transformed into a more modern view—in which husbands and wives both participate in economic activities to support the family. The types of activities in which men and women are engaged have also changed, particularly in rural sectors, where husbands are leaving home for extended periods to work in industry, leaving women to take over most of the farm-based work. Yet changes in attitudes and household practices have come slowly, and as in most other parts of the world, women are still responsible for the bulk of household production, including housework and childcare, even if they are employed in the formal labor market.

Legal Reforms to Promote Gender Equality

Women in Asia Pacific have benefited from a host of legal reforms in recent decades, protecting their health and well-being, granting them more freedom and rights, and promoting their labor market equality with men. Legal reforms have occurred in response to domestic pressure as well as international pressure through the forces of globalization and increased interaction with international agencies. Since the 1970s, a series of influential conferences and publications sponsored by various United Nations organizations—particularly the World Health Organization and the United Nations Children's Fund—have publicized the extent of gender inequities and developed new initiatives to boost women's health, nutrition, and education status. Women's health and education rights have been addressed head-on at large international women's conferences in Mexico City (1975), Nairobi (1985), and Beijing (1995), and at the 1994 International Conference on Population and Development in Cairo.

Participants at the 1995 Beijing conference constructed an action platform to guide policymakers and agencies around the world in better meeting women's health needs. This platform recognizes that women have unequal access to health resources, and in addressing this problem identifies a number of objectives to help women attain improved health status. These objectives include passing legislation that targets behaviors that contribute toward the spread of HIV/AIDS among females, tackling social norms that subordinate women, designing programs for men to help them increase their involvement in the household, encouraging men to engage in responsible sexual and reproductive behavior, and ending the exploitation of female sex workers (Mellor and Rodgers 2001). International agencies have placed a similarly high priority on improving school enrollment rates for girls and on raising female literacy rates. In practice, strategies based on universal education requirements rather than more targeted attempts to educate girls have generally been the most successful in closing the gender educational gap. The current focus on reforming women's health and education policies across Asia Pacific mirrors the focus of these international efforts on gender equity in health and education. The region has been particularly successful compared with the world's other developing regions in closing the gender gap in educational attainment—particularly at the primary school level—by implementing universal schooling requirements.

In addition to advances in legal reforms that improve women's access to health services and education, women have experienced increased autonomy from legal reforms in family law and landownership. Because family law covers personal issues such as marriage, divorce, custody of children, and property ownership, it is contentious and politically charged. Traditionally, family law in Asia Pacific has been highly skewed toward rights favoring men, fully sanctioning practices such as arranged marriages, polygyny, child marriage, unequal rights to divorce, and female exclusion from inherited property. At times, radical legal reforms have made these traditions less egregious, and inequalities less severe, in numerous countries. A notable example is China's marriage law of 1950, which aimed to eliminate bride-price and child marriage, allow women the right to choose their own spouses and demand a divorce, grant women the right to share control of their children, and allow women to inherit property. The marriage law successfully reduced the frequency of arranged marriages and polygyny, and improved young women's domestic autonomy. However, its implementation caused widespread protests, particularly among males and older women, and may have been responsible for tens of thousands of female suicides and murders (Das Gupta et al. 2000). Closely related, blatant gender inequalities in the right to own and inherit land still exist in the region. Some governments are attempting to rectify gender inequalities in customary laws by replacing them with statutory reforms, such as in land registration and titling, but the reforms are slow and problems remain, particularly in the region's lower-income economies (Tinker and Summerfield 1999).

Women in Asia Pacific have also succeeded in gaining a stronger political voice. A fundamental set of rights that women in all but one of the region's economies acquired during the 1900s are the rights to vote and to stand for election on a universal and equal basis (UNDP 2001). Most often these rights were granted at the same time. Only in Brunei have women not yet gained the rights to vote and to stand for election. Brunei shares this distinction with just one or two other countries in the world. Women in North Korea are allowed to vote and to stand for election, but it is unclear when women gained these rights. With its political change to a constitutional monarchy in 1932, Thailand became the first Asia Pacific country to grant these rights to women. Myanmar gave women the right to vote just two years later, but in this country women did not receive the right to stand for election until more than a decade later. The only other country that gave women these political rights in the 1930s was the Philippines. A large group of countries, including China and Japan, followed in the 1940s, and the final countries to pass this legislation (Cambodia, Malaysia, and Laos) did so in the 1950s.

In addition to political reforms, Asian governments in recent decades have implemented a host of labor market reforms protecting worker rights. These reforms have sometimes been prompted by pressures put on governments by the activities of women's rights groups, domestic and international labor movements, and international agencies. Further pressures have come from demographic changes and growth of the work force. As a result of reduced child mortality rates, lower fertility rates, and the slowdown in population growth, a relatively large share of the population across Asia Pacific is now of working age. New labor market laws across the region have included regulations aimed specifically at protecting female workers and promoting their equality with male workers. Most common across the region are working-hour restrictions for women, mandated maternity benefits, and equal-protection legislation.

Provisions on women's working hours, which include both night-work prohibitions and overtime limits, are widespread in formal sector labor markets across Asia Pacific (Nataraj, Rodgers, and Zveglich 1998). As of the mid-1990s, only Singapore, Vietnam, and China had no working-hour restrictions for women. Night-work prohibitions constrain the time of day when workers can be employed, whereas overtime limits constrain the total number of hours that workers may work within a day. Governments typically implement such legislation with the objective of safeguarding women's family time at home and ensuring their physical safety late at night. In Asia Pacific economies, night-work prohibition is relatively more common than are overtime limits, although the severity of the legislation varies considerably across countries. At one extreme, Myanmar restricts women to end their work by six o'clock in the evening, not to resume again until six o'clock the next morning. No exceptions are allowed. At the other extreme, restricted hours in Thailand do not begin until midnight and last for just six hours, with an allowance for occupational exceptions (such as managers or health professionals). Overtime limits that are more restrictive for women than for men occur in fewer than half of the Asia Pacific economies. Again, the most severe limits are found in Myanmar, where women are simply not allowed to work overtime. Overtime limits in economies such as Japan and South Korea are more lenient. In Japan, women are restricted to 150 hours of overtime per year, while men have no restrictions, and in South Korea, women have six fewer hours of overtime per week than men.

Critics of women's working-hour restrictions have argued that these policies are discriminatory and contribute to the persistence of occupational segregation. Because the measures make women's working-hour options less flexible, they hamper women's ability to compete with men for certain jobs.

This criticism is supported by findings for Taiwan (Zveglich and Rodgers 2003). Taiwan's 1984 labor-standards law included both a night-work prohibition and overtime limits for women. These provisions have been shown to significantly dampen women's employment, suggesting that firms' demand for female workers dropped. However, advocates of such policies argue that they limit employer exploitation of female workers and encourage more women who have household responsibilities, and who value shorter workdays, to enter the labor force.

Even more prevalent across Asia Pacific are mandated maternity benefits. Many nations either meet or exceed international guidelines by stipulating at least twelve weeks of paid maternity leave, often compensated fully and financed directly by employers. Among the few countries where employers are not required to pay for leave benefits—including Japan, the Philippines, and Myanmar—women's compensation is financed through social security funds or insurance. Leave benefits in the region's more industrialized economies are among the least generous in the region. For example, Singapore and Taiwan call for just eight weeks of maternity leave, albeit at full pay. At the other extreme, Vietnam's legislation calls for four to seven months of fully paid leave, which is a generous benefit by any standard. The maternity-leave legislation in most countries includes employment protection clauses whereby, at a minimum, women cannot be fired during the leave period. Many countries also have a policy that allows women to take paid nursing breaks. A common provision is two thirty-minute breaks per day for up to a year.

Maternity-leave benefits can facilitate the realization of important labor market and social objectives. In particular, maternity benefits strengthen women's attachment to the labor force and increase their firm-specific tenure and training, which in turn can enhance the productivity of female workers (Waldfogel 1998). More broadly, maternity-leave benefits can also improve the well-being of babies by enabling working mothers to spend more time with their infants in the crucial early months (Ruhm 2000). On a cautionary note, these benefits entail pecuniary costs that may be passed along to female workers in the form of lower wages, particularly if the mandated benefits are financed by employers. In addition, even though maternity-leave legislation is widespread across Asia Pacific, a considerable number of female workers are employed in firms or job categories that are not covered by maternity-leave legislation, are unaware of their rights to maternity leave, or are employed in covered firms that do not comply with the law. For example, in Malaysia, among those cases when women employed in the covered formal sector gave birth and were eligible for a maternity leave, less than half resulted in a maternity leave that was actually taken (Bernasek and Gallaway 1997). Priority should be given in future rounds of labor-law reforms across the region to providing a wider range of women workers with maternity-leave benefits. Steps such as removing sectoral and firm-size exemptions, raising worker awareness of their leave entitlements, and improving enforcement will all work toward this objective.

More "family-friendly" labor market policies are needed to help address the needs of working parents and their children. Parental-leave statutes alongside maternity-leave legislation will support fathers in their efforts to take on more responsibility for childcare. Also, some governments have already increased their attempts to shift the financial burden of childcare provision away from individual families and to extend access to quality childcare services. For example, the South Korean government provides subsidies to employers that have childcare centers to help them cover operational expenses. Government involvement in childcare provision and support is becoming more appropriate for economies in Asia Pacific as family structures move away from the extended-family system, fertility rates decline, and the share of women employed in paid jobs grows. Childcare assistance serves as a useful complement to maternity- and parental-leave statutes in supporting working parents.

In an effort to raise women's relative wages and improve their labor market opportunities, numerous Asia Pacific governments have adopted legislation that promotes equal treatment of women and men in the workplace. The two most common types of such policies are equal-pay and equal-opportunity measures. These measures do not single out women for protection or special treatment, but they do have the explicit goal of enhancing women's labor market outcomes by eliminating discrimination against women in pay and employment. The "equal pay for equal work" clause requires employers to provide the same pay for workers who perform the same job with equal effort, regardless of gender. In theory, the equal-pay clause should increase the earnings of women relative to men with similar qualifications who work in the same job categories. The majority of countries in the Asia Pacific region have adopted legislation mandating equal pay for equal work. However, the legislation is often not enforced, because governments do not have enough resources to create viable enforcement mechanisms. For example, Taiwan implemented an equal-pay clause when it enacted its labor-standards law of 1984, but firms were less likely to comply with the equal-pay clause than they were with other measures of the labor law (Chiu 1993).

In addition to enforcement problems, employment segregation by gender will limit the effectiveness of an equal-pay clause. In particular, legislation that requires equal pay for equal work within an occupation and enterprise will have little impact on women's relative wages if women are segregated by occupation and industry (Blau and Kahn 1995). Fewer than half of the Asia Pacific governments have attempted to tackle the occupational segregation problem with policies that improve women's access to occupations in which they formerly had few opportunities. These provisions prohibit sex-based discrimination in many aspects of employment, including hiring, training, promotion, and firing. Economies with such legislation include Hong Kong, Japan, South Korea, the

Philippines, Vietnam, and China. In theory, equal-opportunity policies should contribute positively to women's relative earnings and to their range of job options. However, in practice, equal-opportunity legislation has had a rather lackluster performance in the Asian economies (Behrman and Zhang 1995). For example, South Korea's gender-equality employment act of 1987 created new opportunities for women in higher-paying professional and technical jobs, but the legislation does not appear to have helped women break through the more formidable "glass ceiling" in administrative and supervisory positions. Summary statistics constructed from detailed information on employment in South Korea's occupational wage surveys for 1986 and 1992 indicate that women did not experience much progress in obtaining higher-ranking and better-paying occupations. Although the female share of professional and technical jobs rose from 17 percent in 1986 to 28 percent in 1992, the female share of administrative positions remained stagnant, at 1 percent, and the female share of supervisor positions actually dropped, from 5 percent to 3 percent.

While they are not explicitly designed to target women's well-being or equality in the labor market, seemingly "gender-blind" policies can also have labor market outcomes that differ for women compared with men. For example, a minimum-wage policy may have no gender content in its stated aims, yet in practice it can affect female and male workers differently. The minimum-wage policy is highly prevalent around the world, including in Asia Pacific, and it can have disproportionately negative effects on women's labor market outcomes. In particular, the minimum wage primarily protects workers in the urban formal sector, whose earnings already exceed by a wide margin the earnings of workers in the rural and informal sectors. Any employment losses caused by an increase in the minimum wage in the regulated formal sector translate into more workers seeking jobs in the unregulated informal sector. The end result could actually be lower, not higher, wages for most poor workers.

To the extent that female workers are relatively concentrated in the informal sector and men in the formal sector, few women will gain from minimum wages that are bound to the formal sector, while more women will suffer lower wages in the informal sector. If the minimum wage does discourage formal sector employment, a disproportionate number of women will experience decreased access to formal sector jobs. In support of these arguments, cross-country evidence, including data on a number of Asia Pacific economies, indicates that labor force participation rates drop more for women than for men when the minimum wage rises relative to income per adult (Schultz 1990). Among individual countries, the Indonesian government tripled the minimum wage in nominal terms during the first half of the 1990s. Although the overall decline in urban sector employment was modest in Indonesia, at no more than 5 percent, small firms and cottage industries experienced larger employment declines in the face of higher labor costs (Rama 2001). If anything, women are relatively concentrated in these smaller firms, implying that they experienced the brunt of employment cutbacks that firms made in order to maintain competitiveness.

Conclusion

Women in Asia Pacific have made great strides in closing the gender gap in health, education, and labor market outcomes. Progress for achieving gender equity has occurred largely as a result of overall economic development, but also as a result of concerted efforts by governments, activist groups, and international organizations to design and implement effective legal reforms. In a virtuous circle, women's relative gains in their health, education, and labor market productivity have increasingly empowered them to stand up for their rights and push for continued legal reforms. At the same time, women's activism and legal reforms focused on gender equity have contributed positively to closing the gender gap in health status, educational attainment, and labor market performance. Where rights are more equal between women and men, gender differentials in well-being are smaller (World Bank 2001).

Yet more progress must be made, and the areas needing work are numerous. As just one example, most legal reforms in the labor market have been limited to formal sector workers. Addressing the problems faced by female workers in the rural and informal sectors has proven far more difficult precisely because these women are employed in small-scale, unregulated operations that remain economically viable due to the low labor costs. Policy changes are crucial for better supporting women in rural and unregulated jobs and for providing them with greater access to formal sector jobs. These policy efforts include—but are certainly not limited to—providing girls and women with more education and job-specific training, extending labor standards and their enforcement to smaller-scale operations whenever feasible, targeting agricultural extension services and technologies to women, and increasing women's access to credit and financial services. As specific examples, women can be encouraged to participate in community-based labor rights groups, or they can be provided with small loans in microcredit initiatives that focus on lending to women. These policy changes can help women to become more independent, engage in new entrepreneurial activities, and build their qualifications for new job opportunities.

More broadly, the erosion of social norms and traditional values favoring men, the maintenance of sound macroeconomic environments, and the continued reform of policies addressing gender equity are all crucial for sustained progress in improving women's well-being. Asia Pacific already stands out among other regions for the remarkable macroeconomic progress recorded by many countries in the region. This growth record, when combined with continued strong commitments by communities, employers, and governments to addressing women's rights, gives the region the potential to also stand out for achieving gender equity on all fronts.

▩ Bibliography

Aslanbeigui, Nahid, Steven Pressman, and Gale Summerfield, eds. 1994. *Women in the Age of Economic Transformation: Gender Impact of Reforms in Post-Socialist and Developing Countries.* London: Routledge.

Aslanbeigui, Nahid, and Gale Summerfield. 2000. "The Asian Crisis, Gender, and the International Financial Architecture." *Feminist Economics* 6, no. 3: 81–103.

Balakrishnan, Radhika, ed. 2002. *The Hidden Assembly Line: Gender Dynamics of Subcontracted Work in a Global Economy.* Bloomfield, Conn.: Kumarian.

Becker, Gary. 1959. *The Economics of Discrimination.* Chicago: University of Chicago Press.

Behrman, Jere, and Elizabeth King. 2002. "Competition and Gender Gaps in Wages: Evidence from 16 Countries." Mimeo. Philadelphia: University of Philadelphia Press.

Behrman, Jere, and Zheng Zhang. 1995. "Gender Issues and Employment in East Asia." *Asian Development Review* 13, no. 2: 1–49.

Berik, Günseli, Yana Rodgers, and Joseph Zveglich. 2004. "International Trade and Gender Wage Discrimination: Evidence from East Asia." *Review of Development Economics* 8, no. 2: 237–254.

Bernasek, Alexandra, and Julie Gallaway. 1997. "Who Gets Maternity Leave? The Case of Malaysia." *Contemporary Economic Policy* 15, no. 2: 94–104.

Blau, Francine, and Lawrence Kahn. 1995. "The Gender Earnings Gap: Some International Evidence." In Richard Freeman and Lawrence Katz, eds., *Differences and Changes in Wage Structures,* pp. 105–143. Chicago: University of Chicago Press.

Brown, Lynn, and Lawrence Haddad. 1995. "Time Allocation Patterns and Time Burdens: A Gendered Analysis of Seven Countries." Working paper. Washington, D.C.: International Food Policy Research Institute.

Cagatay, Nilufer, and Sule Ozler. 1995. "Feminization of the Labor Force: The Effects of Long-Term Development and Structural Adjustment." *World Development* 23, no. 11: 1883–1984.

Cheng, Lucie, and Hsiung Ping-chun. 1994. "Women, Export-Oriented Growth, and the State: The Case of Taiwan." In Joel Aberbach, David Dollar, and Kenneth Sokoloff, eds., *The Role of the State in Taiwan's Development,* pp. 321–353. Armonk, N.Y.: Sharpe.

Chiu, Su-fen. 1993. "Politics of Protective Labor Policy-Making: A Case Study of the Labor Standards Law in Taiwan." PhD diss., University of Wisconsin at Madison.

Chou, Bih-er, Cal Clark, and Janet Clark. 1990. *Women in Taiwan Politics: Overcoming Barriers to Women's Participation in a Modernizing Society.* Boulder: Lynne Rienner.

Coale, Ansley. 1991. "Excess Female Mortality and the Balance of the Sexes in the Population: An Estimate of the Number of 'Missing Females.'" *Population and Development Review* 17, no. 3: 517–523.

Das Gupta, Monica, et al. 2000. "State Policies and Women's Autonomy in China, the Republic of Korea, and India 1950–2000: Lessons from Contrasting Experiences." Policy Research Report on Gender and Development, Working Paper no. 16. Washington, D.C.: World Bank.

Dollar, David, Paul Glewwe, and Jennie Litvack, eds. 1998. *Household Welfare and Vietnam's Transition.* Regional and Sectoral Study. Washington, D.C.: World Bank.

Goldin, Claudia. 1995. "The U-Shaped Female Labor Force Function in Economic Development and Economic History." In T. Paul Schultz, ed., *Investment in Women's Human Capital,* pp. 61–90. Chicago: University of Chicago Press.

Hill, Kenneth, and Dawn Upchurch. 1995. "Gender Differences in Child Health: Evidence from the Demographic and Health Surveys." *Population and Development Review* 21, no. 1: 127–151.

Horton, Susan, ed. 1996. *Women and Industrialization in Asia.* London: Routledge.

Ilahi, Nadeem. 2000. "The Intra-Household Allocation of Time and Tasks: What Have We Learnt from the Empirical Literature?" Policy Research Report on Gender and Development, Working Paper no. 13. Washington, D.C.: World Bank.

Inglehart, Ronald, and Pippa Norris. 2003. *Rising Tide: Gender Equality and Cultural Change Around the World.* Cambridge: Cambridge University Press.

International Labour Organization. Various years. *Yearbook of Labour Statistics.* Geneva.

Johnson, Kay. 1996. "The Politics of the Revival of Infant Abandonment in China, with Special Reference to Hunan." *Population & Development Review* 22, no. 1: 77–98.

Kidd, Michael, and Xin Meng. 2001. "The Chinese State Enterprise Sector: Labour Market Reform and the Impact on Male-Female Wage Structure." *Asian Economic Journal* 15, no. 4: 405–423.

Kim, Young Ok, et al. 1998. "Women in South Korea." In Nelly Stromquist, ed., *Women in the Third World,* pp. 593–600. New York: Garland.

Klasen, Stephan, and Claudia Wink. 2003. "'Missing Women': Revisiting the Debate." *Feminist Economics* 9, nos. 2–3: 263–299.

Lim, Joseph. 2000. "The Effects of the East Asian Crisis on the Employment of Women and Men: The Philippine Case." *World Development* 28, no. 7: 1285–1306.

Manning, Chris, and Peter van Diermen. 2000. *Indonesia in Transition: Social Aspects of Reformasi and Crisis.* London: Zed.

Mellor, Jennifer, and Yana Rodgers. 2001. "Gender Dimensions of Sustainable Development." In United Nations, ed., *Encyclopedia of Life Support Systems.* Oxford: EOLSS. http://www.eolss.net.

Meng, Xin. 1996. "The Economic Position of Women in Asia." *Asian-Pacific Economic Literature* 10, no. 1: 23–41.

Nam Jeong-lim. 1994. "Women's Role in Export Dependence and State Control of Labor Unions in South Korea." *Women's Studies International Forum* 17, no. 1: 57–67.

Nataraj, Sita, Yana Rodgers, and Joseph Zveglich. 1998. "Protecting Female Workers in Industrializing Countries." *International Review of Comparative Public Policy* 10: 197–221.

Oostendorp, Remco. 2004. "Globalization and the Gender Wage Gap." Policy Research Working Paper no. 3256. Washington, D.C.: World Bank.

Rama, Martin. 2001. "The Consequences of Doubling the Minimum Wage: The Case of Indonesia." *Industrial and Labor Relations Review* 54, no. 4: 864–881.

———. 2002. "The Gender Implications of Public Sector Downsizing: The Reform Program of Vietnam." *World Bank Research Observer* 17, no. 2: 167–189.

Rodgers, Yana. 1998. "A Reversal of Fortune for Korean Women: Explaining the 1983 Upward Turn in Relative Earnings." *Economic Development and Cultural Change* 46, no. 4: 727–748.

Rozelle, Scott, Xiao-Yuan Dong, Linxiu Zhang, and Andrew Mason. 2002. "Gender Wage Gaps in Post-Reform Rural China." *Pacific Economic Review* 7, no. 1: 157–179.

Ruhm, Christopher. 2000. "Parental Leave and Child Health." *Journal of Health Economics* 19: 931–960.

Schultz, T. Paul. 1990. "Women's Changing Participation in the Labor Force: A World Perspective." *Economic Development and Cultural Change* 38, no. 3: 457–488.

———. 1993. "Investments in the Schooling and Health of Women and Men: Quantities and Returns." In T. Paul Schultz, ed., *Investment in Women's Human Capital,* pp. 15–50. Chicago: University of Chicago Press.

Seguino, Stephanie. 1997. "Gender Wage Inequality and Export-Led Growth in South Korea." *Journal of Development Studies* 34, no. 2: 102–132.

Sen, Amartya. 1989. "Women's Survival as a Development Problem." *Bulletin of the American Academy of Arts and Sciences* 43, no. 2: 14–29.

Taiwan Directorate-General of Budget, Accounting, and Statistics. 2000. *Population and Housing Census.* Preliminary report. Taipei.

———. Various years. *Social Indicators.* Taipei.

Taiwan Ministry of Education. Various years. *Education Statistical Indicators.* Taipei.

Tinker, Irene, and Gale Summerfield, eds. 1999. *Women's Rights to House and Land: China, Laos, and Vietnam.* Boulder: Lynne Rienner.

United Nations Conference on Trade and Development (UNCTAD). 2005. *World Investment Report, 2005.* New York.

United Nations Development Programme (UNDP). 2001. *Human Development Report, 2001.* New York: Oxford University Press.

———. 2005. *Human Development Report, 2005.* New York: Oxford University Press.

United Nations Educational, Scientific, and Cultural Organization (UNESCO). Various years. *World Education Indicators.* Geneva.

Waldfogel, Jane. 1998. "Understanding the 'Family Gap' in Pay for Women with Children." *Journal of Economic Perspectives* 12, no. 1: 137–156.

Waldron, I. 1987. "Patterns and Causes of Excess Female Mortality Among Children in Developing Countries." *World Health Statistics Quarterly* 40: 194–210.

World Bank. 2001. *Engendering Development: Through Gender Equality in Rights, Resources, and Voice.* Oxford.

———. Various years. *World Development Indicators.* Washington, D.C.

World Health Organization. 2005. *World Health Report, 2005.* Geneva.

Xiaojiang, Li, and Liang Jun. 1998. "Women in China." In Nelly Stromquist, ed., *Women in the Third World,* pp. 593–600. New York: Garland.

Zveglich, Joseph, William Rodgers, and Yana Rodgers. 1997. "The Persistence of Gender Earnings Inequality in Taiwan, 1978–1992." *Industrial and Labor Relations Review* 50, no. 4: 594–609.

Zveglich, Joseph, and Yana Rodgers. 2003. "The Impact of Protective Measures for Female Workers." *Journal of Labor Economics* 21, no. 3: 533–556.

12

Religion in Asia Pacific

Keri Cole

Discussing the religious world of contemporary Asia Pacific in a single chapter is a daunting task. My intent is not to give the reader a complete understanding of the nuances of religious life in Asia Pacific, but rather to provide the tools for imagining the possibilities of that life, ebullient and various as it may be. Becoming aware of the factors that have shaped and continue to shape the religious experiences of this region's peoples is much more important than hurriedly touching on a plethora of contemporary particulars. Presenting a montage of data and statistics would only provide a boring glimpse at meaningless facts; indeed, mild curiosity and Internet access can provide an infinite supply of "facts," of varying degrees of factuality. Thus, primarily, I will consider the large currents that have contributed to the present religious milieu of Asia Pacific. Refraining as much as possible from the generalities that have plagued this field of study, I seek to provide a useful model that can either be placed in the service of more specific pursuits or be cultivated for a better, richer conception of the religious diversity in Asia.

It seems productive to dispense first with a few stereotypes, so that their absence here will cause no surprise or duress. The categories that seem so endemic to the ordering of perceptions of the East quite often cement misconceptions that undermine and prevent a fuller understanding of the diversity of traditions, beliefs, and peoples of Asia and the larger world. Maintaining a bifurcated list of East/West adjectives insults the similarities and diversities of the peoples and traditions on both sides of the globe. This predilection for neat categories, though it makes for easier discussion, does not celebrate the glorious messiness of the enterprises of humanity.

"Eastern religion" is variously construed as holistic, spiritual, mystical, anti-individualistic, irrational, ineffable, nondual, or esoteric; and in some circles,

"Western religion" seems to monopolize fragmentation, individualism, materialism, orthodoxy, and rationality. While both of these "traditions" can be legitimately characterized by these qualities at different points, they do not operate exclusively within them. Certain aspects of "Eastern religion" are just as fragmented, individualistic, and rational as those of "Western religion," which in turn is frequently inclined toward the ineffable. While it is a productive endeavor to understand what general attributes characterize a tradition or group of traditions, essentializing them to rarified modifiers is a dangerous and vainglorious affair that I hope to avoid and discourage.

Many works, much larger and more ambitious than this one, have only had moderate success in providing a lucid summary of East Asian religions, an inevitability of working with such a dynamic and multifaceted topic. To complicate matters, the diversity that has always been present in the religious world of Asia Pacific is becoming ever more overt and pronounced. For example, while "God" is generally characterized as a more impersonal entity in the "East," many Asians nonetheless maintain very personal conceptions of God and the ways in which that God interacts with the human world. Likewise, though the stereotypical "East" is permeated by the spiritual, a notable contingent of Asian thinkers find the idea of a higher power, personal or transcendent, a ludicrous proposition. I recall one conversation about religion with a Chinese friend, during which she shocked my romantic sensibilities by declaring that the very exercise of religiosity was a cumbersome and impractical endeavor. Increasingly, the sheer number of traditions functioning within the Asian religious matrix, and the individual dispositions of those within it, reflect a global character—one that is resistant to many general assumptions.

Another difficulty inherent in this discussion is the partial accuracy of some of the generalizations eschewed above, and, for the moment, some of these generalizations will have to stand. Nonetheless, I caution the reader as to their ultimate inadequacy. If we attempt to locate religion itself within a neat area of discourse, we will fail to appreciate the extent of the religious presence in Asia Pacific. The religion we seek is not restricted to church, orthodoxy, or those realms more traditionally reserved for religious discourse. The boundaries of religions in Asia are remarkably fluid and permeable. "Religion" can be found in, and is often inseparable from, all aspects of life, at times operating on a nearly unconscious level. This milieu facilitates a unique environment in which to practice religion (or irreligion). Ian Reader relates one of his experiences with self-proclaimed nonreligious friends in Japan that points to the practical ramifications of this type of environment:

> At the Shinto shrine we first visited, my friends both tossed a coin into the offertory box, clapped their hands twice—the standard way of greeting the *kami,* the deities of the Shinto tradition—and, bowing their heads, held their hands together in prayer. Next, we visited a Buddhist temple, where they

went through exactly the same performance, offering, bowing, clapping and praying earnestly. [Even though] technically one does not clap one's hands before praying at a Buddhist temple. . . . I was taken aback and naïve enough to point out their mistake. They were mystified by my claim to know what they should have done, for each . . . had hardly considered that there might be any differentiation in the ways that one treated *kami* and Buddhas, at least on the level of encountering and making entreaties to them. (1991:1)

On a more doctrinal level, the pervasive strands of nondual thought that have emerged from Buddhist philosophy and the more indigenous Shinto and Daoist traditions have been conducive to and have contributed to constructing a worldview that, while not always holistic, is often more hesitant to separate religion from other areas of discourse.

In order to provide the reader with enough information to encourage further exploration without an abundance of ponderous detail, this chapter will introduce the five major categories of religious traditions that have shaped the religious experiences of Asia Pacific: Buddhism, Confucianism and the family, shamanism and popular religions, Christianity, and Islam. The generalities and particularities will be illuminated where appropriate, and sufficient caveats will always be provided to keep the reader wary of the true nature of those generalities. These five categories have been chosen because each has contributed to the shaping of the modern religious experience in specific ways. Buddhism has had the largest influence on the Asian religious world; it has moved across geographical boundaries and left indelible marks on all aspects of Asian religion and society. Without a basic understanding of Buddhism— its history, its nature, and its doctrine—the possibilities and peculiarities of the Asian religious world will be difficult to imagine. Belief systems involving Confucianism and the family inform many of the ways in which Asian peoples understand the role of religion in their lives and how they determine its relative importance in lived experience. This tradition has also had quite an effect on the acceptance of Christianity in Asia and the ingression of modernity. Counterbalancing and enriching more orthodox traditions, shamanism and mysticism provide some of the depth and inconsistency that make the Asian religious experience such a multifaceted and remarkable area of discourse. As a more recent import, the introduction of Christianity has compelled Asian cultures to reevaluate their religious lives in the face of new ideas, forcing other traditions to define and articulate their niches within the religious and social world of Asia. Despite the pervasive misconceptions about Islam being a religion located primarily in the Middle East, the world's largest community of Muslims is located in Indonesia, and smaller but thriving populations exist throughout Asia Pacific. Other traditions will be mentioned insofar as they interact with these broad categories and contribute to the religious nexus of Asia Pacific. Geographically, this discussion will focus primarily on China, Japan, and the Koreas. Time and space necessitate this limited discussion; though all states of the Association of Southeast Asian Nations (ASEAN) make unique contributions to the religious life of Asia Pacific, this basic construct of religious discourse should provide the student with the necessary tools for understanding the greater religious community.

A Note on Religion

What exactly does it mean to discuss the religious life of a people and place? Are we discussing the officially sanctioned "religions" that provide institutional influence and a measure of social control? Surely that is too narrow and cynical a construction to detect the religious life in Asia adequately. Should we focus on the more informal traditions that imbue daily activities with significance through ritual and history? That too seems to leave some gaps through which important cultural and religious phenomena could slip. The problem of defining religion in Asia is complicated by the nature of some of the traditions that we will be examining, as there seems to be a large element of what we might functionally consider "philosophy" inherent in the ways these "religions" are implemented in the lives of practitioners. Perhaps religion is more usefully characterized as a system of beliefs that people rely on to help make life choices; however, this seems too inclusive, leaving room for ideologies that are more strictly political, social, or economic.

It seems that our definition refuses to be neat or orderly, perhaps reflecting the diversity present in the Asian religious landscape—or any religious landscape, for that matter. Ninian Smart proposes a model for analyzing behavior that recognizes the multiple functions and facets of traditions that can be characterized as religious. He entreats examiners of "religion" to consider seven dimensions that contribute to the nature of a tradition: (1) the practical and ritual, (2) the experiential and emotional, (3) the narrative or mythic, (4) the doctrinal and philosophical, (5) the ethical and legal, (6) the social and institutional, and (7) the material (1993:19). While we will not rigidly adhere to this system of analysis and classification, these categories provide a useful framework from which we can begin our inquiry. As the religious world that we seek to understand is not located in a discreet compartment, situating our understanding of what it means to be religious within these dimensions of religious experience may help us understand the more pervasive character of religious life in Asia without robbing it of its inherent structure and diversity.

The Difficulty with Gods

Monism, monotheism, polytheism, and *henotheism* are terms with which the student of religion should learn to become facile; those more generally interested in Asian culture would be wise to be able to maneuver through them, as they provide one perspective from which Asian religious experience can begin to be understood. *Monism* implies a belief in the unity and oneness of all creation; the very fabric of reality itself is composed of only one substance. This is not a form of theism, as, technically, there is no god-figure involved in this belief system that is separate from creation. If a religion ascribes to a *monotheistic* worldview, then it propounds belief in the existence of one supreme god, who is separate from humanity and creation. Christianity and Islam are examples of religions that espouse such an understanding of the divine. *Polytheism* is a term that often incorrectly describes Asian religions; it denotes a belief in the existence of multiple gods and goddesses. An underutilized but perhaps more useful and nuanced term is *henotheism*. Someone who practices within a henotheistic tradition acknowledges the existence of multiple gods, but privileges one in particular, usually in accordance with devotional tendencies or pragmatic considerations. These are important concepts to keep in mind when investigating the religious world of Asia Pacific. However, becoming too attached to any of these terms is ill-advised, as their doctrinal meanings are incessantly occluded by actual practice.

For example, strictly speaking, the universe as imagined by Buddhism is monistic in nature. There is no god-figure separate from creation; the only thing that exists is a sort of buddha-mind; all else is an appearance or the illusion of separateness. This monism has been complicated by several developments within the tradition; in many sects, the Buddha has come to represent a cosmic figure of suprahuman proportions, even to the extent that he has become the divine object of veneration for many Buddhists. Moreover, other buddhas and bodhisattvas have become the recipients of devotional actions, often understood to be endowed with superhuman capabilities and attributes. They have come to represent specific types of deities that are beneficial for particular needs and circumstances, even though in strict doctrinal terms they are ontologically no different from any other facet of existence. To make the matter more complex, there has long existed a Buddhist pantheon, which includes many gods that have been appropriated from other traditions. These "gods" maintain some vestiges of their original significance and are generally considered powerful deities; however, Buddhist doctrine maintains that these "gods" are just another class of creatures, prone to rebirth, suffering, and death.

Buddhism in practice, then, could be described as a monism with a penchant for the henotheistic. Practitioners pray to specific deities, or are devoted to particular buddhas, even though they are aware of the existence of multiple gods, buddhas, and bodhisattvas. In more strict ontological terms, however, Buddhist doctrine does not posit the existence of a god that is separate from creation; while extraordinarily in touch with higher realms of reality, buddhas are fundamentally no different from any other humans. To add to this complexity, some Buddhists would not agree with this analysis; they might argue for a more concrete notion of divinity or "otherness." Unfortunately, this is neither the time nor the place for a more detailed discussion. The reader must simply keep in mind the possibilities created by this level of intricacy and ambiguity for imagining the incredible richness of religious life in Asia.

▓ Buddhism: A Pan-Asian Phenomenon

Though Buddhism as a practiced religion in modern Asia has grown in ways not always reflective of its origins, a grasp of its historical development and movement across Asia is crucial to understanding the ways in which the religious atmosphere has developed. Buddhism is the first world religion to have utilized missionaries. Its influence spread from India, where it began, to China, Korea, Japan, and the larger Asian community by way of enthusiastic monks and practitioners. In addition to this, the period during which Buddhism began its dissemination was one in which cultural exchange was encouraged by movement along trade routes, the Silk Road in particular. Monks and practitioners traveling along the route brought with them ideas and innovations that influenced science, art, and religion. Though what is now Asia Pacific was already home to a vigorous religious milieu, it proved to be a fertile ground, ready and conducive to the spread and acceptance of Buddhist ideas.

Buddhist monks in Chiang Mai, Thailand.

Historical Overview

The cultural nexus from which Buddhism emerges is characterized by a period of dissatisfaction and unrest in India. During this time, priests dominated the religious life of the Vedic tradition; they controlled the ceremonies, sacrifices, and the sacred texts. The Vedic tradition has evolved into what is now loosely and problematically called "Hinduism." It should be noted that Hinduism did disseminate into Southeast Asia, particularly in the region now known as Bali. Disagreements about orthodoxy and propriety encouraged a movement away from the authority of the priests and their sacred texts, the Vedas. Traditions like Jainism and Buddhism emerged from this period of upheaval. These movements de-emphasized priestly authority, sacrifice, and caste and moved toward a model of religious practice that privileged renunciation and nonviolence.

Specifically, the story of Buddhism begins, on a rudimentary level, with one man. Though most historical facts about his life have become occluded by legend, there are a few about which scholars are generally in agreement. Sometime between the late sixth and early fourth centuries B.C.E., a young man was born in northern India, near what is today the border that separates India and Nepal. His name was Siddhartha Gautama. The son of a wealthy village chieftain, his family was of the Kshyatria caste, a traditional social group that comprised warriors and rulers. Though he lived a life of relative luxury, traditional sources and hagiographies tell us that he became acutely aware of the suffering and dissatisfaction that seemed to permeate existence early in his adult life. His life was full of advantage, but the realization that old age, sickness, and death are inevitable laid heavily on Siddhartha's awareness. Disillusioned with his life of luxury, he abandoned his family and his obligations and left to seek a more meaningful life.

He spent six years wandering and practicing with renowned sages and yogis of his time. Easily mastering the teachings of each, Siddhartha was left unfulfilled by these experiences, which he felt presented incomplete visions of the truth. During his quest for the ultimate, he was driven to severe asceticism and nearly starved after an extended period of fasting. Siddhartha realized that such extreme behavior could not be conducive to discovering facts any more profound than hunger and discomfort, so he set about finding an alternate means of discovering the truth. Siddhartha engaged in moderate meditation and fasting until he intuited the ultimate truths about the nature of reality and became a buddha, an enlightened being.

As a result of the insights acquired through his experiences, Siddhartha posited what he felt were the essential truths that must be understood about the nature of reality in order to escape from the suffering that seems endemic to this-worldly existence. This realm of suffering is called *samsara;* it is the vicious, endless wheel of birth and death in which all beings are entrenched. The reason for entrapment in this cyclic existence is explained by the Buddhist understanding of karma and rebirth. All actions create positive or negative karma, and the accumulation of this karma determines the character of one's future existences. Until all negative karma is eradicated, one is bound to the cycle of samsara. The Buddhist doctrine, which leads to the liberation of beings from samsara, is based on the four noble truths; they are the basic conceptions about reality that move the consciousness away from the suffering of this world and toward liberation from it. The first noble truth acknowledges the presence of suffering; it permeates life in this world, and without proper understanding, is inescapable. In other words, suffering is what characterizes this-worldly existence. The second noble truth asserts that there is a direct cause of this suffering. Namely, it is the irrational desire for impermanent things that is born from our ignorance about the illusory nature of reality. This misdirected desire keeps us bound to the experience of dissatisfaction; until humans recognize all phenomena as illusory and temporal, attachments to things that cannot last will create suffering. Fortunately, the third noble truth assures us that there is indeed a way to overcome this suffering. By following the eightfold path delineated in the fourth noble truth, all beings can see the ultimate nature of reality and escape from the bonds of samsara. This path represents what is called the "middle way," a balance between the extremes of asceticism and indulgence that facilitates a correct understanding of the world and moves each being toward enlightenment. Though we will not delve further into Buddhist doctrine, an awareness of its basic concepts is productive insofar as it allows for a greater capacity to truly appreciate the more nuanced aspects of the Asian religious experience.

The Dissemination of Buddhism in Asia

It will be beneficial to our discussion to mention two large movements within Buddhist tradition, and the different models of religious life emphasized by each. Early in the life of Buddhism, the devout practitioner aspired to be an *arhat,* a being whose energies and actions were put toward attaining personal enlightenment and liberation. Later, certain thinkers within the tradition came to see this goal as too personal and limiting, and emphasized the ideal of the *bodhisattva,* one who dedicates his or her existence to the liberation of all sentient beings. This person postpones personal buddhahood until every other sentient being is released from the bonds of samsara and this-worldly suffering. The tradition of Buddhists who emphasized the bodhisattva ideal came to be known as Mahayana, and it was this form of Buddhism that made its entrance into China during the first century of the common era. From there it traveled to Korea, Vietnam, and Japan, though it has since manifested into a variety of more discrete forms. The school of Buddhism that today maintains the arhat ideal is called Theravada, and is still practiced in Sri Lanka, Burma, Cambodia, Laos, and Thailand (Carbine and Reynolds 2000:10–12). Along other routes, Buddhism moved into Tibet, Nepal, and Mongolia. Though it received varying amounts of privilege, patronage, and support in India throughout the first millennia, Buddhism enjoyed a period of marked influence between the second and the ninth centuries, and this marks the height of Buddhism's pan-Asian influence.

A Civilizing Influence

Most pertinent to our discussion here are the ways that Buddhism has shaped the religious landscape of Asia Pacific. The manner in which other indigenous religions across Asia reacted to or were articulated by Buddhism provides many of the intricacies and much of the religious foment that have come to characterize this region. Primarily through the medium of the trade route, Buddhism made its way through Asia, assimilating indigenous traditions it encountered along the way. Some of these traditions, among them Shinto, Japan's only indigenous system, did not have an official name or coherent doctrine until the introduction of Buddhism forced its articulation. More than simply adopting the indigenous terms, concepts, and beliefs of indigenous religions, Buddhist monks and scholars utilized these terms in ways that, though distinctly Buddhist, maintained some of their original character. In this way Buddhism managed to attract followers through the reappropriation of familiar terms. For example in China, *dao* was the term used to describe the "middle way"—a term that was laden with familiar meaning, as it was borrowed from the Daoist lexicon. In Japan the Shinto gods, or *kami,* were often claimed as bodhisattvas, and were subordinated by being placed in the service of Buddhism. In this way, Buddhism utilized the familiar to increase its foreign appeal.

This type of interaction sets the stage for our later discussion and aids in a more comprehensive understanding of the religious milieu that still characterizes much of Asia Pacific. As Ninian Smart correctly asserts, Buddhism has never been a "particularly jealous religion" (1993:232). Moreover, the atmosphere was such that the boundaries between religions were never overtly drawn. I do not mean to imply that people never identified with one specific tradition, nor do I want to paint a picture of peaceful pluralism that did not exist. I would, however, like to point to one of the subtleties of religious life in Asia that does not essentialize one tradition but does provide a useful tool for understanding one way in which the peoples of Asia generally understand their religious lives.

One of the crucial Buddhist innovations that contributed to the spread and influence of Buddhism was the establishment of a monastic community. Monasteries came to function much like universities, acting not only as the religious anchors of lay communities, but also as centers of science, literature, art, and culture. The creation of a monastic community served to "both confirm and restrict certain degrees of religious legitimacy and authority" (Buswell, quoted in Carbine and Reynolds 2000:73). The dynamic that developed between the monastic and lay communities significantly impacted the evolution and influence of Buddhism. Each monastic society was completely dependent on a community of lay supporters, as monks were required to renounce money and other worldly pursuits. As such, they were incapable of supporting themselves without a body of generous and loyal laity, which included both royal or aristocratic patronage and more general community devotion. However, the symbiotic relationship that developed between the monastic elite and those belonging to the upper echelons of the ruling class placed Buddhism in a uniquely influential position. Often the monastery was seen as a beneficial entity, helping its supporting community by providing a sort of spiritual currency of merit in return for material support (see Hallisey and Reynolds, in Kitagawa 1989:17–20). Through this relationship of reciprocity, the act of giving to the monastery became a spiritually meritorious endeavor, thus encouraging continued support from the lay community.

The practice of renunciation, however, often presented an ideological quandary for the communities into which Buddhism was introduced. Many of the more indigenous religions and philosophies, like Confucianism, emphasized the importance of family and social responsibility. As a monk, one was not only supposed to be celibate and renounce family ties, but one was also to be exempt from taxes and live off the support of the surrounding lay community. This tension has manifested in multiple ways throughout the history of Buddhist influence in Asia, often finding expression in lay animosity toward monks (Teiser, in Lopez 1999:101–102).

▨ Confucianism and the Family

One of the influences that shaped the way Buddhism and monasticism were perceived was, as implied above, the presence of indigenous traditions that did not encourage the renunciation or abandonment of traditional family roles. In this section I discuss those indigenous traditions very generally, illuminating the crucial points of interaction with other religions, and emphasizing the ways in which the attitudes and worldviews they produced are still present in the religious consciousness of Asia Pacific. The kinds of traditions that will be placed in this category are numerous and important—certainly deserving of more extensive and exclusive attention. However, for the sake of brevity and cogency, only the most overtly influential will be discussed in this section: Confucianism, ancestor traditions, and Shinto. The successive section more carefully examines shamanism and popular religions.

Confucius and Confucian Thought

Depending on how one chooses to define religion, Confucianism may be more correctly characterized as a philosophy or an ideology than as a religion. Though its emphasis is often pragmatic and this-worldly, it does establish a hierarchical structure that is based on its value systems. Moreover, and critical to our exploration of the religious life of Asia Pacific, it fulfills all seven dimensions of Ninian Smart's model. The practical and ritual, experiential and emotional, narrative, philosophical, ethical and legal, social and institutional, and material dimensions are all addressed by Confucian doctrine. The model of social behavior and interaction put forth by Confucian doctrine still informs the way many East Asians understand themselves in relation to the greater social and cosmic order:

> Confucianism has been and still is a vast, interconnected system of philosophies, ideas, rituals, practices, and habits of the heart that informs the lives of countless people in East Asia and now the whole inhabited world. Although known in the West mostly as a philosophic movement, Confucianism is better understood as a compelling assemblage of interlocking forms of life for generations of men and women in East Asia that encompassed all the possible domains of human concern. Confucianism, at various times and places, was a primordial religious sensibility and praxis; a philosophic exploration of the cosmos; an ethical system; an educational program; a complex of family and community rituals; dedication to government service; aesthetic criticism; a philosophy of history; the debates of economic reformers; the intellectual background for poets and painters; and much more. (Berthrong and Berthrong 2000:1)

Like Buddhism, Confucianism is historically based on the teachings of one man, Kong Fuzi, who lived in China from 551 to 479 B.C.E.; however, the tradition that developed can hardly be said to have been the product of one man's thought. In Confucius's thought, he was simply a transmitter and a caretaker for a way of life that already had an impressive history; moreover, many determined people were necessary to continue and strengthen the tradition after the death of Confucius (Yao 2000:17). Though he was born into the aristocracy, his father died when he was a baby and left Confucius and his mother with little material wealth. From an early age he was seized by the desire to study the classics, and he showed more than a natural aptitude for studies, which he avidly pursued. He felt that family, society, and politics had degenerated into a state of horrible disarray. Characterized by pervasive impropriety, disorder, disharmony, and poor scholarship, the times in which Confucius lived were part of the impetus for his cultivation of a system that stressed harmony and order. Though he married and had a son, his passions remained with his philosophies, and he gathered a body of students to whom he imparted his ideas. During his lifetime, Confucius achieved only a modicum of political success; he did not manage to maintain either government support or a consistent following. However, after his death, his ideas were seized by an ardent group of posthumous followers and became some of the defining features of Asian religious thought. Confucius "developed his thought around two central theses: that goodness can be taught and learned, and that society can only be in harmony and at peace under the guidance of wisdom" (Yao 2000:26). Supported by and building on these two crucial points, Confucius set forth what have come to be the four traditionally recognized precepts of

Confucian thought: the Way, ritual and propriety, humanness, and virtue. From these four guiding principles, a person can achieve the highest levels of human functioning and live in accordance with the Mandate of Heaven. Movement along the Way was understood to be a progression through which the qualities of a good human were cultivated, a process Confucius described in his own life (quoted by Ames and Rosemont, in Berthrong and Berthrong 2000:25–26):

> From fifteen, my mind-heart was set upon learning;
> From thirty I took my stance;
> From forty I was no longer doubtful;
> From fifty I realized the propensities of [heaven];
> From sixty my ear was attuned;
> From seventy I could give my mind-heart free rein without
> overstepping the boundaries [of propriety].

Confucian thought does not delve deeply into the spiritual; its reliance on the Mandate of Heaven, a primordial ordering of the cosmos, is practical and worldly in orientation. This mandate emphasizes the way in which people should behave with propriety and virtue; this "way" is understood to be "a reflection of the . . . pattern inherent in the physical and social universe" (Fry et al. 1984:93). Confucius's teachings are deeply situated within the family and strongly encourage proper education, thereby stressing a return to and veneration of classical texts and philosophies. By paying careful attention to family relations, learning, and tradition, we can "become full human beings, fully ethical persons within the larger human family" (Berthrong and Berthrong 2000:27). Humanistic in nature, Confucius's philosophies and social ideologies set forth a way of being in the world that is conducive to optimum human performance.

Though considered highly literary in orientation, Confucianism helped construct a framework through which many East Asians have come to understand what behaviors are appropriate to particular social positions. For example, one's social position is composed of concentric circles of relationships. These circles represent a hierarchy of reciprocity; in order to function at one's highest capacity, one must maintain harmonious relationships with each "circle of relatedness." The relationship to the self comprises the innermost circle, while relationships with family, community, nation, world, and heaven respectively situate the self in the context of the larger order. Specifically, this hierarchy of interaction moves through five categories of relationships—those between ruler and subject, father and son, husband and wife, elder and younger brother, and friend and friend. In these five relationships, reciprocity, brotherly love, and filial conduct should inform the way in which one behaves. This type of arrangement privileges a socially engaged model of behavior, as maintaining external order and creating personal happiness and prosperity are direct functions of appropriate interactions.

This is an important religious phenomenon for myriad reasons; the most important for our purposes is the extent to which it has shaped and continues to shape religious life in East Asia. One can see the tension that exists between the Confucian emphasis on social engagement and responsibility and the Buddhist ideal of renunciation. This has indeed contributed to the more active role of the laity in forms of Buddhism practiced in China, Japan, and Korea.

Confucianism also shapes the way in which those operating beneath its rubric order their experiences; religion and social structure are firmly placed within circles of relatedness, as part of the larger emphasis on family that imbues Asian religion with some of its uniqueness. However, while practices like ancestor veneration are part of Confucianism, other ritual acts involving dead family members extend beyond Confucianism and inform social and religious practice at large. In Confucianism, it is not only important to cultivate harmonious relationships with one's immediate, living family members, but it is also necessary to continuously maintain good rapport with one's deceased relatives. They are powerful entities, able to exert influence over the fortunes of the living. Propitiating the ancestors is understood to be conducive to good health and prosperity; neglecting the appropriate family and ritual duties or failing to display proper reverence toward the dead could result in sickness and financial difficulties.

Ancestor worship is practiced differently throughout Asia, and its presence in some form permeates most of the religious traditions. This "ancestor cult" influences the way Asians understand and participate in both Buddhism and Christianity, as, at least symbolically, the dead play a large role in the lives of many East Asians. Insofar as Asian veneration of the dead has been appropriated by these nonindigenous traditions, the dead have been variously construed to become both bodhisattvas and saints. In Japanese traditions, after appropriate rituals have been performed, the deceased are generally understood to be inducted into the realms of the kami. In the case of some encounters with Christianity, ancestor worship has proven a problematic phenomenon (discussed more fully below).

The tradition of ancestor veneration and rituals for the deceased is Confucian insofar as it looks to maintain harmony within a specific circle of relatedness. Family patriarchs are often seen as deserving of deference and ritual appeasement. Within the larger Confucian framework, sages and benevolent rulers are also accorded obligatory rites after their deaths as a way of ensuring their continued benevolence and support. Without proper ritual attention, these ancestors may very well manifest their displeasure in plagues or natural disasters; thus, placating the dead becomes a way of ensuring one's own well-being in this life. Ideas of relatedness and reciprocity motivate much of the ritual practice surrounding death and funeral rituals. In Japanese practice, the dead depend on the successfully completed rituals of the living to fully join with the ancestors or become a kami, just as much as the living benefit from the ritual action by protecting themselves from the vengeance of ill-disposed ancestors.

A Final Note on Family

Family is an institution rich with religious significance. Familial relationships are defined by religious codes of propriety. As a physical location, the home itself is quite frequently a center for religious meaning. Though it has already been made clear that some of the tension between monasticism and secular responsibility manifested itself in hostility and disagreement, it also was expressed positively in the ordering of the monastic communities: "Patrilineage exercises its influence as a regulating concept even in religious organizations where normal kinship—men and women marrying, having children, and tracing their lineage through the husband's father—is impossible. The Buddhist monkhood is a prime example. . . . Monks create for themselves a home—or a family—away from home" (Earhart 1997:185).

Thus the importance of the family is not simply something that worked against Buddhism, but it is also something that Buddhism inculcated and internalized, a characteristic of Asian society that shaped Buddhist practice in much the same way that Buddhist practice shaped other Asian religions.

▓ Shamanism and Popular Religions

The more esoteric echelons of death rituals are often intricately connected with shamanism. For our purposes, *shamanism* will function as a blanket term beneath which most practices that involve communication with otherworldly spirits and the dead will be placed. In more ancient times, shamanism was an acceptable mainstream practice. In Chinese imperial courts, there has long been a tradition of "reading" shoulder bones or tortoiseshells. In such cases, the diviner poses a simple question, heats the bone or shell, and then consults and interprets the cracks that develop. In more contemporary Asia Pacific, these more localized cults are replete with possessions, exorcisms, and spiritual mediums (for additional reading, see Teiser, in Lopez 1999:116–120; Blacker, in Earhart 1997: 130–135). Shamans or shamanesses are individuals believed to have special connections with other realms—their special relationship with the supramundane is often used to diagnose misfortune or make prognostications. Frequently, these powerful people are physically exceptional; they may be blind or crippled, or they may be children. In China, shamanism has functioned alongside more orthodox traditions, though considered a more local, spontaneous, and eclectic phenomenon. Whereas venerating ancestors in the Confucian sense has more rational, mainstream overtones, shamanism and spirit cults are often seen as no more than popular religious aberrations, and receive little official sanction. In China shamans are often described as "spirit mediums," individuals who "are folk healers; more rarely they teach religious ideas, drawing on a deep tradition of popular literature and textual works of the 'three doctrines'—Buddhism, Daoism, and Confucianism" (DeBernardi, in Lopez 1996:229). Shamanism is generally pragmatic, as practitioners are seeking immediate counsel about daily ills. The tradition is largely oral, unlike more overtly elite and literate traditions of Buddhism and Confucianism.

In Japan, women usually serve in the capacity of spiritual medium; they are often blind and begin their careers at an early age. In their training, they are forced to endure extensive hardships, such as exhaustion and near starvation, in order to become conduits for spiritual communication (Blacker, in Earhart 1997:131). These mediums function in multiple capacities, but foremost among them is making contact with the dead: "The shamanesses of the Tohoku area are usually requested to communicate with and transmit the will of superhuman beings and the spirits of the dead. They are often invited to visit a family in mourning, because the first communication with the spirit of the newly dead person is thought to be an important part of the funeral" (Earhart 1974:98).

Shamanism in Korea may hold a more influential position than in either Japan or China. As a religious practice, it has become imbued with national significance as a tradition that is distinctively Korean. Though in the past shamanism was held in much the same disregard as it is in China and Japan, it has come to represent "Korea's cultural independence from domineering external powers, especially the West." Moreover, Korean shamanism is enjoying a revival of sorts, as it has been recognized as a valuable cultural heritage, and in some cases shamans are seen as "official carriers of Intangible Cultural Properties" (Choi, in Lancaster and Payne 1997:19).

At various points, shamanism has enjoyed a confluence with both Buddhism and Confucianism. The lack of official structure has made for an often easy convergence between Buddhism and shamanism. Ancestor veneration provided a point of contact with Confucian traditions. Similarly, there are strains in shamanistic thought that teach that the goal of life is to become as fully human as possible; though the emphases were a bit different in orientation, this also provided another point of convergence with Confucianism. Again, the reader is reminded of the function that shamanism serves as a religious experience; it fulfills Ninian Smart's categories and expands the imaginative space for constructing the possibilities of religious life in Asia.

Christianity and Modernity

While not synonymous, Christianity has come to represent much of what characterizes modernity. From the perspective of many Asians, it follows on the heels (or heralds the impending arrival) of industrialization and development, technology and urbanization. The introduction of Christianity in China, Japan, and Korea has proven to be a variously problematic enterprise. Before more fully accounting for the success, or lack thereof, Christianity has experienced in Asia, a brief sketch of both its doctrine and its historical progression may be helpful.

A Thumbnail Sketch of Christianity

Though many readers may be more familiar with this tradition, for the sake of consistency, I will briefly discuss what it means to be a Christian, noting the resonances and differences with the other traditions that have shaped the religious landscape of Asia Pacific. Christianity is a "monotheistic" religion, though this appellation is somewhat muddied by what is called the Holy Trinity. God in the singular is actually God the Father, God the Son, and the Holy Spirit. While it is not the business of this chapter to delve too far into theology, the peculiarities of religions are often the very things that impart the most character. Nonetheless, like Islam, Buddhism, and Confucianism, the founding of Christianity is credited to a single man, Jesus of Nazareth. The man who was to be the Messiah, or the deliverer, emerges from the Jewish tradition at the turn of the millennium, a time when the religiously fertile Middle East was producing a fair number of cults and messianic figures. Jesus, a young Nazarene, was but one of the figures to emerge from this period. He preached a message of forgiveness, salvation, brotherly love, and a personal relationship with the Lord. Though Jesus was crucified, his message was recorded by his closest followers, called apostles; it is the longevity and the popularity of Jesus' message that makes the Christian tradition unique. Jesus' followers and the group that rallied around them went about establishing the new Christian church across the Middle East, Europe, and Asia. Though they maintained that the Jewish text, the Torah, was a sacred text, the early Christians reinterpreted it through the lens of Jesus and the new set of writings based on or inspired by his teachings. This collection of writings, which achieved a fixed status several hundred years after the death of Jesus, is now known as the New Testament.

Today, the Christian church represents the largest of the world's religions. Though there are many different sects within the church, one may broadly divide it into two different branches, the Catholic Church and the Protestant Church. Initiation into the Christian church often involves baptism and, unless the baptized is an infant, a confession of faith in the tenets of the church—that Jesus was the son of God, that he died for the sins of man, and that he will return. Though the church is important to the Christian life, a personal relationship with God is emphasized as a unique part of the Christian tradition. The personal nature of the Christian god is very influential to the ways in which Christianity is received in Asia Pacific.

The Introduction of Christianity

The presence of Christianity in China stretches back almost as far into history as the tradition itself. Christianity entered China long before it entered Japan or Korea, and "the story of Christianity in China extends from the time of a

legendary visit of Thomas to China right down to the very questionable present—nearly two thousand years" (Fry et al. 1984:205). Thus its interface with
other religions in China has gone through various stages of failure and success.
In Japan, Jesuit missionaries heralded the arrival of Christianity in the middle
of the sixteenth century; however, this initial presence only lasted for a hundred years before it was outlawed, and Christianity did not reappear until the
last half of the nineteenth century (Earhart 1997:140–141). Attempts to establish a Christian church have been more successful in Korea than in either
China or Japan. Korea has proved a more fertile ground for the growth of
Christianity; the Korean Catholic Church was established in 1784 (Baker, in
Lancaster and Payne 1997:129). The presence of Christianity is also notable in
the Philippines and Southeast Asia.

Christianity in Practice

Christianity has become accepted as a part of the religious landscape in most
areas of Asia Pacific during the past century, particularly in Korea. Nonetheless, many still consider it a foreign religion. Three major tensions have developed between Christianity and the other traditional religions. The first among
these seems to be Christianity's hesitance to integrate fully with the native customs and ways of life of the peoples it seeks to convert. Second, a resurgence
of traditional attitudes toward spirituality has prevented more than a marginal
openness to new religious ideas. Finally, the Confucian ethic and Christian
ideology have often been interpreted as divergent and incompatible, and the
focus on the heavenly realm rather than the earthly realm works to frustrate
further the ingression of Christian thought into the Asian consciousness.

Many smaller dialectics are subsumed beneath the larger rubric of the first
tension, Christianity's resistance to adopt, appropriate, or include traditional
customs. We have seen how the success of Buddhism was, to a large extent,
dependent on its temperament; it was generally not a jealous religion, at least
overtly. Buddhism moved rather fluidly through the natural religious landscape of Asia, accreting those traditions and practices that were helpful along
the way. This type of religious expansion was particularly well suited to the religious milieu of Asia; though it was not an environment of unencumbered
pluralism, it was one wherein religious boundaries were less opaque and overt.
For multiple reasons, Christianity has resisted mixing with the native cultures
in which its missions are ensconced, though it seems that the missionaries
themselves have been less reticent to mesh with the native cultures than the
churches they represent. During the growth of Roman Catholic influence in
China, Christian missions were embroiled in the "rites controversy," which
was a "debate over whether to allow the Chinese Christians to worship their
ancestors and to use various Chinese words to refer to God." After an extended
dispute, Catholic authorities finally decreed that "the church could not compromise its customs nor adapt itself to Chinese life" (Fry et al. 1984:206). This

sort of attitude has made it difficult for Christianity to emerge with much emphasis onto the religious scene in much of Asia.

Moreover, the way in which Christianity has often marketed itself to the Asian audience does not account for some of the attitudes that generally characterize the religious dispositions present in Asia Pacific. For example, George Elison provides several conjectures as to the reasons for Christianity's marginal acceptance in Japan:

> Japanese thought held no preconception corresponding to the Christian predicate. The Japanese critic found the notion of an omnipotent personal deity specious, its consequence disastrous. The foreign religion could be accused of otherworldliness; for the Christians removed the justification of human action from the social sphere to an extraterrestrial locus. The Christian dictate of a supernal loyalty pre-empted loyalty to a secular sovereign. Philosophy, ethics, and politics rejected the Christian claim that the One God existed and acted to determine the moral order. (quoted in Earhart 1997:142)

Though the preceding analysis of why Christianity initially failed to appeal to a Japanese audience does utilize some of the generalities this chapter hopes to avoid, it points to some well-founded characteristics of the religions of Asia Pacific that would complicate the introduction of Christianity. The religious society of Japan is built on duty, ritual, and propriety; in other words, the underlying assumption is that certain actions are powerful and lend the actor a measure of control over reality. Christian notions have failed to provide space for this characteristic of Japanese religion and have thus failed to attract more than 1 percent of the population.

Another reason for the less-than-sweeping presence of Christianity in Asia Pacific concerns the ramifications of the reactions Christianity elicited from traditional religions. As earlier noted, a spiritual revivalism of sorts is taking place. "Reinvigorated by contact with Christianity, many of the ancient faiths . . . are now awakening" (Fry et al. 1984:217). This resurgence is interesting for several reasons. All of Asia Pacific has made a pronounced effort toward modernization in the past century. At different points along their modernizing journeys, each country blamed their adherence to antiquity as one of the primary reasons for the difficult transition. Thus Buddhism, Confucianism, Taoism, Shintoism, and all the indigenous, popular religions have been variously labeled "hindrances" to modernity. However, we are now seeing a concerted movement to maintain and celebrate traditional attitudes toward spirituality (Berthrong and Berthrong 2000:180). We have already discussed the burgeoning role of shamanism in Korea as a beacon of cultural identity, and religions in both China and Japan are being imbued with similar significance. John Berthrong and Evelyn Berthrong point out that, after experiencing many of the negative side effects that have seemed to accompany Christianity and modernity, Asia experienced "a renewal in the humane and spiritual values of the great Asian traditions" (2000:182).

Some of the more specific changes that Christianity has tried to implement directly infringe on traditional Confucian concepts. One of the most general is the Christian focus on the next life; such thought encourages putting all of one's efforts into ensuring a place in heaven. While this has some resonance with Buddhist doctrine and ideas of rebirth, it is overshadowed by the intensely pragmatic worldviews that are shared by most of the Asian religions. Don Baker relates the experience of this phenomenon by the early Korean Christians: "The priests from France were more concerned with producing Catholics than with educating the future leaders of modern Korea. They were also more concerned with healthy souls than with healthy bodies" (quoted in Lancaster and Payne 1997:141). Clearly, the Confucian principles of maintaining harmony and promoting social order in this life are quite opposed to placing all of one's energies into the service of a mysterious goal.

The emphasis on the separation of church and state that often accompanies Christianity has also proved incongruous with more traditional conceptions about the location of religion; some have said that it is "totally alien to Confucian political philosophy" (Baker, quoted in Lancaster and Payne 1997:132). As we have seen, the locus of Confucianism, and much of Asian religious discourse, has been the family and the community at large. Thus the Christian penchant for placing all structures of religious authority outside of that nexus has never quite correlated with the more localized religious settings to which much of Asian thought is accustomed.

One of the most significant factors contributing to Christianity's disharmony with Confucian thought, however, has been the failure of Christianity to respect notions of ancestor veneration. Though some well-known ancestors are now called saints in the Christian tradition, the smaller, more intimate associations that peoples of China, Korea, and Japan have with the dead have not successfully translated into Christian thought or practice. To nuance this phenomenon further, the Christian (and more specifically Catholic) conception of individuality—and an individual relationship with his or her creator—runs adversely to the more Confucian tendency to situate oneself within a lineage of ancestors and family. It is through one's proper social and ritual practice that heaven is encountered in the Confucian tradition.

However, models of successful integration are present in the Asian Christian experience. Korea, as previously mentioned, has been home to a thriving Catholic community for many decades. While the Christian success stories are not as overt in China and Japan, they are present nonetheless. For example, even though only 1 percent of the Japanese population is Christian, they "make up well above one percent of the physicians, college professors, legislators, judges, and corporate and government managers" (Fry et al. 1984:212). The following excerpt from a story illustrates the possibilities that are present for the modern Christian experience in Asia, though this speaks specifically of a Japanese experience:

When he was in his mid-teens Sadao Watanabe, a well-known Japanese print artist, first visited a Christian church, introduced by a neighbour who was a school teacher. He had lost his father when he was ten years old, and tended to live a closed and isolated life. He described his first impression of Christianity as follows, "In the beginning I had a negative reaction to Christianity. The atmosphere was full of 'the smell of butter,' so foreign to the ordinary Japanese."

Now in his print work he joyfully depicts the celebration of the holy communion with sushi, pickled fish and rice, a typical Japanese dish, served on traditional folk art plates. For him rice is a more natural and a more fitting symbol of daily food than bread which is foreign. (Cakenaka 1986:2–3)

Even though Christianity has encountered challenges, it is prudent to remember that a single chapter in a single book cannot capture fully the religious potential or life of a tradition, particularly in such a diverse and dynamic community. The on-the-ground reality of Christianity both within the physical community and within the diaspora is perhaps more resilient and vibrant than the weaknesses discussed here would lead one to believe. The student of religion should remain open to the many possibilities that can be imagined for the religious realities of modernity.

Islam

Islam is a more recent import to the religious world of Asia Pacific, making its first appearance in the seventh century; nonetheless, it has proven to be a persistent and influential presence in much of the region. While the common (and largely American) public perception tends to construe Islam as a Middle Eastern phenomenon, primarily Arab in orientation and popularity, the "most populous Islamic countries are in South and Southeast Asia: Indonesia, Pakistan, Bangladesh, and the Republic of India" (Smart 1993:139). In addition to the Sunni Muslim population who reside in Indonesia, the largest on the planet, many other countries in Asia Pacific are home to significant numbers of Muslims. For example, Islam is the dominant religion in Malaysia. Though Muslims represent only 1.2 percent of the Chinese population, there are more Muslims in China than there are in Saudi Arabia. Additionally, Islam is an important minority religion in Thailand and the Philippines. Thus the Asian scholar should think critically about the ways in which Islam has been integrated into the religious landscape of Asia Pacific. To do that, we must consider both its assimilation into, and its impact on, the previously extant religions in the area.

Though there is a diversity of thought operating within the world of Islamic theology and practice, there are a few general points from which we can build a more specific understanding of the Muslim culture in Asia. The word itself, *islam,* literally means "submission" or "surrender," and one who surrenders to and endeavors to follow the will of God is called a Muslim. As earlier noted, Islam is a monotheistic religion; according to doctrine, there is but one God—Allah. "The duty of human beings is to surrender to this unique, omnipotent God, the Merciful, the Compassionate; to surrender from the bottom of one's heart, with one's whole soul and one's entire mind" (Schimmel 1992:14). Thus it might seem that the fundamental tenets of Islam, compared with the tenets of some of the other traditions considered here, are by their nature perhaps less conducive to the syncretism that characterizes much of the religious life of Asia Pacific.

Islam is the only major world religion whose inception came later than that of Christianity. According to its adherents, the message of Islam has been proclaimed by the prophets since the beginning of man—namely by the important patriarchal figures from Christianity: Adam, Abraham, Moses, and Jesus. The most recent and greatest of that lineage of prophets is Muhammad (ca. 570–632), and Islam originated as a distinct religion through Allah's revelation to Muhammad in 610. Though not much is known about Muhammad's life before he was a prophet, we do know the circumstances that are traditionally thought to surround his first prophetic experience. When Muhammad was forty, he heard an angel command him to recite. For the next twenty-three years, Muhammad recited what was to become the sacred text of Islam, the Quran. However, the Quran is not simply the message of a man; rather, it is believed to be the divine word of God revealed through the pure vehicle of Muhammad.

According to the laws put forth by the Quran, Muslims are responsible for five major religious duties, the Five Pillars of Islam. *Shahada,* the profession of faith, is the duty that is fundamental and in some ways prior to the rest of the pillars. In fact, "whoever confesses in public: 'I testify that there is no deity save God and that Muhammad is the messenger of God' has accepted Islam" (Schimmel 1992:34). The other pillars are ritual prayer, an alms tax, a fast during Ramadan (a holy month), and pilgrimage to Mecca.

The beginnings of Islamic influence in Southeast Asia can be traced back to missionary activity; its introduction is similar to the ways in which Buddhism and Christianity were imported into the religious world. While merchants and traders brought the first wave of the Islamic faith to East and Southeast Asia along the Silk Road as early as the seventh century, Islam enjoyed no real influence or position of power until a new wave of immigration and missionary activity in the twelfth and thirteenth centuries. Though there are records of an early Muslim presence in China, most of the contact occurred in Indonesia and in surrounding areas of the Philippine archipelago.

Islamic scholars and historians disagree about what motivated the first importers of the Muslim faith to proselytize in Asia, but there is little doubt that the nature of the Islamic expansion was to some degree encouraged by doctrinal concerns. As John Esposito remarks, "Muslims believe that Islam was revealed by God to guide the personal and public life of all humankind. . . . The Islamic community is to be the dynamic vehicle for realization of God's will in history, calling all to worship and serve God" (1999:11–12). Thus the movement of Islam into Asia Pacific not only represented the ingression of new religious ideas, but also signified a novel political agenda—one wherein the faithful believed that Islamic law, *sharia,* was the proper law for all of humankind to follow.

However, the religious world of Asia Pacific has long been multifaceted and malleable, often capable of incorporating new religions with ease, at least as seen through the lens of history. In Indonesia and on the Philippine archipelago, an amalgam of Hindu, Buddhist, and animist traditions was already flourishing and active. J. C. van Leur describes the introduction of Islam to Indonesia thus:

> Islam was a missionary community in the early Christian sense, with every believer a potential missionary for spreading its doctrine. However, though it had already been present for centuries in the foreign colonies in the East— on the west coast of Sumatra circa 674, in China arriving along the sea route in the seventh century, in Java and farther India known from the tombstones dated for the years 1082 and 1039—Islam began to exert wider influence only in the fourteenth century. . . . The expansion of the new religion did not result in any revolutions or any newly arrived foreign colonists coming to power—the Indonesian regime did not undergo a single change due to it. (quoted in McAmis 2002:14–15)

Practically and socially, Islam's penetration into the Southeast Asian religious scene evinces much of the tendency toward acculturation that is prevalent throughout the religious history of the region. "Indian Moslem merchants from Gujarat and Bengal also brought Islam to Southeast Asia, and the creed adapted itself to the new environment. It syncretized with earlier Brahmanism and Buddhism or fused with local mysticism, and it is an Islam that few Arabs would recognize" (Karnow, quoted in McAmis 2002:15). Esposito further supports this contention by positing: "In a very real sense an Arab Islam was transformed into Persian, South Asian, and Southeast Asian Islam through the process of assimilation and synthesis. Despite the common core of belief and practice epitomized by the Five Pillars of Islam, Muslim societies differed in the extent and manner to which religion manifested itself in public life—politics, law, and society" (1999:15).

Nonetheless, adherents tend to define themselves rather stringently through the religious lens of Islam. Thus, while one might be culturally Chinese or ethnically Indonesian, one is still strongly identified as religiously Muslim.

Modern Islam

Ibn Battutah, a Muslim living in Tangiers in the fourteenth century, set out for a pilgrimage to Mecca in the summer of 1325. He reached Mecca during the first year of his journey, then proceeded to travel across the Muslim world (*ummah* in Arabic), acting as a judge *(qadi)* in various settlements during his travels. He was but one among a larger movement of Muslims across the Islamic world, all traveling for various purposes such as trade, scholasticism, or professional posts (Waines 2003:175–176). Battutah, uniquely, left an extensive and detailed record of his twenty-five-year sojourn, and his writings provide a tantalizing record of the flourishing, diverse, and surprisingly mobile Muslim world of the time. Ibn Battutah's journey led him from "Andalusia to northern Africa, then across the Mediterranean, the Red Sea, and the Indian Ocean until he reached the Malay archipelago en route to China" (Esposito 1999:421). That travelers of that day would be able to enter geographically divided lands, locate discrete groups of homogeneously religious people, and successfully interact with these peoples on the sole basis of religious identity is truly remarkable.

Though Ibn Battutah was able to move among the Islamic peoples throughout Central and East Asia with relative ease and familiarity, he encountered significant differences among the communities he visited. The traveler witnessed the ways that the "Islams" he encountered had been influenced by indigenous religious and cultural practices. In Indonesia, Battutah encountered an Islam that differed from "the Muslim cultures of the Middle East, India and Africa, owing to the influences upon it of the pre-Islamic Indonesian traditions and folkways strongly influenced by Hinduism and Buddhism" (Waines 2003:180). Battutah was impressed by the well-ordered Muslim societies that he found in China; each city he visited had a recognizable and respected Muslim quarter that boasted individual mosques, hospices for travelers, markets, "a Shaykh al-Islam, who acts as intermediary between the government and the Muslim community, and a *quadi* to decide the legal cases between them" (Waines 2003:180). Even though these tightly knit and advanced communities impressed Ibn Battutah, he was significantly distressed by their markedly Chinese cultural character. The traders who brought Islam to Asia in the seventh and eighth centuries, while maintaining adherence to the tenets of their faiths, had married Chinese women and had become culturally Chinese, save where those customs directly violated Islamic law, such as in the consumption of pork. During the seventeenth and eighteenth centuries, however, "Muslim movements in the provinces of Yunnan and Kansu broke into open rebellion. . . . Muslims were concerned with the heavy concessions made over the centuries which had diluted the distinctive nature of Muslim belief" (Waines 2003:209). Prior to these movements, the Islamic community in China was often described as "Muslim indoors, Chinese outdoors."

If Ibn Battutah were to travel today, he would doubtlessly be awed by the breadth and diversity of Muslim cultures in Asia Pacific (and around the globe). Over 90 percent of the Indonesian population and 40–52 percent of the Malaysian population self-identify as Muslim, depending on the source of the statistics. In both of these countries, Islam is not only the dominant religion, but also a "growing dimension of mainstream political life" (Isaacson and Rubenstein 2002:iv).

In China, the Hui minority is the largest of ten recognized Muslim minorities. Though the word *Hui* originally and simply meant "Muslim," the appellation has arrived at a richer meaning. "As a result of state-sponsored nationality identification campaigns over the course of the last thirty years, they (Hui) have begun to think of themselves as a national ethnic group, something more than just 'Muslims'" (Gladney, quoted in Esposito 1999:444). Another important Muslim minority, the Uighurs, live in the northwest province of Xinjiang. The Uighurs share a "common Islamic, linguistic, and pastoralist heritage with the peoples of the Central Asian states"; accordingly, the Uighurs feel more culturally and ethnically familiar with Turkic peoples (Gladney, quoted in Esposito 1999:468). This distinction has been the cause of much unrest between the minority, which wants its independence, and the Chinese government.

The political influence of Islam has waxed and waned since its beginnings in Southeast Asia. Though the political power it achieved in the thirteenth and fourteenth centuries declined significantly by 1511, its influence in modernity has been rather pronounced. Though Islam exists as part of a matrix composed of several religious traditions, the large communities who thrive in Indonesia and on the Philippine archipelago exert political, social, and economic influence over the area, and are a vibrant part of the Islamic world. Though disagreements and skirmishes have resulted from the tensions present between the different religious traditions in the region, Southeast Asian Muslims have managed to maintain the tenets of Islam while living in relative peace with Buddhist and Hindu practitioners. The presence of Muslim minorities in Malaysia, Thailand, China, and the Philippines speaks to the increasingly modern and pluralistic religious world of Asia Pacific.

■ Conclusion

This chapter has omitted discussing many of the minority religions of Asia Pacific, like Hinduism and the myriad smaller traditions practiced by a thriving population of peoples. These religious experiences are certainly deserving of attention, as they inform the ways in which the region will continue to develop religiously. These traditions allow for and demand growth and change within the more established traditions of Buddhism, Confucianism, shamanism, Christianity, and Islam. But while the minority traditions are important to the Asian religious experience, they are more localized and are perhaps better taken up in a more specific study.

Detailed discussion of some of the more famous Asian traditions—Taoism and Shintoism in particular—has been omitted from this chapter for several reasons. Taoism, while in many ways influential to Confucian ideology, is more characteristically Chinese and does not have the pan-Asian presence of the other traditions discussed. Shintoism is an exclusively Japanese religious phenomenon that was only coherently articulated in response to Buddhism. Nevertheless, both Taoism and Shintoism embody and interact in productive ways with many larger traditions, and account for much of the character of the Asian religious landscape.

There are also numerous social issues related to the current religious foment of Asia Pacific, such as economic reform, political liberties, women's rights, international relations, palliative care, childcare, environmental policy, and abortion, to name just a few. Hopefully this chapter will provide a fertile ground upon which such discussions can flourish.

The religious world of Asia Pacific is too opulent and diverse to be laid upon a foundation of generalities and stereotypical characterizations. In order to study this region's religious life, we must broaden what we imagine the potential of that life to be. Settling into the ancient dynamics of religious conception while directing our sights toward the modern allows us to begin to see, through a different set of lenses, what might be possible for Asia Pacific. We are no longer forced to look through the constructs of things we have taken for granted, but we are free to create a space for imagining the infinite diversity present in one of the oldest religious milieus on the planet.

▓ Bibliography

Basabe, Fernando M. 1972. *Japanese Religious Attitudes.* Maryknoll, N.Y.: Orbis.

Berthrong, John H., and Evelyn Nagai Berthrong. 2000. *Confucianism: A Short Introduction.* Oxford: Oneworld.

Cakenaka, Masao. 1986. *God Is Rice: Asian Culture and Christian Faith.* Geneva: World Council of Churches.

Carbine, Jason A., and Frank E. Reynolds, eds. 2000. *The Life of Buddhism.* Berkeley: University of California Press.

Covell, Alan Carter. 1986. *Folk Art and Magic: Shamanism in Korea.* Elizabeth, N.J.: Hollym.

Cummings, Mark D., and Joseph M. Kitagawa, eds. 1989. *Buddhism and Asian History.* New York: Macmillan.

Earhart, H. Bryan. 1974. *Japanese Religion: Unity and Diversity.* Encino, Calif.: Dickenson.

———. 1997. *Religion in the Japanese Experience: Sources and Interpretations.* Belmont, Calif.: Wadsworth.

Ellwood, Robert S., and Richard Pilgrim. 1985. *Japanese Religion.* Englewood Cliffs, N.J.: Prentice Hall.

Esposito, John L., ed. 1999. *The Oxford History of Islam.* New York: Oxford University Press.

Foltz, Richard C. 1999. *Religions of the Silk Road: Overland Trade and Cultural Exchange from Antiquity to the Fifteenth Century.* New York: St. Martin's.

Fry, C. George, James R. King, Eugene R. Swanger, and Herbert C. Wolf. 1984. *Great Asian Religions.* Grand Rapids, Mich.: Barker.

Gethin, Rupert. 1998. *The Foundations of Buddhism.* Oxford: Oxford University Press.

Guisso, Richard W. I., and Yu Chai-shin. 1988. *Shamanism: The Spirit World in Korea.* Berkeley: Asian Humanities Press.

Isaacson, Jason F., and Colin Rubenstein, eds. 2002. *Islam in Asia.* New Brunswick, N.J.: Transaction.

Kasulis, T. P. 1981. *Zen Action, Zen Person.* Honolulu: University of Hawaii Press.

Kendall, Laurel. 1985. *Shamans, Housewives, and Other Restless Spirits: Women in Korean Ritual Life.* Honolulu: University of Hawaii Press.

Keyes, Charles F., Laurel Kendall, and Helen Hardacre. 1994. *Asian Visions of Authority: Religion and the Modern States of East and Southeast Asia.* Honolulu: University of Hawaii Press.

Kim, Kyoung Jae. 1994. *Christianity and the Encounter of Asian Religions.* Zoetermeer, Netherlands: Uitgeverij Boekencentrum.

Kitagawa, Joseph M., ed. 1989. *The Religious Traditions of Asia.* New York: Macmillan.

———. 1990. *Spiritual Liberation and Human Freedom in Contemporary Asia.* New York: Lang.

Kwok, Man-ho, Martin Palmer, and Jay Ramsay, trans. 1993. *Tao Te Ching.* Rockport, Mass.: Element.

Lancaster, Lewis R., and Richard K. Payne, eds. 1997. *Religion and Society in Contemporary Korea.* Berkeley: Institute of East Asian Studies, University of California.

Lopez, Donald S., ed. 1996. *Religions of China in Practice.* Princeton: Princeton University Press.

———. 1999. *Asian Religions in Practice.* Princeton: Princeton University Press.

MacInnis, Donald E. 1989. *Religion in China Today: Policy and Practice.* Maryknoll, N.Y.: Orbis.

Martinez, D. P., and Jan van Buren. 1995. *Ceremony and Ritual in Japan: Religious Practices in Industrialized Society.* London: Routledge.

McAmis, Robert Day. 2002. *Malay Muslims: The History and Challenge of Resurgent Islam in Southeast Asia.* Grand Rapids, Mich.: Eerdmans.

Murakami, Shigeyoshi. 1980. *Japanese Religion in the Modern Century.* Translated by H. Byron Earhart. Tokyo: University of Tokyo Press.

Nakamura, Hajime. 1964. *Ways of Thinking of Eastern Peoples: India, China, Tibet, Japan.* Honolulu: University of Hawaii Press.

Overmyer, Daniel L. 1986. *Religions of China.* San Francisco: Harper and Row.

Reader, Ian. 1991. *Religion in Contemporary Japan.* Honolulu: University of Hawaii Press.

Reader, Ian, and George J. Tanabe Jr. 1998. *Practically Religious: Worldly Benefits and the Common Religion of Japan.* Honolulu: University of Hawaii Press.

Ruthven, Malise. 2006. *Islam in the World.* New York: Oxford University Press.

Schimmel, Annemarie. 1992. *Islam: An Introduction.* Albany: State University of New York Press.

Smart, Ninian. 1993. *Religions of Asia.* Englewood Cliffs, N.J.: Prentice Hall.

Smith, Huston. 1991. *The World's Religions: Our Great Wisdom Traditions.* San Francisco: HarperCollins.

Spencer, Robert F., ed. 1971. *Religion and Change in Contemporary Asia.* Minneapolis: University of Minnesota Press.

Stoesz, Willis. 1989. *Kurozumi Shinto: An American Dialogue.* Chambersburg, Pa.: Anima.

Tetsuro, Watsuji. 1996. *Watsuji Tetsuro's* Rinrigaku: *Ethics in Japan.* Translated by Yamamoto Seisaku and Robert E. Carter. Albany: State University of New York Press.

Waines, David. 2003. *An Introduction to Islam.* Cambridge: Cambridge University Press.

Williams, Paul, and Anthony Tribe. 2000. *Buddhist Thought: A Complete Introduction to the Indian Tradition.* London: Routledge.

Yao, Xinzhong. 2000. *An Introduction to Confucianism.* Cambridge: Cambridge University Press.

13

Asia Pacific Literature

Fay Beauchamp and Ely Marquez

n response to the ideas of Edward Said's *Orientalism* (1978), contemporary literary critics of Asia have been concerned about the biases of those attempting to define a literary canon—those works considered worthy of attention and analysis. Even concepts such as "Asia" have been challenged. How can there be any generalizations made about an area so vast, heavily populated, and remarkably varied? This chapter is divided into two main parts, the first on East Asia and the second on Southeast Asia. For over a thousand years, East Asia intertwined Buddhist and Confucian ideas, which led to a reverence for literature written in standardized and distinct Chinese, Korean, and Japanese languages. The archipelagic Southeast Asian countries considered here, Indonesia, Malaysia, the Philippines, and Singapore, remain much more culturally varied yet share the experience of Western colonial rule that arbitrarily grouped islands and peninsulas as nations; the question of national language is a current literary issue struggled over by these Southeast Asian authors and characters.

Despite the immense differences among Asian countries, tentative generalizations about their contemporary literature reveal similarities to recent literature in Africa, Latin America, Europe, and the United States. The worldwide "modern" movement, which began in the 1880s, has been replaced by new trends, increasingly evident after the 1980s: (1) Increased universal education has decreased domination by literary elites of production and consumption of literature; social equality has gained ground as a cultural value. (2) Influence from and resistance to European ideologies have been replaced by vibrant self-criticism of current cultures and nations. (3) More women are writing works of literature and gaining respect; both male and female authors often question gender roles. (4) The language of literature has become more colloquial, open, explicit, harsh; experimental literature has become more fragmented and subjective. (5) National boundaries are transcended by writers who move freely among Asian, European, and American countries. (6) Personal voices are more direct, and less filtered through metaphor, image, persona, and other fictional techniques.

As this chapter is intended for an audience who reads English, references are to primary and secondary texts available in English. It is expected that in the future, the works of more authors will be made available in English, and that different criteria, possibly more elitist or nationalistic or revolutionary, will lead to different authors being highlighted.

▓ East Asia

East Asia has a shared literary history due to the adaptability of Chinese characters to countries with quite different oral languages. Although the spread of literacy from China through Korea to Japan followed interest in reading Buddhist religious texts, secular poetry quickly followed, with Japan's early anthologies being modeled after the Chinese *Shi Jing* (Book of Odes). The prefaces to these early anthologies describe perspectives toward literature that resonate through to the twenty-first century: because literature was seen as a natural expression of the *xin* ("heart-mind-soul") of the people, government leaders, and ultimately the emperor, could evaluate the well-being of the country by collecting and analyzing literature. Thus the national identities of East Asian nation-states are intrinsically linked to secular literature, with the odd result that in the 1900s both Mao Zedong and the Japanese emperors wrote poetry; both China and Japan feature their most revered modern writers, Lu Xun and Natsume Soseki, on currency.

As the twentieth century began, Japanese, Chinese, and Koreans shared one literary world, soon to be shattered. The introduction of Western works came primarily through Japan, with Chinese and Korean students going to Japan and retranslating from Japanese such writers as Jules Verne, Nikolai Gogol, and Henrik Ibsen. A dramatic break in attitudes toward literature occurred after 1919, when the Treaty of Versailles exposed the economic, military, and political weaknesses of China, and the relative strength of Japan after the Meiji Restoration of 1868. The student protests of May 4, 1919, galvanized a literary movement in China to break with the past, and 1919 also marked the failed independence movement in Korea.

While the purposes of "modern," or post-1919, literature in Japan and mainland China seem diametrically opposed, with literature in Korea and Taiwan falling in between, there has been a movement toward convergence in "contemporary" literature, here defined as post-1976. Chinese communists controlled modern literature to enforce social reforms for the group. Taiwan and Korea also saw government scrutiny and censorship of literature, though to a much lesser extent than in China. In Japan, modern authors celebrated the individual by most highly valuing personal expression and subtle aesthetic qualities, though they, too, had to deal with censorship by the Japanese militarist government prior to World War II, and then by the US occupation forces. Contemporary literature, however, demonstrates a shift of values. In the decades after Mao's death in 1976, there has been an explosion of ostensibly nonpolitical Chinese fiction; expressive and aesthetic values soar with experimentation, embracing the techniques of the French existentialists. In Japan there has been a countermovement, with the canonical authors of aesthetic modernism dying off and being replaced with a later generation who discuss social issues such as gender roles, consumerism, and acts of war. The situations in North and South Korea are quite different from one another, with poetry and short stories in South Korea being produced by thousands of university-trained writers, while creative literature is tightly controlled in North Korea. Taiwan resembles South Korea in having an urban and international society both critiqued and celebrated in literature since the 1987 end of martial law.

With more open borders between most of East Asia and the West, it has become difficult to draw a line between Asian literature and the immense field of Asian American or Asian European writers. This part of the chapter, therefore, arbitrarily excludes those who originally write in English, such as Kazuo Ishiguro, who was born in Japan and emigrated to England, and Ha Jin, who was born in the People's Republic of China (PRC) and emigrated to the United States. To compare their complex critiques of both Asian and Western societies, expressed in lyrical English, would alone deserve a chapter.

China

Modern short fiction. One writer dominated attitudes in China toward literature throughout the twentieth century, despite the fact that he lived from 1881 to 1936: Lu Xun. His most famous passage occurs in the preface, "Call to Arms," to his 1923 short-story collection, beautifully translated by Yang Xianyi and Gladys Yang (see Lu 1981). He compares life in China to life in an iron box, and questions the wisdom of awakening the light sleepers within, because they would feel the terror of their condition. Then he concludes that without this awakening there is no hope, and that only literature, not technological advances such as Western medicine, can cure the ills of his people. In twenty-first-century China, Lu Xun's stories are commonly taught in school, and the expanded museum dedicated to him in Shanghai is complete with a room with iron floors and walls for visitors to notice that they are in an "iron box."

Lu Xun's primary genres, the short story and the novella, dominated Chinese literature throughout the twentieth century, rather than poetry or drama. While Lu Xun uses a form of social realism that meticulously documents abuses of widows and drunkards alike, his symbolism and irony invite differing interpretations. In "A Madman's Diary," an unreliable narrator moves to the perception that Confucianism has turned his countrymen into cannibals who destroy and consume the youth. Lu Xun's satirical allegories influence much of contemporary Chinese literature; an example is Bei Dao's 1985 "13 Happiness Street," whose narrator has found construction workers making boxlike bunkers for the masses, and who ends in a "lunatic asylum" (Biddle, Bien, and Dhanwadker 1996:281–292).

For over two thousand years, China has had a recorded history of scholar-officials interpreting poetry, with topics such as lovers' complaints read as allegorical complaints against the state. Lu Xun's essays and allegorical stories influenced Mao Zedong in his Yanan talks on literature; the recognition of literature's power justified Mao's establishment of government offices from 1949 to 1976, which both provided state publication and subsidies for writers and enforced literary censorship.

Authors who reflect communist ideology. Lao She (1899–1966) illustrates the social criticism that followed the May Fourth Movement of 1919. The humorous and realistic novel *Rickshaw* (translated 1936) depicts years in the life of one member of the "working proletariat," and ends with a description of the main character as "selfish, unlucky offspring of society's diseased womb, a ghost caught in Individualism's blind alley" (Lao 1979:249). The ironic inability of the protagonist to overcome his obstacles makes the work more than communist propaganda. Official scrutiny of Lao She's plays may have contributed to his suicide in 1966, at the beginning of the Cultural Revolution.

Ding Ling (1904–1986) was a direct protégée of Lu Xun, and had audited his university classes. Lu Xun had written an essay asking what Ibsen's character Nora did after leaving her tradition-bound home. Ding Ling answered through her 1928 novella "Miss Sophie's Diary." Similar to "A Madman's Diary" in theme and technique, this novella can be interpreted as a psychological study of a woman deciding between two lovers, or as an allegory of China torn by communist and nationalist factions. Ding Ling joined Mao after the Long March and began to write communist literature such as *The Sun Shines over the Sanggan River,* about land reform. This ideological writing did not keep her from being sentenced to house arrest for long periods of her life; however, she surfaced in the post-Mao period, traveled to the United States, and then became a well-known figure on Chinese television in the 1980s. In numerous works, critic Tani E. Barlow has explored how Ding Ling could be both "a sexual, literary, and cultural radical" and a writer who conformed to communist ideology (Barlow and Bjorge 1989:31).

Another survivor, who lived to be 100, was Ba Jin (1904–2005). Like Lao She, he was widely respected in the PRC as a person of steadfast integrity. His most famous novel, *The Family* (1933), attacks the traditional hierarchy underlying arranged marriage; he explicitly blames Confucianism as Lu Xun did, yet with less textual complexity. Ba Jin was president of the Chinese Writers

Association after 1984, and declared his support for the student protesters in Tiananmen Square in 1989.

Transition to contemporary literature. With perhaps the exception of Mao Zedong as a poet, from 1949 to 1976 the PRC produced virtually no new widely respected author, perhaps due to state control that could without warning turn lethal. After Mao's death there was a flood of new writing, dominated at first by nonfictional "scar literature" recording the sufferings caused by the Cultural Revolution. One author from this transitional period was Chen Jo-hsi (1938–), born and published in Taiwan. *The Execution of Mayor Yin and Other Stories from the Great Proletarian Cultural Revolution* (1978) draws on her seven years living in mainland China during the Cultural Revolution; the wry and understated stories focus on naive dissidents, such as a child who calls Mao a "rotten egg." In the 1980s, however, leading up to the Tiananmen Square incident of 1989, Chinese literature took off into an unprecedented diversity of approaches.

A major writer well known in the People's Republic of China is Wang Meng (1934–), who survived exile during the Cultural Revolution and emerged with greater wit, humor, and emotional depth. The main character of "The Young Newcomer in the Organization Department" (1956) appears ordinary, earnest, and cautious, with straightforward concern for his country. Yet this piece led to the labeling of Wang Meng as a "rightist" and his exile to Xinjiang province for twenty years. Wang Meng's fiction in *The Butterfly and Other Stories* (1983) refers to his youthful amazement at being exiled, and strains at optimistic endings. In *The Stubborn Porridge and Other Stories* (1994), Wang Meng acknowledges the humiliation and physical suffering of the Cultural Revolution, yet also admires the Uighurs of Xinjiang, whose kindness matched communist idealism. His more recent writing shows a humorous reaction to current capitalist successes.

Representatives of the "root-seeking school." Authors of the root-seeking school question positive assumptions about human nature and the potential for social change with an ambiguity of time and place that defies single interpretation. Fiction writer Han Shaogong (1953–) is credited with characterizing this movement in 1985 and renewing interest in Chinese identity. In the 1980s, writers Shen Congwen (1902–1988) and A Cheng (1949–) accordingly received critical attention in China because of their interest in ethnic identity.

Jia Pingwa (1953–) is a prolific and commercially successful author who turned to historical fiction with roots in Ming and Qing tales of bandits, warriors, and sexual exploits. His novel *Abandoned Capital,* about old Changan, sold 500,000 copies in China in one year alone. The symbolic resonance of the work, however, distinguishes it from the older tradition. In Jia Pingwa's writing, seduction, murder, and emasculation can follow one another with an abruptness that approaches the surreal but can also captivate a broad audience.

Mo Yan (1956–) for a while was one of the most famous contemporary Chinese authors in the United States, due to the early translation (and editing) of *Red Sorghum* (1986) by Howard Goldblatt and the acclaim given to the film version of the novel. Set over a forty-year period starting in the 1930s, when Japanese soldiers roamed rural China, *Red Sorghum* shows how the ability to commit atrocities crosses national boundaries and political ideologies. The skinning alive of Uncle Arhat is a graphic description of horror. While Jia Pingwa allows violence to occur out of genuine, if weird, altruism, Mo Yan's violence and sexuality give a bleaker picture of human potential.

Su Tong (1963–) has acquired fame for reasons similar to those responsible for Mo Yan's fame; the Oscar-nominated 1992 film version of *Raise the Red Lantern,* directed by the exceptionally talented Zhang Yimou, is frequently taught in US college film courses. The novella *Raise the Red Lantern* has a structural balance and even tone that masks the mysteries hidden by the various wings, courtyards, and gardens of the Chen family's traditional house. At first defiant and aloof, the protagonist, Lotus, thinks she sees a third wife murdered for adultery; Lotus ends as the familiar figure of the mad unreliable narrator. Su Tong critiques gender relations in a way that defies solution; the evil caused by power, vanity, or sexual desire transcends cultural boundaries.

"Experimental" authors. While the "root-seeking school" mixed exotic details of sex and violence into a coherent narration that could appeal to a general Chinese audience, the related "experimental school" pushed sexual and violent description to surrealism both repellent in substance and beautiful in style. The authors and their small intellectual audiences are aware of postmodern theory, which values the irrational and fragmented, and which denies that there can be one true version of reality. Images are not easily explained by being dreams or metaphor; on the other hand, the references to events such as the Cultural Revolution invite the conclusion that the authors are still saying, as Lu Xun was, that this nightmare, this madman's dream, is China. These authors take pride in being independent from state support (personal interview with Gu Yizheng 2002).

Yu Hua (1960–) has earned respect among the literary avant-garde for his early work, collected in *The Past and the Punishments* (1996). The story "Classical Love" is set during a time of imperial examinations; however, the constant demolition and rebuilding in a village resemble change in contemporary China. The cannibalism in the story, however, is shocking in its grisly details of flesh and sinew and goes qualitatively beyond what Lu Xun did with the same trope. The title story's "punishment expert" explicitly refers to the relentless interrogations of the Cultural Revolution. The film *To Live,* based on a Yu Hua story, is useful in the classroom as commentary on modern Chinese history; the contrast of story and film reveals biases of the director, Zhang Yimou, who idealized resilient family ties (see Giskin and Walsh 2001:204–207).

Can Xue (1953–) goes even beyond Yu Hua's linguistic experimentation, with disjunctions between sentences interrupting and questioning meaning. Can Xue's bleak view of humanity allows for none of the romantic gestures of Jia Pingwa, let alone the emotional loyalties of Wang Meng. For example, in *Old Floating Cloud,* the characters love to set traps, including "old lady Qi who always hung a huge kettle of boiling water above the door frame" (Can 1991:7). The constant paranoia is given without explanation. With the "experimental" writers, political allegory and a deeper despair of mankind seem joined.

Mystery thriller as philosophical text. Wang Shuo (1958–) has sometimes been dismissed as a commercial author who plays to the desire of young people to be cool and cynical. Bonnie McDougall considers Wang Shuo to have a philosophy that "there is nothing more to life than self-indulgence" (McDougall and Louie 1997:417). But the 1989 novel *Playing for Thrills* definitely goes beyond that summary. On the surface, Wang Shuo spoofs Lu Xun, the Boxer uprising, Katharine Hepburn, and himself; he is self-described as an author of books with a "larger print run than the Selected Works of Chairman Mao" (Wang 1997:45). But what begins as a search for the identity of a killer ends with a surprising dream sequence of redeeming lost love and hope. It is not surprising that Wang Shuo, attacked in China as frivolous, was defended by the sincere, if also commercially successful, Wang Meng. Since 1988, Wang Shuo has been involved in adapting his novels for film and has increasingly channeled his popular appeal into film producing and screenwriting.

Contemporary poetry. Modern poetry in the Western world owes a great debt to traditional Chinese poetry, as translated by Ezra Pound using Ernest Fenollosa's extensive notes. Without knowing oral Chinese, Pound made no attempt to follow the intricate patterns of tone, rhyme, and formal vocabulary of classical Chinese; he left the poetry concise, concrete, and elliptical without supplying the abstractions that help to fix meaning in English. Through Pound's admonishments to T. S. Eliot and W. B. Yeats, modern poetry in English began to sound like Pound's deft and exact translations of Tang dynasty poet Li Bai (Li Po). Ironically, to Chinese speakers, modern Western poetry seemed a total break from tradition. Modern Chinese poetry, using vernacular language endorsed by Hu Shi after 1919, is called "Westernized" without recognition of the reciprocal dynamic at work. In the post–World War II period, translations proliferated, with Stephen Owen's and Burton Watson's work recommended for both accuracy and beauty.

The contemporary Chinese poet best known in the West is Bei Dao (1949–), who declared himself a dissident: "Listen. I don't believe / OK. You've trampled / a thousand enemies underfoot. Call me / a thousand and one" (Barnstone 1993:17). Bei Dao's poetry also expresses personal feelings of love and loss, using traditional Chinese symbols such as "sundered lute-strings" and "the bamboo pipes of the past" (Bei 1988:63, 84). Both political poetry and *menlong* (misty/obscure) poetry were deemed dangerous to the state after a brief period in 1979–1980, when the literary journal *Jintian* (Today) flourished in Beijing. In 1989, Bei Dao supported student protesters immediately before the Tiananmen Square incident, which occurred when he was out of the country. Since 1989, Bei Dao has remained in exile in the West, although in 2006 was considering the opportunity to return to China permanently.

Contemporary drama. The May Fourth Movement of 1919 was punctuated by Chinese performances of Ibsen's *The Doll's House,* which challenged Confucian ideals of family by portraying an exemplary husband caging the wife he treasures and patronizes. Such realistic drama illustrating social wrongs became the norm in China for the next sixty years. First, what became known as the "Gang of Four," headed by Mao's wife, promoted communism through plays and film, and then, after 1976, "anti–Gang of Four" plays used the same didactic techniques.

China's most famous dramatist, Gao Xingjian (1940–), was first recognized by intellectuals within China for a handful of plays. After studying at the Beijing Foreign Languages Institute, being a Red Guard, and then being exiled to provincial life during the Cultural Revolution, in 1981 he was assigned to the Beijing People's Art Theater. His plays were given limited productions intermittently in China until 1987, when his self-exile in France became permanent; he has produced plays in Europe since.

Through his themes, techniques, and self-reflection, Gao has attracted comparison to Albert Camus, Jean-Paul Sartre, and Samuel Beckett. Gao's early play *Bus Stop* resembles *Waiting for Godot.* The 1995 play *Weekend Quartet* can be compared to Sartre's *No Exit,* with a similar claustrophobia of personal relationships that create an endless hell. The physical riddles of the 1992 play *Dialogue and Rebuttal* suggest an East-West comparison of existentialist thought and Chan (Zen) Buddhism.

Soul Mountain was begun in 1983 while Gao Xingjian was avoiding political persecution by roaming southwest China. This "postmodern" novel contains a satirical description of its own form and content; a publisher complains that the author has just "slapped together travel notes, moralistic ramblings, feelings, notes, jottings, untheoretical discussions, unfable-like fables, copied out some folk songs" (Gao 2000:453). The fictional author also protests being categorized in the commercially successful "searching-for-roots" school. Since winning the Nobel Prize for Literature in 2000, Gao has continued to live as a citizen of France, and more novels and short stories have been translated into English.

Women writing about women. Despite the success of authors such as Ding Ling and Can Xue, women writing in China have had a harder time than men in being considered as serious rather than popular authors. Wang Anyi (1954–), however, has gained respect with her novels of personal experience. Tie Ning (1957–) has been a council member of the Chinese Writers Association since the 1980s. Her short stories, collected in *Haystack* (1990), have a freshness and optimism not seen in much of contemporary Chinese literature. "Ah, Fragrant Snow" ends with the youthful female protagonist greeted by friends who are "warm and spontaneous" (Tie 1990:25). More recent publications reflect economic changes. In the novel *Shanghai Baby* (2001), Wei Hui (1974–) creates a glamorous world of urban apartments, love affairs, and champagne parties where the woman protagonist becomes a popular writer resembling the author. In Taiwan, sisters Zhu Tianwen (1956–) and Zhu Tianxin (1958–) have been publishing since the 1970s, and have recently gained wider recognition through screenwriting. In Hong Kong, which retains a distinct literary world, Xi Xi (1938–) has had a long career also leading to recent popularity through film.

Taiwan

Some anthologies present mainland (PRC) and Taiwanese literature together, positing "a new image of China . . . defined not by geopolitical boundaries and ideological closure but by overlapping cultures" (Wang and Tai 1994:238), but the issue of separation versus unity is highly politically charged. With its economic prosperity and close relationship to the United States, Taiwan has often produced writers with blurred identities, a mixture of Asian and Asian American; an early example was S. K. Chang (1944–), who wrote in Chinese for Taiwanese audiences while a professor of computer science at the University of Pittsburgh. David Wang (Wang and Tai 1994) notes that Su Tong, Yu Hua, and Mo Yan were often published in Taiwan before they were published in the PRC, guaranteeing a market in the Chinese language for writers who criticize the communist past.

In his 2000 book *Contemporary Taiwanese Cultural Nationalism*, A-chin Hsiau describes three influences on Taiwan's distinct literary history: an "aboriginal" group who intermarried with immigrants from the mainland during the few hundred years before 1895, Japanese who colonized the island from 1895 to 1945, and Kuomintang nationalists who dominated the island economically and politically after 1945. Those from the first group designate themselves as ethnic Taiwanese, and have promoted *hsiang-tu* (village-local) literature since the 1930s. One well-known writer in the *hsiang-tu* group, Chen Ying-chen (1936–), who was imprisoned for dissent, criticizes life in Taiwan under the US-backed Kuomintang. He describes in his 1978 short story, "One Day in the Life of a White-Collar Worker," the thwarted ambitions of his protagonist, who is outmanipulated by his superiors who have ties to overseas Chinese (Tam, Yip, and Dissanayake 1999:50–75). The 1983 short story "Mountain Path" is more overtly political, with Chen idealizing an altruistic woman who is true to her communist lover for over thirty years (Perng and Wang 1994:1–22). A reference to the 1979 Kaohsiung incident enriches the political layers of the story. The imprisonment of protesters against the authoritarian Taiwanese government in 1979 is compared to the harsh treatment of communist dissidents in the 1950s.

Wang Wen-hsing (1939–) represents a "mainlander" group, since his family moved to Taiwan in 1947. For this cohort, it is not surprising that Wang went from a bachelor of arts at the Taiwan National University, to a master of fine arts from the University of Iowa, to being an editor of the journal *Modern Literature* back in Taiwan. The journal's experiments of form and personal expression are credited to direct Western influence. Wang's 1972 novel *Family Catastrophe* shows the disintegration of Confucian values, such as filial piety, in a series of vignettes that are spare, puzzling, lyrical, and eventually very moving. While Wang Wen-hsing resembles contemporary writers in the PRC in moving toward a postmodern style, his underlying message sometimes seems more idealistic or romantic than the messages of his ostensibly communist counterparts.

Japan

The modern novel. While an economically and politically weak China started the twentieth century with its intellectuals attacking its Confucian traditions, Japan, buoyed by military successes, embraced new ideas without rejecting its aesthetic past, associated with both Shinto and Zen Buddhist beliefs. Modern aesthetics, celebrating nature, transience, simplicity, and suggestion, can be traced to traditional art, architecture, poetry, and drama, but it was the novel that flourished after the Meiji Restoration (launched in 1868) and combined Western and Japanese ideas. Writing at the same time as Henry James, Virginia Woolf, and William Faulkner, and when Arthur Waley was translating Murasaki's ca. 1000 *The Tale of Genji* as the world's first novel, Japanese authors perfected the modern novel, with its stream of consciousness, symbolism, lyrical intensity, and psychological depth.

The most famous Japanese novels that exemplify "modern" aesthetics include Mori Ogai's *The Wild Goose;* Nobel Prize–winning Yasunari Kawabata's *Snow Country, Thousand Cranes,* and *The Sound of the Mountain;* Junichiro Tanizaki's *Some Prefer Nettles;* Natsume Soseki's *Kokoro;* Yukio Mishima's *The Sound of the Waves* and *The Temple of the Golden Pavilion;* and Osamu Dazai's *The Setting Sun* and *No Longer Human.* Published between 1911 and 1967, these intensely personal accounts of ordinary daily life build to moments that suggest universal truths of the human condition. Fleeting moments of joy, however, do not last. Suicides of characters in earlier decades gave way to suicides of authors Dazai and Mishima after World War II.

In the 1911–1967 period, while these personal "*I* novels" were highly esteemed, the world of Japanese literature was much broader. Newspapers and journals brought fiction of all sorts into the homes of a population moving toward universal literacy. Even the canonical writers published humorous, rambling, and self-mocking pieces, such as *Botchan* and *I Am a Cat,* written by famous novelist Natsume Soseki (1867–1916). Shimazaki Toson (1872–1943) wrote naturalistic novels that sharply criticized traditional Japanese attitudes, for example, toward the *burakumin,* the hereditary outcast class. A transition to novels of complex, critical social commentary is exemplified by *The Makioka Sisters,* by Junichiro Tanizaki (1886–1965); the novel's serial publication was suspended by Japanese censors in 1943, but in 1948 it was published in its entirety.

Contemporary novelists. Contemporary Japanese fiction is marked not only by diversity of subject matter and narrative style, but also by a new sense of social responsibility and the need to influence public opinion. In these features, Japanese contemporary literature is perhaps now closer to Chinese literature than to the earlier self-absorbed "*I* novel." Masuji Ibuse (1898–1993) and Yasushi Inoue (1907–1991), two authors who outlived some of their younger protégés to survive to the 1990s, illustrate the range of fictional work in postwar Japan. The independent political stance of Ibuse led him to write the historical novel *John Manjiro, the Castaway: His Life and Adventures,* in 1937, which chronicles the hero's kind treatment at the hands of American whalers in the early 1800s. Ibuse's most famous novel, however, is *Black Rain* (1966), based on interviews and diaries of survivors of the nuclear-bombing of Hiroshima and Nagasaki. The events are described in brutal realism, but the first-person accounts reveal how horror can be relieved by miscellaneous small successes such as finding one's spectacles among the rubble.

Inoue also turned historical fiction into high art. The autobiographical novel *Shirobamba* (1962; translated 1991) is loved by many Japanese as a boyhood story of warm yet painful family relationships. While Ibuse relied on documentary sources to comment on the best and worst of American-Japanese relations, Inoue created new Japanese interest in Chinese history of the Silk Road through his novels *Tun-huang* (1959; translated 1979) and *Lou-lan* (1959; translated 1979).

Kenzaburo Oe (1935–), as well as being a novelist and short-story writer, is a skilled essayist who deftly analyzes contemporary Japanese literature. In his acceptance speech for the 1995 Nobel Prize for Literature, Oe distinguished his work from a previous generation of writers' veneration of aesthetics. He placed himself in a "'post-war school' of writers who came onto the literary scene deeply wounded by the catastrophe of war yet full of hope for a rebirth. They tried with great pain to make up for the atrocities committed by Japanese military forces in Asia" (Oe 1995:118). Oe began his Nobel speech by praising the protagonists of *Huckleberry Finn* and the Swedish novel *The Wonderful Adventures of Nils,* because they move from an amoral life to ethical decisions defying society's rules.

In his Nobel speech, Oe connected his fictional writing to such pivotal decisions in his own life. His novel *A Personal Matter* concerns the moment when the narrator makes a decision to commit himself to his deformed child. Oe made clear the autobiographical elements: "My realization that life with a mentally handicapped child has the power to heal the wounds that family members inflict on one another led me to the more recent insight that the victims and survivors of the atomic bombs have the same sort of power to heal all of us who live in this nuclear age" (Oe 1995:34).

Oe distanced himself not only from Kawabata and Mishima on the grounds of humanistic ideology, but also from popular contemporary authors Haruki Murakami and Banana Yoshimoto, whom he associated with the consumer culture of Tokyo. In a 1990 lecture, "On Modern and Contemporary Japanese Literature," Oe criticized the latter two authors, who "convey the experience of a youth politically uninvolved or disaffected, content to exist within a late adolescent or post-adolescent subculture" (quoted in Oe 1995:50).

Haruki Murakami (1949–), like Kenzaburo Oe, has embraced motifs from Western culture to voice an individualist's response to contemporary Japanese society; Murakami acknowledges the influence of Raymond Chandler and Ross Macdonald on his fiction from 1979 to 1994. Murakami says of these writers' detectives, "No matter what happened to them, they were always able to live their own way, working in a way they like and never complaining about their misfortunes. I love that" (quoted in Gregory, Miyawaki, and McCaffery 2002:4). In novels written in the 1980s, such as *A Wild Sheep Chase, Hard-Boiled Wonderland and the End of the World,* and *Dance, Dance, Dance,* a consistent first-person narrator responds with cool composure and ironic humor to surrealistic urban landscapes of disappearing walls, people, and memory; *Norwegian Wood,* with explicit sexual scenes, led to worldwide sales in the millions.

Whether because of the faltering Japanese economy or because of criticism from Oe, who was a "hero" to Murakami as a young man, Murakami's writing changed dramatically in the mid-1990s. In 1995 he undertook research on Japanese involvement in Manchuria, which led to the novel *The Wind-Up Bird Chronicle.* Its accounts of atrocity in Manchuria and the metamorphosis of Japanese fascist power into contemporary politics and television marked a new concern with Japan's recent history. Murakami continued this trend with his nonfiction book *Underground* (2001), about the 1995 subway gas attack.

A different strand in Murakami's writing is a more positive attitude toward women compared to that of Chandler or Kawabata. From early stories collected in *The Elephant Vanishes* to *Sputnik Sweetheart* (translated 2001), the Murakami narrator sympathetically listens to women talk about their childhoods, writing, and infatuations. In the last story in *After the Quake,* Murakami's protagonist declares, "I want to write stories that are different from the ones I've written so far. . . . I want to write about people who dream and wait for the night to end, who long for the light so they can hold the ones they love" (Murakami

2002:181). It may be this understated romanticism under a restrained veneer that makes Murakami so popular.

Women writing about women. Despite the respect given to the literary masterpieces written by Murasaki and other court women of a thousand years ago, there are often no women authors included in anthologies of "modern" Japanese literature. This exclusion reflects the male-dominated literary world where women were objects of natural beauty; for example, Yasunari Kawabata, in two elegant pages in *Snow Country,* compares a woman to autumn sunlight, mountain paths, grasses, moths, and other insects (Kawabata 1957:92–93). The male dominance of canonical fiction was challenged by two women authors who gained recognition in the postwar years. The first was Fumiko Enchi (1905–1986), an extremely well-educated daughter of a famous Meiji scholar. Enchi used her knowledge of classical Japanese to translate *The Tale of Genji* into modern Japanese; her novel *Masks* (1958) has multiple narrators who discuss and resemble female characters in Murasaki's story. Enchi's *The Waiting Years* (1957) also explores themes of jealousy while challenging the male point of view; readers are asked to identify with an aging wife forced to invite women into her household for her husband. With themes that can be compared to Su Tong's *Raise the Red Lantern,* Enchi gives more voice to women's solidarity and bitterness.

Sawako Ariyoshi (1931–1984), the second major woman author of postwar Japan, shows an even broader range of topics centered on women's lives, past and present. Ariyoshi uses historical research to ground her novels. *The River Ki* (1959) begins in 1897 and follows three generations of women to postwar Japan. The remarkable novel *The Doctor's Wife* (1967) describes experimental surgery for breast cancer in the early nineteenth century; although women's family relations are strained, the women contribute to the successful treatment of a woman's disease. The *Kabuki Dancer* (1972) is set two centuries earlier, when Hideoshi was a shogun planning attacks on China; the novel contrasts a woman's artistic talent with the folly of military aggression. *The Twilight Years* (1972) sees family unity in even more positive terms, through a woman caring for her senile father-in-law. While Fumiko Enchi gives a harsh view of the male promiscuity that "*I* novelists" often idealized, Ariyoshi's view of family relations is more complex in recognizing relationships that are physically and emotionally satisfying over a lifetime.

Kyoko Hayashi (1930–), less prolific than the previous two authors, became a short-story writer, gaining authority from her experience as a child in Shanghai as well as her survival of the Nagasaki bombing. Her 1978 story "Yellow Sand" pairs the themes of sexual and military aggression by describing with lyrical restraint the death of a Japanese prostitute in 1930s Shanghai. "The Empty Can" describes directly the pain of Nagasaki survivors over a thirty-year period (Oe 1985:127–143).

Yuko Tsushima (1946–) puts a woman's perspective firmly in the center of her fiction. Her novel *Child of Fortune* (1978, translated 1983) is a third-person narration of an older single mother who defies convention, only to find herself isolated and self-deluded. Tsushima has said that she began the story through her interest in society's forces that lead some women to imagine they are pregnant. The stories collected in *The Shooting Gallery* (translated 1988) have different female protagonists, but have common elements of a single mother whose painful memories of being deserted by a father, lover, or husband are mitigated by a woman's desire to be independent; these themes have an extra interest, since they parallel Tsushima's life as the daughter of novelist Osamu Dazai, who committed suicide when she was an infant.

Banana Yoshimoto (1964–) heralded a new generation of Japanese writers when she began to publish and win literary prizes in her twenties. Her novels defied convention in both their language and their subject matter. In the 1988 novel *Kitchen,* her colloquial Japanese drew both scorn and praise among Japanese critics. Yoshimoto is a strikingly unusual writer in Japan, perhaps not so much because of her characters who cross-dress and establish unconventional family structures, but because she writes serious literature while allowing her characters to overcome grief and isolation and not succumb to despair and suicide. She has been prolific since 1988.

The variety of fiction now produced by Japanese women might also be well represented by Miyuki Miyabe (1960–). With more than ten novels adapted into films, Miyabe is categorized in Japan as a popular writer. The murder mystery *All She Was Worth* (1992) concerns credit card and bankruptcy policies as well as a woman's search for independence and identity.

Poetry. Older Japanese poetry, like Chinese poetry, helped to create modernism throughout the world. The innovative haiku of Matsuo Basho (1644–1694) introduced new elements of surprise, linguistic delight, daily realism, and philosophic depth that energized Japanese poets in the Tokugawa period and Western poets in the twentieth century. The difference between Basho's poetry and contemporary poetry is more apparent in Japanese than in English translation, due to the new use of colloquial Japanese and a more direct first-person expression of feeling (see Rimer, in Sato and Watson 1986:xliv). Three poets who helped make a transition to modern Japanese poetry were Takamura Kotaro (1883–1956), Hagiwara Sakutaro (1886–1942), and Miyazawa Kenji (1896–1933). In a poem written to his mentally ill wife, Kotaro introduced a new personal directness to Japanese poetry when he wrote, "No, no, I don't like it / your going away" (quoted in Sato and Watson 1986:462), yet he still drew on traditional Japanese symbols such as cherry blossoms. In contrast to these early-twentieth-century poets, contemporary poet Kazuko Shiraishi (1932–) jauntily compares the Flying Dutchman and the trains of the JRline "shaking upside down . . . thought and grief . . . like a bunch of fleas" (Shiraishi 2002:2). Like other contemporary writers, Shiraishi blurs national boundaries due to her birth in Vancouver, study in Iowa, and frequent international travel. Despite these poets' successes, however, no Japanese poet after 1900 has approached Basho's stature, either in Japan or in the West.

One type of poetry that is of course unique to the postwar era is that of survivors of the Hiroshima and Nagasaki bombings. Called *hibakusha* (bomb-victims), some of the survivors were already poets and some turned to poetry to express their intense reactions and to call for world peace. One of the first poems to arise from the Hiroshima devastation was "Let Us Be Midwives," written by Sadako Kurihara (1912–2005) in August 1945. Describing a baby's birth in Hiroshima's wreckage, Kurihara calls for commitment to the future in the midst of disaster (Treat 1995:162). The poem "Give Me Back My Father," by Toge Sankichi (1917–1953), is carved into a monument in Hiroshima's Peace Park. A poet already known for his interest in language, Toge joined the Communist Party and defied censorship under the US occupation, deciding to use his experience in the bombing to work for world peace. Toge's experience as a *hibakusha* and his early death in 1953 are inseparably linked to the power of his writing.

Contemporary theater. Japan's most esteemed modern playwright was arguably Yukio Mishima (1925–1970), whose one-acts translated in 1957 as *Five Modern No Plays* have a canonical status as written texts. The 1960s, however, saw a movement in Japan that challenged the conventions of modern theater. Theater in Japan after the 1960s is noted for being experimental and diverse.

Hisashi Inoue (1934–) is associated with a form of theater called *shingeki,* a modern theater influenced by Western twentieth-century innovations and a break with Japan's unique traditional forms of theater, *kabuki, noh,* and *bunraku.* With 150 works published, beginning with the 1969 play *The Belly Button of the Japanese* and the 1970 novel *Boon and Phoon,* Inoue is a linguistically adventuresome satirist. A 1997 play, *Kamiya-cho Sakura Hotel,* reveals Inoue's combination of irony, fantasy, and historical commentary. In this play, set during World War II, an admiral of the Japanese navy debates the use of kamikaze pilots with a youthful amateur theater troupe in Hiroshima. After the admiral survives the war and the acting troupe dies in Hiroshima, he asks to be convicted as a war criminal because he helped to delay Japan's surrender until after utter destruction (see Iwanami 1998:74–78).

Tadashi Suzuki (1939–), an "artistic director" rather than an author, has put on experimental plays in various locations, including above coffee shops; the town of Toga became the site of an annual international festival in the 1980s and 1990s (Brandon 1993:168–169). Ironically, as Japanese theater became more radical, it resembled *kabuki* and *noh* in being a combined form of language, costume, music, and dance. One playwright associated with Suzuki is Minoro Betsuyaku (1937–), who has an established reputation based on more than seventy plays (see Sorgenfrei in Mostow 2003:270). His play *The Little Match Girl* has been one of his most performed. The symbolism of this play is readily apparent, as the Hans Christian Andersen heroine lives and dies in a postwar Japan that is indifferent to her suffering. Currently, Japanese troupes perform internationally, and directors such as Suzuki have worked in the United States.

Political commentary through historical realism. The literary world recently suffered a loss with the death of Akira Yoshimura (1927–2006). He was a highly respected and bestselling author of twenty novels in Japan, but translation of his work into English, and critical attention abroad, began only in the 1990s. The novel *One Man's Justice,* written in 1978 and translated in 2001, is the most explicit in political commentary. The main character, Takuya, kills a US airman who had parachuted into Tokyo during the World War II air raids that destroyed the city. The novel compares military tribunals in Japan, the Philippines, and elsewhere. Takuya's attitude against the Americans is bitter. Yet he changes during the course of the novel to contemplate not only the morality of his own actions, but also that of Japanese involved in "vivisections at the Kyushu Imperial University" (Yoshimura 2001:227). While Yoshimura is often praised for his historical research and realism, his novels *Shipwrecks* (1982; translated 1996) and *On Parole* (1988; translated 1999) can also be read as scathing political allegories of World War II and its aftermath. He also challenges American assumptions about the possibility of a just war and postwar justice.

Korea
Modern Korean literature is commonly divided into an "enlightenment" period (mid–nineteenth century to 1919), the years of the Japanese colonial rule (1910–1945), and the period of national division (1945–present). The first period saw the growth of literacy through Western-style schools. Even elite authors began using a vernacular prose style, and widely read newspapers published serial novels. These elements of Korean modernization were similar to changes occurring in China and Japan. After 1910, Korean literature under the Japanese shared the Japanese "modern" interest in individual self-discovery and experimentation with form, with social realism being considered a minor form. A retrospective view of life in Korea under Japanese colonial rule can be seen in the writing of Richard E. Kim (1932–), who was born in North Korea and fought in the South Korean forces (1950–1954) before coming to the United States. His novel *Lost Names: Scenes from a Korean Boyhood* creates a world from 1932 to 1945; from a child's point of view, the Japanese colonizers are seen as weak bullies.

The period after 1953 is primarily marked by the extreme difference between North Korea (Democratic People's Republic of Korea) and South Korea

(Republic of Korea). Though North Korean literature is rarely translated into English, US readers can glean an understanding of contemporary literature of North Korea from commentators such as Stephen Epstein, who provides a bibliography of secondary sources in his article "Encountering North Korean Fiction." According to Epstein, literature in North Korea is tightly controlled by the government to serve ideological purposes. *Juche* ideology, defined as nationalist pride and self-determination, calls for problems delineated in fiction to be solved by optimistic endings extolling future possibility. Epstein analyzes the literary mechanisms that move readers "from social reality to social ideals" (2003:2), and one expects that as this literature becomes more available in English translation, theories compatible with socialist concerns will emerge to explore it, much as Chinese Ding Ling's communist writings have received sympathetic attention in recent years.

Fiction. A history of twentieth-century Korean fiction can be read through the collected works of highly regarded, prolific, and long-lived author Hwang Sun-won (1915–2000). Hwang's realism, modern methods of achronological narrative, and humanistic idealism stem from Korea's "enlightenment" period of the very early 1900s. His college education at Waseda University in Japan reflected Japan's occupation of Korea from 1910 to 1945. Hwang began writing in the late 1930s, creating stories of disparity among educated and noneducated classes. A representative early story, "Mantis," portrays moral decay through imagery of blind and dying animals. In "Reeds," the political message, muted at a time of Japanese censorship, is conveyed through symbols such as "shards of celadon ceramic buried in the dirt shone green in the sunlight" (Hwang 1990:43). The pottery evokes the height of Korean aristocratic civilization in the twelfth century, when the glaze of the pottery, like jade, could represent purity, graciousness, restraint, and happiness.

While short stories refer to Japanese occupation, modern Korean literature is distinctive in its retention in form and content of a past when the kingdoms of the Korean peninsula paid voluntary tribute to China while absorbing Chinese literary values. Korea's own Confucian scholar-officials, called *yangban,* were like their Chinese counterparts in highly valuing the production and appreciation of poetry.

When Hwang wrote "Cranes" in 1953, he described overcoming the divisions of war and the Thirty-eighth Parallel by remembering a childhood in an idyllic countryside of hill and river. His image of freeing cranes uses a common East Asian symbol of longevity. One of Hwang's last stories to be anthologized, "Masks," written in 1983, draws on Buddhist beliefs: a soldier becomes a reed, a bull, and the other soldier who killed him. Such a story of reincarnation gives warriors who kill one another a chance at redemption.

For short-story writers born in South Korea in the 1940s, the shift to contemporary literature, as opposed to modern, occurred gradually in the 1970s, in response to dislocating rapid industrialization and urbanization. New fiction began to flourish after the end of the Park Chung Hee era in 1987, with the fall of the Fifth Republic after popular resistance.

Sehui Cho (1942–) reflects the social stress occasioned by the industrialization and urbanization under Park Chung Hee's rule (1961–1978). Bruce Fulton considers Cho's *A Dwarf Launches a Little Ball* to be "the most important postwar Korean novel" (quoted in Mostow 2003:721). The surreal mood of this work is captured by the image of father, called a "dwarf," standing in the moonlight on top of a tall smokestack and launching a paper airplane (Cho 2002:34). Efforts to keep family and home together prove futile against the aggression of destructive entrepreneurs; reality and fantasy blur in a series of vignettes told from different points of view.

Most of the younger Korean writers translated into English are South Korean and urban, despite the single word "Korean" in the anthologies' titles (see Biddle, Bien, and Dhanwadker 1996; Sallee 1993; Fulton and Fulton 1997). These younger, university-educated writers claim fame through literary prizes such as the Tongin and the Yi Sang. Women writers are well represented.

The life depicted in these contemporary stories is typically bleak. While Chinese stories after Lu Xun frequently use surrealism that distances the reader from horror, the Korean stories relentlessly strip away human ties. One story, "Wayfarer," by a prominent woman author, O Chong-hui (1947–), leaves the woman protagonist isolated, beset with memories of killing a man with a soldering iron (Fulton and Fulton 1997:205). O Chong-hui published seven volumes of fiction between 1968 and 1997. Her translators, Bruce Fulton and Ju-Chan Fulton, say that O reveals "nightmarish family constellations warped by divorce, insanity, abandonment, and death" (quoted in Grayson and Tennant 1999:47). All six stories in the anthology *The Snowy Road,* by different authors, end terribly: advice on how to "wail for a dead person"; a narrator "incapacitated with shame"; an old lady who "had been caught in a trap and had bled to death"; a narrator who sinks into a "mood of loneliness"; a narrator shamed "so much that I couldn't even attempt to take a single step"; and a narrator who finds her life "meaningless" (Sallee 1993:23, 63, 81, 110, 141, 164). These quotes may reflect more the revelations and protesting attitudes that led to literary prizes in the 1980s and 1990s rather than the totality of South Korean life of the university-trained authors.

Poetry. There is general agreement that So Chongju (1915–2000) was the most important Korean poet of the twentieth century, famous for his humanistic faith in literature's power. Peter Lee praises So Chongju's exploration of the Korean language to express "emotional states ranging from sensual ecstasy to spiritual quest, from haunting lyricism to colloquial earthiness" (1990:xxi). So Chongju's early poems from the 1940s make the transition to modernity marked by the more direct and personal style perceived in the modern Japanese poets of the

1880s. Traits of traditional Chinese poetry, which formed both Korean and Japanese traditional poetry, are still retained, such as pairing structurally opposed elements and using traditional symbols, for example the chrysanthemum. Brother Anthony of Taize reports that it is difficult to keep track of poetic tendencies in contemporary Korea, since over two thousand poets "published at least one volume" in the 1990s (quoted in Grayson and Tennant 1999:74). Postwar Korean poets can be divided into three groups: those who are traditional, those who value linguistic experimentation, and those who try to better social conditions. Suyong Kim (1927–), who was captured by UN forces and released from a prisoner-of-war camp in 1953 (Lee 1990:272), is prominent in the third group. Suyong Kim's most famous poem is "The Grass," in which the grass, although flattened, has determination to survive. Irony intensifies in poetry by Hwang Tonggyu (1938–), who is the son of Hwang Sunwon but represents a generation familiar with the University of Iowa's writing program as well as with Seoul University. His poetry is explicitly antiwar, with the traditional symbol of flying wild geese viewed from the perspective of a soldier "forgetting dog-tags, frost-bite, even my life" (Biddle, Bien, and Dhanwadker 1996:464). His poem "Four Twilights" also juxtaposes images of ancient Korea with a contemporary view in which "drunken sailors scuffle / Under blossoming clouds" (quoted in Lee 1990:296). Also part of this group is Kim Chi-ha (1941–), whose arrest for political protest led to an international campaign to keep him from being executed under the death penalty. Kim's long poem "The Story of a Sound" is a bitter political satire that compares political suppression in Korea to the dropping of an atom bomb and to the 1989 Tiananmen Square killings in China. The poem describes attempts to quiet the protagonist through beheading, amputation, and castration, but the protester continues "ceaselessly hurling himself against the walls" of a prison (Biddle, Bien, and Dhanwadker 1996:474). The grimness of the poetry parallels that of contemporary Korean short stories.

Comparison of Chinese, Japanese, and Korean Contemporary Literature

Comparing Chinese, Korean, and Japanese contemporary literature translated into English after the 1970s, one is struck by the vast differences in mood across the three countries. Japan, having had over six decades to recover from World War II, is reengaging in political commentary, and facing its own past aggression as well as that of the United States against it. Skepticism over political decisions seems balanced by new considerations of the possibility of love and commitment. The People's Republic of China, recovering from its own turmoil of the Cultural Revolution and the current turmoil of transition to a capitalist economy, is energetically exploring linguistic experimentation and philosophical interpretations of the meaning of life; politics and gender relationships seem equally open to new choices. Korea, divided by an unresolved war, yet with capitalist growth and change in South Korea, seems almost surprisingly the most restricted to images of despair and pain, particularly evident in the writing of younger authors rather than in the more canonical writing of authors born early in the twentieth century. One hopes that the combined political and artistic power of the East Asian nations will lead to further change; one hopes that suppression, based on old gender relationships and twentieth-century hatred of communism and hatred of capitalism, will be replaced with new harmony and positive creativity.

Southeast Asia

Mainland and peninsular Southeast Asian countries share a colonial experience that dominated them and left a common legacy of linguistic hegemony, racial inequality, and often-weak national identities. The British in Myanmar, Brunei, Malaysia, and Singapore, the Dutch in Indonesia, the French in Cambodia, Laos, and Vietnam, and the Spanish and later the Americans in the Philippines, at various times in varying ways and degrees, affected these countries in their native literatures and their literary output during and after their colonizers' departure. In addition, they are also similar in having had their respective precolonial oral indigenous native literatures. Indonesia, Malaysia, and Singapore had the *hikayat,* Cambodia, Laos, Myanmar, and Thailand the *jataka,* and the Philippines its folk-epics. Upon contact with the West, these traditional narrative forms merged easily with the Western genres of the novel and the short story (Kintanar 1994).

Our discussion of Southeast Asian literature concentrates on Indonesia, Malaysia, Singapore, and the Philippines, largely because all have sizable amounts of published literature in English, both nationally and internationally, and because translations of non-English publications from these areas are readily available. Earliest published work in English starts from about 1910 in the Philippines, and about the 1950s in Malaysia and Singapore. In Indonesia, the period considered here starts from after World War II, or the overthrow of the Dutch, with a brief mention of earlier poets to provide a historical perspective on the "new generation" of writers, who are discussed at length. Most of the literary output from the Southeast Asian nations not discussed here is in native languages, and few English translations are easily available, making them largely inaccessible for most Western audiences.

The focus here is on language, which plays a prominent role in any discussion of empire today: the colonial power's language as a hegemonic or oppressive agent of empire, which may lead to language loss or even linguicide; the colonial power's language as appropriated by the colonized and remade to its own uses and purposes; and the language of the colonized and how it is nurtured and developed in opposition to the colonial language for purposes of constructing a national identity or asserting a national voice. In the case of Indonesia, writers played a vital role in the creation, valorization, and nurture of Bahasa Indonesia. Their conscious and concerted efforts toward the abrogation of Dutch, the colonial language, and its replacement by the native language, contrast with the same intensity of concerted efforts in Malaysia, Singapore, and the Philippines toward the appropriation of English, the colonial language in those countries. Instead of allowing it to be an instrument of oppression, writers turned English into a potent weapon of decolonization, cultural assertion, and artistic equality.

Indonesia

Much of modern Indonesian literature is written in Bahasa Indonesia, based on the Malay language, spoken both in Indonesia and Malaysia. Indonesia had a large ethnically Malay population, though the country became extremely diverse linguistically and culturally, as Katherine Kaup presents in more detail in Chapter 10. Bahasa Indonesia is the mother language of only a small minority of the population, with most speaking one of several hundred regional languages. Some of the main local languages include Javanese in central and eastern Java, Sundanese in inland western Java, Minangkabau and Balinese in western Sumatra, and Malay in Kalimantan. Burton Raffel (1967:4) wrote that before the Dutch arrival, around 1600, "there was no uniform culture, no uniform language." Out of about 200 languages, mutually unintelligible to one another, Malay had become dominant by about the fifteenth century. In 1928 it became the official national language, and was named Bahasa Indonesia, which writers have cultivated and developed, both as the language of literature and the language of the people.

Prose fiction. Each region in Indonesia is culturally distinct from the others, but a strong national unity has emerged in literature because of the pervasive use of Bahasa Indonesia. From the very beginning, the country's nationalist writers, most prominently Pramoedya Ananta Toer (1925–2006), strongly supported the dissemination and acceptance of the language. In an interview in 1996, Pramoedya said that his "writing in Indonesia is aimed at popularizing *Bahasa Indonesia,* and making it a living, modern language."

In *This Earth of Mankind,* Pramoedya used his keen awareness of the power of language, especially its hegemonic power over its own speakers, to call attention to the many social inequalities among his own people, exacerbated by the Dutch language. Javanese, the language of the novel's characters, has a high form and a low form. According to Clifford Geertz, "it is nearly impossible to say anything without indicating the social relationship between speakers and the listeners in terms of status and familiarity" (1968:283). Pramoedya rejected this tyranny of Javanese, with its built-in sociolinguistic markers that force its speakers to position themselves according to the complicated Javanese social order. Similarly, he comments on Dutch hegemony toward Javanese and Malay.

Pramoedya, a left-wing writer from the early 1940s to his death, was born in Java in 1925. Active in demanding independence from the Dutch after World War II, he was imprisoned, then released just before independence was granted in 1957. A journalist and an open supporter of communist ideas, he was arrested again by Suharto in 1965 and imprisoned for fourteen years. Long deprived of pen and paper, he dictated four novels to his fellow prisoners to keep the works alive in his memory: *The Earth of Mankind, Child of All Nations, Footsteps,* and *A House of Glass.*

This Earth of Mankind traces the evolution of protagonist Minke's Indonesianization as it proceeds slowly, starting from young Minke's thoroughly Dutch-dominated mentality, to his teenage adoration for the queen of the Netherlands, and his fascination with all Western technological advances, such as the printing press and the steamship. Gradually, as he encounters characters who are less Dutch-enamored and more Malay-conscious, he realizes his own denial of his inferior ascribed status, and finally recognizes and accepts the tyranny of the system and the helplessness and powerlessness of those caught within it.

The first three books narrate Minke's gradual mental decolonization and his gradual acceptance of his responsibility toward his own people as he learns about them and their oppressed lives. He becomes a doctor, later an editor, who eventually writes in Malay, abandoning the Dutch language that he so loved originally. In the last book, *A House of Glass,* Pramoedya switched his focus from Minke to Pangemanann, a police officer who is monitoring Minke. Representing the colonial who has aligned himself thoroughly with his colonizer and realizing he has done so, Pangemanann is torn between the interests of his own people and his own comfort earned by his work for the colonizers.

The Mute's Soliloquy, a collection of "fragments of work" written while in prison, is an introspective examination of Pramoedya's life, his relationship with his family, his views on religion and Indonesian people, and a description of his prisoner existence. Pramoedya also wrote several short stories, especially in his earlier years, when fervor for nation building was at its height. During this time, writers and other artists were debating the value of the Indonesian *adat* (traditions), which some saw as detrimental to the construction of a new and solid Indonesia. Calls for the abolition of some traditional practices, such as arranged marriages, were common.

One Indonesian writer who debated with Pramoedya over the years and writes in English is Mochtar Lubis (1922–2004). In an interview with Francisco Sionil José (see the section on the Philippines, p. 411), Lubis said that his novel *Tiger, Tiger* (1964), a translation from Bahasa Indonesia and one of his more recognized works, "made a strong statement against the abuse of power by our leaders—lying to the people, betraying them, and using beautiful words to impress them, but in reality, the leader works only for himself" (Lubis 1991:149). Talking about another work, *Twilight in Djakarta,* in the same interview, he said that "our freedom is not complete yet. We still have to fight for others" (1991:159–160).

Both Pramoedya and Lubis are concerned with serious national social issues, placing their works within the definition of "literary novel" as opposed to the "popular novel," which flourished in Indonesia in the 1970s. According to Jacob Sumardjo the "literary novel stands out because of its searching and original approach; new themes emerge even with the use of conventional techniques or old themes are tackled by new techniques. Its originality and uniqueness make it a literary work. The popular novel, while deserving of its own place, is more the achievement of a craftsman and not a product of creativity" (quoted in Heraty 1994:124).

Poetry. According to Burton Raffel, the first three modern Indonesian poets were Mohammad Yamin (1903–1962), Sanusi (Sanoesi) Pané (1905–1968), and Rustam (Roestam) Effendi (1903–1979?), whose work "is almost totally unknown outside Indonesia and not well known even there; many Western and Indonesian critics tend to denigrate the achievement of Sanusi Pane and Rustam Effendi, but Indonesian critics have tended to overpraise Yamin" (1967:28). They wrote romantic, patriotic, but "thin" and "tepid" sonnets for political reasons. After publishing his last volume of poems in 1928, Yamin became a politician and stopped writing poetry.

Sanusi Pané wrote in what Raffel called the "Oriental strain," "a way of looking out at the world that poets in England, France, Russia and the United States" do not share, a different sensitivity, a different perception and feeling (1967:45). This oriental strain is best illustrated by Pané's poem "Mentajarii" (Seeking) (quoted in Raffel 1967:44):

I have wandered
All over the West.
And in the end
I came to this garden
In my heart.
There is Happiness
It has been waiting for me
All along.

In contrast, Effendi wrote in the "Westernized strain," which Raffel does not define, but seems to imply as meaning "innovative," both in language and in form, and moving away from traditional forms, such as the *pantun*. "What he did with *Bahasa Indonesia* was utterly unlike the sentimentalities of Yamin, or the simple, limited purity of Sanusi: Effendi wrestled with his country's developing language and pulled it this way and that, trying to find the key to new and better modes of expression. Much of his poetry is awkward, not fully formed, but there are passages that astonishingly prefigure that later greatness others achieved" (Raffel 1967:47). Effendi exploited linguistic structures such as reduplication and affixation, as well as "regional words" and "everyday words," colloquialisms, and literary vocabulary (Raffel 1967:52).

Pané, Sanusi, and Effendi were succeeded by Amir Hamzah (1911–1945), characterized by Raffel as "the greatest Indonesian poet of the 1930s," a "superb craftsman, a wonderfully skilled poetic technician who made *Bahasa Indonesia* do things no one before him had been able to manage." Hamzah "remains the culmination of the 'Oriental strain' in modern Indonesian poetry, but he is also its first great individual, its first great poet; no label fits him satisfactorily" (1967:75). A short poem (quoted in Raffel 1967:79) illustrates this:

But my heart is always sad:
I long for the secret
Of that hidden black valley
Which separates being and non-being.

Following these poets was Chairil Anwar (1922–1949), considered an "art for art's sake" poet and Indonesia's best. He lived life exuberantly and freely, and died young. He subscribed to "universal humanism," in contrast to Pramoedya's "proletarian humanism," which advocated that "the worker is the primary target of poetry." He is best acknowledged for his experiments in language and his extensions of its use and imagery. In one of his public lectures, Anwar said: "The tools and devices with which the poet can express himself are the materials of language, which he uses intuitively. By 'manipulating' the lofty and the low he can achieve a pattern, an organization, and then he can create variations within the pattern—using rhythm as a unifying element" (quoted in Raffel 1967:230). Anwar's most famous and oft-quoted poem is "Aku" (Me), with its famous last line: "I want to live a thousand years" (Anwar n.d.:31; also quoted in Raffel 1970:21).

Anwar "remains Indonesia's greatest literary figure: he deserves a significant and lasting place in Asian and in world literature" (Raffel 1970:xxii). His poetry, though slim in volume, was very influential. A group of writers who called themselves "Angkatan 45" (Generation 45 [in reference to the year 1945]) functioned around him and emulated his work, but their "universal humanism" was derided by Pramoedya as "universally subversive humanism" and "valueless." At one time Pramoedya called Anwar's work "bourgeois" (Raffel 1967:140–141).

Following Generation 45 was "Angkatan Baru" (New Generation), also known as the "Generation of 1966" (Aveling 2001). Ajio Rosidi (1938–) and W. S. Rendra (1935–) were to the Generation of 1966 what Chairil Anwar was to Generation 45. Rendra wrote protest poetry and later protest plays. He was forbidden by Suharto's New Order, the military-dominated regime that wrestled power from Sukarno's "Guided Democracy" in 1965, to perform his plays in some parts of Indonesia, but he continued to write and read his work in public, and managed to have his voice heard during this era of severe artistic repression and censorship. One of his more well-known protest poems is "I Hear Voices" (quoted in Aveling 2001:143):

> There are men shooting at the moon
> There are no birds falling from their nests
> It is time to rise
> To bear witness
> To protect life.

After the initial preoccupation with political issues following the change of government, the Generation of 1966 generally concentrated on an exploration of "the existential significance of the world of nature, the difficulties of human relationships, and a wide range of personal experience," and did so well into the 1990s (Aveling 2001:xii).

The Generation of 1966 was followed by the "Post-Indonesian Generation," a second generation of writers whose work was marked by an interest in and the use of Islamic verse and by a relative "openness," especially toward the end of the 1980s (Aveling 2001:225). Harry Aveling speaks of the "renewal of Islam" and "the emergence of a new group of Muslim poets," such as Emha Ainum Nadjib (1953–), Ahmadun Yosi Herfada (1956–), and Acap Zamzam Noor (1960–), as well as the confrontational openness of Dorothea Rosa Herliany (1963–) and the intellectual work of Toeti Heraty (1937–). It is this generation of writers who Aveling hopes "will continue to write in different and more complex ways in the new millennium" (2001:276).

Drama. Indonesia probably has the oldest and most revered indigenous plays in Southeast Asia, in the form of *wayang* (shadow puppet), a term for various theatrical forms found mostly in Java, Bali, and Sunda, major islands of Indonesia. A *dalang* (puppeteer) manipulates leather or wooden puppets while narrating a story, generally an episode from the Mahabharata or the Ramayana, to the musical accompaniment of the *gamelan,* an orchestra of percussion instruments. Each play generally lasts for nine hours, has five character types, including the clown-servant, and an established dramatic structure that the *dalang* follows assiduously. It uses Kawi (Old-Javanese), with some Sanskrit and colloquial language, following sociolinguistic rules dependent on the characters in the *wayang*. Thus, there are several levels of expressing politeness, depending on the character types, frequent honorifics, and titles. The clown-servant type, who has the most freedom in language use, may use Bahasa Indonesia, or even borrow foreign words and phrases, including English, as the *dalang* sees fit.

A traditional wooden
puppet from Indonesia.

Paulus Rusyanto. Image from BigStockPhoto.com.

The *wayang kulit* (shadow puppet drama) used to be performed at auspi-
cious occasions, such as harvests, births, and marriages, at the request of a pa-
tron, rather than in regular theaters, but the more recent *wayang topeng*
(masked human performers) and *wayang orang* (unmasked human performers) are performed today in commercial theaters, basically for tourists.

It is a big leap from the *wayang* to W. S. Rendra, the poet whose social consciousness turned to political activism in the 1970s. Preceded by older poets who
were also playwrights—such as Effendi (who wrote *Bebasair* [Free] in 1926, an
allegorical play about the abduction of Princess Bebasari [Indonesia] by Rawana
[Holland] and rescued by Buyangga [Indonesian youth]), Sanusi Pané (whose
ideal man in *Manusia Baru* [New Man], written in 1960, is the synthesis of East
and West), and Utuy Tatang Sontani (regarded as "the father of Indonesian realistic drama" [Brandon 1993:131])—Rendra challenged the previous literary tradition and created and produced innovative and politicized plays. Starting with
Bip Bop in 1968, his innovations in theater include productions of Western plays
with *wayang* elements, such as his introduction of the clown in Beckett's *Waiting for Godot* (1969), or his use of Balinese masks and costumes in Sophocles'
Oedipus Rex (1969). His explicitly political play *The Struggle of the Naga Tribe*
(1970), produced in the framework of the *wayang kulit,* landed him a six-month
detention in 1978 and a seven-year ban from the stage.

Another playwright who used traditional forms was Arifin Noer
(1941–1995), whose *Kapai-kapai* (Moths, 1970), "the best known of all mod-

ern Southeast Asian plays" (Brandon 1993:182), and *Sumur Tanpa Dasar* (The Bottomless Well, 1971) have both been translated into English; the latter was performed by the company Noer in the United States in 1992. Arifin also works in film, as do other playwrights like Putu Wiyaya (1944–) and Teguli Karya. There are several native theater companies in Indonesia, including Rendra's Bangkel Teater (Jogjakarta), Teater Koma (Jakarta), and Teater Ganduk (Yogyakarta), most of which continue to deal with political and social issues and themes. There is an active "theater of liberation" in the country, with playwrights actively teaching young people in towns and villages how to create plays of social conscience and political responsibility.

From the *wayang,* with its ultimate fusion of dance, music, drama, and spectacle and its stylized, formal structure, to the contemporary play, with its fusion of *wayang* elements and Western autonomy of the arts, and from ancestral, traditional themes to politicized and nationalistic definitions of identity, Indonesian drama seems to be evolving into an original fusion of East and West.

Malaysia and Singapore

Until 1965, Malaysia and Singapore were intimately intertwined, historically, politically, culturally, and ethnically. From 1826 to 1957, both Malaysia (formerly Malaya) and Singapore were part of the British Straits Settlements. Malaya became the independent Federation of Malaya in 1957, and Singapore became self-governing in 1959. The two joined to form the Malayan Federation in 1963, though they split into two separate states just two years later. Both countries are multiracial and multicultural. Their populations are Malay, Chinese, and Indian (mostly Tamil), all of whom have their own literary traditions, out of which the countries' present-day literatures have developed.

Poetry in English. A cursory examination of almost any bibliography or catalog of Malaysian and Singaporean literary production generally reveals the dominance of poetry over other genres, at least in terms of output. Koh Tai Ann comments that "it is poetry in English that has been privileged and universalised as the expressive vehicle of national identity and situated firmly in the first rank (Koh 1994:67). She writes that "the existing prose work in English is generally lacking literary merit compared to the fairly sophisticated body of poetry in English" (Koh 1981:177).

The "privileged status" of poetry started mostly as student work at the University of Malaya in Singapore shortly after World War II, when the surge of nationalism and clamor for independence from over 130 years of British rule became stronger than ever. The nationalist fervor took many forms and awakened social consciousness, especially to an awareness that English was part of a Eurocentric education with Western assumptions and perceptions. Among the most vocal and productive of the young poets at the time was Edwin Thumboo (1933–). His poem "May 1954" (1988:132–133) encapsulates this nationalism and declares the first challenge to and abrogation of the English language. Addressing the "white man," he wrote:

> Depart:
> You knew when to come;
> Surely know when to go.
> . . .
> We know your language.

The conquest of English in Malaysia and Singapore was undertaken with exuberance and determination. Some poets plunged into a conscientious study of native cultural images to be expressed in English syntax and lexicon; others delved into the intricacies of the English language itself and strove toward complete mastery over it.

One of the leading poets of the 1950s was Ee Tiang Hong (1933–1990). He was not as confrontational as Thumboo, but commented quietly on the colonizers' assumed proprietorship of English: "So you write your poems—in English?" someone, presumably an Englishman, asks him in his short poem "O to Be in England" (Thumboo 1973). According to Thumboo, Ee's "exacting craftsmanship" included a penetrating look at the multiethnic issues of his time, and analyzes the Malaysian Baba and questions of migrant identity in Malaysia. Of Chinese descent but Malaysian in outlook, Ee explored questions of identity, assimilation, linguistic hegemony, and modernization. Another poet of this time period was Muhammad Haji Salleh (1942–), who dealt with aspects of Malay culture and tradition and aspects of village life and its character. Not unlike Ee, he too wrote of migration and his personal history and ancestry.

Most of the poets before the mid-1960s were men, but a few were women, among them Wong May, Lee Tzu Pheng (1946–), Hilary Tham (1947–2005), and Chung Yee Cheng. These poets brought to poetry a more personal sensibility, even as they participated in some of the common issues of the day. Combining issues of personal history, multiethnicity, and linguistic hegemony, Lee Tzu Pheng wrote (quoted in Thumboo 1976:161–162):

> My country and my people
> I never understood.
> I grew up in China's mighty shadow,
> with my gentle, brown-skinned neighbors
> but I keep diaries in English.

In the beginning, the appropriation of the English language was mostly devoted to mastery of its syntax, lexicon, and symbolic connotations. Gradually, writers realized that English was a native language for them that had molded their assumptions, perceptions, and perspectives, and that it was theirs to do with as they wanted. According to Ee Tiang Hong: "If the Malaysian writer cannot take some liberties with his adopted language, extend its connotative range, even suppress or distort its traditional associations, where the occasion warrants, and his expertise enables, then the legacy he has inherited from his erstwhile tutors must be of dubious value" (Ee 1988).

Prose fiction and drama in English. Although poetry may have been privileged as the primary genre expressing and defining Malaysian and Singaporean national identity, it is in the novel and the play that artists have "taken liberties" with English to its utmost, both as a literary device and as a political statement. The most famous of these artists include Catherine Lim (1942–), short-story writer and novelist, and Stella Kon (1944–), playwright and novelist. Lim started her career with short stories. In 1978 she published *Little Ironies: Stories of Singapore.* In this collection of seventeen short stories, Lim's triumph over the English language is very quietly but beautifully understated, especially in "The Taximan's Story," a short-story monologue told completely in a subvariety of Singaporean English by a taxicab driver. The driver tells his silent passenger about himself, his family, and his experiences as a taxicab driver, especially about teenage girls who prostitute themselves to tourists after school without their parents' knowledge. Lim uses differences in the educational levels of her characters to display her mastery over the English language, as in "A. P. Velloo" and "The Teachers." Structural simplifications that characterize the subvarieties of Singaporean English include the omission of the word *be,* for example, and the omission of the past-tense or present-tense marker after a singular subject, which are all found in the taxi driver's speech.

Catherine Lim's first novel was *The Serpent's Tooth* (1982), but her second, *The Bondmaid* (1990), is better known and more easily accessible. Rich in the use of Chinese folklore, superstitions, and stories about gods, it grimly introduces a Chinese family of several children whose poverty forces the mother to sell her four-year-old daughter Han into servitude to the House of Wu, a rich family with a five-year-old son. The novel follows the wealthy family's filial and religious traditions and culminates in a passionate but tragic love affair between Han, now grown into a beautiful young woman, and Master Wu, the handsome, educated son of the family. *The Bondmaid* is more than merely a tragic poor girl–rich boy romance; it is a critique of the exploitation of the powerlessness of children by parents, servants by masters, churchgoers by their ministers. It is also a reexamination of the Chinese traditional arranged marriage and concubinage.

Stella Kon, playwright and novelist, is another important Singaporean writer in English today. Her monodrama *Emily of Emerald Hill* (2001), about a strong-willed Chinese *pernakan nonya* (lady looking back at her life), best illustrates Singaporean English. Emily, the main and only character, converses with various unseen characters, from a baker to a driver, from her son to her best friend, to her sister-in-law and her party guests. She even addresses the audience directly at times. As each interlocutor changes, so does Emily's speech, shifting from one subvariety of Singaporean English to another as the situations shift, from playful to angry to tragic, climaxed by a scene in which Emily receives news of her son's suicide in England.

Until the 1970s, before such novelists as Catherine Lim and Stella Kon, in both Malaysia and Singapore "there [was] not enough either collectively or by any single author from which to select a canon" of English-language writings, according to Tham Seong Chee in his book *Essays on Literature and Society in Southeast Asia* (1981). Probably contributing to this state of writing in English in Malaysia (but not in Singapore, which officially became independent of Malaysia in 1967) was the official declaration, in the late 1960s, of Bahasa Malay as the official language of Malaysia. Henceforth, only literary production in Malay was considered part of the national literature. All other creative works in English, Chinese, Tamil, and other minority languages were considered "sectional literature" and were ineligible to enter literary competitions and win prizes and awards. There were vocal protests against what was perceived as Malay hegemony stemming from these official declarations. The protests came from deeply committed writers in English, such as Ee Tiang Hong, whose native tongue was Pernakan Malay, a marketplace variant of the Malay language. In defense of the use of English, Ee declared that writers "can no more surrender their language now than they can renounce part of themselves, the only tool they have. For most of them, the motivation is not one of nostalgia for things past, still less a colonial 'cultural cringe,' but the national wish to write in the best way they can, using whatever language they please, or what they feel comfortable with" (Ee 1988:21).

The bitter debate was not merely about the medium used in literary works, but also about their content. One group of writers was of the opinion that only works in Malay, on Malay themes, constituted Malay literature, while another group was more linguistically pluralism-oriented.

A positive result of this hegemonic Malay policy may be what Tahir Ungku Maimunah Mohd considers "the heyday of Malay novels" in the 1960s, a period when there was a strong demand for reading materials in Malay. The demand was partly answered by numerous female novelists whose works appeared in magazines and weeklies. The "orientation towards the 'domestic scene,' its perceived viability and continued relevance," was common among the writers. The literary production at this time, however, was still dominated by male writers. According to Tahir, about 10 percent of novels in the 1960s and 1970s were authored by women (Tahir 1995:27).

Malaysia opted for a national language for its national literature. This monolingualism has dampened creative production in the other languages spoken by its multicultural and linguistically diverse population, but has encouraged and nurtured writing in Malay. In contrast, Singapore has opted for multilingualism, encouraging the use of English and other languages spoken in the city-state. Writers have been responsive. The first novel in English was published in 1973, by Goh Poh Seng (1936–), called *If We Dream Too Long.* The first novel by a woman was written by Minfong Ho (1951–) in 1975. Catherine Lim, discussed earlier, came about ten years later. Stella Kon's novel, *The Scholar and the Dragon,* was published in 1986, and her prize-winning novel *Elton* in 2001. Creative writing in English continues to be produced vigorously at the same time that other authors continue writing in their native languages.

Philippines
Spanish colonial rule in the Philippines lasted nearly four centuries, from 1521 to 1898, US rule from 1898 to 1946, and Japanese occupation from 1943 to 1945. US teachers landed on Philippine soil almost simultaneously with US soldiers, to teach English to Filipinos. Unlike the Spanish colonizers, who withheld their language from the Filipinos until late in the nineteenth century, the United States dispensed its language openly throughout the country, achieving perhaps one of the most thorough and successful colonizations of the mind, in the shortest amount of time, in the history of colonialism.

From the very beginning of Philippine writing in English, the use of native themes, experiences, and images was never an issue with the writers, but was perceived as natural. This view was encouraged by their earliest mentors, Dean Fansler and Harriet Fansler, US professors who joined the University of the Philippines almost as soon as it was founded in 1908. The Fanslers urged the budding writers "to look at their own people with pride, with unprejudiced eyes; to study their native customs, to applaud their own folk-wisdom to collect and record basic material as a store for future historians, anthropologists and writers." With several recognized predecessors who wrote in Spanish on themes Philippine, it did not seem necessary for the Fanslers to have "cautioned them not to ape indiscriminately the English and American writers that they were studying, and counseled them to write of their people truthfully and well" (Serrano and Ames 1975:22).

Thus, writing in English was not perceived as incompatible with nationalistic desire and need for a national language. It developed side by side with writing in the native languages, published mostly in weekly magazines. To Filipino writers, it was a matter of choosing the language they were most comfortable with, not what language was more faithful to the native culture or to the nationalist endeavors, both of which could be achieved in either English or the native languages.

Mastery of the English language, therefore, was the main concern of the early writers. Mastery did not come quickly, but by the mid-1930s and early 1940s, writers had gained full control of the English language and could manipulate it successfully as a literary medium (Serrano and Ames 1975:124).

Unlike their counterparts in Singapore and Malaysia, Filipino writers did not participate actively in the discussion of appropriation of the English language until the 1970s, the period of student activism during the time of Philippine dictator Ferdinand Marcos.

Poetry. Early Philippine poetry was mostly lyrical, imitative of US and British classroom models, probably because the Thomasites (the first US teachers in the Philippines, who arrived on the USS *Thomas,* hence the appellation) chose to teach not the liberal and liberating works of Walt Whitman and Henry David Thoreau but the "saccharine poetry" of Edgar Allan Poe and Henry Wadsworth Longfellow (Soliongco 1964).

Romantic and Victorian traditions of writing became prevalent and proceeded well into the late 1950s and 1960s, despite the work of José García Villa (1908–1997), the best known of the poets of this time, who introduced Whitman to the Philippines and wrote like Whitman and later like E. E. Cummings, with whom he formed a friendship while in the United States. The standards of "new criticism" were introduced by US writers who traveled to the Philippines, such as Ernest Hemingway in 1949, Wallace Stegner in 1950, and William Faulkner in 1956, and by Filipino writers who attended US institutions on scholarship, like the University of Iowa through its writing workshops, and then returned home to influence other writers.

Ricaredo Demetillo (1920–1998), in his epic poem "Barter in Panay," wedded English language and metrics on the one hand with native oral tradition on the other: by using the pre-Hispanic epic "Maragtas," he created a model for younger poets to produce longer work. Later poets were influenced either by third world poets like Pablo Neruda and Octavio Paz or by "the lyrical-realist mode . . . of American writing, spawned by imagism and neo-Aristotelianism" (Abad n.d.).

Poets and other writers became preoccupied with their craft, following "new criticism" injunctions on form and craftsmanship. However, the ivory-tower insistence on self-expression and the responsibility-to-self approach gave way to social realities during the Marcos dictatorship. Writers had to simultaneously confront two issues that they had not directly acknowledged in a long time: the place and importance of language in one's creative production and the need to call attention to social injustice and repression. Several poets turned to writing poetry in their native languages at this time.

Perhaps as a result of the tumultuous 1970s, after Marcos was deposed, and the early 1980s, the question of language has now become more prominent, not so much how to deal with English per se, which, after all, has been fully mastered and has been assumed to be a natural vehicle for artistic creation, but whether to use it at all rather than the national language. The question becomes very much like the Achebe-Ngugi debate in Africa. Compare this with Ngugi's passionate assertion that struggling oppressed colonials of all nations have to wield firmly the weapons of the struggle contained in their languages: "The poet writing in English . . . may not be completely aware that to do so is to exclude himself from certain subjects, themes, ideas, values, and modes of thinking and feeling in many segments of the national life that are better expressed—in fact, in most cases, can only be expressed—in the vernacular" (quoted in Abad and Hidalgo 1996:3).

Other poets and writers did not share this view, naturally, resulting in a "schism between writers writing in English, on the one hand, and those whose brand of nationalism demanded that they write in their own tongue, Filipino, on the other" (Pantoja 2002). Partly a consequence of the call for native writing, creative literary production in the major languages in the Philippines, whether novel or short story, poem or play, continues to be vigorous. Poets like Alejandro Hufana (1926–2003), a devout "new criticism" disciple of the 1960s, turned to writing in Ilocano. There are, of course, several important writers who have not written in English at all, but who continue to produce work in their respective native languages. One outcome of the demand in the 1970s for vernacularization in literature has been the native translation of several Western plays.

The play. The play has been the least popular among the different genres, from the earliest period of Filipino writing in English to the present. Early plays were mostly historical, based perhaps on the lives of heroes or incidents during the revolution. Later playwrights used more contemporary themes, like Wilfrido Ma. Guerrero (1911–1995), who wrote either about social ills in society or about Filipino middle-class intellectuals coping with Americanization (Lumbera 1997). Nick Joaquin (1917–2004) combined traditions of Filipino pre-Hispanic and Hispanic pasts with American contemporaneity in his work. Joaquin's best-known play, *Portrait of the Artist as Filipino* (1954), looks at a family who is clinging to Spanish traditions as these are gradually disintegrating in the face of modernization.

Perhaps as part of the awakening responsibility to society for the artist to reach the largest audience possible, and definitely as a consequence of the debate on language (as discussed earlier), some playwrights have shifted from English to their native languages. Leading the playwrights in this shift is Alberto Florentino (1931–2001), creator of *The World Is an Apple and Other Short Plays* (1959), who turned to Tagalog playwriting in the 1970s (Lumbera 1997:45). Amelia Lapena-Bonifacio, who started as a playwright with her award-winning play *Sepang Loka,* now writes in Tagalog. An indirect result of the weakness in playwriting in English is the translation of several plays by playwrights from around the world into Philippine languages, for example, Tennessee Williams's *The Glass Menagerie,* Federico García Lorca's *The House of Bernardo Alba,* Samuel Beckett's *Waiting for Godot,* and some of William Shakespeare's dramas, all translated by Rolando S. Tinio (1937–1997), a highly regarded English and Tagalog playwright in his own right.

Prose fiction. Paz Marquez Benitez (1894–1983) was one of the early Filipino short-story writers, and is recognized even today as a writer whose mastery of form was better than any writer of her day. Her story "Dead Stars" captures Filipino cultural traditions and values in courtship and marriage; in the story, Alfredo marries Esperanza, the unattainable, but longs for Julia, the real, a woman he met one summer. Prominent short-story writers since the days of Paz Marquez Benitez include Francisco Arcellana (1916–2002), Kerima Polotan, Amador Daguio (1912–1966), and Manuel Arguilla (1910–1944). Arguilla is noted for being unequaled in his ability to create "local color" in his stories and his ability to use English "like a Filipino dialect." His best-known short story, "How My Brother Leon Brought Home a Wife," is widely anthologized and still acknowledged as the best-constructed model of how English could be molded to embody the Filipino rural spirit.

The novel. One astonishing quality of Philippine writing in English is the versatility of its writers, most of whom worked in more than one or two genres, much like Indonesia's W. S. Rendra. For example, Nick Joaquin was a short-story writer, playwright, novelist, essayist, and also a poet. José García Villa, recognized as a poet, also wrote short stories. Three major writers—N. V. M. Gonzalez (1915–1999), Bienvenido Santos (1911–1996), and Francisco Sionil José (1924–)—wrote both short stories and novels, as well as some poetry, and critics praise equally their writing in all genres.

N. V. M. Gonzalez, dean of Philippine letters, started writing in the 1940s and continued writing in English until his death in 1999. He wrote several collections of short stories, among them *Children of the Ash-Covered Loam* (1954), *Look Stranger on an Island Now* (1963), and *Bread of Salt and Other Stories* (1993). Most mentioned among his short stories are "A Warm Hand," "Bread of Salt," and "Hunger in Barok."

A close scrutiny of his numerous stories and his novels, *Bamboo Dancers* (1953) and *A Season of Grace* (1963), reveals that Gonzalez exploited and innovated, usually accepted but often defied or challenged, the rules of the English language. His work includes use of several of the processes displayed in Malaysian and Singaporean writing, processes that exploit standard English structures, such as combining native with English terminology and creating hybridized vocabulary (e.g., "tuba-yielding trees," "palay-filled baskets"), and compounding words, which results from condensation (e.g., "kaingin-burning," "tuba-gatherers"). His syntax is marked by several noticeably frequent constructions: inversion (e.g., "farther away glimmered the light from Grandmother's window"), nominalized constructions (e.g., "all I had been able to tell him was that I had my school work in mind"), and cleft and pseudocleft constructions (e.g., "that he did now know who the women were pleased him"). His work is also characterized by its frequent use of periodicity, by which sentences build toward their last words.

Gonzalez's seeming fondness for these constructions—inversion, nominalization, cleft and pseudocleft, and periodicity—might be explained partly by the nature of focus and emphasis in Philippine languages. While focus and emphasis are generally expressed by stress in English, without a change in the structure of the sentence, the usual way in Philippine languages is by inversion of the normal Philippine verb-object-subject word order. Because of this structural noncorrespondence between the two languages, Gonzalez resorted to infrequently used structures in English to express ideas and create images generally expressible in what is structurally natural in Philippine languages.

Bamboo Dancers recounts the odyssey of Gonzalez's protagonist as a government scholar to the United States and his personal, inner development as he meets others like and unlike him. Gonzalez's more memorable work can be found in his short stories, however. Strongly influenced by the "new criticism" pervading the American literary world at the time, he was a craftsman who worked painstakingly on both plot and character, writing of the hardships of the farmer and the struggles of the poor and the oppressed.

The other most commonly acknowledged fictionist in the Philippines is Bienvenido Santos. Unlike Gonzalez, who acknowledged awareness of the language question but did not deal with it directly in any of his writing, Santos created characters who dealt with the language issue in different ways. In "The Wise Man Who Was Not There," the first story in the collection *You Lovely People* (1953), one of his characters asks a Filipino writer, "Why must you write in English? It's the worst language in the world for telling the truth. Besides, haven't you got a language of your own?"

The question remains unanswered, but Santos dealt with it indirectly, in the many ways his characters talk about the English language and the ways they use it. In his novel *Villa Magdalena* (1986), he informs the reader, through the story's protagonist, of differences between English and his native language; the protagonist tells his father of what he is learning in English at school. In the short story "Woman Afraid," from the collection *A Scent of Apples* (1954), Santos comments on the language differences by describing the native language and using a variant of English to make a comparison.

Santos deployed English similarly to Gonzalez, using native vocabulary when appropriate, creating native imagery, making utmost use of the creative English derivational processes, and exploiting periodic sentences as well as inversions. Even as he created within the structural bounds of his borrowed language, Santos exploited differences in the English register in much of his work, not too different from Singapore's Stella Kon. One of Santos's characters, Ambo, tells stories "in the dialect," and the English rendering of his speech is florid and sentimental, to show the author's attempt to represent the "dialect." Ambo's speech in English, however, is characterized by simple sentences and idiomatic expressions. In contrast, another character, Ben, who is highly educated, uses an English characterized by much embedding and periodicity.

Santos's mastery over English discourse differs from Kon's in the latter's novel *Emily of Emerald Hill*. He manipulated English not by using attested subvarieties of the language, but by taking advantage of its varied sentence structures and vocabulary, to distinguish registers from one another. His writing goes from colloquial to informal to formal. Both techniques illustrate how English as a tool of struggle has served its purpose well to fight its hegemonic control over those it has dominated. In some of his writing, Santos reproduced a variety of English spoken by elderly Filipinos in the United States, an interlanguage representative of an incompletely acquired foreign language that has fossilized with time.

Francisco Sionil José is another internationally recognized Filipino writer in English. He is best known for his Rosales saga, a series of five novels that record Philippine history, from colonization to the Hukbalahap movement, to Ferdinand Marcos's dictatorship to the present. The Rosales saga starts with *Dusk* (1992; originally titled *Poon* and written last among the novels), which details Estaquio (Istak) Samson's family history of poverty and flight from oppression by the Spanish clergy in a language that is both imagery-laden and emotionally controlled. It follows Istak's life, from his boyhood in the service of the town parish priest into the armed revolution against Spain and the coming of the Americans. To indict the agents of oppression and social injustice, Sionil José contrasts characters whose awareness of social issues surrounding them is almost nil and pathetic (*Tree,* 1978) with others whose awareness and commitment to fight social injustice are total and complete. The characters range from colonial oppressors (*Dusk*) to landed *illustrados* who have inherited land and acquired their colonial masters' oppressive, exploitive ways toward their rural *kasama,* or tenants (*Tree,* 1978; *My Brother, My Executioner,* 1976; *The Pretenders,* 1962). *Mass* (1991) brings the Rosales saga to a climax in a contemporary period of political corruption and self-interest. The exploitation of the masses and the abuse of power for purposes of self-aggrandizement and acquiring more power are no longer seen as consequences of foreign exploitation, but as an endemic illness in a society where violence seems to be the only way out.

Among the many collections of Sionil José's short stories are *God Stealer and Other Stories* (1983), *Waywaya: Eleven Filipino Short Stories* (1985), *Olvidon and Other Stories* (1988), and *Puppy Love and Thirteen Short Stories* (1998).

Despite the large number of short-story writers in the Philippines, very few have sustained themselves as long and as consistently as have N. V. M. Gonzalez, Bienvenido Santos, and Francisco Sionil José. All three started writing just before the coming of the Japanese in the 1940s, went on to study in the United States after the war, and continued writing uninterruptedly for decades. All three wrote sizable collections of short stories. All three continued writing during the age of repression under Marcos, but Gonzalez and Santos did so at a distance, teaching in US universities. Sionil José remained in the Philippines, balancing his writing between being assertively vocal enough to be heard and tame enough to keep himself out of jail. Several writers who chose to be activists either were jailed or went underground. As previously mentioned, several Filipino writers in English reverted to writing in their native languages at this time. Gonzalez, a short time before his death, was reported to have said that writers should write in their native languages. Sionil José laments the fact that he cannot write in his native Ilokano as he continues to write in English.

The future of Philippine writing in English is uncertain, as more and more of the younger authors opt to write in their native languages. Whatever the eventual outcome, the Filipino writers in English will always retain their important place in Philippine literature. They remain creative and active, seeking to find their place among writers of the world, re-creating and restructuring English to their purposes in almost gleeful vengeance.

Conclusion

Is there a canon in the English-language literatures of Southeast Asia? The idea of "canon" implies several presuppositions, most of which rest on Western criteria of significance and literary value, which differ from non-Western evaluation criteria. Rather than refer to a "canon," it would be more appropriate to look at writers who have gained recognition in their countries and abroad.

In Philippine literature in English: N. V. M. Gonzalez for the short story. In Indonesian literature in English: Pramoedya Ananta Toer and Mochtar Lubis for the novel, Chairil Anwar for poetry, and W. S. Rendra for poetry and drama (though there are several young writers following close behind them). In Malaysian and Singaporean literature in English: Edwin Thumboo and Ee Tiang Hong for poetry, Catherine Lim for the novel, and Stella Kon for playwriting. In all four countries, creativity continues to flow.

■ Bibliography

General

Bernad, Miguel. 1991. *Conversations with F. Sionil José.* Quezon City: Vera Reyes.
Biddle, Arthur W., Gloria Bien, and Vinay Dhanwadker. 1996. *Contemporary Literature of Asia.* Englewood Cliffs, N.J.: Prentice Hall.
Brandon, James R. 1967. *Theatre in Southeast Asia.* Cambridge: Harvard University Press.
———, ed. 1970. *On Thrones of Gold: Three Javanese Shadow Plays.* Cambridge: Harvard University Press.
———. 1993. *The Cambridge Guide to Asian Theatre.* Cambridge: Cambridge University Press.
Herbert, Patricia, and Anthony Milner. 1989. *Southeast Asian Languages and Literatures: A Select Guide.* Honolulu: University of Hawaii Press.

Kachru, B. 1992. *The Other Englishes: English Across Cultures.* Urbana: University of Illinois Press.

Kintanar, Thelma B. 1994. *Emergent Voices: Southeast Asian Women Novelists.* Quezon City: University of the Philippines Press.

Kratz, Ulrich E. 1996. *Southeast Asian Languages and Literatures: A Bibliographic Guide to Burmese, Cambodian, Indonesian, Javanese, Malay, Minangkabu, Thai, and Vietnamese.* London: Tauris.

Lim, Shirley Geok-lim. 1998. *Writing Southeast/Asian English: Against the Grain.* London: Skoob.

Loh, C. Y., and I. K. Ong, eds. 1994. *The Pen Is Mightier Than the Sword.* Skoob Pacifica Anthology no. 2. London: Skoob.

Mostow, Joshua, ed. 2003. *The Columbia Companion to Modern East Asian Literature.* New York: Columbia University Press.

Roskies, D. M. 1993. *Text/Politics in Island Southeast Asia: Essays in Interpretation.* Athens: Ohio University Center for International Studies.

Said, Edward. 1978. *Orientalism.* New York: Vintage.

Singh, Kirpal. 1987. *The Writer's Sense of the Past: Essays on Southeast Asian and Australian Literature.* Singapore: Singapore University Press.

Tam Kwok-kan, Terry Siu-han Yip, and Wimal Dissanayake, eds. 1999. *A Place of One's Own: Stories of Self in China, Taiwan, Hong Kong, and Singapore.* Oxford: Oxford University Press.

Tham Seong Chee, ed. 1981. *Essays on Literature and Society in Southeast Asia: Political and Sociological Perspectives.* Singapore: Singapore University Press.

Thumboo, Edwin, ed. 1988. *Literature and Liberation: Five Essays from Southeast Asia.* Manila: Solidaridad Publishing House.

Yamada, Teri Shaffer, ed. 2002. *Virtual Lotus: Modern Fiction of Southeast Asia.* Ann Arbor: University of Michigan Press.

China and Taiwan

Barlow, Tani E., and Gary J. Bjorge, eds. 1989. *I Myself Am a Woman: Selected Writings of Ding Ling.* Boston: Beacon.

Barnstone, Tony, ed. 1993. *Out of the Howling Storm: The New Chinese Poetry.* Hanover: Wesleyan University Press.

Bei Dao. 1988. *The August Sleepwalker.* Translated by Bonnie S. McDougall. London: Anvil.

Can Xue. 1991. *Old Floating Cloud: Two Novellas.* Translated by Ronald R. Janssen and Jian Zhang. Evanston: Northwestern University Press.

Chen Jo-hsi. 1978. *The Execution of Mayor Yin and Other Stories from the Great Proletarian Cultural Revolution.* Translated by Nancy Ing and Howard Goldblatt. Bloomington: University of Indiana Press.

Gao Xingjian. 1999. *The Other Shore: Plays.* Translated by Gilbert C. F. Fong. Hong Kong: Chinese University Press.

———. 2000. *Soul Mountain.* Translated by Mabel Lee. New York: HarperCollins.

Giskin, Howard, and Bettye S. Walsh. 2001. *An Introduction to Chinese Culture Through the Family.* Albany: State University of New York Press.

Goldblatt, Howard, ed. 1995. *Chairman Mao Would Not Be Amused: Fiction from Today's China.* New York: Grove.

Hsiau A-chin. 2000. *Contemporary Taiwanese Cultural Nationalism.* London: Routledge.

Lao She. 1979. *Rickshaw: The Novel Lo-t'o Hsiang Tzu.* Translated by Jean M. James. Honolulu: University of Hawaii Press.

Lu Xun. 1981. *The Complete Stories of Lu Xun.* Translated by Yang Xianyi and Gladys Yang. Bloomington: Indiana University Press.

McDougall, Bonnie S., and Kam Louie. 1997. *The Literature of China in the Twentieth Century.* New York: Columbia University Press.

Mo Yan. 1993. *Red Sorghum: A Novel of China.* Translated by Howard Goldblatt. New York: Viking.

Perng Ching-hsi and Wang Chiu-kuei, eds. 1994. *Death in a Cornfield and Other Stories from Contemporary Taiwan.* Hong Kong: Oxford University Press.

Su Tong. 1993. *Raise the Red Lantern: Three Novellas.* Translated by Michael S. Duke. New York: William Morrow.

Tie Ning. 1990. *Haystacks.* Beijing: Panda.

Wang, David Der-wei, and Jeanne Tai, eds. 1994. *Running Wild: New Chinese Writers.* New York: Columbia University Press.

Wang Meng. 1983. *The Butterfly and Other Stories.* Translated by Rui An. Beijing: Panda Books.

———. 1994. *The Stubborn Porridge and Other Stories.* Translated by Zhu Hong et al. New York: George Braziller.

Wang Shuo. 1997. *Playing for Thrills: A Mystery.* Translated by Howard Goldblatt. New York: William Morrow.

Wang Wen-hsing. 1995. *Family Catastrophe.* Translated by Susan Wan Dolling. Honolulu: University of Hawaii Press.

Yu Hua. 1996. *The Past and the Punishments.* Translated by Andrew F. Jones. Honolulu: University of Hawaii Press.

Indonesia

Anwar, Chairil. n.d. *Selected Poems.* Translated by Burton Raffel and Nurdin Salam. New York: New Directions.

Aveling, Harry, ed. and trans. 1976. *From Surabaya to Armageddon: Indonesian Short Stories.* Singapore: Heinemann.

———. 2001. *Secrets Need Words: Indonesian Poetry, 1966–1998.* Athens: Ohio University Center for International Studies.

Geertz, Clifford. 1968. "Linguistic Etiquette." In Joshua Fishman, ed., *Readings in the Sociology of Language,* pp. 282–295. The Hague: Mouton.

Hatley, Barbara. 1999. "Cultural Expression and Social Transformation in Indonesia." In Arief Budiman, Barbara Hatley, and Damien Kingsbury, eds., *Reformasi Crisis and Change in Indonesia,* pp. 267–286. Clayton, Australia: Monash Asia.

Heraty, Toeti. 1994. "Women's Issues in a Patriarchal Society: Novels by Indonesian Women." In Thelma B. Kintanar, ed., *Emergent Voices: Southeast Asian Women Novelists,* pp. 121–165. Quezon City: University of the Philippines Press.

Lingard, Jeannette, trans. 1995. *Diverse Lives: Contemporary Stories from Indonesia.* Kuala Lumpur: Oxford University Press.

Lubis, Mochtar. 1968. *Twilight in Djakarta.* Translated by Claire Holt. New York: Vantage.

———. 1988. "Literature and Liberation: An Awareness of Self and Society." In Edwin Thumboo, ed., *Literature and Liberation: Five Essays from Southeast Asia,* pp. 71–104. Manila: Solidaridad.

———. 1991. "Art and Freedom." In Miguel Bernad, *Conversations with F. Sionil José,* pp. 138–175. Quezon City: Vera Reyes.

McGlynn, John H., and E. U. Kratz. 1990. *Walking Westward in the Morning: Seven Contemporary Indonesia Poets.* Introduction by Muhammad Haji Salleh. Indonesia: Lontar.

Pramoedya, Ananta Toer. 1996a. *Child of All Nations.* Translated with an introduction by Max Lane. New York: Penguin.

———. 1996b. *Footsteps.* Translated with an introduction by Max Lane. New York: Penguin.

———. 1996c. *House of Glass.* Translated with an introduction by Max Lane. New York: Penguin.

———. 1996d. *This Earth of Mankind.* Translated with an introduction by Max Lane. New York: Penguin.

———. 1999. *The Mute's Soliloquy: A Memoir.* Translated by Willem Samuels. New York: Hyperion East.

Raffel, Burton. 1964. *Anthology of Modern Indonesian Poetry.* Berkeley: University of California Press.

———. 1967. *The Development of Modern Indonesian Poetry.* New York: State University of New York Press.

———, ed. and trans. 1970. *The Complete Poetry and Prose of Chairil Anwar.* Albany: State University of New York Press.

Rendra, W. S. 1974. *Ballads and Blues: Poems Translated from Indonesia.* Translated by Burton Raffel, Harry Aveling, and Derwent May. Kuala Lumpur: Oxford University Press.

Tham Seong Chee. 1981. "The Social and Intellectual Ideas of Indonesian Writers, 1920–1940." In Tham Seong Chee, ed., *Essays on Literature and Society in Southeast Asia: Political and Sociological Perspectives,* pp. 97–124. Singapore: Singapore University Press.

Japan

Ariyoshi, Sawako. 1978. *The Doctor's Wife.* Translated by Wakako Hronaka and Ann Siller Kostant. Tokyo: Kodansha.

———. 1984. *The Twilight Years.* Translated by Mildred Tahara. Tokyo: Kodansha.

Enchi, Fumiko. 1971. *The Waiting Years.* Translated by John Bester. Tokyo: Kodansha.

———. 1983. *Masks.* Translated by Juliet Winters Carpenter. New York: Vintage.

Gregory, Sinda, Toshifumi Miyawaki, and Larry McCaffery. 2002. "It Don't Mean a Thing, If It Ain't Got That Swing: An Interview with Haruki Murakami." Dalkey Archive.

Ibuse, Massuji. 1969. *Black Rain.* Translated by John Bester. Tokyo: Kodansha.

———. 1987. *Castaways: Two Short Novels.* Translated by Anthony Liman and David Aylward. Tokyo: Kodansha.

Inoue, Yasushi. 1979. *Lou-lan and Other Stories.* Translated by James T. Araki and Edward Seidensticker. Tokyo: Kodansha.

———. 1991. *Shirobamba: A Childhood in Old Japan.* Translated by Jean Oda Moy. New York: Weatherhill.

Iwanami, Go. 1998. "Inoue Hisashi's *Kamiya-cho Sakura Hotel.*" *Japanese Literature Today* 23: 74–78.

Kawabata, Yasunari. 1957. *Snow Country.* Translated by Edward G. Seidensticker. Tokyo: Tuttle.

Miyabe, Miyuki. 1996. *All She Was Worth.* Translated by Alfred Birnbaum. Boston: Houghton Mifflin.

Murakami, Haruki. 1997. *The Wind-Up Bird Chronicle.* Translated by Jay Rubin. New York: Vintage.

———. 2002. *After the Quake: Stories.* Translated by Jay Rubin. New York: Knopf.

Oe, Kenzaburo. 1969. *A Personal Matter.* New York: Grove.

————, ed. 1985. *The Crazy Iris and Other Stories of the Atomic Aftermath.* New York: Grove.

————. 1995. *Japan, the Ambiguous, and Myself: The Nobel Prize Speech and Other Lectures.* Translated by Kunioki Yanagishita. Tokyo: Kodansha.

Sato, Hiroaki, and Burton Watson, eds. and trans. 1986. *From the Country of Eight Islands: An Anthology of Japanese Poetry.* Introduction by Thomas Rimer. New York: Columbia University Press.

Shiraishi, Kazuko. 2002. *Let Those Who Appear.* Translated by Samuel Grolmes and Yumiko Tsumura. New York: New Directions.

Tanizaki, Jun'ichiro. 1957. *Makioka Sisters.* Translated by Edward G. Seidensticker. New York: Knopf.

Treat, John Whittier. 1995. *Writing Ground Zero: Japanese Literature and the Atomic Bomb.* Chicago: University of Chicago Press.

Tsushima, Yuko. 1983. *Child of Fortune.* Translated by Geraldine Harcourt. Tokyo: Kodansha.

————. 1988. *The Shooting Gallery.* Translated by Geraldine Harcourt. New York: Pantheon.

Yoshimoto, Banana. 1993. *Kitchen.* Translated by Megan Backus. London: Faber and Faber.

Yoshimura, Akira. 1996. *Shipwrecks.* Translated by Mark Ealey. San Diego: Harcourt.

————. 1999. *On Parole.* Translated by Stephen Snyder. San Diego: Harcourt.

————. 2001. *One Man's Justice.* Translated by Mark Ealey. New York: Harcourt.

Korea

Cho Sehui. 2002. *A Dwarf Launches a Little Ball.* Seoul: Jimoondang.

Epstein, Stephen. 2003. "Encountering North Korean Fiction: The Origins of the Future." http://www.wordswithoutborders.

Fulton, Bruce, and Ju-chan Fulton, eds. 1997. *Wayfarer: New Fiction by Korean Women.* Seattle: Women in Translation.

Grayson, James Huntley, and Agnita Tennant, eds. 1999. *Language, Culture, and Translation: Issues in the Translation of Modern Korean Literature.* Sheffield: School of East Asian Studies.

Hwang Sun-won. 1990. *Shadows of a Sound: Stories.* Edited by J. Martin Holman. San Francisco: Mercury.

Kim, Richard E. 1988. *Lost Names: Scenes from a Korean Boyhood.* Berkeley: University of California Press.

Lee, Peter H. 1990. *Modern Korean Literature: An Anthology.* Honolulu: University of Hawaii Press.

Sallee, Hyun-jae Yee, ed. 1993. *The Snowy Road and Other Stories: An Anthology of Korean Fiction.* Fredonia, N.Y.: White Pine.

So Chongju. 1989. *Selected Poems of So Chongju.* Edited and translated by David R. McCann. New York: Columbia University Press.

Malaysia and Singapore

Ee Tiang Hong. 1988. "Literature and Liberation: The Price of Freedom." In Edwin Thumboo, ed., *Literature and Liberation: Five Essays from Southeast Asia,* pp. 11–42. Manila: Solidaridad.

Fernandez, G. 1983. *Poets of Singapore: 81 Poems by 31 Poets.* Singapore: Society of Singapore Writers.

Fernando, Lloyd. 1964. *Twenty-two Malaysian Stories: An Anthology of Writing in English.* Singapore: Heinemann.

————. 1972. *New Drama One.* Kuala Lumpur: Oxford University Press.

————. 1988. *Malaysian Short Stories.* Singapore: Heinemann.

Koh Tai Ann. 1981. "Singapore Writing in English: The Literary Tradition and Cultural Identity." In Tham Seong Chee, ed., *Essays on Literature and Society in Southeast Asia: Political and Sociological Perspectives,* pp. 160–186. Singapore: Singapore University Press.

————. 1994. "Sing to the Dawn: Novels in English by Singaporean Women." In Thelma B. Kintanar, ed., *Emergent Voices: Southeast Asian Women Novelists,* pp. 66–79. Quezon City: University of the Philippines Press.

Kon, Stella. 1995. *Eston.* Singapore: EPB.

————. 2000. *The Immigrant and Other Plays.* Singapore: SNP.

————. 2002. *Emily of Emerald Hill: A One-Woman Play.* Singapore: Constellation.

Lim, Catherine. 1978. *Little Ironies: Stories from Singapore.* Kuala Lumpur: Heinemann.

————. 1980. *Or Else: The Lightning God and Other Stories.* Kuala Lumpur: Heinemann.

————. 1993. *The Woman's Book of Superlatives.* Singapore: Times Books International.

————. 1995. *The Bondmaid.* New York: Overlook.

Manian, K. S. 1995. *Haunting the Tiger.* London: Skoob.

Pakir, Anne. 1990. *Voices of Singapore: Multilingual Poetry and Prose.* Singapore: National University of Singapore Press.

Rajah, Jothie, and Simon Tay. 1991. "From Second Tongue to Mother Tongue: A Look at the Use of English in Singapore Drama from the 1960s to the Present." In Edwin Thumboo, ed., *Perceiving Other Worlds,* pp. 400–411. Singapore: Times Academic for UNIPRESS.

Salleh, Muhammad Haji. 1991. "The Writer as Asian." In Miguel Bernad, ed., *Conversations with F. Sionil José,* pp. 21–58. Quezon City: Vera Reyes.

Tahir Ungku Maimunah Mohd. 1995. "Women Novelists in Modern Malay Literature." In Thelma B. Kintanar, ed., *Emergent Voices: Southeast Asian Women Novelists,* pp. 17–55. Quezon City: University of the Philippines Press.

Tham Seong Chee. 1981a. "Literary Response and the Social Process: An Analysis of the Cultural and Political Beliefs Among Malay Writers." In Tham Seong Chee, ed., *Essays on Literature and Society in Southeast Asia: Political and Sociological Perspectives,* pp. 253–286. Singapore: Singapore University Press.

————. 1981b. "The Politics of Literary Development in Malaysia." In Tham Seong Chee, ed., *Essays on Literature and Society in Southeast Asia: Political and Sociological Perspectives,* pp. 216–252. Singapore: Singapore University Press.

Thumboo, Edwin, ed. 1970. *The Flowering Tree: Selected Writings from Singapore/ Malaysia.* Singapore: Educational Publications Bureau.

————. 1973. *Seven Poets: Singapore and Malaysia.* Singapore: Singapore University Press.

————. 1976. *The Second Tongue: An Anthology of Poetry from Malaysia and Singapore.* Selected with an introduction by Edwin Thumboo. Singapore: Heinemann.

————. 1979. *Ulysses by the Merlion.* Singapore: Heinemann.

————. 1988. *Literature and Liberation: Five Essays from Southeast Asia.* Manila: Solidaridad.

————. 1990. *Words from the 25th: Readings by Singapore Writers.* Singapore: UNIPRESS.

————. 1991. *Perceiving Other Worlds.* Singapore: Times Academic for UNIPRESS.

Yeo, Fernando, ed. 1993. *Singular Stories: Tales from Singapore.* Vol. 1. Washington, D.C.: Three Continents.

Philippines

Abad, Gemino H. n.d. *One Hundred Years of Philippine Poetry.* http://www.geocities .com/icasocot/articles7.html.

Abad, Gemino H., and Cristina Pantoja Hidalgo. 1996. *The Likhaan Book of Poetry and Fiction 1995.* Quezon City: University of the Philippines Press.

Arguilla, Manuel. 1970. *How My Brother Leon Brought Home a Wife, and Other Stories.* Westport: Greenwood.

Francia, Luis H. 1993. *Brown River, White Ocean: An Anthology of Twentieth-Century Philippine Literature in English.* New Brunswick, N.J.: Rutgers University Press.

Gonzalez, N. V. M. 1963. *A Season of Grace.* Manila: Benipayo.

————. 1977. *Bamboo Dancers.* Manila: Republic Book Supply.

————. 1989. *Mindoro and Beyond.* Quezon City: New Day.

————. 1990. *The Father and the Maid: Essays on Filipino Life and Letters.* Quezon City: University of the Philippines Press.

————. 1993. *The Bread of Salt and Other Stories.* Seattle: University of Washington Press.

————. 1996. *The Novel of Justice: Selected Essays, 1968–1994.* Pasay City: Anvil.

————. 1997. *A Grammar of Dreams and Other Stories.* Quezon City: University of the Philippines Press.

José, F. Sionil. 1962. *The Pretenders.* Manila: Solidaridad.

————. 1978. *Tree.* Manila: Solidaridad.

————. 1979a. *Mass.* Manila: Solidaridad.

————. 1979b. *My Brother, My Executioner.* Quezon City: New Day.

————. 1992a. *Dusk.* New York: Modern Library.

————. 1992b. *Three Filipino Women.* New York: Random House.

————. 1993. *Viajero.* Manila: Solidaridad.

————. 1994. *Sin: A Novel.* Manila: Solidaridad.

Lumbera, Bienvenido. 1997. *Revaluation 1997: Essays on Philippine Literature, Cinema, and Popular Culture.* Manila: University of Santo Tomas Press.

Lumbera, Cynthia Nograles, and G. Maceda, eds. 1977. *Rediscovery: Essays in Philippine Life and Culture.* Quezon City: National Bookstore.

Macasantos, Francis C., and Priscilla S. Macasantos. n.d. *Philippine Literature in the Post-War and Contemporary Period.* http://www.ncca.gov.ph/phil._culture/arts/ literary/literary_post-war.htm.

Santos, Bienvenido N. 1953. *You Lovely People.* Manila: Bookmark.

————. 1955. *Scent of Apples: A Collection of Stories.* Seattle: University of Washington Press.

————. 1986. *Villa Magdalena.* Quezon City: New Day.

————. 1991a. *Brother, My Brother.* Manila: Bookmark.

————. 1991b. *The Day the Dancers Came.* Manila: Bookmark.

Serrano, Josefine Bass, and Trinidad Maño Ames, eds. 1975. *A Survey of Filipino Literature in English: From Apprenticeship to Contemporary with Preview of the Early States of Filipino Literature.* Rev. ed. Quezon City: Phoenix.

Soliongco, I. P. 1964. "On American Literature and Filipino Society." In *Literature and Society: A Symposium on the Relation of Literature to Social Change,* pp. 20–31. Manila: A. S. Florentino.

Tinio, Rolando S. 1990. *A Matter of Language: Where English Fails.* Quezon City: University of the Philippines Press.

Van Erven, Eugene. 1992. "Beyond the Shadows of *Wayang:* Theatre of Liberation in Indonesia." In *The Playful Revolution Liberation in Asia,* pp. 184–206. Bloomington: University of Indiana Press.

14

Trends and Prospects

Brantly Womack

A Hong Kong businesswoman and her Filipina maid may live in the same flat, but they come from different worlds, and despite the intersection of their paths, they are likely to have different futures. Perhaps the maid came from a large, poor family on the outskirts of Clark Air Base, which was the largest overseas US military facility until it closed in 1992 and became a special economic zone. She sends most of her paycheck back to her family and plans to return and settle down in a few years. The parents of her employer may have been even poorer when they arrived illegally from Guangdong in the 1970s, and now the daughter is thriving as an intermediary between the assembly factories of her ancestral village and the global marketing capabilities of Hong Kong. As we address the question of trends and prospects in such a vast region as Asia Pacific, it is well to remember that two people living in such different worlds can every day take the same elevator to the same door.

Much has happened in the world since 1945, but the Asia Pacific region has undergone more than its share of transformation. Sometimes the span of "the foreseeable future" has been only a few months, as when the outbreak of the Korean War in 1950 caught analysts by surprise, who thought that hostilities could be prevented, if not indefinitely, at least for the next few years. In economics, the region has witnessed one Asian "miracle" after another—first the reemergence of Japan, then the rise of the "four tigers" (South Korea, Taiwan, Hong Kong, and Singapore), and last but certainly not least, the rise of China. Thus it is quite a challenge to review the trends of Asia Pacific, and it is even more daunting to gauge the region's prospects.

Three broad categories of trends and prospects will be distinguished in this chapter. First, changes in the conditions of interaction in the region. This includes geography in its broadest sense—not just physical features of the region,

425

but resources, environment, demography, transportation, communication, and so forth. Although this category has seen the least change over time, its trends are significant and it poses some of the most predictable challenges for the future. The second category, society, comprises the decisions that communities in the region have made, the paths they have taken in politics and economics, and their interaction within the region. The third category, external interaction, includes the interactions between Asia Pacific and the rest of the world. While it is impossible to disentangle these trends completely—global warming, for instance, involves geography, society, and external interaction—these broad categories should be useful in sketching the overall dynamics of a complex region.

Geography

As Ron Hill notes in Chapter 2, geography is anything but constant, and even the land itself is in flux. What does Asia Pacific have to work with in terms of resources and people? How have these capacities changed since World War II, and what are the prospects for further change? Addressing these questions is an important prerequisite to understanding the political and economic options of the region.

Geology is well known for changing at its own slow pace, but even in this respect Asia Pacific moves rather quickly. The Himalayas are rising one centimeter each year as the Indian tectonic plate continues to push under the Eurasian landmass. More dramatic are the region's many earthquakes, volcanoes, tsunamis, and typhoons. The most spectacular recent disaster was the Asian tsunami of December 26, 2004, caused by the second most powerful earthquake ever recorded and killing 230,000 people on the coasts of South and Southeast Asia. The region remains vulnerable to such events, and the only confident prediction is that they will continue to occur.

Global warming poses more general problems for the region. The resulting rise in sea levels would flood not only some of the smaller islands of the Philippines and Indonesia, but also many rich and productive urban areas, located on flat deltas, along the region's coast. Moreover, global warming is likely to increase aridity in the South Pacific, leading to more droughts, forest fires, and typhoons. Further inland, the melting of the Tibetan glaciers is causing a temporary increase in water supply, but at the cost of a severe shortage in the future. Despite regional vulnerability, the Asia Pacific states in general have been slow to adjust their national policies to reduce greenhouse gases, and even slower to cooperate regionally on global warming issues. China is the second largest producer of greenhouse gases in the world, after the United States.

One might think that natural resources would be a stable feature of geography, but such resources must be discovered and utilized, and ultimately they can be exhausted. Royal Dutch/Shell, the world's second largest oil company, was founded in 1890 to exploit Indonesia's oil. However, declining production and reserves made Indonesia a net oil importer by 2004. China's oil fortunes have been more volatile. China was not thought to have oil when the People's Republic of China was founded in 1949, but discoveries led to the development of the Daqing and other oil fields, and oil fueled China's growth and was an important export in the 1980s. By the mid-1990s, rapidly rising domestic consumption made China a net oil importer, and by 2005 it was importing 45 percent of its oil needs. In general, the region is becoming increasingly dependent on oil from the Middle East, Central Asia, and Africa.

The regional shortage of oil increases the significance of other energy sources. Asia has a quarter of the world's coal reserves, and China has the world's third largest reserves, after the United States and Russia (World Energy Council 2004). Nevertheless, Asia is a net importer of coal. Since coal has the highest carbon density at point of combustion, it is a major contributor to greenhouse gases, and Chinese coal has a high percentage of sulfur, which contributes to acid rain and pollution. Nuclear energy is quite important for developed countries in the region, supplying almost half of South Korea's energy, one-third of Japan's, and one-quarter of Taiwan's. The lack of other energy options contributes to North Korea's interest in the nuclear option.

Asia has the world's largest potential for hydropower, and electricity generated from dams currently supplies one-fourth of the region's power. One of the purposes of the Three Gorges dam project in China is to supply 84.7 billion kilowatt-hours of electricity, equivalent to over 10 percent of China's total electrical demand (Asian Development Bank 2006:4). Although hydroelectric energy is clean, is inexpensive to manage, and has the longest factory life of any mode of energy production, the environmental and demographic disruption caused by the building of large dams makes such projects controversial.

Besides energy, the problem of freshwater resources in Asia Pacific deserves special mention. The regional water problem is not as severe as that of the Middle East, which has only 1 percent of the world's water resources, but monsoonal variations create a seasonal flood and drought cycle that is particularly noticeable in the Mekong River basin. The seasonal change is detrimental to transportation and land use, but it sustains a unique ecology. One of the more interesting natural events in Cambodia is the semiannual change of direction of the river that connects the Mekong to the Tongle Sap, the country's largest lake. North China is experiencing an increasingly severe water shortage that is beginning to threaten industry and agriculture, prompting the massive "South Waters North" project to divert 5 percent of the Yangzi's flow into the Yellow River basin.

The population of Asia Pacific was not decimated and displaced by the "guns, germs, and steel" of the imperialists. In contrast to the labor shortage reflected in slavery and immigration policies in the Americas, the first problems of most new states in Asia Pacific were population control and increasing food production. In recent years, three major famines have occurred in the region: the Tonkin famine of 1944–1945 in Vietnam, the Great Leap Forward famine in China in 1960–1961, and the famine of 1997 in North Korea.

Indonesia and China have been world leaders in population control among developing countries, and the main justification is to avoid future overpopulation. The reduction in dependent children and corresponding rise in working-age adults as a percentage of the total population contributed to rapid economic growth rates. Overall, 10 percent of the countries' economic growth can be attributed to population control, and in the 1980s the higher percentage of workers contributed 16 percent to China's growth (Hofman, Ishihara, and Zhao 2007). But as the current working population ages, the advantage will turn into a severe disadvantage. As we can see now in the case of Japan, there will be fewer children to support their parents in old age. Other problems associated with population control are government coercion and gender imbalance, especially in China.

On the more positive side of regional demographics, there have been widespread increases in health and literacy in Asia Pacific. National languages have become almost universal. This was a major development especially in Indonesia, where only 7 percent of the population spoke Bahasa Indonesia (literally, "language of Indonesia") when it was proclaimed the national language on Independence Day in 1945. More recently there is greater attention to minority languages and cultures throughout the region.

For most of the Asia Pacific region, the most striking geographical changes of the second half of the twentieth century have occurred in transportation and communication. The region's rugged terrain had created subcommunities who had little contact with national affairs. In some cases, identity was defined more by elevation—mountain, highland, and lowland groups—than by political borders (Leach 1965). The creation of road and rail networks has been a prerequisite of national integration. The most recent major project of this sort is the railway linking Tibet to the rest of China, opened in 2006, the first-ever all-weather mass transit to Tibet from anywhere.

The communications revolution in the region is equally profound and ongoing. In the case of China, wired radios reached most villages only in the early 1960s, and their novelty enhanced the leftist propaganda of the Cultural Revolution. Television became a new form of community entertainment before each family could afford their own. Telephones were generally slow to become universal, but land lines have now been overtaken by omnipresent mobile phones. In the region's developed countries, two-thirds of the population are now Internet users, and Internet usage is increasing rapidly everywhere else in the region. China in 2006 had over 130 million Internet users, representing one-tenth of its population and half the number of Internet users in the United States (Pace 2006). Together, the transportation and communication revolutions have made possible more intense national, regional, and global interaction and integration.

Society

The most basic social trend in Asia Pacific over the past six decades has been a transformation in national identities, but regional integration is a more likely prospect for the future than further national transformation. Although the divisions imposed by Western domination in Asia Pacific were not as artificial as those in Africa, the problems of constructing postcolonial national identities were tremendous (for details, see Chapter 4). In its presence in Asia, the West combined domination with modernization, and it was the difficult task of new regimes to assert independence and at the same time continue modernization. The most radical transformations occurred in China and Vietnam, where popular mobilization in rural-based revolutions created a new social base and brought to power new, revolutionary leaderships. In Myanmar and Indonesia, national figures emerged to personify new national identities, but societal development proved to be difficult, and succeeding governments became obsessed with maintaining order. On the Korean peninsula and in Taiwan, identity remains an issue. Japan has had the unique problem of adjusting to a postimperial context in which it remains strategically dependent on the United States while having to negotiate new relationships with neighbors that it once dominated.

There have been a series of spectacular economic successes in Asia Pacific, beginning with Japan's recovery from World War II and followed by the rise of the four tigers: South Korea, Taiwan, Hong Kong, and Singapore. Last and most spectacular has been the "peaceful rise" of China since 1980. The success of Japan and the four tigers was related, directly and indirectly, to the US presence in the Pacific. The Cold War in Asia involved US assistance to anticommunist allies, and the two wars fought there, though destructive for Korea and Vietnam, brought more US money into the region. Until the 1980s, the United States allowed its allies to pursue mercantilist strategies of protecting their domestic markets while maximizing exports to the United States. By contrast, China's economic growth has had a greater domestic dynamic and more diverse external stimuli. China's trade and foreign investment have been more balanced than those of its predecessors, mostly because developed Asian countries are active partners.

Not all regional economic trends have been positive. Myanmar remains desperately poor despite its rich potential, and the Philippines has not developed as fast as expected. The stagnation of the Japanese economy in the 1990s raises questions about plateaus of Asian development, and the Asian financial crisis of 1997 demonstrated the vulnerability of regional prosperity.

The region's pattern of domestic politics has shown a general strengthening of governance capacity, but with a variety of political forms. South Korea and Taiwan have seen democratic transformations, while Japan's politics became more contested in the 1990s. The mass-based party-states of China and Vietnam have performed well in delivering basic services, better than some states that have more resources (Kerkvliet 2005). Even more impressive, they have proved flexible and capable of guiding market economies (Lai 2006). Whether they can institutionalize a form of government satisfactory to a modern society remains an open question. Meanwhile, the potential role of the military in Myanmar, the Philippines, Indonesia, and Thailand remains a shadow over civilian government.

Intraregional relations have seen many divisions and fluctuations since 1945, but since the 1990s a trend toward greater economic integration and political accommodation can be seen. The greatest fluctuation has been in relations between China and Vietnam (Womack 2006). From 1945 to 1975, they were "as close as lips and teeth." They became hostile from 1978 to 1991, and since then have developed a close but normal relationship. On a larger scale, the Korean War confirmed the regional split between communist and noncommunist states, and the US war in Vietnam exacerbated divisions and turmoil in Southeast Asia. Since the late 1980s, however, there has been a powerful trend toward regional economic integration.

Economic integration in Asia Pacific started from a very low point. Under the influence of disparate colonial powers, Southeast Asian countries provided agricultural goods and raw materials to their "mother countries." They did not trade with their neighbors. Indeed, the major economic links within Southeast Asia were the immigrant Chinese, who kept in contact with family members in various ports. The Japanese empire was the exception that proved the rule, because when Japan was dissolved in 1945, it was hardly welcome as a peacetime partner. China, the traditional central power of the region, pursued self-sufficiency, and in any case was shunned because of its revolutionary politics.

Things began to change in the 1980s. Japan's generous foreign assistance improved its image and accessibility, and China's new policy of openness benefited first "greater China" and then the region as a whole. Ironically, a major impetus to regional economic integration was supplied by the United States. As the United States began to penalize Japan and other states for trade imbalances in the late 1980s, the more developed states evaded the sanctions by moving the final stages of product assembly to other countries, especially China. The multinational production network has been enormously successful ever since, and has contributed to the "Asianization" of Asia Pacific. Besides multinational production for other markets, Asia's own markets have stimulated a rapidly increasing amount of intraregional trade.

Regional institutions have developed more slowly, but they have picked up momentum in the last few years. The Association of Southeast Asian Nations

(ASEAN) was founded in 1967 by Indonesia, Thailand, Malaysia, Singapore, and the Philippines, and it expanded into an inclusive regional association only in the 1990s. At that time, ASEAN took the lead in exploring cooperation in the larger Asia Pacific as well. The ASEAN Regional Forum (ARF) was established as a venue for informal dialogue among twenty-five members on both sides of the Pacific (including the United States and the European Union), and joint meetings were held between ASEAN and various other states. The most important of these joint meetings have been the ASEAN Plus Three, among China, Japan, and South Korea, which began in 1997.

The Asian financial crisis of 1997 gave special impetus to relations between ASEAN and China. ASEAN was quite impressed and grateful that China was able to hold steady the value of its currency and the Hong Kong dollar, and over the next decade rapid improvements in ASEAN-China relations were made. An ASEAN-China Free Trade Area was agreed on in 2002 and has made rapid progress since then. At the same time, both sides signed a declaration of conduct in the South China Sea, which contributed to avoiding conflict over the Spratly Islands despite several states' competing territorial claims to the islands. The following year, China became the first non-ASEAN signatory of the Southeast Asian amity and cooperation treaty, which generalized commitments to peaceful and mutually beneficial relations. Following China's lead, Japan and India became more active in multilateral diplomacy with Southeast Asia, resulting in the East Asia Summit of 2006 (which did not include the United States).

Regional integration in Northeast Asia is of course a different story, given the rogue state status of North Korea and the mutual aversion of China and Japan. There is no regional organization, and the six-party talks regarding North Korea's nuclear weapons have been inconclusive. Nevertheless, trade does unite the region. In 2006, China was the largest trading partner of both Koreas and almost the equal of the United States in trade with Japan. Although trade does not automatically induce political integration, it does create an inertia of mutual interest that at a minimum weighs heavily in favor of the status quo and against crises. The function of trade and investment as a ballast to the status quo can also be seen in relations between China and Taiwan. Although there have been no breakthroughs in the cross-strait relationship, serious breakdowns appear unlikely. Increasing integration of the region is more likely to generate minor crises resulting from the friction of greater contact and to decrease the likelihood of major crises.

Since 2002, the standoff between the United States and North Korea over the latter's nuclear weapons program has riveted global attention on this issue, but the deeper and more lasting problem for Northeast Asia is the reintegration of the Korean peninsula. The nuclear issue is a question of policy, and it could be resolved by a significant move from either side. The reintegration problem is more complex. The social and economic differences between the two Koreas are enormous, much greater than those between East and West Germany before their reunification. Moreover, South Korea cannot bear the costs of reunification on its own. With the burden of North Korea, it cannot maintain its competitive edge in world markets. And powerful neighbors such as China and Japan, as well as the United States, are not likely to sit quietly on the sidelines. Thus the Korean peninsula is likely to remain the focus of regional attention for Northeast Asia.

Regional integration in Asia Pacific does not hold prospects for an "Asian Union" mirroring Europe, but the activities centered on Southeast Asia seem more promising than current regional efforts in Africa and Latin America. Trade, investment, and production relationships have created patterns of regional interaction that touch the daily lives of many of Asia's citizens. Given the relative stability of regional governments and the reduction of ideological divides, regional normalcy is likely to continue and to grow stronger. The openness of the region to external influences creates vulnerabilities to global influences, both political and economic. However, it is possible that, like the Asian financial crisis, global crises will bring countries of the region closer together rather than creating new divisions.

External Interaction

The countries of Asia Pacific, whether colonized or not, were dominated by the West for the century preceding World War II. But the war in Asia demonstrated the bankruptcy of the imperialist system. First, the Japanese defeated the old imperialists or subordinated them (in the case of the Vichy France regime in Indochina). Then, Japan's "Greater East Asia Co-Prosperity Sphere" fostered some local anti-Western elites, but turned out to be an even harsher form of international exploitation, and then it too was defeated. After these experiences, it was impossible for the old imperial powers to return to their old privileges, though they made the attempt.

Asia Pacific became the venue for the two hot wars of the Cold War because, unlike Europe, its regional structure was unclear. The United States wanted to draw the dividing line of the bipolar world as close as it could to the borders of territory already conceded to the communist world—to contain communism. Meanwhile China saw itself as the vanguard of a third world revolution, though from 1970 its diplomacy became much more pragmatic. Despite these very real regional divisions, the notion of the Cold War as a bipolar struggle between the United States and the Soviet Union did not fit well in Asia. By the early 1960s, China was openly critical of Soviet "revisionism" and "social imperialism," and the Siberian border clashes of 1969 underlined the possibility of war between communist countries. This eventuality, impossible in a monolithic "communist world," became a reality in 1978–1979 when

Vietnam overthrew the communist government of Pol Pot in Cambodia and then itself was invaded by China. While divisions between communist and noncommunist countries remained important into the 1980s, the specifics of each division were not simply proxies of the US-Soviet confrontation, as Derek McDougall explains in Chapter 6.

Nixon's visit to China in 1972 and the US withdrawal from Vietnam in 1973–1975 changed the significance of US strategic presence in Asia Pacific. US military installations remained in Japan, South Korea, and the Philippines, but US attention shifted elsewhere and the likelihood of another intervention in the region diminished. The inertia of the inactive presence of the United States in the region created a global climate favorable to the reduction of divisions and the emergence of regional integration. The role of the United States as the relatively passive and distant guarantor of the regional status quo continues to be an important factor, since otherwise Japan would feel a more urgent need to develop its military, and ASEAN would have to cope with new security tensions.

In the post–Cold War world, there is no clear demarcation between the regional situation of Asia Pacific and its global environment. Regionalization is more intense than globalization, but it has not excluded outsiders, and it has been driven by the same global forces. In contrast to the European Union, Asia Pacific has been a region without boundaries. The internationalization of information, investment, and finance has brought the Asia Pacific states closer together because they are neighbors in a shrinking world.

Contrary to Thomas Friedman's famous claim (2005), however, the world as experienced by Asia Pacific is not flat. It is lumpy. All states are exposed to the horizonless world of globalization, but some are more exposed than others. Moreover, states with greater capacities, with more to offer others in terms of both opportunities and risks, naturally attract more attention from their neighbors and from the rest of the world. The United States is on the front page of the world's news almost every day, and on a smaller scale there is a standing interest in the activities of Europe, Japan, China, and India that exceeds the attention paid to smaller neighbors. When China held its Africa Summit in November 2006, officials from forty-eight of fifty-two states were in attendance.

Despite unequal attention, states increasingly deal directly with one another rather than through dominating "metropolitan" states. The Asianization of Asia is not the result of exclusivism, but rather reflects the transformation of the artificial wagonwheel patterns of colonial trade into the more natural patterns of trading most conveniently with neighbors. In the post–Cold War world, the United States is the center of the world economy, but not everything moves through the center. Global interaction is not equal, but it is dispersed. The world is neither flat nor an empire; it is multinodal (Womack 2007).

There is no self-destruction mechanism built into the current multinodal regional and world orders, but neither are they impervious to crises and to major policy changes. Though crises are by their nature difficult to predict, the possible effects of two potential economic crises should be considered.

The first possible crisis would be the slowing and stagnation of the Chinese economy. The most probable cause would be the failure to adequately adjust to the requirements of sustainability, which include controlling environmental damage, upgrading infrastructure, and balancing opportunities across regions and classes. Sustainability is itself likely to slow growth, but blind growth is more likely to hit a wall and to collapse. Even if China's percentage growth declines, the material increment to its economy will be significant. In 2006, the value added to the Chinese economy in purchasing power parity was more than the entire gross national product (GNP) of Indonesia; with half the growth rate, the increment would have been the equivalent of the GNP of Poland or the Netherlands. The effects of a Chinese economic collapse would of course be strongest in China, but it would not necessarily lead to political change. The most important regional and world effects would be analogous to those of the 1997 Asian financial crisis, namely, acute problems for a couple of years, and a lingering sense of vulnerability and of lowered expectations.

The second possible economic crisis would be a collapse of the value of the US dollar, creating a global financial crisis. Both globally and regionally this would be considerably more serious than the 1997 crisis. The loss of trade, the devaluing of current assets, and the disruption of the international economic system would all affect the Asia Pacific region. Although the United States is no longer the dominant consumer outlet, 22 percent of Asia's trade is still with North America, and much of that trade is in consumer goods whose sales would suffer in a US recession. Moreover, China and the developed countries of Asia Pacific hold trillions in dollar assets. As the value of the dollar would sink, so would the value of these assets. Most important, the dollar is currently the major world currency, and therefore a dollar crisis would destabilize most international transactions, and would increase pressures for a market basket of currencies or for multilateral regulation of currency markets.

No state in Asia Pacific would escape the negative effects of such a crisis, but some would be hit harder than others. Japan and the four tigers were built on the US market and would be hit the hardest. China's trade figures and asset values would be hit, but in fact much of its export to the United States involves the assembly of foreign components by factories owned by other Asians. China's internal economy and the size of its domestic market would reduce the proportional effect of a world economic crisis. As a result, China might be the least damaged major economy not only in the region, but possibly in the world. If this were the case, the Asia Pacific region would also be relatively less damaged, but its economic prospects would be centered even more strongly on China.

Major global policy changes could also result in crises in Asia Pacific. If the United States were to decide that China is a challenger comparable to the Soviet

Union and therefore that an active policy of containment is necessary, then Asia Pacific would become the ultimate focus of a new cold war. But the hotspots of a new cold war might well occur elsewhere. After all, the focus of the Cold War was Europe, but its wars were in Asia. However, it should be remembered that in the Cold War, the Soviet Union effectively contained itself—it sealed off Eastern Europe, it built the Berlin Wall, it frightened Western Europe. China's relationship with its neighbors has been the opposite. In Asia Pacific, the pressures to align on one side or the other would threaten to undermine the inclusiveness of the region. Undoubtedly, most states would try to evade making a choice. Vietnam, for example, has China as its main trading partner and the United States as its main export market—choosing between them would be painful. If one or the other tried to force a choice, then that "join me or else" threat might backfire. A containment strategy, no matter how attractive in the abstract to Americans worried about the "China threat," would be frustrating to implement and might even lead to a reduction of US influence in Asia Pacific. The welcome that the region extends is premised on the United States acting as a passive preserver of the status quo; an active "them or us" strategy would be a very different matter.

$$* \quad * \quad *$$

From the next tsunami to turns in the global economy, the future of Asia Pacific remains unpredictable, but we can be cautiously optimistic. Its progress in the past six decades has been remarkable, and while new problems of sustainability have emerged, regional growth does not appear to have an internal fatal flaw. Likewise, regional economic integration seems solidly based on the mutual interests of neighboring states. Economic interaction is likely to intensify, certainly if the current global climate prevails, but even if the global economy turns sour. The region is too diverse in every respect—geographically, socially, and in global attachments—to move toward political union, but it also appears to have grown out of the external dependencies and wars that scarred its previous century.

Bibliography

Asian Development Bank. 2006. "Country Synthesis Report on Urban Air Quality Management: People's Republic of China." Discussion draft. http://www.adb.org/documents/reports/urban-air-quality-management/prc.pdf.

Friedman, Thomas. 2005. *The World Is Flat.* New York: Farrar, Straus & Giroux.

Hofman, Bert, Yoichiro Ishihara, and Min Zhao. 2007. "Asian Development Strategies: China and Indonesia Compared." *Bulletin of Indonesian Economics and Statistics* (May).

Kerkvliet, Ben 2005. "Political Expectations and Democracy in the Philippines and Vietnam." *Philippine Political Science Journal* 26, no. 49: 1–26.

Lai, Hongyi. 2006. *Reform and the Non-State Economy in China.* New York: Palgrave Macmillan.

Leach, Edmund Ronald. 1965. *Political Systems of Highland Burma.* Boston: Beacon.

Pace, Natalie. 2006. "China Surpasses U.S. Internet Use." Forbes.com, April 3. http://www.forbes.com/2006/03/31/china-internet-usage-cx_nwp_0403china.html.

Womack, Brantly. 2006. *China and Vietnam: The Politics of Asymmetry.* New York: Cambridge University Press.

———. 2007 (forthcoming). "Asymmetry Theory and Regional Powers: The Cases of India, Brazil, and South Africa." In Juan Tokatlian, ed., *Emergent Powers and Regional Security.*

World Energy Council. 2004. *Survey of Energy Resources, 2004.* London.

Acronyms

ADB	Asian Development Bank
AFTA	ASEAN Free Trade Area
AIDS	acquired immunodeficiency syndrome
APEC	Asia-Pacific Economic Cooperation
ARF	ASEAN Regional Forum
ASEAN	Association of Southeast Asian Nations
BN	Barisan Nasional (National Front) (Malaysia)
CCP	Chinese Communist Party
CECC	Congressional-Executive Commission on China
CINCPAC	Commander-in-Chief Pacific
CP	cleaner production
DALY	disability adjusted life year
EMR	extended metropolitan region
EU	European Union
FDI	foreign direct investment
FRETILIN	Frente Revolucionária do Timor-Leste Independente (Revolutionary Front of Independent East Timor)
GAM	Gerakan Aceh Merdeka (Free Aceh Movement)
GATS	General Agreement on Trade in Services
GDP	gross domestic product
GNI	gross national income
GNP	gross national product
HPAE	high-performing Asian economy
HIV	human immunodeficiency virus
IAEA	International Atomic Energy Agency
IISS	International Institute for Strategic Studies
IMF	International Monetary Fund
IPCC	Intergovernmental Panel on Climate Change
ISO	International Standardization Organization

JETRO	Japan External Trade Organization
LDC	less-developed country
LDP	Liberal Democratic Party (Japan)
MCA	Malayan Chinese Association
MIC	Malayan Indian Congress
OPM	Organisasi Papua Merdeka (Free Papua Movement)
PBOC	People's Bank of China
PKI	Partai Komunis Indonesia (Indonesian Communist Party)
PLA	People's Liberation Army (China)
PNI	Partai Nasional Indonesia (Indonesian National Party)
PRC	People's Republic of China
SARS	severe acute respiratory syndrome
SCO	Shanghai Cooperation Organization
SIJORI	Singapore-Johor-Riau
SOE	state-owned enterprise
SME	small and medium-size enterprise
TFR	total fertility rate
UMNO	United Malays Nationalist Organization
UMP	urban megaproject
UN	United Nations
UNCCD	United Nations Convention to Combat Desertification
UNCTAD	United Nations Conference on Trade and Development
UNDP	United Nations Development Programme
UNEP	United Nations Environment Programme
UNESC	United Nations Economic and Social Council
UNESCAP	United Nations Economic and Social Commission for Asia and the Pacific
UNPD	United Nations Population Division
UNTAC	United Nations Transitional Authority in Cambodia
UNTAET	United Nations Transitional Administration for East Timor
VOC	Vereenigde Oost-Indische Compagnie (Dutch United East India Company; Dutch East India Company)
WBCSD	World Business Council for Sustainable Development
WCED	World Commission on Environment and Development
WHO	World Health Organization
WMD	weapons of mass destruction
WTO	World Trade Organization

Basic Political Data

Brunei
Capital City   Bandar Seri Begawan
Date of Independence   January 1, 1984
Population   379,444 (2006 est.)
Current Leader   Sultan Hassanal Bokiah Mu'izzaddin Waddaulah (since 1967)
Type of Government   Constitutional Sultanate

Cambodia
Capital City   Phnom Penh
Date of Independence   November 9, 1953
Population   14 million (2005)
Current Leader   King Norodom Sihamoni (since 2004)
Principal Postindependence Leaders   Norodom Sihanouk (prince then king, 1941–1955, 1960–1970, 1975–1976, 1991–2004); Pol Pot (1976–1979); Heng Samrin (president of People's Revolutionary Council, 1979–1981; chairman, Council of State, 1981–1992); Hun Sen (prime minister, 1985–2007)
Type of Government   Multiparty democracy under a constitutional monarchy

China, People's Republic
Capital City   Beijing
Date of Independence   October 1, 1949
Population   1.3 million (2006)
Current Leader   General Secretary Hu Jintao (since 2002)
Principal Postindependence Leaders   Mao Zedong (CCP chairman, 1949–1976); Hua Guofeng (CCP chairman, 1976–1981); Deng Xiaoping

(acknowledged de facto leader despite lack of official titles, 1978–1997);
Jiang Zemin (general secretary, 1989–2002)
Type of Government Communist regime

East Timor

Capital City Dili
Date of Independence May 20, 2002
Population 947,000 (2005)
Current Leader President Kay Rala Xanana Gusmão (since 2002)
Type of Government Republic

Indonesia

Capital City Jakarta
Date of Independence December 27, 1949
Population 245.5 million (2006)
Current Leader President Susilo Bambang Yudhoyono (since 2004)
Principal Postindependence Leaders Sukarno (president, 1946–1967);
    Suharto (president, 1967–1998); Bacharuddin Jusuf Habibie (1998–1999);
    Abdurrahman Wahid (president, 1999–2001); Megawati Sukarnoputri
    (president, 2001–2004)
Type of Government Republic

Japan

Capital City Tokyo
Date of Independence Never colonized
Population 127.5 million (2006)
Current Leader Emperor Akihito (since 1989)
Principal Postindependence Leaders Showa (Hirohito) (emperor, 1926–
    1989); Shigeru Yoshida (prime minister, 1946–1947, 1948–1954); Hayato
    Ikeda (prime minister, 1960–1964); Kakuei Tanaka (prime minister, 1972–
    1974); Yasuhiro Nakasone (prime minister, 1982–1987); Kiichi Miyazawa
    (prime minister, 1991–1993); Murayama Tomiichi (prime minister,
    1994–1996); Obuchi Keizo (prime minister, 1997–2000); Junichiro Koizumi
    (prime minister, 2001–2006); Shinzo Abe (prime minister, 2006–2007)
Type of Government Constitutional monarchy with a parliamentary govern-
    ment

Laos

Capital City Vientiane
Date of Independence July 19, 1949 (from France); December 2, 1975
    (proclamation of Lao People's Democratic Republic)
Population 6.4 million (2006)

Current Leader   General Secretary Choummaly Sayasone (since 2006)
Principal Postindependence Leaders   Sisavang Vong (king, 1946–1959); Savang Vatthana (king, 1959–1975); Kayson Phomvihan (1975–1991); Khamtay Siphandon (general secretary, 1991–2006); sixteen prime ministers (1945–1975)
Type of Government   Communist regime

Malaysia
Capital City   Kuala Lumpur
Date of Independence   August 31, 1957
Population   26.9 million (2006)
Current Leader   Prime Minister Abdullah Ahmad Badawi (since 2003)
Principal Postindependence Leaders   Tunku Abdul Rahman Putra (prime minister, 1957–1970); Tun Abdul Razak bin Hussein (prime minister, 1959, 1970–1976); Hussein bin Onn (prime minister, 1976–1981); Mahathir bin Mohamad (prime minister, 1981–2003)
Type of Government   Constitutional monarchy with a parliamentary government

Myanmar (Burma)
Capital City   Yangon
Date of Independence   January 4, 1948
Population   54.3 million (UNESCAP 2004 est.; last official census was taken in 1983)
Current Leader   Chairman Than Shwe (State Peace and Development Council) (since 1997)
Principal Postindependence Leaders   Ne Win (union president, 1974–1981; chairman, Revolutionary Council, 1962–1974); Saw Maung (chairman, SLORC, 1988–1992); Than Shwe (chairman, State Law and Order Restoration Council [SLORC], 1992–1997)
Type of Government   Military regime

North Korea
Capital City   Pyongyang
Date of Independence   August 15, 1945 (from Japan); September 9, 1948 (proclamation of Democratic People's Republic of Korea)
Population   23.1 million (2006)
Current Leader   General Secretary Kim Jong Il (since 1994)
Principal Postindependence Leader   Kim Il Sung (general secretary, 1948–1994)
Type of Government   Authoritarian socialist dictatorship

Philippines

Capital City   Manila
Date of Independence   July 4, 1946
Population   85.2 million (2005 est.)
Current Leader   President Gloria Macapagal-Arroyo (since 2001)
Principal Postindependence Leaders   Ferdinand Emmanuel Edralin Marcos
   (president, 1965–1986); Maria Corazon Cojuangco Aquino (president,
   1986–1992)
Type of Government   Republic

Singapore

Capital City   Singapore
Date of Independence   August 9, 1965
Population   4.48 million (2006)
Current Leader   Prime Minister Lee Hsien Loong (since 2004)
Principal Postindependence Leaders   Lee Kuan Yew (prime minister,
   1959–1990); Goh Chok Tong (prime minister, 1990–2004)
Type of Government   Parliamentary republic

South Korea

Capital City   Seoul
Date of Independence   August 15, 1948
Population   48.8 million (2006)
Current Leader   President Roh Moo Hyun (since 2003)
Principal Postindependence Leaders   Syngman Rhee (president,
   1948–1960); Park Chung Hee (president, 1963–1979); Chun Doo Hwan
   (president, 1980–1988); Roh Tae Woo (president, 1988–1993); Kim
   Young Sam (president, 1993–1998); Kim Dae Jung (president,
   1998–2003)
Type of Government   Republic

Thailand

Capital City   Bangkok
Date of Independence   Never colonized
Population   62.4 million (2005)
Current Leader   King Phumiphon Adunyadet (since 1946)
Principal Postindependence Leaders   Plaek Pibulsongkram (prime minister,
   1948–1957); Thanom Kittikachorn (prime minister, 1963–1973); Prem
   Tinsulanonda (prime minister, 1980–1988); Chuan Leekpai (prime minis-
   ter, 1997–2001); Thaksin Shinawatra (prime minister, 2001–2006);
   Surayud Chulanout (prime minister, 2006–2007)
Type of Government   Constitutional monarchy

Vietnam

Capital City   Hanoi

Date of Independence   September 2, 1945

Population   83.1 million (2005)

Current Leader   General Secretary Nong Duc Manh (since 2001)

Principal Postindependence Leaders   Truong Chinh (general secretary, 1941–1956); Ho Chi Minh (general secretary, 1956–1960; president, 1930–1969); Le Duan (general secretary, 1960–1986); Ngyuyen Van Linh (general secretary, 1986–1991); Do Muoi (general secretary, 1991–1997); Le Kha Phieu (general secretary, 1997–2001)

Type of Government   Communist state

The Contributors

Fay Beauchamp is professor of English and humanities coordinator at the Community College of Philadelphia.

Keri Cole is a doctoral student in religion at Harvard University.

Dean Forbes is professor of geography and vice chancellor (international) of Flinders University, Adelaide, Australia.

Ron D. Hill is professor of geography and geology at the University of Hong Kong.

Peter Hills is professor and director of the Center of Urban Planning and Environmental Management at Hong Kong University.

Katherine Palmer Kaup is associate professor of political science and chair of Asian studies at Furman University, Greenville, South Carolina.

Kailash Khandke is associate professor of economics and Asian studies at Furman University, Greenville, South Carolina.

Colin Mackerras is professor emeritus in Asian studies at Griffith University, Queensland, Australia.

Ely Marquez is professor of English at the Community College of Philadelphia.

Derek McDougall is associate professor of political science at Melbourne University.

Yana Rodgers is associate professor of women's and gender studies at Rutgers University.

Robert Sutter is professor in the School of Foreign Service at Georgetown University, Washington, D.C.

Brantly Womack is professor of politics at the University of Virginia, Charlottesville.

Index

About the Book

Covering China, Japan, the Koreas, and all member states of the Association of Southeast Asian Nations, *Understanding Contemporary Asia Pacific* provides a comprehensive introduction to one of the most complex and rapidly changing regions in the world today.

This accessible, up-to-date volume is designed to be used as a core text for "Introduction to Asia" and "Asian Politics" courses, and also as a supplement in a variety of discipline-oriented curriculums. The authors cover history, politics, economics, and international relations, as well as such topics as the role of the military, population and urbanization, environmental issues, women and development, ethnicity, and religion. Maps, photographs, bibliographies, and an appendix of basic political data enhance the text.

Katherine Palmer Kaup is associate professor of political science and chair of the Asian Studies Department at Furman University. She is author of *Creating the Zhuang: Ethnic Politics in China*.